Maintaining Biodiversity in

Forest Ecosystems

The maintenance of the earth's biological diversity is necessary for ecosystem health as well as being aesthetically desirable. In ecosystems such as forests, which provide a range of resources that can be exploited by humans, the theory and practice of maintaining biodiversity are now seen as fundamental to successful management. This book focuses on how biodiversity can be maintained in forested ecosystems, particularly in those forests that are subject to timber harvesting. At the core of the book lies the concept that diversity should be conserved in all its forms, from the smallest microbes to the largest trees, and at all levels of organization, from genes, through species to whole ecosystems. Introductory chapters on biodiversity and ecological forestry provide a solid foundation for the reader, leading on to sections dealing with management at the macro (landscape) and micro (stand) levels. A concluding section considers socioeconomic and policy perspectives which inform an overall synthesis and framework for the implementation of successful management practices. Thirty-three experts from ten countries contribute to this thorough and comprehensive account, providing a broad-based perspective which will be of interest to graduate students in natural resources (in particular forestry, wildlife, and conservation biology), practicing forest scientists, and forest managers with a keen interest in forest ecology research.

MALCOLM 'MAC' HUNTER is the Libra Professor of Conservation Biology in the Department of Wildlife Ecology at the University of Maine. His research covers a wide range of organisms and ecosystems, although his major focus is on forests. He is author of two other volumes: Fundamentals of Conservation Biology, a textbook which reflects his broad conservation interests, and Wildlife, Forests, and Forestry.

Maintaining Biodiversity in

Forest Ecosystems

EDITED BY MALCOLM L. HUNTER JR

CAMBRIDGE
UNIVERSITY PRESS

PUBLISHED BY THE PRESS SYNDICATE OF THE UNIVERSITY OF CAMBRIDGE
The Pitt Building, Trumpington Street, Cambridge CB2 1RP, United Kingdom

CAMBRIDGE UNIVERSITY PRESS
The Edinburgh Building, Cambridge CB2 2RU, UK   http://www.cup.cam.ac.uk
40 West 20th Street, New York, NY 10011–4211, USA   http://www.cup.org
10 Stamford Road, Oakleigh, Melbourne 3166, Australia
Ruiz de Alarcón 13, 28014 Madrid, Spain

First published 1999
Reprinted 2000

Printed in the United Kingdom at the University Press, Cambridge

Typefaces FF Quadraat & Mezz   System QuarkXPress ®   [SE]

A catalogue record for this book is available from the British Library

Library of Congress cataloguing in publication data

Maintaining biodiversity in forest ecosystems / edited by Malcolm L.
   Hunter, Jr.
       p.   cm.
     Includes bibliographical references and index.
     ISBN 0 521 63104 1 (alk. paper). – ISBN 0 521 63768 6 (pbk.: alk. paper)
       1. Biological diversity conservation. 2. Forest conservation.
     3. Ecosystem management. 4. Forest management. 5. Forest ecology.
     I. Hunter, Malcolm L.
     QH75.M32125   1999
     639.9–dc21   98-40458 CIP

ISBN 0 521 63104 1 hardback
ISBN 0 521 63768 6 paperback

Contents

Contributors

H. LEE ALLEN, Department of Forestry, Box 8008, North Carolina State University, Raleigh, NC 27695-8008, USA

PER ANGELSTAM, Grimso Wildlife Research Station, Department of Conservation Biology, Forest Faculty, Swedish University of Agricultural Sciences, S-730 91 Riddarhyttan, Sweden

B. BRUCE BARE, College of Forest Resources, Box 352100, 292 Bloedel Hall, University of Washington, Seattle, Washington, 98195-2100, USA

JOSHUA T. BISHOP, International Institute for Environment and Development (IIED), 3 Endsleigh Street, London, WC1H oDD, United Kingdom

MARK BRINSON, Dept of Biology, East Carolina Univ., Greenville, NC 27858, USA

MELIH BOYDAK, Faculty of Forestry, University of Istanbul, Buyuk Dere, Istanbul, Turkey

NICHOLAS BROKAW, Manomet Center for Conservation Sciences, Box 1770, Manomet, MA 02345, USA

ARAM CALHOUN, Department of Plant, Soil, and Environmental Sciences, University of Maine, Orono, ME 04469, USA

R. TODD ENGSTROM, Tall Timbers Research Station., Rt 1, Box 678, Tallahassee, FL 32312-9712, USA

LEE FRELICH, Department of Forest Resources, University of Minnesota, 115 Green Hall, 1530 N. Cleveland Ave., St. Paul, MN 55108-1027, USA

YRJÖ HAILA, Department of Regional Studies and Environmental Policy, University of Tampere, P.O. Box 607, 33101, Tampere, Finland

ANDREW HANSEN, Department of Biology, 310 Lewis Hall, Montana State University, Bozeman, MT 59717-0346, USA

MALCOLM HUNTER, JR., Department of Wildlife Ecology, University of Maine, Orono, ME 04469-5755, USA

RICHARD LENT, Harvard Forest, P.O. Box 68, Harvard University, Petersham, MA 01366-0068, USA. Present address: College of the Holy Cross, One College Street, Worcester, MA 01610-2395, USA

DAVID LINDENMAYER, CRES, Australia National University, Canberra, ACT 0200, Australia

BRUCE LIPPKE, College of Forest Resources, University of Washington, Box 352100, Seattle, WA 98195-2100, USA

JOHN LITVAITIS, Department of Natural Resources, Pettee Hall, University of New Hampshire, Durham, NH 03824, USA

LYNN A. MAGUIRE, Nicholas School of the Environment, Box 90328, Duke University, Durham, NC 27708-0328, USA

GLENN MATLACK, Department of Biological Sciences, University of Southern Mississippi, Box 5018, Hattiesburg, MS 39406, USA

WILLIAM MCCOMB, Department of Forestry and Wildlife Management, University of Massachusetts, MA 01003, USA

CONSTANCE I. MILLAR, USDA Forest Service, Pacific Southwest Research Station, P.O. Box 245, Berkeley, CA 94701, USA

SUSAN E. MOORE, 5420 Knightdale-Eagle Rock Road, Knightdale, NC 27545-8414, USA

DAVID A. NORTON, Conservation Research Group, School of Forestry, University of Canterbury, Private Bag 4800, Christchurch, New Zealand

CHADWICK D. OLIVER, College of Forest Resources, Box 352100, University of Washington, Seattle, WA 98195-2100, USA

BRIAN PALIK, Forestry Sciences Lab, USDA Forest Service, 1831 Hwy. 169 E., Grand Rapids, MN 55744-3399, USA

KLAUS PUETTMANN, University of Minnesota, Department of Forest Resources, 1530 N. Cleveland Ave., St. Paul, MN 55108, USA

JAY ROTELLA, Biology Department, 310 Lewis Hall, Montana State University, Bozeman, MT 59717, USA

GERARDO SEGURA, Centro de Ecologia, Universidad Nacional Autonoma de Mexico, Apdo Postal 70-275, 04510, Mexico D.F., Mexico

ROBERT SEYMOUR, Department of Forest Ecosystem Science, University of Maine, Orono, ME 04469-5755, USA

THOMAS A. SPIES, Forestry Sciences Lab, 3200 Jefferson Way, Corvallis, OR 97331, USA

JACK WARD THOMAS, School of Forestry, University of Montana, Missoula, Montana, USA

IAN THOMPSON, Canadian Forest Service, Great Lakes Forestry Centre, P.O. Box 490, Sault Ste. Marie, Ontario, P6A 5M7, Canada

MONICA TURNER, Department of Zoology, University of Wisconsin, Madison, WI 53706, USA

JOS T.A.VERHOEVEN, Department of Plant Ecology and Evolutionary Biology, University of Utrecht, Postbus 80084, 3508 TB Utrecht, The Netherlands

Foreword

At last, a volume that relates the goal of the retention of biodiversity in managed forests to ecosystem management through the integrated considerations of the attributes of the 'macro management'. Some of these attributes include tree species, dynamic forest mosaics, environmental gradients, edges, 'forest islands' and fragments, riparian zones, and wetlands in the context of forested landscapes.

The authors, then, delve into the 'micro management' of some important attributes of individual forest stands such as dying, dead, and down trees; vertical within-stand diversity; special species emphasis; retention of genetic diversity; and silviculture for both wood production and retention of biodiversity.

These approaches include restoration ecology, establishment and maintenance of forest reserves, and the preparation of forest management plans built on producing wood fiber while maintaining biodiversity. This discussion of planning and management includes the critical elements of consideration of economic and socio-political perspectives.

Every once in a while, I pick up a book and think, 'I wish I had done this book.' This is such a book. This effort is both thorough and most timely. The editor and authors have done a most excellent job of weaving various related ideas, concepts, philosophies, and technical attributes of managing to retain biodiversity into a tapestry of interwoven relationships.

When I was Chief of the U.S. Forest Service, the agency had embarked upon 'ecosystem management' in response to the recognition that the overriding objective of the management of the Federal Lands had become the preservation of biodiversity. The 'prod' that drove me to that conclusion was the interaction of the Endangered Species Act and the 'diversity clause' of the regulations issued pursuant to the National Forest Management Act. Clearly, achieving the goal of preserving biodiversity in the course of forest management through the route of developing and executing 'recovery plans' for one threatened or endangered species after another was untenable in the longer term. Further, this approach serves poorly to achieve the stated purpose of the Endangered Species Act to . . .

'provide a means whereby the ecosystems upon which endangered species and threatened species may be conserved . . .'

Of course, anything so new and radical as the retention of biodiversity as an overriding forest management objective to be achieved through 'ecosystem management' could be expected to set off a wave of consternation. That would be followed by the inevitable demand from critics for exact definitions and a 'rule book' to guide application. Both expectations have been fulfilled. My response to both reactions was to note that ecosystem management and the coincident preservation of biodiversity were concepts that were rapidly evolving and, always, had to be placed in context of time, place, and human circumstance.

My concept was that, compared with traditional approaches, ecosystem management involved more inclusive thinking at larger scale, over a longer time frame, and considering more variables with the full recognition that people and the satisfaction of the needs and desires of people were part of that approach. Inherent in the approach was the recognition that humans must exploit their environment in order to live. The question, then, was not whether to exploit the forest but how to do so while saving what Aldo Leopold called all 'the cogs and wheels'.

The time for such a management approach has arrived and, in fact, cannot be avoided if resource extraction from managed forests is to continue considering the requirement for obedience to the myriad applicable laws. During a hearing in Washington during my time as Chief, a United States Senator challenged me as to the legal basis for ecosystem management. When I answered that question in a fashion that he could not successfully challenge, he said (I am paraphrasing), 'Well, there are a number of us who don't like it and we may just make it clear, in law or budget language that you shouldn't proceed along this path.' I did not make it a custom to make flippant comments to Senators. But, there are times for exceptions. I replied, 'Senator, this is a concept whose time has come. Ecosystem management will evolve no matter what you do. If you choose to draft legislation to outlaw ecosystem management, I suggest that you go to the beach and practice by shouting at the tide to go back.'

Now, this book has emerged that places the concept of ecosystem management into context at both landscape and stand level. And, that context, most appropriately, includes the needs and desires of people and the reality of economic and socio-political considerations in ecosystem management.

I believe that this pioneering effort will find its way into the classrooms of the Academy and into the libraries of scholars of forestry and wildlife management. More important yet, I predict that this book will significantly influence practitioners of the rapidly evolving art and science of ecosystem management. This approach to forest management that is built upon the recognition that our 'intelligent tinkering' of ever evolving forest management involves 'every cog and wheel' of the forest ecosystems that fascinate us all. This book is one large step on the road to applied ecosystem management – and it has come none too soon.

JACK WARD THOMAS

Boone and Crockett Professor of Wildlife Conservation

University of Montana

Missoula

Preface

Ecosystem management, sustainable forestry, ecological forestry, and similar terms are waxing stronger and stronger in the language of forest managers, reflecting a growing realization that society wants much more than timber products from forests. Recreation, wildlife, and water often come to mind first. They have been the big three 'other values' for many years and they remain a driving force for forest management. However within the last ten years or so, even this list of four values has seemed inadequate; the core ecological or biological values of a forest seem to be missing. For some people the term 'wildlife' captures this issue; for most people 'wildlife' is too closely associated with a small portion of our biota, especially the birds and mammals. Consequently, a number of terms have developed around this issue – biotic integrity, ecosystem health, and others – but arguably the most prominent is 'biological diversity' or 'biodiversity'. This book is about maintaining biodiversity in forests, a set of ecosystems that occupy only about 6% of the earth's total surface area, but which harbors a greatly disproportionate share of the earth's biological diversity.

This book is intended to reach a broad audience with the latest thinking about maintaining forest biodiversity, especially in forests managed for timber production. Among all the people interested in forests, those who are managing forests on a day to day basis and the students who will soon be joining the ranks of professional natural resource managers are our particular focus. The book is global in scope but, with over half of its contributors coming from North America, there is a clear North American bias. Assiduously avoiding this bias would be difficult and not necessarily desirable given that a majority of the scientists focused on forest biodiversity issues are probably North American.

This book originated in a Conservation Fellowship awarded by the Pew Charitable Trusts to Bob Seymour and me and thus the first acknowledgment must go to the Trusts and their staff, and to Bob, a superb colleague in all respects. Many people reviewed various manuscripts for the book; these include George Peterken, Jerry Franklin, Bob Seymour (these three read the entire manuscript) plus Andy Hansen, Mark Ashton, J. A. Baker,

B. Bruce Bare, Lenny Brennan, Mark Brinson, Nick Brokaw, Aram Calhoun, Jiquan Chen, Meredith W. Cornett, Ron Davis, Richard DeGraaf, Phillip DeMaynadier, David Field, Lee Frelich, Tom Fox, Alisa Gallant, Charles Goebel, Frank Golet, Andrew Gray, David Guynn, Yrjö Haila, Mitschka Hartley, John Hayes, Robert Healy, Steve Henderson, Sharon Herman, George Hess, Richard Hobbs, Elizabeth Jacqmain, Matt Kelty, Al Kimball, Jari Kouki, Marc Kramer, Matt Kraska, Richard A. Lent, Guadalupe Williams Linera, Bruce Lippke, John Litvaitis, Craig G. Lorimer, Janet McMahon, Lynn Maguire, Curt Meine, David Mladenoff, Jari Niemelä, P. H. Nienhuis, David Norton, Brian Palik, John Perez-Garcia, Andrew Plantinga, Douglas Reagan, Deborah Rogers, Guy Rotella, F. N. Scatena, Harris Sondak, Tom Spies, Toddi Steelman, Fred Swanson, Ian Thompson, Steve Trombulak, Monica Turner, Staffan Ulfstrand, Robert Westfall, Alan White, and Richard H. Yahner. Working with Alan Crowden, Maria Murphy, and all the staff at Cambridge University Press has been a great pleasure. Saving the best for last, working with the ever-talented and always cheerful Andrea Sulzer was the most enjoyable part of the overall effort.

MALCOLM L. HUNTER JR

Part I

Introduction

1   Biological diversity

MALCOLM L. HUNTER, JR.

For over a decade the mail has brought a steady stream of flyers announc-
ing new books and conferences with the terms 'biological diversity' or
'biodiversity' featured prominently. Apparently 'biodiversity' is here to
stay, holding an important position in the vocabulary of natural resource
management. It arrived just as people were becoming sensitive to the
entire spectrum of life with which we share the planet and the myriad
threats facing it. Despite this prominence the term still confuses many
people. In large part this is because biodiversity seems like something that
we should be able to quantify, like biomass or population density, but in
practice only limited components of biodiversity can be measured easily.
This constraint pushes biodiversity toward being more of a conceptual
entity, analogous to aesthetics or ecosystem integrity, than a tangible
thing. In this chapter we will first try to sort through the confusion to
provide a clear idea of what biodiversity is. In the second part we will sum-
marize the many reasons why it is important to maintain biodiversity.
Finally, in the third part we will discuss the relationship between biodiversity and related concepts such as ecosystem integrity and sustainability.

What is biodiversity?

Biodiversity could be defined simply as 'the diversity of life', but a
fuller definition is generally preferable. A definition such as 'the diversity
of life in all its forms and at all its levels of organization' (Hunter 1990)
reminds us that biodiversity includes the microbes and fungi that are often
overshadowed by plants and animals. It also compels us to look beyond
species to the genetic and ecosystem components of life on earth (Figure
1.1).

Biodiversity is easiest to understand in terms of the millions of species
that inhabit the earth. This form of diversity is very tangible. Although tax-
onomists can argue at length about how to distinguish species x from

Fig. 1.1. Biodiversity exists at three primary levels, genes, species, and ecosystems.

species y, most people make basic distinctions routinely and recognize that the differences among species are reflected in our value systems. A carpenter values both the red pine (*Pinus resinosa*) and the red oak (*Quercus rubra*) because they can be used for different purposes, and a birdwatcher values the differences between the red grouse (*Lagopus lagopus*) and the black grouse (*Lyrurus tetrix*) primarily just because they are different.

Genetic diversity, at its simplest level, lies in the patterns of cytosine, guanine, adenine, and thymine that make one strand of DNA different from another. Of course the key issue is how these patterns shape organisms. To understand this it is useful to think of genetic diversity as occurring at four levels: among species, among populations, among individuals within a population, and within individuals. The first level, among species, simply recognizes that the differences that separate species have a genetic basis. Genetic diversity at the second level, among populations, can be quite substantial too. Consider the manifold shapes, sizes, and colors of dogs or squashes. These differences often allow different populations of the same species to occupy a wider range of environments than a single population could: for example by having different tolerances to temperature extremes. At the third level, differences among individuals are the primary basis for natural selection and thus are critical in allowing a species to evolve and persist in response to environmental change. Finally, within an individual, genetic diversity exists whenever there are two alleles for the same gene: for example an allele for red flowers and an allele for white flowers. Differences at the allele level are the basis for quantifying genetic diversity as we will see in Chapter 14.

The diversity of ecosystems is apparent to even the most casual observer of the natural world: forests, meadows, lakes, lagoons, and so on. Nevertheless, ecosystems can be difficult to define. We might readily agree that a forest 90% dominated by oaks is a different type of ecosystem from a forest 90% dominated by pines, but is an oak–pine forest 60% dominated by oaks different from a pine–oak forest 60% dominated by pines? Out on the ground, how do you decide just where the red maple forest ends and the red maple swamp begins? One might arrive at a reasonable definition based on hydrology or the distribution of certain plants, but what about all those animals that will move back and forth across any arbitrary boundary? Defining ecosystems can be a rather arbitrary exercise, but this does not make it invalid. There are real patterns to the distributions of organisms across various physical environments, and defining ecosystems is a way of organizing our understanding of these patterns. We will return to another issue that confounds defining ecosystems – spatial scale – in the next chapter.

This discussion of biodiversity has placed a heavy emphasis on the structure of life on earth and said little about all the processes that maintain life. Of course these are inseparable and thus any complete discussion of biodiversity must recognize the extraordinary diversity of ecological and evolutionary processes. These processes far outnumber the structural elements of biodiversity because they include the evolution of every species, all the ecological interactions among species, and myriad ecosystem and genetic processes. Nevertheless, conservationists tend to focus their actions on the structural elements of biodiversity rather than the processes because it is usually simpler to do so. Note that some ecologists split the structural aspects of ecosystems into two parts: composition (chiefly the species that constitute the ecosystem) and structure (dominant physical features such as tall trees and logs).

MEASURING AND MISMEASURING BIODIVERSITY

Imagine that you were asked to compare the impacts on biodiversity of clearcuts and shelterwood cuts. Our simple conceptual definition of biodiversity would be of limited value for this task. You would want to make quantitative comparisons of a series of clearcuts and shelterwood cuts and this would require both volumes of data and a quantitative definition of biodiversity. Both of these are problematic.

	Described Species	Estimated Species Richness
Viruses	4,000	400,000
Bacteria	4,000	1,000,000
Fungi	72,000	1,500,000
Protozoa	40,000	200,000
Algae	40,000	400,000
Plants	270,000	320,000
Arthropods	1,065,000	8,9000,000
Other animals	255,000	900,000

Fig. 1.2. Roughly 1.7 million species have been described by scientists, with arthropods, primarily insects, constituting almost half this number. The estimated number of species is far greater, especially for smaller life forms. The data presented here are summarized from table 3.1–2 of Heywood and Watson 1995.

First, gathering data on the elements of biodiversity is no easy task. Yes, we can readily survey species of vascular plants and most vertebrates, but from here on the task becomes quite difficult. From a global perspective the difficulties are apparent when you compare the number of species that have been described, about 1.7 million, to the gross estimates of the number of species that exist, from 10 million to 100 million (Wilson 1992) (Figure 1.2). Locally, no one has done a complete inventory for even a single forest ecosystem, and they are not likely to any time soon given the unknowns of microbe taxonomy (Torsvik *et al.* 1990). In contrast, ecosystems are easy to survey but you do have to resolve the issue of how to define them first. In terms of genetic diversity, technology is improving all the time, but to date we have described the complete genome of only a few species of bacteria (Fraser *et al.* 1995).

Moving to the second problem, quantitative definitions of biodiversity do exist and are commonly used, but they are often misleading in a conservation context. (See Box 1.1 for the basic ideas behind diversity indices.)

BOX 1.1 **Measuring diversity**

In Table 1.1, ecosystem A is easily recognized as more diverse than B or C because it has four tree species instead of three. This characteristic is called *species richness* or just *richness* and it is sometimes used as a simple measure of diversity. There is a second component of diversity called *evenness* that is based on the relative abundance of different species. In Table 1.1 ecosystem C is more diverse than B because in C the three species have similar levels of abundance, or high evenness. The concept of evenness is not as intuitively obvious as the idea of richness. Think of a jury that has five women and five men versus one that has nine women and one man; the five plus five jury is more diverse because it is more even.

Table 1.1. *Abundance of species (number/hectare) in three ecosystems and measures of richness, evenness, and the Shannon diversity index (H)*

Ecosystem	A	B	C
Black oak	40	120	80
White pine	30	60	60
Red maple	20	2	60
Yellow birch	10		
Richness	4	3	3
Evenness	0.92	0.88	0.99
H	0.56	0.39	0.47

Notes:
$H = -\Sigma p_i \log p_i$ where p_i is a measure of the importance of the ith species.
Evenness $= H/H_{max}$ where H_{max} is the maximum possible value of H.

Richness and evenness are often combined into a single index of diversity using mathematical formulas such as the Shannon index shown in Table 1.1. Sometimes they are both plotted together on a graph to represent diversity patterns visually. Diversity indices are commonly used to quantify the species diversity of ecosystems and occasionally used to quantify the ecosystem diversity of landscapes. For more information on quantifying diversity see Magurran (1988).   Adapted from Hunter (1996a)

It is easiest to use an example to explain why diversity indices can lead you astray if your goal is maintaining biodiversity. Imagine that you were managing a longleaf pine (Pinus palustris) stand in the southeastern United States and you decided that you wanted to do something beneficial for biodiversity. You might decide that by modifying the fire regime you could encourage various species of oaks to grow in the stand. Not only would you increase your species richness with oaks, but you would also gain many animal species associated with oaks, several insects and a few vertebrates. However, at least one species is likely to disappear from the stand the red-cockaded woodpecker (Picoides borealis): a species at risk of extinction (Walters 1991). Red-cockaded woodpeckers avoid stands with a midstory of hardwood trees, perhaps because these stands attract southern flying squirrel (Glaucomys volans) which may usurp nesting cavities from the woodpeckers. In this case increasing the diversity of longleaf pine stands at the local scale could lead to diminishing global diversity, and conservationists would argue that this is a very poor trade.

A generic example can be found almost everywhere there is a large tract of old forest. Some people will argue that clearcutting a portion of this forest will create new habitat for a whole suite of species that require an early successional stage and thereby increase the overall diversity of the tract. This is usually true but there is another side to the story. In most regions of the world, large tracts of old forest have become very uncommon, along with the species that need these old forests. In contrast, early successional species are often quite common in these regions. Consequently, converting late successional habitat to early successional habitat in such a region is likely to decrease the diversity of the region by lowering evenness (i.e., making common species more abundant and uncommon species rarer) and possibly reducing richness (if some late successional species disappear from the region for lack of habitat).

The bottom line here is that when evaluating the effects of management on biodiversity we need to take a large-scale perspective. Conservationists often speak of 'maintaining gamma diversity' or 'protecting global biodiversity' to make this point. (See Figure 1.3 for an explanation of scales of diversity.) When biodiversity conservation at a local scale is viewed in a large-scale context there are only two basic goals: (a) to maintain the biodiversity of ecosystems that are in a reasonably natural condition, and (b) to restore the biodiversity of ecosystems that have been degraded. We need to be wary of applying verbs such as 'increase' and 'enhance' to biodiversity for they often indicate a small-scale focus that may not be desirable in the

Fig. 1.3. Whittaker (1960) described three scales at which diversity occurred: alpha, beta, gamma – A, B, C in Greek. Alpha diversity is the diversity that exists within a habitat. In this figure two hypothetical moth species, spotted moths and banded moths, illustrate alpha diversity by coexisting in the same forest, living at different heights within the forest. A third species, speckled moths, illustrates beta diversity (among habitats diversity) by occurring in a nearby field. Finally, if you imagine spotted, banded, and speckled moths living on one island, and a fourth species, gray moths, living a thousand kilometers away on another island, this would represent gamma diversity, or geographic scale diversity.

big picture; indeed a verb like 'maximize' raises the spectre of importing exotic species (Hunter 1996a).

Why is biodiversity important?

'Variety is the spice of life' and it seems intuitive that diversity is generally a good thing. Nevertheless it is not hard to find some people who doubt the necessity of maintaining biodiversity: 'Who cares about yellow-bellied sapsuckers and hairy-nosed wombats!' or 'That swamp is nothing but a festering pit of snakes and mosquitoes!' The most fundamental response to such exhortations is a philosophical and moral one. Many people believe that every species has a right to exist because it has *intrinsic value*, value that is completely independent of its usefulness to people or any other species (Callicott 1990). It has value simply because it is a part of life. Even an ecosystem may have intrinsic value. This idea is easier to embrace if you accept a synergistic view of ecosystems (i.e., ecosystems are much more than the sum of their parts) but even in a reductionist view of ecosystems one might think of an ecosystem's intrinsic value as a summation of all the intrinsic values of its constituent species. The concept of intrinsic value is not universally accepted (Hargrove 1989). Far easier to accept is the idea of *instrumental values*, that a species' or ecosystem's value is measured by how useful it is. In the next seven sections we will outline some types of instrumental value.

ECONOMIC VALUES

'Money makes the world go round', and the instrumental values of biodiversity are easiest to grasp when we think about things that are bought and sold. In the language of economics these are the elements of biodiversity that provide goods and services that are traded in the market place. First and foremost is food; everything we eat is derived from a living organism except for salt and a few other additives. Of course most of our food comes from domestic species and agricultural ecosystems, but these too are part of biodiversity and derived from wild species. It is also surprising how directly important wild species and natural or semi-natural ecosystems are. In many parts of the world, rural people consume significant quantities of fruits, nuts, game, etc. gathered from the wild, and even the most urban urbanite is likely to eat seafood prepared from wild species.

Medicines are one of the favorite topics of biodiversity advocates because so many of our drugs are derived from a diverse array of organisms. Most of the world's people live in developing nations where about 80% of the population relies primarily on herbal medicines (Farnsworth 1988); in the United States about 41% of medicines have an active ingredient derived from an organism (Oldfield 1984). More importantly, it is widely recognized that there is an enormous potential for finding important new medicines among all the species (the large majority) that have not been tested for their pharmacological traits. The best known example in forestry circles comes from the Pacific yew (*Taxus brevifolia*), a tree of virtually no commercial value, until taxol, a chemical extracted from its bark, was found to be a promising treatment for ovarian and breast cancer (Joyce 1993).

When we think of the economic value of biodiversity in forest ecosystems, wood and its uses for fuel, fiber, and building material are always prominent. Some of these values are quite species-specific (e.g., guitar makers consider the acoustic qualities of Brazilian rosewood [Dalbergia nigra] to be unique) while others are rather general (e.g., virtually any tree species is a reasonably suitable source of fuel). Outdoor recreation is also a very big business with people spending billions of dollars to enjoy time in diverse ecosystems, often seeking interactions with particular species through hobbies like hunting, fishing, and birdwatching (USFWS 1993). Some hobbies based on biodiversity are pursued closer to home like gardening, keeping tropical fish, and collecting shells or butterfly stamps, but still can involve sizable sums of money.

SPIRITUAL VALUES

People love life, a phenomenon called 'biophilia' (Wilson 1984). They love interacting with diverse species; they love being in ecosystems where the hand of humanity is absent or hard to detect. Sometimes these relationships are revealed in our recreational spending but often they are not. They may be evident in the biotic symbols we choose to represent our nations, religions, and sports teams, or to decorate our jewelry and T-shirts. There are many people who care deeply about the forests of Amazonia even though they have never been there and never will. They derive pleasure out of just knowing that these forests exist; such feelings are called *existence values*. These values are often overlooked because they are difficult to measure, but they are very real and potentially very important. People who hold these spiritual values can have a significant impact when they act to protect what they cherish; witness the success of environmental groups like the World Wide Fund for Nature.

SCIENTIFIC AND EDUCATIONAL VALUES

Whether it is children understanding the cycles of reproduction by raising tadpoles from frog eggs, or early engineers being stimulated to fly by watching birds, life on earth is a rich lode of inspiration and information for science and education. Science and education are two of the most important arenas for improving the well-being of people. To take one example, imagine the current state of medicine and agriculture without our understanding of genetics and evolution. This understanding is due in part to finches in the Galapagos, peas in an Austrian monastery, and fruit flies in labs all over the world.

ECOLOGICAL VALUES

'Biodiversity has ecological value' may seem like the ultimate truism but there are some interesting complexities here. First, although every species in an ecosystem may have its particular ecological role, it does not follow that all of these roles are of equal importance. For example, while recognizing that an uncommon species of bark-dwelling lichen may have a special role in an oak forest ecosystem, most ecologists would be ready to say that the oaks are more important because of their greater biomass. Species that are important because of their great abundance or biomass are called *dominant species*. Furthermore, ecologists recognize that some species have a greater ecological impact than you would predict from their abundance or biomass (Power *et al.* 1996). For example, if the removal of barred owls (*Strix varia*) from a forest led to a population explosion of rodents, and this led to overconsumption of tree seeds and a failure of tree regeneration, we would refer to the owls as a *keystone species*. Beavers (*Castor* spp.), which profoundly shape streams, forests, and wetlands by building dams, are a great example of a keystone species (further details will be covered in Chapter 13).

The importance of biodiversity is also tied to an old controversy: the relationship between ecosystem stability and ecosystem diversity (Pimm 1991). Is a diverse ecosystem more likely to be stable, or conversely is a stable ecosystem more likely to be diverse? Or is there no relationship between the two? Some experimental evidence suggests that indeed, an ecosystem with many species is more likely to be stable (Tilman and Downing 1994). To understand one plausible mechanism think about a natural disturbance that removed some species from an ecosystem. A diverse ecosystem might be little changed by this loss because other species with similar ecological niches may perform most of the functions of the missing species. Although the details of the relationship between ecosystem diversity and stability require much more research, most ecologists would not argue with the basic truth of a metaphor proposed by Paul and Anne Ehrlich (1981). Imagine that you were flying in a plane and looked out the window just as a rivet fell out of the wing. You might not be too panicked because there are many thousands of rivets holding a plane together and several could fall out without threatening the plane. Nevertheless at some point, if enough rivets fell out, a catastrophe would ensue. Similarly, the loss of a few species may not jeopardize an ecosystem, especially if they were not keystone or dominant species, but at some point loss of species has to jeopardize the overall structure and function of an ecosystem.

STRATEGIC VALUES

Professional conservationists often aggressively exploit certain species and ecosystems to advance their overall conservation goals. Of course this exploitation is usually benign and indirect. The clearest manifestations are all the posters, calendars, T-shirts, and other propaganda that bear the images of eagles, whales, rainforests, and so on. Conservationists call the charismatic species that win the hearts and purses of the general public, *flagship species*. A similar concept, *umbrella species*, refers to the idea that some species have such broad habitat requirements and large home ranges that if you protect their populations you will inevitably protect many other elements of biodiversity as well. The consummate example of an umbrella species is the tiger (*Panthera tigris*), which require large tracts of forests ranging from wet tropical forests in southern India to boreal forests in eastern Russia. Finally, *indicator species* are used to monitor the state of the environment as a whole; for example, lichen populations are often monitored to keep track of air pollution.

REALIZED VERSUS POTENTIAL VALUES

Discussions of instrumental values almost always focus on what is useful here and now, but this is very shortsighted given the enormity of our ignorance. Millions of species have not even been identified, let alone assayed for their potential values. Who would have guessed that the Pacific yew would become of such great interest to pharmacologists? In the face of all that we do not know about the potential, future values of biodiversity it is critical to follow one of the favorite mottos of biodiversity advocates: keep options alive. We can never say of any species that it lacks value.

GENETIC DIVERSITY

Understanding the value of genetic diversity requires a different perspective because basically genes are just chemicals that have no value in and of themselves. Genes have value only because of what they do – control the structure and function of life – rather than what they are. The value of genetic diversity will be covered in Chapter 14; for now it will be sufficient to make three main points. First, the world is constantly changing and this requires species to evolve if they are to survive. Genetic diversity (as expressed through variability in the fitness of different individuals) is one of the basic prerequisites for evolution. Second, populations that lack genetic diversity are likely to suffer from a lack of fitness. Third, genetic diversity can allow a variety of instrumental values to be obtained from the same species. Our domestic species provide many wonderful examples of this: for example, horses bred for racing, cattle herding, or logging.

THE HISTORY OF BIODIVERSITY

To round out our discussion of why biodiversity is important we need to take an historical perspective. People who question the importance of maintaining endangered species often do this, pointing out that extinction is a natural process and that therefore we should not worry about the imminent loss of many species. It is true that about 99.9% of all the species that have ever lived on earth are now extinct and one can reasonably assume that all existing species will become extinct eventually too (Raup 1991). Furthermore, an examination of the fossil record (Figure 1.4) indicates that the overall number of species has been increasing quite steadily – but not absolutely steadily. Close examination of Figure 1.4 reveals a good news–bad news story. The good news is the overall rise of species richness despite some periods (e.g., 245 million years ago) when the number of species dropped dramatically. The bad news is that after each of these episodes of mass extinction it has taken tens of millions of years to recover as new species have evolved (Jablonski 1995). Most conservation biologists believe that we are in the midst of another episode of mass extinction generated by humans. For example, Pimm *et al.* (1995) estimated that the current rate of species extinction is about 1000 times greater than the normal, background rate of extinction. If this is true, none of us, or our children, or our great, great, great . . . great grandchildren is likely to see a recovery. This is a gloomy prospect but we can work to slow the tide of extinction and that is one of the major aspirations of this book.

Biological integrity, ecosystem integrity, and sustainability

'Biodiversity' is not the only term that has waxed strongly in the language of natural resource managers in recent years: 'sustainability', 'eco-

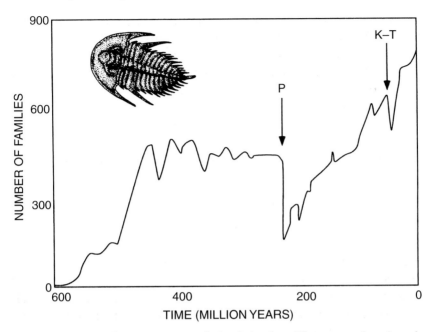

Fig. 1.4. The number of species in existence during the last 600 million years can be estimated using the fossil record and an index based on the number of families of marine organisms. (Marine organisms at the family level are used because their fossil record is likely to be relatively complete.) The overall trend is upward but there have been at least five major extinction events that have led to a recovery period of over 10 million years. (Reproduced from Hunter 1996a; redrawn from Sepkoski 1982; reproduced with permission of Blackwell Science, Inc.)

system integrity', 'biological integrity', and similar terms are also prominent now. In this section we will attempt to clarify the linkages and differences between these terms and biodiversity because this is fundamental to understanding how and why this book focuses on biodiversity.

BIOLOGICAL INTEGRITY

Biological or biotic integrity is a term that is well known among people who manage aquatic ecosystems and it is gaining currency among terrestrial resource managers as well. It refers to the completeness or wholeness of a biological system, including presence of all the elements at appropriate densities and occurrence of all the processes at appropriate rates (Angermeier and Karr 1994). Clearly there is a great deal of similarity between this concept and biodiversity. Perhaps the biggest difference is that biological integrity explicitly includes biological processes whereas in many definitions of biodiversity these are only implicit. Consequently, a person who was evaluating the status of an ecosystem from a biological integrity perspective would probably be more sensitive to a change in the ecosystem's productivity (to take one example) than would a person who was focusing on biodiversity. A biological integrity perspective might also be less vulnerable to some of the misunderstandings about biodiversity described earlier in this chapter. For example, no one would ever claim that they had increased biological integrity by adding an exotic species to an eco-system. Although biological integrity is a broader, more encompassing concept, under some circumstances focusing on biodiversity rather than integrity would be advantageous. For example, a person who was judging the integrity of an ecosystem would be likely to focus on the ecosystem's key species and processes and might overlook the disappearance of a rare species. The well-being of rare things – species, ecosystems, and sometimes genes – is always in the spotlight from a biodiversity perspective. In sum, the difference here is primarily a matter of emphasis with biotic integrity emphasizing the overall balance and completeness of biological systems and biodiversity emphasizing that all the biotic elements are present.

ECOSYSTEM INTEGRITY

Next we find a cluster of four terms that differ by shades: ecosystem health, ecosystem integrity, ecological health, and ecological integrity. Both 'ecosystem' and 'ecological' imply a relationship between communities of organisms and their physical environments: chiefly water, air, soil, and climate. 'Health' and 'integrity', as used in these terms, are nearly synonymous as well, although 'health' tends to emphasize the absence of any signs of ecosystem distress. 'Health' is an easier concept to grasp because everyone has a personal understanding of the difference between being healthy and unhealthy (Rapport 1989, 1995). On the other hand, the analogy between human health and ecosystem health can be misleading (to take just one example, an ecosystem that is profoundly affected by a native pathogen is not necessarily unhealthy) (Suter 1993, De Leo and Levin 1997) and thus 'integrity' may be the preferred word. For simplicity's sake we will use 'ecosystem integrity' as a synonym for all four terms.

There is a substantial link between the concepts of biodiversity and eco-system integrity; for example, any assessment of an ecosystem's integrity should include an appraisal of its biological diversity. However, there are some key differences too. These are easiest to explain by building on the differences between biotic integrity and biodiversity described in the preceding section. In one important way, ecosystem integrity is broader than biological integrity because it encompasses the physical environment. Soil erosion and sedimentation, for example, are primarily physical processes that are directly part of ecosystem integrity but only linked, albeit strongly sometimes, to biological integrity. On the other hand, in theory the concept of biotic integrity is broader because it includes genes and evolutionary processes that are quite tangential to ecosystem structure and function. In practice, the biotic integrity concept is usually applied to ecosystems and only rarely to genetic systems.

In sum, a person who is evaluating ecosystem integrity will focus on the biological and physical structures and processes of ecosystems, and biodiversity is a critical component of this array. That same person will probably not address any of the genetic issues that are part of biodiversity, and like the person focusing on biotic integrity, may overlook the rare species within an ecosystem.

SUSTAINABILITY

In its most general form, 'sustainability' is simply the ability to maintain something over a period of time without diminishing it (Lélé and Norgaard 1996). In a natural resource management context, the main goal for many people is to sustain the availability of resources that are important to the well-being of humanity: timber, water, recreational opportunities, and so on. The technical term here is 'intergenerational equity', or in plainer language, not messing things up for our children and grandchildren. For people who are less centered on human needs, the goal is to sustain biological structures and processes (which may or may not be of direct economic value to people). For this latter group, sustaining biodiversity will always be a major goal, perhaps their primary goal. For the former group, sustaining biodiversity will be important to the extent that it is tied to sustaining natural resources as described in the section 'Why is biodiversity important?' Some people are reluctant to focus on sustainability because it implies that the status quo is satisfactory; many conservationists would argue that we should be restoring ecosystems to a previous state, one less degraded by humans. A focus on sustainability can also be misleading if we fail to recognize that most ecosystems are highly dynamic, and that this dynamism should form a background against which we seek sustainability. In other words, ecosystems are always changing and thus our goals for them must be flexible to some degree (Chapin *et al.* 1996).

VALUES

Differences in people's values are clearly reflected in their ideas about what should be the focus of sustainability. It is also true, but less obvious, that the ways we evaluate biological integrity and ecosystem integrity are also shaped by values (Lackey 1995, Lélé and Norgaard 1996, De Leo and Levin 1997). Proponents of the biological integrity concept are quite explicit that their ideas about 'all appropriate elements and occurrence of all processes at appropriate rates' are based on using natural systems as benchmarks, i.e., those with little or no human influence (Angermeier and Karr 1994, Hunter 1996b). For example, they would decide whether or not a particular species of trout belongs in a given lake by whether or not it would be there without human intervention. This is a reasonable standard that many biologists would share, but there is nothing sacred about using a natural system as the basis for comparison. Indeed ecologists who write about ecosystem integrity often appear willing to accept alternative benchmarks (Rapport 1989). For example, Robert Lackey (1995) has argued that 'An undiscovered tundra lake and an artificial lake at Disneyland can be equally healthy'; for him the key question is whether or not the lake is in a desired state. In other words, is it satisfying human expectations? Of course values or expectations differ dramatically from one person to the next as witnessed by the strife of environmental politics. The bottom line is that to use any of these concepts – including biodiversity – requires some kind of benchmark and the selection of benchmarks inevitably reflects human values.

Summary

Biodiversity refers to the diversity of life in all its forms (animals, plants, fungi, and microorganisms) and at all levels of organization (genes, species, and ecosystems). The complexity of biodiversity makes it a conceptual entity, virtually impossible to define quantitatively in its entirety. Limited components of biodiversity can be measured (for example the number of vascular plant species found in a given ecosystem and their relative abundance or evenness), but these measures of diversity can be profoundly misleading if your goal is to maintain biodiversity. For example, introducing exotic plant species could increase the species richness of a given ecosystem but diminish regional biodiversity if the exotic plants reduced the abundance of rare native plants.

The importance of biodiversity can be understood most readily in terms of instrumental values: the utility that species, ecosystems, and genes have because of the vast array of goods and services that they provide. Many of these goods and services have direct economic impacts but some, such as ecological, spiritual, and aesthetic values, do not. Many conservationists also accept the idea that species and ecosystems have intrinsic value, value independent of their usefulness.

The goal of maintaining biodiversity is closely related to some other goals such as maintaining ecosystem or biotic integrity, or assuring sustainability of natural resource management, but there are some key differences. Maintaining ecosystem integrity is a broader concept that largely subsumes maintaining biodiversity; it also includes biogeochemical cycling, hydrologic regimes, and other features that are tangential to biodiversity. Maintaining biological integrity and maintaining biodiversity are similar undertakings; the primary difference is in emphasis. A biological integrity approach focuses on maintaining the natural species composition and processes of ecosystems whereas retaining the complete array of species is often the emphasis of a biodiversity approach. Sustainability highlights the idea that current use of natural resources should not diminish the options of future generations, and maintaining biodiversity is clearly one of the requirements for meeting this goal.

Further readings

Many of the ideas presented here about what biodiversity is and why it is important have been distilled from longer treatments in two books (Hunter 1990, 1996a). See the *Global Biodiversity Assessment* (Heywood and Watson 1995) for a massive treatment on biodiversity and DeLong (1996) for a review of definitions of biodiversity. Costanza *et al.* 1992 is a good compilation of papers on ecosystem health.

Literature cited

Angermeier, P. L., and J. R. Karr. 1994. Biological integrity versus biological diversity as policy directives. *BioScience* **44**:690–7.

Callicott, J. B. 1990. Whither conservation ethics? *Conservation Biology* **4**:15–20.

Chapin, F. S. III, M. S. Torn, and M. Tateno. 1996. Principles of ecosystem sustainability. *American Naturalist* **148**:1016–37.

Costanza, R., B. G. Norton, and B. D. Haskell (eds). 1992. *Ecosystem Health.* Island Press, Washington, DC. 269 pp.

De Leo, G. A., and S. Levin. 1997. The multifaceted aspects of ecosystem integrity. *Conservation Ecology* [online] 1(1): 3. URL: http://www.consecol.org/vol1/iss1/art3

DeLong, D. C., Jr. 1996. Defining biodiversity. *Wildlife Society Bulletin* 24:738–49.

Ehrlich, P., and A. Ehrlich. 1981. *Extinction.* Random House, New York. 305 pp.

Farnsworth, N.R. 1988. Screening plants for new medicines. Pp. 83–97 in E. O. Wilson and F. M. Peter (eds). *Biodiversity.* National Academy Press, Washington D.C. 521 pp.

Fraser, C. M. *et al.* 1995. The minimal gene complement of *Mycoplasma genitalium. Science* 270:397–403.

Hargrove, E. C. 1989. An overview of conservation and human values: are conservation goals merely cultural attitudes? Pp. 227–31 in D. Western, and M.C. Pearl (eds). *Conservation for the Twenty-first Century.* Oxford University Press, New York. 365 pp.

Heywood, V. H., and R. T. Watson (eds). 1995. *Global Biodiversity Assessment.* Cambridge University Press, Cambridge. 1140 pp.

Hunter, M. L., Jr. 1990. *Wildlife, Forests, and Forestry: Principles of Managing Forests for Biological Diversity.* Prentice-Hall, Englewood Cliffs, New Jersey. 370 pp.

1996a. *Fundamentals of Conservation Biology.* Blackwell Science, Cambridge, Massachusetts, 482 pp.

1996b. Benchmarks for managing ecosystems: are human activities natural? *Conservation Biology* 10:695–7.

Jablonski, D. 1995. Extinctions in the fossil record. Pp. 25–44 in: J. H. Lawton and R. M. May (eds). *Extinction Rates.* Oxford University Press, Oxford. 233 pp.

Joyce, C. 1993. Taxol: search for a cancer drug. *BioScience* 43:133–6.

Lackey, R. T. 1995. Ecosystem health, biological diversity, and sustainable development: research that makes a difference. *Renewable Resources Journal* 13(2):8–13.

Lélé, S., and R. B. Norgaard. 1996. Sustainability and the scientist's burden. *Conservation Biology* 10:354–65.

Magurran, A. E. 1988. *Ecological Diversity and its Measurement.* Princeton University Press, Princeton, New Jersey. 179 pp.

Oldfield, M. L. 1984. *The Value of Conserving Genetic Resources.* U.S. Department of the Interior, National Park Service, Washington, D.C. 360 pp. (Republished by Sinauer in 1989.)

Pimm, S. L. 1991. *The Balance of Nature?* University of Chicago Press, Chicago. 434 pp.

Pimm, S. L., G. J. Russell, J. L. Gittleman, and T. M. Brooks. 1995. The future of biodiversity. *Science* 269:347–50.

Power, M. E., D. Tilman, J. A. Estes, B. A. Menge, W. J. Bond, L. S. Mills, G. Daily, J. C. Castilla, J. Lubchenko, and R. T. Paine. 1996. Challenges in the quest for keystones. *BioScience* 46:609–20.

Rapport, D. J. 1989. What constitutes ecosystem health? *Perspectives in Biology and Medicine* **33**:121–32.

  1995. Ecosystem health: an emerging integrative science. Pp. 5–31 in Rapport, D. J., C. L. Gaudet, and P. Calow (eds). *Evaluating and Monitoring the Health of Large-scale Ecosystems.* Springer-Verlag, Berlin. 454 pp.

Raup, D. M. 1991. *Extinction: Bad Genes or Bad Luck?* Norton, New York. 210 pp.

Sepkoski, J. J., Jr. 1982. Mass extinctions in the Phanerozoic oceans: a review. Pp. 283–9 in L. T. Silver, and P. H. Schultz (eds). *Geological implications of impacts of large asteroids and comets on the Earth.* The Geological Society of America Special Paper 190, Boulder, Colorado. 528 pp.

Suter, G. W. II. 1993. A critique of ecosystem health concepts and indexes. *Environmental Toxicology and Chemistry* **12**:1533–9.

Tilman, D., and J. A. Downing. 1994. Biodiversity and stability in grasslands. *Nature* **367**:363–5.

Torsvik, V., J. Goksoyr, and F. L. Daae. 1990. High diversity in DNA of soil bacteria. *Applied and Environmental Microbiology* **56**:782–7.

USFWS (U.S. Fish and Wildlife Service). 1993. *National Survey of Fishing, Hunting, and Wildlife-associated Recreation.* U.S. Government Printing Office, Washington, D.C. 124 pp.

Walters, J. R. 1991. Application of ecological principles to the management of endangered species: the case of the red-cockaded woodpecker. *Annual Review of Ecology and Systematics* **22**:505–23.

Whittaker, R. H. 1960. Vegetation of the Siskiyou Mountains, Oregon and California. *Ecological Monographs* **30**:279–338.

Wilson, E. O. 1984. *Biophilia.* Harvard University Press, Cambridge, Massachusetts. 157 pp.

  1992. *The Diversity of Life.* Harvard University Press, Cambridge, Massachusetts. 424 pp.

2 Principles of ecological forestry

ROBERT S. SEYMOUR AND MALCOLM L. HUNTER, JR.

Ecologically sound stewardship has long been a cornerstone of the forestry profession. But just what does 'ecologically sound' mean in practice? Historically, foresters were often taught that forest ecosystems could be engineered at will for human benefit. Ensuring ecological integrity meant not violating 'constraints' associated with soil, water quality, and wildlife (implicitly defined as well-known birds and mammals). Recently, the definition of ecological integrity has expanded; clearly, a primary focus is now on maintaining, and even restoring, native biological diversity. At the same time, a growing worldwide demand for forest products has encouraged foresters to expand traditional high-yield practices, amidst growing evidence that such systems often conflict with biodiversity.

While not discounting the difficulty of these conflicts, we believe there is a vision of ecological forestry that offers hope. To set the stage for the rest of this book, we define ecosystems, stands, and landscapes. Next, we review various incarnations of forestry, with emphasis on North American practice and the strong influence of the U.S. Forest Service. Hopefully, this will help readers to place the current discussion of ecological forestry into an historical, scientific, and professional context. Important principles of ecological forestry are defined and discussed, and related to traditional timber production forestry. Finally, a balanced forestry paradigm, which blends elements of traditional and ecological forestry, is described.

Ecosystems, stands, and landscapes

Asked to define *ecosystem*, a politician who was espousing the importance of protecting ecosystems hesitated for a long time then finally said, 'Well...they're kind of like an aquarium...they have plants and animals...and other stuff.' In fairness to the politician, ecosystems can be rather hard to define. Ecologists readily construct definitions such as 'a community of interacting species plus the physical environment that they occupy', but, as we saw in Chapter 1, it is not always easy to move from a conceptual definition to defining ecosystems in the real world. Separating a lake and a forest is easy but where do you draw the boundary between a spruce forest ecosystem and a spruce swamp ecosystem? Is a spruce–fir forest that is 80% dominated by spruce (Picea spp.) a different type of ecosystem from one that is 80% dominated by fir (Abies spp.)?

One of the things that makes defining ecosystems particularly difficult is the fact that they can occur at any spatial scale. The examples used above (a forest, a lake, a forested wetland) imply a spatial scale that is commonly used: patches of vegetation that one can easily see from a small plane – patches one would usually measure in hectares, rather than square kilometers or square meters. However, ecosystems can be much smaller or larger. Aquariums are indeed small, artificial ecosystems. One could even argue that all the invertebrates and microorganisms that occupy a single fallen acorn constitute a tiny ecosystem (Winston 1956). On the other hand, we could argue that because all the organisms on earth interact with one another and their physical environment (through global carbon and oxygen cycles for example) that the whole earth is one ecosystem (a concept close to the Gaia hypothesis of James Lovelock, 1979). In recent years there has been a growing tendency, especially among natural resource managers, to define ecosystems at quite large scales, as in the 'Greater Yellowstone Ecosystem' (Mattson and Reid 1991). This tendency can probably be traced to the increasing emphasis on ecosystem management, a key principle of which is thinking at larger spatial scales.

Because ecosystem is a scaleless term we will avoid using it in this book except where the emphasis is on the general concept of ecosystems and not on any particular scale. For patches of forest vegetation that are reasonably homogeneous in terms of species composition, age, and density, we will use the traditional forestry term, stand. Stands are usually defined at scales that make them roughly equivalent to communities (although in fact, community is really a scaleless term like ecosystems) and we will use this as a generic term for forests and non-forests. For the arrays of forest stands, grasslands, wetlands, and so on that form heterogeneous mosaics across the land we will use the term landscape (Forman 1995). In recent years landscape ecology has emerged as an important subdiscipline of ecology that focuses on the ecological patterns and processes that emerge at spatial scales where vegetation is seen as a heterogeneous mosaic (Figure 2.1). The distinction between forest stands and forest landscapes is the basis for delineating two major parts of the book: Part II: The macro approach,

Fig. 2.1. Ecosystems can be defined at many scales; they are often recognized in terms of distinct patches of vegetation such as forest stands, wetlands, fields, etc.

managing forest landscapes; and Part III: The micro approach, managing forest stands.

Different models of forestry

Forestry in the broadest sense involves the science, art, and business of managing forests for human benefit. Forestry began at different times and different places throughout the world as societies' demand for wood outgrew the volumes obtainable by exploiting wild forests (Fernow 1913, Sedjo 1996). The earliest forms of forestry could be characterized as *custodial* (focusing on protecting the forest from overexploitation and fire), usually followed by *sustained yield timber production* (focusing on assuring a continuous supply of timber). More recently, explicit efforts to manage forests for a broad array of resources led to *multiple-use* forestry on many lands, while in other forests intensive efforts to maximize timber production following an agricultural paradigm led to *production* forestry. Some forests continue to be managed *extensively*, with little investment other than protection. Many believe we have entered an era of *ecological* forestry, in which maintenance of ecological integrity will be paramount.

CUSTODIAL FORESTRY

The earliest roots of custodial forestry are obscure but it was no doubt well established in Europe during the middle ages. It took the form of increasingly restrictive laws that limited widespread unsustainable forest exploitation and conversion to agriculture (Fernow 1913, Plochmann 1992). Custodial forestry reached the United States in the late nineteenth century. In the western United States, forests were set aside from the remaining unsettled, unlogged public domain and later these became national forests. In the eastern and Midwestern United States, where lands had largely been logged over, the U.S. Forest Service began to buy them back in strategically chosen watershed protection zones. Custodial management emphasized fire protection, with low harvest levels; silviculture focused on natural regeneration. Planting was limited mainly to restoring trees to severely understocked lands. Owing to limited markets and a strong professional aversion to clearcutting, harvests tended to focus on large trees of valuable species.

The effect of custodial forestry on ecological integrity of public forests was probably mixed. On heavily exploited lands, the strong emphasis on protection and restoration has been undeniably positive. For example, 50–80 years later, many hardwood forests throughout the eastern United States are again beginning to resemble their earlier composition (minus the American chestnut, *Castanea dentata*, that was extirpated by an introduced fungus). Where custodial forestry was applied to old-growth, virgin stands, the focus on removing only large trees may have simplified stand structures, but the overall effect was fairly benign due to low harvest levels.

SUSTAINED-YIELD TIMBER-PRODUCTION FORESTRY

As timber demands increased and unexploited wild forests became scarce, it became clear that management needed to become more sophisticated in order to ensure that harvests could be sustained. Custodial forestry was thus supplanted by sustained-yield timber-production forestry. Key concepts of sustained-yield forestry are rotation (harvest) ages set at the point where average annual yield is maximum (the 'culmination of mean annual increment') and the regulated or 'normal' forest structure with equal areas of age classes up to the rotation age (Sedjo

1996). Although foresters promoting sustained-yield forestry clearly had a strong stewardship ethic, this model tended to predate, at least in Europe, the recognition of ecology as a science (Toumey 1928), and thus was generally devoid of any ecosystem perspectives.

MULTIPLE-USE FORESTRY

It has long been recognized that forests provide more than timber, and should be managed as such. To some extent the origins of managing forests for other resources are very old indeed; certainly European land managers have long been sensitive to the needs of various game species. However, it is only relatively recently that this perspective has been codified in law and pursued scientifically. For example it was in 1960 that U.S. National Forests were mandated to link multiple use with the traditional sustained-yield paradigm in the seminal Multiple Use-Sustained Yield Act. Opinions vary widely on the success and legacy of National Forest management under the Multiple Use-Sustained Yield paradigm; however, most agree that timber tended to remain the dominant output. Other values tended to be viewed as constraints, not equally important objectives (SAF 1993), despite an apparent legislative mandate to maximize social value of both market and non-market values (Krutilla and Haigh 1978, as cited in Sedjo 1996). Generations of foresters were educated under a philosophy that equated forest management with efficient timber production. Indeed, the index of Davis and Johnson's (1986) widely used text, 'Forest Management', refers to 'multiple use' only once (a cryptic paragraph in the introduction about laws governing forestry in the United States).

PRODUCTION SILVICULTURE

The implementation of sustained-yield forestry has become increasingly sophisticated, paralleling scientific advances in forest biology and technology. In the 1960s, just as forest management at the landscape level was equated with timber production, silviculture was often equated with maximizing timber yields at the stand level. Nowhere was this attitude more apparent than in the second paragraph of the influential text, 'The Practice of Silviculture', where David Smith (1962) characterized silviculture as '. . . somewhat analogous to . . . agronomy in agriculture, in that it is concerned with the technical details of crop production.'

'High-yield' silvicultural systems patterned after an agricultural model are common throughout the world. Beginning early in the nineteenth century, German foresters began a widespread and ultimately very effective effort to replace degraded mixed-species forests with conifer plantations, a program which has long been regarded as a national model of forest rehabilitation (Plochmann 1992). In other regions such as the British Isles, Chile, New Zealand, and the southern United States, conifer plantations were established over vast areas of abandoned crop or pasture lands, often with major government subsidies. In the southern United States, 20% of the softwood growing stock and 15% of timberland are now in pine plantations, 55% of which is owned by the forest industry (Rosson 1995). Production silviculture uses intensive practices to achieve high yields of economically valuable, genetically improved species (see Chapter 12). Any non-crop plants are viewed as competition to be controlled, usually by herbicides (Walstad and Kuch 1987). High timber yields demand close control and simplification of naturally diverse plant communities, and thus conflict inherently with promoting stand-level biodiversity.

EXTENSIVE FORESTRY

Another form of forestry has persisted on some private and industrial lands which have not adopted the above models. Often called *extensive* forestry to contrast it with the intensive nature of production forestry, this type of management tends to be characterized by opportunistic timber harvesting driven mainly by product demands. Silviculture usually consists of crude, broad-brush harvesting treatments with little investment in non-commercial treatments. Harvest levels typically are low relative to potentials under intensive management, but can still be non-sustainable relative to the actual (i.e., low or non-existent) level of investment. Allowable cuts are rarely determined with any reliability, however, so its timber sustainability is difficult to assess.

Some environmentalists tolerate or even support extensive forestry because its 'low-budget' approach tends to eschew practices such as clear-cutting and herbicide spraying that they find objectionable. They may not realize that protracted extensive forestry has tended to reduce age diversity (by discriminating against old trees and stands) and to favor aggressive, often early- successional species. Over time, forest regions dominated by multi-cohort stands of valuable late-successional forests may be gradually replaced by younger, single-cohort communities that are neither ecologically well adapted nor economically productive. This conversion can be somewhat insidious, because it happens over time horizons that span human generations and may thus be imperceptible. An example is the red spruce (*Picea rubens*) forests of the Acadian region of northeastern North America: the short-lived, aggressive balsam fir, red maple, and aspen have become increasingly common at the expense of the spruce and long-lived northern hardwoods such as yellow birch and sugar maple (Seymour 1992).

ECOLOGICAL FORESTRY

By the late 1980s widespread dissatisfaction within the forestry profession and scientific community with traditional sustained-yield multiple-use forestry in the United States was publicly manifested in three prominent critiques. In 1989, Jerry Franklin published an influential article in which he argued for a 'New Forestry' on U.S. national forests. A year later, a distinguished panel of forest scientists issued a visionary report calling for a new approach to studying and managing forest ecosystems, distinct from traditional commodity approaches (NRC 1990). Shortly thereafter, another task force of scientists and professionals convened by the Society of American Foresters issued a controversial indictment of traditional sustained-yield forestry, also calling for a revamped, ecologically based approach (SAF 1993).

Only history can judge whether we are witnessing an historic revolution to a profoundly new era of 'ecological forestry', or just an incremental evolution of the multiple-use doctrine. We do not intend to contribute to the lengthy debate about the exact meaning of 'ecological forestry', 'forest ecosystem management', 'new forestry', and similar terms (cf. Grumbine 1994, Irland 1994, Salwasser 1994). We accept their inherently fuzzy nature (More 1996), recognizing that broadly accepted definitions will only come after future implementation by practitioners. We will use the term *ecological forestry* as a collective heading for the concepts and practices which constitute this new brand of forestry.

We do not mean to suggest that sustained-yield forestry and production silviculture are devoid of ecological underpinnings. Clearly, these practices manipulate ecosystems, albeit simplified ones, and ecological processes provide the sideboards that bound silvicultural possibilities. Nor has traditional, timber-oriented silviculture ignored natural stand development processes. The seventh edition of Smith's (1962:6–7) silviculture text captures quite well the attitudes prevailing among American foresters until perhaps a decade ago. Under the heading 'Silviculture as an Imitation of Nature', Smith wrote:

> The fact that [the forester] must know the course of natural succession does not indicate that he should necessarily allow it to proceed. Economic factors ultimately decide the silvicultural policy on any given area; the objective is to operate so that the value of benefits derived... exceeds by the widest possible margin the value of efforts expended.

What distinguishes ecological forestry, as we define it here, is the emphasis placed on natural patterns and processes: understanding them, working in harmony with them, and maintaining their integrity, even when it becomes financially difficult or inconvenient to do so.

In this chapter, we limit our treatment to the *biological* concepts that characterize ecological forestry. We recognize that ecosystem management in the broad sense also involves many administrative and socio-political issues (Grumbine 1994, More 1996) which are dealt with in Part IV of this book. We also recognize, but do not discuss, the prominent ecological role of physiographic factors which govern below-ground processes (hydrology, geology, nutrient cycling) and create above-ground gradients in productivity.

Natural disturbance regimes

It is easy to endorse the premise of sustaining ecological integrity, but just what does this mean in practice? We believe that the central axiom of ecological forestry is that *manipulation of a forest ecosystem should work within the limits established by natural disturbance patterns prior to extensive human alteration of the landscape.* The key assumption here is that native species evolved under these circumstances, and thus that maintaining a full range of similar conditions under management offers the best assurance against losses of biodiversity. This is analogous to the 'coarse-filter' approach (i.e., conserving diverse ecosystems and landscapes), in that it should maintain habitats for the vast majority of species (Hunter *et al.* 1988). With an effective coarse-filter strategy in place, the more costly and information-intensive fine-filter management can be focused on the few species of special concern.

Ecological forestry that maintains an effective coarse filter differs markedly from the 'engineering' approach common under sustained-yield timber management. Under that model, foresters try to define precise objectives for specific ecosystem components (e.g., trees, water, habitat for a particular endangered species) and use sophisticated quantitative methods to determine optimal management strategies. Though it can be considered appropriate for certain narrowly defined problems, we believe that there is a certain arrogance to such an approach to managing forests for biodiversity. It assumes a near-perfect understanding of the ecosystems under management.

EMULATING DISTURBANCES WITH MANAGEMENT

The fact that all forests are profoundly shaped by natural disturbances is now so widely accepted by ecologists and foresters that it is hard to imagine a time when things were otherwise. Yet, only a few decades ago, disturbances were viewed as extraordinary events – unnatural deviations from the normal successional development of equilibrium communities (Chapter 4 in this book, Oliver 1981, Pickett and White 1985, Oliver and Larson 1996). As a consequence, our knowledge of disturbances – along with our ability to use them as a template for managed stands and landscapes – is limited to relatively recent research, unlike the classical scientific underpinnings of sustained-yield forestry, which often go back a century or more.

Ecologists define *disturbances* as 'any relatively discrete event in time that disrupts ecosystem, community, or population structure and changes resources, substrate availability or the physical environment' (Pickett and White 1985). To describe a specific disturbance *regime* and its effect on plant communities, three important parameters must be quantified (Chapter 4 in this book, Pickett and White 1985):

- *return interval*: the average time between occurrences in a given stand. Sometimes this is expressed as the *frequency*, which is simply the inverse of the return interval. For example, a regime with a 50-year return interval means that 2% (the frequency) of the landscape will, on the average, be disturbed in a given year.
- *severity*: the amount of vegetation killed, and the type of growing space made available for new plants, relative to that present before disturbance. A closely related, complementary concept is the *biological legacy* (Hansen *et al*. 1991), or the biomass that survives the disturbance in various forms, ranging from unaffected trees to dead and down material.
- *spatial pattern*: distribution of disturbance effects at various scales, from within-stand to large landscapes.

Important disturbance *agents* include fire, wind, herbivore outbreaks (Attiwill 1994a), as well as floods, avalanches, ice storms, landslides, volcanic eruptions, and glaciers (Oliver and Larson 1996:99–126).

Disturbance parameters often have high variability about average values. When this variability is coupled with many different disturbance

Table 2.1. *Some important forestry decisions typically made with a timber production emphasis but which also have strong ecological underpinnings, with examples*

Stand-level decisions (= silviculture)	Examples
Age structure (of trees in stands)	*single-cohort (= even-aged); multiple-cohort (= uneven-aged).*
Harvest timing	*50-year rotation; 10-year cutting cycle*
Regeneration method	*shelterwood; seed-tree*
Landscape-level decisions (= forest management)	
Annual harvest	*volume control: 200k m³/year* *area control: 300 ha/year*
Age structure (of stands in landscapes)	*areas by 10-year age classes*
Area in production silviculture	*25% of land in strategic timber base*
Area in ecological reserves	*10% of land not managed*
Location of harvest operations	*concentrated or dispersed cutting blocks*

agents operating in the same forest, the potential array of disturbance regimes can seem bewildering, defying meaningful categorization. Nevertheless, even broad groupings can be useful. For example, British Columbia has classified their forests into five broad 'natural disturbance types' (B.C. Ministry of Forests 1995) based largely on the return interval.

Foresters have found it useful to separate major, or *stand-replacing* disturbances, which kill virtually all of the overstory, from minor or *partial* disturbances which leave much of the stand alive (Oliver and Larson 1996: 95). Silviculturists have further subdivided lethal stand-replacing disturbances into *releasing* disturbances that kill the overstory only (releasing understory vegetation) or *severe* disturbances that have progressively more lethal effects on the understory vegetation and forest floor (Smith *et al.* 1997:163–4). Hurricanes are an example of the former, whereas most fires fall into the latter category. Such classifications have long been used by silviculturists to choose appropriate age structures and regeneration methods.

To provide an initial framework for discussion, we have listed some of the most important forestry decisions in terms typically understood by production foresters (Table 2.1). The remainder of this chapter will explain how to use an understanding of natural disturbance regimes when making these decisions. Forestry decisions are typically made at either the stand or landscape scale. In general, stand-level issues involve details of the silvicultural systems employed, whereas landscape-level decisions involve allowable cuts, harvest schedules, and protection strategies.

The next two sections will describe ecological forestry in the context of stand and landscape-level age structure, with their associated silvicultural systems and harvest levels.

Stand-level decisions

CHOOSING THE APPROPRIATE AGE STRUCTURE

The most defining feature of a silvicultural system is the age structure of the stand. Until quite recently, only two alternatives were recognized in North America: even-aged or *single- cohort* stands in which the trees are more or less the same age, and uneven-aged or *multi-cohort* stands which contain at least three distinct age classes (Smith 1986). Until c. 1960, uneven-aged or *selection* silviculture was the prevailing doctrine in North America, in part because clearcutting was still closely associated with exploitative logging, and because planting was limited to old-field reforestation. Then, an abrupt shift to even-aged management occurred, in recognition that many early attempts at selection silviculture had been failures (Seymour et al. 1986) and to implement high-yield silvicultural systems. Much highly polarized debate, both within and outside the forestry profession, has since focused on the merits of two extreme (and uncommon) endpoints of this silvicultural continuum – clearcutting with intensive site preparation and planting of monocultures, versus balanced single-tree selection cutting – ignoring the fact that the most logical silvicultural solutions to forest management problems often lay between (Smith 1972).

Happily, modern American silviculture is diverging from its earlier self-imposed rigidity surrounding the four classical systems of clearcutting, shelterwood, seed tree, and selection. Increasingly, silvicultural systems are viewed as a means of producing a virtually infinite array of stand structures to address an equally varied set of societal objectives (O'Hara et al. 1994). One example is the much wider use of *two-aged* silvicultural systems – essentially variants of even- aged systems where *reserve* trees or *standards* are left after the regeneration period. Although two-aged structures have very old lineage in Europe, actually predating more uniform systems (Troup 1955:121–8), only recently were they 'legitimized' in American terminology (Helms et al. 1994). These systems are treated extensively in two recently published American silviculture texts (Smith et al. 1997, Nyland 1996), and Franklin et al. (1997) feature such variable-retention systems prominently in their discussion of ecologically based harvesting.

An important development with respect to strengthening silviculture's ecological basis has been to use the concept of cohorts to describe silvicultural systems (Oliver and Larson 1996, Smith et al. 1997:22–3), rather than mensurationally based age classes. In silviculture, cohorts are populations of trees that originate after some type of disturbance (natural or silvicultural) that makes growing space available, regardless of whether they differ in age by more than 20% of the rotation. For example, foresters can now speak of growing irregular 'three-cohort' stands without worrying about the fact that such a system might not fit some standard cookbook.

Even-aged silviculture is popular mainly because it is easy and economical to understand and implement, and, in the case of high-yield production forestry, because the specific stand establishment practices require it. It is tempting for overworked foresters to extend these administrative advantages to the treatment of natural stands. Whether this is justified ecologically depends critically upon the interaction of disturbance severity and return interval, relative to the life span of the tree species under management.

Where stand-replacing disturbances have a high probability of occurring within the typical life span of the dominant trees, single- or two-cohort structures best emulate natural patterns. Here, it is extremely important to distinguish disturbances that cause complete overstory mortality – creating true single-cohort stands – from events where a few members of the predisturbance cohort (large legacy trees) survive to form two-cohort structures. Some examples will clarify this distinction.

Single-cohort stands

Prominent examples of truly complete mortality events come from forests of fire-adapted species such as Eucalyptus regnans in southeastern Australia (Attiwill 1994b), boreal forests of spruces and pines (Cogbill 1985), and serotinous-coned conifers such as lodgepole pine (Pinus contorta). In these forests, individual trees usually do not survive the severe crown fires that naturally regenerate these forests, so single-cohort stands accurately emulate natural disturbances, as long as spatial patterns and the percentage of the landscape affected also resemble those of natural disturbances (Hunter 1993).

Other, extremely severe disturbances such as very hot fires in high-fuel situations which consume much of the forest floor (e.g., after an extensive blowdown or insect outbreak), and severe erosional events such as land-slides and volcanic eruptions, also create single-cohort stands, although the stand initiation stage may well extend for many decades. Such events are arguably so rare and so destructive that one would not consciously per-petuate them. In other words, natural forces will produce enough of these without human assistance. However, important silvicultural analogues to these disturbances do exist, in the form of conifer monocultures that pioneer on abandoned agricultural lands. The prominence of this succes-sional pattern in New England a century ago (Whitney 1994), where the only natural analogue would have been the post-glacial environment, tes-tifies to the resiliency of these forest ecosystems. Indeed, these unnatural old-field monocultures have proven to be so productive that high-yield sil-vicultural systems essentially emulate this disturbance regime (Smith et al. 1997:163). Aspen forests in the Lake States, which originated after severe, repeated fires following logging of the old-growth pine, are now valuable enough that foresters consciously perpetuate a severe disturbance regime that was quite uncommon before human exploitation (Johnson 1995).

Two-cohort stands

Often, severe disturbances do not completely eliminate the mature forest. Virtually all the disturbed area regenerates to a new cohort, but

Fig. 2.2. (a) Fire origin lodgepole pine–spruce forest in central Alberta, Canada, showing clearcut blocks with 'islands' of unharvested trees reserved to simulate the natural fire pattern. (Robert Seymour photo)

Fig. 2.2. (b) Reserved patches would eventually develop an old-growth structure like that shown, unlike the matrix which either burns or is harvested on a 80- to 100-year rotation. (Robert Seymour photo)

scattered veterans of the older, predisturbance cohorts remain. Two cases can be distinguished: survival as small patches under a few hectares in size (often too small to be considered separate stands), and survival as scattered, large individual stems. Such living *legacies* can be very important in such obvious ways as seed sources and refugia for recolonization, and very likely serve a myriad other ecosystem functions not fully understood (Chapter 11).

Both fire and stand-replacing windstorms tend to produce patterns in which trees survive in small patches owing to natural fuel breaks, microsite or topographic variation, chance occurrences, and other phenomena. Where such patches are large enough to be considered separate stands, then the disturbed area can be considered a separate single-cohort stand. Smaller patch sizes, however, should be treated as the older of two cohorts and the silvicultural system designed to perpetuate this structure. Here, studies of natural disturbance patterns are extremely valuable as landscape templates. For example, in northern Alberta Eberhart and Woodard (1987) found that fires of 41–200 ha (a typical harvest block) had 0.4 unburned islands per 100 ha, averaging 2.3 ha each. (Islands under 1 ha were not recorded.) Emulating this with a two-cohort 'clearcutting with patchy reserves' silvicultural system would be quite straightforward (Figure 2.2).

Cases where legacy trees tend to occur as individuals include: (a) wildfires in old-growth stands where older trees or certain species have thick bark and thus are more likely to survive the severe fires than others, and (b) insect outbreaks in mixed stands, in which tree species differ in susceptibility. Species exhibiting the first pattern include Scots pine (*Pinus sylvestris*) and coastal Douglas-fir (*Pseudotsuga menziesii*). A well-studied example of the second case is the spruce budworm (*Choristoneura fumiferana*) in the fir–spruce forests of the subboreal region of eastern Canada, in which the budworm periodically defoliates and eventually kills the susceptible mature balsam fir (*Abies balsamea*). Scattered black or white spruces (*Picea mariana, P. glauca*) tend to survive, however, thereby perpetuating a two-cohort structure dominated in numbers by the regenerating fir (Baskerville 1975; Figure 2.3). The exact choice of silvicultural systems here depends on the appropriate silvicultural *regeneration method* (see below) and should recognize the possibility of multiple successional pathways that maintain landscape species diversity (Bergeron and Harvey 1997). For example, one would likely use a 'seed tree with reserves' system for the fire-resistant species that establish after the fire, and a 'shelterwood with reserves' system for the fir–spruce forest that depends on advance regeneration.

Fig. 2.3. Surviving individual white spruce legacy tree in a stand formerly dominated by balsam fir that was completely killed by spruce budworm defoliation during the 1970s outbreak in northern Maine, USA. Though not apparent in the photograph, the stand is well regenerated with advance conifer seedlings. (Robert Seymour photo)

Fig. 2.4. Old-growth ponderosa pine stand in eastern Oregon, USA; different tree sizes represent different cohorts. The preponderance of small trees is an unnatural condition induced by decades of fire suppression. (Robert Seymour photo)

Multi-cohort stands

Where stand-replacing disturbances are very infrequent (several times the life span of the late-successional tree species), but partial, gap-creating disturbances are dominant, then creating multi-cohort structures will most closely emulate this pattern. Multi-cohort structures are also most appropriate in dry conifer forests such as ponderosa pine (*Pinus ponderosa*; Figure 2.4) and inland Douglas-fir, where frequent patchy ground fires continually recruit new cohorts but prevent fuel buildup that would allow crown fires to kill the dominant trees (White 1985, Covington and Moore 1994, Agee 1991).

Some forest types exhibit more complex patterns that tend to grade into two-cohort structures. For example the Acadian forest characterized by the long-lived red spruce tends to develop multi-cohort structures on deep soils, sheltered locations, or in mixture with hardwoods (Figure 2.5). On poorly drained 'flats', however, or where the shorter-lived balsam fir dominates stand composition, chronic windthrow and spruce budworm outbreaks appear to prevent the buildup of more than two or three distinct cohorts (Seymour 1992, Cogbill 1996). Single-cohort structures evidently were quite rare in the presettlement forest, however, as return intervals for

Fig. 2.5. Old-growth multi-cohort stand of red spruce in western Maine, USA. (Robert Seymour photo)

stand-replacing fires and windstorms ranged from 1000 to nearly 2000 years in northern Maine (Lorimer 1977).

Silvicultural literature about the treatment of multi-cohort (formerly uneven-aged) stands historically has emphasized the idealized balanced stand structure, in which a reverse-J-shaped diameter distribution is maintained indefinitely through carefully controlled *selection cuttings* (Nyland 1996, O'Hara 1996). Although common in Swiss mixed conifer forests, successful applications in North America over long time frames are rare and limited mainly to northern hardwood forests (Seymour 1995, Lorimer 1989) and the loblolly–shortleaf pine (*Pinus taeda–P. echinata*) forests on the Crossett Research Forest in Arkansas (Baker *et al.* 1996; Figure 2.6). Many silviculturists (e.g., Smith *et al.* 1997) have long considered the goal of maintaining balanced size or age distributions to be an unduly constraining feature of traditional selection silviculture. More importantly from the standpoint of disturbance regimes, such a finely balanced age structure rarely has a natural analogue. Rather, it serves mainly as a timber management construct aimed at sustaining frequent, equal harvests from individual stands.

Given the popularity of selection cutting among the public and many environmentalists, it is worthwhile to recount why this system became discredited within American forestry circles in about 1960, so that foresters do not reinvent a square wheel in well-meaning attempts to practise ecologically based forestry. Typical misapplications of multi-cohort silviculture are harvests that: (a) remove just large trees; and (b) reduce density uniformly throughout the stand to a level that regenerates a new cohort virtually everywhere instead of in discrete gaps. These practices usually result from financial pressures to cut too many large trees; few natural analogues for such a disturbance pattern exist (Lorimer 1989). Such cuttings actually are a crude form of two-cohort silviculture; they differ from the previous examples by virtue of the fact that the older cohort is represented by numerous medium-size trees rather than a few larger ones. Often short-sighted management causes such 'selective' cuttings (*sensu* Nyland 1996:502–8) to be repeated more frequently than the natural disturbance intervals, each time discriminating heavily against the oldest or largest trees. The unfortunate result is typically a reduction in age, size, and species diversity, with the cohort structures becoming more uniform over time and economically valuable species being lost.

Importance of legacy trees

The distinctions among different naturally occurring age structures highlight the point that vegetation (living and dead) that survives the dis-

Fig. 2.6. Multi-cohort stand of loblolly and shortleaf pines that has been under selection management since the 1930s, Crossett Experimental Forest, Arkansas, USA. (Robert Seymour photo)

turbance is the critical issue in creating the appropriate silvicultural analogue. To be ecologically justified, disturbance mimicry must be more than superficial; it cannot be applied selectively just where it happens to suit some timber-management purpose but ignored where it is inconvenient or costly. For example, too often in the past, foresters have endorsed complete clearcutting as emulating all kinds of severe natural disturbances, even though this argument is valid only in certain specific cases of truly lethal mortality events. In other cases where cuttings were not complete, reserve trees were chosen not because they resembled those that would have survived natural disturbances, but simply because they were too small. Because the large Douglas-firs and pines that survive disturbances invariably are the most valuable trees in the stand, serious conflicts can arise between financial demands and ecological integrity.

Dead trees are just as important to retain as part of the biological legacy as are living ones (Chapter 10). In fact, a very important reason for reserving mature, living individuals is to ensure that during the next generation of the young cohort, there will be a continual supply of large dead trees for cavities and other habitat (Woodley and Forbes 1997). As such, reserve trees may have merit even in otherwise very artificial systems such as high-yield plantations.

An excellent illustration of the dangers of overly superficial mimicry comes from Hutto's (1995) study of bird communities in 34 post-fire sites in western Montana and Wyoming. Hutto noted that recent U.S. Forest Service 'green retention' practices, which leave scattered living lodgepole pines after clearcutting but destroy most standing dead stems, do not emulate natural patterns as well as complete clearcuts that leave all standing dead snags. To emulate natural fire regimes in this forest, Hutto advocated leaving some living trees then killing them after harvest with a prescribed fire, in order to ensure adequate nesting and foraging habitat for certain birds that depend on this particular post-fire structure.

HARVEST TIMING

Rotations for single and two-cohort stands

Where stand-replacing disturbances dominate and single- or two-cohort stands are the prevailing structure, foresters must decide how long the stands will be allowed to develop between regeneration harvests – the rotation. Under sustained-yield timber management, rotations are set using biophysical or economic criteria that maximize commodity outputs or present net worth (Davis and Johnson 1986). It is rare to encounter a forest where this is actually done routinely, however, due to unbalanced age structures, mill demands, and other overriding factors. If the forest composition is simple and a single disturbance agent predominates, then ecologically based rotations clearly depend on the disturbance return interval. Because this is largely an issue of setting an appropriate age structure at the landscape scale, it will be discussed later under that heading.

In situations where multiple disturbance agents affect forests of mixed species with very different natural life spans, it is a gross oversimplification to view the rotation as a single number. A variety of species may initiate during the same year after a severe stand-replacing disturbance, but these same species will reach their average life spans at different times, perhaps centuries apart. Community composition will thus naturally vary, until all pioneering individuals die off and autogenic succession takes over, or another stand-replacing disturbance occurs. This initial floristics view of plant succession (Egler 1954) has been widely adopted by silviculturists as a model of natural development for stratified, mixed-species stands (Oliver and Larson 1996, Smith et al. 1997:164).

If species mature at very different rates in the same stand, a single rotation – i.e., removing most or all of the stand in a single regeneration cutting – is clearly inappropriate. If the rotation is based on the shorter-lived members of the community, later-successional individuals may never reach maturity, and the next generation community composition will be simplified in favor of the early-successional species. North America has numerous examples of forests that have been profoundly altered by unusually severe stand-replacing disturbances at unnaturally short intervals. The original pine forests of the Lake States that are now largely dominated by aspen (Populus tremuloides), and the northern hardwood–hemlock (Tsuga) forests of the Allegheny plateau in Pennsylvania that are now cherry–maple (Prunus–Acer) forests, are two prominent examples. Conversely, setting the rotation at the life span of the longest-lived species would emulate disturbance well, but would sacrifice substantial economic production from the shorter-lived species. A reasonable compromise in such stands is to use multiple, species-specific rotations when incomplete removal cuttings are made. Such silvicultural systems can be effective in maintaining species diversity while also restoring single-cohort forests to their naturally diverse, multi-cohort structures. Smith et al. (1997:391–419) and the chapters in Kelty et al. (1992) outline many creative approaches to this common problem.

Cutting cycles for multi-cohort stands

Unlike single- and two-cohort systems, multi-cohort stands are never affected by severe disturbances and thus have no rotation *per se*. Yet, the basic principle is the same: periodic partial harvest cuttings must regenerate cohorts at approximately the same rate as the relevant partial disturbance regime. This is quite a different approach from the typical way multi-cohort stands are managed, which focuses on sizes and volumes of trees harvested. For example, Runkle (1985) noted that disturbance frequencies for a wide variety of agents and severities ranged only from 0.5% to 2% per year throughout temperate forests. This equates to average return intervals of 50–200 years, which in turn represents the average time an individual tree would be expected to reside in the canopy – essentially equivalent to the *rotation* of a single-cohort stand.

To emulate this regime with multi-cohort silviculture, one sets a *cutting cycle* (time between silvicultural disturbances for the stand *as a whole*), and multiplies by an appropriate annual disturbance frequency to obtain the total area to be created in canopy gaps at each stand entry. The inverse of this number equals the number of cohorts to be maintained (Nyland 1996:200). For example, to emulate a 1% frequency (= 100 year return interval) on a constant 20-year cutting cycle, one would need to limit gaps to 20% of the stand at each entry, with the aim of maintaining a 5–cohort stand. Additionally, one would need to ensure that, on the average, trees are harvested after approximately 100 years canopy residence time. Holding the cutting cycle and disturbance rate constant over time, as in this example, produces a perfectly balanced age structure within the stand. Of course, nature is almost never so perfect and the cutting cycle and disturbance frequency could be varied (in complementary ways) to produce a more irregular structure with fewer cohorts that occupied different amounts of area. Legacy trees of long-lived species should also be reserved well beyond the 100-year limit to replenish large cavities and woody debris.

SILVICULTURAL REGENERATION METHODS

Well before the discipline of ecology even existed, foresters were devising regeneration methods by close observation of vegetation response to disturbances. Natural patterns and their silvicultural analogues can be usefully grouped into two distinctly different categories: releasing disturbances such as wind or insect outbreaks that kill from the 'top down,' and those (mainly fire) that kill trees from the 'bottom up' (Smith *et al.* 1997:162–4).

The shelterwood method

Releasing disturbances, even those that kill the entire overstory, tend to favor mid- to late-successional, shade-tolerant species that persist as advance regeneration or perennial rootstocks in the understory. The clear silvicultural analogue here is the *shelterwood* method, the defining feature of which is the establishment of seedlings under protective over-story cover *before* the overstory is removed. By varying the timing of establishment and removal cuttings, as well as the overstory density during the regeneration stage, conditions can be created to favor virtually all but the most disturbance-dependent species. By varying spatial pattern of the cuttings and leaving permanent reserve trees, vertical and horizontal diversity can be greatly enhanced compared with more uniform treatments.

The uniform shelterwood method traditionally has been associated with single-cohort structures, because the regeneration period occurs during a relatively short period near the end of the rotation of the older cohort. Smith *et al.* (1997:347–63) now refer to shelterwood cuttings as an example of a 'double-cohort' system, presumably because the old and new cohorts overlap, however briefly, during the regeneration phase. This is unconventional usage of the two-cohort terminology; here and elsewhere (Helms *et al.* 1994), two-cohort stands are those in which the older cohort is more or less permanently represented in the form of *reserve trees* left after the rest of the overstory is removed. Irregular shelterwood systems with more protracted regeneration periods fall in a gray area between the uniform and distinctly two-aged cases. An excellent example is the German Femelschlag (irregular group shelterwood) method (Spurr 1956), in which the regeneration period may extend up to half the rotation.

Seed tree and clearcutting methods

Fires which kill from the ground up tend to favor two categories of species: shade-intolerant pioneers that establish best in open environ-ments with exposed mineral soil; and species which reproduce vegeta-tively as stump sprouts or root suckers. The appropriate silvicultural analogue depends on the specific source of propagules. Where severe fires leave only scattered large trees that are important sources of seed for a new cohort – such as the Douglas-fir and Scots pine examples discussed above – the *seed tree* method is clearly most appropriate. Smith *et al.* (1997:347) treat seed tree and shelterwood cuttings similarly; the main distinction is that seed tree cuttings do not provide shade and protection to the new seedlings.

Where fires or other severe disturbances kill virtually all vegetation, the appropriate silvicultural analogue is the clearcutting method. Unlike the terms 'seed tree' and 'shelterwood' which accurately convey the ecological intent of the cuttings, clearcutting is a timber harvesting term that has a wide variety of meanings within forestry. In a strict silvicultural sense, clearcutting applies only to cases where seedlings develop *after* the complete harvest. Seeds can come from surrounding stands, the crowns of trees harvested, or the seed bank in the forest floor. Where new plants arise from vegetative sources (e.g., stump sprouts), this is known as the coppice method. Great semantic confusion arises because clearcutting as a *harvesting* term is used by both foresters and the public to describe a wide variety of operations where most or all the merchantable timber is removed in a single entry. These include removal cuttings in the shelterwood method, seed tree cuttings, and heavy selective cuttings ('commercial clearcuttings') with no silvicultural intent. Silviculturists have thus found it necessary to use the modifier *true* or *silvicultural* clearcut when speaking of a regeneration harvest (Smith *et al.* 1997:327–8). When the intent is to release advance regeneration, the correct term is *overstory removal* cutting, even if there were no prior harvests and the advance seedlings are of purely natural origin.

Selection silviculture

The *selection* regeneration method is yet another source of confusion. Technically, this method applies to any type of harvest designed to create regeneration under a multi-cohort silvicultural system. From an ecological standpoint, most selection cuttings resemble the shelterwood method; the only difference is that with selection, only a small portion of the stand is regenerated in a single entry in order to perpetuate the multi-cohort structure.

Artificial regeneration

If one were beginning to implement ecological forestry in a forest unaffected by past human exploitation, then there would be no need for any 'artificial' practices. Unfortunately, centuries of human use has often reduced tree species diversity on scales that make natural reintroduction unlikely. Here, planting and direct seeding can play a useful role in augmenting natural methods; these practices in the context of restoration forestry are covered in Chapter 15.

A COMMENT ON SILVICULTURAL TERMINOLOGY

The preceding section highlights the fact that silviculture is in a state of evolution. Important new terms are replacing old, because silviculturists have become frustrated with the *prescriptive* implications of the old language and its inability to *describe* creative, ecologically based practices and systems. Foresters should not worry about whether a particular practice has a convenient traditional pigeonhole somewhere in the silviculture textbooks. The key is to create the appropriate overstory and microenvironmental conditions for tree growth, seedling establishment and habitat for other species, within the confines of the chosen cohort structure. If traditional silvicultural terminology cannot readily describe novel or unconventional combinations, this is a weakness of the terminology, not of the person prescribing the treatment or the treatment itself.

Landscape-level decisions

HARVEST LEVELS AND AGE STRUCTURES

The volume of wood harvested annually is probably the single most important decision affecting a forest property or region. Forest managers have typically used one of two forest regulation methods: *volume control*, typically associated with forests under uneven-aged management; or *area control* used in forests of single- or two-cohort stands. Area-based approaches have one outcome in mind: a perfectly rectangular age distribution, with equal areas in each age class up to the rotation, and none older – the so-called 'normal' or perfectly regulated forest. As computer technology has evolved, complex harvest scheduling models have emerged which combine both methods. Forest regulation under sustained-yield timber management has always attempted to maximize wood volumes harvested over time, subject to long-run sustainability constraints that may or may not include ecological parameters.

The best way to determine an ecologically sustainable harvest level is with an area-based approach that attempts to maintain (or recreate) a natural landscape age structure. Under this modification of area regulation, the harvest is the sum of all timber volumes derived by applying the appropriate silvicultural systems to the appropriate areas at a sustainable pace. It is *not* calculated as function of actual forest growth or growing stock volumes, as is done with various volume control methods. First, we will consider the simpler case of stand-replacing disturbances in forests composed of single-cohort stands, then extend this reasoning to partial disturbances in forests of predominantly multi-cohort stands.

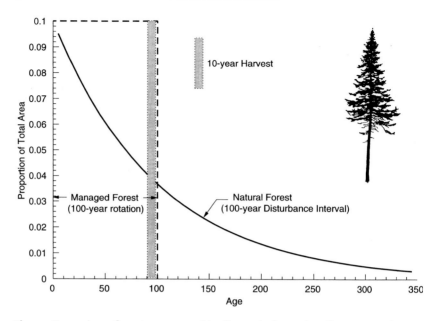

Fig. 2.7. Comparison of age structures resulting from a single rotation of 100 years vs. the natural distribution produced by random disturbances (after Van Wagner 1978).

Stand-replacing disturbance regimes

Simply setting a managed forest rotation equal to the disturbance interval does not accurately emulate a natural disturbance regime. To understand why, compare a forest with a 1% annual stand-replacing fire disturbance regime with a forest managed on a 100-year rotation (Figure 2.7). In nature, the quasi-random spatial pattern of disturbances results in some stands burning repeatedly on short cycles while others escape for long periods. Under certain conditions (see Van Wagner 1978), such a forest will approach a negative exponential (not rectangular) age distribution:

$A(x) = p \exp(-px)$
where $A(x)$ = area of age x; and
p = annual disturbance frequency = inverse of the return interval.

Under sustained-yield timber management, no stands 'escape' harvest and reach old age, nor are any young ones intentionally disturbed. Importantly, the area burned or harvested (and thus regenerated) annually is equal in both forests, but the natural forest has twice the mean age as the managed one. Over 37% of the natural forest is older than the 100-year

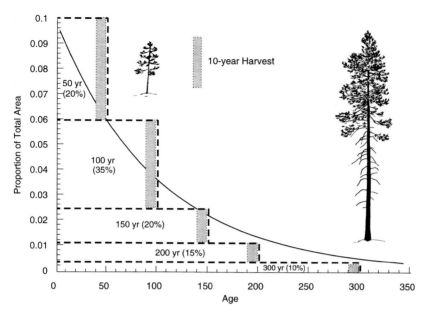

Fig. 2.8. Approximating the natural, negative exponential landscape age structure by managing different portions of the forest on varying rotations.

timber rotation. If the disturbance is 'shared' equally among natural causes and harvest (0.5% each), the resulting age structure will simply be a truncated exponential that resembles the timber-regulated forest much more closely than the natural structure, with no old-growth stands (Van Wagner 1983). Clearly, the problematical issue in mimicking natural patterns is the 'tail' (Chapter 4) of old growth that does not exist with harvesting.

The most straightforward way to emulate this pattern under management would be to allocate different portions of the forest to successively longer rotations, ranging from age 50 for short-lived species up to 300 years for late-successional habitat. This would appear as a series of rectangular distributions, each stacked on top of one another (Figure 2.8). For example, we could emulate the example above by harvesting 10% of the forest on a 300-year rotation, 15% at age 200, 20% at age 150, 35% at age 100, and 20% at age 50. Sixteen percent would be harvested at a younger age than the classic normal forest (Figure 2.7), whereas 45% would be managed on rotations longer than 100 years. About 10% of the forest would be harvested and regenerated each decade, distributed among age classes as shown, just as in the natural situation.

The foregoing example presumes that all natural disturbances can be preempted through management. In reality, some natural disturbances will occur, creating early successional forests, so the challenge of managers is to *complement*, not replace, the natural pattern. If substantial areas of older stands existed in ecological reserves where disturbance patterns were not altered by harvesting, then the age structure of the managed forest could be configured to complement that of the reserves (B.C. Ministry of Forests 1995). However, if reserves were small or isolated such that a single disturbance could eliminate the old forests completely, this approach could ultimately prove unsatisfactory.

Yet another option would be simply to let some disturbance occur and salvage mortality afterward (with due consideration for biological legacy issues), thereby letting natural events control the age structure. Although appealing ecologically, such an approach would be highly impractical in situations where the forest is fully utilized and a stable annual cut is needed, but the area annually affected by disturbance is highly variable.

Partial disturbance regimes

Where partial disturbances dominate, only a small portion of the landscape naturally occurs in single-cohort stands to which a single age can be readily assigned. Here, foresters should consider the forest not as a distribution of clearly defined age classes, but as a matrix of multi-cohort stands, each of which is continually regenerating in relatively small patches. Studies of disturbance regimes in such forests (e.g., Runkle 1991, Frelich and Lorimer 1991, Frelich and Graumlich 1994, and Dahir and Lorimer 1996 for northern hardwood temperate forests) provide excellent management templates to design multi-cohort systems. The key issues are: (a) average disturbance frequency, or the area regenerated annually within the stand, (b) the size distribution of gaps, and (c) how the gaps are configured spatially. When such parameters are known, incorporating them into multi-cohort silvicultural systems is conceptually straightforward. Just as with single-cohort systems, legacy issues must also be kept in mind by allowing some trees to reach their natural lifespans. For example, in a northern hardwood forest that averages a 1% partial disturbance frequency, one must allow some sugar maple trees to exceed 100 years of age, just as they would in nature.

SPATIAL PATTERNS OF HARVESTS

Matching the temporal patterns and intensity of harvests and natural disturbances may be the key issue in ecological forestry, but we also need to consider spatial patterns. Specifically, we need to ask: How do the size, shape, and distribution of harvests compare with the spatial characteristics of natural disturbances? This question is relevant from a biodiversity perspective for at least three reasons. First, a large stand represents different habitat for some species than a small stand. Second, stands with irregular shapes have relatively more edge than regularly shaped stands and edges represent a different type or quality of habitat for some species. Finally, the spatial distribution of stands can affect the ability of organisms to move across the landscape (e.g., a carnivore patrolling its home range, or a plant propagule dispersing). All of these issues are particularly germane when managing landscapes that are a mosaic of single- and two-cohort stands. In landscapes covered by extensive multi-cohort stands, the question is probably less critical because it is unlikely that organisms are highly sensitive to the spatial configurations of small groups of trees.

The spatial patterns generated by natural disturbances can be complex. At a minimum they will be shaped by: (a) the unique attributes of a specific event (e.g., velocity of a particular hurricane or wind direction during a particular fire); (b) the topography of a given site (e.g., is there a hill to provide a wind break or a river to provide a fire break?), and (c) the vegetation itself (e.g., are the trees relatively vulnerable or invulnerable to being burned, blown over, killed by insects, etc.?). This variability might seem terribly daunting for foresters trying to emulate it with their harvest plans, but in a sense it also provides considerable latitude. The key is to understand the general pattern of past natural disturbance events and to use this as a template for laying out harvests. It is preferable if this information can be specific for a particular landscape. However, it is not possible to achieve perfection. In the big picture, one is always trying to hit a moving target; for example, global climate change will always be shifting the patterns of fires and wind storms (Clark 1988). Certainly, most forest operations have enormous scope for improvement when it comes to emulating the spatial patterns of natural events (Hunter 1993). Many landscapes managed for timber production look like someone has been at work with a square cookie cutter of about 10 hectares, punching a regular pattern of holes across the landscape (Figure 2.9). Spatial issues are covered in detail in Chapters 4, 5, 6, and 7.

Balanced forestry

In this book many prominent forest scientists have been asked to formulate a working hypothesis of how to maintain biodiversity in

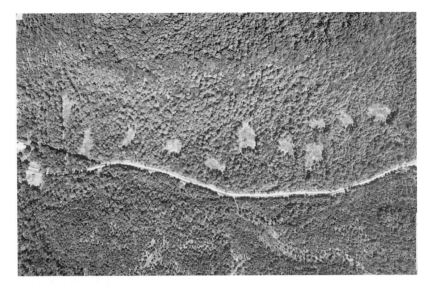

Fig. 2.9. Landscapes dominated by single- and two-cohort stands are often harvested in a series of patches that are quite uniform in size and shape and regularly distributed. This pattern bears little resemblance to the spatial pattern generated by natural disturbances. (The example shown here comes from the shortleaf pine forest type on the Ouachita National Forest, Arkansas, USA. Jim Guldin, USDA Forest Service photo.)

managed forests. The implicit assumption here is that forest ecosystems function to conserve biodiversity just fine on their own. To put this another way, a conservative person must assume that, until proven otherwise, any human manipulation represents a compromise between ecological integrity and society's demand for forest products. The disciplines of ecology and conservation biology help us to understand the biological consequences of human manipulation, but it falls upon the profession of forestry to balance these often-conflicting demands in practice. As human populations grow in numbers and affluence, this balancing act becomes more and more difficult, and it becomes clear that no single approach to forestry will meet all of society's needs.

It was this recognition – that society's competing demands were on a collision course – that led us to propose a fundamental change in our home state of Maine, where there is little public forest land and where industrial landowners have managed over 3 million contiguous hectares under a mixture of custodial, extensive, and sustained-yield approaches for nearly a century. At first, the situation seemed hopeless. Conservation biologists had become concerned that only very small, non-representative areas were protected from harvesting, and thus there were few credible benchmarks against which to judge ecological consequences of forest management activities. At the same time, forecasts of timber shortfalls suggested that any agenda for withdrawing forest land from harvest would meet stiff opposition on economic grounds.

While writing a review of ecological forestry in the Acadian spruce-fir forest (Seymour and Hunter 1992), we realized that simply replacing extensive forestry with ecological forestry – while clearly a very positive step from the standpoint of biodiversity – would not solve the larger problem. Setting aside adequate, representative areas for ecological reserves without reducing timber harvests would require a compensatory increase in production silviculture. Such a scenario is feasible in Maine because extensive forestry has produced such low timber yields; substituting production silviculture can raise per-hectare yields from threefold to fivefold (Seymour 1993). Consequently one could, in theory, set aside 3–5 ha of ecological reserves for every hectare shifted into production forestry, with no net loss in overall timber production. This rationale has also been advocated as a global forest conservation strategy (Gladstone and Ledig 1990, Sedjo and Botkin 1997), in grassland and aquatic ecosystems (Hunter and Calhoun 1996), and is supported by economists (Vincent and Binkley 1993) and some conservation geneticists (Libby 1993).

Where such increases in timber yields are possible, it is easy to see that timber lost from setting aside 10% of the landscape in ecological reserves could, in the long run, be replaced by timber from a small area of land dedicated to production silviculture. In this scenario, ecological forestry would supplant extensive forestry, and constitute the predominant matrix into which reserves and production forestry would be embedded. We call this vision a landscape triad, in order to highlight the three, fundamentally different, objectives to which forest land would be dedicated on the landscape. Designing and managing such a landscape that attempts to provide for all societal demands would be an example of *balanced forestry* (after Kimmins 1992), a term chosen to acknowledge explicitly that all uses have inherent worth and thus must be balanced against one another in practice.

The triad does not, as some have inferred, suggest an *equal* allocation; exact values in each sector must come from case-specific analyses. For example, consider the United States South where most of the landscape was once cleared for agriculture and land is inherently quite productive. Here, the forest industry is actively converting abandoned agricultural lands to high-production loblolly pine plantations, and it is probably inevitable that the landscape will be dominated by production forests. Nevertheless, ecologically viable blocks and corridors of natural forest, wetlands and riparian zones could be established to maintain critical bio-diversity functions. Alternatively, rather than convert all degraded lands to commodity production, innovative silviculture could be used to restore more natural communities (e.g., longleaf pine) where necessary to ensure landscape connectivity and maintain critical habitats not provided by the production-oriented matrix. In contrast, consider New Zealand, where plantations of exotic species are extremely productive and native forests are difficult to manage on short rotations. Here, the approach has been to produce almost all timber from plantations and to set aside the vast major-ity of the remaining native forest.

IMPLEMENTING A LANDSCAPE TRIAD

The first and perhaps most critical step in practicing balanced forestry is to accept and support the premise that some of the landscape must be left alone. This is a difficult step for many foresters who have been inculcated with a 'manage everywhere' mentality that assumes virtually any forest can be improved through careful human intervention, and that good silviculture must be good for biodiversity. This may be true, but given our current state of ignorance about biodiversity, a conservative ethic dictates that we regard it as an hypothesis, not an established fact. Importantly, this hypothesis cannot be tested without adequate experi-mental controls from which to learn and adapt management accordingly; hence the need for a scientifically designed system of reserves (see Chapter 16).

Once a system of reserves is in place, one needs to assess the commod-ity-production potential of the unreserved landscape. Where timber demands are relatively low, intensive application of ecological forestry will likely sustain them. If, however, demands are relatively high, it is likely that some portion of the landscape will need to be managed under production silviculture to offset the reserves. Foresters would naturally seek to estab-lish high-yield plantations on the most productive sites. Conservation biologists would advocate locating them where they would do the least damage; i.e., the most degraded communities (such as lands formerly converted to agriculture, repeatedly high-graded, etc.). Often these are the same lands, so decisions should be straightforward. If plantations do not disrupt key features such as landscape connectivity and riparian zones, are limited to a minority of the total forest, and are managed on sufficiently long rotations without whole-tree harvesting in order to maintain the integrity of nutrient cycles, then there should be little cause for alarm.

DO WE REALLY NEED PLANTATIONS?

Advocates of ecological forestry often question whether growing trees under an agricultural paradigm is really necessary in order to achieve high timber yields. They argue that by managing natural forests more intensively and sensitively, both timber yields and ecological values could both be increased. We accept this premise up to a point; it is certainly true where sophisticated ecological forestry replaces low-budget extensive forestry. However, the success of production silviculture, as in intensive agriculture, derives from the fact that canopy leaf areas are carefully controlled to maximize carbon fixation in merchantable stemwood of economically useful species, all of which is eventually harvested. Ecological forestry, in contrast, demands that a significant portion of the carbon fixed by photosynthesis be left on site in the form of various structural elements, and further, relies on manipulating canopy structure for purposes other than maximum leaf areas.

A related issue that has come under intense discussion in Europe and parts of North America is whether certain features of ecological forestry can be incorporated in production silvicultural systems. Clearly, practices such as leaving dead snags and conserving downed woody debris which do not result in competition to the crop trees, should be used wherever possible, regardless of the stand-level objective. Lengthening rotations may be another valuable option, especially if doing so actually results in higher production of more valuable products (Peterken 1996:425–63). Leaving living reserve trees, which may compete with the developing stand, is a more problematical issue. Is there some sort of hybrid silviculture that achieves both high timber output and high levels of diversity? We have few answers, though there is reason to be skeptical, for the more an ecosystem is simplified through production silvicultural practices, the more likely we are to lose some elements of biodiversity that depend on its natural complexity. However, this is not to discourage creative foresters from attempting innovative modifications to plantation silviculture, for we will undoubtedly learn much from this experience (Chapter 12).

Summary

Forestry has evolved many different models such as custodial forestry, sustained-yield timber production, multiple-use forestry, production forestry, and extensive forestry. One of the newest forms focuses on maintaining the ecological integrity of forest ecosystems; it is known by many terms – we call it 'ecological forestry'. The central axiom of ecological forestry is that any manipulation of a forest ecosystem should emulate the natural disturbance patterns of the region prior to extensive human alteration of the landscape. This axiom is based on the assumption that native species have evolved under these natural disturbance regimes and will be better able to cope with human-induced disturbances such as logging if these are designed to imitate the key characteristics of natural disturbances: the return interval between disturbances, disturbance severity, and the spatial pattern of disturbances.

Stand structures maintained under ecologically based silvicultural systems can be either single-cohort, two-cohort, or multi-cohort, depending on the disturbance agent, its severity, and return interval. Emulating disturbances at the stand level should pay close attention to providing biological legacies (typically large, old trees and dead snags) similar to those that survive natural disturbances. Silvicultural regeneration methods should also be patterned after natural disturbance processes; the critical difference is whether seedlings originate prior to, or after, the disturbance. At the landscape level, the crucial point is to regenerate areas of new cohorts at approximately the same rate as the natural disturbance cycles would have, and to ensure that the natural diversity in age and structure are conserved and maintained. To emulate large-scale stand-replacing disturbances, single- or two-cohort stands managed under several different rotations should be employed. Special attention should be given to ensuring that some forests reach at least twice the age of the average disturbance interval. In forests with patchy, partial disturbances dominated by gap processes, having multi-cohort stand structures managed under variable cutting cycles best emulates natural patterns.

Ultimately, human demand for timber is likely to make it impossible to practise ecological forestry in all forests, especially if we want to set aside larger areas of forests to serve as ecological reserves. This reality will likely dictate that we practise balanced forestry, represented by a triad of production forestry and ecological reserves embedded in a matrix of ecological forestry.

Further readings

Traditional silviculture texts such as Smith (1962), Smith *et al.* (1997), Nyland (1996) and Matthews (1989) are good starting points for understanding the context and evolution of ecological forestry. Peterken (1981) and Hunter (1990) are early syntheses of ecological forestry ideas; more recent treatments include Alverson *et al.* (1994) and Kohm and Franklin (1997). Recent forest ecology texts such as Perry (1994), Kimmins (1997), and Barnes *et al.* (1998) provide excellent coverage of biophysical process and how they interact with disturbances.

Literature cited

Agee, J. K. 1991. Fire history of Douglas-fir forests in the Pacific Northwest. Pp. 25–33 in Ruggiero, L. F. *et al.*, (eds). *Wildlife and vegetation of unmanaged Douglas-fir forests*. USDA Forest Service General Technical Report PNW-GTR-285. Portland, Oregon. 520 pp.

Alverson, W. S., W. Kuhlmann, and D. M. Waller. 1994. *Wild Forests: Conservation Biology and Public Policy*. Island Press, Washington, D.C. 300 pp.

Attiwill, P. M. 1994a. The disturbance of forest ecosystems: the ecological basis for conservative management. *Forest Ecology and Management* **63**:247–300.

　　1994b. Ecological disturbance and the conservative management of eucalypt forests in Australia. *Forest Ecology and Management* **63**:301–46.

Baker, J. B., M. D. Cain, J. M. Guldin, P. A. Murphy, and M. G.Shelton. 1996. *Uneven-aged silviculture for the loblolly and shortleaf pine forest cover types*. USDA Forest Service General Technical Report SO-118. Asheville, N.C. 65 pp.

Barnes, B. V., D. R. Zak, S. R. Denton, and S. H. Spurr 1998. *Forest Ecology*. 4th edn. John Wiley and Sons, N.Y. 774 pp.

Baskerville, G. L. 1975. Spruce budworm: super silviculturist. *Forestry Chronicle* **51**:138–40.

B.C. Ministry of Forests. 1995. *Forest Practices Code of British Columbia – Biodiversity Guidebook*. Victoria, B.C., Canada. 99 pp.

Bergeron, Y. and B. Harvey. 1997. Basing silviculture on natural ecosystem dynamics: an approach applied to the southern boreal mixedwood forest of Quebec. *Forest Ecology and Management* **92**:235–42.

Clark, J. S. 1988. Effect of climate change on fire regimes in northwestern Minnesota. *Nature* **334**:233–5.

Cogbill, C. V. 1985. Dynamics of the boreal forests of the Laurentian Highlands, Canada. *Canadian Journal of Forest Research* **15**:252–61.

　　1996. Black growth and fiddlebutts: the nature of old-growth red spruce. Pp. 113–25 in Davis, M. B., (ed.). *Eastern Old-growth Forests: Prospects for Rediscovery and Recovery*. Island Press, Washington, D.C. 383 pp.

Covington, W .W. and M. M. Moore. 1994. Southwestern ponderosa pine forest structure: changes since European settlement. *Journal of Forestry* **92**(1):39–47.

Davis, L. S. and K. N. Johnson. 1986. *Forest Mangement.* 3rd edn. McGraw-Hill, New York. 790 pp.

Dahir, S. E. and C. G. Lorimer. 1996. Variation in canopy gap formation among developmental stages of northern hardwood stands. *Canadian Journal of Forest Research.* **26**:1875–92.

Eberhart, K. E. and P. M. Woodard. 1987. Distribution of residual vegetation associated with large fires in Alberta. *Canadian Journal of Forest Research* **117**:1207–12.

Egler, F. E. 1954. Vegetation science concepts: I. Initial floristic composition: a factor in old-field vegetation development. *Vegetatio* **4**:412–17.

Fernow, B. E. 1913. *A Brief History of Forestry in Europe, the United States, and Other Countries.* 3rd edn. University Press of Toronto. 506 pp.

Forman, R. T. T. 1995. *Land Mosaics.* Cambridge University Press, Cambridge, United Kingdom. 632 pp.

Franklin, J. F. 1989. Toward a new forestry. *American Forests* (Nov–Dec issue). 37–44.

Franklin, J. F., D. R. Berg, D. A. Thornburgh, and J. C. Tappeiner. 1997. Alternative silvicultural approaches to timber harvesting: variable retention harvest systems. Pp. 111–39 in K. A. Kohm and J. F. Franklin (eds). *Creating a Forestry for the 21st Century.* Island Press, Washington D.C. 475 pp.

Frelich, L. E. and L. J. Graumlich. 1994. Age-class distribution and spatial patterns in an old-growth hemlock-hardwood forest. *Canadian Journal of Forest Research* **24**:1939–47.

Frelich, L. E. and C. G. Lorimer. 1991. Natural disturbance regimes in hemlock-hardwood forests of the upper Great Lakes region. *Ecological Monographs* **61**(2):145–64.

Gladstone, W. T. and F. T. Ledig. 1990. Reducing pressure on natural forests through high-yield forestry. *Forest Ecology and Management* **35**:69–78.

Grumbine, R. E. 1994. What is ecosystem management? *Conservation Biology* **8**:27–38.

Hansen, A. J., T. A. Spies, F. J. Swanson, and J. L. Ohmann. 1991. Conserving biodiversity in managed forests: lessons from natural forests. *BioScience* **41**:382–92.

Helms, J. A. (Chair.) *et al.* 1994. *Silviculture Terminology,* with appendix of draft ecosystem management terms. Society of American Foresters, Bethesda, MD.

Hunter, M. L., Jr. 1990. *Wildlife, Forests, and Forestry: Principles of Managing Forests for Biological Diversity.* Prentice-Hall, Englewood Cliffs, N.J. 370 pp.

   1993. Natural fire regimes as spatial models for managing boreal forests. *Biological Conservation* **65**:115–20.

Hunter, M. L., Jr. and A. Calhoun. 1996. A triad approach to land-use allocation. Pp. 477–91 in R. C. Szaro and D. W. Johnston (eds). *Biodiversity in Managed Landscapes.* Oxford University Press, New York. 778 pp.

Hunter, M. L., Jr., G. L. Jacobson, and T. Webb. 1988. Paleoecology and coarse-filter approach to maintaining biological diversity. *Conservation Biology* 2:375–85.

Hutto, R. L. 1995. Composition of bird communities following stand-replacement fires in northern Rocky Mountain (USA) conifer forests. *Conservation Biology* 9:1041–58.

Irland, L. C. 1994. Getting from here to there: implementing ecosystem mangement on the ground. *Journal of Forestry* 92(8):12–17.

Johnson, J. E. 1995. The Lake States Region. Pp. 81–127 in J. W. Barrett (ed.). *Regional Silviculture of the United States.* 3rd edn. Wiley and Sons, New York 643 pp.

Kelty, M., B. C. Larson, and C. D. Oliver, (eds) 1992. *The Ecology and Silviculture of Mixed-species Forests.* Kluwer Publishers, Norwell, MA. 287 pp.

Kimmins, H. 1992. *Balancing Act: Environmental Issues in Forestry.* University of British Columbia Press, Vancouver. 244 pp.

   1997. *Forest Ecology: A Foundation for Sustainable Management.* 2nd edn. Prentice-Hall, Inc. 596 pp.

Kohm, K. A. and J. F. Franklin. 1997. *Creating a Forestry for the 21st Century.* Island Press, Washington, D.C. 475 pp.

Krutilla, J. V. and J. A. Haigh. 1978. An integrated approach to national forest management. *Environmental Law* 8(2):57–68.

Libby, W. J. 1993. Mitigating some consequences of in-situ genetic conservation. In P. Baradat, (ed.). *Proceedings INRA/IUFRO International Symposium on Population Genetics and Gene Conservation of Forest Trees.* Carcans Maubuisson.

Lorimer, C. G. 1977. The presettlement forest and natural disturbance cycle of northeastern Maine. *Ecology* 58:139–48.

   1989. Relative effects of small and large disturbances on temperate hardwood forest structure. *Ecology* 70:565–7.

Lovelock, J. E. 1979. *Gaia.* Oxford University Press, Oxford. 157 pp.

Matthews, J. D. 1989. *Silvicultural Systems.* Oxford University Press, Oxford. 284 pp.

Mattson, D. J., and M. M. Reid. 1991. Conservation of the Yellowstone grizzly bear. *Conservation Biology* 5:364–72.

More, T. A. 1996. Forestry's fuzzy concepts: an examination of ecosystem management. *Journal of Forestry* 94(8):19–23.

NRC (National Research Council). 1990. *Forestry Research: a Mandate for Change.* National Academy Press, Washington, D.C.

Nyland, R. D. 1996. *Silviculture: Concepts and Applications.* McGraw-Hill, New York. 633 pp.

O'Hara, K. J., R. S. Seymour, S. D. Tesch, and J. M. Guldin. 1994. Silviculture and our changing profession. Leadership for shifting paradigms. *Journal of Forestry* 92(1):8–13.

O'Hara, K. L. 1996. Dynamics and stocking-level relationships of multi-aged ponderosa pine stands. *Forest Science Monograph* 33. (42:4) 34 pp.

Oliver, C. D. 1981. Forest development in North America following major disturbances. *Forest Ecology and Management* 3:153–68.

Oliver, C. D. and B. C. Larson. 1996. *Forest Stand Dynamics* Wiley and Sons, New York. 520 pp.

Perry, D. A. 1994. *Forest Ecosystems*. Johns Hopkins University Press, Baltimore, MD. 649 pp.

Peterken, G. F. 1981. *Woodland Conservation and Management*. Chapman and Hall, London.

    1996. *Natural Woodland: Ecology and Conservation in Northern Temperate Regions*. Cambridge University Press. 522 pp.

Pickett, S. T. A. and P. S. White. 1985. *The Ecology of Natural Distrubance and Patch Dynamics*. Academic Press, Orlando, FL. 472 pp.

Plochmann, R. 1992. The forests of central Europe: a changing view. *Journal of Forestry* **90**(6):12–16, 41.

Rosson, J. F., Jr. 1995. *Forest plantations in the midsouth, USA*. USDA Forest Service Research Paper SO-290. 30 pp.

Runkle, J. R. 1985. Disturbance regimes in temperate forests. Pp. 17–33 in S. T. A. Pickett, and P. S. White. *The Ecology of Natural Disturbance and Patch Dynamics*. Academic Press, Orlando, FL. 472 pp.

    1991. Gap dynamics of old-growth eastern forests: management implications. *Natural Areas Journal* **11**:19–25.

SAF (Society of American Foresters). 1993. *Task force report on sustaining long-term forest health and productivity*. SAF Publ. 93–02. Bethesda, MD. 83 pp.

Salwasser, H. 1994. Ecosystem management: can it sustain diversity and productivity? *Journal of Forestry* **92**(8):6–10.

Sedjo, R. A. 1996. Toward an operational approach to public forest management. *Journal of Forestry* **94**(8):24–7.

Sedjo, R. A. and D. Botkin. 1997. Using plantations to spare natural forests. *Environment* **39**(10):14–20, 30.

Seymour, R. S. 1992. The red spruce-balsam fir forest of Maine: evolution of silvicultural practice in response to stand development patterns and disturbances. Pp. 217–44 in M. J. Kelty, B. C. Larson, and C. D. Oliver (eds.). *The Ecology and Silviculture of Mixed-species forests*. Kluwer Publishers, Norwell, MA. 287 pp.

    1993. Plantations or natural stands? Options and tradeoffs for high-yield silviculture. Pp. 16–32 in R. D. Briggs, and W. B. Krohn (eds). *Nurturing the Northeastern forest*. *Proceedings New England Society American Foresters, March 3–5, 1993*. Portland, ME. Maine Agricultural and Forestry Experiment Station Miscellaneous Report 382.

    1995. The Northeastern Region. Pp. 31–79 in J. W. Barrett (ed.). *Regional Silviculture of the United States* 3rd edn. Wiley and Sons, New York 643 pp.

Seymour, R. S. and M. L. Hunter, Jr. 1992. *New Forestry in eastern spruce-fir forests: principles and applications to Maine*. Maine Agricultural and Forestry Experiment Station Miscellaneous Publication 716. 36 pp.

Seymour, R. S., P. R. Hannah, J. R. Grace and D. A. Marquis. 1986. Silviculture: the next 30 years, the past 30 years. Part IV. The Northeast. *Journal of Forestry* **84**(7):31–8.

Smith, D. M. 1962. *The Practice of Silviculture*. 7th edn. Wiley and Sons, New York. 578 pp.

1972. The continuing evolution of silvicultural practice. *Journal of Forestry* 70:89–92.

1986. *The Practice of Silviculture*. 8th edn. Wiley and Sons, New York. 527 pp.

Smith, D. M., B. C. Larson, M. J. Kelty, and P. M. S. Ashton. 1997. *The Practice of Silviculture: Applied Forest Ecology*. 9th edn. Wiley and Sons, New York. 537 pp.

Spurr, S. H. 1956. German silvicultural systems. *Forest Science* 2:75–80.

Troup, R. S. 1955. *Silvicultural Systems*. 2nd edn. Oxford University Press. 216 pp.

Toumey, J. W. 1928. Preface to: *The Foundations of Silviculture* John Wiley and Sons, New York.

Van Wagner, C. E. 1978. Age-class distribution and the forest fire cycle. *Canadian Journal of Forest Research* 8:220–7.

1983. Simulating the effect of forest fire on the long-term annual timber supply. *Canadian Journal of Forest Research* 13:451–7.

Vincent, J. R. and C. S. Binkley. 1993. Efficient multiple-use forestry may require land-use specialization. *Land Economics* 69:370–6.

Walstad, J. D. and P. J. Kuch. 1987. *Forest Vegetation Management for Conifer Production*. John Wiley and Sons, New York. 523 pp.

White, A. S. 1985. Presettlement regeneration patterns in a southwestern ponderosa pine stand. *Ecology* 66:589–94.

Whitney. G. G. 1994. *From Coastal Wilderness to Fruited Plain: a History of Environmental Change in Temperate North America*. Cambridge University Press, New York. 451 pp.

Winston, P. W. 1956. The acorn microsere, with special reference to arthropods. *Ecology* 37:120–32.

Woodley, S. and G. Forbes (eds.). 1997. *Forest management guidelines to protect native biodiversity in the Fundy model forest*. New Brunswick Cooperative Fish and Wildlife Research Unit, University of New Brunswick, Fredericton. 35 pp.

Part II
The macro approach, managing forest landscapes

3　Species composition

BRIAN PALIK AND R. TODD ENGSTROM

When many people look at a forest they see only the trees. This is understandable, as trees are substantially larger than any other organism in the forest. Yet despite their physical dominance, overstory trees generally are not the most species-rich, nor numerically abundant, taxonomic group in a forest. Richness and population sizes of many other organisms, especially herbs, invertebrates, and microbes, may be several orders of magnitude greater than overstory trees.

The 'other taxa' of forest ecosystems may outnumber trees, but in many ways the overstory has a profound influence on their existence. In this context, the overstory provides a fabric to the forest that controls the types, richness, and abundance of other biota through regulation of key functions and provision of critical resources. The compositional fabric varies across physical and chemical gradients of landscapes. Tree composition also changes over time with succession after disturbances. Forest management can cause equally important changes in the fabric of overstory composition.

In this chapter, we review the relationships that exist between overstory trees and other organisms in a forest and assess the ecological consequences of altering these relationships through forest management, namely, changing the compositional fabric. This understanding is essential to devise management strategies that both maintain biological diversity and sustain timber production. Methodologies for managing overstory composition often have a stand-level focus, but they also need to include a larger-scale perspective that considers the distribution and abundance of stand compositions across landscapes. To this end we discuss challenges and recommendations for developing and pursuing compositional goals for landscapes.

How overstory composition changes naturally

Despite the public's assertions otherwise, foresters are not the sole force causing changes in overstory composition. Rather, overstory composition changes both spatially and temporally in response to a number of natural factors that influence a species' ability to establish, survive to maturity, and reproduce. The spatial factors are hierarchical, with upper levels in the hierarchy constraining lower levels (Rowe and Sheard 1981). At large spatial scales (e.g., continents and subcontinents) forest composition varies with climate and large-scale physiographic features (Bailey 1996).

Within climatic and physiographic regions, composition relates to mesoscale geomorphic features, such as glacial or marine deposited landforms (Bailey 1996). Topography and soil-forming processes vary within mesoscale geomorphic features, affecting microclimate, soil water-holding capacity, drainage characteristics, nutrient availability, and natural disturbance regimes (Pregitzer et al. 1983). Patterns in forest composition within landscapes relate to these hierarchical controls, as has been demonstrated in different regions (Barnes et al. 1982, Goebel et al. 1996).

Overstory composition in stands also changes over time as species migrate in response to long-term climate change, and during succession following disturbance (secondary succession) or colonization of new substrate (primary succession). The mechanisms causing composition changes during succession are complex (Chapter 4). Yet understanding successional pathways within ecosystem-types is important because management often depends on having informed predictions about future composition of forests.

How foresters change overstory composition

It is an unavoidable fact that forest management alters overstory composition. Usually these changes are intentional and sometimes they can be extreme, as in replacement of natural forest with plantations of exotic species. Plantations of all kinds comprise only around 3% of world forest area (Gauthier 1991), presumably not a significant threat to global biodiversity. However, in some regions, plantations are being established at the expense of old-growth or minimally disturbed forests. For example, between 1980 and 1990, 77% of new tropical plantations were established

Table 3.1. *Industrial plantation area (thousand hectares) in the tropics and subtropics in 1975 and 2000 (projected)*

Region	1975	2000
Central and South America	2786	10705
Africa south of Sahara[a]	997	2180
Developing Asia and the Far East[b]	2892	8265
Total	6675	21150

Notes:
[a] Excludes South Africa.
[b] Includes Pakistan eastward excluding the People's Republic of China, Mongolia, and Japan.
Source: Lanly and Clement (1979).

on land cleared of natural closed-canopy forest (FAO 1995). Additionally, plantations often consist of non-native species, such as lodgepole pine (*Pinus contorta*) in Great Britain (Docherty and Leather 1997), or Monterey pine (*Pinus radiata*) in Australia (Disney and Stokes 1976). These two points suggest that the potential impacts of plantations on forest biodiversity can be extreme, when an introduced species replaces natural forest. Additionally, the global extent of plantations may be increasing at a substantial rate. The projected increase of industrial plantations in the tropics, for instance, is from a 1975 total of 7 million ha to over 21 million ha by 2000 (Table 3.1).

In addition to complete replacement with plantations, forestry practices can inhibit or promote species changes as they occur naturally during succession. This represents the predominant means by which management alters overstory composition. In this chapter, we refer to such taxonomic changes as managed successional pathways. Managed successions use a variety of techniques, including harvesting, prescribed fire, herbicides, and mechanical manipulation of soil and forest floor. Plantation management uses these techniques as well; the distinction in managed successions is that the goal is manipulation of natural regeneration and persistence of at least a portion of species occurring in the local flora.

Silviculture used to manage successional pathways may result in dramatic changes in species composition. Systems that increase light availability at whole-stand scales, such as clearcutting or a shelterwood, coupled with prescribed surface fire or herbiciding, promote dominance by early successional taxa. Management of longleaf pine (*Pinus palustris*) in the southeastern United States is a good example. A shelterwood increases light availability and maintains a longleaf pine seed source. Prescribed fire prepares a mineral seedbed and kills more shade tolerant, later succession hardwood species (Wahlenberg 1946, and see the case study in this chapter).

Sometimes, shifts in composition are less noticeable, but still significant from the standpoint of biological diversity. Multi-cohort silviculture, for instance, may result in subtle changes in composition, particularly if it involves some form of selection harvesting that removes a particular species preferentially. If the selection system creates only small openings in the forest canopy, then species composition may shift towards greater abundance of shade tolerant species. This can occur at the expense of mid-tolerant and intolerant species that require larger openings to establish or grow (Miller and Smith 1993).

Does overstory composition affect other species?

The intuitive answer to this question is yes, but with some important caveats. The extent that it is true depends on the degree of structural and functional similarity between different tree taxa. Also important is the level of specificity between a plant or animal and a particular tree species. Finally, the composition of the surrounding landscape matrix may determine whether or not changes in tree composition of individual stands affect other organisms.

Establishing single-species plantations at the expense of natural mixed-species stands can result in significant changes in forest biota because of structural and functional dissimilarities between the native and replacement forest. This is true for a variety of taxa (Table 3.2). As an example, consider a comparison of bird communities in Australian wet sclerophyll forest, and in exotic Monterey pine plantations (Disney and Stokes 1976). Almost all birds encountered in the native forest foraged in the planted pine, but few actually bred in the plantations (30 breeding species in native forest versus 9 in the plantation). Densities for most species were also higher in native forest than in pine (e.g., 105 pairs of grey fantails [Rhipidura fuliginosa] per 40 ha versus 5 pairs per 40 ha, respectively). Additionally, the introduced European goldfinch (Carduelis carduelis) bred only in the plantation.

Not all comparisons of unmanaged forests to plantations have found an impoverished flora or fauna in the latter. Plantations may have characteristic species richness and abundance of native birds, canopy invertebrates, vascular plants, and large mammals (Duff et al. 1984, Tickell 1994,

Table 3.2. *Negative effects of plantations on species diversity*

Taxa	Effect	Source
1. Rare understory plants	Reduced abundance	Bernáldez et al. 1989 in Sawyer 1993
2. Interior forest birds	Reduced richness or abundance	Disney and Stokes 1976; Carlson 1986; Mitra and Sheldon 1993; Thiollay 1995; Gjerde and Sætersdal 1997.
3. Insects	Reduced richness	Holloway et al. 1991; Vun Khen et al. 1992;
4. Mammals	Reduced richness or abundance	Duff et al. 1984; Henson 1994

Clout and Gaze 1994). But the frequent absence in plantations of rare native taxa or inferior forest specialists strongly tempers these results (Duff et al. 1984). For instance, densities of interior forest birds were two to three orders of magnitude greater in Kenyan Brachylaena–Croton forest than in replacement Monterey pine plantations (Carlson 1986).

Similarities in biotic diversity between plantations and the native forest they replace may depend on composition of the surrounding landscape matrix. Plantations located in a matrix of native forest may have minimal reduction in species richness and abundance of taxa that move easily across large distances, such as birds, insects, and bats (Duff et al. 1984, Holloway et al. 1991). The plantations may attract species from the surrounding matrix because they provide a particular resource in abundance, but they do not necessarily provide all habitat features required by these species (Duff et al. 1984, Mitra and Sheldon 1993).

Forestry practices that alter successional pathways, especially by homogenizing overstory composition, can change communities of other taxa. Even subtle simplifcation in overstory composition may cascade into loss of other taxa, particularly when there is a close functional relationship between a particular tree and another species. In a particularly compelling argument for maintaining uncommon tree species in managed forests, Kuusinen (1994) found that high lichen species richness and specialist lichen taxa were associated with goat willow (Salix caprea), a deciduous tree found occasionally in conifer-dominated boreal ecosystems in Finland. This hardwood has little commercial value and often is actively eliminated by foresters. Data from selectively logged tropical forests suggest similar relationships. Some frugivorous and folivorous vertebrates, for instance, depend closely on rarer overstory taxa, which are cut or damaged in selective logging operations (Johns 1988). Reductions in large hornbills (Bucerotidae) with loss of strangler figs (*Ficus* spp.) in Bornean rainforests is an example of this relationship (Leighton and Leighton 1983).

As with plantations, the landscape matrix may affect biotic composition within managed natural forests. Many interior forest animals occasionally use forests with altered overstory composition if the surrounding matrix is favorable to them, but they may not breed in the altered forests. This occurs for a number of bird species, e.g., large-billed blue flycatcher (*Cyornis caerulatus*) and red-naped trogon (*Harpactes kasumba*), in selectively logged Bornean rainforests (Lambert 1992). Presumably it may also be true for additional taxa in other types of forests.

Comparisons of understory plant communities in similar-aged conifer and broadleaf forests growing on similar sites provide additional examples of dependent relationships between overstory composition and other species. It seems that most understory plants occur in both compositional-types. This is seen in comparisons of jack pine (*Pinus banksiana*) and mixed hardwood stands in New Brunswick, Canada (MacLean and Wein 1977), as well as eastern white pine (*Pinus strobus*)–eastern hemlock (*Tsuga canadensis*) and mixed hardwood forests in New England, USA (Whitney and Foster 1988). However, in these cases, total species richness and population sizes often are higher in broadleaf forests, and they may contain more rare or infrequent taxa.

Understory plant and animal communities may differ even within broadly similar forest-types (e.g., within conifer or hardwood forests). For example, Docherty and Leather (1997) found greater cover of ground layer plants, as well as higher plant species richness, under Scots pine (*Pinus sylvestris*) compared with lodgepole pine forests in Scotland. Correspondingly, they found higher species richness of spiders, and higher abundance of individual spider taxa.

The examples we have given illustrate the correlative relationships that can occur between overstory composition and other taxa in a forest. We cannot possibly cover all such examples in this space. We can, however, provide a framework for understanding why these relationships occur; that is, what are the mechanisms that link overstory trees to other species of plants and animals in a forest. Armed with this framework, foresters can begin to understand their own examples of dependent relationships between overstory trees and forest biodiversity. Moreover, they can begin to think more creatively about ways of sustaining these links. We address many of these mechanisms in the next section.

How overstory composition affects species diversity

As mentioned, overstory trees influence the structural and functional characteristics of ecosystems and, consequently, shape the biota of a forest. Overstory trees regulate ecosystem structure and function by virtue of their physical dominance (Bond 1994) and in so doing control the distribution and abundance of other taxa in the forest (Figure 3.1). Specifically, trees affect forest biota through provision of resources, such as food and substrates. Further, they alter light environments and microclimate in the forest understory through their crown characteristics (Chapter 11). Trees also affect ecosystem processes like nutrient cycling and disturbances, which, in turn, can affect the type, number, and abundance of other species. The point to remember, when thinking about these functional links, is that when overstory composition changes, the nature of the links that trees provide to other taxa also changes.

FOOD

Obviously, the reduction or elimination of a particular tree species will negatively affect organisms that specialize on consumable resources produced by that tree, e.g., roots, sap, shoots, pollen, and seeds. Many phytophagous insect groups are host specific, at least to the family level. Among North American butterflies for which host-plant data exist, more than 80% are restricted to a single plant family (Ehrlich and Murphy 1988), and >90% of the species in several well-studied phytophagous insect faunas feed on three or fewer plant families (Bernays and Graham 1988). Within a temperate deciduous forest, however, most tree species do not appear to have distinctive host-specific insect faunas (Futuyma and Gould 1979).

Among vertebrates, few mammals or birds feed specifically on resources from a single tree species. Even species traditionally considered to be specialists feed on more than one species. One of the most specialized mammals, the koala (*Phascolarctos cinereus*), browses exclusively on *Eucalyptus* foliage, but will eat leaves of three different species within the genus (Eberhard 1978). Another specialist, the red tree-mouse (*Phenacomys longicaudus*), feeds primarily on Douglas-fir (*Pseudotsuga menziesii*) needles in coastal forests in the Pacific Northwest (Maser *et al.* 1981), although other foods are consumed. A notable specialist among birds may be the Clark's nutcracker (*Nucifraga columbiana*), which appears to have a mututalistic relationships with whitebark pine (*Pinus albicaulis*) (Lanner

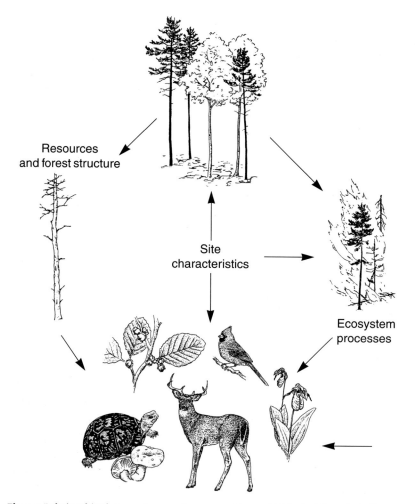

Resources
and forest structure

Site
characteristics

Ecosystem
processes

Fig. 3.1. Relationships between tree species composition and biological diversity in forest ecosystems. Characteristics of a site influence composition of both plant and animal communities, but because of their physical dominance, overstory trees provide strong additional controls over other biota. Trees provide resources for other organisms and they influence characteristics of ecosystems through their physical structure. Trees also affect ecosystem processes that, in turn, control the abundance and diversity of other organisms.

1996). The large, lipid-rich pine seeds provide the primary food for the nutcracker. The nutcracker, in turn, disperses the pine by caching more than three-quarters of the seeds collected in the soil. Apparently few other animal species disperse whitebark pine seeds, although many feed on them.

Seasonality of food resources can have a strong impact on the community of primary consumers, particularly in tropical forests. For example, just a few tree species in a rich Peruvian flora provide critical resources for five primate species during the height of the dry season (Terborgh 1983). Seasonality of resource production by different taxa can be important in temperate forests as well. For example, when the yellow-bellied sapsucker (*Sphyrapicus varius*) first arrives on its breeding grounds in mixed forests in northern Michigan, deciduous trees that provide sugar-rich sap for the bird have not yet leafed out and phloem channels have not developed. During this critical part of its annual cycle, the sapsucker relies on sap from native conifers, e.g., balsam fir (*Abies balsamea*) and white spruce (*Picea glauca*). The sapsucker switches to angiosperm trees e.g., aspens (*Populus* species) and paper birch (*Betula papyrifera*) as leaf-out proceeds. The sapsucker frequently forages for insects on conifers during the breeding season, but returns to deciduous trees to dip the captured insects in sap wells before feeding the bolus to its young (Tate 1973). As this example suggests, tree species that produce consumable resources during annual periods of scarcity deserve special attention in forest management plans (Lugo 1995).

LIGHT AND MICROCLIMATE

Forest canopies alter the quantity of light reaching the forest floor through their crown structure and foliar arrangement. So-called mono-layered species (Horn 1971), which have horizontally arranged leaves concentrated on the crown periphery, cast deep shade. Multilayered species, in contrast, have leaves arrayed vertically in several layers and transmit more light. Differences in light transmittance among species also arise from variation in crown depths. Species with deep crowns cast more shade because low branches block incident radiation across a greater range of angles (Canham *et al.* 1994).

Crown architecture and light transmittance parallel successional status. In cool temperate forests of eastern North America, for example, stands dominated by late successional species, such as sugar maple (*Acer saccharum*) and eastern hemlock, transmit less than 1% of full sunlight. In contrast, stands of earlier successional species, such as yellow birch (*Betula alleghaniensis*) and northern red oak (*Quercus rubra*), transmit more than 5% of full sunlight (Messier and Bellefleur 1988, Canham *et al.* 1994).

Overstory composition also affects light quality. For instance, red:far red light ratios differ between early and late successional species, such as pin cherry (*Prunus pensylvanica*) and sugar maple. They also differ between species of similar successional status, like sugar maple and American beech (Fagus americana) (Messier and Bellefleur 1988). Red:far red ratios affect growth and development of plants in the forest understory, and understory species differ in their response to different ratios (Morikawa and Asakawa 1976).

Striking changes in understory light regimes, that affect other forest biota, result when needle-leaved taxa replace whole stands of broadleaf trees. Light regimes also change when forests of late successional species replace early successional trees, or even with changes in the relative abundance of tree species within stands. For instance, a spring leafless condition links deciduous forest trees to carbon assimilation of ephemeral herbs (Sparling 1967); conversion of these forests to evergreen species breaks this link. Moreover, some herbaceous and shrub species closely associate with tree species that cast deep shade. For example, in forests of the Pacific Northwest, USA, bunchberry (Cornus canadensis) occurs preferentially under western hemlock (Tsuga heterophylla), a late successional species that casts deep shade (Halpern and Spies 1995).

Compared with species that cast deep shade, forests composed of trees that transmit more light often have increased understory productivity and standing crop (e.g., Mitra and Sheldon 1993). Understory productivity, in turn, affects forage availability and habitat complexity. This may, in part, control animal communities, such as spider abundance and species richness in Scots pine plantations (Docherty and Leather 1997) and bird diversity in tropical Albizia falcataria groves (Mitra and Sheldon 1993).

Light environments within tree crowns themselves vary among taxa and can affect epiphyte communities (McCune and Antos 1982). The unique epiphyte community found on goat willows in boreal Finland may result at least partially from characteristics of the crown light environment in this species (Kuusinen 1994).

Overstory composition can also affect forest microclimate, including air and soil temperatures, relative humidity, rain interception, snow loadings, and wind velocities. Conifers in northern latitudes, for instance, intercept greater amounts of snow and reduce wind speeds to a greater degree than deciduous hardwoods. Consequently, deer (Cervidae family) favor conifers for winter yarding because of their tempered microclimate (Verme 1965). Variation in stand microclimate may affect plants as well. For example, epiphyte communities may differ between drier lodgepole pine (Pinus contorta) and wetter Douglas-fir (Pseudotsuga mensiensii) forests in western North America (McCune and Antos 1982).

TREES AS SUBSTRATES

Distinctive structural characteristics of tree species, such as bark texture, leaf architecture, and branch arrangement, provide shelter and foraging substrates that affect animal abundance, distribution, and behavior. For phytophagous insects, plant structural characteristics affect predator risks and moisture regimes and are critical factors in host selection (Janzen 1985). In northern hardwood forests of New Hampshire, Holmes and Robinson (1981) found that 10 common insectivorous bird species exhibited distinct preferences among tree species as foraging sites. Compared with what would be expected by chance, yellow birch was favored as a site for foraging by all bird species; and, with the exception of two abundant species, red-eyed vireo (*Vireo olivaceous*) and American redstart (*Setophaga ruticilla*), sugar maple was avoided. Greater density of arthropods and foliar structure (small leaves on short petioles) may make yellow birch a superior foraging substrate in this forest.

The substrate that is used for foraging or hiding interacts with the morphology of the organisms involved to affect habitat selection. For instance, the goldcrest (*Regulus regulus*) has specialized pads, papillae, and folds on the soles of the feet that allow it to cling effectively to spruce needles and it therefore prefers conifer forests (Winkler and Leisler 1985). By contrast, the closely related firecrest (*Regulus ignicapillus*) does not have specialized structures on the soles of its feet; it shows a preference for American beech over spruce in experimental chambers.

SOIL RESOURCE AVAILABILITY

Composition of a forest can have a marked influence on soil resource availability, in turn affecting the distribution and abundance of other species in an ecosystem, particularly plants. Some of the mechanisms behind this linkage include: effects of litter quality on soil pH, rates of organic matter decomposition and nutrient mineralization; differences among species in stemflow chemistry; and the addition of nitrogen by symbiotic fixation.

Nitrogen mineralization and availability differ under different overstory species. For example, Klemmedson (1991) found that availability of nitrogen in soils of ponderosa pine (*Pinus ponderosa*) forests in Arizona, USA, increased concurrently with basal area of co-occurring gambel oak (*Quercus gambelii*). In another study, available nitrogen varied positively with the presence of eastern hemlock in the canopy of mixed-hardwood forests in the eastern United States (Beatty 1984).

Litter composition correlates with nutrient availability because decomposition of the dominant foliage type controls mineralization rates (McClaugherty et al. 1985). Species having high quality litter increase nutrient availability in a forest because organic forms of nutrients in their litter turn over rapidly. Decomposition varies with ratios of carbon and lignin to different nutrients, which differ among species (Vitousek 1982).

Litter quality also affects forest floor pH and base concentrations (e.g., Alban 1967, Messenger 1975). Species influences on these factors may be greatest when taxa differ greatly in the physical and chemical characteristics of their litter, as with conifers and hardwoods. In contrast, base concentrations may be similar when litter characteristics are similar (Kalisz and Stone 1984). The chemistry of stemflow, however, can differ significantly even among similar species. For instance, Crozier and Boerner (1984) found higher concentrations of calcium and sulfate, and lower concentration of hydrogen, in stemflow of white oak (Quercus alba), compared with red maple (Acer rubrum), black birch (Betula lenta), and American beech. Soil around oaks had correspondingly higher calcium and sulfate concentrations and lower pH.

The addition or removal of nitrogen-fixers can influence nitrogen availability in the forest. Sometimes foresters discourage nitrogen-fixing trees (e.g., red alder [Alnus rubra] in coastal conifer forests of western North America) to minimize competition with crop species (Franklin 1988). This may be quite short-sighted because the loss of nitrogen-fixers may undermine sustainable timber production.

These examples illustrate how differences in overstory composition cause changes in nutrient availability and soil chemical characteristics. This linkage may explain differences in understory species richness and composition among forest-types, or even under the crowns of different tree species that occur on similar sites (Parker and Parker 1983, Beatty 1984, Whitney and Foster 1988). For example, in an eastern North American hardwood forest, soil calcium concentration was highest under white oak (Crozier and Boerner 1984), as was the abundance of wild geranium (Geranium maculatum).

The longleaf pine ecosystem: a case study

The longleaf pine ecosystem once dominated the Atlantic and Gulf Coastal Plains of the southeastern United States (Ware et al. 1993).

Estimates place the original extent of longleaf pine at somewhere between 22 and 37 million ha, but currently little remains. The longleaf pine ecosystem is a good example of how overstory composition affects virtually all other forest biota through control of an ecosystem process in this case, natural disturbance from fire. Natural fire regimes in longleaf pine ecosystems consist of low to mid-intensity growing season surface fires occurring every two to 10 years, depending on site conditions (Ware et al. 1993). Fuels for these fires are primarily highly pyrogenic longleaf pine needles. Fires favor persistence of longleaf pine on a site by exposing mineral seedbeds that favor longleaf pine germination (Wahlenberg 1946). By contrast, regular fires reduce the abundance of herbaceous and woody species. Moreover, regular burning controls brown-spot needle blight (Scirrhia acicola), a deadly pathogen of longleaf pine seedlings (Wahlenberg 1946). Despite its famed fire tolerance, burning does kill longleaf pines, particularly new germinants and saplings that have just begun height growth (Maple 1975). Fire-caused mortality of smaller stems maintains low population densities in the overstory. The end result of regular fires is an open canopy structure (Platt et al. 1988), with few hardwoods in the overstory (Figure 3.2a).

A remarkable feature of longleaf pine ecosystems is their high richness of herbaceous and shrub species. Plant richness may reach 140 species per 1000 m². This value exceeds any yet reported for temperate ecosystems in the western hemisphere (Peet and Allard 1996). Richness of animal taxa is also high. Herpetofaunal diversity is roughly twice that of other pine ecosystems at similar latitudes (Guyer and Bailey 1993). Xeric longleaf pine forests contain approximately 4000 to 5000 species of arthropods (Folkerts et al. 1993). Some old-growth longleaf pine forests have as many bird species as more structurally complex hardwood forests within the region (Engstrom 1993). Some longleaf pine ecosystems, particularly those on xeric sites, do not have such high diversity, but they contain many endemic species (Folkerts et al. 1993, Peet and Allard 1996).

Studies have shown that fire controls plant diversity and persistence of endemic species. Altering components of the fire regime, including seasonality, frequency, and intensity of burning, favors different suites of species (Walker and Peet 1983). Longleaf pine needle input controls fire regimes; intensity of fire with needle fuels is greater than with leaves of co-occurring tree species, particularly hardwoods (Williamson and Black 1981). Elimination or reduction of fire results in rapid hardwood recruitment (Figure 3.2b). This initial change in the fire regime initiates a positive feedback mechanism whereby an increase in hardwood fuels further

Fig. 3.2. Alternative compositional states for a longleaf pine ecosystem. (a) An old-growth forest maintained by fire. Note that there is little hardwood encroachment into the midstory and longleaf pine is regenerating in a canopy gap (Thomas County, Georgia, USA). (b) Longleaf pine forest with fire exclusion. Hardwoods rapidly fill lower strata, limiting opportunities for longleaf pine regeneration (Thomas County, Georgia, USA).

Fig. 3.2. (c) Thinned loblolly pine plantation on a former longleaf pine site (Grady County, Georgia, USA). (R. Todd Engstrom photos)

reduces fire intensity, favoring additional hardwood encroachment (Rebertus *et al.* 1993).

Animal taxa also respond to altered fire regimes. Loss of native herbs eliminates browse for herbivores such as the endangered gopher tortoise (*Gopherus polyphemus*), which feeds primarily on fire-maintained legumes (Garner and Landers 1981). Encroachment of hardwoods into the lower canopy reduces excavation of new cavities, and use of existing cavities, by the endangered red-cockaded woodpecker (Walters 1991).

Thus, a fire regime that shifts composition from longleaf pine toward more hardwoods has a dramatic and conspicuous negative impact on the characteristic biota of these ecosystems. A more subtle, but perhaps just as profound, shift occurs when congeners replace longleaf pine. Conversion to slash pine (*Pinus elliottii*) or loblolly pine (*Pinus taeda*), either through natural regeneration or through planting (Figure 3.2c), is common in much of the longleaf pine region. The forest industry relies heavily on slash and loblolly pines, mostly because these species produce higher yields over short rotation lengths than does longleaf pine.

An important question is whether different pines can substitute functionally for longleaf pine by maintaining linkages to other species via fire. Few studies have compared the characteristics of fire regimes among these ecosystems, and few have tried to determine how the forest biota reacts to changes in fire that result from differences in pine species. In addition to differences in the physical and chemical characteristics of their needles, there are differences in the way managers can burn forest of these taxa. Seedlings of slash and loblolly pines are highly sensitive to fire, much more so than longleaf pine. Burning in young single-cohort stands of loblolly and slash pine cannot occur until regeneration reaches a fire-tolerant size: about 3 to 5 m in height or 2 to 3 cm in basal diameter. Such a change in fire frequency alone will alter animal and plant species composition in the ecosystem. Further, to burn in multi-cohort stands, foresters must protect regeneration from fire, adding to management complexity and cost. These uncertainties need addressing, to answer the question of functional equivalence among pine species.

Challenges and recommendations

MANAGING OVERSTORY COMPOSITION

Foresters need to ask themselves certain questions when evaluating the effects of their management on overstory composition. Are population sizes of species that are characteristic of certain ecosystems being greatly changed by management? Is overstory diversity being reduced in favor of one or a few commercial species? Is management for early successional trees impairing the potential for late successional species to dominate afterwards, i.e., is successional potential being lost? Are early successional species being eliminated from forests when managing principally for later successional trees? If the answer to any of these questions is yes, then the larger question is whether the degree of alteration is acceptable given other management objectives. If the answer to this larger question is no, then obviously a reassessment of management objectives is in order, with actions taken to shift composition towards a condition more in line with broader management goals.

In reality, the demand for wood fiber dictates the answer to the first suite of questions; providing commodities in profitable ways alters overstory composition in many forests. Early successional species may get preference because of high growth and yield over short rotation lengths. If these species are natural seral components of an ecosystem, then management may be truncating succession in ways that are analogous to many types of natural disturbances (Chapters 2 and 4). Unfortunately, by favoring early successional taxa foresters often do more than truncate succession. Instead, they simplify composition in the overstory by, for instance, increasing the abundance of economically important taxa at the expense of non-commercial species (Seymour and Hunter (1992).

In light of potential ecological benefits, managers should try to maintain species mixtures in patterns that better reflect conditions in unmanaged ecosystems, even in forests managed principally for early successional taxa (Franklin 1992). There are numerous ways to do this, but to be successful, managers may need to experiment outside the confines of traditional silvicultural systems, and rely more on their imaginations as guided by scientific data. For example, residuals of windfirm later-successional and non-commercial species can be maintained during regeneration harvests, i.e., legacy trees. These trees add immediately to compositional, structural, and functional diversity of the new stand. They also are a seed source for new establishment, helping to maintain the potential to shift composition in a different direction in the future. For example, conversion of many pine-dominated forests in the northern Great Lakes region to aspen followed turn-of-the century logging and wildfires (Palik and Pregitzer 1992). The widespread commercial use of aspen helps to perpetuate the type. However, by maintaining some seed sources for pines, along with aspen, a forester also maintains the potential to increase pine abundance in the future (Palik and Pregitzer 1994, Figure 3.3). Eliminating later successional species also eliminates this potential.

Advance regeneration of later successional species may require protection during harvesting of early successional forests. Protection is important. The amount of protection depends on the desired mix of early and late successional taxa in the regenerating stand. Light-on-the-land harvesting methodologies, such as cut-to-length processors, skidding on designated trails, or aerial yarding systems, can all reduce damage to residual vegetation during harvesting (Gingras 1995). For species that establish on moist decomposing wood, as on nurse logs (Harmon and Franklin 1989), regeneration depends on having a sufficient supply of downed coarse woody debris in the forest (Chapter 10).

Managing forests for later successional taxa also may cause a decline in tree species diversity. Here, less favored trees often include early successional species that are present only in low numbers in mature and old-growth forests. One approach to maintaining the wider array of canopy species in these forests is to vary the size and intensity of silvicultural disturbances. This can increase the number of distinctive environments

Fig. 3.3. This trembling aspen ecosystem is an example of maintaining seed sources and compositional potential in a managed early successional forest. The primary management goal for this forest is fiber production. Retention of the large eastern white pine in the background helps to maintain some compositional diversity in the overstory. This tree functions as a seed source for new pine establishment later in stand development. Retention of compositional diversity provides managers with the option of shifting composition toward longer-lived species in the future (Alcona County, Michigan, USA). (Kurt Pregitzer photo)

available for establishment and growth of different species (Seymour and Hunter 1992). Tree species differ in their adaptation to resource levels and substrate conditions found in disturbances of different sizes and intensities (e.g., Hannah 1991). Foresters also should consider mode of regeneration, and how harvesting and site preparation can inhibit or enhance species that establish by different means. For example, removing or disrupting the forest floor and upper soil profile may adversely affect species that regenerate from a buried seed pool (Roberts and Dong 1993).

LANDSCAPE CONSIDERATIONS

Determining the appropriate composition of stands in landscapes is a great challenge. Rarely will maintaining biological diversity in patterns resembling those in less managed forests be the sole force behind decisions about composition. In landscapes where timber production is a central objective, management deliberately favors certain species over others. Consequently, the linkages they provide to other taxa will increase at the expense of linkages provided by rare or non-commercial tree species. Managers must assess and weigh the tradeoffs that exist between timber production and sustainability of populations of species other than trees and, in so doing, decide which taxa (including overstory trees) they will favor.

Management of ecological reserves to maintain linkages between overstory composition and biological diversity may seem an easy task, compared with achieving this same goal in landscapes managed primarily for timber (Chapter 16). Management goals for large natural areas may be to maintain composition in patterns similar to unharvested landscapes, or at least move closer to this model. In reality, achieving overstory compositions that reflect unharvested conditions is a difficult and elusive goal. To do so requires large areas where natural disturbances can occur with the intensity, frequency, and extent needed to generate species compositions characteristic of presettlement conditions (Frelich and Lorimer 1991, Roovers and Rebertus 1993). There are few areas of the planet where this is still possible. Additionally, there probably are uncertainties about the appropriate compositional targets for these landscapes. Part of this uncertainty arises from poor historical documentation and a lack of intact models for comparison. More fundamentally, the compositional target is always moving as species distributions shift with changes in climate (Delcourt and Delcourt 1987). Consequently, even in management of ecological reserves, managers must make decisions about appropriate composition. In so doing, they set the stage for determining the types and abundance of other organisms that will occur in these forests.

There are tools that managers can use to help with their decisions about tree composition in both ecological reserves and production forests. These tools do not solve conflicts between competing land uses or avert the ill effects they may have on biodiversity. They can, however, assist foresters in making informed decisions by organizing information about current and potential forest composition, as it varies along environmental gradients (Tool 1) and with past land use (Tool 2).

TOOL NUMBER 1: ECOSYSTEM CLASSIFICATION

Determining the potential composition of forest stands within landscapes is a complex task. Heterogeneous soil and geologic characteristics result in large variation in vegetation-types at relatively small spatial scales (100s to 1000s of ha). Quantifying and mapping this variation has engrossed ecologists and resource managers for decades. Approaches to classification that incorporate the hierarchical structure of landscapes have proven valuable for delineating differences in overstory vegetation among ecosystems. The premise behind ecological classifications is that repeatable and mappable hierarchical combinations of climate, geomorphology, soils, topography, and vegetation exist on the ground (Barnes et al. 1982). Other features, e.g., primary productivity, nutrient cycles, and animal communities, vary in parallel with the same factors that distinguish ecosystems (Zak et al. 1986, Host et al. 1988, Zou et al. 1992). Thus, ecologically based classifications inherently capture a number of the important linkages that occur between trees and other components of biological diversity.

Classifying forest ecosystems using a hierarchical approach can aid with the complexity that succession adds to management of overstory composition. Field studies demonstrate predictability in successional pathways among ecosystem-types (Host et al. 1987, Fralish 1988), despite the importance of historical factors in determining the specifics of succession (Pickett 1989). Perhaps this is because the historical factors that influence these specifics, e.g., human disturbances, and proximity to seed sources, also vary consistently in response to hierarchical landscape controls. As such, ecosystem classifications are not only useful for understanding factors controlling spatial variation in current overstory vegetation, they also are a tool for quantifying potential composition within managed landscapes. Equipped with this tool, resource managers can make informed decisions about composition of forest landscapes from both spatial and temporal perspectives.

TOOL NUMBER 2: DISTURBANCE GRADIENTS

Human settlement and natural resource use have altered overstory composition in many forested landscapes. In many forests some element of the overstory flora is missing, or its abundance is greatly altered from more natural conditions. As our overview illustrates, these compositional changes may be extreme, as in some plantations, or they may be subtle, such as in some selectively logged forests. All levels of compositional change, however, can have important consequences for biodiversity of forests.

For any landscape where management has caused compositional change, foresters can array the current composition of stands within each ecosystem-type along a disturbance gradient. This gradient reflects the range of potential compositional states for that ecosystem. Complete compositional replacement is one end point on this gradient; a forest replaced by a shopping mall or an agricultural field, for example. The other end of the gradient is a condition of no human impact (Hunter 1996), or some other model used to define 'natural' (Figure 3.4). The actual array of states along the gradient mirrors the effects of past land use and management on composition. This gradient is a tool for quantifying the degree and frequency of compositional changes that have occurred within each type of ecosystem in a landscape. It also is useful for assessing the acceptability of these compositional states given current management objectives.

The distribution of ecosystems along the disturbance gradient will depend on past management objectives. In landscape managed intensively for timber production, compositional states are likely to fall to the left on the gradient: for instance, a landscape of eucalyptus plantations in place of mixed-species tropical forest. Compositionally, the plantations are quite different from the unmanaged condition, but they still are an improvement over a shopping mall. Plantations of native species also differ from natural forests, but they still are superior, compositionally, from states farther to the left on the gradient. Replacement of longleaf pine by planted slash or loblolly pine in the southeastern United States is an example. Annual row crops, an important alternative land use in much of the longleaf pine region, obviously provide even fewer of the controlling functions of overstory strees than do the pine plantations.

These contrasts continue to the far right on the gradient where management of ecological reserves is important. A forest managed for this purpose may differ from the ideal natural condition because a particular species is reduced in abundance. Elimination of American elm (Ulmus americana) by an introduced pathogen from even old-growth North America forests is an example (Parker 1989). From a compositional standpoint, this condition still is superior to any state to the left on the gradient, since it likely maintains a high number of important linkages between overstory trees and other species.

As these examples suggest, arranging ecosystems along gradients of disturbance and compositional states can be an important conceptual tool for assessing the desirability of a particular compositional pattern in a landscape, given current management objectives. For example, a large number of plantations are not ideal when a landscape is being managed as an ecological reserve, but this condition may be sufficient when maximizing timber production. Also, these gradients are useful for inferring cause

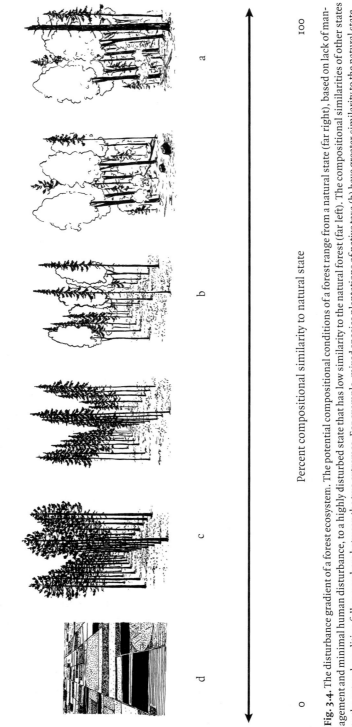

d   c   b   a

Percent compositional similarity to natural state

0   100

Fig. 3.4. The disturbance gradient of a forest ecosystem. The potential compositional conditions of a forest range from a natural state (far right), based on lack of management and minimal human disturbance, to a highly disturbed state that has low similarity to the natural forest (far left). The compositional similarities of other states to the natural condition fall somewhere between the two extremes. For example, mixed species plantations of native taxa (b) have greater similarity to the natural state than do plantations of exotic species (c).

and effect relationships between current composition and past management. If the desired composition differs from the current composition (for instance, because of new goals for biodiversity), then managers must devise new objectives that shift the distribution of compositional states in the appropriate directions along the gradient. Looking at ecosystems along disturbance gradients will not solve conflicts between competing land uses. However, this tool does provide a framework for quantifying the potential tradeoffs that exist between managing for populations of native species and managing for commodities. More importantly, a disturbance gradient allows managers to assess current composition of stands relative to the full array of potential states for each ecosystem. This allows judging a particular state for its desirability, relative to all other potential conditions on the gradient. Many of these potential compositional states could be a lot worse from the standpoint of overall biodiversity.

Summary

The biota of a forest includes much more than the trees that capture our immediate attention. Other organisms in a forest may be inconspicuous, yet their diversity and population sizes can be staggering compared with trees. Concerns for biodiversity often focus on these less conspicuous taxa, yet management for commodities focuses primarily on trees. The two are inseparably linked; changes in overstory composition have important consequences for forest biodiversity because of the causal linkages that exist between trees and other species. Trees affect forest biota through the resources they produce (e.g., food) or regulate (light) and through the physical structures they provide. Trees also influence other taxa through their effects on ecoystem processes such as nutrient cycles, disturbances, and understory productivity. Different tree taxa provide different structures and resources, and influence ecosystem processes in different ways. Thus, by changing composition to meet specific objectives, foresters alter the linkages that exist between the overstory and other taxa. Managers must be cognizant of these linkages if they are to make informed decisions about the consequences of managing for specific stand compositions. Moreover, understanding these links will help them to better balance the tradeoffs that occur when managing for competing values. It is a daunting task to manage ecosystems in a way that minimizes negative impacts of forestry on tree composition. The task can be simpler through use of innovative silvicultural approaches that maintain overstory species diversity in patterns more similar to unmanaged forests, even in intensively managed ecosystems. Further, management tools, such as ecological land classification, and assessments of stand compositions along disturbance gradients, can be useful for understanding physical and cultural controls on composition. They also will help managers identify desired future conditions in the managed setting.

Further readings

Bond's (1994) views on the controlling functions of dominant and keystone taxa in ecosystems shaped our thinking about mechanistic links between overstory composition and other taxa. More broadly, Franklin (1988, 1992) highlights interrelationships among compositional, structural, and functional diversity in forests and discusses ways in which management can either reduce or sustain biotic diversity. Finally, Hunter (1996) provides a definition of a 'natural' ecosystem for the purposes of identifying benchmarks for conservation. This definition has relevance for defining the least disturbed endpoint along a gradient of potential disturbance states and for assessing the effects of management on forest composition relative to the natural state.

Literature cited

Alban, D. H. 1967. The influence of western hemlock and western redcedar on soil properties. Dissertation. Washington State University, Pullman, Washington.

Bailey, R. G. 1996. *Ecosystem Geography*. Springer-Verlag, New York.

Barnes, B. V., K. S. Pregitzer, T. A. Spies, and V. H. Spooner. 1982. Ecological forest site classification. *Journal of Forestry* **80**:493–8.

Beatty, S. W. 1984. Influence of microtopography and canopy species on spatial patterns of forest understory plants. *Ecology* **65**:1406–19.

Bernays, E., and M. Graham. 1988. On the evolution of host specificity in phytophagous arthropods. *Ecology* **69**:886–92.

Bond, W. J. 1994. Keystone species. Pp. 237–53 in E.-D. Schuluze and M. A. Mooney (eds). *Biodiversity and Ecosystem Function*. Springer-Verlag, Berlin.

Canham, C. D., A. C. Finzi, S. W. Pacala, and D. H. Burbank. 1994. Causes and consequences of resource heterogeneity in forests: interspecific variation in light transmission by canopy trees. *Canadian Journal of Forest Resources* **24**:337–349.

Carlson, A. 1986. A comparison of birds inhabiting pine plantation and indigenous forest patches in a tropical mountain area. *Biological Conservation* **35**:195–204.

Clout, M. N., and P. D. Gaze. 1984. Effects of plantation forestry on birds in New Zealand. *Journal of Applied Ecology* **21**:795–815.

Crozier, C. R., and E. J. Boerner. 1984. Correlations of understory herb distributions patterns with microhabitats under different tree species in a mixed mesophytic forest. *Oecologia* **62**:337–43.

Delcourt, P. A., and H. R. Delcourt. 1987. Long-term Forest Dynamics of the Temperate Zone. Springer-Verlag, New York.

Disney, H. J., and A. Stokes. 1976. Birds in pine and native forests. *Emu* **76**:133–138.

Docherty, M., and S. R. Leather. 1997. Structure and abundance of arachnid communities in scotch and lodgepole pine plantations. *Forest Ecology and Management* **95**:197–207.

Duff, A. B., R. A. Hall, and C. W. Marsh. 1984. A survey of wildlife in and around a commercial tree plantation in Sabah. *The Malaysian Forester* **47**:197–213.

Eberhard, I. H. 1978. Ecology of the koala, *Phascolarctos cinereus* (Goldfuss) Marsupialia: Phascolarctidae, in Australia. Pp. 315–27 in G. G. Montgomery, editor. *The Ecology of Arboreal Folivores*. Smithsonian Institution Press, Washington, D.C.

Ehrlich, P. R., and D. D. Murphy. 1988. Plant chemistry and host range in insect herbivores. *Ecology* **69**: 908–9.

Engstrom, R. T. 1993. Characteristic mammals and birds of longleaf pine forests. Pp. 127–38 in S. M. Hermann (ed.). *The Longleaf Pine Ecosystem: Ecology, Restoration and Management*. Proceedings of the 18th Tall Timbers Fire Ecology Conference. Tallahassee, Florida.

Food and Agriculture Organization. 1995. *Forest Resources Assessment 1990: Global Synthesis*. FAO United Nations, Rome. Forestry Paper 124.

Folkerts, G. W., M. A. Deyrup, and D. C. Sisson. 1993. Arthropods associated with xeric longleaf pine habitats in the southeastern United States: a brief overview. Pp. 159–92 in S. M. Hermann (ed.). *Proceedings of the 18th Tall Timbers Fire Ecology Conference*. Tallahassee, Florida.

Fralish, J. S. 1988. Predicting potential stand composition from site characteristics in the Shawnee Hills forest of Illinois. *The American Midland Naturalist* **120**:79–101.

Franklin, J. F. 1988. Structural and functional diversity in temperate forests. Pp. 166–75 in E. O. Wilson (ed.). *Biodiversity*. National Academy Press, Washington, D.C.

———— 1992. Scientific basis for new perspectives in forests and streams. Pp. 25–72 in *Watershed Management*. Springer-Verlag, New York.

Frelich, L. E., and C. G. Lorimer. 1991. Natural disturbance regimes in hemlock-hardwood forests of the upper Great Lakes region. *Ecological Monographs* **61**:145–64.

Futuyma, D. J., and F. Gould. 1979. Associations of plants and insects in a deciduous forest. *Ecological Monographs* **49**:33–50.

Gauthier, J. J. 1991. Les bois de plantations dans le commerce mondial des produits forestiers. In L'Emergence des Nouveaux Potentiels Forestiers dans le Monde. AFOCEL, Paris, France.

Garner, J. A., and J. L. Landers. 1981. Foods and habitat of the gopher tortoise in southwestern Georgia. Proceedings of the Annual Conference of the Southeastern Association of Fish and Wildlife Agencies 35:120–34.

Gingras, J-F. 1995. Partial cutting in boreal mixedwoods: a comparison of productivity and site impacts with different harvesting systems. Forest Engineering Research Institute of Canada Field Note: Partial Cutting-4.

Gjerde, I. and Sætersdal, M. 1997. Effects on avian diversity of introducing spruce (Picea spp.) plantations in the native pine (Pinus sylvestris) forests of western Norway. Biological Conservation 79:241–50.

Goebel, P. C., B. J. Palik, L. K. Kirkman, and L. West. 1996. Geomorphic influences on riparian forest composition and structure in a karst landscape of southwestern Georgia. Pp. 110–14 in K. M. Flynn (ed.). Proceedings of the Southern Forested Wetlands Ecology and Management Conference. Consortium for Research on Southern Forested Wetlands, Clemson University, Clemson, South Carolina.

Guyer, C., and M. A. Bailey. 1993. Amphibians and reptiles of longleaf communities. Pp. 139–58 in S. M. Herman (ed.). Proceedings of the 18th Tall Timbers Fire Ecology Conference. Tallahassee, Florida.

Halpern, C. B., and T. A. Spies. 1995. Plant species diversity in natural and managed forests of the pacific northwest. Ecological Applications 5:913–44.

Hannah, P. R. 1991. Regeneration of northern hardwoods in the northeast with the shelterwood method. Northern Journal of Applied Forestry 8:99–104.

Harmon, M. E., and J. F. Franklin. 1989. Tree seedlings on logs in Picea–Tsuga forests of Oregon and Washington. Ecology 70:48–59.

Henson, I. E. 1994. Environmental Impacts of Oil Palm Plantations in Malaysia. Occasional Paper of the Palm Oil Research Institute of Malaysia No. 33.

Holloway, J. D., A. H. Kirk-Spriggs, and C. Vun Khen. 1991. The response of some rain forest insect groups to logging and conversion to plantation. Pp. 425–36 in A. G. Marshall and M. D. J. Swaine, (eds). Proceedings of the Conference on Tropical Rain Forest: Disturbance and Recovery. Philosophical Transactions of the Royal Society of London, United Kingdom, Biological Sciences 335.

Holmes, R. T., and S. K. Robinson. 1981. Tree species preferences of foraging insectivorous birds in a northern hardwoods forest. Oecologia 48:31–5.

Horn, H. S. 1971. The Adaptive Geometry of Trees. Monographs in Population Biology 3. Princeton University Press, New Jersey.

Host, G. E., K. S. Pregitzer, C. W. Ramm, J. B. Hart, and D. T. Cleland. 1987. Landform-mediated differences in successional pathways among upland forest ecosystems in northwestern lower Michigan. Forest Science 33:445–57.

Host, G. E., K. S. Pregitzer, C. W. Ramm, D. P. Lusch, and D. T. Cleland. 1988. Variation in overstory biomass among glacial landforms and ecological land units in northwestern lower Michigan. *Canadian Journal of Forest Research* **18**:659–68.

Hunter, M., Jr. 1996. Benchmarks for managing ecosystems: are human activities natural? *Conservation Biology* **10**:695–7.

Janzen, D. H. 1985. A host plant is more than its chemistry. *Illinois Natural History Survey Bulletin* **33**:141–74.

Johns, A. D. 1988. Effects of 'selective' timber extraction on rain forest structure and composition and some consequences for frugivores and folivores. *Biotropicia* **20**:31–7.

Kalisz, P. J., and E. L. Stone. 1984. The longleaf pine islands of the Ocala national forest, Florida: a soil study. *Ecology* **65**:1743–54.

Klemmedson, J. O. 1991. Oak influence on nutrient availability in pine forests of central Arizona. *Soil Science Society of America Journal* **55**: 248–53.

Kuusinen, M. 1994. Epiphytic lichen diversity on *Salix caprea* in old-growth southern and middle boreal forests of Finland. *Annales Botanici Fennici* **31**:77–92.

Lambert, F. R. 1992. The consequences of selective logging for Bornean lowland forest birds. Pp. 443–57 in A. G. Marshall and M. D. J. Swaine (eds). *Proceedings of the Conference on Tropical Rain Forest: Disturbance and Recovery.* Philosophical Transactions of the Royal Society of London, United Kingdom, Biological Sciences 335.

Lanly, J. P., and J. Clement. 1979. Present and future natural forest and plantation areas in the Tropics. *Unasylva* **31**:12–20.

Lanner, R. M. 1996. *Made for Each Other: a Symbiosis of Birds and Pines.* Oxford University Press, Oxford.

Leighton, M., and D. R. Leighton. 1983. Vertebrate responses to fruiting seasonality within a Bornean rainforest. Pp. 181–96 in S. L. Sutton, T. C. Whitmore and A. C. Chadwick (eds). *Tropical Rain Forest: Ecology and Management.* Blackwell Scientific Publications, Oxford.

Lugo, A. E. 1995. Management of tropical biodiversity. *Ecological Applications* **5**: 956–61.

Maclean, D. A., and R. W. Wein. 1977. Changes in understory vegetation with increasing stand age in New Brunswick forests: species composition, cover, biomass, and nutrients. *Canadian Journal of Botany* **55**:2818–31.

Maple, W. R. 1975. *Mortality of longleaf pine seedlings following a winter burn against brown-spot needle blight.* USDA Forest Service Research Note SO-195.

Maser, C. O., Mate, B. R., Franklin, J. F., and Dryness, C. T. 1981. *Natural history of Oregon coast mammals.* USDA Forest Service General Technical Report PNW-133.

McClaugherty, C. A., Pastor, J., Aber, J. D., and Melillo, J. M. 1985. Forest litter decomposition in relation to soil nitrogen dynamics and litter quality. *Ecology* **66**:266–75.

McCune, B., and J. A. Antos. 1982. Epiphyte communities of the Swan Valley, Montana. *The Bryologist* **85**:1–12.

Messenger, A. S. 1975. Climate, time, and organisms in relation to podzol development in Michigan sands. II. Relationships between chemical element concentrations in mature tree foliage and upper humic horizons. *Soil Science Society of America Proceedings* **39**:698–702.

Messier, C., and P. Bellefleur. 1988. Light quantity and quality on the forest floor of pioneer and climax stages in a birch –beech–sugar maple stand. *Canadian Journal of Forest Research* **18**:615–22.

Miller, G. W., and H. C. Smith. 1993. A practical alternative to single-tree selection. *Northern Journal of Applied Forestry* **10**:32–8.

Mitra, S. S., and F. H. Sheldon. 1993. Use of an exotic tree plantation by Bornean lowland forest birds. *Auk* **110**:529–40.

Morikawa, Y., and S. A. Asakawa. 1976. Growth of pine and birch seedlings under lights with different spectral compositions and intensities. *Journal of Japanese Forestry Society* **58**:174–8.

Palik, B. J., and K. S. Pregitzer. 1992. A comparison of presettlement and present-day forests on two bigtooth aspen-dominated landscapes in northern Lower Michigan. *The American Midland Naturalist* **127**:327–38.

1994. White pine seed-tree legacies in an aspen landscape: influences on post-disturbance white pine population structure. *Forest Ecology and Management* **67**:191–201.

Parker, A. J., and K. C. Parker. 1983. Comparative successional roles of trembling aspen and lodgepole pine in the southern Rocky Mountains. *Great Basin Naturalist* **43**:447–55.

Parker, G. R. 1989. Old-growth forests of the central hardwood region. *Natural Areas Journal* **9**:5–11.

Peet, R. K., and D. J. Allard. 1996. Longleaf pine vegetation of the Southern Atlantic and Eastern Gulf Coast regions: a preliminary classification. Pp. 127–38 in S. M. Herman (ed.). *Proceedings of the 18th Tall Timbers Fire Ecology Conference*. Tallahassee, Florida.

Pickett, S. T. A. 1989. Space-for-time substitutions as an alternative to long-term studies. Pp. 110–56 in G. Likens (ed.). *Long-term Studies in Ecology: Approaches and Alternatives*. Springer-Verlag, New York.

Platt, W. J., G. W. Evans, and S. L. Rathbun. 1988. The population dynamics of a longlived conifer (*Pinus palustris*). *American Naturalist* **131**:491–525.

Pregitzer, K. S., B. V. Barnes, and G. D. Lemme. 1983. Relationship of topography to soils and vegetation in an Upper Michigan ecosystem. *Soil Science Society of America Journal* **47**:117–23.

Rebertus, A. J., G. B. Williamson, and W. J. Platt. 1993. The impact of temporal variation in fire regimes on savanna oaks and pines. Pp. 215–26 in S. M. Hermann (ed.). *Proceedings of the 18th Tall Timbers Fire Ecology Conference*. Tallahassee, Florida.

Roberts, M. R., and H. Dong. 1993. Effects of soil organic layer removal on regeneration after clear-cutting a northern stand in New Brunswick. *Canadian Journal of Forest Research* **23**:2093–100.

Roovers, L. M., and A. J. Rebertus. 1993. Stand dynamics and conservation of an old growth Engelmann spruce–subalpine fir forest in Colorado. *Natural Areas Journal* **13**:256–66.

Rowe, J. S., and J. W. Sheard. 1981. Ecological land classification: a survey approach. *Environmental Management* **5**:451–64.

Sawyer, J. 1993. *Plantations in the Tropics: Environmental Concerns.* International Union for Conservation of Nature and Natural Resources. Gland, Switzerland and Cambridge, UK.

Seymour, R. S., and M. L. Hunter. 1992. *New forestry in eastern spruce-fir forests: principles and applications to Maine.* Maine Agricultural Experiment Station Miscellaneous Publication 716. University of Maine, Orono.

Sparling, J. H. 1967. Assimilation rates of some woodland herbs in Ontario. *Botanical Gazette* **128**:160–8.

Tate, J. 1973. Methods and annual sequence of foraging by the sapsucker. *Auk* **90**:840–56.

Terborgh, J. 1983. *Five New World Primates: a Study in Comparative Ecology.* Princeton University Press, Princeton, New Jersey.

Thiollay, J. M. 1995. The role of traditional agroforests in the conservation of rain forest bird diversity in Sumatra. *Conservation Biology* **9**:335–53.

Tickell, O. 1994. Conifer forests are not the 'deserts' they seem. *New Scientist* **144**:16.

Verme, L. J. 1965. Swamp conifer deeryards in northern Michigan: their ecology and management. *Journal of Forestry* **63**:523–9.

Vitousek, P. M. 1982. Nutrient cycling and nutrient use efficiency. *The American Naturalist* **119**: 553–72.

Vun Khen, C., M. R. Speight, and J. D. Holloway. 1992. Comparison of biodiversity between rain forest and plantations in Sabah using insects as indicators. In F. R. Miller and K. L. Adam (eds). *Proceedings of the Oxford Conference on Tropical Forests: Wise Management of Tropical Forests.* Oxford Forestry Institute, Oxford.

Wahlenberg, W. G. 1946. *Longleaf Pine: its Use, Ecology, Regeneration, Protection, Growth and Management.* Charles Lathrop Pack Forestry Foundation, Washington, D.C.

Walker, J., and R. K. Peet. 1983. Composition and species diversity of pine-wire-grass savannas of the Green Swamp, North Carolina. *Vegetation* **55**:163–79.

Walters, J. R. 1991. Application of ecological principals to the management of endangered species: the case of the red-cockaded woodpecker. *Annual Review of Ecology and Systematics* **22**:505–23.

Ware, S., C. Frost, and P. D. Doerr. 1993. Southern mixed hardwood forest: the former longleaf pine forest. Pp. 447–93 in W. H. Martin, S. G. Boyce and A. C. Echternacht (eds). *Biodiversity of the Southeastern United States.* John Wiley and Sons, New York,.

Whitney, G. G., and D. R. Foster. 1988. Overstory composition and age as determinants of the understory flora of woods of central New England. *Journal of Ecology* **76**:867–76.

Williamson, G. B., and E. M. Black. 1981. High temperature of forest fires under pine as a selective advantage over oaks. *Nature* **293**:643–4.

Winkler, H., and B. Leisler. 1985. Morphological aspects of habitat selection in birds. Pp. 415–34 in M. L. Cody (ed.). *Habitat Selection in Birds*. Academic Press, Orlando, Florida.

Zak, D. R., K. S. Pregitzer, and G. E. Host. 1986. Landscape variation in nitrogen mineralization and nitrification. *Canadian Journal of Forest Research* **16**:1258–63.

Zou, X., C. Theiss, and B. V. Barnes. 1992. Pattern of Kirkland's warbler occurrence in relation to the landscape structure of its summer habitat in northern lower Michigan. *Landscape Ecology* **6**:221–31.

4 Dynamic forest mosaics

THOMAS A. SPIES AND MONICA G. TURNER

A stand of forest trees is quite tangible to us; however, many of the processes that shape the biological diversity of that stand are invisible because they relate to events that have happened during some distant past or because they occur in the landscape beyond the area of forest we can see. Some scientists have called this phenomena 'the invisible present' and the 'invisible place' (Magnuson 1990, Swanson and Sparks 1990) meaning that the wrong temporal and spatial perspectives can produce erroneous conclusions. Humans and their management systems have typically perceived ecosystems at short distances and over short time frames. However, processes such as dispersal, disturbance, and succession, which control the state and dynamics of ecosystems and biological diversity, operate across a much wider range of spatial and temporal scales. This chapter is about seeing these large-scale temporal and spatial phenomena and understanding how they relate to the conservation of biological diversity.

Understanding the dynamics and heterogeneity of natural forest landscapes has become very important as management objectives for forests increasingly include the maintenance of biological diversity. Using natural or semi-natural ecosystems as a template for management is quite challenging, requiring understanding not only the patterns of forest change, but also the processes that underlie them. Recent advances in theory and empirical studies of vegetation ecology and landscape ecology indicate that if goals of maintaining biological diversity across landscapes are to be achieved in the long run, then management and conservation need to broaden their focus to include variability, scale, pattern, disturbance, and biotic processes. This is a daunting task that requires both a conceptual framework to organize and simplify ecosystem complexity and knowledge of the details of particular systems.

Our overall objective in this chapter is to synthesize some of the more recent findings about the temporal and spatial variability in forests and examine their implications for maintaining biological diversity. Our specific objectives are: (a) to review recent advances in the concepts and understanding of vegetation dynamics and spatial patterns at stand and landscape scales; (b) identify the major physical and biotic processes that are responsible for vegetation dynamics and pattern; (c) briefly review some of the major ecological consequences of forest dynamics and heterogeneity; (d) review ways in which temporal and spatial ecosystem complexity can be simplified for management and conservation purposes; and (e) examine three case studies that illustrate different natural systems and different management problems.

Forest dynamics: a complex of causes and patterns across time and space

SPATIAL AND TEMPORAL SCALES OF CHANGE

Forest structure, composition, and ecological processes change over a vast range of spatial and temporal scales. For example, at fine spatial scales sunflecks beneath a forest canopy create variation in carbon fixation and microclimate, at the scale of leaves or small gaps, which changes in a matter of seconds or minutes. At the very coarse scales, forests have changed over thousands or millions of years over entire continents as a result of climate change, evolution, and continental drift. A positive relationship exists between the spatial scale or extent of physical and biological processes and the temporal variability of those processes – small events and processes occur more frequently than large ones (Figure 4.1) (Delcourt and Delcourt 1987, Johnson 1996). Biotic processes such as establishment and competition occur frequently at microscales, whereas succession and dispersal occur over larger spatial scales. Although relatively infrequent, long-distance dispersal events can have important consequences to population viability and community dynamics. Disturbances occur across a wide range of microscales to mesoscales and frequently set the spatial and temporal context for biotic processes which are nested within the disturbances.

Forest management activities and policies operate within a limited range of mesoscales (Figure 4.1). Human activities typically range from the scale of individual trees to entire landscapes or regions and the time frames range from years to decades to centuries. The temporal scale is frequently set by political and planning cycles (2–10 years), economic timber rotations (30–80 years), and span of professional careers (40–50 years), and not by natural disturbances intervals (1–1000 years) and life spans of

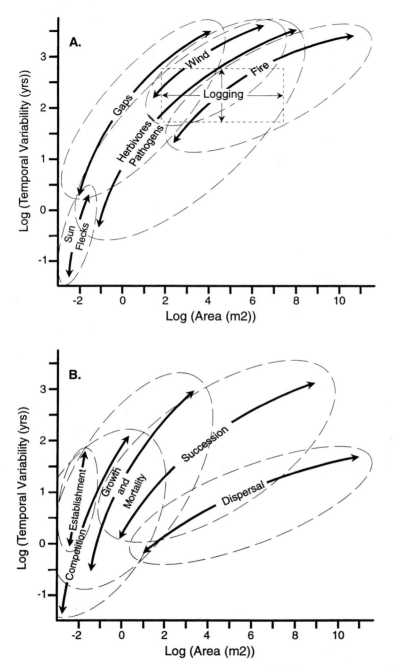

Fig. 4.1. Relation between spatial scale and temporal variability for micro to meso scale forest disturbance (A) and biotic development (B).

dominant tree species (100 to 1000 years). Similarly, economic feasibility typically determines the size of human forest disturbances, which can range from single trees in selection systems to hundreds or thousands of hectares for large clearcutting operations. In general, forest management disturbance events do not occur at large spatial scales and low frequencies relative to the domain of natural disturbances (Figure 4.1). While individual forest harvesting events occur over relatively small areas they may, however, accumulate over large areas defined by ownership boundaries and large planning and jurisdictional units.

DRIVERS OF FOREST DYNAMICS

The condition of the vegetation in a stand, landscape, or region is a product of the interplay of forces of disturbance and biotic development on a stage set by patterns and dynamics of climate, soil, and landforms. Understanding and managing forest dynamics is a major challenge that requires knowledge of complex interactions among these process at multiple scales.

Disturbance

Disturbances are a major driver of vegetation change and not necessarily rare events that are 'outside' the system (Pickett and White 1985, Pickett et al. 1989). The sudden destruction or death of plants and/or animals can result in a cascade of biotic and physical changes in ecosystems that can play out over centuries and large landscapes. Episodic disturbances appear to control tree regeneration in most forest types (Crawley 1990). However, definitions of disturbance vary and these differences can lead to confusion with regard to understanding and managing vegetation dynamics. For example, disturbance can be defined in terms of changes in physical environment, effects on biota, mechanisms or type, and uniqueness or rarity in system history. Some authors have described disturbance as changes that are not normal or are outside of some natural range of variation (Rykiel 1985). While this concept may be useful for some purposes it creates a problem by requiring detailed knowledge of history of disturbances which is lacking for most ecosystems or landscapes. We use the definition of Pickett and White (1985, p. 7) who define disturbance as 'any relatively discrete event in time that disrupts ecosystem, community, or population structure and changes resources, substrate availability, or the physical environment.' This broad definition includes both destructive events and severe or prolonged environmental fluctuations that result in disruptions to ecosystems and it avoids interpretation of whether the disturbance is 'endogenous' or 'exogenous' or within the range of natural variability. Such interpretations can still be made and can still be useful in the context of a particular ecosystem or species. Disturbance definitions that emphasize physical changes in ecosystem components such as light, moisture, nutrients, substrates, and biotic effects on community and population structure, can be readily linked to the biotic processes that drive change following the disturbance. Of course, this definitional approach still requires subjective decisions about the degree of disruption that constitutes 'disturbance'.

Physical attributes of disturbances include type, magnitude, and intensity, timing and spatial distribution (Heinselman 1981, Pickett and White 1985). Because of the high variability of disturbances in space and time a single disturbance event at a specific site has limited value as a predictor of future disturbances and as a model for conservation. Consequently, disturbances are described in terms of a disturbance regime which is the aggregate behavior of disturbance over long time frames and large areas. Aggregating disturbance behavior over large scales reduces variability in disturbance, making it more feasible to compare and predict ecosystem dynamics. Disturbance regimes can explain differences in biological diversity among landscapes and regions. For example, Bunnell (1995) found that regions in western Canada with higher natural fire frequencies have a larger proportion of species that breed in early successional conditions than regions with lower fire frequencies.

Disturbance type is one of the most important characteristics of a disturbance regime. The effects of disturbance from fire, wind, logging, and landslides can be quite different. For example, fire can kill all vegetation over very large areas but the effects of wind and pathogens can be very specific to particular canopy layers or species in the forest (White 1979). The most severe disturbances are those such as landslides and agriculture that destroy vegetation and alter soil and landform characteristics. Since forests are highly layered ecosystems, disturbances can affect one layer and leave other layers relatively intact. For example, surface fires may kill only the shrub and herb layer but not the tree layer, whereas crown fires will kill all the trees in a stand but may allow root systems of shrubs and herbs to survive, enabling these species to dominate in the early stages of vegetative regrowth (Stickney 1986). Wind damage that uproots trees and churns the mineral soil has a different effect on ecosystems than wind breakage which only disturbs the above-ground portions of ecosystems. In some cases different types of disturbance can have similar effects. For example, dense understories of shade-tolerant conifers on dry sites in the western United States can be selectively killed either by low intensity fire or by insects and disease (Campbell and Liegel 1996). In many cases, interactions occur between disturbances (Veblen *et al.* 1994). For example, following fire, forests in the Pacific Northwest are frequently susceptible to bark beetle outbreaks that result from the accumulation of large amounts of dead trees (Agee 1993) and landslides that result from loss of root strength on steep slopes (Swanson 1981). Because variability within types of disturbances is high the evaluation and prediction of disturbance effects is more dependent on the actual characteristics of the disturbance (e.g., frequency and severity) than the general classification of its type (e.g., fire, wind, human vs. natural) (Bazzaz 1983).

The relative importance of different disturbance regimes varies across biomes and regions. Fire has been a major large-scale disturbance in almost every major biome including tropical forests (Spurr and Barnes 1980, White 1979, Heinselman 1981, Attiwill 1994b) and has affected the evolution of many life history characteristics of the component species. Fire occurrence within biomes is typically quite variable – most frequent in flammable vegetation types and dry regions, landscapes, and topographic positions and least frequent or essentially absent where vegetation is resistant to fire and conditions are moist (Zackrisson 1977, Mueller-Dombois 1981, Whitney 1994, Syrjänen *et al.* 1994). In regions such as the northeastern United States, Pacific coastal forests of Canada and southeastern Alaska, the British Isles, boreal spruce forests of northeastern Europe, and tropical rainforests, wind is the a dominant disturbance (Webb 1958, Bormann and Likens 1979, Ruth and Harris 1979, Peterkin 1996, Syrjänen *et al.* 1994, Attiwill 1994a).

The magnitude of the disturbance is usually expressed as either intensity, or physical force, or as severity, the amount of live organic matter killed or removed. Severity is more easily related to biological responses than the force (amount of energy per unit area per unit time) of the disturbance event which may be hard to measure and relate to physical characteristics. Fire severity can range from little or no death of forest trees to almost complete destruction of all above and below-ground vegetative parts (Agee 1993). Hurricane disturbances vary in severity according to elevation, topography, and forest composition. For example, the highest severity windthrow from Hurricane Hugo in Puerto Rico occurred at lower elevations on northwest and north aspects in tall broadleaf forest types (Foster and Boose 1995). While attention is often focused on the death and destruction caused by disturbances, the recovery of ecosystems following disturbance is strongly controlled by the organisms and structures that survive disturbances. This 'legacy' of disturbance can determine the speed and direction of vegetation succession following disturbance. The effects of biological legacies have been documented in many ecosystems (Perry 1994). The eruption of Mt St Helens and destruction of thousands of hectares of forest vegetation provided many good examples of how legacies of surviving plants and structures formed the basis of recovery patterns in this severe disturbance (Franklin *et al.* 1985).

The timing of disturbances can have profound effects on ecosystem composition and structure. Timing can be viewed in three primary ways: seasonality (time during the year) duration, and frequency which is usually expressed as return interval, or rotation time (time required to disturb an area equivalent to the area of study). The timing of disturbance during the year is important in ecosystem response. For example, flooding during a dormant season will have very different effects on trees than floods during the growing season (Oliver and Larson 1990), and fire during moist springs may damage developing plant parts, such as buds and fine roots, more than in the fall (Agee 1993). Many disturbances such as fire and windthrow are short-lived events; however, others such as drought, flooding, and insect outbreaks can persists for months or years, and the severity of their effects, of course, increases with duration. Prolonged drought can lower chemical defenses in tree foliage leading to widespread insect outbreaks (Perry 1994). Dry years and multi-year droughts related to global weather cycles may account for most of the large fires and periods of frequent fires in boreal and temperate forest ecosystems (Bonan and Shugart 1989, Swetnam and Betancourt 1990, Swetnam 1993). The disturbance characteristic with the most profound influence on vegetation may be frequency. As intervals between fires, wind, or defoliation decrease, species composition and life history characteristics can shift toward dominance by shade-intolerant, rapidly colonizing species with early ages of sexual maturity (Agee 1993), or species with abilities to sprout and recover following destruction of above-ground parts. Where high winds are frequent, such as at high elevations and coastal areas, wind can kill or damage some species, shifting the competitive balance toward lower-stature, wind-resistant vegetation (Oliver and Larson 1990). High frequencies of fire can shift vegetation from trees to shrubs or grasses in many areas of the world, including Australia, Africa and North America (Pyne 1992, Belsky 1995, Whitney 1994).

The spatial distribution, extent, and shape of disturbances is also an important feature of disturbance regimes. Disturbances often occur more frequently in some parts of landscapes than others: e.g., floods in riparian areas and fires on dry sites and exposed topographic positions (Swanson *et al.* 1988). In Labrador, for example, fire and topography jointly influenced patterns of forest vegetation with nearly all patches of birch (*Betula*) forest occurring on steep slopes or ridges with high moisture (Foster and King 1986). Lightning would ignite fires on ridge tops covered by spruce–fir (*Picea–Abies*) forest, sweep down the ridges, and stop at existing birch stands or wetter areas in the valley bottoms. The newly burned areas along the slopes would then provide opportunities for birch to colonize. However, when fire intensity becomes extreme, topography may not influence fire distribution (Turner and Romme 1994). Wind and fire disturbances can have characteristic patch size distributions depending on the landscape and disturbance regime (Figure 4.1) (Forman 1995). Disturbances resulting from lower intensity wind events create gaps in the range of 50 to 500 m^2 for tropical forests, and fires in boreal ecosystems are typically large, ranging from a few thousand hectares to over 200 000 ha in Alaska (Dyrness *et al.* 1986, Attiwill 1994a, Essen *et al.* 1997). The ecological effects of disturbance size are largely a function of biological and physical edge effects between disturbed patches and the surrounding undisturbed forest. Large disturbance patches have lower edge to interior area ratios and will have lower densities of seed rain from the surrounding forest (Oliver and Larson 1990) and more extremes of microclimate (Geiger 1965). Absolute disturbance patch size may be less important to microclimate than the ratio of the diameter of the disturbance patch to the height of the surrounding vegetation (Geiger 1965).

Natural vs. anthropogenic disturbances

The direct and indirect effects of human disturbances on biological diversity and ecosystems are subjects of considerable debate and interest. It is no wonder that there is concern over the role of human disturbance, given the intensity and extent of direct human disturbances including: clearcutting; road building; flood control; drainage of wetlands; fire control; hunting; thinning and salvage logging; recreation; forest clearing for agriculture and development; application of chemical for fertilizer and pest and pathogen control; and indirect effects of non-forest activities on climate and atmosphere. While much of the concern derives from directly observed effects of specific forest management activities on biological diversity (FEMAT 1993) additional worries come from the more general issue of whether humans are part of nature or not. This is ultimately a philosophical debate (Hunter 1996) for several reasons including the evidence that humans are part of the same evolutionary process that produced the 'nature' we value. Furthermore, it is difficult to find a forest or landscape where humans have not had some direct or indirect influence and the concept of 'natural' may be more realistically thought of as a continuum of 'naturalness' (Peterken 1996). We try to avoid this debate by focusing not on the source of the disturbance, human or nature, but on the characteristics of the disturbance regime as described above. Bazzaz (1983) argues that 'the distinctions between natural and man-made disturbances are less important and what matters is not what caused the disturbance but what are the nature and consequences of disturbance and how do species and populations respond to them over ecological and evolutionary times.'

Using a framework of disturbance ecology, it is possible to evaluate how well disturbances that derive from direct and indirect human sources match disturbance regimes of the past which have shaped many ecosystems and to which many species are adapted. In many cases anthropogenic disturbances do not match well with natural disturbance regimes, especially in terms of frequency, size (Figure 4.1) and severity. Given our increasing awareness of the important role of disturbance in ecosystems it is possible to design management plans on the basis of natural disturbance regimes (Spies et al. 1991, Hansen et al. 1991, McComb et al. 1993, Attiwill 1994a). This approach has limitations, however, because we lack detailed knowledge of past disturbance regimes and ecological effects of current ones. This lack of understanding should be a caution against applying an ecological engineering approach everywhere in the landscape. However, in landscapes where human activity is a reality and threats to biological diversity are high, using natural disturbance regimes as a model for management may be the best way of maintaining biodiversity while meeting other human needs (Attiwill 1994a).

Biotic processes

Just as landscape-scale phenomena may not be apparent at the stand scale, the fine-scale biotic processes that gradually change vegetation following disturbance may also be invisible at the landscape scale. Early research on forest succession focused on endpoints, such as climax, and classifications of stages or pathways; recent research has emphasized successional mechanisms and the biotic drivers of successional change. This has been valuable in that it has helped to demystify the process of succession, taking it out of the realm of some sort of organismic community into the realm of population dynamics and interactions of individual species.

Many models of the mechanisms or causes of succession have been put forth (Glenn-Lewin *et al.* 1992). We will briefly mention a few here. In the classical model of Clements (1916) succession was a temporal sequence of plant communities, each of which changed the local environment and facilitated invasion by the next community. The processes that drove this model included disturbance, migration, ecesis or establishment, biotic reaction or environmental change, and competition. The endpoint of these processes was a stable climax vegetation that was the same for nearly all sites in a climatic region. Ecologists challenged this classical model almost from the beginning with alternative ideas including: (a) plants respond individualistically rather than as a community (Gleason 1917); (b) the sequence of succession is not fixed or predictable but was often determined by the first species ('intial floristics') to occupy a site following disturbance (Egler 1954); and (c) several different alternative mechanisms of vegetation change occur including facilitation (Clement's biotic reaction), tolerance (new species take over a site by tolerating the environment created by other species and growing through them) and inhibition (new species take over a site only after the inhibition of existing species has been broken by small canopy gap disturbances) (Connell and Slayter 1977). 'Vital attributes' or differences in life history traits among species, such as growth rates, longevity, age at reproduction, and response to disturbance have also proved valuable in explaining the process of successional change (Noble and Slayter 1980). The combination of life history characteristics and disturbance leads to successions that follow multiple pathways. Pickett *et al.* (1987) have proposed a hierarchical framework for vegetation dynamics that includes disturbance and biotic processes (Figure 4.2). Particularly important biotic processes are colonization, competition, and growth rate and longevity/mortality. We describe these processes in more detail below.

The most limiting stage of plant succession occurs at the beginning. Succession begins with colonization, which consists of dispersal and establishment, and is a function of seed source patterns, site availability and environmental patterns. For colonization to occur, seeds or propagules (including vegetative parts) must be present on a site (stored in soil or canopy) or disperse in from source areas. Succession may be most closely linked to environmental patterns during the early stages when plants are small and highly sensitive to the environment. The spatial and temporal variation of forest composition is strongly linked to dispersal and establishment in many ecosystems (Hobbs 1994, Masaki *et al.* 1994, Clark and Ji 1995, Pacala *et al.* 1996). The absence of a plant species from a site may not be a result of lack of suitable environment but simply of the

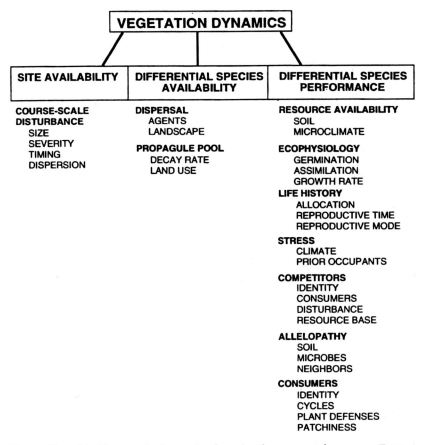

Fig. 4.2. Hierarchical framework of vegetation dynamics phenomena and processes. (From Pickett *et al.* 1987.)

fact that not enough time has elapsed since a disturbance or loss of the species for new propagules to reach the site and become established (Busing *et al.* 1995, Poage and Spies 1996, Sillett 1994, Duffy and Meier 1992, Halpern and Spies 1995). Conversely, the presence of plants on a site, which may otherwise not be optimal habitat, may be a result of 'mass effects' of an abundant local seed source (Cody 1989, Tilman 1988).

Once plants have established on a site, competitive interactions among forest plants become the primary drivers of forest succession and stand development in many environments (Oliver and Larson 1990, Glenn-Lewin *et al.* 1992). However, other biotic interactions such as herbivory and mutualism can also play important roles (Crawley 1990, Oliver and Larson 1990). Where mixes of species initiate succession following disturbance, changes in forest structure over time can be accounted for simply by differences in growth rates (Oliver 1978). Differences in shade tolerance also play an important role. Early successional plants are typically less competitive for light resources and put more of their energy into fecundity, early seed production, rapid growth, and 'escaping' succession to find new sites than late successional species (Harper 1977). Stands formed by early successional species are often subject to invasion by shade-tolerant trees that are more competitive than shade-intolerant species for scarce light and nutrient resources. Traits that allow a tree to persist and regenerate repeatedly in the absence of large disturbances include shade tolerance, longevity, clonal growth, and internal cycling of nutrients. What late successional species gain in competitive traits they apparently lose in fecundity, early sexual maturity, growth rates, and sometimes in seed size and dispersal capability (Harper 1977, Tilman 1988). While early successional species are not well adapted to persisting through succession (in the absence of large disturbances), it is not true that late successional species are absent from early successional environments. Shade-tolerant species can colonize early successional environments if seed sources are nearby, suitable germination sites are present, and climatic conditions are suitable (Oliver and Larson 1990).

By combining a diversity of species, life history traits with environmental heterogeneity we can see how succession can be resistant to explanation by simple models. Tilman (1988) argues that differences in multiple resources such as soil nutrients, moisture, and light control long-term successional dynamics. In his model, competitive abilities of different species shift across resource gradients, making the distinction between early and late successional species dependent on environmental context. This can help us understand why it can be very difficult to predict the spatial patterns and rates of succession across a landscape: spatial heterogeneity of resources can alter competitive abilities of species and patterns of seed rain can result in species persisting on sites where they are not very competitive or being absent from sites on which they are competitive. Add disturbance to the system and vegetation dynamics become wonderfully complex!

PATTERNS AND PATHWAYS OF VEGETATION CHANGE AT LANDSCAPE SCALES

The diversity of processes involved in succession can produce an incredible variety of patterns and pathways of vegetation over time and landscapes. The classical model of succession had great appeal because of its simplicity. More recent models that emphasize processes, unpredictability, and complexity, are more realistic but may be less appealing from a management perspective, where simplicity and efficiency are valued. Landscape ecologists typically view landscapes as populations of patches of different types (Forman 1995). Biotic processes operating at the scale of individual plants or interplant interactions may be too fine scale for coarse-scale spatial models of landscapes (Johnson 1996). Is there some way to reduce the complexity of the current models for applied purposes? Are there general patterns that help us understand, communicate, and manage these dynamics at landscape scales? We think the answer is yes. Instead of viewing succession from only an ontological perspective (i.e., emphasis on process and causal mechanisms), a phenomenological perspective (i.e., a description of patterns, pathways, and probabilities), can be useful in management and landscape-scale applications. Repeating patterns of change emerge at landscape scales and some order can be found through descriptions of successional pathways, patch mosaics, and seral stages that facilitates the understanding and management of vegetation at landscape scales. The challenge and art is to simplify without losing important attributes and to work with simplifications without losing sight of the underlying complexity.

Successional pathways and climax

As mentioned above, Clements (1916) classical model of successional processes did not match the reality that ecologists were observing. The same is true of his description of successional patterns and pathways across landscapes. Whittaker (1953, 1973) pointed out that within a climatic region, instead of one climax vegetation type, many are possible depending on soil and local climate variations. His classic study (Whittaker 1956) in the Great Smoky Mountains demonstrated the intricate relationships between the mosaic of forest communities and gradients of elevation and moisture. Cove forests that include beech (*Fagus gradifolia*), tulip tree (*Liriodendron tulipifera*), basswood (*Tilia americana*), sugar maple (*Acer saccharum*) and hemlock (*Tsuga* spp.) develop in sheltered areas at lower elevations; dry exposed sites tend to be occupied by pines and oaks. Thus, the idea that vegetation converges on the same equilibrium endpoint across landscapes is inadequate for understanding and managing vegetation dynamics (Glenn-Lewin *et al.* 1992). The concept of climax as a stable end point is also misleading. It is uncommon for vegetation or ecosystems to reach an equilibrium point or condition of no net change, which requires a perfect balance between opposing forces of disturbance and biotic development (Pickett and McDonnell 1989). The failure of equilibrium models to represent adequately the reality of vegetation dynamics has led to alternative theoretical formulations based on multiple pathways, non-equilibrium theory, and chaos theory (Cattelino et al. 1979, Wu and Loucks 1995, Stone and Ezrati 1996). These new formulations focus more on dynamics and variability than single endpoints. Rather than equilibrium it is more realistic to think in terms of 'quasi-equilibrium', 'dynamic equilibrium', or slowly changing systems, and to recognize that the rate and direction of change in vegetation is dependent on spatial and temporal scale.

Classifications of successional patterns can help us visualize how landscape composition and diversity will change over time. If we can assign probabilities to different patterns or pathways then we can project potential outcomes of different management actions using simple models. At least five different, phenomenological classifications of successional pathways have been identified. They include convergence (different sites become more similar), divergence (similar sites become more different), cyclical (repeating and alternating vegetation types), and multiple pathways (Frelich and Reich 1995). While these may sometimes appear to be mutually exclusive hypotheses, they may be viewed as variations of a generalized, multiple pathways model in which vegetation can follow different pattern types depending on the diversity of species in a landscape, their life history characteristics, the disturbance regime, and the environment. To some degree the differences between these characterizations of vegetation change are a function of spatial and temporal scale. For example, succession in hardwood forests in the northeastern United States has been described as cyclical (Forcier 1975) (yellow birch to sugar maple to beech and back to yellow birch again following gap disturbances) but early succession following stand replacement disturbances in these forests follows multiple pathways based on the presence or absence of pin cherry which, in turn, depends on bird dispersal and time since last disturbance (Marks 1974).

The term 'climax' no longer has value to many plant ecologists because it is associated with the Clementsian climax of superorganism and stable end points. However, 'climax' does not have to be a Clementsian term if it is put in the context of contemporary views of multiple dynamic equilibria (climaxes) within a particular spatial and temporal scale. Some ecologists still find it useful to use 'climax' or the potential natural vegetation(s) in a less formal way with the caveats that disturbance will intervene, and that communities based on too precise a listing of species may be nothing but random, ephemeral assemblages (Shrader-Frechette and McCoy 1993). Most applied ecologists who deal with real pieces of ground still need to use some way of classifying and mapping the potential vegetation assemblages that could occur over time on a site (Peterken 1996).

Vegetation as a dynamic mosaic

Another useful way of understanding vegetation dynamics is to characterize it as a shifting mosaic of patches of different ages and developmental stages (Watt 1947, Bormann and Likens 1979). This concept is a particularly useful abstraction at landscape levels (Remmert 1991) where the units are patches of vegetation that change like a kaleidoscope. The power of the shifting mosaic idea lies in three areas. First, it helps to illustrate one of the paradoxes of vegetation dynamics – the fact that vegetation can be both highly dynamic and yet appear to be slowly changing or even unchanging if the overall pattern stays the same but the spatial distribution of individual patches changes. This, of course, results from the fact that individual plants or patches of plants can change quite dramatically over time and space but when viewed over a large enough area, such as a large stand or landscape, these patches can be sufficiently out of synchrony that the net effect is a shifting mosaic of patches whose aggregate characteristics (e.g., biomass, species diversity, patch type and size distribution) may change very slowly (Figure 4.3). Second, the emphasis on population dynamics of patches and the disturbances that destroy and create them provide a framework for nesting process studies of population ecology of plants within more phenomenological approaches (i.e., description of patches, pathways and transition probabilities) (Forman 1995). For example, the population dynamics of patches of even-aged plants can be used to estimate rates of canopy gap formation (Clark 1991, 1992). Third, the spatial aspect of this concept provides a framework for how spatial characteristics such as patch sizes or juxtaposition of patches can affect overall system behavior. For example, systems with fine-grained patch structure may favor shade-tolerant species whereas systems with coarse-scale disturbances may favor shade-intolerant species (Spies and Franklin 1996). The spatial nature of this concept also allows it to be represented in maps which help humans to understand and manage natural systems.

The shifting mosaic concept has typically been applied to relatively small canopy gaps in forests, although there is no theoretical reason why it must be restricted to this size of patch. The importance of canopy gap

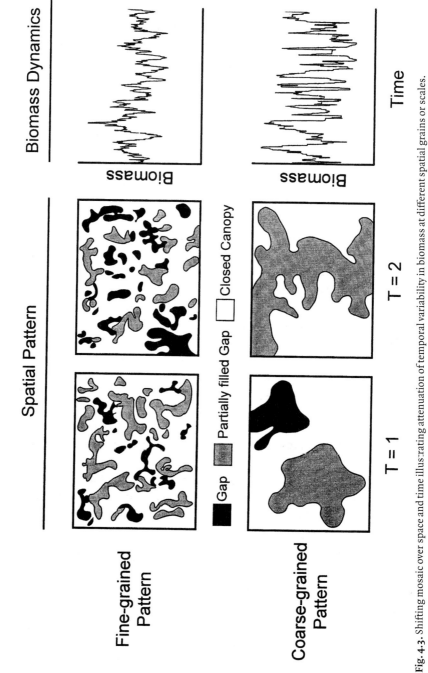

Fig. 4.3. Shifting mosaic over space and time illustrating attenuation of temporal variability in biomass at different spatial grains or scales.

dynamics to forest dynamics has been identified in many forests, especially in temperate forests in eastern North America and the New World tropics (Shugart 1984, Runkle 1985, Platt and Strong 1989, Attiwill 1994a). However, the importance of gap dynamics has been recognized in other regions including temperate Asia (Yamamoto 1992) and boreal Scandanavia (Leemans 1991). Most canopy gaps are small, ranging from single trees covering a few tens of square meters to small groups of trees covering hundreds of square meters (Attiwill 1994a). Gap creation rates range between 0.2% to 2.0% of a stand each year, which is equivalent to a rotation period of 50 to 500 years (Runkle 1985, Spies *et al.* 1990). Although canopy gaps may be relatively small they may cover 5% to 30% of a forest, and influence more than 50% of a forest, if canopies bordering the gaps ('expanded gap', Runkle 1982, 1992) are taken into account (Lertzman *et al.* 1996). Canopy gaps do not have the same effect on resources or vegetative response in all forests. For example, Canham *et al.* (1990) found that single-tree gaps do not produce the same amount or pattern of resources in forests with different canopy heights and from different latitudes. At low latitudes single-tree canopy gaps can provide significant levels of light resources; at high latitudes, single-tree gaps in tall forests transmit very little direct radiation to the forest floor.

Many forest mosaics are driven by large patches created by fire or large windstorms (Attiwill 1994a). Coarse-scale disturbances can create patches of 50 to 1000 ha in the case of windstorms (Canham and Loucks 1984) and over 200 000 ha in the case of fire in boreal systems (Dyrness *et al.* 1986). Where these coarse-scale disturbances occur more frequently than the life spans of the trees, canopy-gap dynamics may be relatively unimportant in explaining forest dynamics and biological diversity (Denslow 1987, Yamamoto 1992). In other landscapes fine-scale disturbances can be superimposed on patches originating from coarse-scale disturbances that occur with similar or lower frequencies (Spies and Franklin 1989, Clark 1991).

Vegetation states in time

Emphasis on process, quasi-equilibria, and multiple pathways may appear to argue against the development of classification schemes for succession. These classifications will invariably be subjective and the results of analyses and models based on these schemes will be more or less a function of the classification definitions (Usher 1992). However, for practical applications in which relatively simple questions are being addressed, the development and use of seral stage or developmental phase classifications

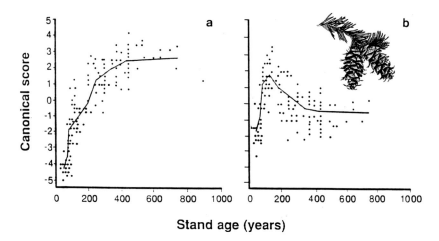

Fig. 4.4. Relationship of canonical variates of stand structure to age in a 1000-year chrono-sequence of Douglas-fir stands. (From Spies and Franklin 1991.)

can be quite appropriate. A classification approach is especially needed where spatial analysis is done and successional stages must be mapped as patch, stand or cover types.

Most classifications of forest successional stages recognize four to six major types and potentially many more if these are stratified by different environments, or potential natural vegetation types (e.g., based on climate or soil). The primary stages are: (a) stand initiation or establishment; (b) stem exclusion or thinning; (c) understory reinitiation; (d) transition or transition old-growth; and (e) shifting mosaic ('true old-growth') (Bormann and Likens 1979, Oliver 1981, Oliver and Larson 1990, Peet and Christensen 1987). Additional classes have been sometimes added to the early and late stages (Thomas 1979, Spies 1997). These stages can be distinguished based on either population processes (the origin and status of different tree population cohorts) (Oliver and Larson 1990) or on structural differences in live and dead forest vegetation that are expressions of the population and disturbance processes (Spies 1997). Changes in structure and composition tend to be rapid during the first stages and then gradually decline in later stages (Figure 4.4) (Spies and Franklin 1991, Spies and Franklin 1996, Peterken 1996). However, slow changes in old growth resulting from successional and disturbance processes may continue for centuries if the species are long lived and if shade-tolerant species are slow to colonize and grow into the canopy.

Ecological characteristics of late-successional and old-growth stages

Few issues have been more controversial in forest management and conservation circles than those surrounding late succession and old growth. Old growth is probably the only stage of forest development to have been the subject of congressional hearings in the United States (House of Representatives, 1990). Yet, it may be the least-studied stage of succession (Oliver and Larson 1990). The lack of scientific understanding of old growth is probably a result of emphasis of forestry research on earlier stages of forest development associated with economic rotations, and the lack of late-successional stands in most landscapes. In addition, the relatively rapid compositional changes that occur in early succession make younger stages more suitable for study during the course of a research grant than older more slowly changing stages.

Old-growth forests have been defined from a variety of ecological and social perspectives (Oliver 1981, Hunter 1990, Spies 1997, Davis 1996, Peterken 1996). Old growth is frequently associated with absence of evidence of human activity (Leverett 1996); however, this meaning is more accurately described by the term 'virgin' forest which is a commonly used term in Europe and elsewhere (Peterken 1996). The term 'primary forest' is also used to describe the original forests of an area prior to cutting for agriculture or settlement and seems to be favored by ecologists working in tropical regions as well as Europe. Old-growth definitions based on absence of human influence are problematic for several reasons, including the fact that many forests have been influenced by indigenous or premodern humans at least indirectly (Foster *et al.* 1996). Defining old growth based on the structure of current old-growth stands may also present problems if those definitions are used to set goals for old-growth restoration. It may not be possible to grow future old growth that is similar to current old growth because many present-day old-growth stands can comprise anomalous or unique assemblages in comparison with their predecessors (Foster *et al.* 1996) or are relics of past climates and disturbance regimes (Spies and Franklin 1988).

Ecological definitions of old growth have typically been based on age, live and dead stand structure, or population processes. A common denominator in many of these definitions is the presence of a population of old trees and their associated structures (e.g., dead trees, tree canopy gaps). The age at which this occurs and the associated structures that would develop would depend on the life history characteristics of the tree species and the disturbance regimes that create and maintain old growth (Spies and Franklin 1996). In the broadest sense all tree species or forest types can develop an old-growth stage as populations of trees age, develop large crowns, become damaged, deformed, diseased, die, create gaps for new establishment or release of regeneration, and produce relatively large (for the species) standing dead and fallen trees. In this sense, a short-lived species like aspen (*Populus* spp.), with a potential life span of around 100 years, will develop an old-growth stage as well as long-lived species like giant sequoia (*Sequoia gigantea*) which has a potential life span of over 2000 years. It is, however, the old-growth types from long-lived species (those trees whose expected life spans exceed 200 years) that are least common in forest landscapes.

Although net rates of change in old-growth forest attributes may be small at stand and landscape scales, these forests are far from static. The degree of change in old-growth stands is a function of the attributes which are measured, the particular ecosystem studied, and the spatial scale of investigation. Mortality rates within old-growth stands can range between 0.3 and 1.1% per year (Peterken 1996). Overall biomass may remain steady despite relatively high levels of mortality (Franklin and DeBell 1988). At landscape scales, pollen diagrams from temperate forests often reveal relatively stable forest composition over hundreds of years (Foster and Zebryk 1993, Worona and Whitlock 1995). Pollen studies generally show less stability at stand scales than landscape scales (Peterken 1996) but some old-growth stands have been relatively stable in composition for thousands of years at relatively fine spatial scales (Davis *et al.* 1994). Unfortunately while pollen studies can characterize long-term compositional changes fairly well, they are not able to detect long-term structural changes in age and stand structure which may be more distinctive in old growth than are compositional changes (Spies and Franklin 1991).

The relative frequency, severity, and size of disturbance determines the amount and kind of old growth in a landscape (Spies and Franklin 1996, Johnson *et al.* 1995). Old-growth forests in which the canopy trees can regenerate in small canopy-gap disturbances will frequently develop a fine-grained patch structure and will theoretically develop a 'reverse-J' age-class distribution or become multi-cohort over long time periods. However, few old-growth stands actually show this; they are more typically characterized by irregularities in age distributions as a result of intermediate-scale or moderate-severity disturbances (Peterken 1996). Old growth in landscapes characterized by large disturbances such as fire will have a coarse-grained mosaic of age classes, which will eventually require large disturbances to maintain the landscape age-class pattern and distribution. In old-growth systems with large trees that survive low to moderate severity fires, such as pine (*Pinus* spp.) and Douglas-fir (*Psuedotsuga menziesii*), fire, instead of wind, may create gaps and heterogeneity.

Landscape dynamics and age/seral class distributions

The proportion of different age classes or seral stages across a landscape and over time is one of the fundamental characteristics of the vegetation mosaic. Under natural disturbance regimes these proportions will vary over time and across landscapes depending on the frequency, intensity, and pattern of disturbances and the rates of development of different seral stages. The age-class distributions of large landscapes under natural or semi-natural disturbance regimes are generally not well known (Hemstrom and Franklin 1982, Johnson *et al.* 1995). In many cases the amounts of different age classes over time do not appear to be constant but fluctuate over time. A steady-state condition of relatively constant proportions of different age classes appears to be uncommon, even for large landscapes (Hemstrom and Franklin 1982, Baker 1989, Turner *et al.* 1993). Quasi-equilibrium conditions seem to be most common where small-scale wind and treefall disturbances dominate the regime and fire is rare, such as in parts of New England (Bormann and Likens 1979), and the north central United States (Frelich and Lorimer 1991). Rather than search for the elusive equilibrium it is more realistic to evaluate the relative variability of different landscapes. Turner *et al.* (1993) evaluated disturbance regimes from several different types of landscapes based on four factors: (a) interval between disturbances; (b) rate of recovery of a seral stage; (c) spatial extent of the disturbance; and (d) spatial extent of the landscape. They found that variability increased as the ratio of the disturbance interval to the recovery interval decreased and as the ratio of the disturbance extent to the landscape extent increased (Figure 4.5). In other words, where disturbances were frequent and landscapes were relatively small, variability in older age classes was high. Shugart (1984) also observed that when the disturbance size approached the size of the landscape, amounts of different patch types became quite variable over time. This general finding is, of course, one reason (but not the only one) why nature reserve design puts a premium on large areas (Chapter 16). Large habitat areas are more stable than small ones. However, it must be remembered that few landscapes, even under 'natural' conditions, were ever constant in the amount of different age/seral classes over time.

The rarity of constancy in natural landscapes does not necessarily argue for the view that whatever humans do will produce the same ecological

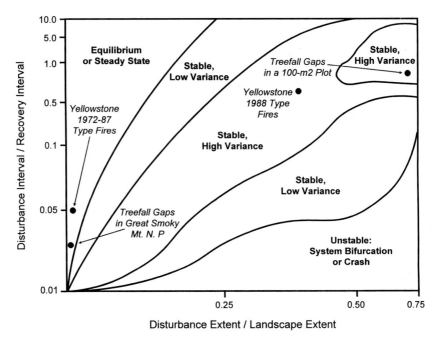

Fig. 4.5. State-space diagram of the temporal and spatial characteristics of disturbances and landscapes illustrating different types of landscape dynamics. (From Turner *et al.* 1993.)

outcomes (Sprugel 1991). One of the distinctive features of natural land-scape age-class distributions, regardless of how variable they may be, is the presence of a 'tail' in the forest age-class distribution that extends into older ages. The tail results from the fact that natural disturbances, such as fire, insect outbreaks and large windstorms do not always remove the oldest age classes in a landscape – they typically disturb young stands as well. In fact, in some cases young stands with green fuels close to the ground may be more likely to burn than older stands with higher canopies (Agee and Huff 1987). In addition, lakes and soil and topographic variabil-ity create areas where stands may escape fire and wind disturbances for long periods (Bergeron 1991, Syrjänen *et al.* 1994, Foster and Boose 1995). The fact that natural disturbances do not remove all stands and do not nec-essarily only destroy older stands leads to landscapes in which some older stands survive. It is possible to estimate what the age-class distributions of landscapes would look like under these natural disturbance regimes using a well-accepted fire-frequency model (Van Wagner 1978, Johnson and Gutsell 1994). The cumulative survivorship distribution is determined from the following equation:

$$A(t) = \exp - (t/b)$$

where t is the time since last disturbance and A(t) is the survivorship distribution, and b is the disturbance cycle (time required to disturb an area equal to the study area), the inverse of which is the disturbance frequency at any given point in the landscape. Applying this model, which assumes equal probability of disturbance among the age classes, produces the expected distribution shown in Figure 4.6 for different fire frequencies and ages of old growth.

The age-class distributions of forest landscapes almost never fit this model distribution exactly and may deviate from it considerably (Van Wagner 1978, Johnson et al. 1995) Forest landscapes may deviate from expected model age-class distributions as a result of either changes in disturbance frequencies over time or the lack of validity of the assumption of uniform flammability with age. The model can be modified using a Weibull formula to estimate the distribution where disturbance probabilities are not uniform across the age classes (Johnson and Gutsell 1994). This model can then be used to estimate the amount of landscape that occurred in an old-growth condition if old growth can be defined in terms of age since the last major disturbance. For example, if old-growth forests develop in around 150 years, and the average stand replacement disturbance frequency is 300 years, then the expected long-term amount of old growth will be about 61% (Figure 4.6).

Compositional responses to forest dynamics

The ecological changes resulting from disturbances and vegetation development vary by species and ecological process. Disturbances themselves kill both animals and plants; however, we confine our focus on the direct effects on vegetation and the indirect effects on animal habitat and ecosystem functions.

The differences in vegetation structure and species composition between early successional forest conditions and later stages when tree canopies close and increase in height have been documented in many studies (Gashwiler 1970, Helle 1985, Haila et al. 1994). Of course, the structural and compositional changes that occur when forests change to meadows, prairies, fields, and recent clearcuts, or vice versa, are greater than changes that occur with transitions among various stages of closed-canopy forest development. Early stages of forest succession are characterized by species with high colonization abilities and later stages by species better adapted to slowly changing habitats or, in the case of plants, by shade-tolerant species that can compete well for light resources but

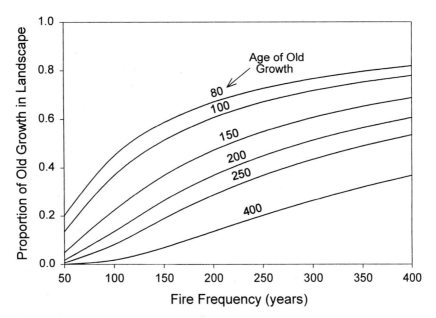

Fig. 4.6. Theoretical proportions old growth forests in landscapes in relation to disturbance frequency and age at which old growth develops.

may have poor dispersal abilities (Tilman *et al.* 1994). Landscapes in which early and late successional habitat are intermixed may provide conditions suitable for species such as various deer species which require both foraging and cover habitat (Thomas 1979). Conversely, the quality of habitat of the remaining forest patches may decline through fragmentation effects, such as microclimate changes (Chen *et al.* 1995) herbivory, predation at edges (Alverson *et al.* 1988), higher rates of mortality in dispersing juveniles, and increased rates of disturbance (Franklin and Forman 1987) (Chapters 6 and 7).

Although changes from late to early stages of forest development are most drastic and may account for the greatest alterations of biological diversity, changes in the quality and diversity of mid to late successional forests through management for wood production can also alter biological diversity and threaten the viability of species and ecosystems (Heliövaara and Väisänen 1984, FEMAT 1993, Essen *et al.* 1992). Forest management for wood production typically decreases the interval between disturbances, alters landscape age-class distributions, decreases the diversity of forest structure and composition at stand and landscape scales, and results in forest fragmentation. These changes may not result in much change in forest cover in a landscape; however, they may alter forest quality and affect species and processes that are sensitive to it.

Few studies have documented the differences in the fauna and flora of managed and unmanaged forests. However, a comprehensive study of differences in natural forests of mid to late seral stages has been made in the Pacific Northwest (Ruggiero et al. 1991). The plant and animal communities of closed canopy forests in over 200 stands ranging in age from 40 years to over 900 years were studied across the entire region. The stands in this chronosequence range in development from stem-exclusion stage through old-growth stages. Forest structure varied dramatically (Spies et al. 1988, Spies and Franklin 1991) (Figure 4.4). Diversity of plant and animal species tended to be higher in old growth than in earlier closed canopy stages, although differences in diversity were small. Community overlap, the proportion of species not showing statistical differences among forest age classes, typically ranged from 56% for trees and amphibians to 91% for shrubs and herbs (Hansen et al. 1991). Sensitivity of bird species abundance to age class differences was highest in the Coast Range subregion (Huff and Raley 1991) where disturbance history created a greater difference in forest structure among the age classes than in other subregions (Spies et al. 1988). No species of plant or vertebrate occurred exclusively in the old-growth forests, although many occurred more frequently there than in younger forests. Plant species showing the greatest abundance in older forests were small shade-tolerant forest herbs, canopy lichens (*Lobaria* spp.) and Pacific yew (*Taxus brevifolia*), all of which may be less abundant in younger stands because of slow rates of colonization (Halpern and Spies 1995, Sillett 1994). Vertebrate species with greater abundances in older forests included the northern spotted owl (*Strix occidentalis caurina*), which appears to prefer multi-layer canopies for foraging and large trees for nesting, bats (*Myotis* spp.) which use snags and large damaged or diseased trees for roosting. Brown creepers (*Certhia americana*), a bark-gleaning bird, and shrew-moles (*Neurotrichus gibbsii*), which apparently prefer sites with deep accumulations of fine and coarse litter, were also more abundant in the old-growth stage (Aubry et al. 1991). Although these studies in the Pacific Northwest have provided much valuable information about changes in species composition during succession, it must be remembered that the results do not necessarily apply to managed stands in heavily managed landscapes.

Spatial heterogeneity

As we mentioned at the beginning of this chapter forest dynamics and spatial heterogeneity are closely linked (Figure 4.1). In many ways forest dynamics and spatial patterns are just two sides of the same coin. They are often generated by the same forces, are highly variable both spatially and temporally, are systematically described to help us understand, communicate, and manage them, and they both can have strong effects on the abundance and distribution of organisms and functions of ecosystems. In this section we focus specifically on the causes, characterizations and effects of spatial pattern. We are just beginning to understand spatial patterns in forests. The recent development of high-speed computing, GIS (geographical information systems), remote sensing, and spatial statistics now gives tools to help us see patterns that we could not see before and evaluate their ecological effects.

CAUSES OF SPATIAL PATTERNING

The forces that cause forest dynamics also result in spatial patterning. However, spatial pattern will occur even in the absence of disturbance and successional processes. Spatial variation in environmental factors such as elevation, slope, aspect, and soil type creates complex abiotic templates upon which forest communities develop (Chapter 5). Many studies have described these types of relationships in a variety of landscapes (e.g., Whittaker 1956, Reiners and Lang 1979, Spies and Barnes 1985).

We have already given some examples of how biotic interactions can influence forest succession. Another interaction that may strongly influence dynamics and spatial pattern is herbivory by dominant organisms. Beavers (*Castor canadensis*) create openings and impose a strong spatial pattern on the distribution of forest and non-forest communities across a landscape (e.g., Johnston and Naiman 1990). Selective foraging by moose (*Alces alces*) in boreal forests creates distinct patterns in the distribution of deciduous and coniferous species (e.g., Pastor *et al.* 1988, McInnes *et al.* 1992). Herbivory by ungulates such as elk (*Cervus elaphus*) on aspen (*Populus tremuloides*) in the northern Rockies may be one of many factors influencing the spatial distribution of aspen (e.g., Romme *et al.* 1995). Pests and pathogens also generate spatial patterns in the distribution of species and of age classes of trees (e.g., Sprugel 1976, Sato and Iwasa 1993, Castello *et al.* 1995).

Human activities create strong spatial patterns in many forests. Patterns of land use and forest harvest are two conspicuous human influences on spatial pattern, although there are many others. The dispersed cutting patterns implemented in forests of the Pacific northwestern United States has resulted in a sharp decline in the average patch size and connectivity of older forests and a dramatic increase in edge habitat (Franklin and Forman 1987, Li *et al.* 1993, Spies *et al.* 1994, Wallin *et al.* 1994). Similar results have been observed in Swedish boreal forests (Edenius and Elmberg 1996). In general, disturbance suppression, the use of small prescribed disturbances, and fragmentation from clearcutting all tend to produce landscapes with smaller more numerous patches that are closer together; restoration of a natural disturbance regime following fragmentation or disturbance suppression tends to produce the opposite trends (Baker 1995). Because forests take a long time to develop, the patterns created by human activities may be very persistent, even after the activity ceases (e.g., forest harvest patterns, Wallin *et al.* 1994). Simulation studies have suggested that landscapes require one-half to two rotations of a new disturbance regime for their structure to adjust to that new regime, regardless of how the disturbance regime has been altered (Baker 1995).

Patterns of human settlement have profoundly influenced forest structure and heterogeneity for millennia (e.g., Ellenberg 1988, Burgess and Sharpe 1981, Turner *et al.* in press, Essen *et al.* 1997). For example, forest covered about half of the conterminous U.S. at the time of European settlement. Although the forests had been influenced for centuries by Native American land-use practices, forest clearing for fuel, timber and other wood products, and cropland lasted through the 1920s and led to profound changes in abundance and spatial distribution of forest communities (e.g., Whitney 1994, Meyer 1995). Old-growth eastern hemlock and mature hardwoods dominated northern Wisconsin in the 1800s. By 1931, following extensive cutting and burning of slash, young forests covered more than 50% of the landscape, and by 1989 a mixture of second-growth hardwood and conifer communities dominated (White and Mladenoff 1994). Although the total area covered by forest has increased since 1900 (following cropland abandonment) across much of the eastern United States, the composition of these forests is often quite different from those in the 1700s (Turner *et al.* in press).

Thus, forest landscape patterns result from the interplay of abiotic constraints, biotic interactions, and disturbances. The pattern is not simply a constraint imposed on the ecological system by topography and soils.

Instead, there is an intimate tie between pattern and process that forms an important core to the understanding of forest landscapes (Urban *et al.* 1987).

CHARACTERIZING SPATIAL HETEROGENEITY

Quantitative methods are required to describe spatial patterns: (a) to relate patterns to ecological processes; (b) to monitor changes through time; (c) to compare different forests, and (d) to evaluate the effects of alternative forest management options within a spatial context. Overviews of the various metrics for quantifying spatial pattern are readily available elsewhere (e.g., O'Neill *et al.* 1988; Turner 1989, 1990; Baker and Cai 1992; Turner and Gardner 1991; McGarigal and Marks 1995), and we will not review these here. Rather, we will briefly discuss some of the important factors that must be considered in performing or interpreting such analyses.

A landscape is typically represented as a grid of cells, and this grid then provides the basis for quantitative analysis. (Data may also be represented in vector format, but the gridded form is more common and is consistent with remotely sensed imagery.) The spatial scale of these data strongly influences the numerical results of any pattern analysis (Turner *et al.* 1989). Spatial scale encompasses both the *grain*, or resolution of the data – e.g., the size of the grid cells or the minimum mapping unit – as well as the *extent*, or size of the area to be analyzed. Recent analyses suggest that the grain of the data used for spatial analyses should be two to five times smaller than the spatial features of interest (O'Neill *et al.* 1996). In addition, the spatial extent should be two to five times larger than landscape patches to avoid bias in calculating landscape metrics (O'Neill *et al.* 1996).

The choice of what categories to include in a spatial analysis is critical, as the classification strongly influences the numerical results. For example, when describing a forested landscape, one might classify the forest based on dominant species or by successional stage. The patches identified by these two schemes would usually be very different, and the metrics describing them would also be dissimilar. The classes must be selected for the particular question or objective. For example, general categories (e.g., deciduous vs. coniferous forest) might be appropriate to study landscape patterns in the eastern United States, but various forest community classes would be needed to study patterns within a particular landscape such as the Great Smoky Mountains National Park.

There is no single metric that is, by itself, sufficient for quantifying spatial pattern. The choice of which metrics are 'best' must be based upon the question at hand. Many metrics of spatial pattern are strongly correlated with one another, containing much redundant information. Riiters et al. (1995) examined the correlations among 55 different landscape metrics by means of a factor analysis and identified only five independent factors. Thus, many typical landscape metrics are not measuring different qualities of spatial pattern, and the set of metrics to be used in concert should be carefully selected.

ECOLOGICAL CONSEQUENCES OF SPATIAL PATTERN

Spatial pattern can exert a strong influence on population dynamics and ecosystem processes, and many effects have been described (e.g., Forman 1995, Chen et al. 1995). Indeed, understanding spatial ecological dynamics has been labeled 'the final frontier' for ecology (Kareiva 1994). Despite the recent interest and progress, it remains challenging to determine for various processes or organisms the conditions under which spatial heterogeneity is and is not important. We highlight here several of the well-described ecological consequences of spatial pattern, focusing on the importance of habitat connectivity for species, the influence of landscape context on local processes, land–water interactions, and the spread of disturbance.

Habitat connectivity has important effects on the persistence and abundance of species (Chapter 7). It is clear that the actual spatial arrangement – not simply the variance – of habitat and barriers affects the location, movement patterns, foraging dynamics, and persistence of organisms. To understand connectivity (or its inverse, fragmentation), one must characterize suitable habitat from the perspective of the particular species of interest (Wiens 1976). 'Perspective' here refers to describing the physical and biological environment at an appropriate spatial scale (Wiens 1989, Pearson et al. 1996); simply identifying what is connected or fragmented from a human perspective may not be relevant to another species. In forested landscapes, stand age often interacts with community composition to define suitable habitat. For example, in the southeastern coastal plain of the United States, suitable habitat for Bachman's sparrow includes both early- and late-successional forest, but not the middle seral stages (Pulliam et al. 1992). This leads to rather complex interactions between habitat connectivity for this species and forest management (Liu 1993). Habitat connectivity for species requiring old-growth forest has received considerable attention (e.g., FEMAT 1993) and is clearly an important consideration for forest mosaics.

Local ecological processes may respond not only to local conditions but also to the landscape context (Turner *et al.* 1995), and this is another consequence of spatial patterning. For example, some species respond more to the pattern of forest and non-forest communities in the surrounding landscape than to the local habitat structure. In his study of wintering birds, Pearson (1993) found that the occupancy of a habitat patch may depend on other surrounding patches, and occupancy may be enhanced if the patch is surrounded by additional suitable habitat. Thus, the landscape context must be considered along with site-specific attributes when considering species abundance and biodiversity (Franklin 1993).

Land–water interactions are strongly influenced by the spatial patterns of vegetation, especially the presence and integrity of riparian communities (Chapter 8). Riparian forests along streams can filter undesirable excess nutrients in landscapes in which forests are mixed with agricultural or urban land uses. In a Maryland watershed, dramatic reductions in water-borne nutrient loads (C, N and P) occurred within riparian forest (Peterjohn and Correll 1984). Riparian buffers can reduce nitrate-N concentrations by up to 90% in shallow groundwater (Osborne and Kovacic 1993). The coupling of natural and managed forests within a watershed has important implications for water quality. For example, shading of streams by trees can help maintain cool temperatures required by salmonids (Chamberlin *et al.* 1991). Landslides originating in steep forested headwall areas can deliver large wood and sediment to streams that may have positive or negative effects, depending on the kind and size of trees and size and amount of the sediment delivered to the stream. Thus, riparian forests are important not only for the functions they provide as live intact vegetation, but also for the large organic matter they deliver when disturbance occurs near streams.

Spatial patterning may also influence the spread of disturbances and the patterns of succession. Various spatial locations across a landscape may be differentially susceptible to disturbances, though this is by no means uniform. In forests of central New England, for example, slope position and aspect strongly influence probability of disturbance (Foster 1988a, 1988b). Exposed hilltops and southeastern slopes tend to be more susceptible to storm-related hurricane damage. However, disturbance in forests in the upper Midwest showed no significant response to topographic features (Frelich and Lorimer 1991). Beyond the influence of landscape position, connectivity of forest habitat may influence the spread of pests or pathogens. In northern Ontario, Canada, the best predictor of the duration of outbreaks of forest tent caterpillars was the amount of forest edge per km^2 of forest (Roland 1993). As succession proceeds following a disturbance, the spatial patterning of the disturbed and undisturbed areas within a forested landscape can influence community structure by influencing local site conditions (e.g., temperature, light availability) and seed sources. The effect of disturbance size and spatial configuration is probably most important when the biotic residuals (e.g., in situ propagules or surviving plants) are low and when disturbance size is large (Turner *et al.* in prep).

Implications for management

GENERAL PRINCIPLES

The 'new ecology' or new paradigm of ecology that has emerged in recent years (Botkin 1990, Zimmerer 1994, Pickett and Ostfeld 1995, Christensen 1997) has replaced 'balance of nature' with 'ecosystem dynamics' or 'flux of nature' as the dominant metaphor of ecology. According to Pickett and Ostfeld (1995) the classical paradigm leads to many false assumptions that undermine many, but not all, of the principles that management systems have been based on. These are: (a) systems are closed to outside influences and therefore management can ignore changes outside management boundaries; (b) systems are self-regulating, will remain relatively stable in the face of environmental change, and therefore management can rely on benign neglect; (c) systems possess a single end point at which they are at equilibrium and therefore a management strategy of benign neglect will allow systems to maintain stability or return to the same compositional and functional state they were at in the past; (d) succession always proceeds through the same pathway so temporal changes are predictable and will take care of themselves; (e) disturbance is something that is outside the system so management can ignore it or try to stop it if it occurs; and (f) humans are not components of ecosystems so, for example, past impacts of Native Americans on current ecosystem conditions can be ignored.

The new paradigm is based on the assumptions that: (a) ecosystems and landscapes are dynamic, (b) disturbance is a critical component of systems; (c) ecosystems are controlled by biotic and physical processes that occur at different spatial scales and levels of the biological hierarchy; (d) succession does not necessarily follow the same path and end at the same equilibrium point; (e) spatial pattern is important to biological diversity; (f) pattern–process interactions are organism specific; and (g) human activities of the recent and distant past have had strong influences on many ecosystems that we may perceive as 'natural' today (Pickett and Ostfelt 1995, Turner et al. 1995). The new metaphors of ecology may help us to sustain biological diversity but they probably make management more complex and difficult. Incorporation of these new principles into management must be based on understanding of the ecological limits or domains where successional and evolutionary processes can sustain biological diversity. In addition managers must have some idea of how these limits are distributed across landscapes and spatial scales and how they can vary over time.

DISTURBANCE

One of the foundations for conservation of biological diversity in forest landscapes is understanding and managing the disturbance regimes of a landscape under past natural or semi-natural conditions. The alteration of landscape disturbance regimes by humans has had four major effects: (a) exclusion of fire from fire-dependent ecosystems; (b) reduction in structural and compositional diversity through intensive forest management; (c) conversion of forests to other land-cover types such as agriculture and development; and (d) alteration of hydrological processes and disturbance regimes. Ultimately, the effects of human activities on climate and atmospheric conditions may produce the most pervasive changes of all.

Human alteration of fire regimes has had profound effects on the structure, composition, and function of many forest ecosystems. In some cases, human activity has increased fire frequency and intensity causing losses in species diversity and ecosystem productivity. For example, fire frequency and severity increased during the period of European settlement and logging of virgin forests in many areas of the world including Australia (Attiwill 1994a) and eastern North America, where pine and hemlock populations were depleted from many landscapes in the Great Lakes region. Losses of organic matter and nitrogen from soils have also resulted from hot and frequent slash fires associated with logging and land clearing (Whitney 1994) and slash and burn agriculture in tropical areas (Ramakrishnan et al. 1981, Mueller-Dombois 1981). On the other hand, suppression of fire by humans has drastically changed successional pathways, forest composition and structure, and increased the incidence of disease and insect outbreaks in many forest ecosystems including boreal forests

(Heinselman 1981), temperate coniferous forests in western North America (Kilgore 1981), oak forests in eastern North America (Abrams 1992), Mediterranean vegetation types (Naveh 1974) and fire-adapted eucalypt forests in Australia (Attiwill 1994b). The implications to managers are clear: if you change the fire regime you change the ecosystems and the landscape.

Intensive forest management for timber and wood fiber production has altered disturbance regimes by increasing the frequency and severity of disturbances in many landscapes relative to natural and semi-natural disturbance regimes (Spies and Cline 1988, Franklin and Forman 1987, Hansen et al. 1991, McComb et al. 1993, Swanson et al. 1993, Essen et al. 1992, Hunter 1990). In addition, the size and pattern of cutting units typically results in dissection from roads and perforation and fragmentation of remaining forest patches, thereby increasing edge effects (Chen et al. 1995) and decreasing the ability of some organisms to move around the landscape (Forman 1995, Spies et al. 1994, Hunter 1997). Increased frequency and severity of management disturbance has resulted in losses of old-growth forests and threats to species associated with old growth in the Pacific Northwest (FEMAT 1993) and reduction in structural (e.g., large trees, snags, decayed fallen trees) and compositional (deciduous trees in coniferous plantations) diversity and associated plant and animal species in intensively managed boreal forests (Essen et al. 1992, Angelstam 1997). Some foresters have stated that clearcutting imitates severe wildfire. While this may be true in some landscapes for some disturbance regime attributes (e.g., opening size and frequency), the degree of similarity with wildfire is typically low because of the high level of biomass removal from traditional clearcuts, the uniformity of structure within clearcuts, the low diversity of patch sizes, and the high cutting frequency (in landscapes where natural fire return intervals exceed 100 years). In landscapes with low to moderate severity fire regimes, logging practices can be made more similar to the natural disturbance regime by leaving live and dead trees as individuals and in groups (Franklin 1989, Attiwill 1994a) and altering cutting unit sizes and patterns (Franklin and Forman 1987). In landscapes with high severity fires, variation in severity probably left patches of relatively unburned forest especially near wetlands, rock outcrops or other fire breaks and in moist topographic positions. In this type of landscape logging frequency and severity can be varied across the landscape to imitate potential natural variation in fire frequency associated with different landscape units (Angestam 1997).

Conversion of forests to agriculture and development has had enormous impacts on the loss of forest biodiversity throughout history

(Williams 1989). The conversion from forest management to intensive agriculture results in drastic semi-permanent changes at stand and landscape scales. Much of the losses of virgin forest in the eastern United States can be attributed to clearing of forest for agriculture (Whitney 1994). Landscape effects of conversion to agriculture include rapid and severe forest fragmentation (Curtis 1959). Some forest landscapes such as New England have been able to recover to some degree from conversion to agriculture (Foster 1995). Many forest animals such as bear (Ursus euartos), cougar (Felis concolor), and moose (Alces alces) have begun to repopulate these former agricultural landscapes as forest cover has reached high levels. However, subtle changes in soil and species composition still remain over 150 years following abandonment of farming in this region. The message to management is that restoration of forests from loss and severe disturbances in agricultural landscapes is possible even where forests have been removed and soils altered, but it will be a slow process and will probably not return to the same structure and composition that occurred before the disturbance.

Human effects on the hydrology of rivers and wetlands is another example where humans have altered the frequency and severity of disturbance regimes causing declines in some species and changes in community structure (Johnson et al. 1976, Nilsson et al. 1991). In the case of rivers, logging operations which used rivers as transportation corridors frequently produced log jams and splash dams which when broken caused severe floods that removed riparian vegetation and aquatic habitat (Whitney 1994, Sedell et al. 1991). Conversely, channelization and damming of rivers has often resulted in fewer floods and narrower, less complex river channels and floodplains (Chamberlin et al. 1991). The effects of altered flow and meandering rate can reduce the abundance of early successional species (Populus spp. and Salix spp.) reducing species diversity and habitat complexity (Johnson et al. 1976). The message to management is that floods are critical disturbances in maintaining the diversity and function of riparian forests.

VEGETATIVE PROCESSES

Management of landscape dynamics must not only be based on disturbance regimes, but also vegetation processes that underlie the ecosystem response to disturbances. Following disturbance, vegetation composition and structure may not change in desirable ways or at desirable or expected rates because of biotic interactions. The existence of alternative stable states of vegetation (where some alternatives do not meet bio-diversity goals) has been linked not only to disturbance regimes but also to regeneration and establishment stages, and competitive ability and longevity of vegetation (Hobbs 1994). The absence of plants in many landscapes may be a result of loss of propagule sources rather than absence of suitable habitat (Duffy and Meier 1992, Sillett 1994). Understanding potential bottlenecks in vegetation processes that lead to particular vegetation states is an important part of managing landscape dynamics. For example, loss of inputs of large dead conifer trees into streams as a result of logging along streams has been associated with declines in the quality of salmonid habitat in the Pacific Northwest (FEMAT 1993). Consequently, one goal of management for biodiversity in this region is to increase the supply of large conifer trees along streams. This goal may not be achieved by simply setting up riparian reserves. Many existing riparian areas lack conifer regeneration today probably because of lack of seed sources for some shade-tolerant conifer species and because of competition from aggressive deciduous shrubs and trees in moist streamside environments (Minore and Weatherly 1994, Pabst and Spies 1998). As a result, achieving aquatic conservation goals in this region is dependent on finding ways to establish conifers in the face of biotic constraints. Management practices that may be required to deal with vegetation processes include planting of desirable species, elimination of undesirable species, and manipulating stand density. The vegetation process that is probably most sensitive to landscape-scale alterations by humans is dispersal. Managers can actively disperse propagules (e.g., through planting or seeding) but to provide for the entire suite of species that may have mobility problems it may be more cost effective to retain source areas for natural dispersal within landscapes. Source areas can take the form of individual retention trees with complements of epiphytes, small patches of trees with both epiphytes and protected forest floors, or riparian zones and larger patches that contain species with low capacities for dispersal.

SOME RECOMMENDATIONS FOR MAINTAINING TEMPORAL AND SPATIAL HETEROGENEITY OF LANDSCAPES

Maintain the tails of age class and patch size distributions
Under typical forest management plans which are based on the concept of a 'fully regulated' forest the tails of age-class distributions are cut off, beyond the rotation age. Very young stages may be cut off as well if

silvicultural practices accelerate canopy closure. Consequently, conservation of biological diversity in forest landscapes would be promoted by maintaining a broad range of age classes including a significant portion of old stands and old structures. The exact amount would depend on the disturbance regime and other factors.

As with old stands, very large patches are typically lost from managed landscapes (Spies *et al.* 1994). A variety of authors (e.g., Wright 1974, Pickett and Thompson 1978) have suggested that natural areas should be sufficiently large to include a mosaic of all normal stages in community development, and that natural processes of perturbation and recovery should be allowed to occur without intervention. The argument for large patches is not restricted to strict forest reserves, but applies to more actively managed areas. In landscape lacking reserves, harvest scheduling and road building can be modified to create large blocks of forest that may slowly change across the landscape. The size and number of large forest blocks, whether actively managed or reserves, will be a function of disturbance regime, biodiversity goals, and practical considerations. By knowing the frequency and extent of disturbances within a landscape, the spatial extent necessary to incorporate this disturbance could be determined. Obviously, landscapes characterized by very large scale patterns of disturbance and recovery would necessitate a much larger natural area than might be required under systems in which perturbations are small and frequent. The importance of infrequent disturbances, especially if they are large in size, is noteworthy (Turner and Dale in prep). If the rare disturbances which affect a large portion of a system are neglected, our understanding of landscape dynamics as well as species persistence, energetics, soil, and nutrient relations will be impeded (Franklin and Hemstrom 1981). Management strategies that retain large forest blocks are a common element of many forest landscape management designs (Harris 1984, FEMAT 1993, Crow *et al.* 1994). Less common are conservation designs that allow large-scale disturbances to occur (Hunter 1993).

Develop goals for spatial pattern

Landscapes managed with uniform cutting unit sizes and spatial distributions can develop into relatively homogeneous mosaics despite apparent diversity in forest conditions. In other words, pattern diversity can be low which could result in loss of some species and processes. Elements of spatial pattern include amount, proportion, size, interpatch distance, variation in patch size and interpatch distances, and landscape connectivity (Harrison and Fahrig 1995). Strictly speaking, absolute or relative amount of a forest type is not spatial because it does not require knowledge of the distribution of habitat across space. Many of these characteristics are dependent on each other; for example interpatch distance is related to amount of a particular forest type in the landscape. The amount of a forest type may be the single most important attribute; however, spatial patterning that affects edge density and connectivity can also be important to species and processes that depend on flows between landscape elements and through landscapes (Franklin and Forman 1987). Maintenance of some large patches in landscape will reduce edge density. Connectivity can be provided through corridor-like features, 'stepping stones', or reduced contrast between the habitat type of interest and its surrounding matrix. Since organisms perceive landscapes differently, no one design will be best for all (Hunter 1990). However, in general, spatial designs that provide for the most specialized species with the largest home ranges or large area needs should provide for the spatial needs of organisms with more general habitat needs or small area needs.

Altering spatial pattern of cutting may compensate for 'high' rates of cutting for some components of biological diversity

The effects of cutting pattern on species and landscape pattern and process are generally dependent on disturbance rate and amount of suitable habitat (Spies *et al.* 1994, Harrison and Fahrig 1995). At high rates of cutting amounts of interior forest habitat are low no matter what the spatial pattern of cutting and at low rates of cutting, varying spatial pattern has little effect on amount of edge or interior forest. At intermediate rates of cutting, different patterns of cutting can result in very different proportions of edge and interior forest conditions. Some cutting patterns preserve interior conditions and connectivity more than others (Franklin and Forman 1987) so that for a constant rate of disturbance (or commodity outputs) different levels of edge or interior habitat may be achieved through different disturbance patterns. Managers may be able to take advantage of this compensation to meet goals of interior or edge condition while maintaining the same rate of cutting on an area basis. However, there is a limit to which changing cutting pattern can compensate for relatively high rates of cutting. The effects of spatial pattern are also dependent on the proportion of habitat in a landscape (Andrén 1994, McGarigal and McComb 1995). Where habitat is very abundant or very low, spatial pattern may not be as important. However, where habitat is moderately low in a landscape the condition of the landscape matrix may become even more important (Franklin 1993). This may be especially true in intensively managed landscapes where only a few isolated older forest islands exist. In this situation, retention of elements of natural forest (e.g., large trees, snags, fallen trees, hardwoods) in the managed matrix may provide important refugia or dispersal habitat.

Landscape locations are important and processes vary across environmental gradients within landscapes

Landscapes are fundamentally structured by the physical template of the earth's surface (Swanson *et al.* 1988, Rowe and Barnes 1994). The physiographic template should serve as the basis of managing landscapes for biological diversity (Barnes *et al.* 1982, Lapin and Barnes 1995). Elements of location that are important include: position along topo-climatic and topo-edaphic gradients, watersheds, riparian areas, wetlands, cliffs, talus and caves and special soils and geological formations (Chapter 5). One important implication to management is that allocation of reserves, and other management practices across landscapes should correspond to the physical template as much as possible so that management is working with nature and not against it. For example, Angelstam (1997) has proposed a landscape conservation scheme for boreal forests in which reserves and management intensity are tailored to site types with different frequencies of fire based on their topographic and soil conditions.

Three case studies

While general concepts and theories provide a framework for understanding and managing forest mosaics, the knowledge required to understand the dynamics of a particular landscape and to achieve particular conservation goals must also come from a solid empirical knowledge of the environmental patterns, disturbance regimes and vegetation processes of specific places. In the following section we present three case studies to illustrate the diversity and complexity of landscape dynamics and to show how information about disturbance and succession can form the basis of conservation plans and practices for different management goals.

MIXED HARDWOOD–CONIFER REGION OF NORTHERN LAKE STATES

The landscapes of the northern lake states region of the United States are a mosaic of hemlock–hardwood forests, white and red pine forests, and boreal spruce–birch–fir forests (Frelich and Reich 1996).

Although topographic relief in this area is low, there are strong physiographic controls over vegetation patterns as a result of differences in soil drainage and texture (Pregitzer and Barnes 1984, Spies and Barnes 1985). Both wind and fire are major natural disturbances in the region but the two disturbance types differ in their dominance across the region and within landscapes. Fire frequencies increase from east to west. Heinselman (1973, 1981) estimates that natural fire rotations ranged from 50 to 100 years in the 'near boreal' pine, spruce and fir forests of the western and northern parts of the region, to 150 years in white/red pine forests, and from 350 to over 1400 years for the northern hardwood–hemlock forests on mesic soils (Stearns 1949, Whitney 1986, Frelich and Lorimer 1991). Where fire is infrequent, wind becomes an important disturbance agent. Frelich and Lorimer (1991) estimate that rotation periods range from 69 years for low severity disturbance (<10% canopy removal) to almost 2000 years for high severity disturbances (>60% canopy removal) at the scale of their sample plots (0.5 ha). Many of these larger disturbances were apparently associated with thunderstorm downbursts which produce patches ranging from a few meters to over 1 km in widths (Canham and Loucks 1984). The relatively fine scale of the disturbance regime of the northern hardwood forests creates forests with uneven-age distributions in contrast to the more even-aged distributions found in jack pine and red pine forests which are typically of fire origin. Consequently, the hemlock–hardwood forests of this region are characterized as 'quasi-equilibrium' landscapes (Frelich and Lorimer 1991), whereas the fire-prone boreal forest types of the region with high frequencies of large fires are not equilibrium landscapes (Baker 1989). Successional pathways within these forests can be relatively simple in the case of hemlock–hardwood forests which may cycle between dominance by different hardwood species in small gap disturbances to complex in the case of white pine dominated forests which can move between at least three different types depending on the disturbance frequency and intensity (Frelich and Reich 1996).

The juxtaposition of wetlands, mesic moraines, and dry outwash plains, results in a relatively fine-grained mixture of boreal, pine and northern hardwood forests (Barnes *et al.* 1982, Pregitzer and Barnes 1984, Spies and Barnes 1985). The particular pattern of ecosystem types may influence disturbance and vegetation dynamics in these mosaic landscapes. Fire-resistant hardwood forest types may experience more fires if they are adjacent to dry fire-prone pine forests. Wetlands and lakes may act as fire breaks and islands may be isolated from large fires but more exposed to lightning strikes and smaller fires (Bergeron 1991). Mass effects (Cody 1989) of local seed sources may also play a role in maintaining species on sites where they are not most competitive. For example, drier deciduous forests adjacent to hemlock-dominated wetlands may be more susceptible to invasion by hemlock than when they are further away from hemlock seed sources (Spies 1983, Frelich *et al.* 1993). Spatial pattern development does not necessarily require variability in disturbance and environment. A shifting mosaic of hemlock patches and sugar maple patches may arise simply as a result of competitive interactions of the species and operate within the coarser scale patterns set up by disturbances (Frelich *et al.* 1993).

Logging and logging related fires in the 1800s and early 1900s removed almost all of the original forest cover. Areas that have escaped human disturbance in the last 150 years exist in one large wilderness area (Boundary Waters Canoe Area) and several smaller wilderness areas and small set asides. Today, areas are dominated by forests less than 150 years old. Given the long return intervals between severe disturbances in hemlock–hardwood forests, almost any forest management regime that uses clearcuts larger than a few hectares and rotations under 200 years is probably larger, much more severe, and more frequent than the natural disturbance regime dominated by wind and small gap disturbances. Under natural disturbance regimes more than 90% of the hemlock–hardwood landscape type was probably in an old-growth state ($>$120 years) (Frelich and Reich 1996). Under timber management (40 to 120 year rotations), very little of the hardwood landscape would be in an old-growth condition. In contrast, in boreal landscapes of wilderness areas where fire rotations were 50 years, human fire suppression has decreased disturbance frequency relative to presettlement disturbance regimes. This change of disturbance regime is changing successional pathways toward shade-tolerant species and the role of small canopy gap disturbances in succession is becoming more important than it was in presettlement times (Frelich and Reich 1995). Jack pine, a fire-dependent species, may be lost from these landscapes. Even if fire occurs in the future, seed sources of jack pine may not be available to colonize burns and composition may shift more to aspen.

Human disturbances can either increase or decrease landscape heterogeneity in these landscapes depending on the focus and scale (Baker 1992, Mladenoff *et al.* 1993). A clear signature of forest cutting on landscape patterns was observed in the upper Midwestern United States (Mladenoff *et al.* 1993): the disturbed forest landscape had significantly more small forest patches and fewer large, matrix patches than the intact landscape, and forest patches in the disturbed landscape were simpler in shape (Figure

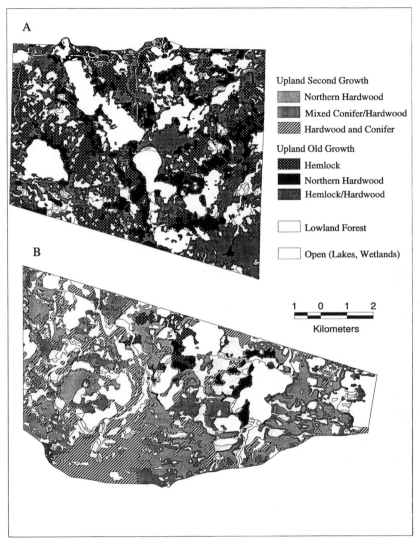

Fig. 4.7. Spatial pattern of forest communities in northern Michigan, USA: (A) Sylvania Wilderness Area, an intact forested landscape, and (B) Border Lakes, a similar region which has been subjected to forest harvesting. (From Mladenoff et al. 1993, p. 297.)

4.7). In addition, certain types of juxtapositions between different forest community types (e.g., hemlock–lowland conifers) were present in the intact landscape but absent in the disturbed landscape.

The implications to management in this region are that: (a) human alterations of disturbance regimes relative to natural and semi-natural systems have produced different landscape dynamics leading to losses of biological diversity at landscape scales; (b) the diversity of ecosystems and forest dynamics along climatic and species gradients makes it impossible to apply the same practices to maintain biological diversity across the region; (c) landscape management designs for conservation goals will need to be based on restoring disturbance processes such as fire, and recreating or maintaining the important older age classes, larger patch sizes, and connectivity (Crow et al. 1994).

FIRE-DOMINATED LANDSCAPES OF THE NORTHERN ROCKIES: YELLOWSTONE NATIONAL PARK

Yellowstone National Park (YNP) offers a good case study of a fire-dominated landscape and the problems of managing fire in a landscape where commodity extraction does not exist and ecological goals are paramount. The park encompasses 9000 km² in the northwest corner of Wyoming and is primarily a high, forested plateau. Approximately 80% of the park is covered with coniferous forests dominated by lodgepole pine (Pinus contorta var. latifolia). Fire has long been an important component of this landscape, and, as in most other parts of the Rocky Mountains, fire has profoundly influenced the fauna, flora, and ecological processes of the Yellowstone area (e.g., Houston 1973, Loope and Gruell 1973, Taylor 1973, Arno 1980, Romme 1982, Romme and Despain 1989, Despain 1991). Reconstructions of fire history demonstrated that extensive fires had occurred in the early 1700s and that the landscape was a non-equilibrium mosaic of forest stands in differing successional stages (Romme 1982). With the initiation of a natural fire program in Yellowstone, 235 lightning-caused fires were permitted to burn without interference. Most of these fires went out by themselves before burning more than a hectare, and the largest fire burned about 3100 ha in 1981. However, fires in 1988 affected more than 250 000 ha in YNP and surrounding lands as a consequence of unusually prolonged drought and high winds (Renkin and Despain 1992, Bessie and Johnson 1995). The enormous extent and severity of the 1988 fires surprised many managers and researchers, and such large fires may represent a major disturbance event that occurs at 100 to 300 year intervals in this landscape (Romme and Despain 1989) (Figure 4.8).

Fires in Yellowstone have created a mosaic of burn severities across the landscape as a result of variations in wind, topography, vegetation, and time of burning (Rowe and Scotter 1973, Wright and Heinselman 1973, Van Wagner 1983). The 1988 fires provide an ideal opportunity to study the ecological effects of fire size and pattern (Christensen *et al.* 1989, Turner *et al.* 1994). Some areas of Yellowstone experienced stand-replacing crown fires, other areas experienced stand-replacing severe-surface burns, and still other areas received light-surface burns in which trees were scorched but not killed. Understanding the effect of fire on landscape heterogeneity is important because the kinds, amounts, and spatial distribution of burned and unburned areas may influence the re-establishment of plant species on burned sites. Although the fires were quite large, the majority of severely burned areas were within close proximity (50 to 200 m) to unburned or lightly burned areas, suggesting that few burned sites are very far from potential sources of propagules for plant re-establishment (Turner *et al.* 1994).

How has the fire-created mosaic influenced the developing forest community? Burn severity and patch size both had significant effects on initial postfire succession (Turner *et al.* 1997). Severely burned areas had higher cover and density of lodgepole pine seedlings, greater abundance of opportunistic species, and lower richness of vascular plant species than less severely burned areas. Larger burned patches had higher cover of tree seedlings and shrubs, greater densities of lodgepole pine seedlings and opportunistic species, and lower species richness than smaller patches. Surprisingly, dispersal into the burned areas from the surround-

Fig. 4.8. View across the landscape of Yellowstone National Park, Wyoming, following the 1988 fires that affected about 45% of the park. (Monica Turner photo, October 1988).

ing unburned forest has not been an important mechanism for re-establishment of forest species thus far. Most plant cover in burned areas consisted of resprouting survivors during the first three years after the fires, and the seed from these residuals effectively filled in much of the burned area.

The patterns of initial postfire succession were surprisingly more variable in space and time than current theory would have suggested (Turner *et al.* 1997). Although succession across much of YNP appears to be moving toward plant communities similar to those that burned in 1988, primarily because of extensive biotic residuals even within large burned areas, there are some profound differences in plant re-establishment. For example, forest re-establishment is questionable in large burned areas that were old (>400 years) forests with low pre-fire serotiny (Turner *et al.*, unpublished data). Even where forests are regenerating, there is tremendous spatial variation in succession across the landscape – ranging from dense 'doghair' stands of lodgepole pine to sparse lodgepole pine stands. Thus, the 1988 fires may have initiated multiple successional pathways related to differential fire severity, fire size, pre-fire community structure. These alternative pathways include development of non-forest communities in some areas previously characterized by coniferous forest.

Unanticipated recruitment of seedling aspen in areas of Yellowstone previously dominated by lodgepole pine also followed the 1988 fires (Romme *et al.* 1997). Tree-sized aspen have not regenerated since park establishment in 1872 (Kay 1993, Romme *et al.* 1997) and aspen occupied only about 1% of YNP prior to the 1988 fires (Despain 1991), occurring almost exclusively on the low-elevation sagebrush–grasslands in northern YNP. However, abundant aspen seedlings were observed in 1989 across widely distributed burned areas of the Yellowstone Plateau, and these seedlings, though browsed by ungulates, were still persisting eight years after the fire. The flush of post-fire aspen seedling establishment may enhance the long-term ability of this species to persist in YNP by providing sources of seedling and vegetative reproduction. The increased genetic diversity in the seedling populations (Tuskan *et al.* 1996) may enhance the ability of aspen to withstand current climate conditions, levels of interspecific competition, and ungulate browsing (Jelinski 1993).

Future forest conditions in the regions with very low tree seedling densities are least predictable in Yellowstone. Continued measurement will be necessary to determine whether succession there is simply proceeding at a much slower rate toward a coniferous forest or whether a non-forest community will persist. Little is known about how long-term dynamics will influence indicators of ecosystem function at landscape scales.

Given the persistent spatial variation in post-fire stand densities and herbaceous cover across the YNP landscape, implications for long-term ecosystem function are substantial. If fire management policies do not allow a full range of patch sizes and severities the structure and composition of the Yellowstone landscape will change and with uncertain effects on species populations that may cascade across several trophic levels. The essential debate in management at Yellowstone is whether a more active prescribed fire management scheme is needed than the current policy allows. Under the current policy lightning-caused fires are permitted to burn, prescribed fires are used to a limited extent to reduce fuel levels around human settlements, and non-intentional human-caused fires are suppressed (Knight 1991). Some scientists argue that more prescribed burning is necessary to counteract the effects of fire suppression prior to the 1970s which may have created abnormally high fuel loads that now threaten to create much larger and more intense fires than have occurred in the past (Bonnicksen 1989). The fact that fires that start outside the park are typically suppressed probably means that fire frequency has decreased within the park. On the other hand, the presence of humans within the park may produce higher frequencies of ignition of fire. The 2.5 million hectare area of the National Park and adjacent National Forest Wilderness areas may be large enough to maintain a more passive approach to fire management. However, without a better understanding of the fire regimes of the past, it will be difficult to determine just how well either more passive or more active management strategies will achieve park goals.

PACIFIC NORTHWEST CONIFER FOREST LANDSCAPES

The coastal (west of the crest of the Cascade Mountain Range) forests of the Pacific Northwest are dominated by Douglas-fir and western hemlock and are characterized by variable fire-dominated natural disturbance regimes. Wind can be an important disturbance in immediate coastal areas in sitka spruce (*Picea sitchensis*)/western hemlock forests which experience episodic, catastrophic windstorms (Ruth and Harris 1979). However, fire still occurs in near-coast areas of Washington, Oregon and northern California. Fire frequencies in this region range from 90 years on dry sites or drier parts of the region to over 900 years in the moist coastal and northerly parts. Fire occurrences are irregular and difficult to predict (Agee 1993). Fires can be very large – over 200 000 ha – and severe, killing all trees in very large patches (Agee 1993). Moderate sized landscapes (100 000 ha) such as Mt Rainier National Park do not appear to be in a quasi-equilibrium (Hemstrom and Franklin 1982). Given the large size of many fires, it appears that quasi-equilibrium conditions would not occur in areas of less than a million hectares and perhaps much larger. However, in the long term average amount of old-growth forests (>200 years) is estimated to range from about 40% to 80% (Spies and Franklin 1988, Booth 1991, Fahnestock and Agee 1983, Ripple 1994). Fire severity increases and frequency and patchiness appear to decrease with increasing moisture, which promotes fuel accumulation. Fire can set up large (10^3 to 10^4 ha) patches of similar-aged forest in the landscape and subsequent small gap disturbances and patchy low to moderate severity fires diversify and propel these cohorts into old-growth stages of development. In the drier interior parts of the region, where mixed forests of ponderosa pine (*Pinus ponderosa*), Douglas-fir and white fir (*Abies concolor*) and other conifers occur, high natural fire frequencies (<20 years) maintained many forests in ponderosa pine with relatively open understories and low fuel accumulations. With fire suppression many of these stands have developed dense understories of shade-tolerant Douglas-fir and white fir and higher fuel accumulations, changing the fire regimes from low-severity surface fires to high-severity crown fires (Seidel and Cochran 1981, Agee 1993).

Successional development in the coastal region is relatively slow and long – a function of long establishment periods and long-lived seral dominants (>750 years). Structural differentiation can require over 400 years to level off (Spies and Franklin 1991) (Figure 4.4). Successional pathways are relatively simple, converging on a variety of shade-tolerant conifer forests depending on elevation and climatic gradients (Franklin and Dyrness 1973, Franklin and Hemstrom 1981, Ohmann and Spies 1998). Small canopy-gap disturbances from wind and disease, which occur every 100 to 200 years and average 300 m² in size, play an important role in the development of old-growth forest structure (Spies *et al.* 1990). In wetter parts of the region, particularly in moist riparian zones where deciduous trees and shrubs are competitive, hydrological and logging disturbances can result in the development of relatively stable patches of deciduous shrubs that resist invasion by conifer seedlings (Minore and Weatherly 1994). This state is potentially undesirable from an aquatic habitat perspective, especially in watersheds lacking large conifers that were removed by extensive logging. Large conifer wood helps to create stream habitat complexity and lack of large conifers in watersheds reduces the inputs to streams from individual treefalls and landslides.

The disturbance regime imposed by humans in this region is typically based on intensive forest management with relatively short rotations (40 to 80 years), clearcut logging and preference for conifers, especially Douglas-fir. On public forest lands, which occupy about half of the forest area, the rate of cutting has been substantially reduced since the early 1990s (FEMAT 1993). Despite these recent changes, 30–40% of public forest landscapes contain a legacy of a patchwork of forest plantations that were established in the 1950s through the 1980s. Relative to natural disturbance regimes, logging disturbances have typically been more frequent, more severe, left fewer biological legacies (i.e., structures and species that survive disturbances) and created more edge and fragmented landscapes (Spies and Cline 1988, Hansen *et al.* 1991, McComb *et al.* 1993, Franklin and Forman 1987, Chen *et al.* 1995, Spies *et al.* 1994). Interestingly, the typical patch size clearcuts (10–20 ha) may be similar to that of wildfires in the southern part of the region, where fires tend to be patchy (Morrison and Swanson 1990, Spies *et al.* 1994). However, the range of clearcut sizes is much narrower than the range of wildfire sizes. The high frequency of clearcutting on private lands (40–50 years) and the relatively high rate on public lands (80 years) until the early 1990s results in larger patches (100s to 1000s of ha) of young plantations as clearcut units coalesce over 10 to 20 year periods.

Recent changes in forest management policies on public lands have reduced rates of cutting and, where logging is still allowed, have increased the amount of live and dead trees that are left on the site (FEMAT 1993). On private lands, intensive forestry is still practiced, although state forest policies require retention of some trees in riparian and upslope stands. It is unlikely that wildfire regimes will be allowed to spread except in some wilderness areas. The area of old-growth forest has declined by over 50% in the last 50 years (Bolsinger and Wadell 1993). The only remaining old forest is on public lands and concern over species viability and historical losses of old-growth forests means that further losses of old forest, even from natural events such as wildfire, are not desirable.

The Northwest Forest Plan (FEMAT 1993) is one of the most comprehensive regional forest conservation plans that relies on application of conservation biology, landscape ecology and ecosystem management. The plan, whose goals are the protection of terrestrial and aquatic species associated with late successional and old-growth forests and conservation of old-growth ecosystems and watersheds, relies on a set of strategies including species-based conservation, reserve-based ecosystem conservation, and active management and restoration. Under this plan 80% of a 10 million hectare federal landbase (out of a total of 57 million ha of public and private land) in western Washington, Oregon, and northern California is in some form of high-level protection including national parks and wilderness areas (29%), late successional reserves (29%), riparian reserves (9%), special management areas (e.g., scenic areas, natural areas and adaptive management areas [13%] where no existing old-growth can be cut [FEMAT 1993, p. II-26]). The remaining 20% of the landscape forms the 'matrix' where most of the scheduled timber harvesting will occur (Figure 4.9).

The land allocations within this plan are based on many principles of forest ecology, landscape ecology and conservation biology. For example, the protection of many existing old-growth stands in late successional reserves is based on the understanding that these older age classes were relatively common in these landscapes under natural fire regimes and that land clearing and intensive forest management have reduced the abundance of these ecosystems across all ownerships. Thus, the federal landbase is the only area where this type of ecosystem occurs and is allowed to develop. In addition to providing for the tails of the age-class distributions, the federal lands also now provide for some of the largest patches (10^4 to 10^5 ha) of continuous forest in the region. The design of the Northwest Forest Plan also took spatial pattern of forest practices into account through consideration of spacing of reserves to facilitate dispersal of the northern spotted owl and use of riparian reserves to provide for land–water interactions (e.g., inputs of large conifer wood) and contribute to connectivity of forest cover across the landscape. Where management is more intense in the matrix lands, patchy fires are simulated in logging operations by leaving at least 15% of the logging unit in small patches (0.2 to 1.0 ha) of large live trees and existing standing dead trees and retaining existing large wood on the forest floor. These retention guidelines are intended to provide for disturbance-sensitive elements of biological diversity that can use old-forest structures through cutting cycles. Finally, the importance of vegetative processes is recognized in the plan for managing existing plantations within the late successional reserves. The development of trees in these relatively dense stands does not follow the same pathway as old-growth stands which developed under lower densities and through a series of partial disturbances (Tappeiner et al. 1997). As a result, it may be that trees in these stands will develop old-growth characteristics (e.g., large limbs and epi-

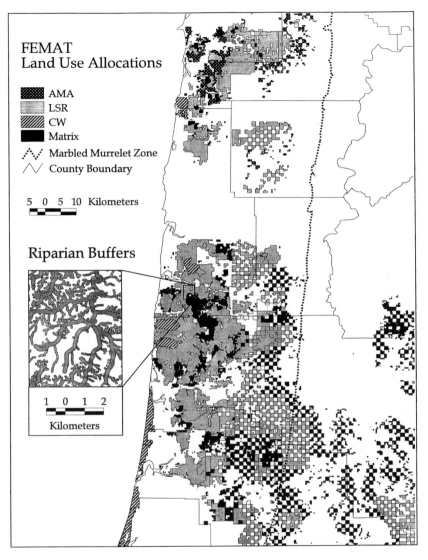

Fig. 4.9. Spatial distribution of late-successional (old-growth) reserves (light gray), key watersheds (stripped) and matrix lands (dark gray) in western Oregon on Federal lands and examples of riparian reserve strategy. (Adapted from FEMAT 1993.)

cormic branch fans) more slowly than under natural conditions. Consequently, thinning may be needed in young plantations (<80 years old) to facilitate their development into late-successional and old-growth forest structure.

Summary

Forests are dynamic mosaics driven by disturbance and biotic processes. The patterns and rates of temporal and spatial change vary with scale of observation and may differ across forest types and regions. The regime of a disturbance can be used to evaluate its potential ecological effects and evaluate how changes in management practices might affect forest dynamics and biological diversity. Scientific perspectives on disturbance and forest succession have changed in recent decades from emphasis on equilibrium and end points to emphasis on process, pathway and heterogeneity. Although forest dynamics is a complex process, it can be divided into several stages that are useful in management and mapping of forest mosaics. Because of past land-use and forest management practices the later stages of succession, especially old-growth forests, are lacking in many landscapes. The absence of old age classes and associated habitats has resulted in loss of biological diversity in many regions.

Forest landscapes are rich in spatial heterogeneity from a variety of causes, including environment, biotic interactions and disturbance and succession. Spatial patterns can have strong influences on population dynamics and ecosystem processes including the spread of disturbance. Human activities have had a profound effect on forest structure and pattern. In managed forest landscapes, cutting patterns often result in reduction in patch sizes and increases in edge densities. Spatial heterogeneity can be described using a variety of metrics. No single metric alone is sufficient for quantifying spatial pattern and the choice of metrics will depend on the question and process at hand.

Maintenance of temporal and spatial heterogeneity in landscapes can help to conserve biological diversity. Specific recommendations include: (a) maintain tails of age class and patch size distributions; (b) develop goals for spatial pattern; (c) take advantage of tradeoffs between rates of cutting and spatial pattern; (d) incorporate important locations on the physical template of the landscape into planning and management. Three case studies are presented which illustrate the diversity of landscape dynamics, the importance of disturbance, succession, and spatial pattern in biological diversity and challenges and solutions to managing dynamic forest mosaics.

Further readings

Attiwill, P. M. 1994. The disturbance of forest ecosystems: the ecological basis for conservative management. *Forest Ecology and Management* **63**:247–300.

Glenn-Lewin, D. C., R. K. Peet, and T. T. Veblen (eds). 1992. *Plant succession: theory and prediction.* Chapman & Hall, London.

Hansson, L. (ed.). 1997. Boreal ecosystems and landscapes: structures, processes, and conservation of biodiversity. *Ecological Bulletins* **46**.

Hansson, L., L. Fahrig and G. Merriam (eds). 1995. *Mosaic Landscapes and Ecological Processes.* Chapman and Hall London.

Peterken, G. F. 1996. *Natural woodland.* Cambridge University Press, Cambridge.

Ruggiero, L. F., K. B. Aubry, A. B. Carey, and M. H. Huff (tech. coords). 1991. *Wildlife and vegetation of unmanaged Douglas-fir forests.* United States Forest Service, Pacific Northwest Research Station General Technical Report PNW-GTR-285.

Literature cited

Abrams, M. D. 1992. Fire and the development of oak forests. *BioScience* **42**:346–53.

Agee, J. K. 1993. *Fire Ecology of Pacific Northwest Forests.* Island Press, Washington, D.C.

Agee, J. K., and M. H. Huff. 1987. Fuel succession in a western hemlock/Douglas-fir forest. *Canadian Journal of Forest Research* **17**:697–704.

Alverson, W. S., D. M. Waller, and S. L. Solheim. 1988. Forests too deer: edge effects in northern Wisconsin. *Conservation Biology* **2**:348–58.

Andrén, H. 1994. Effects of habitat fragmentation on birds and mammals in landscapes with different proportions of suitable habitat: a review. *Oikos* **71**:355–66.

Angelstam, P. 1997. Landscape analysis as a tool for the scientific management of biodiversity. *Ecological Bulletins* **46**:140–70.

Arno, S. F. 1980. Forest fire history in the northern Rockies. *Journal of Forestry* **78**:460–5.

Attiwill, P. M. 1994a. The disturbance of forest ecosystems: the ecological basis for conservative management. *Forest Ecology and Management* **63**:247–300.

1994b. Ecological disturbance and the conservative management of eucalypt forests in Australia. *Forest Ecology and Management* **63**:301–46.

Aubry, K. B., M. J. Crites, and S. D. West. 1991. Regional patterns of small mammal abundance and community composition in Oregon and Washington. Pp. 284–94 in L. F. Ruggiero, K. B. Aubry, A. B. Carey, and M. H. Huff (tech. coords). *Wildlife and vegetation of unmanaged Douglas-fir forests.* United States Forest Service, Pacific Northwest Research Station General Technical Report PNW-GTR-285. Portland, Oregon.

Baker, W. L. 1989. Landscape ecology and nature reserve design in the Boundary Waters Canoe Area, Minnesota. *Ecology* **70**:23–35.

—— 1992. Effects of settlement and fire suppression on landscape structure. *Ecology* **73**:1879–87.

—— 1995. Long-term response of disturbance landscapes to human intervention and global change. *Landscape Ecology* **10**:143–59.

Baker, W. L., and Y. Cai. 1992. The r.le programs for multiscale analysis of landscape structure using the GRASS geographic information system. *Landscape Ecology* **7**:291–302.

Barnes, B. V., K. S. Pregitzer, T. A. Spies, and V. Spooner. 1982. Ecological forest site classification. *Journal of Forestry* **80**:493–8.

Bazzaz, F. A. 1983. Characteristics of populations in relation to disturbance in natural and man-modified ecosystems. Pp. 259–75 in H. A. Mooney and M. Godron (eds). *Disturbance and Ecosystems: Components of Response*. Ecological Studies 44. Springer-Verlag, Berlin.

Belsky, A. J. 1995. Spatial and temporal landscape patterns in arid and semi-arid African savannas. Pp. 31–56 in L. Hansson, L. Fahrig, and G. Merriam (eds). *Mosaic Landscapes and Ecological Processes*. Chapman & Hall, London.

Bergeron, Y. 1991. The influence of island and mainland lakeshore landscapes on boreal forest fire regimes. *Ecology* **72**:1980–92.

Bessie, W. C., and E. A. Johnson. 1995. The relative importance of fuels and weather on fire behavior in subalpine forests. *Ecology* **76**:747–62.

Bolsinger, C. L., and K. L. Waddell, 1993. *Area of old-growth forests in California, Oregon, and Washington*. United States Forest Service, Pacific Northwest Research Station Resource Bulletin PNW-RB-197.

Bonan, G. B., and H. H. Shugart. 1989. Environmental factors and ecological processes in boreal forests. *Annual Review of Ecology and Systematics* **20**:1–28.

Bonnicksen, T. 1989. Fire gods and federal policy. *American Forests* **95**:14–166, 66–68.

Booth, D. E. 1991. Estimating prelogging old-growth in the Pacific Northwest. *Journal of Forestry* **89**:25–9.

Bormann, F. H., and G. E. Likens. 1979. *Pattern and Process in a Forested Ecosystem: disturbance, development, and the steady state based on the Hubbard Brook ecosystem study*. Springer-Verlag, New York.

Botkin, D. B. 1990. *Discordant Harmonies: a New Ecology for the Twenty-first Century*. Oxford University Press, New York.

Bunnell, F. L. 1995. Forest-dwelling vertebrate faunas and natural fire regimes in British Columbia: patterns and implications for conservation. *Conservation Biology* **9**:636–44.

Burgess, R. L., and D. M. Sharpe (eds). 1981. *Forest Island Dynamics in Man-dominated Landscapes*. Springer-Verlag:New York.

Busing, R. T., C. B. Halpern, and T. A. Spies. 1995. Ecology of Pacific yew (*Taxus brevifolia*) in western Oregon and Washington. *Conservation Biology* **9**:1199–207.

Campbell, S., and L. Liegel (tech. coords). 1996. *Disturbance and forest health in Oregon and Washington*. United States Forest Service, Pacific Northwest Research Station and Pacific Northwest Region; Oregon Department of Forestry; and Washington Department of Natural Resources General Technical Report PNW-GTR-381.

Canham, C. D., and O. L. Loucks. 1984. Catastrophic windthrow in the presettlement forests of Wisconsin. *Ecology* **65**:803–9.

Canham, C. D., J. S. Denslow, W. J. Platt, J. R. Runkle, T. A. Spies, and P. S. White. 1990. Light regimes beneath closed canopies and tree-fall gaps in temperate and tropical forests. *Canadian Journal of Forest Research* **20**:620–31.

Castello, J. D., D. J. Leopold, and P. J. Smallidge. 1995. Pathogens, patterns, and processes in forest ecosystems. *BioScience* **45**:16–24.

Cattelino, P. J., I. R. Noble, R. O. Slatyer, and S. R. Kessell. 1979. Predicting the multiple pathways of plant succession. *Environmental Management* **3**:41–50.

Chamberlin, T. W., R. D. Harr, and F. H. Everest. 1991. Timber harvesting, silviculture, and watershed processes. *American Fisheries Society Special Publication* **19**:181–207.

Chen, J., J. F. Franklin, and T. A. Spies. 1995. Growing-season microclimatic gradients from clearcut edges into old-growth Douglas-fir forests. *Ecological Applications* **5**:74–86.

Christensen, Jr., N. L. 1997. Managing for heterogeneity and complexity on dynamic landscapes. Pp. 167–86 in S. T. A. Pickett, R. S. Ostfeld, M. Shachak, and G. E. Likens (eds). *The Ecological Basis of Conservation: Heterogeneity, Ecosystems, and Biodiversity*. Chapman and Hall, New York.

Christensen, N. L., J. K. Agee, P. F. Brussard, J. Hughes, D. H. Knight, G. W. Minshall, J. M. Peek, S. J. Pyne, F. J. Swanson, J. W. Thomas, S. Wells, S. E. Williams, and H. A. Wright. 1989. Interpreting the Yellowstone fires of 1988. *BioScience* **39**:678–85.

Clark, J. S. 1991. Disturbance and population structure on the shifting mosaic landscape. *Ecology* **72**:1119–37.

1992. Density-independent mortality, density compensation, gap formation, and self-thinning in plant populations. *Theoretical Population Biology* **42**:172–98.

Clark, J. S., and Y. Ji. 1995. Fecundity and dispersal in plant populations: implications for structure and diversity. *American Naturalist* **146**:72–111.

Clements, F. E. 1916. *Plant Succession: an Analysis of the Development of Vegetation*. Carnegie Inst. Pub. 242. Washington, D.C.

Cody, M. L. 1989. Discussion: structure and assembly of communities. Pp. 227–41 in J. Roughgarden and R. M. May (eds). *Perspectives in Ecological Theory*. Princeton University Press, Princeton, New Jersey.

Connell, J. H., and R. O. Slayter. 1977. Mechanisms of succession in natural communities and their role in community stability and organization. *American Naturalist* **111**:1119–44.

Crawley, M. J. 1990. The population dynamics of plants. *Philosophical Transactions of the Royal Society of London B* **330**:125–40.

Crow, T. R., A. Haney, and D. M. Waller. 1994. *Report on the scientific roundtable on biological diversity convened by the Chequamegon and Nicolet National Forests.* United States Forest Service, North Central Forest Experiment Station General Technical Report NC-166.

Curtis, J. T. 1959. *The Vegetation of Wisconsin: an Ordination of Plant Communities.* University of Wisconsin Press, Madison, Wisconsin.

Davis, M. B. (ed.). 1996. *Eastern Old-growth Forests: Prospects for Rediscovery and Recovery.* Island Press, Washington, D.C.

Davis, M. B., S. Sugita, R. R. Calcote, J. B. Ferrari, and L. E. Frelich. 1994. Historical development of alternate communities in a hemlock–hardwood forest in northern Michigan, USA. Pp. 19–39 in P. J. Edwards, R. M. May, and N. R. Webb (eds). *Large-scale Ecology and Conservation Biology.* Blackwell Scientific Publications, Oxford.

Delcourt, P. A., and H. R. Delcourt. 1987. *Long-term Forest Dynamics of the Temperate Zone.* Springer-Verlag, New York.

Denslow, J. S. 1987. Tropical rain forest gaps and tree species diversity. *Annual Review of Ecology Systematics* **18**:431–51.

Despain, D. G. 1991. *Yellowstone Vegetation: Consequences of Environment and History.* Roberts Rinehart Publishing Company.

Duffy, D. C., and A. J. Meier. 1992. Do Appalachian herbaceous understories ever recover from clearcutting? *Conservation Biology* **6**:196–201.

Dyrness, C. T., L. A. Viereck, and K. Van Cleve. 1986. Fire in Taiga communities of interior Alaska. Pp. 74–86 in K. Van Cleve, F. S. Chapin III, P. W. Flanagan, L. A. Viereck, and C. T. Dyrness (eds). *Forest Ecosystems in the Alaskan Taiga: a Synthesis of Structure and Function.* Springer-Verlag, New York.

Egler, F. E. 1954. Vegetation science concepts, I: initial floristic composition – a factor in old field vegetation development. *Vegetatio* **4**:412–17.

Ellenberg, H. 1988. *Vegetation Ecology of Central Europe.* Cambridge University Press, Cambridge.

Essen, P. A., B. Ehnström, L. Ericson, and K. Sjöberg. 1992. Boreal forests – the focal habitats of Fennoscandia. Pp. 252–325 in L. Hansson (ed.). *Ecological Principles of Nature Conservation.* Elsevier, Amsterdam

Essen, P., B. Ehnström, L. Ericson, and K. Sjöberg. 1997. Boreal forests. *Ecological Bulletins* **46**:16–47.

Fahnestock, G. R., and J. K. Agee. 1983. Biomass consumption and smoke production by prehistoric and modern forest fires in western Washington. *Journal of Forestry* **81**:653–7.

FEMAT 1993. *Forest ecosystem management: an ecological, economic, and social assessment.* Report of the Forest Ecosystem Management Assessment Team, July 1993. U.S. Government Printing Office: 1993 794–478.

Forcier, L. K. 1975. Reproductive strategies and co-occurrence of climax tree species. *Science* **189**:808–10.

Forman, R. T. T. 1995. *Land Mosaics: the Ecology of Landscapes and Regions*. Cambridge University Press, Cambridge.

Foster, D. R. 1988a. Disturbance history, community organization and vegetation dynamics of the old-growth Pisgah Forest, southwestern New Hampshire, USA. *Journal of Ecology* **76**:105–34.

1988b. Species and stand response to catastrophic wind in central New England, USA. *Journal of Ecology* **76**:135–51.

1995. Land-use history and four hundred years of vegetation change in New England. Pp. 253–319 in B. L. Turner II, A. G. Sal, F. G. Bernáldez, and F. de Castri (eds). *Global Land Use Change: a Perspective from the Columbian Encounter*. Consejo Superior de Investigaciones Científicas, Madrid.

Foster, D. R., and E. R. Boose. 1995. Hurricane disturbance regimes in temperate and tropical forest ecosystems. Pp. 305–39 in M. P. Coutts and J. Grace (eds). *Wind and Trees*. Cambridge University Press, Cambridge.

Foster, D. R. and G. A. King. 1986. Vegetation pattern and diversity in southeastern Labrador, Canada: *Betula papyrifera* (Birch) forest development in relation to fire history and physiography. *Journal of Ecology* **74**(2):465–83.

Foster, D. R., and T. M. Zebryk. 1993. Long-term vegetation dynamics and disturbance history of a *Tsuga*-dominated forest in New England. *Ecology* **74**:982–98.

Foster, D. R., D. A. Orwig, and J. S. McLachlan. 1996. Ecological and conservation insights from reconstructive studies of temperate old-growth forests. *Tree* **11**:419–24.

Franklin, J. F. 1989. Toward a new forestry. *American Forestry* **11**:37–44.

1993. Preserving biodiversity: species, ecosystems, or landscapes. *Ecological Applications* **3**:202–5.

Franklin, J. F., and D. S. DeBell. 1988. Thirty-six years of tree population change in an old-growth *Pseudotsuga-Tsuga* forest. *Canadian Journal of Forest Research* **18**:633–9.

Franklin, J. F., and C. T. Dyrness. 1973. *Natural vegetation of Oregon and Washington*. United States Forest Service, Pacific Northwest Research Station General Technical Report PNW-8. Portland, Oregon.

Franklin, J. F., and R. T. T. Forman 1987. Creating landscape patterns by forest cutting: ecological consequences and principles. *Landscape Ecology* **1**:5–18.

Franklin, J. F., and M. A. Hemstrom. 1981. Aspects of succession in the coniferous forests of the Pacific Northwest. Pp. 212–39 in D. C. West, H. H. Shugart, and D. B. Botkin (eds). *Forest Succession: Concepts and Application*. Springer-Verlag, New York.

Franklin, J. F., J. A. MacMahon, F. J. Swanson, and J. R. Sedell. 1985. Ecosystem responses to the eruption of Mount St. Helens. *National Geographic Research* (Spring):198–216.

Frelich, L. E., and C. G. Lorimer. 1991. Natural disturbance regimes in hemlock–hardwood forests of the Upper Great Lakes region. *Ecological Monographs* **61**:145–64.

Frelich, L. E., and P. B. Reich. 1995. Spatial patterns and succession in a Minnesota southern-boreal forest. *Ecological Monographs* **65**:325–46.

———. 1996. Old growth in the Great Lakes region. Pp. 144–160 in M. B. Davis (ed.). *Eastern Old-growth Forests: Prospects for Rediscovery and Recovery*. Island Press, Washington, D.C.

Frelich, L. E., R. R. Calcote, M. B. Davis, and J. Pastor. 1993. Patch formation and maintenance in an old-growth hemlock––hardwood forest. *Ecology* **74**:513–27.

Gashwiler, J. S. 1970. Plant and mammal changes on a clearcut in west-central Oregon. *Ecology* **51**:1018–26.

Geiger, R. 1965. *The Climate Near the Ground*. Harvard University Press, Cambridge, Massachusetts.

Gleason, H. A. 1917. The structure and development of the plant association. *Bulletin of the Torrey Botanical Club* **43**:463–81.

Glenn-Lewin, D. C., R. K. Peet, and T. T. Veblen (eds). 1992. *Plant Succession: Theory and Prediction*. Chapman & Hall, London.

Haila, Y., I. K. Hanski, J. Niemelä, P. Punttila, S. Raivio, and H. Tukia. 1994. Forestry and the boreal fauna: matching management with natural forest dynamics. *Annales Zoologici Fennici* **31**:187–202.

Halpern, C. B., and T. A. Spies. 1995. Plant species diversity in natural and managed forests of the Pacific Northwest. *Ecological Applications* **5**:913–34.

Hansen, A. J., T. A. Spies, F. J. Swanson, and J. L. Ohmann. 1991. Conserving biodiversity in managed forests: lessons from natural forests. *BioScience* **41**:382–92.

Harper, J. L. 1977. *Population Biology of Plants*. Academic Press, London.

Harris, L. D. 1984. *The Fragmented Forest: Island Biogeography Theory and the Preservation of Biotic Diversity*. University of Chicago Press, Chicago, Illinois.

Harrison, S., and L. Fahrig. 1995. Landscape pattern and population conservation. Pp. 293–308 in L. Hansson, L. Fahrig, and G. Merriam (eds). *Mosaic Landscapes and Ecological Processes*. Chapman & Hall, London.

Heinselman, M. L. 1973. Fire in the virgin forests of the Boundary Waters Canoe Area, Minnesota. *Quaternary Research* **3**:329–82.

———. 1981. Fire intensity and frequency as factors in the distribution and structure of northern ecosystems. Pp. 7–57 in H. A. Mooney, T. M. Bonnicksen, N. L. Christensen, J. E. Lotan, and W. A. Reiners (tech. coords). *Fire regimes and ecosystem properties: proceedings of the conference*. United States Forest Service General Technical Report WO-26.

Helle, P. 1985. Effects of forest regeneration on the structure of bird communities in northern Finland. *Holarctic Ecology* **8**(2):120–32.

Heliövaara, K., and R. Väisänen. 1984. Effects of modern forestry on northwestern European forest invertebrates: a synthesis. *Acta For. Fennica* **189**:1–32.

Hemstrom, M. A., and J. F. Franklin. 1982. Fire and other disturbances of the forests in Mount Rainier National Park. *Quaternary Research* **18**:32–51.

Hemstrom, M., R. Kiester, P. McDonald, C. Palmer, T. Spies, J. Teply, and R. Warbington. (in press). Late-successional and old-growth forest effectiveness monitoring plan for the Northwest Forest Plan. United States Forest Service, Portland, Oregon.

Hobbs, R. J. 1994. Dynamics of vegetation mosaics: can we predict responses to global change? *Ecoscience* **1**:346–56.

House of Representatives. 1990. *Management of Old-growth Forests of the Pacific Northwest*. United States Government Printing Office Serial No. 101–35, Washington, D.C.

Houston, D. B. 1973. Wildfires in northern Yellowstone National Park. *Ecology* **54**:1111–17.

Huff, M. H., and C. M. Raley. 1991. Regional patterns of diurnal breeding bird communities in Oregon and Washington. Pp. 176–205 in L. F. Ruggiero, K. B. Aubry, A. B. Carey, and M. H. Huff (technical coordinators). *Wildlife and vegetation of unmanaged Douglas-fir forests*. United States Forest Service, Pacific Northwest Research Station General Technical Report PNW-GTR-285. Portland, Oregon.

Hunter, Jr., M. L. 1990. *Wildlife, Forests, and Forestry: Principles of Managing Forests for Biological Diversity*. Prentice-Hall, Inc., Englewood Cliffs, New Jersey.

1993. Natural disturbance regimes as spatial models for managing boreal forests. *Biological Conservation* **65**:115–20.

1996. Benchmarks for managing ecosystems: are human activities natural? *Conservation Biology* **10**:695–7.

1997. The biological landscape. Pp. 57–67 in K. A. Kohm and J. F. Franklin (eds). *Creating a Forestry for the 21st Century: the Science of Ecosystem Management*. Island Press, Washington, D.C.

Jelinski, D. E. 1993. Associations between environmental heterogeneity, heterozygosity, and growth rates of *Populus tremuloides* in a Cordilleran landscape. *Arctic and Alpine Research* **25**:183–8.

Johnson, A. R. 1996. Spatiotemporal hierarchies in ecological theory and modeling. Pp. 451–6 in M. F. Goodchild, L. T. Steyaert, B. O. Parks, C. Johnston, D. Maidment, M. Crane, and S. Glendinning (eds). *GIS and Environmental Modeling: Progress and Research Issues*. GIS World, Inc., Fort Collins, Colorado.

Johnson, E. A., and S. L. Gutsell. 1994. Fire frequency models, methods and interpretations. *Advanced Ecological Research* **25**:239–87.

Johnson, E. A., K. Miyanishi, and J. M. H. Weir. 1995. Old-growth, disturbance, and ecosystem management. *Canadian Journal of Botany* **73**:918–26.

Johnson, W. C., R L. Burgess, and W. R. Keammerer. 1976. Forest overstory vegetation and environment on the Missouri River floodplain in North Dakota. *Ecological Monographs* **46**:59–84.

Johnston, C. A., and R. J. Naiman. 1990. The use of a geographic information system to analyze long-term landscape alteration by beaver. *Landscape Ecology* **4**:5–19.

Kareiva, P. 1994. Space: the final frontier for ecological theory. *Ecology* **75**:1.

Kay, C. E. 1993. Aspen seedlings in recently burned areas of Grand Teton and Yellowstone National Parks. *Northwest Science* **67**:94–104.

Kilgore, B. M. 1981. Fire in ecosystem distribution and structure: western forests and scrublands. Pp. 58–89 in H. A. Mooney, T. M. Bonnicksen, N. L. Christensen, J. E. Lotan, and W. A. Reiners (technical coordinators). *Fire regimes and ecosystem properties: proceedings of the conference.* United States Forest Service General Technical Report WO-26.

Knight, D. H. 1991. The yellowstone fire controversy. Pp. 87–103 in R. B. Keiter and M. S. Boyce (eds). *The Greater Yellowstone Ecosystem: Redefining America's Wilderness Heritage.* Yale University Press, New Haven and London.

Lapin, M., and B. V. Barnes. 1995. Using the landscape ecosystem approach to assess species and ecosystem diversity. *Conservation Biology* **9**:1148–58.

Leemans, R. 1991. Canopy gaps and establishment patterns of spruce (*Picea abies* (L.) Karst.) in two old-growth coniferous forests in central Sweden. *Vegetatio* **93**:157–65.

Lertzman, K. P., G. D. Sutherland, A. Inselberg, and S. C. Saunders. 1996. Canopy gaps and the landscape mosaic in a coastal temperate rain forest. *Ecology* **77**:1254–70.

Leverett, R. 1996. Definitions and history. Pp. 3–17 in M. B. Davis (ed.). *Eastern Old-growth Forests: Prospects for Rediscovery and Recovery.* Island Press, Washington, D.C.

Li, H., J. F. Franklin, F. J. Swanson, and T. A. Spies. 1993. Developing alternative forest cutting patterns: a simulation approach. *Landscape Ecology* **8**:63–75.

Liu, J. 1993. An introduction to ECOLECON: a spatially explicit model for ECOLogical ECONomics of species conservation in complex forest landscapes. *Ecological Modelling* **70**:63–87.

Loope, L. L., and G. E. Gruell. 1973. The ecological role of fire in the Jackson Hole area, northwestern Wyoming. *Quaternary Research* **3**:425–43.

Magnuson, J. J. 1990. Long-term ecological research and the invisible present. *BioScience* **40**:495–501.

Marks, P. L. 1974. The role of pin cherry (*Prunus pensylvanica* L.) in the maintenance of stability in northern hardwood ecosystems. *Ecological Monographs* **44**:73–88.

Masaki, T., Y. Kominami, and T. Nakashizuka. 1994. Spatial and seasonal patterns of seed dissemination of *Cornus controversa* in a temperate forest. *Ecology* **75**:1903–10.

McComb, W. C., Spies, T. A., and Emmingham, W. H. 1993. Douglas-fir forests: managing for timber and mature-forest habitat. *Journal of Forestry* **91**:31–42.

McGarigal, K., and B. J. Marks. 1995. FRAGSTATS: *Spatial pattern analysis program for quantifying landscape structure.* United States Forest Service, Pacific Northwest Research Station General Technical Report PNW-GTR-351.

McGarigal, K., and W. C. McComb. 1995. Relationships between landscape structure and breeding birds in the Oregon Coast Range. *Ecological Monographs* **65**:235–60.

McInnes, P. F., R. J. Naiman, J. Pastor, and Y. Cohen. 1992. Effects of moose browsing on vegetation and litter of the boreal forest, Isle Royale, Michigan, USA. *Ecology* **73**:2059–75.

Meyer, W. B. 1995. Past and present land use and land cover in the USA. *Consequences* (Spring) 25–33.

Minore, D. and Weatherly, H.G. 1994. Riparian trees, shrubs, and forest regeneration in the coastal mountains of Oregon. *New Forests* 8:249–63.

Mladenoff, D. J., M. A. White, and J. Pastor. 1993. Comparing spatial pattern in unaltered old-growth and disturbed forest landscapes. *Ecological Applications* **3**:294–306.

Morrison, P., and F. J. Swanson. 1990. *Fire history and pattern in a Cascade Range landscape*. United States Forest Service, Pacific Northwest Research Station General Technical Report PNW-GTR-254.

Mueller-Dombois, D. 1981. Fire in tropical ecosystems. Pp. 137–76 in H. A. Mooney, T. M. Bonnicksen, N. L. Christensen, J. E. Lotan, and W. A. Reiners (technical coordinators). *Fire regimes and ecosystem properties: proceedings of the conference*. United States Forest Service General Technical Report WO-26.

Naveh, Z. 1974. Effects of fire in the Mediterranean region. Pp. 401–34 in T. T. Kozlowski and C. E. Ahlgren (eds). *Fire and Ecosystems*. Academic Press, New York.

Nilsson, C., Ekblad, A., Gardfjell, M., and Carlberg, B. 1991. Long-term effects of river regulation on river margin vegetation. *Journal of Applied Ecology* **28**:963–87.

Noble, I. R., and R. O. Slayter. 1980. The use of vital attributes to predict successional changes in plant communities subject to recurrent disturbance. *Vegetatio* **43**:5–21.

Ohmann, J. L., and T. A. Spies. 1998. Regional gradient analysis and spatial pattern of woody plant communities of Oregon forests. *Ecological Monographs* **68**:152–82.

Oliver, C. D. 1978. *Development of northern red oak in mixed species stands in central New England*. Yale University School of Forestry and Environmental Studies Bulletin 91.

    1981. Forest development in North America following major disturbances. *Forest Ecology and Management* **3**:153–68.

Oliver, C. D., and B. C. Larson. 1990. *Forest Stand Dynamics*. McGraw-Hill, New York.

O'Neill, R. V., J. R. Krummel, R. H. Gardner, G. Sugihara, B. Jackson, D. L. DeAngelis, B. T. Milne, M. G. Turner, B. Zygmunt, S. Christensen, V. H. Dale and R. L Graham. 1988. Indices of landscape pattern. *Landscape Ecology* **1**:153–62.

O'Neill, R. V., C. T. Hunsaker, S. P. Timmins, B. L. Jackson, K. B. Jones, K. H.

Riitters, and J. D. Wickham. 1996. Scale problems in reporting landscape pattern at the regional scale. *Landscape Ecology* 11:169–80.

Osborne, L. L., and D. A. Kovacic. 1993. Riparian vegetation buffer strips in water-quality restoration and stream management. *Freshwater Biology* 29:243–58.

Pabst, R.J., and T.A. Spies. 1998. Distribution of herbs and shrubs in relation to landform and canopy cover in riparian forests of coastal Oregon. *Canadian Journal of Botany* 76:298–315.

Pacala, S. W., C. D. Canham, J. Saponara, J. A. Silander, Jr., R. K. Kobe, and E. Ribbens. 1996. Forest models defined by field measurements: estimation, error analysis and dynamics. *Ecological Monographs* 66:1–43.

Pastor, J., R. J. Naiman, B. Dewey, and P. McInnes. 1988. Moose, microbes, and the boreal forest. *BioScience* 38:770–6.

Pearson, S. M. 1993. The spatial extent and relative influence of landscape-level factors on wintering bird populations. *Landscape Ecology* 8:3–18.

Pearson, S. M., M. G. Turner, R. H. Gardner, and R. V. O'Neill. 1996. An organism-based perspective of habitat fragmentation. Pp. 77–95 in R. C. Szaro (ed.). *Biodiversity in Managed Landscapes: Theory and Practice*. Oxford University Press, Covelo, California.

Peet, R. K., and N. L. Christensen. 1987. Competition and tree death. *BioScience* 37:586–95.

Perry, D. A. 1994. *Forest Ecosystems*. The Johns Hopkins University Press, Baltimore and London.

Peterjohn, W. T., and D. L. Correll. 1984. Nutrient dynamics in an agricultural watershed: observations on the role of a riparian forest. *Ecology* 65:1466–75.

Peterken, G. F. 1996. *Natural Woodland*. Cambridge University Press, Cambridge.

Pickett, S. T. A., and M. J. McDonnell. 1989. Changing perspectives in community dynamics: a theory of successional forces. *Tree* 4:241–5.

Pickett, S. T. A., and R. S. Ostfeld. 1995. The shifting paradigm in ecology. Pp. 261–78 in R. L. Knight and S. F. Bates (eds). *A New Century for Natural Resources Management*. Island Press, Washington, D.C.

Pickett, S. T. A., and J. N. Thompson. 1978. Patch dynamics and the design of nature reserves. *Biological Conservation* 13:27–37.

Pickett, S. T. A., and P. S. White (eds). 1985. *The Ecology of Natural Disturbance and Patch Dynamics*. Academic Press, New York.

Pickett, S. T. A., S. L. Collins, and J. J. Armesto. 1987. Models, mechanisms and pathways of succession. *Botanical Review* 53:335–71.

Pickett, S. T. A., J. Kolasa, J. J. Armesto, and S. L. Collins. 1989. The ecological concept of disturbance and its expression at various hierarchical levels. *Oikos* 54:129–36.

Platt, W. J., and D. R. Strong. 1989. Special feature – treefall gaps and forest dynamics. *Ecology* 70:535–76.

Poage, N., and T. A. Spies. 1996. Tale of two riparian forests. *Cope Report* 9:6–9.

Pregitzer, K. S., and B. V. Barnes. 1984. Classification and comparison of the upland ecosystems of the Cyrus H. McCormick Experimental Forest, Upper Peninsula, Michigan. *Canadian Journal of Forest Research* **14**:362–75.

Pulliam, H. R., J. B. Dunning, and J. Liu. 1992. Population dynamics in complex landscapes: a case study. *Ecological Applications* **2**:165–77.

Pyne, S. J. 1992. *Burning Bush: a Fire History of Australia*. Allen & Unwin, North Sydney, New South Wales.

Ramakrishnan, P. S., O. P. Toky, B. K. Misra, and K. G. Saxena. 1981. Slash and burn agriculture in northeastern India. Pp. 570–86 in H. A. Mooney, T. M. Bonnicksen, N. L. Christensen, J. E. Lotan, and W. A. Reiners (technical coordinators). *Fire regimes and ecosystem properties: proceedings of the conference*. United States Forest Service General Technical Report WO-26.

Reiners, W. H., and G. E. Lang. 1979. Vegetational patterns and processes in the balsam fir zone, White Mountains, New Hampshire. *Ecology* **60**:403–17.

Remmert, H. (ed.) 1991. *The Mosaic-cycle Concept of Ecosystems*. Springer-Verlag, Berlin.

Renkin, R. A., and D. G. Despain. 1992. Fuel moisture, forest type and lightning-cause fire in Yellowstone National Park. *Canadian Journal of Forest Research* **22**:37–45.

Rjitters, K. H., R. V. O'Neill, C. T. Hunsaker, J. D. Wickham, D. H. Yankee, S. P. Timmons, K. B. Jones, and B. L. Jackson. 1995. A factor analysis of landscape pattern and structure metrics. *Landscape Ecology* **10**:23–40.

Ripple, W. J. 1994. Historic spatial patterns of old forests in western Oregon. *Journal of Forestry* **92**:45–8.

Robertson, P. A., G. T. Weaver, and J. A. Cavanaugh. 1978. Vegetation and tree species patterns near the northern terminus of the southern floodplain forest. *Ecological Monographs* **48**:249–67.

Roland, J. 1993. Large-scale forest fragmentation increases the duration of tent caterpillar outbreak. *Oecologia* **93**:25–30.

Romme, W. H. 1982. Fire and landscape diversity in subalpine forests of Yellowstone National Park. *Ecological Monographs* **52**:199–221.

Romme, W. H., and D. G. Despain. 1989. Historical perspective on the Yellowstone fires of 1988. *BioScience* **39**:695–9.

Romme, W. H., M. G. Turner, L. L. Wallace, and J. Walker. 1995. Aspen, elk and fire in northern Yellowstone National Park. *Ecology* **76**:2097–106.

Romme, W. H., M. G. Turner, R. H. Gardner, W. W. Hargrove, G. A. Tuskan, D. G. Despain, and R. A. Renkin. 1997. A rare episode of sexual reproduction in aspen (*Populus tremuloides*) following the 1988 Yellowstone fires. *Natural Areas Journal*, **17**:17–25.

Rowe, J. S., and B. V. Barnes. 1994. Geo-ecosystems and bio-ecosystems. *Bulletin of the Ecological Society of America* **75**:40–1.

Rowe, J. S., and G. W. Scotter. 1973. Fire in the boreal forest. *Quaternary Research* **3**:444–64.

Ruggiero, L. F., K. B. Aubry, A. B. Carey, and M. H. Huff (tech. coords). 1991. *Wildlife and vegetation of unmanaged Douglas-fir forests*. United States Forest Service, Pacific Northwest Research Station General Technical Report PNW-GTR-285.

Runkle, J. R. 1982. Patterns of disturbance in some old-growth mesic forests of eastern North America. *Ecology* 63:1533–46.

    1985. Disturbance regimes in temperate forests. Pp. 17–34 in S. T. A. Pickett and P. S. White (eds). *The Ecology of Natural Disturbance and Patch Dynamics.* Academic Press, New York.

    1992. *Guidelines and sample protocol for sampling forest gaps.* United States Forest Service, Pacific Northwest Research Station General Technical Report PNW-GTR-283. Portland, Oregon.

Ruth, R. H., and A. S. Harris. 1979. *Management of western hemlock–sitka spruce forests for timber production.* United States Forest Service, Pacific Northwest Forest and Range Experiment Station General Technical Report PNW-88.

Rykiel, E. J. 1985. Towards a definition of ecological disturbance. *Australian Journal of Ecology* **10**:361–5.

Sato, K., and Y. Iwasa. 1993. Modeling of wave regeneration in subalpine *Abies* forests: population dynamics with spatial structure. *Ecology* **74**:1538–50.

Sedell, J. R., F. N. Leone, and W. S. Duval. 1991. Water transportation and storage of logs. *American Fisheries Society Special Publication* **19**:325–68.

Seidel, K. W., and P. H. Cochran. 1981. *Silviculture of mixed conifer forests in eastern Oregon and Washington.* United States Forest Service, Pacific Northwest Forest and Range Experiment Station General Technical Report PNW-121. Portland, Oregon.

Shrader-Frechette, K. S., and E. D. McCoy. 1993. *Method in Eecology: Strategies for Conservation.* Cambridge University Press, New York.

Shugart, H. H. 1984. *A Theory of Forest Dynamics.* Springer-Verlag, New York.

Sillett, S. C. 1994. Growth rates of two epiphytic cyanolichen species at the edge and in the interior of a 700-year-old Douglas-fir forest in the western Cascades of Oregon. *Bryologist* **97**:321–4.

Spies, T. A. 1983. Classification and analysis of forest ecosystems of the Sylvania Recreation Area, upper Michigan. Ph.D. dissertation. University of Michigan.

    1997. Stand structure, function, and composition. In K. A. Kohm and J. F. Franklin (eds). *Creating a Forestry for the 21st Century: the Science of Ecosystem Management.* Island Press, Washington, D.C.

Spies, T. A., and B. V. Barnes. 1985. A multifactor ecological classification of the northern hardwood and conifer ecosystems of Sylvania Recreation Area, Upper Peninsula, Michigan. *Canadian Journal of Forest Research* **15**:949–60.

Spies, T. A., and S. P. Cline. 1988. Coarse woody debris in forests and plantations of coastal Oregon. Pp. 5–24 in C. Maser, R. F. Tarrant, J. M. Trappe, and J. F. Franklin (technical editors). *From the forest to the sea: a story of fallen trees.* United States Forest Service, Pacific Northwest Research Station General Technical Report PNW-GTR-229.

Spies, T. A., and J. F. Franklin. 1988. Old growth and forest dynamics in the Douglas-fir region of western Oregon and Washington. *Natural Areas Journal* **8**:190–201.

1989. Gap characteristics and vegetation response in coniferous forests of the Pacific Northwest. Pp. 543–5 in W. J. Platt and D. R. Strong (eds). Special feature – treefall gaps and forest dynamics. *Ecology* **70.**

1991. The structure of natural young, mature, and old-growth Douglas-fir forests. Pp. 91–110 in L. F. Ruggiero, K. B. Aubry, A. B. Carey, and M. H. Huff (tech. coords). *Wildlife and vegetation of unmanaged Douglas-fir forests.* United States Forest Service, Pacific Northwest Research Station General Technical Report PNW-GTR-285. Portland, Oregon.

1996. The diversity and maintenance of old-growth forests. Pp. 296–314 in R. C. Szaro and D. W. Johnston (eds). *Biodiversity in Managed Landscapes.* Oxford University Press.

Spies, T. A., J. F. Franklin, and T. B. Thomas. 1988. Coarse woody debris in Douglas-fir forests of western Oregon and Washington. *Ecology* **69**:1689–702.

Spies, T. A., J. F. Franklin, and M. Klopsch. 1990. Canopy gaps in Douglas-fir forests of the Cascade Mountains. *Canadian Journal of Forest Research* **20**:649–58.

Spies, T. A., J. Tappeiner, J. Pojar, and D. Coates. 1991. Trends in ecosystem management at the stand level. Pp. 630–41 in *Transactions 56th North American Wildlife and Natural Resources Conference.*

Spies, T. A., W. J. Ripple, and G. A. Bradshaw. 1994. Dynamics and pattern of a managed coniferous forest landscape in Oregon. *Ecological Applications* **4**:555–68.

Sprugel, D. G. 1976. Dynamic structure of wave-regenerated *Abies balsamea* forests in the north-eastern United States. *Journal of Ecology* **64**:889–911.

1991. Disturbance, equilibrium, and environmental variability: What is 'natural' vegetation in a changing environment? *Biological Conservation* **58**:1–18.

Spurr, S. H., and B. V. Barnes. 1980. *Forest Ecology.* Third edition. Wiley, New York.

Stearns, F. W. 1949. Ninety years change in a northern hardwood forest in Wisconsin. *Ecology* **30**:350–8.

Stickney, P. 1986. *First decade plant succession following the Sundance forest fire, northern Idaho.* United States Forest Service, Intermountain Research Station General Technical Report INT-197. Ogden, Utah, USA.

Stone, L., and S. Ezrati. 1996. Chaos, cycles and spatiotemporal dynamics in plant ecology. *Journal of Ecology* **84**:279–91.

Swanson, F. J. 1981. Fire and geomorphic processes. Pp. 401–20 in H. A. Mooney, T. M. Bonnicksen, N. L. Christensen, J. E. Lotan, and W. A. Reiners (technical coordinators). *Fire regimes and ecosystem properties: proceedings of the conference.* United States Forest Service General Technical Report WO-26.

Swanson, F. J., and R. E. Sparks. 1990. Long-term ecological research and the invisible place. *BioScience* **40**:502–8.

Swanson, F. J., T. K. Kratz, N. Caine, and R. G. Woodmansee. 1988. Landform effects on ecosystem patterns and processes. *BioScience* **38**:92–8.

Swanson, F. J., J. A. Jones, D. O. Wallin, and J. H. Cissel. 1993. Natural variability
– implications for ecosystem management. Pp. 89–103 in M. E. Jensen
and P. S. Bourgeron (eds). *Eastside forest ecosystem health assessment*. Volume
II: *Ecosystem management: principles and applications*. United States Forest
Service Pacific Northwest Research Station, Portland, Oregon.

Swetnam, T. W. 1993. Fire history and climate change in giant sequoia groves.
Science **262**:885–9.

Swetnam, T. W., and J. L. Betancourt. 1990. Fire-Southern Oscillation relations
in the southwestern United States. *Science* **249**:1017–20.

Syrjänen, K., R. Kalliola, A. Puolasmaa, and J. Mattsson. 1994. Landscape structure and forest dynamics in subcontinental Russian European taiga.
Annales Zoologici Fennici **31**:19–34.

Tappeiner, J. C., D. Huffman, D. Marshall, T. A. Spies, and J. D. Bailey. 1997.
Density, ages, and growth rates in old-growth and young-growth forests
in coastal Oregon. *Canadian Journal of Forest Research* **27**:638–48.

Taylor, D. L. 1973. Some ecological implications of fire control in Yellowstone
National Park. *Ecology* **54**:1394–6.

Thomas, J. W. (tech. ed.). 1979. *Wildlife habitats in managed forests: the Blue
Mountains of Oregon and Washington*. United States Department of
Agriculture Agriculture Handbook Number 553.

Tilman, D. 1988. *Plant Strategies and the Dynamics and Structure of Plant Communities*.
Princeton University Press, Princeton, New Jersey.

Tilman, D., R. M. May, C. L. Lehman, and M. A. Nowak. 1994. Habitat destruction and the extinction debt. *Nature* **371**:65–6.

Turner, M. G. 1989. Landscape ecology: the effect of pattern on process. *Annual
Review of Ecology and Systematics* **20**:171–97.

1990. Spatial and temporal analysis of landscape patterns. *Landscape Ecology*
4:21–30.

Turner, M. G., and V. H. Dale. (in prep) Comparing large, infrequent disturbances: what have we learned? *Special Feature in Ecology*.

Turner, M. G., and R. H. Gardner (eds). 1991. *Quantitative Methods in Landscape
Ecology*. Springer-Verlag, New York.

Turner, M. G., and W. H. Romme. 1994. Landscape dynamics in crown fire ecosystems. *Landscape Ecology* **9**:59–77.

Turner, M. G., R. V. O'Neill, R. H. Gardner, and B. T. Milne. 1989. Effects of
changing spatial scale on the analysis of landscape pattern. *Landscape
Ecology* **3**:153–62.

Turner, M. G., W. H. Romme, R. H. Gardner, R. V. O'Neill, and T. K. Kratz. 1993.
A revised concept of landscape equilibrium: disturbance and stability on
scaled landscapes. *Landscape Ecology* **8**:213–27.

Turner, M. G., W. H. Hargrove, R. H. Gardner, and W. H. Romme. 1994. Effects
of fire on landscape heterogeneity in Yellowstone National Park,
Wyoming. *Journal of Vegetation Science* **5**:731–42.

Turner, M. G., R. H. Gardner, and R. V. O'Neill. 1995. Ecological dynamics at
broad scales. *BioScience*: Supplement S-29 to S-35.

Turner, M. G., W. L. Baker, R. K. Peet, and C. Peterson. (in prep) Factors influencing succession: lessons from large, infrequent disturbances. *Special Feature in Ecology.*

Turner, M. G., W. H. Romme, R. H. Gardner, and W. W. Hargrove. 1997. Effects of fire size and pattern on early succession in Yellowstone National Park. *Ecological Monographs,* **67**:411–33.

Turner, M. G., S. R. Carpenter, E. J. Gustafson, R. J. Naiman, and S. M. Pearson. (in press) Land use. In M. J. Mac, P. A. Opler, P. Doran, C. Haecker, and L. Huckaby Stroh (eds). *Status and Trends of our Nation's Biological Resources.* Volume 1. National Biological Service, Washington, D.C.

Tuskan, G.A., K.E. Francis, S.L. Russ, W.H. Romme, and M. G. Turner. 1996. RAPD markers reveal diversity within and among clonal and seedling stands of aspen in Yellowstone National Park, USA. *Canadian Journal of Forest Research,* **26**:2088–98.

Urban, D. L., R. V. O'Neill, and H. H. Shugart. 1987. Landscape ecology. *BioScience* **37**:119–27.

Usher, M. B. 1992. Statistical models of succession. Pp. 215–48 in D. C. Glenn-Lewin, R. K. Peet, and T. T. Veblen (eds). *Plant Succession: Theory and Prediction.* Chapman & Hall, London.

Van Wagner, C. E. 1978. Age-class distribution and the forest fire cycle. *Canadian Journal of Forest Research* **8**:220–7.

    1983. Fire behaviour in northern conifer forests and shrublands. Pp. 65–80 in R. W. Wein and D. A. MacLean (eds). *The Role of Fire in Northern Circumpolar Ecosystems.* John Wiley & Sons, New York.

Veblen, T. T., K. S. Hadley, E. M. Nel, T. Kitzberger, M. Reid, and R. Villalba. 1994. Disturbance regime and disturbance interactions in a Rocky Mountain subalpine forest. *Journal of Ecology* **82**:125–35.

Wallin, D. O., F. J. Swanson, and B. Marks. 1994. Landscape pattern response to changes in pattern generation rules: land-use legacies in forestry. *Ecological Applications* **4**:569–80.

Watt, A. S. 1947. Pattern and process in the plant community. *Journal of Ecology* **35**:1–22.

Webb, L. J. 1958. Cyclones as an ecological factor in tropical lowland rainforest, North Queensland. *Australian Journal of Botany* **6**:220–8.

White, M. A., and D. J. Mladenoff. 1994. Old-growth forest landscape transitions from pre-European settlement to present. *Landscape Ecology* **9**:191–205.

White, P. S. 1979. Pattern, process and natural disturbance in vegetation. *Botanical Review* **45**:229–99.

Whitney, G. G. 1986. Relation of Michigan's presettlement pine firests to substrate and disturbance history. *Ecology* **67**:1548–59.

    1994. *From Coastal Wilderness to Fruited Plain: a History of Environmental Change in Temperate North America, from 1500 to the Present.* Cambridge University Press, Cambridge.

Whittaker, R. 1956. Vegetation of the Great Smoky Mountains. *Ecological Monographs* **26**:1–80.

Whittaker, R. H. 1953. A consideration of climax theory: the climax as a population and pattern. *Ecological Monographs* **23**:41–78.

   1973. Climax concepts and recognition. *Handbook of Vegetation Science* **8**:137–54.

Wiens, J. A. 1976. Population responses to patchy environments. *Annual Review of Ecology Systematics* **7**:81–120.

Wiens, J. A. 1989. Spatial scaling in ecology. *Functional Ecology* **3**:385–97.

Williams, M. 1989. *Americans and their Forests: a Historical Geography.* Cambridge University Press, Cambridge.

Worona, M. A., and C. Whitlock. 1995. Late quaternary vegetation and climate history near Little Lake, central Coast Range, Oregon. *Geological Society of America Bulletin* **107**:867–76.

Wright, H. E., Jr. 1974. Landscape development, forest fires, and wilderness management. *Science* **186**:487–95.

Wright, H. E., Jr., and M. L. Heinselman. 1973. Introduction to symposium on the ecological role of fire in natural coniferous forests of western and northern America. *Quaternary Research* **3**:319–28.

Wu, J., and O. L. Loucks. 1995. From balance of nature to hierarchical patch dynamics: a paradigm shift in ecology. *Quarterly Review of Biology* **70**:439–66.

Yamamoto, S. 1992. The gap theory in forest dynamics. *Botanical Magazine, Tokyo* **105**:375–83.

Zackrisson, O. 1977. Influence of forest fires on the north Swedish boreal forest. *Oikos* **29**:22–32.

Zimmerer, K. S. 1994. Human geography and the 'new ecology': the prospect and promise of integration. *Annals of the Association of American Geographers* **84**:108–25.

5   Abiotic factors

ANDREW HANSEN AND JAY ROTELLA

The western edge of Yellowstone National Park (YNP) is one of North America's most striking borders between a natural landscape and a human-altered one. Within YNP, vast stands of centuries-old coniferous forest are broken only by paths of recent wildfires. Outside the park, numerous clearcuts fragment what forest remains. Yellowstone's old-growth forests and wildfire patches are rich in structural complexity, with many canopy layers, tree sizes, and/or abundant snags. West of the park, structural complexity has been greatly reduced by clearcutting and fire suppression. Most modern ecologists would predict that the structural complexity in YNP supports a diverse community of animals and plants, while fewer native species are expected to occur in the human-impacted lands outside of the park. Science, however, is full of surprises.

When we sampled the bird community in this area, we found as expected that individual bird species differed in abundance among natural old-growth forests, wildfire patches, and clearcuts. However, bird species richness and total bird abundance did not differ among these stand types (Hansen and Harting, in prep). Moreover, bird density was low in all three stand types; only about 25% of what we had found in similar stands in western Oregon. Why is bird richness not strongly related to structural complexity in this landscape and bird abundance low compared with other biomes?

Nineteenth-century ecologists would likely not have been surprised at our observations in Yellowstone. They might have suggested that abiotic factors like topography, climate, and soil can exert a stronger influence on species than structural complexity. While many modern ecologists have focused on the important relationships between natural disturbance, structural complexity, and species diversity (Chapter 4), classical ecologists looked more towards the role of abiotic factors in controlling communities. Early biogeographers like Merriam (1894) were struck by how well the distributions of broad vegetation classes correlated with altitude, and referred to elevational bands as 'life zones'. Clements (1936) and

Holdridge (1967) formalized these ideas into a classification system to predict biome type based on climate alone. By the mid 1900s, vegetation ecologists such as Whittaker (1956, 1960) and Daubenmire (1956, 1968) had quantified the strong influence of soils, climate, and topography on the spatial patterns of abundance of individual plant species. More recently, a few vertebrate ecologists have become interested in abiotic factors. Currie (1991), for example, found that climate variables explained over 90% of the variation in vertebrate species richness across North America.

Currie's findings, and the availability of new tools to measure climate, topography, and soils, have generated a resurgence of interest in how abiotic factors affect organisms. We suggest in this chapter that modern concepts of patch dynamics, species diversity, and forest management can be enriched by integration of traditional thinking on abiotic factors. In analogy to the theater, a landscape may be viewed as a biophysical stage and organisms as the actors (Harris et al. 1996). The drama of the interactions among ecological processes and organisms reflects the setting or spatial patterning of the biophysical stage. While ecologists have learned much about abiotic effects on the distribution of plant species, similar studies are needed on animals. Both plant and animal ecologists will benefit from a better understanding the interactions between abiotic factors, ecological processes like disturbance, and community characteristics like species diversity. Most pressing of all is the need to incorporate thinking about abiotic and biotic interactions into ecosystem management and conservation. In this chapter we explore how the changing stage of climate, topography, and soils influences ecological processes like disturbance and energy flow and the consequences for biodiversity.

We first examine how abiotic factors (e.g., climate, topography, soil, substrate, and water) influence organisms directly as components of species' niches, and indirectly by modifying ecological processes. Next, we consider how abiotic factors interact with disturbance, vegetation structure, and primary productivity to cause spatial variation in habitat suitability across landscapes. The influence of this spatial heterogeneity on species abundance, demography and richness is considered next. Implications for management are then drawn out, with an emphasis on how human land use has been arrayed along abiotic gradients relative to the spatial patterning of biodiversity. The aspects of biodiversity we emphasize here are the demography and abundance of individual species and the richness and total abundance of species in the community. All these ideas are illustrated in a concluding section on the Greater Yellowstone Ecosystem.

Returning to the birds of Yellowstone, it is likely that the high elevations and harsh winters along the western boundary of YNP cause energy to limit bird abundance and diversity in both clearcuts and in structurally complex old-growth stands. 'Hot spots' for birds are mostly found at lower elevations outside of YNP (Hansen *et al.* in press), where longer growing seasons and better soils allow higher levels of primary productivity and greater energy availability. Many of the hot spots are on private lands, and cooperative management across land ownerships offers promise for maintaining native biodiversity across greater ecosystems like Yellowstone.

In reading this chapter, you will become aware that simple explanations for biodiversity are elusive. Abiotic and biotic factors often interact in complex ways, and analyses that consider both will likely be the most revealing. Many of the hypotheses on abiotic factors and biodiversity mentioned here have not yet been well tested. Yet, these concepts offer bright new opportunities for understanding, and managing biodiversity.

Abiotic limits on organisms

How might abiotic factors influence an organism such as an annual plant or a small mammal? Climate, topography, and soils may be resources or conditions (e.g., Begon *et al.* 1990) that affect the fitness of an organism. They also may drive other components of the ecosystem such as vegetation structure or primary productivity, which, in turn, bear on the organism.

Hutchinson (1957) used the term 'niche' to describe the range of abiotic and biotic conditions and resources required by an organism for survival, growth, and reproduction. The niche of most organisms includes many dimensions or axes, each of which is defined by a limiting abiotic or biotic factor. The niche of a salamander, for example, may include an ambient temperature axis which limits metabolic rates, a humidity axis which influences body moisture, and a vegetation structure axis which influences predator avoidance. Rates of growth and reproduction for an organism vary along a niche axis, generally peaking at some intermediate level within the range where survival is possible. Members of a species have similar niche requirements. Consequently, a species is most likely to be present at those places in a landscape that contain the appropriate suite of niche attributes, and the abundance of the species is likely to peak where values for the niche dimensions allow maximum rates of growth and reproduction. To the extent that abiotic and biotic limiting factors vary across a landscape, we expect survival, reproduction, and abundance of a species to vary accordingly.

DIRECT EFFECTS OF ABIOTIC FACTORS ON ORGANISMS

You could observe direct effects of abiotic factors on organisms by walking along a transect from a valley bottom to a mountain top. Notice how elements of topography such as elevation, slope, aspect, and slope position change along the transect. These topographic changes influence climate and soils. Mean annual temperature generally decreases with elevation, while precipitation increases. Soils on valley bottoms and toe slopes are often deeper, contain more organic matter, and have higher water-holding capacity than those on mid-slopes and ridge tops.

Plants respond strongly, of course, to these gradients in climate and soil (Daubenmire 1956, 1968; Hack and Goodlet 1960). Rates of plant photosynthesis and growth, for example, vary with ambient temperature, radiant energy, and soil moisture (Begon et al. 1990). Thus, the distributions of plant species vary with elevation such that each reaches maximum abundance at particular elevational and topographic settings (Whittaker 1956, 1960). Notice the very strong effects of abiotic factors on plants at mountain tree-line, above which lethal temperatures, water stress, and/or physical damage by storms prevent tree growth (Slatyer and Noble 1992).

Even though animals are often more mobile than plants, they are still constrained by abiotic factors. Poikilotherms are unable to regulate body temperature via metabolism and are therefore limited by ambient temperatures. Thus, invertebrates, amphibians, and reptiles are often less common at higher elevations and northerly latitudes. Even homeotherms like mammals may die from hypothermia in extreme climates (Coughenour and Singer 1996). The structure and nutrient status of soils also influences some animals (Robinson and Bolen 1989). Burrowing animals are often found where soil texture has sufficient sand content to permit digging but not so much sand as to allow burrow collapse. Many ungulates are attracted to 'salt licks', places where essential minerals are concentrated in exposed soils. Also, some animal species specialize on rock outcroppings, which provide protection from predators (e.g., pikas, Ochotona spp.), or hot, dry microclimates (e.g., reptiles). As you walk to the mountain top, your rapid breathing is evidence of how topography may

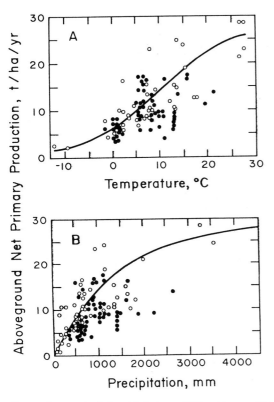

Fig. 5.1. Proposed relationship between NPP and temperature (A) or precipitation (B) fitted to the original data (open circles), with supplemental data (closed circles) from the International Biological Program. (From Waring and Schlesinger 1985.)

constrain organism movement. Some species cannot negotiate steep slopes and are restricted to valley bottoms. Others may orient their movements along ridge tops or through mountain passes. Beyond these direct effects, abiotic factors may limit organisms indirectly by altering ecological processes like energy flow and disturbance rates.

PRIMARY PRODUCTIVITY

Green plants fix energy from sunlight, of course, and fuel the food chain. Rates of net primary productivity (NPP) by green plants set constraints on secondary production by herbivores, tertiary production by predators, and rates of decomposition by detritovores. NPP is affected by climate, soil, and topography and consequently varies over the landscape (Waring and Schlesinger 1985) (Figure 5.1). For example, slopes with aspects facing the sun experience relatively higher levels of solar radiation and evapotranspiration than aspects shaded from the sun, often reducing NPP. Even relatively subtle differences in soil depth and drainage within a forest can create observable differences in forest biomass (Perry 1994).

How might NPP influence species abundance and diversity? Many studies have found that species richness is positively associated with NPP (see Huston 1994, Rosenzweig 1995). Higher levels of NPP are thought to allow rare species to achieve larger population sizes and a reduced chance of extinction (Abrams 1995). Hence, more species are able to persist in energy-rich environments (Currie 1991, Kerr and Packer 1997). However, species diversity is sometimes reduced where NPP is very high, possibly because a few species are able to out-compete others and dominate under these conditions (Huston 1994). Thus, a landscape that is patchy in climate, soils and topography is likely to also be patchy in plant growth rates and in the spatial distribution of species abundances and species richness.

VEGETATION STRUCTURE AND DISTURBANCE

We opened the chapter suggesting that many ecologists would expect structurally complex forests in YNP to be relatively high in species abundance and diversity. Studies from many forest ecosystems have found that the abundance of some organisms and richness is positively correlated with the diversity of vegetative architecture within stands and with variation in vegetation structure across landscapes (Chapter 4). Elements of vegetation structure such as canopy layers, tree density, or snag density are important axes in the habitat niches of many species (James 1971). Thus, the abundance of individual species and species richness should be highest in forests with high structural complexity because of the variety of niches represented there (Urban and Smith 1989). The same idea also holds at the landscape scale. Landscapes that have a greater variety of stand types, sizes, and shapes generally support more species than more homogeneous landscapes. Hence, managers striving to maintain viable populations of many native species often attempt to maintain or restore structural complexity at the stand and landscape levels (Hunter 1990, Hansen et al. 1991). Even here, however, abiotic factors cannot be ignored, because they influence the plant growth rates that build vegetation structure and the expression of ecological disturbance that, in turn, destroys and/or transforms vegetation structure.

One way that abiotic factors affect vegetation structure is by constraining NPP. As plants are the fundamental building blocks of vegetation structure, the rate of plant growth sets an upper limit on the rate of biomass accumulation in a forest. Sites with favorable climate and soils and high NPP can build vegetation structure faster than harsher sites. Vegetation also alters microclimate, soil, and nutrients (Begon *et al.* 1990). Thus there are strong feedbacks between abiotic factors and vegetation.

Another way that abiotic factors can drive vegetation structure is by influencing ecological disturbance. Disturbances such as fire, windthrow, and landslides tend to destroy, transform, or transport elements of vegetation structure. Wildfire, for example, may destroy live tree biomass by converting it to inorganic materials in ash and smoke or transform it into coarse woody debris. Disturbances like avalanches and floods can transport biomass from one location to another. Thus, high-severity disturbance may reduce vegetation structure by destroying vegetation structure or moving it off site, while mild or moderate severity disturbance may enhance structural complexity by increasing the diversity of structural types (Franklin 1992).

What is the link between abiotic factors and ecological disturbance? Climate is a primary driver of many types of disturbance such as hurricanes, windthrow, and wildfires (Pickett and White 1985). Consequently, broad-scale disturbance regimes often reflect continental climatic patterns. Along the west coast of North America, for example, precipitation amount and seasonality drive patterns of fire frequency and severity (Agee 1993). The dry summers and frequent lightning in the Siskiyou Mountains of Northern California result in light- to moderate-severity surface fires with a frequency of 50–90 years. Summer precipitation is higher and lightning less frequent farther north in western Washington, where stand-replacement fires recur every 250–450 years on average. Still farther north in southeast Alaska, summer rains are so heavy that wildfire is very rare.

Climate and topography can interact to influence disturbance at regional and local spatial scales. For example, fire frequency varies from about 50 years at lower elevations in the Rocky Mountains to more than 250 years at higher elevations, due to the increasing moisture higher in the mountains (Turner and Romme 1993). In the western Cascades of Oregon, wildfire is more frequent and intense on steep south-facing slopes than in valley bottoms (Morrison and Swanson 1990). This is because fuels are drier and more combustible on south-facing slopes and because convective forces cause fires to burn uphill and with increasing intensity. Similarly, landslides tend to be initiated in moderately steep headwalls within mountainous landscapes (Swanson *et al.* 1988).

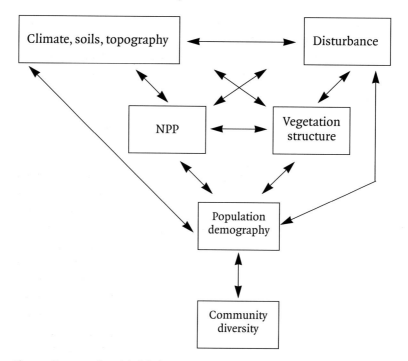

Fig. 5.2. Conceptual model of the interactions between abiotic factors, ecological processes, and biodiversity. See text for explanation.

Topography may also alter the movement of disturbance. Ridgelines, stream bottoms, and lakes or wetlands may act as fire breaks that slow or stop fire expansion (Turner and Romme 1993). Alternatively, insect outbreaks are often spread by winds channeled along constricted valley bottoms or through mountain passes (Despain 1990).

You can begin to imagine the complexity of the interactions among physical factors, primary productivity, ecological disturbance, vegetation structure, and species diversity. While some modern ecologists have emphasized the influence of abiotic factors on plant distributions, it is clear that we have a great deal to learn about the interactions among abiotic factors and other elements of the ecosystem. It is now increasingly apparent that we must think about the biophysical stage on which the ecological drama unfolds. A conceptual model of these linkages is presented in Figure 5.2. The model illustrates that abiotic factors may directly influence the population dynamics and community diversity. Abiotic factors may also influence organisms indirectly by modifying rates of NPP or by affecting disturbance regimes which, in turn, have consequences for vegetation structure. Disturbance and vegetation also provide feedbacks that modify abiotic factors. To the extent that the physical conditions vary from place to place, we should be able to make predictions about how ecological processes and biodiversity are distributed across landscapes.

Spatial interactions among abiotic factors and ecological processes

If a landscape is a biophysical stage, how are abiotic factors distributed across the stage, what are the consequences for the actors, and for the ecological drama they weave? The spatial patterns of abiotic factors were mapped by classical ecologists primarily at the biome level. More recently, the spatial distributions of climate, topography, and soils, and vegetation have been quantified at continental, regional, and local scales (Bailey 1978, Barnes et al. 1982, Ohmann and Spies 1998). These studies reveal considerable spatial heterogeneity in abiotic factors and species distributions at all of these spatial scales. Such spatial heterogeneity in abiotic factors can strongly influence the distribution, abundance, and population dynamics of species (Neilson and Wullstein 1983). The emergence of landscape ecology (Turner 1989) over the last few decades, however, offers an excellent context for addressing spatial heterogeneity of abiotic factors.

Landscape ecology has largely focused on the spatial interactions between natural disturbance, human land-use, vegetation cover, and organisms. This body of work has revealed that landscapes are more than the sum of the patch types they comprise. The spatial arrangement of the patches, their sizes, shapes, and juxtapositioning, also strongly influence the types of organisms that live in the landscape (Chapter 6) and the rates of processes like succession, nutrient cycling, and energy flow (Turner 1989). Landscape ecologists are also beginning to consider the spatial patterning of abiotic factors across landscapes (e.g., Ohmann and Spies 1998) and this approach shows considerable promise for improving our ability to understand and manage landscapes.

Below we offer an example where knowledge of spatial patterning of abiotic factors provided new insights into landscape function. The effects of thresholds in abiotic factors on landscape dynamics are then examined. We end the section with consideration of how to classify abiotic factors across landscapes.

WINDTHROW AND STAND STRUCTURE IN SOUTHEAST ALASKA

Kuiu is one of a multitude of mountainous islands in southeast Alaska that is draped with lush temperate rainforest (Figure 5.3a). Rainfall is so high here that wildfire does not occur. The productive coniferous forests on Kuiu island are naturally fragmented by bogs or 'muskegs' where soils are so saturated that tree growth is restricted (Figure 5.3b) (Kramer et al. in prep.). Where forests do occur, wind is the primary agent of disturbance. Windthrow was thought to be sufficiently infrequent and small in area to allow most of the forests here to succeed to the old-growth stage (Deal et al. 1991). These localized wind events were thought to enhance the structural complexity of old-growth forests (Lertzman et al. 1996).

Our understanding of windthrow and forest dynamics in this system has started to change as a result of the work of graduate student Marc Kramer from Montana State University (Kramer et al. in prep.). Kramer developed a statistical model to predict probability of windthrow based on wind exposure (Figure 5.3c), slope, and elevation. The resulting map of windthrow probability shows that a surprising proportion of the island is susceptible to intense windthrow (Figure 5.3d). He found that intense storms approach the island from the south; hence probability of windthrow is highest at higher elevations on south-facing slopes and on ridgetops. Valley bottoms, north-facing slopes, and other places 'shadowed' from the wind by topography have low probability of windthrow. He then compared the model predictions to field measurements and found that the model accurately predicted windthrow intensity 70% of the time.

These windthrow patterns strongly influence forest structure. Areas of low probability of windthrow were found to be dominated by structurally complex old-growth forests, as was previously believed. However, areas of high probability of windthrow were found to support forests in the younger stem exclusion and understory reinitiation seral states. These seral stages are relatively low in structural complexity.

These findings have important implications. First, much less of Kuiu Island supports old-growth forest that previously believed. The windthrow regime is sufficient to inhibit the development of old growth in more exposed landscape settings. Many species of plants and animals are associated with late-seral forests in southeast Alaska (Suring et al. 1993). Hence, this important habitat type is naturally less abundant and more fragmented than land managers thought. Interestingly, Sitka black-tailed

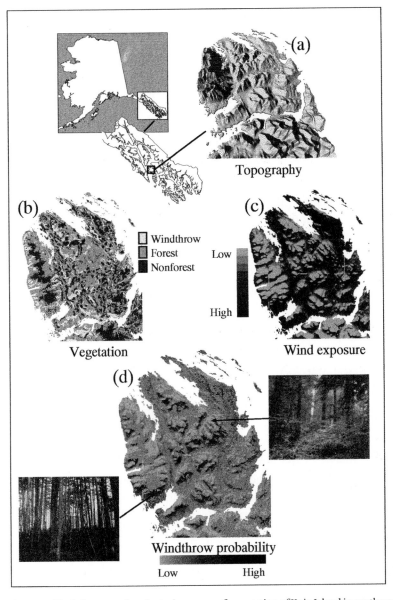

Fig. 5.3. Abiotic factors and ecological processes for a portion of Kuiu Island in southeast Alaska. (a) Location of the focal area and elevation zones. (b) Distribution of forest cover as derived from aerial photograph interpretation by the USDA Forest Service. (c) Exposure to wind as based on wind direction, elevation, and slope. (d) Probability of windthrow as predicted by a logistic function based on wind exposure, elevation, and slope. Typical forest stand structures in areas of high (stem exclusion and reinitiation stages) and low windthrow probability (old-growth gap phase state) are depicted in the photographs. (Photographs by Marc Kramer. From Kramer et al. in prep.)

deer (*Odocoileus hemionus sitkensis*) prefer old-growth forests on south-facing slopes where snow accumulation is reduced. On Kuiu Island, however, old growth is less likely to be found on such slopes due to wind-throw. Given this new understanding of the ecosystem, conservation plans (e.g., Suring *et al.* 1993) to maintain late-seral species, like the Sitka black-tailed deer, may have to be revised accordingly.

The work also has implications for timber harvest. Logging in the region has mostly involved clearcutting of old-growth stands on valley bottoms and toe slopes. Kramer's work suggests that a more ecologically based approach would focus timber harvest on the mid-seral stands found in locations of higher wind exposure. Rather than clearcutting these stands, harvest strategies that retain live trees, snags, and fallen trees would better promote the ecological processes that are typical of these stands. In the wind-protected, old-growth stands, smaller 'gap' cuts would better retain current levels of forest complexity. This case study demonstrates how the consideration of abiotic factors can dramatically improve our understanding of how ecosystems work and can provide a template for effective management strategies.

THRESHOLDS IN ABIOTIC CONTROLS

Initial studies on interactions among abiotic factors and ecological processes are finding that the relationships are often nonlinear. Ecological processes like disturbance regime or NPP may change abruptly with increasing spatial heterogeneity of topography or climate. For example, ecologists have observed that topography often 'constrains' disturbance to certain places in the landscape (Swanson *et al.* 1988). Wildfire, for instance, may be constrained to topographic settings like south-facing slopes where fuel moisture is sufficiently low to allow ignition, and be unable to spread across other parts of the landscape (Figure 5.4a). Extreme meteorological conditions, however, may sometimes cause disturbance to 'override' the effects of topography (Turner and Romme 1993). Under hot, dry, and windy weather conditions, fire may burn across all parts of the landscape regardless of topographic settings (Figure 5.4b). Hence, topography constrains fire only under a subset of weather conditions. The 1988 wildfires in YNP produced examples of each of the fire regimes, depending on the weather conditions at the time of burning (Turner and Romme 1993).

Such thresholds in interactions among abiotic factors can have important implications for vegetation patterns across landscapes. When topog-

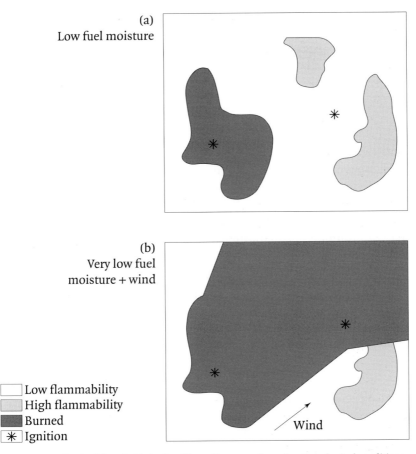

(a)
Low fuel moisture

(b)
Very low fuel
moisture + wind

Low flammability
High flammability
Burned
✳ Ignition

Wind

Fig. 5.4. Hypothesized thresholds in the effects of topography and meteorological conditions on fire spread. (a) Topography constrains the spread of fire to certain topographic settings with flammable fuels. Flammability is high only in certain topographical settings (e.g., south-facing slopes) and fire occurs only in such settings that have ignition sources. (b) Extreme weather conditions cause fire to override topographic constraints and spread across the landscape. High winds and very low fuel moisture cause fire to spread over a variety of topographical settings. (Modified from Turner and Romme 1993.)

raphy does constrain disturbance, vegetation structure will be heterogeneous because disturbance severity will vary with topographic position (Swanson *et al.* 1988). This heterogeneity often promotes high levels of niche and species diversity (Franklin 1992). When disturbance overrides the topography, the vegetation structure may be homogenized over the landscape, reducing species diversity. Also, ecosystem recovery is likely to be slower in landscapes experiencing large, severe disturbance compared with those where undisturbed patches provide colonization sources for adjacent disturbance patches (Turner and Romme 1993). Knowledge of such thresholds is obviously important to managers trying to determine which disturbance regime to allow or prescribe to achieve desired vegetation patterns and resource objectives in a given landscape.

QUANTIFYING ABIOTIC FACTORS ACROSS LANDSCAPES

If knowledge of abiotic factors can improve our understanding of landscape function, which abiotic factors should be quantified across landscapes to better understand controls on biodiversity? Examples of the climatic, topographic, soil, geographic, and aquatic variables used in published studies are presented in Table 5.1. Any of these variables can be used to describe heterogeneity across the landscape and some of these variables may be strongly correlated with particular ecological processes or organisms. A powerful approach to studying controls on biodiversity is to quantify several of these variables across the landscape and determine which of the variables explain significant spatial variation in species abundance or the richness of a community. In the next section we explore some of the abiotic factors that strongly influence the abundance, reproduction, and diversity of biota.

Species demography and diversity over the landscape

Earlier we asserted that abiotic factors may represent important axes describing the niche of a species and that the performance of the species will vary along the niche axis. Thus, species demography and diversity across a landscape should reflect the spatial patterning of limiting conditions and resources. How good is the evidence that species abundance, survival, reproduction, and ultimately the species richness of a community, vary with abiotic factors? What are some of the consequences of the resulting spatial patterns for the dynamics of populations and communities? Can we make predictions about patterns of diversity from one biome to another based on abiotic factors? These are some of the questions examined in this section.

SPECIES ABUNDANCE

We all suspect that species are not randomly distributed over the landscape. But a major question is how patchy is the abundance of

Table 5.1. *Examples of abiotic factors that have been used to predict patterns of species abundance and richness*

Variable	Organisms studied	Authors
Temperature		
Means annual and monthly, all-time recorded max and min	Woody plants	Ohmann and Spies 1998
Mean annual, variability	Trees	Currie and Paquin 1987
Degree days, absolute min.	Trees	Lenihan 1993
Mean annual	Trees	Austin *et al.* 1996
Mean Jan. & June CV, absolute max and min, annual range	Mammals	Owen 1990
Mean annual, min-coldest month, max-hottest month, annual range, mean-wettest quarter, mean-driest quarter	Kangaroos	Caughley *et al.* 1987
Precipitation		
Mean annual and monthly	Woody plants	Ohmann and Spies 1998
Mean annual, seasonality	Trees	Austin *et al.* 1996
Mean annual, variability	Trees	Currie and Paquin 1987
Annual snowfall	Trees	Lenihan 1993
Intermonthly variability	Mammals	Owen 1990
Total annual	Large herbivores	Coe *et al.* 1976
Mean annual, annual range, total-wettest month, total-driest month, total-wettest quarter, total driest quarter	Kangaroos	Caughley *et al.* 1987
Evapotranspiration		
Mean annual, variability	Trees	Currie and Paquin 1988
Cumulative-summer	Trees	Lenihan 1993
Actual, potential	Birds, angiosperms, mammals	Wylie and Currie 1993
Actual	Mammals	Shvarts *et al.* 1995
Solar radiation		
Potential	Woody plants	Ohmann and Spies 1998
Mean annual and variability of insolation	Trees	Currie and Paquin 1987
Mean annual	Trees	Austin *et al.* 1996

Table 5.1. (cont.)

Variable	Organisms studied	Authors
March and June	Trees	Turton and Sexton 1996
Clear sky irradiance, annual cloud cover	Coral	Fraser and Currie 1996
Annual	Birds, angiosperms, mammals	Wylie and Currie 1993
Topography		
Slope, aspect, elevation	Woody plants	Ohmann and Spies 1998
Median and variability of elevation	Trees	Currie and Paquin 1987
Altitude, aspect, slope, topographic position	Trees	Burns 1995
Topographic position	Trees	Austin et al. 1996
Elevation	Fish	Reyes-Gavilan et al. 1996
Elevational variance	Mammals	Owen 1990
Geology		
Lithology, geologic age	Woody plants	Ohmann and Spies 1997
Rock type	Trees	Austin et al. 1996
Geography		
Latitude, longitude	Woody plants	Ohmann and Spies 1998
Latitude, longitude, quadrat area, geographic position	Trees	Currie and Paquin 1987
Plot size	Trees	Austin et al. 1996
Latitude, continental shelf area, reef length, up-current island density	Coral	Fraser and Currie 1996
Distance from sea	Fish	Reyes-Gavilan et al. 1996
Latitude	Birds	Emlen et al. 1986
Soil		
Exchangeable cations, pH, phosphorus, organic matter	Plants	Enright et al. 1994
Annual moisture deficit	Trees	Lenihan 1993
Drainage	Trees	Burns 1995
Nutrient index	Trees	Austin et al. 1996
March and June temperature, pH, total nitrogen, organic carbon, leaf litter	Trees	Turton and Sexton 1996

Table 5.1 .(cont.)

Variable	Organisms studied	Authors
Primary productivity		
Primary productivity	Coral	Fraser and Currie 1996
Net	Birds, angiosperms, mammals	Wylie and Currie 1993
Net above ground	Large herbivores	Coe *et al.* 1976
Net above ground	Mammals	Owen 1990
Hydrology		
Stream order, width depth, substrate	Fish	Reyes-Gavilan *et al.* 1996
Oceanic		
Mean, max and min surface, salinity variation, mean salinity, secchi depth	Coral	Fraser and Currie 1996
Disturbance		
Timber harvest history	Woody plants	Ohmann and Spies 1998
Fire history	Plants	Enright *et al.* 1994
Cyclone frequency	Coral	Fraser and Currie 1996

individual species. Brown *et al.* (1995) addressed this question for several groups of organisms and found that their abundances were significantly more clumped than expected by chance for the majority of species. For example, 77 of 90 North American bird species studied had more than 50% of their individuals in less than 25% of the places where that species occurred. A likely explanation for this is that relatively few places across a species' range contain the biotic and abiotic factors that allow high levels of abundance. Well-designed studies are needed to determine which abiotic and biotic factors best explain species abundances. The studies below provide examples of organism abundance and distribution being strongly associated with abiotic factors.

One of the most striking cases of abiotic controls on species distributions is the response of tree species to deglaciation. In eastern North America, the grip of the last ice age eased 16 000 years ago as the Laurentide ice sheet began to recede northward from its southern extreme in Pennsylvania. Mean global temperature has increased some 4.5 °C since then. Davis (1981) used fossil pollen as a basis for plotting the range expansions of several tree species during this period of warming. American chestnut (*Castanea dentata*) expanded its range over 2000 km to the northeast over the last 15 000 years (Figure 5.5). In contrast to chestnut, eastern hemlock (*Tsuga canadensis*) expanded to the northwest into the Great Lake States (Figure 5.5). This demonstrates that each species responded to climate change according to its individual tolerances. The strength of association between modern climate and tree distributions was quantified by Lenihan (1993). Using five measures of climate, he was able to predict the spatial distribution of dominance for eight tree species across Canada with a classification accuracy of 88–98%, depending upon species. The strong relationship between climate and plant distributions described in these two studies provides a basis for predicting how vegetation is likely to respond to possible future global warming resulting from human-caused greenhouse-gas emissions (e.g., Overpeck *et al.* 1991).

Abiotic factors such as climate can also limit animal distributions. In analyzing the ranges of 113 avian species wintering in North America, Root (1988) found that 60% of these species have northern range limits associated with a particular temperature regime. The range limits of each of these species were within one degree of latitude (115 km) of a particular average minimum temperature isotherm (Figure 5.6). Energy budgets developed for 14 species with adequate physiological data revealed a surprising consistency. The resting metabolic rate at the northern range limit was about 2.49 times greater than the basic metabolic rate (BMR) for all the species. (BMR is the metabolic rate of a night-resting individual at an ambient temperature above that at which an individual must increase its metabolic rate to maintain heat balance.) These findings suggest that the winter ranges of many bird species are limited by energy expenditures necessary to compensate for colder ambient temperatures. Energy relationships were associated with the abundances of 7 of these 14 species (Figure 5.6). Similarly, Emlen *et al.* (1986) found that the abundances of some species of breeding birds were also related to climate, and Caughley *et al.* (1987) were able to predict successfully the distributions of three species of kangaroos based on temperature and precipitation regimes.

An example of climate influencing animal abundance by altering NPP comes from work by Coe *et al.* (1976) on African herbivores. They compiled data on biomass for up to 36 species of large herbivores and rainfall data for 24 locations in the savannas of southern and eastern Africa. Mean annual rainfall explained 88% of the variation in total biomass of large herbivores (Figure 5.7a). Herbivore biomass was also strongly correlated with aboveground NPP (Figure 5.7b). This suggests that rainfall limits plant growth

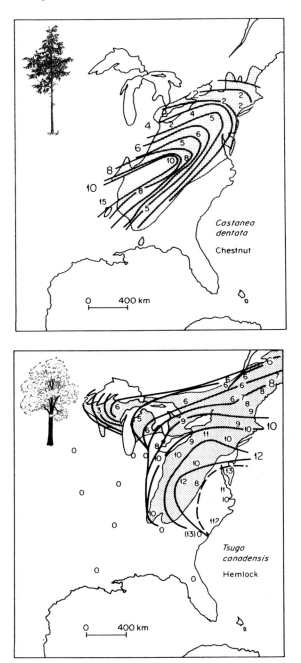

Fig. 5.5. Migration maps for American chestnut and eastern hemlock as reconstructed from analyses of fossil pollen. Numbers refer to the radiocarbon age (years before present) of the first appearance of the species at the site after 15 000 years ago. Isopleths represent the leading edge of the expanding population distribution. The stippled area represents the modern range of the species. (From Davis 1981.)

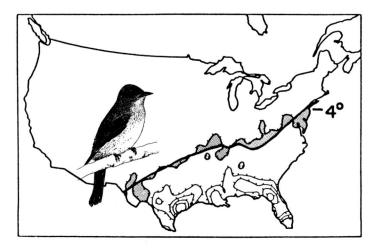

Fig. 5.6. Contour map of the winter distribution and abundance of eastern phoebe (*Sayornis phoebe*). The bold line is the edge of the species range and the four contour intervals are 20%, 40%, 60% and 80% of maximum abundance. The northern range limit is associated with the $-4°$ C isotherm of average minimum January temperature. The stippling indicates the area of deviation between the range boundary and the isotherm. (From Root 1988.)

rates and energy availability to herbivores. Soil nutrients may modify the relationship between rainfall and ungulates. Ecosystems with nutrient-rich volcanic and alluvial soils had herbivore biomasses higher than predicted based on rainfall alone, presumably due to higher forage quality (Coe *et al.* 1976). Rainfall and soil nutrients vary in space and time in many ecosystems, and the dispersal of ungulates often reflects this. Many herbivores move to patches with the highest plant productivity within seasons and the major herbivore migrations in Africa are driven by the spatial distribution of forage productivity among seasons (McNaughton 1985).

These examples demonstrate that the abundance and distribution of species sometimes varies with abiotic factors, due either to direct effects on organism fitness or to indirect effects through ecosystem processes such as primary productivity. What are the relative strengths of abiotic and biotic factors in driving intraspecific distribution and abundance? Relatively few studies have systematically addressed this question across several species and a comprehensive synthesis is not yet possible.

THE DEMOGRAPHY OF SPECIES

Although biotic factors such as competition and predation can clearly have strong impacts on survival and reproduction, abiotic factors

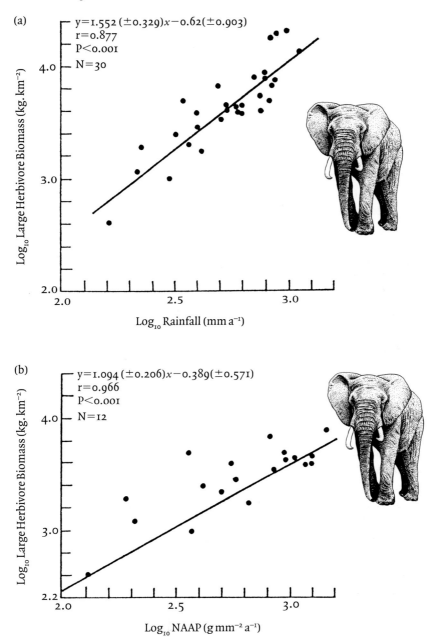

Fig. 5.7. Relationship between African large-herbivore standing-crop biomass and (a) precipitation and (b) aboveground net primary productivity. (Modified from Coe *et al.* 1976.)

are also important and often overlooked. Specifically, temporal and spatial variation in abiotic factors can cause survival and reproductive success to vary among years, seasons, and locations, which in turn causes population dynamics to vary temporally and spatially. Knowledge of the types of locations that allow higher rates of survival and reproduction is vital for managing population viability.

Survival of many species is greatly influenced by climate (Lack 1966). For example, in ungulates, survival rates of moose (*Alces alces*) (Ballard et al. 1991), elk (*Cervus canadensis*) (Sauer and Boyce 1983), mule deer (*Odocoileus hemionus*) (Bartmann and Bowden 1984), and white-tailed deer (*Odocoileus virginianus*) (Fuller 1990) are negatively affected by severe winter weather. Ungulate mortality is generally thought to be high in areas or years with severe weather because deep snow decreases access to preferred foods and increases vulnerability to predators, while low temperatures increase energy expenditures and lead to starvation. The impacts can be substantial: in a Minnesota study of white-tailed deer, 89% of fawns survived during winters with relatively shallow snow, whereas only 60% survived in winters with moderate snow depths (Fuller 1990). Similarly, a gray partridge (*Perdix perdix*) population declined by 72% from October to March in eastern Washington during a winter with record-breaking snow depths (Rotella and Ratti 1986).

Climate may also affect reproduction in populations. For example, in Nevada autumn precipitation was found to be an important determinant of bighorn sheep (*Ovis canadensis*) reproductive success in the following year (Douglas and Leslie 1986). Similarly, in south-central Canada, the amount of precipitation during the previous year strongly impacts the number of wetland basins containing water and thereby affects reproductive success of a number of duck species. North American mallard (*Anas platyrhnchos*) populations ranged between 7.1 and 14.4 million birds during 1955–72, with population highs and lows generally coinciding with annual wetland conditions in prairie Canada. (Pospahala et al. 1974).

Although it is clear that abiotic factors such as climate can affect survival and reproduction, few studies have investigated spatial patterning of survival or reproduction rates across landscapes. Knowledge of such patterns could prove fruitful however. For example, in Maine the abundance of earthworms, the primary food of American woodcock (*Philohela minor*), and in turn the rate of woodcock chick survival were highest on forested sites with lightly textured, moderately drained soils that had been previously farmed (Owen and Galbraith 1989, Rabe et al. 1983). Therefore, efforts to restore declining woodcock populations should consider the mosaic of soil types and past land use across landscapes.

A study of black bears (*Ursus americanus*) in the Great Smoky Mountains National Park, Tennessee, indicates how abiotic factors like climate and elevation interact with vegetation structure and habitat management to influence the quality of various sites to populations. Johnson and Pelton (1981) found that bears prefer above-ground tree cavities to ground dens during winter. Bears using tree dens are better protected from wind and rain and have reduced energy demands, which may allow females to achieve higher reproductive and survival rates. However, due to low-elevation logging that occurred before the Park was established, trees suitable for denning occur in clumps at higher elevations where weather conditions may be more severe. Thus, past management, which ignored the important role of abiotic factors, causes many bears to experience low vital rates. To ensure population viability, future efforts must ensure that key habitat features such as tree dens are well dispersed and abundant in locations with favorable abiotic conditions.

These examples show that abiotic factors affect survival and reproductive success to a large extent across a variety of species. Results also indicate that when important abiotic factors are spatially patterned, survival and reproductive rates may vary across the landscape. Under these circumstances, subpopulations living in different portions of the landscape have different population growth rates. In landscapes with strong environmental gradients, some subpopulations may not have adequate reproduction to offset annual mortality. In such cases, source-sink dynamics may occur (Pulliam 1988) and spatial aspects of population dynamics must be considered.

In recent years, spatially explicit population dynamics have received much attention (Hanski 1989, Hanski and Gilpin 1991, Pulliam 1988, 1996). The term 'metapopulation' was coined to describe a set of subpopulations that interact via dispersing individuals (Levins 1970, Hanski 1996). This is important because dispersers from one subpopulation (source) can 'rescue' from extinction another subpopulation (sink) that has relatively few individuals. Such dynamics better maintain the long-term viability of the overall metapopulation. Both habitat heterogeneity and species-specific dispersal abilities influence population dynamics (Harrison 1994) (Figure 5.8). The more patchy the environment, the more animal survival, reproduction, and abundance will differ among patches, leading to source/sink dynamics among subpopulations. If a species can disperse well among habitat patches (patchy populations), then rescue

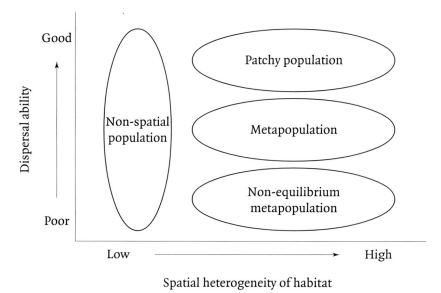

Spatial heterogeneity of habitat

Fig. 5.8. Conceptual model of the effects of landscape heterogeneity and organism dispersal ability on population dynamics. See text for explanation.

effects are likely among subpopulations and risk of extinction is reduced (Chapter 7). As dispersal ability decreases relative to habitat patchiness and the likelihood of movement of individuals among subpopulations decreases (classic metapopulations), then chance of local extinction increases. Where dispersal is very poor and subpopulations do not exchange individuals (non-equilibrium metapopulations), extinction of individual subpopulations and, consequently, the overall metapopulation is more likely. As we come to realize the high level of spatial heterogeneity that abiotic factors impose on organism survival and reproduction, it becomes apparent that such metapopulation dynamics are more common in nature than previously appreciated.

In many cases, maintaining population viability will require identifying source habitats and managing them to maintain suitable levels of survival and reproduction. Careful management of such places in the landscape is important because human activities such as timber harvest, agriculture, or residential development in or near source areas can elevate predation levels and cause them to become sink areas.

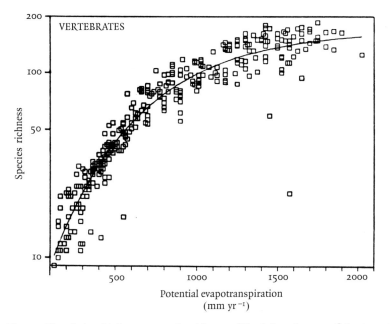

Fig. 5.9. The relationship between species richness of North American non-flying terrestrial vertebrates and annual potential evapotranspiration. (From Currie 1991.)

SPECIES RICHNESS

If the abundances and distributions of individual species are influenced by abiotic factors, then spatial patterns of species diversity should also vary with abiotic factors. A growing number of studies indicates that this is indeed the case.

One of the most striking of these studies is by Currie (1991). He quantified species richness of birds, mammals, amphibians, and reptiles across North America and analyzed patterns of association with 21 environmental variables involving climate, primary productivity, glacial history, and proximity to oceans. Several climate variables were significantly correlated with vertebrate richness, particularly annual potential evapotranspiration (PET), solar radiation, and mean annual temperature. PET alone explained 81–93% of the variation in richness for each of the four animal groups and 92% of the variation for all ground-dwelling vertebrates combined (Figure 5.9). PET reflects the energy of the atmosphere, as measured by the ability of the atmosphere to evaporate water from saturated surfaces. It reflects both the energy available to organisms for thermoregulation and the energy available to fuel NPP and food production for vertebrates (Currie 1991). Species richness is positively related to PET, probably because more species are able to persist in energy-rich environments.

In a follow-up study, Kerr and Packer (1997) reanalyzed Currie's data for mammals and confirmed that PET explained the most variation in mammal species richness in Canada and Alaska where PET is relatively low (<1000 mm/year). Where PET was higher, however, topographic heterogeneity was a better predictor of mammal richness than PET. As mentioned above, knowledge of such thresholds in the effects of abiotic factors is important for understanding and managing biodiversity.

Two recent studies nicely demonstrate the effects of topography, climate, and soils on the spatial distribution of plants across large watersheds. Burns (1995) examined vascular plants in warm temperate mature forests in the Waipoua Forest, New Zealand. Austin et al. (1996) focused on trees in forested habitats of southeastern New South Wales, Australia. Both analyzed associations between species richness and climate, slope position, and soil-nutrient status. Spatial patterns of richness were found to differ among plant life forms and taxonomic groups. Both studies found that total tree-species richness was greatest at low-elevation, warm sites with moderate rainfall and intermediate to high nutrient levels. Maximum richness for eucalyptus trees, however, occurred on ridges with aseasonal rainfall and intermediate nutrient levels, while richness of rainforest trees was highest in gullies with summer rainfall and high nutrient levels (Austin et al. 1996). In contrast to trees, epiphytes achieved highest richness at high elevations due to higher moisture levels there (Burns 1995).

In total, these studies demonstrate that species richness often varies with abiotic factors, but the strengths and directions of these associations differ among spatial scales, geographic locations, and species groupings. To what extent are abiotic factors considered in current theory on the spatial distribution of species richness?

The major hypotheses on species richness are presented in Table 5.2 and are reviewed by Huston (1994) and Rosenzweig (1995). The Available Energy and Habitat Complexity hypotheses were described above. The Disturbance hypothesis suggests that richness will peak at intermediate levels of disturbance, where both early- and late-seral species will be present. The Environmental Stress and Environmental Stability hypotheses are similar in suggesting that relatively few species can persist in places where environmental factors are either especially harsh or variable. The Area hypothesis is supported by several studies showing that species rich-

Table 5.2. *Hypotheses on factors controlling species richness*

Hypothesis	Logic	Examples of independent variables	Hypothesized relationships
Available energy	Supply of energy that is available to be partitioned among species limits richness	Mean heat/moisture Mean productivity Nutrient/food availability	
Habitat complexity	Diversity of habitat niches limits species richness	Mean and variance in: vertical structure horizontal structure species composition	
Disturbance	Intermediate disturbance favors both early and late seral species and prevents competitive exclusion	Mean disturbance: frequency patch size return interval	
Environmental stress	Fewer species are physiologically equipped to tolerate harsh environments	Mean: heat/moisture nutrient/food availability	
Environmental stability	Fewer species are physiologically equipped to tolerate varying environments	Variation in: heat/moisture nutrient/food availability	
Area	Richness reflects sampling effects and environmental heterogeneity	Habitat area	
Biotic interactions	Interactions among species such as competition and predation affect niche partitioning	Niche overlap Covariance in species densities	Various

Note: For the hypothesized relationships, independent variables are depicted on the horizontal (x) axis and species richness on the vertical (y) axis. Broken lines denote possible alternative relationships.
Source: Modified from Fraser and Currie (1996).

ness increases with the area sampled, primarily because of greater variety
in abiotic and/or biotic factors in larger areas. The Biotic Interactions
hypothesis purports that organisms are part of the environment and can
influence resources and conditions for other species via competition, predation, mutualism, etc.

Among the myriad studies on species richness, empirical support can
be found for each of these hypotheses. A sure conclusion from these
studies is that no single factor universally controls species richness
(Begon et al. 1990). The relative strengths of these hypotheses in explaining species richness varies with spatial scale, taxonomic group of organism, and geographic location. If you had to hedge your bets on which
factor is most often associated with species richness, however, Wright et
al. (1993) would suggest that you go with available energy. They analyzed
the vast literature on the topic and reported that NPP (and its correlates)
and habitat diversity were most often found to be significantly associated
with species richness, with NPP accounting for about twice as much variation in richness as any other factor. Wright et al. (1993) concluded '. . . the
most powerful explanation for spatial variation in species richness is that
it depends upon levels of energy'.

What conclusions can we draw from Table 5.2 on the relevance of
abiotic factors to species richness? Climate, topography, and soils cannot
be ruled out as direct or indirect driving factors under any of the hypotheses. Environmental stress and stability directly involve abiotic factors. As
discussed above, physical factors also bear on energy production, disturbance regimes, and habitat complexity. A primary mechanism underlying
the species–area relationship is thought to be heterogeneity in biophysical
factors (Huston 1994). Even species interactions may vary under the influence of abiotic factors. Dunson and Travis (1991) provide several examples
of where the outcomes of competition among species varied with soil type,
salinity levels, and other physical factors.

The conclusion that abiotic factors, especially those related to available
energy, often underlie patterns of species richness may be a bit surprising
to animal ecologists because of the emphasis placed on habitat complexity
in many modern wildlife texts (e.g., Patten 1992, Morrison et al. 1992). One
consequence of this emphasis on habitat complexity is that nearly all ter-
restrial-vertebrate conservation plans are based primarily on vegetation
cover and structure (e.g., Thomas et al. 1990, Suring et al. 1993). Additional
consideration of available energy and abiotic factors may dramatically
improve our ability to identify and conserve sensitive species and hot-spot
locations.

It is important to keep in mind that the relative influence of biotic and abiotic factors in species abundance and richness may differ among biomes. In locations where environmental conditions are well within the range of tolerance of most organisms, species abundance and community diversity are likely to vary less with climate, topography, and soils, than in locations where species are near the limits of their tolerances (Neilson and Wullstein 1983, Ohmann and Spies 1998). We speculate that in biomes with equitable climates and high vegetation productivity (e.g., the Pacific Northwest), vegetation structure may limit species abundance and richness of some taxonomic groups more than climate or NPP. Just the opposite may be true where abiotic factors strongly constrain NPP (e.g., the coniferous forest of the Northern Rockies).

If these hypotheses are correct, they are fundamentally important to managing biodiversity. In biomes where NPP is relatively high and forest structure primarily limits species distributions, the maintenance of vegetation with high structural complexity is important for biodiversity. The position of these stands along abiotic gradients may be of less importance because NPP is relatively high in all parts of the landscape. In biomes with harsher climates, the positioning of vegetation types along abiotic gradients may strongly influence the distribution of organisms within them. In the northern Rockies, for example, species abundance and richness are concentrated in localized settings that are high both in NPP and structural complexity (see Case Study section). Owing to the effects of climate and soils, these are mostly at lower elevations on toe slopes and valley bottoms. Native species could best be maintained here by avoiding intense forest management in these lowland hot spots for biodiversity. Knowledge of such relationships in other parts of the world would lay a foundation for tailoring forest management strategies to groups of biomes based on their biophysical properties.

Human land-use and biodiversity

Like other species, humans generally do not settle randomly on the landscape. Rather, human density and land use are often located to maximize access to critical resources. In our home state of Montana, for example, the first homesteaders selected lands where soils and climate allowed higher agricultural production. Subsequent homesteaders were forced to settle on marginal lands. More than a century later, profitable farms persist on the productive lands. Farms on marginal lands were

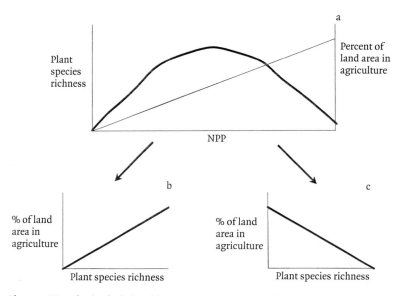

Fig. 5.10. Hypothesized relationships among net primary productivity (NPP), plant species richness, and percentage of the earth's land surface devoted to agriculture. (a) Plant species richness (dark line) shows a unimodal (hump-shaped) relationship with NPP, while the percent of land area devoted to agriculture increases with NPP. (Based on Huston 1993.) (b) In places where NPP is relatively low (left-hand side of the NPP/species richness curve), agriculture is concentrated on the more productive sites where plant species richness is relatively high. (c) Where NPP is relatively high (right-hand side of the NPP species richness curve), agriculture is focused on the more productive sites where species richness is relatively low.

abandoned, and the empty cabins still visible today are a reminder that abiotic factors do influence human economies and well being. Similar trends occurred across North America; the most productive lands are typically privately owned and support agriculture and other intensive land uses (Huston 1994). Public lands generally have harsher climates and less-fertile soils. Most nature reserves were established in such harsh settings because of their scenic grandeur, potential for tourism, and the political expediency of locating reserves on public, rather than private, lands (Newmark 1985). Even in modern non-agricultural societies, humans often choose to live in certain topographic and climatic settings. Waves of people are now moving to the mountainous landscapes of western North America, partially because of the scenery and access to outdoor recreation (Johnson and Rasker 1995).

What are the consequences of these patterns of human settlement for biodiversity? This question has not yet been well studied. Huston (1993, 1994) did a global analysis and concluded that intensive agriculture has not been centered on areas of high plant-species richness. His reasoning is based on numerous studies showing that plant species richness is highest on soils of intermediate fertility and is lowest on both the least and most fertile soils (Figure 5.10a). The reduced richness on fertile soils is thought to be due to a few dominant species being able to out-compete other species and monopolize the site. As humans have preferentially located agriculture on the most productive soils, Huston suggests that agricultural practices have had relatively little influence on global plant-species diversity. Accordingly, he recommends that nature-conservation efforts be focused on less-fertile sites, where many species can be protected with relatively little loss of agricultural productivity. Even though Huston's analysis focused on agriculture, it is highly relevant to the management of forest biodiversity. The distribution of land use across watersheds and regions is a critical component to managing forest species. Where in the landscape to maintain forests and the forest properties to promote biodiversity often needs be evaluated in the context of abiotic gradients. Maintaining forest species will often require management across the full gradients of elevation and soil productivity, regardless of current land use or ownership (see Case Study section).

The conclusions one might draw from this model, however, may differ among regions around the world and taxonomic groups. Herbivore and carnivore richness differ in response to NPP compared with plants. Richness of these animals increases with NPP even in very productive habitats (Huston 1993). Thus, management conclusions for vascular plants may be inappropriate for higher trophic levels. Also, natural disturbance may be more severe in places of high site quality. Such places may build up higher levels of biomass and be more susceptible to fire, windthrow, or insect outbreaks. This could break the competitive advantage of dominant species and allow high species richness at these sites. Most importantly, we need to keep in mind that maximizing local species richness is often not the goal of conservation planning. Rather, the goal is often to maintain viable populations of all native species, including those species that have key habitats outside of places of high local species richness (see Chapter 1). In the United States, for example, endangered species are concentrated in areas of intense land use (Dobson *et al.* 1997). Recovering these species in highly human-modified habitats offers a special challenge to conservationists.

Despite these caveats, Huston's global model of plant species richness and NPP (Figure 5.10a) has interesting implications for management at regional scales. In many regions, plant species richness increases with

NPP or soil fertility (Abrams 1995). This may be because even the best sites in these locations do not allow competitive dominance by a few species. In other words, these locations are on the left-hand side of the NPP/species richness curve (Figure 5.10b), where NPP and species richness are positively correlated. Here, we would predict that intensive agriculture is most likely to occur within hot spots for native species richness. As most nature reserves are located in harsher sites, these reserves and the surrounding lands likely fall on the left-hand side of the NPP species richness curve where human land use is likely to be centered on the places most important for species richness.

Clearly, strategies for maintaining biodiversity should differ among regions depending on the local relationships between abiotic factors, species richness, and human land use. In very productive regions of the world, human activities should, perhaps, be focused on the most productive places. That way a given level of agricultural and forest output can be achieved on the smallest land area with the smallest impact on species richness. In less-productive regions of the world, managers should avoid intense land use within some of the most productive landscape settings to minimize impacts on native species.

The relationships between abiotic factors, NPP, and species richness suggest some counter-intuitive relationships in nature reserves and the lands that surround them. Where nature reserves were placed in relatively harsh locations (Figure 5.10b), NPP, species richness, and intense land use likely overlap in the more productive landscape settings surrounding the nature reserves. Such nature reserves may not adequately protect native species. The rapid growth in human populations around many of the world's nature reserves may have a disproportionally strong negative influence on our last refugia for native species.

Implications for landscape management

Returning to the analogy of the theater, Harris et al. (1996) suggested that if organisms are the actors on a biophysical stage, then landscape managers have focused too heavily on the actors and too little on the play itself. The play represents the interactions among the biophysical setting, such ecological processes as disturbance and energy flow, and the organisms. As suggested in Figure 5.2, we cannot understand the dynamics of the organisms without knowing the ecological and evolutionary drama that links them with the changing biophysical stage. Maintaining the organisms requires that we maintain the processes that sustain them. The challenge to landscape managers is to maintain the spatial and temporal interactions among ecological processes that will perpetuate viable populations of native species (Harris et al. 1996). Our review of abiotic factors leads to the conclusion that many landscapes are even more patchy than we previously appreciated. Underneath the mosaic of vegetation cover types and seral stages lie patterns in topography, climate, and soil that impose spatial heterogeneity on ecological processes and biodiversity. There are several implications of this patchiness for landscape management at local and regional scales.

The issue of how to distribute land uses across regions becomes especially important when spatial patterning of abiotic and biotic factors are considered. In many regions, land use increases in intensity from harsher environments (e.g., high elevations or arid settings) to more mesic environments. Nature reserves often occupy the more extreme end of the environmental gradient, publicly owned multiple-use lands lie in the middle of the gradient, and privately owned agricultural, rural residential, and urban lands are at the mesic end of the gradient. Consideration of the distribution of biodiversity along such environmental and land-use gradients is critical for devising management strategies to optimize biodiversity and resource production objectives. In many locations, land use within nature reserves, multiple-use lands, or private lands will influence patterns of species population viability and community diversity across the entire region. Hence, careful distribution of management strategies and intensities within major land allocations and among allocations may be necessary to maintain native species.

For example, because of the abiotic and biotic patchiness of landscapes, species abundance and diversity are seldom evenly distributed over the landscape. Rather, they are often high only in localized hot spots (we define 'hot spot' as a location where the abundance of individual species and the species richness of a community are disproportionately high) where biophysical conditions allow the persistence of many individuals and species. Because hot spots often contain a large proportion of the individuals of a species and many species in the community, it is important to identify them and set management strategies accordingly (Brown et al. 1995). Knowledge of the factors that cause these places to be hot spots allows managers to maintain or enhance these features. Moreover, mapping abiotic factors may allow us to discover places that have the physical potential to be hot spots so that vegetation and/or human activities can be managed to allow these places to become hot spots.

Where abiotic and biotic factors cause the abundance of a species to be patchy in space there is an increased likelihood of spatially mediated population dynamics (Figure 5.8). In this case, management strategies that alter the spatial patterning of the landscape can have strong effects on population viability. Maintaining population source habitats may be critical to regional population viability. Similarly maintaining connectivity for dispersal among subpopulations increases the chances that emigration will inhibit chance extinctions of subpopulations (Stacey and Taper 1992). It is important to determine which hot spot habitats are population source areas and which, because of human activity, are population sinks. Thus, careful demographic studies should be focused on those places in the landscape and those species that are the greatest viability concerns, and management strategies devised accordingly.

To appropriately distribute land-use type and intensity within and across ownerships, it is necessary to quantify and understand the biophysical stage, the organisms, and the ecological drama that weaves them together. We suggest that it is insufficient to rely on maps of vegetation cover type and seral stage in landscape management. Rather, managers should invest in quantifying key abiotic factors and ecological processes along with vegetation and land use (e.g., Bailey 1978, Omernik 1987, Wiken 1986). Some abiotic factors and/or ecological processes like NPP may be important filters for biodiversity planning that can greatly improve our ability to prioritize the ecological and socioeconomic value of lands and evaluate potential for restoration. Careful analyses of these data are also critical. We pointed out above that generalizing from one region to another is risky and that an understanding of local interactions is necessary. Within a region it is important to keep in mind thresholds in the interaction of abiotic factors and ecological processes. Knowledge of such thresholds allows managers to apply prescribed disturbance at intensities that can best accomplish management objectives.

Within multiple-use lands used for wood production, a major question is where to place timber harvest relative to gradients in abiotic factors and primary productivity. Seymour and Hunter (1992) and Hunter and Calhoun (1995) pointed out that biodiversity might best be maintained by concentrating intensive timber harvest on the most productive sites. This way, a given level of wood production would impact the smallest area of land. As described above, Huston (1993, 1994) also advocates this approach for agriculture. Beyond impacting the smallest land area, this avoids altering the places with intermediate site potential that likely support the highest plant species richness. As emphasized above, however, global generalities about land allocation may be misleading at regional to local scales.

We suggest that it is important to first evaluate spatial patterns of abiotic factors, ecological processes, and biodiversity and then to craft a management approach that is appropriate for the local area. In regions where plant-species richness declines as site potential improves, it may be appropriate to focus intensive forestry or agriculture on the most productive sites. Even here though, it is important to consider other trophic levels, such as herbivores and carnivores, that may achieve highest abundances and species richness on these most productive sites. Moreover, productive sites may be population source areas for some individual species. Thus, strategies that maintain some carefully selected nature reserves and/or areas with less-intense timber harvest on productive sites may best achieve biodiversity and economic objectives in these regions.

In regions where species abundance and diversity are concentrated in the most productive landscape settings, choices are still more difficult. Logging activities that reduce habitat quality or alter biotic interactions (e.g., predation) in these productive settings may have disproportionately strong negative effects on native biodiversity. Perhaps the best alternative here is to use silviculture systems that minimize negative impacts on species. Examples include retention of high levels of structural complexity, small gap-scale harvest units, and helicopter logging to prevent road building (Franklin 1992). Focusing timber harvest on moderately productive sites is another option. However, keep in mind that a larger area must be impacted to achieve a given level of wood production. In places where high productivity sites have already undergone intensive logging, there may be a good opportunity for restoration (Chapter 15). Because primary productivity is high in these sites, plants will respond relatively quickly to silvicultural strategies such as thinning, pruning, and underplanting that favor the growth of large trees and multiple canopy layers.

Interaction between abiotic factors and natural disturbance regimes also bear on silvicultural strategies for forest lands. Given that some topographic settings are more prone to natural disturbance, undesired disturbances such as landslides can be minimized by not placing timber harvest units in such settings. Alternatively, more intensive timber harvest may be most appropriate in disturbance-prone settings because the organisms there are adapted to disturbance. The south-facing slopes and ridgetops on Kuiu Island, Alaska, that undergo frequent blowdown may be appropriate settings for relatively large harvest units with moderate to high levels of live tree and snag retention (Kramer *et al.* in prep.). Alternatively, the old-growth properties of the places on Kuiu protected from windthrow could best be maintained through no logging or through small, infrequent gap cuts.

Similarly, Cissel *et al.* (1994) organized forest management around topography and disturbance in western Oregon. They reconstructed fire history and stand structure for the past 300–400 years across the planning area and used these historic patterns as a basis for current management. The rationale was that native species and key ecological processes (e.g., woody debris delivery to streams) persisted under this natural disturbance regime and should continue to exist if modern landscape patterns are maintained within the natural range of variation (Chapter 4). Under this approach, they prescribed long-rotation, low-retention logging for valley bottoms and north-facing slopes because presettlement wildfires were infrequent but intense in these topographic settings. Wildfire was found to be more frequent but less intense on south-facing slopes and ridge tops. Here they prescribed shorter rotation harvests that retained high levels of live and dead forest structure.

Just as in multiple-use lands, biophysical gradients need to be considered in the design and management of nature reserves such as wilderness areas and parks. Harris *et al.* (1996) pointed out the shortcomings of ignoring ecological processes in the design of conservation plans. For example, many species require different habitats at different times of day, seasons of the year, or life stages. Surprisingly often, management strategies do not result in the maintenance of each of the required habitats with connectivity between them. For example, Kruger National Park, South Africa, is situated in the lowlands, which are wet-season habitats for large ungulates, but does not include the adjacent highlands that were traditional dry-season habitats for these species. Consequently, water holes had to be installed to prevent animal die-offs in dry years. Similarly, some locations or topographic settings in a landscape may be initiation zones for disturbance while other places are disturbance runout zones (Baker 1992). Both types of landscape setting are required in a nature reserve to maintain disturbance regimes and the species dependent upon them. The cutover landscape west of YNP described in the introduction was likely a fire-ignition zone for YNP prior to its being logged. The young forests there now have fuel loads too low to carry fire well (Despain 1990). Hence, human activities outside YNP have probably altered the fire regime within the park. Consideration of the spatial patterning and dynamics of landscapes is clearly necessary to maintain key processes and species.

As mentioned above, hot spots for species abundance and richness might not be well represented in our existing nature reserves. After all, maintaining biodiversity was not among the primary objectives for establishing national parks and wilderness areas (Newmark 1985), and our knowledge of the spatial heterogeneity of ecological systems was underdeveloped when these reserves were established. We predict that those nature reserves that are situated at higher elevations, on poor soils, or extreme climates are unlikely to include the landscape settings with more favorable biophysical conditions that are likely to be hot spot habitats. Hence, it may be unreasonable to assume that nature reserves are self-maintaining systems that are best preserved by 'natural regulation' (Boyce 1991). Carefully crafted management strategies will often be needed inside nature reserves and on surrounding lands to achieve biodiversity objectives.

With constraints on reserve size and location, reserve managers may have to alter the distribution and/or spatial scaling of abiotic factors and disturbance to maintain key ecological processes. The installation of water holes in Kruger National Park and use of prescribed fire in prairie reserves (Madden 1996) are examples. Another strategy is to identify and protect key landscape settings adjacent to or near nature reserves. Because hot spots are often small in area, it is often feasible to acquire them through purchase or through conservation easements. The Rocky Mountain Elk Foundation, for example, has obtained rights to some key winter range on private lands that are used by elk that summer in Yellowstone National Park. In this way, the boundaries of nature reserves can be, in essence, redrawn to more closely match biophysical boundaries. Coordinating management among the ownerships bordering nature reserves is often essential (Newmark 1985, Wilcove and May 1986). The extractive public lands that often surround nature reserves can be managed to buffer the reserves from the more intense human land use on private lands. Ecological hot spots will often be located on private lands, however. New partnerships among reserve managers, local government, scientists, and private land owners will likely be needed to develop the educational programs, incentives packages, and planning policies necessary to allow biodiversity objectives to be achieved on private lands.

A classic example of the difficulty of managing biodiversity where key habitats are under different ownership jurisdictions is the Greater Yellowstone Ecosystem. Here two national parks are surrounded by over 30 agency jurisdictions and numerous private land owners. Moreover, gradients in abiotic factors, species richness, and human land use are very pronounced in this ecosystem.

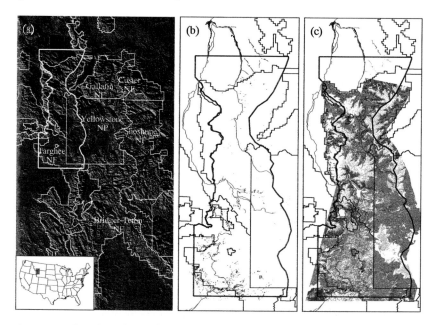

Fig. 5.11. (a) Shaded relief map of the Greater Yellowstone Ecosystem. Our study area in the northwest portion of the Greater Yellowstone Ecosystem is outlined in white. (b) Dark areas denote predicted presence of yellow warblers (*Dendroica petechia*) over a study area predicted from field data based on cover type, seral stage, and elevation. This species specializes on aspen, cottonwood, and willow habitats, which are patchily distributed in the study area. (c) Predicted bird species richness based on cover type, seral stage, and elevation. Darker shades denote higher species richness.

Case study – the Greater Yellowstone Ecosystem

The Greater Yellowstone Ecosystem (GYE) (Figure 5.11a) is in many ways a symbol of the promise and challenge of biodiversity conservation worldwide. Yellowstone was the world's first national park and remains the largest in the conterminous United States (Keiter and Boyce 1991). YNP and the surrounding public lands constitute one of the largest 'intact' native ecosystems in the temperate zones of the globe. All native mammals persist here, including the largest herds of migratory elk and bison (*Bison bison*) in North America. Further, natural disturbance occurs unimpeded by humans over much of the nature reserves in GYE.

As large as the GYE is, however, the biophysical boundaries encompass a still larger area than that in public ownership. The term 'greater ecosystem' was originally used to describe the vast range, including public and private lands, of the Yellowstone grizzly bear population. 'Greater ecosys-

tem' has now come to denote places where linkages between ecological and human communities are especially strong. Surrounding the nature reserves of the GYE are gradients in human land use that culminate in urban areas in the productive lowlands. The myriad public and private ownerships in the GYE bring a special challenge to coordinated management (Harting and Glick 1994). As the human population swells, the need for creative management is increasing. Many human immigrants have been attracted to the GYE because of the scenic beauty and high quality of life the region affords (Johnson and Rasker 1995). This raises the question as to how to maintain both native species and the quality of life that attracted current human residents.

POTENTIAL DRIVERS OF BIODIVERSITY

Among the drivers of biodiversity in the GYE, it is hard to overlook natural disturbance and human activities. The coniferous forest of the GYE is a classic crown-fire system, where large and severe wildfires have traditionally recurred at about 250-year intervals (Romme 1982). The most recent large fire was in 1988, when over 40% of YNP burned (Christensen *et al.* 1989). Many native species are well adapted to tolerate this disturbance regime, and some species require periodic fire. Hence, many of the nature reserves here are managed under a 'let-burn' policy to maintain natural disturbance.

Public lands surrounding the nature reserves have been subjected to intensities of logging ranging from mild to extreme. Most striking, perhaps, is the Targhee National Forest west of YNP where 55% of the landscape has undergone clearcut logging. Compared with wildfire, this logging has left relatively little structural complexity within logged patches and has severely fragmented the remaining forest (A. Hansen, unpublished data). Both of these effects may reduce habitat quality for some native species.

Abiotic gradients are also pronounced in the GYE. Notice that the ecosystem is centered on mountains and high plateaus (Figure 5.11a). These uplands are cut by river valleys that flow out into the surrounding plains. This topography strongly influences climate and soils. In YNP, for example, winter is long and harsh and the growing season is as short as two months (Despain 1990). The young volcanic soils of the Yellowstone Plateau are very infertile and prone to summer drying. Hence, NPP is low across the higher elevations of the GYE. In contrast, the growing season is about five months long at lower elevations, and localized areas with good soils have levels of NPP that are much higher than are found on the Yellowstone Plateau. To better understand the effects of these potential drivers on biodiversity, we have initiated studies of bird populations and communities in the northwest portion of the GYE (Figure 5.11a).

BIRD DIVERSITY IN THE GYE

In 1995 we sampled almost 100 species of breeding birds across 97 stands stratified by vegetation cover type, seral stage, and elevation (Hansen *et al.* in press). Preliminary results suggest that abiotic factors associated with elevation strongly influence bird abundance and diversity. Within a forest type (mature and old-growth lodgepole pine), we found that bird abundance (e.g., Figure 5.11b) and richness were more than twice as high at lower elevations than at higher elevations. Elevation alone explained almost 50% of the variation in bird-species richness and total abundance. We hypothesize that this is because NPP, climate, or both, limit birds at higher elevations, and we are now collecting data to test these possibilities. Across lodgepole stands of different age, disturbance histories, and, thus, structural complexities, elevation explained more variation in bird abundance and richness than did structural complexity. While structural complexity is important in this system, climate and/or energy availability appear to place greater limitations on bird communities.

Considering all vegetation types, we found that cottonwood, aspen, and willow communities had much higher bird abundance and richness than other coniferous and herbaceous stand types. Moreover, 25% of our bird species specialized on these three habitats (e.g., Figure 5.11c). These three stand types occur in localized places at low elevations on the best soils. We suspect that these stand types are high in bird abundance and diversity because they are high both in NPP and in structural complexity, providing high levels of energy availability and habitat diversity. As these stand types are very patchy in distribution, we can think of them as hot spots for bird abundance and richness, and possibly other taxonomic groups. Notice that these hot spots cover only a small portion of the eco-system and are mostly at lower elevations (Figure 5.11c). Moreover, we suspect some of these hot spots are also population source areas for some species and are critical to maintaining population viability over the GYE.

HUMAN POPULATION GROWTH

The vast landscapes of the Northern Rocky Mountains have human population densities that are low relative to most of the temperate world. Over the last decade, however, a wave of immigration to this region has begun. Now the counties surrounding the GYE are some of the fastest growing in the nation (Stolgren 1996). Many of these immigrants are successful business people or professionals who can afford to relocate in semi-remote places like the GYE where quality of life is high. Economists have suggested that the natural ecosystem and recreational opportunities in the GYE are among its greatest economic assets (Johnson and Rasker 1995). However, these immigrants may be dramatically changing the ecology of the GYE, partially by where they settle in the landscape. Most rural residential development is at lower elevations on the most productive sites. Riparian zones and aspen groves on mountain toe slopes are among the most popular settings for home construction. Beyond conversion of these hot-spot habitats, human settlement may also have more subtle effects on biodiversity.

We sampled the reproductive success of birds nesting in two types of hot-spot habitats: cottonwood and aspen. The results were unexpected. Averaging across species, nest success was nearly twice as high in aspen stands as in cottonwoods. Nest success for yellow warblers (*Dendroica petechia*), for example, was only 27% in the cottonwoods versus 68% in the aspen. Combining these data with estimates of clutch size and survival, we calculated that the finite population growth rate for this species in aspen is 1.48, indicating aspen stands are population source areas. In contrast, the growth rate in cottonwood was estimated to be 0.93, slightly below the threshold value of 1.0 that separates population source from sink areas. Hence, cottonwood habitats in the study area appear to be ecological traps for yellow warblers, where birds are attracted in high numbers but suffer poor reproductive success.

Why might one hot-spot stand type be a source area and another a population sink? The cottonwood stands in our study area all lie within a human-dominated landscape and are bordered by farms and subdivisions. Such landscapes favor high densities of nest predators (e.g., black-billed magpie, *Pica pica*) and brood parasites (brown-headed cowbirds, *Molothrus ater*). These predators and parasites penetrate the cottonwoods and exact a heavy toll on the reproductive success of other bird species. In contrast, the aspen stands we studied sit in a forested matrix where human disturbance and predator/parasite densities are lower. So, it appears that where humans choose to settle in the landscape may strongly influence native species in ways that are subtle (trickle-down effects like changing nest success) and not so subtle (converting native habitats into subdivisions).

CONSERVING BIODIVERSITY IN THE GYE

We suspect that the GYE is typical of many greater ecosystems. Abiotic factors strongly structure the region, with hot spots for biodiversity lying mostly at lower elevations in productive landscape settings. Often these hot spots are outside the boundaries of nature reserves. Thus, these reserves, typically thought of as refugia for biodiversity, may be insufficient for maintaining native species. How can we sustain both native species and the growing human community in the GYE and similar greater ecosystems? As described above, it is important to determine the combination of abiotic and biotic factors that control biodiversity and to use that knowledge to design coordinated management that includes strategies for nature reserves, extractive public lands, and private lands. Such analyses are now under way in the GYE (e.g., Noss 1991, Harting and Glick 1994), and the success of such efforts may have considerable implications for the management of other greater ecosystems around the world.

Summary

Modern ecologists have made considerable progress in understanding controls on biodiversity by focusing on disturbance, patch dynamics, and biotic interactions. We suggest that this understanding can be enhanced by also considering the effects of abiotic factors such as topography, climate, and soils. Beyond their direct effects on organism survival, growth, and reproduction, abiotic factors may influence organisms indirectly by altering ecological processes such as disturbance regimes, succession, and energy flow. The interactions between abiotic factors and ecological processes are sometimes nonlinear, and knowledge of thresholds in these relationships is important for landscape management. In landscapes where abiotic factors impose strong spatial patterning, the abundance, reproduction, and survival of organisms may be spatially heterogeneous. Source-sink and other forms of metapopulation dynamics may be typical of such populations. Species richness may also be patchy across landscapes due to the influence of abiotic factors. Management to retain and/or restore population source areas and hot spots for species richness is critical for maintaining viable populations of native species. Human land use is also arrayed along gradients in abiotic factors. In some places, intense land use and hot spots for native biodiversity occupy the same locations along abiotic gradients. In places like the Greater Yellowstone Ecosystem, these biodiversity hot spots are not well protected in existing nature reserves. Consideration of such relationships among abiotic factors, ecological processes, biodiversity, and land use can enhance our ability to better optimize biodiversity and socioeconomic objectives in private, public multiple-use, and nature reserve lands.

Further readings

More information on the spatial distribution and abiotic and biotic controls on population abundance and species richness can be found in Brown (1995) and Rosenzweig (1995). Swanson *et al.* (1996) consider how geomorphic factors and disturbance provide a template for managing ecosystems. Implications of biophysical gradients for managing biodiversity are examined in Huston (1993, 1994) and Hunter and Calhoun (1995).

Literature cited

Abrams, P. A. 1995. Monotonic or unimodal diversity-productivity gradients: what does competition theory predict? *Ecology* 76(7):2019–27.

Agee, J. K. 1993. *Fire Ecology of Pacific Northwest Forests*. Island Press, Washington, D.C.

Austin, M. P., J. G. Pausas, and A. O. Nicholls. 1996. Patterns of tree species richness in relation to environment in southeastern New South Wales, Australia. *Australian Journal of Ecology* 21:154–64.

Bailey, R. W. 1978. *Description of the Ecoregions of the United States*. USDA Forest Service Intermountain Region, Ogden, Utah.

Baker, W. 1992. The landscape ecology of large disturbances in the design and management of nature reserves. *Landscape Ecology* 7(3):181–94.

Ballard, W. B., J. S. Whitman, and D. J. Reed. 1991. Population dynamics of
    moose in south-central Alaska. *Wildlife Monographs* **114**.
Barnes, B. V., K. S. Pregitzer, T. A. Spies, and V. H. Spooner. 1982. Ecological
    forest site classification. *Journal of Forestry*, August, 493–8.
Bartmann, R. M., and D. C. Bowden. 1984. Predicting mule deer mortality from
    weather data in Colorado. *Wildlife Society Bulletin* **12**:246–8.
Begon, M., J. L. Harper and C. R. Townsend. 1990. *Ecology: Individuals,
    Populations and Communities*. Blackwell Scientific Publications, Oxford.
Boyce, M. S. 1991. Natural regulation or the control of nature? Pp. 183–208 in R.
    B. Keiter, and M. S. Boyce (eds). *The Greater Yellowstone Ecosystem*. Yale
    University Press, New Haven, CT.
Brown, J. H. 1995. *Macroecology*. University of Chicago Press, Chicago, Ill.
Brown, J. H., D. W. Mehlman, and G. C. Stevens. 1995. Spatial variation in abun-
    dance. *Ecology* **76**(7):2028–43.
Burns, B. R. 1995. Environmental ccorrelates of species richness at Waipoua
    Forest Sanctuary, New Zealand. *New Zealand Journal of Ecology*
    19(2):153–62.
Caughley, G. J., G. C. Short, and H. Grigg. 1987. Kangaroos and climate: an
    analysis of distribution. *Journal of Animal Ecology* **56**:751–61.
Christensen, N. L., and 12 others. 1989. Interpreting the Yellowstone fires.
    BioScience **39**(10):678–85.
Cissel, J. H., F. J. Swanson, W. A. McKee, and A. L. Burditt. 1994. Using the past
    to plan the future in the Pacific Northwest. *Journal of Forestry* **92**(8):30–31,
    46.
Clements, F. E. 1936. Nature and structure of the climax. *Journal of Ecology*
    24:252–84.
Coe, M., J. D. H. Cumming, and J. Phillipson. 1976. Biomass and production of
    large African herbivores in relation to rainfall and primary production.
    Oecologia **22**:341–54.
Coughenour, M. B., and F. J. Singer. 1996. Elk population processes in
    Yellowstone National Park under the policy of natural regulation.
    Ecological Applications **6**(2):573–93).
Currie, D. J. 1991. Energy and large-scale patterns of animal- and plant- species
    richness. *American Naturalist* **137**(1):27–49.
Currie, D. J., and V. Paquin. 1987. Large-scale biogeographical patterns of
    species richneess of trees. *Nature* **329**:326–7.
Daubenmire, R. 1956. Climate as a determinant of vegetation distribution in
    eastern Washington and northern Idaho. *Ecological Monographs*
    26:131–54.
    1968. Soil moisture in relation to vegetation distribution in the mountains of
    northern Idaho. *Ecology* **49**:431–8.
Davis, M. B. 1981. Quaternary history and the stability of forest communities.
    Pp. 132–53 in D. C. West, H. H. Shugart, D. B. Botkin. *Forest Succession:
    Concepts and Application*. Springer-Verlag, New York.
Deal, R. L., C. D. Oliver, B. T. Borman. 1991. Reconstruction of mixed

hemlock–spruce stands in coastal southeast Alaska. *Canadian Journal of Forest Research* **21**:643–54.

Despain, D. 1990. *Yellowstone Vegetation*. Roberts Rinehart Publishers, Boulder, CO.

Dobson, A. P., J. P. Rodriguez, W. M. Roberts, D. S. Wilcove. 1997. Geographic distribution of endangered species in the United States. *Science* **275**:550–3.

Douglas, C. L., and D. M. Leslie. 1986. Influence of weather and density on lamb survival of desert mountain sheep. *Journal of Wildlife Management* **50**:153–6.

Dunson, W. A., and J. Travis. 1991. The role of abiotic factors in community organization. *American Naturalist* **138**(5):1067–91.

Emlen, J. T., M. J. DeJong, J. Jaeger, T. C. Moermond, K. A. Rusterholz, and R. P. White. 1986. Density trends and range boundary constraints of forest birds along a latitudinal gradient. *Auk* **103**:791–803.

Enright, N. J., B. P. Miller, and A. Crawford. 1994. Environmental correlates of vegetation patterns and species richness in the northern Grampians, Victoria. *Australian Journal of Ecology* **19**:159–68.

Franklin, J. F. 1992. Scientific basis for new perspectives in forests and streams. Pp. 5–72 in R. Naiman (ed.). *Watershed Management: Balancing Sustainability and Environmental Change*. Springer-Verlag, New York.

Fraser, R. H., and D. J. Currie. 1996. The Species Richness-Energy hypothesis in a system where historical factors are thought to prevail: coral reefs. *American Naturalist* **148**(1):138–59.

Fuller, T. K. 1990. Dynamics of a declining white-tailed deer population in north-central Minnesota. *Wildlife Monographs* **110**.

Hack, J. T., and J. C. Goodlet. 1960. Geomorphology and forest ecology of a mountain region in the central Appalachians. *U.S.G.S. Professional Paper* **347**. 66 pp.

Hansen, A. J., and B. Harting. (In prep). Bird habitat associations in natural and anthropogenic landscapes in Greater Yellowstone.

Hansen, A. J., T. Spies, F. Swanson and J. Ohmann. 1991. Conserving biodiversity in managed forests: lessons from natural forests: implications for conserving biodiversity in managed forests. *BioScience* **41**(3):382–92.

Hansen, A. J., J. R. Rotella, and M. L. Kraska. (In press). Dynamic habitat and population analysis: A filtering approach to resolve the biodiversity manager's dilemma. *Ecological Applications*.

Hanski, I. 1989. Does it help to have more of the same? *Trends in Ecology and Evolution* **4**:113–14.

1996. Metapopulation ecology. Pp. 13–43 in O. E. Rhodes, R. K. Chesser, and M. H. Smith (eds). *Population Dynamics in Ecological Space and Time*. University of Chicago Press, Chicago, Ill.

Hanski, I., and M. E. Gilpin. 1991. Metapopulation dynamics: brief history and conceptual domain. *Biological Journal of the Linnean Society* **42**:3–16.

Harris, L. D., T. S. Hoctor and S. E. Gergel. 1996. Landscape processes and their significance to biodiversity conservation. Pp. 319–47 in O. E. Rhodes, R. K. Chesser, and M. H. Smith (eds). *Population Dynamics in Ecological Space and Time*. University of Chicago Press, Chicago, Ill.

Harrison, S. 1994. Metapopulations and conservation. Pp. 111–28 in P. J. Edwards, R. M. May, and N. R. Webb. *Large-scale Ecology and Conservation Biology*. Blackwell Scientific Publications, Oxford.

Harting, A., and D. Glick. 1994. *A Blueprint for Greater Yellowstone*. Greater Yellowstone Coalition, Bozeman, MT.

Holdridge, L. R. 1967. Determination of world plant formation from simple climatic data. *Science* **105**:367–8.

Hunter, M. L. 1990. *Wildlife, Forests, and Forestry: Principles of Managing Forests for Biological Diversity*. Prentice-Hall, Englewood Cliffs, New Jersey.

Hunter, M. L. Jr., and A. Calhoun. 1995. A triad aproach to land use allocation. Pp. 447–91 in R. Szaro, and D. Johnston, (eds). *Biodiversity in Managed Landscapes*. Oxford University Press, New York.

Huston, M. 1993. Biological diversity, soils, and economics. *Science* **262**:1676–80.

Huston, M. A. 1994. *Biological Diversity*. Cambridge University Press, Cambridge.

Hutchinson, G. E. 1957. Concluding remarks. *Cold Spring Habor Symposium in Quantative Biology*. 22:415–27.

James, F. 1971. Ordination of habitat relationships among birds. *Wilson Bulletin* **83**:215–36.

Johnson, J. D., and R. Rasker. 1995. The role of economic and quality of life values in rural business location. *Journal of Rural Studies*. **11**(4):405–16.

Johnson, K. G., and M. R. Pelton. 1981. Selection and availability of dens for black bears in Tennessee. *Journal of Wildlife Management* **45**:111–19.

Keiter, R. B., and M. S. Boyce, (eds). 1991. *The Greater Yellowstone Ecosystem: Redefining America's Wilderness Heritage*. Yale University Press, New Haven, CT.

Kerr, J. T. and L. Packer, 1997. Habitat heterogeneity as a determinant of mammal species richness in high-energy regions. *Nature* **385**:252–4.

Kramer, M. G., A. J. Hansen and E. Kissinger. (In Prep). Abiotic controls on windthrow and pattern and process of forest development on Kuiu Island, Alaska.

Lack, D. 1966. *Population Studies of Birds*. Clarendon Press, Oxford. 341 pp.

Lenihan, J. M. 1993. Ecological response surfaces for North American boreal tree species and their use in forest classification. *Journal of Vegetation Science* **4** : 667–80.

Lertzman, K. P., G. D. Sutherland, A. Inselberg, and S. C. Saunders. 1996. Canopy gaps and the landscape mosaic in a coastal temperate rain forest. *Ecology* **77**(4):1254–70.

Levins, R. 1970. Extinctions. Pp. 75–100 in Some mathematical questions in biology. *Lecture on Mathematics in the Life Sciences*, Vol 2. American Mathematical Society, Providence, RI.

Madden, E., 1996. Passerine communities and bird-habitat relations on prescribed-burned prairie in North Dakota. M.S. Thesis, Montana State University, Bozeman, MT. 153 pp.

McNaughton, S. J. 1985. Ecology of a grazing ecoystem: the Serengeti. *Ecological Monographs* **55**:259–94.

Merriam, C. H. 1894. Laws of temperature control of the geographic distribution of terrestrial plants and animals. *National Geographic Magazine* **6**:229–38.

Morrison, P. H., and F. J. Swanson. 1990. *Fire History and Pattern in a Cascade Range Landscape.* USDA Forest Service, Pacific Northwest Research Station, PNW-GTR-254, Portland OR.

Morrison, M. L., B. G. Marcot, and R. W. Mannan. 1992. *Wildlife-Habitat Relationships: Concepts and Applications.* University of Wisconsin Press, Madison, WI.

Neilson, R. P., and L. H. Wullstein. 1983. Biogeography of two southwestern American oaks in relation to atmospheric dynamics. *Journal of Biogeography* **10**:275–97.

Newmark, W .D. 1985. Legal and biotic boundaries of western North American national pParks: a problem of congruence. *Biological Conservation* **33**:197–208.

Noss, R. 1991. Landscape conservation priorities in the Greater Yellowstone Ecosystem. Unpublished report to The Nature Conservancy.

Ohmann, J. L., and T. A. Spies. 1998. Regional gradient analysis and spatial pattern of woody plant communities of Oregon forests. *Ecological Monographs* **68**:152–82.

Omernik, J. M. 1987. Ecoregions of the conterminous United States. *Annals of the Association of American Geographers* **77**(1) 118–25.

Overpeck, J. T., P. J. Bartlein, and T. Webb III. 1991. Potential magnitude of future vegetation change in eastern North America: comparisons with the past. *Science* **254**:692–5.

Owen, J. G. 1990. Patterns of mammalian species richness in relation to temperature, productivity, and variance in elevation. *Journal of Mammalogy* **71**(1):1–13.

Owen, R. B., and W. J. Galbraith. 1989. Earthworm biomass in relation to forest types, soil, and land use: implications for woodcock management. *Wildlife Society Bulletin* **17**:130–6.

Patten, D. R. 1992. *Wildlife Habitat Relationships in Forested Ecosystems.* Timber Press, Inc. Portland, OR.

Perry, D. A. 1994. *Forest Ecosystems.* The Johns Hopkins University Press, Baltimore, MD.

Pickett, S. T. A., and P. S. White. 1985. *The Ecology of Natural Disturbance and Patch Dynamics.* Academic Press, New York.

Pospahala, R. S., D. R. Anderson, and C. J. Henny. 1974. *Population ecology of the mallard: II. Breeding habitat conditions, size of the breeding populations, and production indices.* U.S. Bur. Sport Fish. Wildl., Resour. Publ. 115. 73 pp.

Pulliam, H. R. 1988. Sources, sinks, and population regulation. *American Naturalist* **132**:652–61.

——— 1996. Sources and sinks: empirical evidence and population consequences. Pp. 45–69 in O. E. Rhodes, R. K. Chesser, and M. H. Smith (eds). *Population Dynamics in Ecological Space and Time.* University of Chicago Press, Chicago, Ill.

Rabe, D. L., H. H. Prince, and E. D. Goodman. 1983. The effect of weather on bioenergetics of breeding American woodcock. *Journal of Wildlife Management* **47**:762–71.

Reyes-Gavilan, F. G., R. Garrido, A. G. Nicieza, M. M. Toledo, and F. Grana. 1996. Fish community variation along physical gradients in short streams of northern Spain and the disruptive effects of dams. *Hydrobiologia* **321**:155–63.

Robinson, W. L., and E. G. Bolen. 1989. *Wildlife Ecology and Management.* Macmillan Publishing Company, New York.

Romme, W. H. 1982. Fire and landscape diversity in subalpine forests of Yellowstone National Park. *Ecological Monographs* **52**(2):199–221.

Root, T. 1988. Energy constraints on avian distributions and abundances. *Ecology* **69**(2): 330–9.

Rosenzweig, M. L. 1995. *Species Diversity in Space and Time.* Cambridge University Press, Cambridge.

Rotella, J. J., and J. T. Ratti. 1986. Test of a critical density index assumption: a case study with gray partridge. *Journal of Wildlife Management* **50**:532–9.

Sauer, J. R., and M. S. Boyce. 1983. Density dependence and survival of elk in northwestern Wyoming. *Journal of Wildlife Management* **47**:31–7.

Seymour, R. S., and M. L. Hunter Jr. 1992. *New forestry in eastern spruce-fir forests: principles and applications to Maine.* Maine Agricultural and Forest Experimental Station Miscellaneous Publication 716.

Shvarts, E. A., S. V. Pushkaryov, V. G. Krever, and M. A. Ostrovsky. 1995. Geography of mammal diversity and searching for ways to predict global changes in biodiversity. *Journal of Biogeography* **22**:907–14.

Slatyer, R. O., and I. R. Noble. 1992. Dynamics of montane treelines. Pp. 346–59 in A. J. Hansen and F. di Castri (eds). *Landscape Boundaries: Consequences for Biotic Diversity and Ecological Flows.* Springer-Verlag, Ecological Studies 92, New York.

Stacey, P. and M. Taper. 1992. Environmental variation and the persistence of small populations. *Ecological Applications* **2**:18–29.

Stohlgren, T. 1996. *The Rocky Mountains.* USDI National Biological Service, Washington, D.C.

Suring, L. and 8 others. 1993. *A proposed strategy for maintaiing well-distributed, viable populations of wildlife associated with old-growth forests in southeast Alaska.* Interagency Committee, USDA Forest Service, Juneau, AK.

Swanson, F. J., T. K. Krantz, N. Caine, and R. G. Woodsmansee. 1988. Landform effects on ecosystem patterns and processes. *BioScience* **38**:92–8.

Swanson, F. J, J. A. Jones, and G. E. Grant. 1996. The physical environment as a basis for managng ecosystems. Pp. 451–67 in K. A. Kohm, and J. F. Franklin, (eds). *Creating a Forestry for the 21ˢᵗ Century: The Science of Ecosystem Management*. Island Press, Washington D.C.

Thomas, J. W., E. D. Forsman, J. B. Lint and others. 1990. *A conservation strategy for the northern spotted owl: a report of the Interagency Scientific Commitee to address the conservation of the northern spotted owl*. USDA Forest Service, Portland, OR.

Turner, M. G. 1989. Landscape ecology: the effect of pattern on process. *Annual Review of Ecology and Systematics* **20**:171–97.

Turner, M. G., and W. H. Romme. 1993. Landscape dynamics in crown fire ecosystems. *Landscape Ecology* **9**:59–77.

Turton, S. M., and G. J. Sexton. 1996. Environmental gradients across four rainforest-open forest boundaries in northeastern Queensland. *Australian Journal of Ecology* **21**:245–54.

Urban, D. U., and T. Smith. 1989. Microhabitat pattern and the structure of forest bird communities. *American Naturalist* **133**(6):811–29.

Waring, R. H., and W. H. Schlesinger. 1985. *Forest Ecosystems: Concepts and Management*. Academic Press, Orlando.

Whittaker, R. H. 1956. Vegetation of the Great Smoky Mountains. *Ecological Monographs* **26**:1–80.

—— 1960. Vegetation of the Siskiyou Mountains, Oregon and California. *Ecological Monographs* **30**:279–38.

Wilcove, D. S., and R. M. May. 1986. National park boundaries and ecological realities. *Nature* **324**:206–7.

Wiken, E. 1986. *Terrestrial Ecozones of Canada*. Ecological Land Classification Series No. 19. Environment Canada, Ottawa.

Wright, D. H., D. J. Currie, and B. A. Mauer. 1993. Energy supply and patterns of species richness in local and regional scales. Pp. 66–74 in R. E. Ricklefs, and D. Schluter, (eds). *Species Diversity in Ecological Communities*. University of Chicago Press, Chicago, Ill.

Wylie, J., and D. J. Currie. 1993. Species energy theory and patterns of species richness. II. Predicting mammal species richness of isolated nature reserves. *Conservation Biology* **63**:145–8.

6 Forest edges

GLENN R. MATLACK AND JOHN A. LITVAITIS

When humans cut a forest, they hardly ever cut it all. We tend to cut in patches leaving isolated remnant stands of varying sizes and shapes scattered across the landscape. An important consequence is the creation of great lengths of stand edge relative to the area of surviving forest. Because patchy cutting is practised globally, forest edges have proliferated in every forest ecosystem.

We define a *forest edge* as an abrupt transition between two relatively homogeneous ecosystems, at least one of which is a forest. Natural forests often include recognizable edges, usually corresponding to physical gradients in topography, hydrology, or substrate (Whittaker 1956, Roman *et al.* 1985) or marking the borders of large disturbances such as fires or hurricanes (Bormann and Likens 1979). In clearcuts, humans have created a novel form of edge that differs from natural edge in several important ways. First, human-generated edges are abrupt. Harvesting operations tend to stop at arbitrary linear boundaries leaving a vertical wall of surviving trees. In northern Europe, where woodlands have been intensively managed for centuries, edges may be defined by ditches and banks with managed hedges. By contrast, natural disturbances generate ragged edges, with individual trees varying in crown structure and degree of damage (Trimble and Tryon 1966, Runkle and Yetter 1987). Human-generated edges differ from natural edges in the size and character of the adjacent clearings. As a consequence of larger size, for example, human-generated clearings tend to experience more severe wind turbulence than natural canopy gaps, a condition that may damage trees in adjacent forests (Geiger 1965, Liu *et al.* 1996). In contrast to natural edges, human-generated edges often cut across complex landscapes without regard for natural landscape features. Finally, human-generated edges are unusual in their great length. Natural disturbance processes rarely generate as much edge in close proximity to such a high proportion of surviving forest.

For decades, forest managers emphasized edge creation in response to the observation that some forms of wildlife (notably popular game species) were abundant at edges (Leopold 1933). Now, however, edge habitat is recognized as being incompatible with the requirements of many forest species, and the proliferation of forest edges has threatened the diversity of many forest communities (e.g., Gates and Gysel 1978, Yahner 1988, Paton 1994). In this chapter, we seek to understand the consequences of edge creation by humans, and make suggestions for the protection of diversity in managed forest ecosystems. We begin by describing the physical character of human-generated edges and then explore the ways in which physical gradients influence the distributions of forest species. We reflect on the direct and indirect consequences for forest biodiversity and management, and look more closely at a tropical example.

First, it is necessary to adopt some terminology. The position of the *forest edge* is a line precisely defined by the limit of the activity that created the clearing. Processes arising in the clearing can influence the microenvironment of forest across this line. For example, air heated in the clearing often moves into the forest lowering humidity, drying leaf litter, and creating drought stress for plant species. Such a physical or biotic phenomenon originating in the clearing and having an influence on the neighboring forest is termed an *edge effect*. The section of forest experiencing edge effects is the *edge zone*. The character of the forest edge may change through successional time as herbs, shrubs, and saplings are recruited at the edge, and surviving trees develop adventitious limbs (Figure 6.1). A *recent edge* typically has a well-developed crown canopy but very little understory vegetation, reflecting its recent formation from intact forest.

As shrubs grow and trees produce adventitious limbs, a curtain of foliage develops at the edge (the *side canopy* – analogous to the crown canopy). Such vegetation closes the edge with respect to light and air movement creating a *closed edge* (Matlack 1993). Unless maintained, the clearing will succeed to young forest. After a few decades, the original edge is only a discontinuity in species composition and age structure, but profound differences may remain in the vegetation. Such an edge is said to be *embedded* in a continuous matrix of canopy trees. These distinctions are important because the character of the edge vegetation strongly influences edge-zone phenomena. Unfortunately, few published studies have been specific about edge location or character, leading to unnecessary ambiguity in their conclusions (Murcia 1995).

clearing   forest

Fig. 6.1. Common types of edges created by human activity: (top) recent edge, (middle) closed edge, (bottom) embedded edge. Through successional time, recent edges may become closed edges and, eventually, embedded edges. The arrow indicates the boundary of the gap-forming disturbance.

Physical effects at forest edges

To a large extent, the physical environment determines plant and animal distributions at forest edges and, thus, underpins many of the distinctive biological properties of edges. Edge zones are typically hotter, drier, windier, and lighter than undisturbed forest, but less extreme than the clearing bordering the edge. As such, edges are transitional between the forest interior microclimate, which is controlled by the crown canopy, and the clearing in which the soil is the thermodynamically active surface. Edge microclimate is more than a simple collection of edge-interior gradients, however, having peculiar patterns of heating, particle deposition, and turbulence. It is useful to compare a forest with a building. Both are physical structures that intercept light and interrupt air movement. In an otherwise cool building, rooms with windows facing the sun are light and warm, at least as far in as the rays shine. People set houseplants on windowsills, and sit near windows to enjoy the warmth. In a similar manner, forests are heated at sun-lit edges, affecting plant growth and animal behavior. Wind may be deflected around the building creating turbulence that cools or warms rooms and piles leaf litter against the foundation (or, in the case of a hurricane, it may tear off the roof!). By the same mechanism, wind moves around the forest stand, heating or cooling at edges, depositing particulates, and (occasionally) tearing down trees.

LIGHT AND ITS CONSEQUENCES

At recently created edges, light enters the forest diagonally, creating a bright zone beneath the crown canopy. Light intensity declines logarithmically with distance into the stand (Figure 6.2; Kapos 1989, Matlack 1993, Chen et al. 1995). In temperate zones, more light enters the forest at edges facing the equator (e.g., south-facing edges in the north-temperate zone), and more light penetrates under a high tree canopy than a low one. These observations arise from simple solar geometry: the larger the edge opening and the closer the sample point to the edge, the more direct-beam radiation it receives (Canham et al. 1990). Note that ecologically significant light penetration also occurs at pole-facing edges because some light is diffused or reflected into the forest from the open sky.

Light entering at the edge drives thermodynamic processes at the forest floor, with direct beam radiation generating high soil temperatures, heating near-ground air, and drying the leaf litter (Geiger 1965, Matlack 1993). Air temperature gradients translate into gradients of vapor pres-

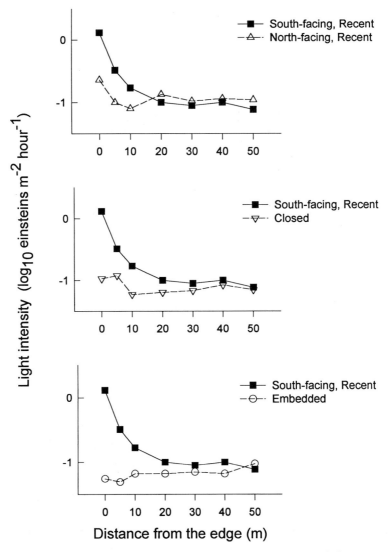

Fig. 6.2. Light at forest edges: four sites in northern Delaware, USA. Sites differ in aspect and openness of the side canopy. Note that data from the south-facing, recent edge are repeated in each graph for comparison. The closed and embedded edges also face south. 'O' distance indicates the forest edge.

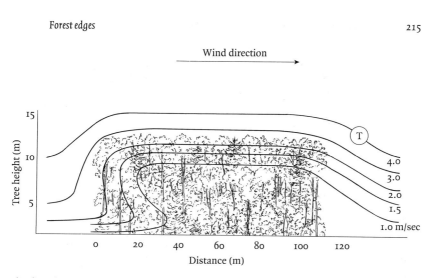

Fig. 6.3. Air movement around a hypothetical forest stand (based on Raynor 1971 and Liu *et al.* 1996). Isolines show wind speed in m/sec. 'T' indicates the area of greatest turbulence.

sure deficit (VPD) – a measure of the drying capacity of air as experienced by plants and animals. Such gradients are more pronounced at edges facing the sun; all are stronger at recent than at closed edges.

AIR MOVEMENT

A forest edge is a wall of vegetation that channels air, creates turbulence, and absorbs kinetic and thermal energy from air bodies. Moving air is forced up over a forest, creating faster wind speeds at edges than observed in the forest interior or the clearing (Ghuman and Lal 1987, Hutchison and Matt 1977). If air approaches the forest from the clearing, there is a small zone of turbulence (an eddy) before the forest (Figure 6.3), whereas wind approaching the clearing from above the forest creates a large zone of turbulence just past the edge. The turbulence can be powerful enough to break or uproot canopy trees (for example, old-growth spruce in northwest Sweden, Esseen 1994, or low-elevation tropical forest in Panama, Williams Linera 1990a).

Of course forests are not solid blocks deflecting air. Wind approaching the edge creates a jet of elevated wind speed which may extend 30–40 m into the forest (Raynor 1971, Miller 1975). Air movement into the stand tends to raise the air temperature and VPD, with a strong drying effect on plants, litter, and woody debris. Probably as a result of air movement, measures of the edge zone defined by relative humidity and VPD often greatly exceed the edge zone defined by light intensity (Kapos 1989,

Matlack 1993, Chen et al. 1995). In an extreme example from the Amazon basin, advective drying was so severe that fires were able to spread into the normally dripping rainforest (Lovejoy et al. 1984). Much particulate material is also carried in the air flowing around the forest. Airborne particles tend to drop out at forest edges in the same way blowing snow forms drifts around fences. Indeed, forest edges collect more snow than interior locations (Geiger 1965, Wales 1967), with the greatest accumulation occurring in brushy microsites. Edge effects have also been observed in the deposition of dust, leaf litter, sea salt, and wind-dispersed seeds (Geiger 1965, Augspurger and Franson 1988, Hardt and Forman 1989, Beier 1991).

Rain and fog droplets collide with foliage at the forest edge leading to increased moisture accumulation up to 40 m into the forest (Geiger 1965, Neal et al. 1991, Weathers et al. 1995). Edges have also been shown to collect pollutants such as NH_4, NO_3, and SO_4, observed at spruce stands in southern Sweden and nearby Denmark (Beier 1991, Balsberg Pahlson and Bergkvist 1995) and lead, recorded in alpine forests in New York (Weathers et al. 1995).

These physical measures often give contrasting estimates of edge zone width at different sites, and differ among themselves at a single site. Contrary to conventional wisdom, there is no easy formula for calculating physical edge zone width – land managers must measure microclimate in their own forests. Fortunately, this is comparatively easy – a shrewd estimate can be made quickly and cheaply with a few basic instruments.

Vegetation at edges

Most of the physical parameters described above affect plant growth, so it is not surprising that plant distributions show strong edge effects. Closed edges are often an impenetrable mass of shrubs and saplings – a nuisance to hikers and well familiar to all forest professionals. Woody species commonly have higher stem densities and basal area at forest edges than in forest interiors, reflecting the dense growth of saplings in the high-light edge environment (e.g., Ranney et al. 1981, Williams Linera 1990a, Palik and Murphy 1990). Trees at the edge extend limbs into the opening giving them a 'one sided' appearance. Herbaceous species show a similar light response, characterized by increased densities of light-demanding species near the edge (Matlack 1994a). Consistent with light availability, edge effects on vegetation are less pronounced in edges facing away from the sun (i.e., facing north in the north-temperate zone) than those receiving direct-beam radiation (Palick and Murphy 1990, Matlack 1994a). As such, the response of vegetation at human-generated edges is very similar to the vigorous growth observed in natural canopy gaps (Moore and Vankat 1986, Reader and Bricker 1992).

Not all vegetational edge effects are related to light levels. In northeastern France the abundance of nitrophilous herb species at edges corresponds to a local peak of nitrogen deposition (Thimonier et al. 1992). It is easy to imagine that the accumulation of leaf litter, snow, or pollutants at forest edges might influence plant growth but this possibility has not been rigorously examined. Advective drying also seems to affect plants at a great distance into forests. In fragmentary stands near Manaus, Brazil, many standing trees up to 50 m from the edge died within 1–2 years of fragment formation, apparently killed by edge-related desiccation (Lovejoy et al. 1984).

There has been a strenuous debate about plant species composition at edges: is dense edge vegetation composed of typical forest species taking advantage of the great increase in light, or is there a suite of 'edge specialist' species only found in this microhabitat (Gysel 1951, Fravers 1994, Matlack 1994a)? Greater species richness has been observed at edges in some studies, and attributed to the addition of edge specialists. In hindsight, however, such effects are probably artifacts of the sampling design and the strong patchiness of forest herb distributions. Indeed, studies with very broad sampling (e.g., Laurence 1991), show occurrence of 'edge species' deep into the forest. It is probably most correct to say that edge effects arise in plant distributions because edges offer good opportunities for species which are normally present, but uncommon, in the intact forest.

DYNAMIC PROCESSES

Too often, the 'edge effect' is understood as a single, static measure of a forest community. In fact, vegetation at edges shows considerable variation among sites, successional stages, and species. The display of vegetation at a forest edge reflects demographic fluxes of a large number of individual plant species, each with a distinctive life history and physical requirements which translate into individualistic edge zone distributions. For example, at mixed hardwood sites in northern Delaware (Matlack 1994a), most species reached their highest concentration at the edge (e.g., *Carex* spp.), but many others thrived at a distance from the edge (e.g., *Smilacina racemosa* consistently peaked at 20 m; *Arisaema triphyllum* at 40 m).

Edge-oriented patterns can arise very quickly in vegetation at newly formed edges (1–2 years at sites in mixed hardwood forest; Matlack 1994a), presumably driven by strong microclimate gradients. With closure of the side canopy (20–30 years), microclimate gradients become indistinct but edge-oriented pattern remains in understory vegetation. At embedded edges, an edge-oriented pattern may still be observable in plant distributions as much as 55 years after canopy closure! Assuming that the longevity of many understory species is an evolutionary response to the frequency of natural gaps, we may expect edge-oriented pattern in the understory to persist as long as the interval between gaps, i.e., *c.* 100 years after side-canopy closure (Canham 1985, Runkle and Yetter 1987).

We still have a very coarse understanding of the community dynamics of plants at forest edges. Thus far, studies have not shown negative impacts on any understory species (but see Lovejoy *et al.* 1984), but few relevant data are available. In the absence of data on individual species, and considering our broad ignorance about community responses to disturbance in forests, managers must fall back on the general knowledge that vegetation is radically reorganized at edges and that such changes can persist for a very long time. The most prudent course of action is to avoid creation of edges near botanically sensitive areas.

Animal responses

Plant composition and structure at edges will inevitably influence animal distributions. It is widely acknowledged that vertical (MacArthur and MacArthur 1961) and horizontal (Roth 1976) heterogeneity of a site has a large influence on the density and diversity of animals because these parameters integrate microhabitat diversity. The assemblage of animals along edges may include species affiliated specifically with the edge, species that require either of the vegetation types that constitute the edge, and habitat generalists. Where edge boundaries are distinct and linear (e.g., recent edges), densities of species that require one vegetation type are likely to be low because edges function as psychological barriers (Chasko and Gates 1982, Bendel and Gates 1987). Where edges are sinuous or structurally complex, territories of these species may cross edges (Chasko and Gates 1982, Hardt and Forman 1989).

As forest edges close and successional vegetation develops in the clearing, edges become the locus for a group of animals that rarely occur in adjacent ecosystems. Among vertebrates, edge-affiliated species include

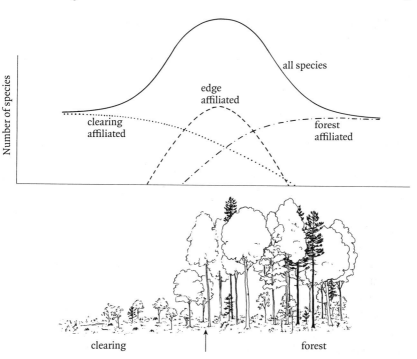

Fig. 6.4. A typical distribution of animal species at a closed forest edge. The arrow indicates the boundary of the gap-forming disturbance.

birds and mammals that are dependent on the dense, shrubby growth at closed forest edges. Medium and large mammals and semi-colonial song-birds that occur along extensive edges and in large patches of scrubby vegetation (e.g., old fields) may also occur in natural canopy gaps, but these gaps are often not large enough for such species. Habitat generalists that can exploit resources found in both of the adjoining ecosystems may not be affected by forest edges. However, if edge vegetation is more productive than surrounding ecosystems, generalists may concentrate their activity at the edge (Yahner 1988, Andren 1995). As a result, the density and diversity of animals may be substantially greater along edges than within any of the adjoining ecosystems (Figure 6.4).

Community interactions at edges

We have presented a fairly simple chain of causation: animal behavior at edges responds to vegetation structure which in turn is determined by physical gradients. More complex biological interactions also occur, fostered by the lush vegetation at edges, the structural complexity of the edge zone, and the proximity of both forest and clearing communities.

GRAZING

Animals respond to edge vegetation and shape it through their impact on plant recruitment and mortality. Aldo Leopold (1936) ascribed the abundance of game species at edges to the strong growth of forage plants. Since then, there have been many qualitative descriptions of intensive grazing at edges, particularly by white-tailed deer (*Odocoileus virginianus*; Alverson et al. 1988, Johnson et al. 1995). Dense populations of deer may prevent forest regeneration (Behrend et al. 1970, Tilghman 1989), reducing local diversity of both herbaceous and woody plants (Alverson et al. 1988, McShea and Rappole 1992, Miller et al. 1992) which, in turn, removes cover for ground and near-ground nesting birds. With less cover, birds and their nests become increasingly vulnerable to predation, even in predominately forested landscapes (DeGraaf et al. 1991, Leimgruber et al. 1994). Herbivorous insects may also be more abundant along edges. Gypsy moths (*Lymantria dispar*, Bellinger et al. 1989) and locust borers (*Megacyllene robiniae*, Harman and Harman 1987) have been observed at higher densities at edges than interior forest or field sites, respectively.

SEED DISPERSAL

Forest plants support bird populations by the production of fruit, and benefit from the interaction through the dispersal of their seeds. Edges are particularly attractive to frugivorous birds due to rich fruit production and abundant perches near the food source. As a result, fruits produced on the edge of canopy gaps are taken significantly faster and in greater numbers than fruit produced under a closed canopy (Thompson and Willson 1978). Edges receive disproportionately many bird-dispersed seeds (Hoppes 1988) because the local pattern of seed deposition strongly reflects the availability of perches (McDonnell and Stiles 1983, McClanahan and Wolfe 1987). Strong avian seed dispersal also reflects the improved cover from predators provided by edge vegetation. To the extent that seed availability is limiting in a plant community, the influx of seed at edges potentially increases plant species number and diversity.

PREDATION

Probably the most contentious issue involving animals at forest edges is the interaction of predators and their potential prey. Structurally complex and food-rich, edges attract a variety of herbivores. This local concentration of prey may attract vertebrate predators from adjoining ecosystems or provide foraging opportunities for those predators that use edges as travel corridors. Foraging success of predators in edges may be high because of their linear nature, making it easy to locate and subdue prey (Brown and Litvaitis 1995). The concentration of predators has led to the now-familiar notion that edges function as 'ecological traps' (Gates and Gysel 1978). But how strong is the evidence supporting this assertion?

Much research has focused on predation of migratory songbirds because many species have declined substantially over the last 20 years (Hagan and Johnston 1992). In review papers, Paton (1994) and Andrén (1995) summarized the results of these studies and concluded that predation rates were elevated along some, but not all forest edges. Edge-related increases in predation were more common in forest patches surrounded by farmland than that in predominately forested landscapes (Andrén 1995). Several factors may contribute to this difference including the abundance of generalist mammals and birds at farm–forest edges (Angelstam 1986, Andrén and Angelstam 1988, Moller 1989, Nour et al. 1993). Among these, corvids were the most frequently identified predator (Paton 1994). While foraging, these birds rely on perches from which to scan for food. Thus, vegetation structure appears to concentrate an open-land predator within the larger agricultural-forest matrix, resulting in a disproportionate level of foraging activity along forest–field edges.

In predominantly forested landscapes, corvids are less abundant and generalist mammals may be the major predator of avian nests (Reitsma et al. 1990, Nour et al. 1993, Leimgruber et al. 1994, Hanski et al. 1996). Mammalian predators probably encounter nests incidentally while searching for more common prey (Roseberry and Klimstra 1970, Crabtree and Wolfe 1988, Vickery et al. 1992, Pasitschniak-Arts and Messier 1995, Hanski et al. 1996). Nest predation rates by mammals, therefore, will be higher in edges than surrounding habitats if either predators or prey are more abundant in edges. Vulnerability of nests also appears to be affected by the structural complexity of edge habitats (Bowman and Harris 1980), nests being more vulnerable along straight rather than irregular edges (Ratti and Reese 1988). It is worth noting that elevated predation rates may not be restricted to human-generated edges. Gates and Giffen

(1991) detected higher concentrations of nesting songbirds along a forest–stream edge and speculated that potential nest predators might be attracted to these sites.

NEST PARASITISM

In North America, the issue of nest parasitism by brown-headed cowbirds (*Molothrus ater*) has generated considerable concern because populations of cowbirds have recently increased in many regions outside their historical range (Brittingham and Temple 1983). Initial research on nest parasitism suggested that this phenomenon may be an edge effect (Gates and Gysel 1978, Brittingham and Temple 1983). However, recent work on this topic has revealed that the prevalence of nest parasitism is largely a consequence of the regional conversion of forest to agriculture and is not directly caused by forest edge (Hahn and Hatfield 1995, Robinson *et al.* 1995). The limited research to date suggests that populations of generalist predators increase as 20% or more of the forested landscape is converted to agriculture or other permanent opening (Robinson *et al.* 1995, Oehler and Litvaitis 1996).

Management for biological diversity

The negative repercussions of edge habitats have prompted changes in forestry practices, especially regulations regarding the size, distribution, and configuration of clearcuts. Yet there is considerable variability in edge response among forest sites and species, which makes it difficult to formulate a consistent edge management policy. The most productive approach is probably to consider the impact of edges on forest communities on a case-by-case basis. We suggest that land managers consider at least two fundamental issues when considering edge creation. First, what is the composition of the landscape that contains the affected forest stand? Second, what is the status of individual species in the edge zone?

CONTROLLING EDGE EFFECTS IN MANAGED FORESTS

Protection of most forest species is best served by uncut forest, well away from the peculiar dynamics of human-generated forest edges. In many regions, however, no large tracts of forest remain or it may not be possible to maintain large tracts. It is now apparent that many of the negative consequences of edges are not only site-specific. Responses to habitat features also need to be described at two additional scales: local (the size of the forest stand), and landscape (composition of the habitat matrix). For example, populations of edge predators and nest parasites respond to edge proximity, but also reflect regional abundance of agriculture or other permanent openings. In such landscapes, management for regional diversity may include efforts to minimize edge effects rather than attempting to avoid edge creation altogether.

Because edge zone area grows as an exponential function of zone width (Figure 6.5), minor variation in edge width can be critical. If one knows edge width, one can calculate the amount of interior (non-edge) habitat remaining in stands of a particular size and shape (e.g., Laurence 1991, Laurence and Yensen 1991). As we have stressed throughout this chapter, there is no standard edge width for any particular forest type. The best advice we can give land managers is to determine edge effects empirically for the most edge-sensitive species, or (better yet) use a conservative maximum width based on many measurements in the local ecosystem. With a width figure in mind, managers can avoid creating small stands that would be dominated by edge habitat.

The amount of edge habitat in a stand is also a function of stand shape (i.e., the perimeter:area ratio). A complex shape will have a greater proportion of edge habitat than a roughly circular stand of similar area (Franklin and Forman 1987). Perimeter is also important because fragmentary stands constantly exchange energy, material, and organisms with the surrounding landscape (contrary to the well-known biogeographic model). By reducing edge length relative to area, such exchange can be minimized (Game 1980, Janzen 1986). Fires are less likely to spread into forest stands with a short edge exposure. There is less edge to collect airborne pollutants and seeds of exotic plant species. Grazing animals have less opportunity to wander into the forest, and there are fewer points of entry for illicit hunting and firewood-gathering. Thus, managers should try to plan cuts and regrowth such that surviving forest is consolidated in approximately circular stands. Narrow peninsulas of forest should be avoided.

In small fragments, edge effects can be moderated somewhat by managing edge vegetation. Because physical gradients are much less pronounced behind closed edges, side canopies should be encouraged. In the eastern United States growth of limbs to form a closed side canopy requires several decades (Trimble and Tryon 1966, Runkle and Yetter

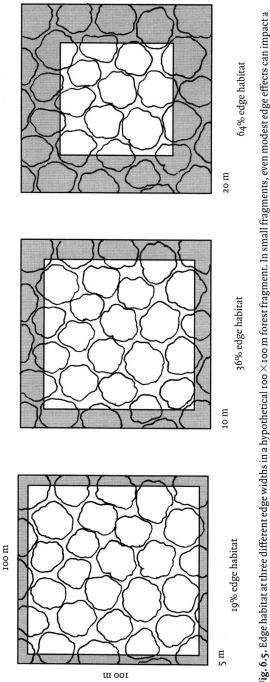

100 m

100 m

5 m

19% edge habitat

10 m

36% edge habitat

20 m

64% edge habitat

Fig. 6.5. Edge habitat at three different edge widths in a hypothetical 100 × 100 m forest fragment. In small fragments, even modest edge effects can impact a large proportion of the stand.

1987), so it is important to keep the existing side canopy intact. Given sufficient time, natural succession may produce a buffer strip of young trees in front of the forest, effectively moving the microclimatic edge outward from the original forest edge. Some authors (Ranney 1977, Ranney et al. 1981) have referred to such buffer strips as 'advancing edge', but this terminology is inaccurate. Although woody species advance into the clearing, few herbaceous species colonize the buffer strip (Matlack 1994b), and soil structure does not resemble the original stand. The buffer strip may be a useful management tool in controlling edge zone microclimate, but it should not be considered part of the forest. Because edge effects are particularly long lived in successional time (Matlack 1994a), the embedded edge will require decades to return to the forest interior condition despite the presence of a buffer strip.

EDGE-AFFILIATED SPECIES

Edges often provide habitat for species not naturally found in intact forest, including exotic species. In most cases, exotic species are only vigorous in a narrow zone a few meters from the edge (e.g., Brothers and Spingarn 1992, Matlack 1994a). This is not to suggest that exotics do not pose a threat to forest biodiversity. A small number of species seem to tolerate heavy shade, allowing them to penetrate deeply into intact forest – up to 60 m into the stand in some cases (Fravers 1994). In the eastern United States, garlic mustard (Alliaria petiolata), bush honeysuckle (Lonicera tatarica), and European ground mint (Glechoma hederacea) are particularly worrisome. In the case of light-requiring exotics, edge populations may serve as seed sources, allowing penetration of forest by rapid invasion of natural canopy gaps. The most effective strategy to control invasive plant species is simply to minimize edge length when cutting, and to allow closure of the side canopy, as described above.

Up to this point, we have emphasized negative edge effects, but edges can also benefit taxa whose habitat is at risk. In the northeastern United States populations of some birds and mammals (e.g., golden-winged warbler, Vermivora chrysoptera; New England cottontail, Sylvilagus transitionalis; and bobcat, Felis rufus) that are dependent on early successional forests or shrubland habitats are declining as succession reduces the abundance of those habitats on a regional scale (Askins 1993, Litvaitis 1993, Hagan 1994). Such species would benefit by increasing the abundance of complex edge habitats that include dense, shrubby vegetation. Concentration of edge habitats in local areas would limit the detrimental effects of edge creation and provide for a greater variety of species at a regional scale (Askins 1994, Litvaitis and Villafuerte 1996).

Premontane Wet Forests of Panama: a case study

No single ecosystem clearly illustrates all of the generalizations made above, but the following example is illuminating. Guadalupe Williams Linera (1990a,b) examined edge sites on the Pacific slope of Panama to determine the impact of recently created edge on tropical forest vegetation. She selected five stands of undisturbed primary forest in the Premontane Wet Forest life zone (220–325 m elevation) each of which were adjacent to a rice field created 1–12 years previously. On transects laid out from the clearing into the forest, she measured light, temperature, and relative humidity, and surveyed forest plant species.

The forest showed a spectacular diversity of tree species consisting mainly of palms and tropical hardwoods, with a high degree of eveness among them (48 tree species constitute 74% of stems). At each site, temperatures were higher in the rice field than in the forest but the heated air extended only 3–15 m into the stands – a relatively shallow physical edge zone. Light levels were highest at recent edges, and declined with successional time. Tree density and basal area were twice as high at the edge as the interior, declining smoothly with increasing distance into the forest. Consistent with shallow physical effects, basal area and density were indistinguishable from background levels only 5–20 m from the edge.

Comparison among the sites suggests that side canopy development was much more rapid than in temperate forests. The greatest stem density occurred at sites c. 5 years old, and edge openness dropped from 42% to 11% in only 12 years (Williams Linera 1990a). Contrary to expectation, the rapidly growing side canopy was composed of palms and dicot trees rather than the lianas that often fill disturbed sites in tropical forests. With time, tree basal area was reduced by increased mortality in the edge zone, apparently related to increased drying adjacent to the clearing (Williams Linera 1990a). Fourteen times more trees died in the edge zone (0–20 m) than in control plots in intact forest.

Where soil was exposed at the edge, there was extensive germination from the seedbank (Williams Linera 1990b). However, most edge vegetation arose from seedlings and saplings present before edge creation. This is in contrast with temperate forest edges, which often appear to close by germination of new individuals and extension of adventitious limbs from

canopy trees (Trimble and Tryon 1966, Runkle and Yetter 1987). This
pattern of vegetation development matches growth in naturally occurring
gaps, which derive principally from seedlings present before gap formation in Central American forests (e.g., Brokaw 1985). Although the demographic mechanism is different, we have the familiar theme of gap-like
vegetational processes expressed at human-generated edges.

Too few edges have been described in tropical ecosystems to recognize
the essentially 'tropical' elements of this example. Indeed, it includes
some marked contrasts with two other tropical studies: Laurence (1991)
working at edges in the Atherton Tableland, northern Australia, found
more climbing species and a much wider edge zone than described by
Williams Linera in Panama; and at a site near Manaus in the Amazon
Basin, Lovejoy et al. (1984) and Kapos (1989), found climatic gradients
extending much further into the stand than reported by Williams Linera. It
is reassuring, however, to recognize a few ecological themes in common
with the temperate zone.

Summary

One artifact of the human modification of forests has been the tremendous increase in forest edges. Historically, land managers considered
the lush plant growth and diversity of animals at edges as beneficial.
However, recent investigations have described radical changes in community structure at edges, suggesting serious problems from a biodiversity
perspective. Edge habitats are advantageous to a variety of exotic plants,
predators, brood parasites, and herbivores that are capable of altering the
composition of local forest communities. Radical changes in the forest
microclimate at edges lead to dramatic changes in plant community structure which may persist several decades, at least. Forest managers can avoid
edge impacts in plant communities by laying out clearcuts to minimize
edge length relative to interior habitat. Side canopy vegetation should be
protected as a microclimate barrier, but cannot be relied on as habitat for
forest species. In contrast to plants, edge effects in animals are likely
dependent on environmental features expressed at spatial scales much
larger than those used to describe the edge. Therefore, forest managers
need to understand how animals use the edge in the spatial and temporal
context of the whole landscape.

Further readings

For those considering an investigation of edge effects Murcia (1995) summarizes some of the difficulties associated with these studies. Geiger (1965) remains the authoritative description of edge microclimate. He presents many clear examples in a lucid, readable style. Laurence and Yensen (1991) describe edge effects in plants and illustrate how edge zone width can be used to evaluate individual forest fragments. Lovejoy et al. (1984) provide an excellent example from a tropical ecosystem, describing edge responses in many taxa.

Literature cited

Alverson, W. S., D. M. Waller, and S. L. Solheim. 1988. Forests too deer: edge effects in northern Wisconsin. *Conservation Biology* **2**:348–58.

Andrén, H. 1995. Effects of landscape composition on predation rates at habitat edges. Pp. 225–55 in L. Hansson, L. Fahrig, and G. Merriam (eds). *Mosaic Landscapes and Ecological Processes.* Chapman & Hall, London.

Andrén, H. and P. Anglestam. 1988. Elevated predation rates as an edge effect in habitat islands: experimental evidence. *Ecology* **69**:544–7.

Angelstam, P. 1986. Predation on ground nesting bird nests in relation to predator densities and habitat usage. *Oikos* **47**:365–73.

Askins, R. A. 1993. Population trends in grassland, shrubland, and forest birds in the eastern North America. Pp. 1–34 in D. M. Power (ed.). *Current Ornithology,* Volume 7. Plenum Publications, New York.

1994. Open corridors in a heavily forested landscape: impacts on shrubland and forest-interior birds. *Wildlife Society Bulletin* **22**:339–47.

Augspurger, C. K. and S. E. Franson. 1988. Input of wind dispersed seeds into light gaps and forest sites in a neotropical forest. *Journal of Tropical Ecology* **4**: 239–52.

Balsberg Pahlsson, A. and B. Bergkvist. 1995. Acid deposition and soil acidification at a southwest facing edge of Norway spruce and European beech in south Sweden. *Ecological Bulletins* **44**:43–53.

Behrend, D. F., G. F. Mattfeld, W. C. Tierson, and J. E. Wiley, III. 1970. Deer density control for comprehensive forest management. *Journal of Forestry* **68**:695–700.

Beier, C. 1991. Separation of gaseous and particulate dry deposition of sulfur at a forest edge in Denmark. *Journal of Environmental Quality* **20**:460–6.

Bellinger, R. G., F. W. Ravlin, and M. L. McManus. 1989. Forest edge effects and their influence on gypsy moth (*Lepidoptera: Lymantriidae*) egg mass distribution. *Environmental Entomology* **18**:840–43.

Bendel, P. R., and J. E. Gates. 1987. Home range and microhabitat partitioning of the southern flying squirrel (*Glaucomys volans*). *Journal of Mammalogy* **68**:243–55.

Bormann F. H., and G. E. Likens. 1979. Catastrophic disturbance and the steady state in northern hardwood forests. *American Scientist* **67**: 660–9.

Bowman, G. B., and L. D. Harris. 1980. Effects of spatial heterogeneity on ground-nest depredation. *Journal of Wildlife Management* **44**:806–13.

Brittingham, M. C. and S. A. Temple. 1983. Have cowbirds caused forest song-birds to decline? *BioScience* **33**: 31–5.

Brokaw, N. V. 1985. Gap-phase regeneration in a tropical rainforest. *Ecology* **66**:682–7.

Brothers, T. S. and A. Spingarn. 1992. Forest fragmentation and alien plant invasion of central Indiana old-growth forests. *Conservation Biology* **6**:91–100.

Brown, A. L., and J. A. Litvaitis. 1995. Habitat features associated with predation of New England cottontails: what scale is appropriate? *Canadian Journal of Zoology* **73**:1005–11.

Canham, C. D. 1985. Suppression and release during canopy recruitment in *Acer saccharum*. *Bulletin of the Torrey Botanical Club* **112**:134–45.

Canham, C. D., J. S. Denslow, W. J. Platt, J. R. Runkle, T. A. Spies, and P. S. White. 1990. Light regimes beneath closed canopies and tree-fall gaps in temperate and tropical forests. *Canadian Journal of Forest Research* **20**: 620–31.

Chasko, G. G. and J. E. Gates. 1982. Avian habitat suitability along a transmission line corridor in an oak-hickory forest region. *Wildlife Monographs* **82**:1–41.

Chen, J., J. F. Franklin, and T. A. Spies. 1995. Growing season microclimatic gradients from clearcut edges into old-growth Douglas fir forests. *Ecological Applications* **5**:74–86.

Crabtree, R. L., and M. E. Wolfe. 1988. Effects of alternate prey on skunk predation of waterfowl nests. *Wildlife Society Bulletin* **16**:163–9.

DeGraaf, R. M., W. M. Healy, and R. T. Brooks. 1991. Effects of thinning and deer browsing on breeding birds in New England oak woodlands. *Forest Ecology and Management* **41**:179–91.

Esseen, P. 1994. Tree mortality patterns after experimental fragmentation of an old-growth conifer forest. *Biological Conservation* **68**:19–28.

Franklin, J. F. and R. T. T. Forman. 1987. Creating landscape patterns by forest cutting: ecological consequences and principles. *Landscape Ecology* **1**:5–18.

Fravers, S. 1994. Vegetation responses along edge-to-interior gradients in the mixed hardwood forests of the Roanoke River Basin, North Carolina. *Conservation Biology* **8**:822–32.

Game, M. 1980. Best shape for nature reserves. *Nature* **297**:630–2.

Gates, J. E., and N. R. Giffen. 1991. Neotropical migrant birds and edge effects at a forest-stream ecotone. *Wilson Bulletin* **103**:204–17.

Gates, J. E. and L. W. Gysel. 1978. Avian nest dispersion and fledgling success in field-forest ecotones. *Ecology* **59**:871–83.

Geiger, R. 1965. *The Climate Near the Ground*. Harvard University Press, Cambridge, Massachusetts.

Ghuman, B. S. and R. Lal. 1987. Effects of partial clearcutting on microclimate in a humid tropical forest. *Agricultural and Forest Meteorology* 40:17–29.

Gysel, L. W. 1951. Borders and openings of beach-maple woodlands in southern Michigan. *Journal of Forestry* 49:13–19.

Hagan, J. M., III. 1994. Decline of the rufous-sided towhee in the eastern United States. *Auk* 110:863–74.

Hagan, J. M., III, and D. W. Johnston (eds). 1992. *Ecology and Conservation of Neotropical Migrant Landbirds*. Smithsonian Institution, Washington, D.C.

Hahn, D. C., and J. S. Hatfield. 1995. Parasitism at the landscape scale: cowbirds prefer forests. *Conservation Biology* 9:1415–24.

Hanski, I. K., T. J. Fenske, and G. J. Niemi. 1996. Lack of edge effect in nesting success of breeding birds in managed forest landscapes. *Auk* 113:578–85.

Hardt, R. A. and R. T. T. Forman. 1989. Boundary form effects on woody colonization of reclaimed surface mines. *Ecology* 70:1252–60.

Harman, D. M., and A. L. Harman. 1987. Distribution pattern of adult locust borers (*Coleoptera: Cerambycidae*) on nearby goldenrod, *Solidago* spp. (*Asteraceae*), at a forest-field edge. *Proceedings of the Entomological Society of Washington* 89:706–10.

Hoppes, W. G. 1988. Seedfall pattern of several species of bird-dispersed plants in an Illinois woodland. *Ecology* 69:320–9.

Hutchison, B. A. and D. R. Matt. 1976. Beam enrichment of diffuse radiation in a deciduous forest. *Agricultural Meteorology* 17:93–110.

Janzen, D. H. 1986. The eternal external threat. Pp. 286–303 in M. E. Soule (ed.). *Conservation Biology*, Sinauer Associates, Sunderland, Massachusetts.

Johnson, A. S., P. E. Hale, W. M. Ford, J. M. Wentworth, J. R. French, O. F. Anderson, and G. B. Pullen. 1995. White-tailed deer foraging in relation to successional stage, overstory type and management of southern Appalachian forests. *American Midland Naturalist* 133:18–35.

Kapos, V. 1989. Effects of isolation on the water status of forest patches in the Brazilian Amazon. *Journal of Tropical Ecology* 5:173–85.

Laurence, W. F. 1991. Edge effects in tropical forest fragments, application of a model for the design of nature reserves. *Biological Conservation* 57:205–19.

Laurence, W. and E. Yensen. 1992. Predicting the impacts of edge effects in fragmented habitats. *Biological Conservation* 55:77–92.

Leimgruber P., W. J. McShea, and J. H. Rappole. 1994. Predation on artificial nests in large forest blocks. *Journal of Wildlife Management* 58:254–60.

Leopold, A. 1933. *Game Management*. Charles Scribners, New York.

1936. Deer and the dauerwald in Germany. *Journal of Forestry* 34:366–75, 460–6.

Litvaitis, J. A. 1993. Response of early successional vertebrates to historic changes in land use. *Conservation Biology* 7:866–73.

Litvaitis, J. A., and R. Villafuerte. 1996. Factors affecting the persistence of New England cottontail metapopulations: the role of habitat management. *Wildlife Society Bulletin* 24:686–93.

Liu, J., J. M. Chen, T. A. Black, and M. D. Novak. 1996. E-e modeling of turbulent air flow downwind of a model forest edge. *Boundary Layer Meteorology* 77:21–44.

Lovejoy, T. E., J. M. Rankin, R. O. Bierregard, K. S. Brown, L. H. Emmons, M. E. Van der Voort. 1984. Ecosystem decay of Amazon rain forest remnants. Pp. 295–325 in M. H. Nitecki (ed.). *Extinctions*. University of Chicago Press, Chicago, Illinois.

MacArthur, R. H. and J. W. MacArthur. 1961. On bird species diversity. *Ecology* 42:594–8.

Matlack, G. R. 1993. Microenvironment variation within and among forest edge sites in the eastern United States. *Biological Conservation* 66: 185–94.

1994a. Vegetation dynamics of the forest edge – trends in space and successional time. *Journal of Ecology* 82:113–24.

1994b. Plant species migration in a mixed-history forest landscape in eastern North America. *Ecology* 75:1491–502.

McClanahan, T. R. and R. W. Wolfe. 1987. Dispersal of ornithochorous seeds from forest edges in central Florida. *Vegetatio* 71:107–12.

McDonnell, M. J. and E. W. Stiles. 1983. The structural complexity of old field vegetation and the recruitment of bird-dispersed plant species. *Oecologia* 56:109–16.

McShea, W. J., and J. H. Rappole. 1992. White-tailed deer as keystone species within forest habitats of Virginia. *Virginia Journal of Science* 43:177–86.

Miller, D. R. 1975. Structure of the microclimate at a woodland/parking lot interface. Pp. 109–14 in *Proceedings of the Conference on the Metropolitan Physical Environment, Syracuse, New York*. U.S. Forest Service Northeast Forest Experiment Station, Technical Report 25.

Miller, S. G., S. P. Bratton, and J. Hadidian. 1992. Impacts of white-tailed deer on endangered and threatened vascular plants. *Natural Areas Journal* 12:67–74.

Moller, A. P. 1989. Nest site selection across field-woodland ecotones: the effect of nest predation. *Oikos* 56:240–6.

Moore, M. R. and J. L. Vankat. 1986. Responses of the herb layer to the gap dynamics of a mature beech maple forest. *American Midland Naturalist* 115:336–47.

Murcia, C. 1995. Edge effects in fragmented forests: implications for conservation. *Trends in Ecology and Evolution* 10:58–62.

Neal, C., A. J. Robson, R. L. Hall, G. P. Ryland, T. Conway, and M. Neal. 1991. Hydrological impacts of hardwood plantation in lowland Britain: preliminary findings on interception at a forest edge, Black Wood, Hampshire, southern England. *Journal of Hydrology* 127:349–65.

Nour, N., E. Matthysen, and A. A. Dhondt. 1993. Artificial nest predation and habitat fragmentation: different trends in bird and mammal predators. *Ecography* 16:111–16.

Oehler, J. D., and J. A. Litvaitis. 1996. The role of spatial scale in understanding responses by medium-sized carnivores to forest fragmentation. *Canadian Journal of Zoology* 74:2070–9.

Palik, B. J. and P. G. Murphy. 1990. Disturbance versus edge effects in sugar maple/beech forest fragments. *Forest Ecology and Management* **32**:187–202.

Pasitschniak-Arts, M., and F. Messier. 1995. Risk of predation on waterfowl nests in the Canadian prairies: effects of habitat edges and agricultural practices. *Oikos* **63**:347–55.

Paton, P. W. C. 1994. The effect of edge on avian nest success: how strong is the evidence? *Conservation Biology* **8**:17–26.

Ranney, J. W. 1977. *Forest island edges – their structure, development, and importance to regional forest ecosystem dynamics.* Environmental Sciences Division Publication No. 1069, Oak Ridge National Laboratory, Oak Ridge, Tennessee. 56 pages, EDFB/IBP-77/1.

Ranney, J. W., M. C. Bruner, and J. B. Levenson. 1981. The importance of edge in the structure and dynamics of forest islands. Pp. 67–96 in R. L. Burgess and D. M. Sharpe (eds). *Forest Island Dynamics in Man-dominated Landscapes.* Springer Verlag, New York.

Ratti, J. T., and K. P. Reese. 1988. Preliminary test of the ecological trap hypothesis. *Journal of Wildlife Management* **52**:484–91.

Raynor, G. S. 1971. Wind and temperature structure in a coniferous forest and a contiguous field. *Forest Science* **17**:351–63.

Reader, R. J. and B. D. Bricker. 1992. Response of five deciduous forest herbs to partial canopy removal and patch size. *American Midland Naturalist* **127**:149–57.

Reitsma, L. R., R. T. Holmes, and T. W. Sherry. 1990. Effects of removal of red squirrels, *Tamiasciurus hudsonicus*, and eastern chipmunks, *Tamias striatus*, on nest predation in a northern hardwood forest: an artificial nest experiment. *Oikos* **57**:375–80.

Robinson, S. K., F. R. Thompson, III, T. M. Donovan, D. R. Whitehead, and J. Faaborg. 1995. Regional forest fragmentation and the nesting success of migratory birds. *Science* **267**:1987–90.

Roman, C. T., R. A. Zampella, and A. Z. Jaworski. 1985. Wetland boundaries in the New Jersey Pinelands: ecological relationships and delineation. *Water Resources Bulletin* **21**:1005–12.

Roseberry, J. L., and W. D. Klimstra. 1970. The nesting ecology and reproductive performance of the eastern meadowlark. *Wilson Bulletin* **82**:243–67.

Roth, R. R. 1976. Spatial heterogeneity and bird species diversity. *Ecology* **57**:773–82.

Runkle, J. R. and T. C. Yetter. 1987. Treefalls revisited: gap dynamics in the southern Appalachians. *Ecology* **48**:546–58.

Thimonier, A., J. L. Duponey, and J. Timbal. 1992. Floristic changes in the herb-layer vegetation of a deciduous forest in the Lorraine Plain under the influence of atmospheric deposition. *Forest Ecology and Management* **55**:149–67.

Thompson, J. N. and M. F. Willson. 1978. Disturbance and the dispersal of fleshy fruits. *Science* **200**:1161–3.

Tilghman, N. G. 1989. Impacts of white-tailed deer on forest regeneration in northwestern Pennsylvania. *Journal of Wildlife Management* **53**: 524–32.

Trimble, G. R. and E. H. Tryon. 1966. Crown encroachment into openings cut in Appalachian hardwood stands. *Journal of Forestry* **64**:104–8.

Vickery, P. D., M. L. Hunter, Jr., and J. V. Wells. 1992. Evidence of incidental nest predation and its effects on nests of threatened grassland birds. *Oikos* **63**:281–8

Wales, B. A. 1967. Climate, microclimate, and vegetation relationships on north and south forest boundaries in New Jersey. *The William L. Hutcheson Memorial Forest Bulletin* **2**:1–60.

Weathers, K. C., G. M. Lovett, and G. E. Likens. 1995. Cloud deposition to a spruce forest edge. *Atmospheric Environment* **6**: 665–72.

Whittaker, R. H. 1956. Vegetation of the Great Smokey Mountains. *Ecological Monographs* **26**:1–80.

Williams Linera, G. 1990a. Vegetation structure and environmental conditions of forest edges in Panama. *Journal of Ecology* **78**:356–73.

1990b. Origin and early development of forest edge vegetation in Panama. *Biotropica* **22**:235–41.

Yahner, R. H. 1988. Changes in wildlife communities near edges. *Conservation Biology* **2**:333–9.

7   Islands and fragments

YRJÖ HAILA

Many forests exist as small stands isolated from other stands by intensively modified land such as fields, pastures, clearcuts, and silvicultural plantations. In many parts of the world isolated patches are all that is left of a formerly continuous forest cover. There is no doubt whatever that such a change in forest structure brings forth harmful ecological changes. My aim in this chapter is to review what is known about such changes and suggest ways to mitigate the consequences through appropriate management.

The process through which formerly continuous forest expanses turn into forest patches of varying size, isolated from each other by tracts of non-forested land, is called *fragmentation*. The resulting configuration often resembles an 'archipelago' in which forest 'islands' are surrounded by a 'sea' of another type of environment. This commonly drawn analogy between forest fragments and real islands has a background in the development of ecological theory: research on the ecology of discrete forest patches has been inspired by research on the ecology of real islands, in particular, by the theory of island biogeography of MacArthur and Wilson (1967) and its predecessors (see Williamson 1981). I will argue later in this chapter that a strict analogy is misleading but, nevertheless, there are similarities that make a comparison fruitful.

The most important factor driving forest fragmentation, by far, has been agriculture. Historically, agriculture has spread unevenly. The rate of conversion of natural vegetation to agriculture reached in many parts of the world record levels in the twentieth century, particularly after World War II. This has created highly fragmented landscapes in which the proportion of forest is miniscule, and the remaining forest patches quite literally resemble 'islands' surrounded by intensively cultivated open fields. Examples familiar to ecologists include the Western Australian wheatbelt (Hobbs and Saunders 1993), eastern United States (Burgess and Sharpe 1981), and the United States Midwest (Curtis 1956), but similar landscapes are found in virtually all intensively cultivated regions of the world.

234

Modern forestry has also changed forest structure, but with more ambiguous consequences as regards fragmentation. The aim of timber harvesting is to remove timber from the forest. This is often done using clearcuts which leave older forest reduced to patches isolated from each other by young stands. However, modern forestry modifies forest ecosystems in various ways, and it is often difficult to distinguish the particular contribution of fragmentation among all types of ecological change that occur in harvested landscapes.

The harmful consequences that follow from fragmentation are amply documented in ecological literature. They are usually divided into three main types: (a) effects of the reduction in area of the remaining fragments; (b) effects of increasing isolation of the fragments from each other; and (c) effects of increasing disturbance from the surroundings (Harris 1984, Wilcove *et al.* 1986, Hunter 1990, Saunders *et al.* 1991, Haila *et al.* 1993b, Noss and Csuti 1994). The question is, does forest fragmentation increase the threat to the ecological diversity and integrity of forest ecosystems through any, or possibly all, of these processes?

I will mainly focus on fragmentation caused by forestry. In the next section I elaborate upon conceptual aspects of forest fragmentation. In the third section I focus on the ecological mechanisms that actually cause relevant ecological change in fragmented environments. In the fourth section I assess the role of theory in understanding fragmentation. In the last section I present a checklist of issues that should be considered when plans are made to manage fragmented forest landscapes.

The multiple faces of 'fragmentation'

In the previous section, 'fragmentation' was understood in a 'phenomenological' way, that is, using change in landscape structure as the defining feature. However, a change in landscape structure induces many different types of ecological change. Consequently, before we can focus upon the consequences of fragmentation, we have to recognize other possible effects. This raises the need to make conceptual distinctions.

FRAGMENTATION VERSUS LOSS

The first distinction to consider is between forest *fragmentation* and forest *loss*. These processes belong together. Forest fragmentation results, by definition, from clearing a substantial portion of a landscape that previously had a continuous forest cover. However, the processes of loss and fragmentation need to be distinguished from each other because forest loss alone is expected to induce changes in the flora and fauna. This occurs for two reasons, both of which can be deduced from common ecological knowledge. First, a reduction in forest area means a reduction in the total amount of resources available for forest organisms. As a consequence, average population sizes of forest species decline and they are faced with an increasing danger of local extinction (MacArthur and Wilson 1967). Second, as no forest is internally homogeneous, a reduction in forest area also results in a decrease in the range of environments available within the forest. Consequently, a species specialized on a particular microenvironment within the forest may be left without any suitable habitat at all. The idea that habitat loss is a major factor driving species into extinction is a well-known principle in conservation biology.

Changes of these two types follow forest cutting irrespective of whether the forest actually is fragmented or not, i.e., whether it is distributed in one block or in many isolated patches after cutting. For the term forest fragmentation to have any definite meaning at all, it must refer to processes that influence forest organisms in addition to forest loss (Haila and Hanski 1984, Wilcove et al. 1986).

In the real world fragmentation and loss go together. Consequently, it is very difficult to identify the relative significance of these two causes of ecological change. One could argue that the distinction is not important for managers who have to deal with both forest fragmentation and forest loss in practice. However, it is definitely important for ecologists who have to understand and explain ecological change in forests. I return to these points below.

SCALING: AN ORGANISM-CENTERED PERSPECTIVE

Natural landscapes are not uniform; in contrast, they comprise mosaics of different environmental types on many different scales of resolution. This fact has been emphasized over and over again in modern ecology (Andrewartha and Birch 1954, Levins 1968, Whittaker and Levin 1977). In other words, natural environments are inherently 'fragmented' – any particular type of environment is surrounded by different types of environment. This is true of forests, too (see Chapter 4). The problem this fact poses for understanding the consequences of forest fragmentation is: When does the fragmentation caused by human activity matter?

This depends on two factors. The first one is scale. The second one is the type of disruption human activity causes in forest structure. I take up scale here and defer discussion of the second factor to the next subsection.

Scaling has become an important issue in ecology in recent years (Delcourt et al. 1983, Wiens 1989). This follows from the recognition that ecological processes have their characteristic spatial and temporal dimensions. For instance, the habitat use of particular birds during the nesting season covers a certain area and this defines the spatial scale. The temporal scale is the length of the nesting period. Scaling of ecological processes and fragmentation are connected to each other. To be specific: fragmentation is of consequence if it modifies the environment on such a spatial scale that ecological processes are disrupted.

In other words, a spatial standard to assess fragmentation can be derived from the ecological processes potentially disrupted. I suggest an organism-centered perspective for specifying the standard: let the important scales be defined by organisms themselves (Haila 1991). The homogeneity vs. heterogeneity of a particular landscape can be evaluated by looking at how particular organisms actually use the environment.

When we humans define fragmentation we resort, of course, to our own perspective. A landscape is fragmented if we perceive it as consisting of one uniform environmental type split into pieces by what we regard as another environmental type. However, for other kinds of organisms the human perspective may be irrelevant. Some bird species may routinely 'patch together' several pieces of land that we perceive as being separate from each other (Haila 1983); for these birds the landscape is 'functionally continuous' (Andrén and Delin 1994). On the other hand, insects may experience as extremely fragmented a forest that we perceive as homogeneous (Niemelä et al. 1992, Siitonen and Martikainen 1994).

An organism-centered view implies that there is no single general perspective to define fragmentation. Organisms differ greatly from each other, and criteria to define fragmentation vary accordingly. Multiple perspectives are needed. For instance, both the capercaillie (Tetrao urogallus), the largest member of the grouse family in the world, and Agonum mannerheimi, a carabid beetle about 1 cm long, require old-growth forest in Fennoscandia to maintain viable local populations, but the former needs tens of square kilometers (Wegge et al. 1992) and the latter needs only hectares (Niemelä et al. 1987). This comparison can also be made in another way: in a particular fragmented landscape different organisms face different types of problems. Thus, in a forest fragmented on the scale of hectares to tens of hectares capercaillies may suffer because individual birds, particularly males, cannot find suitable forage in the winter. In contrast, carabid individuals may thrive well in patches of this size but dispersal among suitable patches may fail, which can eventually lead to loss of local populations.

This multiplicity of perspectives allows a fruitful parallel to real islands. Different islands are not identical with respect to their 'insularity', and the appropriate characterization of the 'insularity' of a particular island depends on the organism one is interested in. Let us compare Skokholm, 1 km² in area and 4 km off the coast of Wales, with, say, Ireland. Soil arthropods such as springtails and mites on Skokholm live in populations that are isolated from populations on the mainland in Wales whereas birds breeding on Skokholm stay there through the nesting period but disperse freely to the mainland in the migration season. On the other hand, several non-migratory bird species of Ireland cross the Irish Sea only rarely and their populations are isolated from the populations in Britain. One can envisage a continuum from smaller to larger islands, or from less isolated to more isolated islands, and the criteria by which a particular island is an 'island' in an ecological sense will change across this continuum (Haila 1990).

The previous comparison brings into focus another factor that is critical in defining an adequate scale, namely, the difference between individual, population, and evolutionary processes (Haila 1990). By and large, the differences between these processes from a fragmentation perspective are as follows:

- On the individual scale, relevant criteria relate to movement patterns of single individuals: a landscape is fragmented if individuals do not move from patch to patch but each individual stays mainly within a single patch.
- On the population scale, relevant criteria relate to population dynamics and differentiation: a landscape is fragmented if local populations in different patches are to some extent dynamically independent of each other.
- On the evolutionary scale, relevant criteria come from factors determining speciation and the divergence of flora and fauna. Speciation and divergence occur on isolated oceanic islands such as the Galapagos and Hawaii. In contrast, forest fragments created by human disturbance are typically far too small and ephemeral to allow for any evolutionary differentiation at all. However, it is quite plausible that indirect evolutionary consequences follow from changes in selection regime which are caused by changes in landscape structure (Williams 1992: 31–7), provided there is genetic variation in populations allowing some adaptation to the new conditions (Dolman and Sutherland 1994).

The distinction between individual, population, and evolutionary scales helps to recognize significant differences between forest fragments and real islands (see also Wiens 1995). Forest fragmentation is most likely to have consequences on the individual scale but also quite often on the population scale, depending on the characteristics of the species in question and the degree of isolation of the fragments from each other. On the other hand, small, exposed islands are likely to differ from mainland because of differences in habitats, as is shown by data from the Åland archipelago in the Baltic (Haila 1983, Haila *et al.* 1983, Niemelä *et al.* 1988). Whether real archipelagoes offer reasonable analogies to fragmented forests is a question to be considered separately in each case.

THE DYNAMICS OF NATURAL FRAGMENTATION

As all environments are naturally heterogeneous they are naturally fragmented as well, in various ways depending on the particular organism and process of interest. Consequently, a proper baseline for understanding fragmentation is not an assumption of homogeneous environments but rather the type of fragmentation that is naturally characteristic of particular landscape types (Noss and Csuti 1994). A critical issue is whether the types of fragmentation brought about by human activity are similar or different from the types of fragmentation occurring naturally. For instance, clearcutting creates openings that resemble those produced by wildfires in some respects but differ from them in other respects. Such similarities and differences relate not only to the mosaic character of the resulting landscape (Chapter 4) and the nature of edges (Chapter 6), but also to the type of fragmentation that characterizes the resulting forest landscape.

Natural heterogeneity on the landscape scale is caused by variation in physical features of the environment such as topography and soil type (Chapter 5). In addition, within a particular type of environment, internal heterogeneity is maintained by natural disturbances. As is well known, characteristic disturbance types vary across environmental types and biogeographic regions. For instance, wildfires are particularly important in dry tropical forests, Australian eucalypt forests and bushlands, pine-dominated Mediterranean forests, and boreal coniferous forests. Windthrows dominate the picture in temperate forests and tropical rainforests, but are also important in some parts of the boreal zone (Syrjänen *et al.* 1994). Another factor creating disturbance on a large scale is insect outbreaks (Holling 1992). A site that has undergone a particular natural disturbance event is by no means structurally uniform. Wildfires, for instance, may leave behind great small-scale heterogeneity depending on the efficiency of the burn (Syrjänen *et al.* 1994, Haila 1994). Consequently, the ecological effects of each type of natural disturbance require careful characterization.

Natural disturbance cycles give one set of standards for assessing human-induced fragmentation (Hunter 1990, 1993). We can expect that forest organisms are to some degree adapted to changes in forest configuration that have occurred frequently under natural conditions. When we want to evaluate the consequences of human-induced fragmentation against natural disturbance, several specific questions arise. First, what is the size distribution of the forest patches produced by each type of disturbance? Second, how strict is isolation among the patches with respect to dispersal of forest organisms? Third, does human-induced disturbance produce new ecological barriers? For instance, the use of alien tree species in plantations creates a stronger contrast to remaining older forests than the use of native species.

Spatial and temporal scales are closely integrated in ecological processes (Preston 1960, Wiens 1981, Delcourt *et al.* 1983). This relationship seems more straightforward in animal than in plant ecology, for three reasons. (a) Plant seeds may remain viable in the seedbank for an extended time, but with the possible exception of some microinvertebrates, animals lack an analogous mechanism. (b) The longevity of plant individuals, particularly of trees, produces time-lags in their response to fragmentation: individuals remain alive in fragments where regeneration has ceased (Bierregaard *et al.* 1992, Hobbs 1993). (c) Variation in the size of animals gives a rough approximation for the characteristic population-level scale of different species: the larger the organism, the broader the scale of habitat use (Calder 1984). However, such a rule is meaningless in plants because size is a poor predictor of their life-history attributes.

The requirements of species often include various elements that are not identically distributed in space for instance, safe nest site vs. feeding grounds for birds and mammals. In such a case the baseline habitat is actually a mosaic of microhabitats, and the degree of fragmentation must be evaluated against this mosaic (Addicott *et al.* 1987). An organism-centered perspective is fruitful also in this context. Critical factors can be quite subtle. For example, in Australian eucalypt forests both folivorous marsupials and birds have patchy distributions that are based on the nutrient content of the foliage: forests that appear homogeneous are actually highly fragmented for these species, and human-induced fragmentation following cutting has quite different consequences depending on whether or not these high-quality habitats are preserved (Braithwaite *et al.* 1988, 1989).

INTERMEDIATE CONCLUSIONS: WHAT IS, AND WHAT IS NOT 'FRAGMENTATION'?

My purpose in this section has been to demonstrate that a merely 'phenomenological' definition of fragmentation is insufficient for three main reasons:

1. The effect of forest loss is, on a phenomenological level, indistinguishable from the effect of fragmentation, but to understand the processes triggered by fragmentation, these must be separated. It is clear that forest loss is a threat to species that require forest but we must also know whether the spatial configuration of the remaining forest is of consequence.

2. Landscapes undisturbed by human activity are not homogeneous but, in contrast, comprise mosaics of different ecosystem types and, furthermore, these mosaics are constantly changing as a consequence of natural disturbances. Such dynamics form a proper baseline for assessing fragmentation.

3. Fragmentation threatens different species in different ways, depending on species-specific characteristics and the type of the environment. This multiplicity can be assimilated in thinking about fragmentation by adopting an organism-centered perspective.

These considerations are summarized in Figure 7.1. We need to understand fragmentation more rigorously than what a mere phenomenological approach allows. Fragmentation is defined through its opposite, which is continuity: a forest that is not continuous is fragmented. But as we saw, there are many possible criteria to use in defining continuity, depending on which organism we are interested in and whether we focus on the individual, population, or evolutionary scale. Furthermore, we can expect that there is variation across biogeographic regions and environmental types in how particular criteria 'translate' on maps, measured in standard units.

This emphasizes the importance of context in understanding fragmentation. Fragmentation is disruption of continuity, but the particular type of continuity that is disrupted is always contextual in a particular situation and should be specified with respect to organisms, or ecological processes, or preferably both (Haila 1990, Lord and Norton 1990, Wiens 1995).

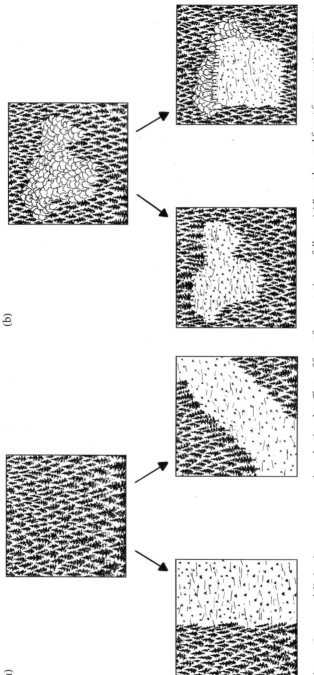

Fig. 7.1. Conceptual distinctions are necessary in evaluating the effects of forest fragmentation, as follows: (a) Forest loss and forest fragmentation are different issues: the former (left-hand side) means reduction of the total area of forest, whereas the latter (right-hand side) means reduction plus isolation of the remaining forest patches from each other. (b) Forests are heterogeneous because of stand type variation. Harvest designed to follow natural landscape features (left-hand side) has less drastic effects than harvest designed without concern for natural landscape features (right-hand side); in the former case the natural patch structure remains intact whereas in the latter case the patch structure becomes fragmented.

(a)

(b)

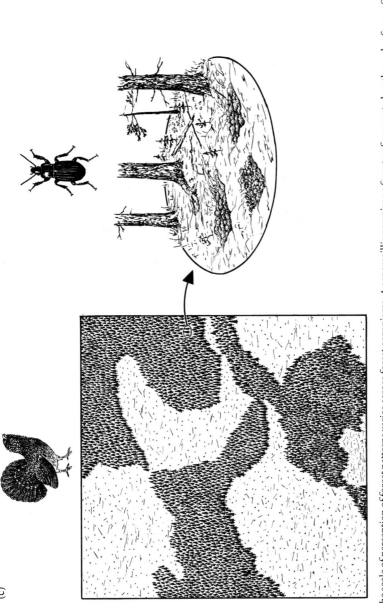

Fig. 7.1. (cont.) (c) The scale of perception of forest patterns varies across forest organisms. A capercaillie perceives a forest as fragmented on the scale of tens of hectares (left-hand side) whereas a forest-dwelling carabid beetle (*Agonum mannerheimi*, a denizen of moist *Sphagnum*-dominated patches within the forest) perceives variation in forest floor vegetation on the scale of tens of square meters (right-hand side).

The mechanisms of fragmentation

To understand ecological change produced by fragmentation we must be able to identify mechanisms driving such change. 'Mechanism' is a synonym for 'cause'. Causes are not immediately visible in the phenomena themselves – if they were, no science would be needed. For instance, a particular orchid may disappear from small rainforest fragments isolated by open pastures because its obligate pollinator bees do not readily cross open country. One clearly cannot explain the disappearance unless this critical mechanism is identified. In biology, in particular, temporal processes have a prominent role in causal explanation because all biological systems are historical, i.e., they are shaped by past events (Depew and Weber 1995).

Observed patterns are usually amenable to alternative explanations which cannot be told apart by investigating the pattern alone. This is one aspect of the 'pattern' vs. 'process' dilemma familiar in ecological research: patterns need to be systematically described but they can only be explained by identifying the underlying causal mechanisms (Watt 1947, Wiens 1984).

In management practice this distinction is not equally critical as in scientific explanation, however. Phenomenological observations and models can be valuable as well. For instance, for preserving the whole suite of species in a particular region, knowing their distribution patterns helps a lot even if one were unable to give a causal explanation to the patterns (Margules 1989, Margules and Austin 1991). Whether knowledge of causal mechanisms is necessary for managers depends on how specific the management task is. If the task were to preserve the orchid used as an example above, recognition of the actual mechanism causing its disappearance from the forest fragments would be useful.

'APPARENT IMPOVERISHMENT' IN FOREST FRAGMENTS

The recent history of fragmentation studies demonstrates that patterns may be deceptive. Many characteristics of ecological assemblages in fragments as well as on real islands are expected to vary systematically with fragment or island area. This is most obvious in the case of species number which is expected to be smaller on a small island or fragment than on a large one just because a small fragment hosts a smaller total number of individuals (Preston 1948, Helliwell 1976, Connor and McCoy 1979, Haila and Järvinen 1981, Haila 1983). For instance, an island of ten hectares in the Åland archipelago in southwest Finland has, on average, 30–40 pairs of breeding birds every summer. One could not possibly find there the whole breeding fauna of the nearby main island of Åland which includes more than 100 species (Haila 1983).

This point was originally raised by Helliwell (1976) as a criticism against contemporaneous authors who concluded on the basis of mere lists of bird species present in British woods of varying size that bird assemblages in small woodlots were 'impoverished'. His point is worth citing in full (p. 412): 'It appears to me that [they] have not asked the relevant question in this connection which is whether a particular species of bird is likely to be found in a standard unit of, say, 10 ha, no matter whether this is isolated or part of a 100 ha wood.' The warning has often gone unnoticed, and the claim has been repeated over and over again that the smaller species number recorded in small forest fragments than in large ones in itself indicates faunal 'impoverishment' (for criticisms, see Haila et al. 1983, Haila et al. 1993a, Andrén 1994).

An analogous problem relates to 'turnover', that is, year-to-year change in the list of species present on a particular small island or fragment. The species list is expected to change to some degree merely because individuals of particular species change their location from year to year although the population level on the regional scale would remain unchanged. This phenomenon concerns primarily vagile species such as birds, and has been documented in northern Europe both on small islands (Haila and Hanski 1987) and in small forest fragments (Haila et al. 1993a).

These examples give another demonstration of the pattern – process distinction. A smaller species number in a small fragment than in a large fragment is a 'pattern'. One possible explanation to this pattern is simply that the total number of individuals is smaller in the small fragment than in the large one. However, there may also be other mechanisms at play, and the challenge is to identify these.

The average rate of the decline in species number with decreasing area is expressed by the well-known species–area curve (Preston 1962, MacArthur and Wilson 1967; for discussions in a conservation biology context see Hunter 1990, Noss and Csuti 1994, and May et al. 1995). To get a concrete idea of the relationship we can envisage small forest fragments as 'taking small samples' from a species 'pool' in the surrounding area (Preston 1960, Connor and McCoy 1979, Haila 1983). The more evenly the abundances of different species are distributed in the 'pool', the steeper the curve. In this way, the shape of the species–area relationship depends on the species–abundance distribution of the total species 'pool' from which the fragment assemblages are derived.

The expected species–area relationship in any particular situation gives a realistic expectation for the 'apparent impoverishment' of assemblages in small fragments. Forest fragmentation is expected to have an additional effect, differentially on different species according to their species-specific characteristics. It is highly likely that the total effect is nonlinear relative to area, i.e., negligible at first when fragmentation of a continuous landscape begins but then getting important after a certain threshold in the degree of fragmentation has been reached.

It is now time to begin a systematic survey of potential mechanisms. Negative effects on particular species are realized through mechanisms on the population level (Wiens 1990, Caughley 1994). The challenge is to specify links between the general effects of fragmentation on the one hand and critical population processes, natality, mortality, and dispersal, on the other hand.

EFFECTS ON NATALITY

If natality of a particular species in a fragmented landscape is consistently too low to compensate for mortality of the reproducing adults, then the population requires continuous immigration from other parts of its range, i.e., the fragmented environment constitutes a 'sink' which is supported by individuals from a 'source' (Wiens and Rotenberry 1981, Pulliam 1988). Considerable evidence suggests that such a 'source–sink' structure holds true in the eastern United States for a set of migratory bird species in which population declines have been observed in recent decades (Robbins et al. 1989, Askins et al. 1990, Sauer et al. 1996).

However, this observed population trend is another pattern that may have several alternative explanations. To attribute the population declines to forest fragmentation, we need data on variation in reproductive success of birds as a function of degree of forest fragmentation (Donovan et al. 1995, Robinson et al. 1995, Villard et al. 1995). The ovenbird (Seiurus aurocapillus) appears to have a greater number of unpaired males and lower breeding success in small fragments in agricultural landscapes than in large continuous forests (Villard et al. 1993). Such evidence is not unanimous across species, however. The wood thrush (Hylocichla mustelina) did not show lowered reproductive success in a fragmented environment compared with a continuous one in the data of Sauer et al. (1996); see also Roth and Johnson (1993).

Two mutually reinforcing explanations are generally given for this source–sink structure, namely, increased predation rate on bird nests in small forest fragments close to fragment edges, and nest parasitism by the brown-headed cowbird (*Molothrus ater*). Ample evidence for both mechanisms is available. Increased nest predation rate in small fragments has been confirmed by experiments using dummy nests; the results of such experiments were reviewed by Paton (1994) and Andrén (1995). Data on cowbird parasitism have also been summarized (Hahn and Hatfield 1995).

However, there is quite a lot of variation in the results of empirical studies on nest predation and parasitism. This variation suggests that the proportion and configuration of forests in the landscape surrounding the fragments studied modify the effect. For instance, a general pattern seems to be that nest predation increases at the edge predominantly in fragments surrounded by farmland (Andrén 1995), while this does not happen near edges separating different forest stands (more about edges in Chapter 6). Similarly for nest paratisitism by the brown cowbird: in Minnesota in a primarily forested environment, no statistically significant difference was detected in an edge vs. interior comparison (Hanski *et al.* 1996).

To understand fragmentation as a conservation problem, studies that do not detect harmful effects are as important as ones that do detect them. As an example, density variation and reproductive success of the black woodpecker (*Dryocopus martius*) were studied in two landscape types in central Sweden (Tjernberg *et al.* 1993). One of the landscapes was dominated by forest (80%) and the other by farmland, forest comprising only 26% of the area. The total density of the black woodpecker was lower in the farmland-dominated landscape. However, when calculated per forest area and not per total land area, the density was the same in both landscapes. The mean number of forest fragments included in the woodpecker home ranges in the farmland-dominated landscape was 76. Furthermore, no differences were detected in reproduction parameters (clutch size, laying date, nesting success, nestling size) between the two landscapes. Thus, in this study the effect of forest fragmentation could be equated with pure habitat loss. Interestingly, the closely related North American species, the pileated woodpecker (*Dryocopus pileatus*), is also able to patch together its home range from a set of small forest patches (Noss and Csuti 1994).

A different pattern was found in a study on the effect of forest fragmentation on tawny owls (*Strix aluco*) in a forest–farmland landscape in Britain (Redpath 1995). Radio-telemetry was used to obtain information on home range and territorial behaviour of the owls. Home ranges were smaller in continuous woods than in the fragmented environment, but the owls occurred in a higher density per unit of woodland in the latter type of environment suggesting that they also utilized open areas in between the forest fragments for hunting. The relationship between woodlot size and breeding success was quadratic, that is, fledging success was higher in intermediate sized fragments (4–10 ha) than in very small (<4 ha) or large (>10 ha) fragments. The turnover of territories was also lowest in the intermediate-sized woodlots.

EFFECTS ON MORTALITY

The most unambiguous type of mortality caused by forest fragmentation occurs when the fragments are so small that physical or biotic disturbance from the surroundings leads to a complete change in the conditions in the fragment: sedentary organisms such as plants just perish. This is what happens in very small fragments both in the tropics (Bierregaard et al. 1992) and in the boreal forest (Esseen 1994). The pressure from surrounding, human-modified areas on small fragments of native forest vegetation is a universal threat, often furthered by disturbance caused by livestock (Janzen 1986, Scougall et al. 1993).

While it is fairly easy to observe increased mortality in plants in small fragments, similar data on animal populations are much more laborious to obtain. John Litvaitis with his coworkers demonstrated in a series of studies that mortality in New England cottontail (*Sylvilagus transitionalis*) increased in small fragments (<2.5 ha) compared with larger ones (>5 ha) (Barbour and Litvaitis 1993, Oehler and Litvaitis 1996). The critical mechanism seems to be predation: several mammalian predators favor fragmented landscapes during some part of the year. Also, the rabbits find less food in small fragments: their feeding niche is broadened (Barbour and Litvaitis 1993) and their physiological condition is more stressed in small than in large fragments (Villafuerte et al. 1997).

Similar results have been obtained in an intensive population study of the snowshoe hare (*Lepus americanus*) in Wisconsin (Keith et al. 1993). A population of hares was monitored over a three-year period in an environment with variable sized fragments of prime habitat (range 5 to 28 ha). Neither density nor reproductive success of the hares differed between small and large fragments but mortality, due to predation by coyotes (*Canis latrans*), was higher in the small ones.

EFFECTS ON DISPERSAL

Dispersal has long been known as one of the main factors influencing population dynamics (e.g., Andrewartha and Birch 1954). Dispersal is also a critical factor in both insular and fragmented environments; after all, isolation was a major variable in the theory of island biogeography of MacArthur and Wilson (1967). Unfortunately, dispersal is a notoriously difficult subject to study empirically.

It is mainly in real island situations that the importance of dispersal has been demonstrated, and usually indirectly, by following population fluctuations on islands compared with a nearby mainland. In species that have pronounced population fluctuations, dispersal to small islands can be expected to vary with population size on the mainland. Small mammals have provided many examples, no doubt because their population variations are fairly easy to monitor. For example, shrews on islands in Finnish lakes (Hanski 1986, Peltonen and Hanski 1991), and field voles (*Microtus agrestis*) in an archipelago on the southern Finnish coast (Pokki 1981) have shown this pattern. Dispersal over ice in the winter has been identified as an important immigration 'filter' in small mammals in the Great Lakes in North America (Lomolino 1986, 1993).

Small mammals favoring forested landscape do not venture into open farmland but use strips of wooded habitat to cross agricultural landscapes (Merriam 1988). There are fewer data on the effect of stand variation on mammal dispersal in forested landscapes. Results of one study on the Eurasian red squirrel (*Sciurus vulgaris*) showed a managed landscape to be 'functionally continuous', i.e., forest fragmentation had little effects on dispersal (Andrén and Delin 1994). Ongoing radio-telemetry research suggests that the flying squirrel (*Pteromys volans*) is more vulnerable to fragmentation caused by cutting (Hanski 1998).

Dispersal across fragmented landscapes may pose problems also for sedentary birds. The significance of roadside vegetation for dispersal in the Western Australian wheatbelt has been demonstrated for many species of birds (Saunders 1989, Saunders and de Rebeira 1991). Such effects are also amply demonstrated in tropical rainforests (Bierregaard and Lovejoy 1989). There is species-specific variation in this case again: honeyeaters in Australia and hummingbirds in the Brazilian Amazon exploit high-quality food patches even in forest fragments isolated by open country (Lambeck and Saunders 1993, Stouffer and Bierregaard 1995).

Linear distance may be a weak measure of isolation and its counterpart, connectivity. A distant fragment in a landscape with high connectivity will be less isolated than a closer fragment within a landscape with low connectivity. The importance of connectivity has been demonstrated using simulations (Andrén 1996, Bascompte and Solé 1996). Simulations show consistently that the relationship between landscape pattern and connectivity is nonlinear: when forest is removed from a formerly continuously forested landscape, the connectivity of landscape pattern drops abruptly when around one half of the original area is destroyed. However, whether this affects particular species depends on their characteristics.

Data on the effects of fragmentation on dispersal are largely limited to birds and mammals, as was the case with natality and mortality, but it may be possible to make enlightened guesses concerning other groups of organisms. Generalizations across biogeographic zones would be unwise; in the following I describe some examples from the northern boreal forest (see also Niemelä 1997). Generally the dispersal ability of northern forest insects may be quite good simply because there is considerable year to year variation in where the most suitable sites are likely to be found, particularly in young forest stands (Niemelä *et al.* 1996). To take an obvious example, insects specialized to colonize recent burns are obliged to be efficient dispersers.

One might draw contradictory conclusions on whether arthropods living in old-growth forests are vulnerable to forest fragmentation. In temperate forests these species often occur in tiny local populations which may be very sedentary, thus suggesting a high degree of vulnerability (Thomas and Morris 1995). In boreal conditions, on the other hand, many rare beetles that are strictly specialized to a specific type of decaying wood show remarkable flexibility with respect to macrohabitat features occurring, for instance, both inside old-growth forest and on recent clearcuts (Kaila *et al.* 1997). Species that 'track' an ephemeral resource such as decaying wood of a particular species and age across the landscape are probably efficient dispersers, but we have no idea about the distances involved. On the other hand, in some cases it is clear that the local continuity of high-quality habitat is critical (Siitonen and Martikainen 1994). Habitat continuity is certainly important for plant taxa that are specialized to old-growth boreal forest such as lichens, mosses and fungi (Esseen *et al.* 1992, Kuusinen 1995). The critical question is: What kind of disruptions break continuity (Haila 1994)?

An interesting but not much investigated question is the significance of social structure and nesting habits in dispersal. For instance, social structure is important for the success of territorial wood-ants (*Formica rufa* group) in fragmented boreal forest in northern Europe: small fragments are inhabited by monogynous species that disperse through nuptial flights, whereas large fragments and continuous forest are dominated by polygynous species that disperse mainly through nest budding (Punttila 1996).

INTERMEDIATE CONCLUSIONS: MULTIPLICITY OF MECHANISMS AND SYNERGISTIC EFFECTS

The effects of fragmentation on different species in different conditions vary enormously, and many alternative causal mechanisms are at play. Furthermore, the mechanisms may interact; for instance, predators may destroy the nests or eat the adults of their prey, or do both. Such complex mechanisms can be evaluated by using organisms themselves as a 'measuring instrument' in assessing fragmentation. Survival is obviously a key criterion; others might include the physiological state of individuals (Villafuerte *et al.* 1997) or individual behavior and movement patterns (Hanski *et al.* 1992).

Synergistic effects are expected also between the two major consequences of forest clearance, namely, fragmentation and loss. Because of such synergisms there is no substitute for investigations which cover several groups of organisms and take into account the whole range of ecological processes; the work done in Western Australia sets a good standard in this respect (Hobbs and Saunders 1993). General surveys can be used for screening larger groups of species to identify those that are probably most vulnerable to fragmentation (Haila and Hanski 1984, Helle 1984). Carefully designed manipulations and experiments are also needed, especially such that cover many different taxa and ecosystem processes (Bierregaard *et al.* 1992, Margules 1992). Experimental work often reveals contrasting responses in ecologically similar species (Margules *et al.* 1994).

Although fragmentation effects are amply demonstrated, their contribution to biodiversity decline in any particular situation is a more open question. For instance, birds, which are among the best known groups of organisms, include no unambiguous cases of extinction caused by fragmentation (Simberloff 1995). Forest loss is the most important process driving population extinctions, by far.

Theoretical perspectives

The previous sections of this chapter seem to suggest that the ecological effects of forest fragmentation are extremely variable from case to case. This raises the question: Is it possible to place these effects within a broader framework of ecological theory? Theory is not a value in itself but a necessary and integral part of scientific work, a tool for making systematic generalizations and predictions (e.g., Hacking 1983). In this context I only point out alternative ways in which theoretical ideas are fruitful in thinking about fragmentation.

Ideas of fragmentation are heavily indebted to two ecological theories, namely, island biogeography (MacArthur and Wilson 1967) and metapopulation dynamics (Levins 1969, Hanski and Gilpin 1991). These are both deductive, formal theories which aim at deriving predictions from a set of assumptions. I have already referred several times to island biogeography. One of the aims of metapopulation theory is to predict what proportion of fragments in a fragment 'archipelago' is inhabited by a particular species, depending on its extinction and colonization rates in single fragments. Were such predictions reliable, this would clearly be an enormous asset in managing particular metapopulations living in fragmented environments.

Both of these theoretical frameworks have been criticized, for similar reasons: they make quite restrictive assumptions about conditions under which they are likely to be relevant; for island biogeography, see Simberloff (1976), Gilbert (1980), Williamson (1989) and Haila (1990) and for metapopulation dynamics see Harrison (1994), Doak and Mills (1994) and Simberloff (1995). However, all deductive theories have a restricted domain of validity; this is not a sufficient reason for rejecting any theory (Van Valen 1976). The critical question is whether or not a particular theory can be applied in a stimulating way in specific situations. Deductive theories in biology show what is possible starting from particular assumptions, not what will actually happen (Lewontin 1985). As an example, Hanski and Thomas (1994) used the metapopulation theory for deriving predictions from census data for the survival of butterflies in systems of habitat patches; it would be virtually impossible to do this from the data alone.

Another stimulating theoretical perspective, albeit less formalized than the previous ones, is provided by ideas on landscape heterogeneity (Chapters 4 and 5). For reasons already stated in this chapter, the overall heterogeneity of the landscape in which particular forest fragments are located has a critical influence on ecological processes in those fragments (Lord and Norton 1990, Fahrig and Merriam 1994). Spatial heterogeneity is inherently stochastic in detail. This has two interesting corollaries as regards the responses of species to fragmentation. First, there is considerable unpredictability in site selection patterns of organisms; for instance, a bird territory which offers singing posts, rich feeding grounds, and a safe nest site can be put together in several possible ways (Haila *et al.* 1996). Second, adequate scaling becomes a critical issue. The influence of broadscale landscape features on ecological processes in small, isolated forest stands is a very difficult problem to address empirically, but evidence of such an effect is accumulating particularly in birds (McGarigal and McComb 1995, Jokimäki and Huhta 1996).

Theoretical thinking can play yet another role in research by helping to draw empirical generalizations. A potentially useful type of generalization would be to explain the ecological characteristics that make some species vulnerable (Lawton 1995). For instance, in northern Fennoscandia, sedentary bird species seem to be particularly at risk compared to migratory species (Järvinen *et al.* 1977, Helle and Järvinen 1986, Väisänen *et al.* 1986, Virkkala 1991), and similar conclusions have been drawn in the Pacific Northwest in the United States (Rosenberg and Raphael 1986). In the eastern United States, in contrast, tropical migrants are considered most vulnerable (Wilcove and Robinson 1990). This difference may reflect different evolutionary histories of the regional bird faunas (Mönkkönen and Welsh 1994). Regionally derived generalizations are not necessarily valid elsewhere; for instance, among Western Australian birds, passerines have been more vulnerable than non-passerines (Saunders 1989), but this observation can certainly not be extended to other areas.

Another, weaker, but still useful, generalization would describe the proportion of species in different taxa that mainly live in old-growth forest. In southern Finland in several taxa such as carabid beetles and ground-living spiders this proportion seems to be around 5–10% (Haila *et al.* 1994, Niemelä 1997); however, in saproxylic beetles the proportion is certainly higher (Väisänen *et al.* 1993).

If no empirical generalization seems adequate, this is also a theoretically interesting result. This implies that processes affecting the phenomenon of interest are complex and context-specific and need to be known in detail. A review by Mark Williamson of the biology of colonization offers an example: no generalizations seem to be at hand on what kind of species are likely to be successful colonists except for a crude estimate of the proportion of successes ('tens rule') (Williamson 1996).

Management implications

The challenge for managers is to realize the potential significance of forest fragmentation and to identify measures to alleviate harmful effects. The context-specific character of fragmentation, emphasized in this chapter, is no new principle for managers: managers always face situations that are unique in some respects but resemble others in other respects. They have to decide which differences matter.

I think it is fruitful to formulate the management challenges as a series of specific questions that should be answered in any particular situation:

1. What is the smallest fragment size at which a fragment is still like a forest? Such a limit is defined by the scale at which fragments are completely changed to a different type of environment. There are probably no absolute rules in this regard – depending on the context, one can argue that almost any patch of original forest type is valuable for some forest organisms, possibly even for the rare ones (e.g., Lord and Norton 1990, Haila 1994). However, some 'target organisms' can be used to derive numerical estimates. In northwest European boreal forests, for example, fragments in the size range of a few hectares to tens of hectares are certainly valuable for birds on the scale of single breeding pairs, and for insects on the scale of local populations. For preserving regional populations of birds or insects larger total areas are naturally needed, but whether these need to be contiguous or not must be assessed separately.

2. What are the forest types in which local habitat continuity is particularly important? In northern Europe these include, for instance, natural fire refugia dominated by old spruce stands (Esseen *et al.* 1992). Such forest types require particular attention.

3. What is the role of corridors, i.e., linear strips of natural or semi-natural vegetation that link larger patches (Hunter 1990), in promoting dispersal across the landscape? In heavily fragmented agricultural landscapes corridors can be important (Saunders and Hobbs 1991). Managed forests, in contrast, are dynamic mosaics of different stand types that probably provide connectivity for many species but are not, strictly speaking, corridors. It is likely that corridors created by natural variation in topography and soils such as riparian habitats are valuable and worth preserving.

4. Is disturbance to the fragments from the outside important? Disturbance can be alleviated by buffer zones or, for instance, by fencing off livestock in agricultural settings. However, in predominantly forested landscapes general rules cannot be given except that the fragments need to be large enough not to be pure edge.

5. What is forest composition on a broader spatial scale? Characteristics such as the area proportion of forest types and age classes as well as distances among old-growth stands need to be monitored (see Chapter 4).

6. What species should we focus upon? There are no differences in the inherent value of different species, but it is simply impossible to consider all species simultaneously. One way to approach this question is to manage for 'umbrella species' which by their existence assure that suitable conditions are maintained for a set of 'target species' as well. For instance, the white-backed woodpecker (*Dendrocopus leucotos*) is a possible umbrella species for saproxylic beetles living in decaying trunks of deciduous trees in northern Europe (Martikainen *et al.* 1998). The 'umbrella species' should represent different characteristic scales. In northern Europe, for instance, the capercaillie might be a good 'umbrella' for managing regional forest composition, the flying squirrel for managing landscape structure, and particular passerine birds and forest insects for managing stand structure. I do not think big predators can be used as 'umbrella species' in forest management because of their large home ranges and catholic environmental requirements. For instance, the recent recovery of the timber wolf (*Canis lupus*) in the western Great Lakes region in the United States can be attributed to discontinuation of persecution, not to any particular features of forest structure (Mladenoff *et al.* 1995).

Summary

The term 'forest fragmentation' refers to a change in the spatial configuration of forests so that formerly continuous forest areas turn into small stands isolated from other stands by intensively modified land such as cropland, pastures, clearcuts and silvicultural plantations. The crux of the matter is disruption of continuity. The harmful consequences that follow from fragmentation are usually divided into three main types: (a) effects of the reduction in area of the remaining fragments; (b) effects of increasing isolation of the fragments from each other; and (c) effects of increasing disturbance from the surroundings. In elaborating the consequences it is, however, necessary to make the following specifications: (a) forest fragmentation and forest loss must be distinguished from each other; (b) the processes which are disrupted because of fragmentation must be specified; and (c) the dynamic heterogeneity of natural landscapes must be acknowledged as a standard for comparison. Real islands can serve to a certain degree as analogues for fragmented environments but they also show important differences with respect to landscape dynamics. Above all, we should understand ecologically harmful mechanisms triggered by fragmentation. I review research on such mechanisms which generally seem to be highly species- and environment-specific. No simple, universal rules can be given to mitigate the effects of fragmentation in forest management, but I formulate a checklist of six questions that should be considered in every management situation.

Further readings

Curtis (1956) is a classical and recommendable natural-history account of the effect of fragmentation on forest vegetation in the United States Midwest; Harris (1984) is a concise overview of fragmentation and forests. In a conservation biology context, the effects of fragmentation have been reviewed by Hunter (1990), Saunders *et al.* (1991), Haila *et al.* (1993b), Fahrig and Merriam (1994) and Noss and Csuti (1994); the essays in Hobbs and Saunders (1993) and Laurance and Bierregaard (1997) give a feel for the variability of the patterns. The important background theories, island biogeography and metapopulation theory, were introduced by MacArthur and Wilson (1967) and Levins (1969), respectively, and later overviews are offered by Williamson (1981) and Hanski and Gilpin (1989), respectively.

Literature cited

Addicott, J. F., J. M. Aho, M. F. Antolin, D. K. Padilla, J. S. Richardson, and D. A. Soluk. 1987. Ecological neighbourhoods: scaling environmental patterns. *Oikos* **49**:199–204.

Andrén, H. 1994. Effect of habitat fragmentation on birds and mammals in landscapes with different proportions of suitable habitat: a review. *Oikos* **71**:355–66.

1995. Effects of landscape composition on predation rates at habitat edges. Pp. 225–55 in L. Hansson, L. Fahrig and G. Merriam (eds). *Mosaic Landscapes and Ecological Processes*. Chapman and Hall, London.

1996. Population responses to habitat fragmentation: statistical power and the random sample hypothesis. *Oikos* **76**:235–42.

Andrén, H., and A. Delin. 1994. Habitat selection in the Eurasian red squirrel, *Sciurus vulgaris*, in relation to forest fragmentation. *Oikos* **70**:43–8.

Andrewartha, H. G., and L. C. Birch. 1954. *The Distribution and Abundance of Animals*. University of Chicago Press, Chicago.

Askins, R. A., J. F. Lynch, and R. Greenberg. 1990. Population declines in migratory birds in eastern North America. *Current Ornithology* **7**:1–57.

Barbour, M. S., and J. A. Litvaitis. 1993. Niche dimensions of New England cottontails in relation to habitat patch size. *Oecologia* (Berlin) **95**:321–7.

Bascompte, J., and R. V. Solé. 1996. Habitat fragmentation and extinction thresholds in spatially explicit models. *Journal of Animal Ecology* **65**:465–73.

Bierregaard, R. O. J., and T. E. Lovejoy. 1989. Effects of forest fragmentation on Amazonian understory bird communities. *Acta Amazonica* **19**:215–41.

Bierregaard, R. O. J., T. E. Lovejoy, V. Kapos, A. A. dos Santos, and R. W. Hutchings. 1992. The biological dynamics of tropical rainforest fragments. A prospective comparison of fragments and continuous forest. *BioScience* **42**:859–66.

Braithwaite, L. W., D. L. Binns, and R. D. Nowlan. 1988. The distribution of arboreal marsupials in relation to eucalypt forest types in the Eden (NSW) Woodchip Concession Area. *Australian Wildlife Research* **15**:363–73.

Braithwaite, L. W., M. P. Austin, M. Clayton, J. Turner, and A. O. Nicholls. 1989. On predicting the presence of birds in Eucalyptus forest types. *Biological Conservation* **50**:33–50.

Burgess, R. C., and D. M. Sharpe (eds). 1981. *Forest Island Dynamics in Man-dominated Landscapes*. Springer Verlag, New York.

Calder, W. A. III 1984. *Size, Function, and Life History*. Harvard University Press, Cambridge, Ma.

Caughley, G. 1994. Directions in conservation biology. *Journal of Animal Ecology* **63**:215–44.

Connor, E. F., and E. D. McCoy. 1979. The statistics and biology of the species–area relationship. *American Naturalist* **113**:791–833.

Curtis, J. T. 1956. The modification of mid-latitude grasslands and forests by man. Pp. 721–36 in W. L. J. Thomas (ed.). *Man's Role in Changing the Face of the Earth*. University of Chicago Press, Chicago.

Delcourt, R. H., P. A. Delcourt, and T. Webb. 1983. Dynamic plant ecology: the spectrum of vegetational change in space and time. *Quaternary Science Reviews* **1**:153–75.

Depew, D. J., and B. H. Weber. 1995. *Darwinism Evolving. Systems Dynamics and the Genealogy of Natural Selection*. MIT Press, Cambridge, Ma.

Doak, D. F., and L. S. Mills. 1994. A useful role for theory in conservation. *Ecology* **75**:615–26.

Dolman, P. M., and W. J. Sutherland. 1994. The response of bird populations to habitat loss. *Ibis* **137**:S38–S46.

Donovan, T. M., F. R. Thompson, J. Faaborg, and J. R. Probst. 1995. Reproductive success of migratory birds in habitat sources and sinks. *Conservation Biology* **9**:1380–95.

Esseen, P.-A. 1994. Tree mortality patterns after experimental fragmentation of old-growth conifer forest. *Biological Conservation* **68**:1–10.

Esseen, P.-A., B. Ehnström, L. Ericson, and K. Sjöberg. 1992. Boreal forests – the focal habitats of Fennoscandia. Pp. 252–325 in L. Hansson, (ed.). *Ecological Principles of Nature Conservation*. Elsevier, London.

Fahrig, L., and G. Merriam. 1994. Conservation of fragmented populations. *Conservation Biology* **8**:50–9.

Gilbert, F. S. 1980. The equilibrium theory of island biogeography: fact or fiction? *Journal of Biogeography* 7:209–35.

Hacking, I. 1983. *Representing and Intervening. Introductory Topics in the Philosophy of Natural Science.* Cambridge University Press, Cambridge.

Hahn, D. C., and J. S. Hatfield. 1995. Parasitism at the landscape scale: cowbirds prefer forest. *Conservation Biology* 9:1415–24.

Haila, Y. 1983. Land birds on northern islands: a sampling metaphor for insular colonization. *Oikos* 41:334–51.

——— 1990. Toward an ecological definition of an island: a northwest European perspective. *Journal of Biogeography* 17:561–8.

——— 1991. Implications of landscape heterogeneity for bird conservation. *Acta Congr. Intern. Ornithol.* 20:2286–91.

——— 1994. Preserving ecological diversity in boreal forests: ecological background, research, and management. *Annales Zoologici Fennici* 31:203–17.

Haila, Y., and I. K. Hanski. 1984. Methodology for studying the effect of habitat fragmentation on land birds. *Annales Zoologici Fennici* 21:393–7.

——— 1987. Habitat and territory overlap of breeding passerines in the mosaic environment of small, northern islands. *Ornis Fennica* 64:37–49.

Haila, Y., and O. Järvinen. 1981. The underexploited potential of bird censuses in insular ecology. *Studies in Avian Biology* 6:559–65.

Haila, Y., O. Järvinen, and S. Kuusela. 1983. Colonization of islands by land birds: Prevalence functions in a Finnish archipelago. *Journal of Biogeography* 10:499–531.

Haila, Y., I. K. Hanski, and S. Raivio. 1993a. Turnover of breeding birds in small forest fragments: the 'sampling' colonization hypothesis corroborated. *Ecology* 74:714–25.

Haila, Y., D. A. Saunders, and R. J. Hobbs. 1993b. What do we presently understand about ecosystem fragmentation? Pp. 45–55 in D. A. Saunders, R. J. Hobbs and P. R. Ehrlich (eds). *Nature Conservation 3. The Reconstruction of Fragmented Ecosystems.* Surrey Beatty & Sons, Chipping Norton, NSW.

Haila, Y., I. K. Hanski, J. Niemelä, P. Punttila, S. Raivio, and H. Tukia. 1994. Forestry and the boreal fauna: matching management with natural forest dynamics. *Annales Zoologici Fennici* 31:187–202.

Haila, Y., A. O. Nicholls, I. K. Hanski, and S. Raivio. 1996. Stochasticity in bird habitat selection: year-to-year changes in territory locations in a boreal forest bird assemblage. *Oikos* 76:536–52.

Hanski, I. 1986. Population dynamics of shrews on small islands accord with the equilibrium theory. *Biological Journal of the Linnean Society* 28:23–36.

Hanski, I. K. 1998. Home ranges and habitat use in the declining flying squirrel, *Pteromys volans*, in managed forests. *Wildlife Biology* 4:33–46.

Hanski, I., and M. Gilpin. 1991. Metapopulation dynamics: brief history and conceptual domain. *Biological Journal of the Linnean Society* 42:3–16.

Hanski, I., and C. D. Thomas. 1994. Metapopulation dynamics and conservation: a spatially explicit model applied to butterflies. *Biological Conservation* 68:167–80.

Hanski, I. K., Y. Haila, and A. Laurila. 1992. Variation in territorial behaviour and breeding fates among male chaffinches. *Ornis Fennica* **69**:72–81.

Hanski, I. K., T. J. Fenske, and G. J. Niemi. 1996. Lack of edge effect in nesting success of breeding birds in managed forest landscapes. *Auk* **113**:578–85.

Harris, L. D. 1984. *The Fragmented Forest: Island Biogeography Theory and the Preservation of Biotic Diversity.* University of Chicago Press, Chicago.

Harrison, S. 1994. Metapopulations and conservation. Pp. 111–28 in P. J. Edwards, R. M. May and N. R. Webb (eds). *Large-Scale Ecology and Conservation Biology.* Blackwell Scientific, Oxford.

Helle, P. 1984. Effects of habitat area on breeding bird communities in north-eastern Finland. *Annales Zoologici Fennici* **21**:421–5.

Helle, P., and O. Järvinen. 1986. Population trends of North Finnish land birds in relation to their habitat selection and changes in forest structure. *Oikos* **46**:107–15.

Helliwell, D. R. 1976. The effects of size and isolation on the conservation value of woodland sites in Britain. *Journal of Biogeography* **3**:407–16.

Hobbs, R. J. 1993. Effects of landscape fragmentation on ecosystem processes in the Western Australian wheatbelt. *Biological Conservation* **64**:193–201.

Hobbs, R. J., and D. A. Saunders (eds). 1993. *Reintegrating Fragmented Landscapes. Towards Sustainable Production and Nature Conservation.* Springer Verlag, New York.

Holling, C. S. 1992. The role of forest insects in structuring the boreal land-scape. Pp. 170–95 in H. H. Shugart, R. Leemans and G. B. Bonan (eds). *A Systems Analysis of the Global Boreal Forest.* Cambridge University Press, Cambridge.

Hunter, M. L. Jr. 1990. *Wildlife, Forests, and Forestry. Principles of Managing Forests for Biological Diversity.* Prentice Hall, Englewood Cliffs, N.J.

1993. Natural disturbance regimes as spatial models for managing boreal forests. *Biological Conservation* **65**:115–20.

Janzen, D. H. 1986. The eternal external threat. Pp. 286–303 in M. E. Soulé (ed.). *Conservation Biology. The Science of Scarcity and Diversity.* Sinauer, Sunderland, Ma.

Järvinen, O., K. Kuusela, and R. A. Väisänen. 1977. Effects of modern forestry on the numbers of breeding birds in Finland in 1945–1975. *Silva Fennica* **11**:284–94.

Jokimäki, J., and E. Huhta. 1996. Effects of landscape matrix and habitat structure on a bird community in northern Finland: a multi-scale approach. *Ornis Fennica* **73**:97–113.

Kaila, L., P. Martikainen, and P. Punttila. 1997. Dead trees left in clear-cuts benefit saproxylic Coleoptera adapted to natural disturbances in boreal forest. *Biodiversity and Conservation* **6**:1–18.

Keith, L. B., S. E. M. Bloomer, and T. Willebrand. 1993. Dynamics of a snowshoe hare population in fragmented habitat. *Canadian Journal of Zoology* **71**:1385–92.

Kuusinen, M. 1995. Cyanobacterial macrolichens on *Populus tremula* as indicators of forest continuity in Finland. *Biological Conservation* **75**:43–9.

Lambeck, R. J., and D. A. Saunders. 1993. The role of patchiness in recon-
    structed wheatbelt landscapes. Pp. 153–61 in D. A. Saunders, R. J. Hobbs
    and P. R. Ehrlich (eds). Nature Conservation 3. *The Reconstruction of
    Fragmented Ecosystems.* Surrey Beatty & Sons, Chipping Norton, NSW.
Laurance, W. F., and R. O. Bierregaard, Jr (eds). 1997. *Tropical Forest Remnants.
    Ecology, Management, and Conservation of Fragmented Communities.* The
    University of Chicago Press, Chicago.
Lawton, J. H. 1995. Population dynamic principles. Pp. 147–63 in J. H. Lawton
    and R. M. May (eds). *Extinction Rates.* Oxford University Press, Oxford.
Levins, R. 1968. *Evolution in Changing Environments.* Princeton University Press,
    Princeton.
    1969. Some demographic and genetic consequences of environmental het-
    erogeneity for biological control. *Bulletin of the Entomological Society of
    America* **15**:237–40.
Lewontin, R. 1985. Population genetics. Pp. 3–18 in P. J. Greenwood, P. W.
    Harvey and M. Slatkin (eds). *Laws of Nature: Essays in Honour of John
    Maynard Smith.* Cambridge University Press, Cambridge.
Lomolino, M. V. 1986. Mammalian community structure on islands: the impor-
    tance of immigration, extinction and interaction effects. *Biological Journal
    of the Linnean Society* **28**:1–21.
Lomolino, M. 1993. Winter filtering, immigrant selection and species composi-
    tion of insular mammals of Lake Huron. *Ecography* **16**:24–30.
Lord, J. M., and D. A. Norton. 1990. Scale and the spatial concept of fragmenta-
    tion. *Conservation Biology* **4**:197–202.
MacArthur, R. H., and E. O. Wilson. 1967. *The Theory of Island Biogeography.*
    Princeton University Press, Princeton, N.J.
Margules, C. R. 1989. Introduction to some Australian development in conserva-
    tion evaluation. *Biological Conservation* **50**:1–11.
    1992. The Wog Wog fragmentation experiment. *Environmental Conservation*
    19:316–25.
Margules, C. R., and M. P. Austin (eds). 1991. *Nature Conservation: Cost Effective
    Biological Surveys and Data Analysis.* Csiro, Australia.
Margules, C. R., G. A. Milkovits, and G. T. Smith. 1994. Contrasting effects of
    habitat fragmentation on the scorpion *Cercophonius squamata* and an
    amphipod. *Ecology* **75**:2033–42.
Martikainen, P., L. Kaila and Y. Haila. 1998. Threatened beetles in white-backed
    woodpecker habitats. *Conservation Biology* **12**:293–301.
May, R. M., J. H. Lawton, and N. E. Stork. 1995. Assessing extinction rates. Pp.
    1–24 in J. H. Lawton and R. M. May (eds). *Extinction Rates.* Oxford
    University Press, Oxford.
McGarigal, K., and W. C. McComb. 1995. Relationships between landscape
    structure and breeding birds in the Oregon coast range. *Ecological
    Monographs* **65**:235–60.
Merriam, G. 1988. Landscape dynamics in farmland. *Trends in Ecology and
    Evolution* **3**:16–20.

Mladenoff, D. J., T. A. Sickley, R. G. Haight, and A. P. Wydeven. 1995. A regional landscape analysis and a prediction of favourable grey wolf habitat in the northern Great Lakes region. *Conservation Biology* 9:279–94.

Mönkkönen, M., and D. A. Welsh. 1994. A biogeographical hypothesis of the effects of human caused landscape changes on the forest bird communities of Europe and North America. *Annales Zoologici Fennici* 31:61–70.

Niemelä, J. 1997. Invertebrates and boreal forest management. *Conservation Biology* 11:601–10.

Niemelä, J., Y. Haila, E. Halme, T. Pajunen, P. Punttila, and H. Tukia. 1987. Habitat preferences and conservation status of *Agonum mannerheimii* Dej. in Häme, southern Finland. *Notulae Entomologiae* 67:175–9.

Niemelä, J., Y. Haila, and E. Halme. 1988. Carabid beetles on isolated Baltic islands and on the adjacent Åland mainland: variation in colonization success. *Annales Zoologici Fennici* 24:179–94.

Niemelä, J., Y. Haila, E. Halme, T. Pajunen, and P. Punttila. 1992. Small-scale heterogeneity in the spatial distribution of carabid beetles in the southern Finnish taiga. *Journal of Biogeography* 19:173–81.

Niemelä, J., Y. Haila, and P. Punttila. 1996. The importance of small-scale heterogeneity in boreal forests: variation in diversity in forest-floor invertebrates across the succession gradient. *Ecography* 19:352–68.

Noss, R. F., and B. Csuti. 1994. Habitat fragmentation. Pp. 237–64 in G. K. Meffe and C. R. Carroll (eds). *Principles of Conservation Biology*. Sinauer Associates, Sunderland, Ma.

Oehler, J. D., and J. A. Litvaitis. 1996. The role of spatial scale in understanding responses of medium-sized carnivores to forest fragmentation. *Canadian Journal of Zoology* 74:2070–79.

Paton, P. W. 1994. The effect of edge on avian nest success: How strong is the evidence? *Conservation Biology* 8:17–26.

Peltonen, A., and I. Hanski. 1991. Patterns of island occupancy explained by colonization and extinction rates in shrews. *Ecology* 72:1698–708.

Pokki, J. 1981. Distribution, demography and dispersal of the field vole, *Microtus agrestis* (L.), in the Tvärminne archipelago, Finland. *Acta Zoologica Fennica* 164:1–48.

Preston, F. W. 1948. The commonness and rarity of species. *Ecology* 29:254–83.
    1960. Time and space and the variation of species. *Ecology* 41:611–27.
    1962. The canonical distribution of commonness and rarity. *Ecology* 43:185–215, 410–32.

Pulliam, H. R. 1988. Sources, sinks, and population regulation. *American Naturalist* 132:652–61.

Punttila, P. 1996. Succession, forest fragmentation, and the distribution of wood ants. *Oikos* 75:291–8.

Redpath, S. 1995. Habitat fragmentation and the individual: tawny owls *Strix aluco* in woodland patches. *Journal of Animal Ecology* 64:652–61.

Robbins, C. S., J. R. Sauer, R. S. Greenberg, and S. Droege. 1989. Population declines in North American birds that migrate to the Neotropics. *Proceedings of the National Academy of Sciences, USA* 86:7658–62.

Robinson, S. K., F. R. Thompson, T. M. Donovan, D. Whitehead, and J. Faaborg. 1995. Regional forest fragmentation and the nesting success of migratory birds. *Science* **267**:1987–90.

Rosenberg, K. V., and M. G. Raphael. 1986. Effects of forest fragmentation on vertebrates in douglas-fir forests. Pp. 263–72 in J. Verner, M. L. Morrison and C. J. Ralph (eds). Wildlife 2000. *Modeling Habitat Relationships of Terrestrial Vertebrates*. The University of Wisconsin Press, Madison, Wi.

Roth, R. R., and R. K. Johnson. 1993. Long-term dynamics of a Wood thrush population breeding in a forest fragment. *Auk* **110**:37–48.

Sauer, J. R., G. W. Pendleton, and B. G. Peterjohn. 1996. Evaluating causes of population change in North American insectivorous songbirds. *Conservation Biology* **10**:465–78.

Saunders, D. A. 1989. Changes in the avifauna of a region, district and remnant as a result of fragmentation of natural vegetation: the wheatbelt of Western Australia. A case study. *Biological Conservation* **50**:99–135.

Saunders, D. A., and C. P. de Rebeira. 1991. Values of corridors to avian populations in a fragmented landscape. Pp. 221–40 in D. A. Saunders and R. J. Hobbs (eds). *Nature Conservation 2: the Role of Corridors*. Surrey Beatty & Sons, Chipping Norton, NSW.

Saunders, D. A., and R. J. Hobbs (eds). 1991. *Nature Conservation 2: the Role of Corridors*. Surrey Beatty & Sons, Chipping Norton, NSW.

Saunders, D. A., R. J. Hobbs, and C. R. Margules. 1991. Biological consequences of ecosystem fragmentation: a review. *Conservation Biology* **5**:18–32.

Scougall, S. A., J. D. Majer, and R. J. Hobbs. 1993. Edge effects in grazed and ungrazed Western Australian wheatbelt remnants in relation to ecosystem reconstruction. Pp. 163–78 in D. A. Saunders, R. J. Hobbs and P. R. Ehrlich (eds). *Nature Conservation 3. The Reconstruction of Fragmented Ecosystems*. Surrey Beatty & Sons, Chipping Norton, NSW.

Siitonen, J., and P. Martikainen. 1994. Occurrence of rare and threatened insects living on decaying *Populus tremula*: a comparison between Finnish and Russian Karelia. *Scandinavian Journal of Forest Research* **9**:185–91.

Simberloff, D. 1976. The significance of species turnover and the status of equilibrium island biogeography. *Science* **194**:572–8.

1995. Habitat fragmentation and population extinction in birds. *Ibis* **137**:S105–S111.

Stouffer, P. C., and R. O. J. Bierregaard. 1995. Use of Amazonian forest fragments by understory insectivorous birds. *Ecology* **76**:2429–45.

Syrjänen, K., R. Kalliola, A. Puolasmaa, and J. Mattsson. 1994. Landscape structure and forest dynamics in subcontinental Russian European taiga. *Annales Zoologici Fennici* **31**:19–34.

Thomas, J. A., and M. G. Morris. 1995. Rates and patterns of extinction among British invertebrates. Pp. 111–30 in J. H. Lawton and R. M. May (eds). *Extinction Rates*. Oxford University Press, Oxford.

Tjernberg, M., K. Johnsson, and S. G. Nilsson. 1993. Density variation and breeding success of the black woodpecker *Dryocopus martius* in relation to forest fragmentation. *Ornis Fennica* **70**:155–62.

Väisänen, R. A., O. Järvinen, and P. Rauhala. 1986. How are extensive, human-caused habitat alterations expressed on the scale of local bird populations in boreal forests? *Ornis Scandinavica* 17:282–92.

Väisänen, R., O. Biström, and K. Heliövaara. 1993. Subcortical Coleoptera in dead pines and spruces: is primeval species composition maintained in managed forests? *Biodiversity and Conservation* 2:95–113.

Van Valen, L. 1976. Domains, deduction, the predictive method, and Darwin. *Evolutionary Theory* 1:231–45.

Villafuerte, R., J. A. Litvaitis, and D. F. Smith. 1997. Physiological responses by lagomorphs to resource limitations imposed by habitat fragmentation: implications for conditions-sensitive predation. *Canadian Journal of Zoology* 75:1–148.

Villard, M.-A., P. R. Martin, and C. G. Drummond. 1993. Habitat fragmentation and pairing success in the Ovenbird (*Seiurus aurocapillus*). *Auk* 110:759–68.

Villard, M.-A., G. Merriam, and B. A. Maurer. 1995. Dynmics in subdivided populations of neotropical migratory birds in a fragmented temperate forest. *Ecology* 76:27–40.

Virkkala, R. 1991. Population trends of forest birds in Finnish Lapland in a landscape of large habitat blocks: consequences of stochastic environmental variation or regional habitat alteration? *Biological Conservation* 56:223–40.

Watt, A. S. 1947. Pattern and process in the plant community. *Journal of Ecology* 35:1–22.

Wegge, P., J. Rolstad, and I. Gjerde. 1992. Effects of boreal forest fragmentation on capercaillie grouse: empirical evidence and management implications. Pp. 738–49 in D. R. McCullough and R. H. Barret (eds). *Wildlife 2001*. Elsevier, London.

Whittaker, R. H., and S. A. Levin. 1977. The role of mosaic phenomena in natural communities. *Theoretical Population Biology* 12:117–39.

Wiens, J. A. 1981. Scale problems in avian censusing. *Studies in Avian Biology* 6:513–21.

1984. On understanding a non-equilibrium world: myths and reality in community patterns and processes. Pp. 439–57 in D. R. J. Strong, D. Simberloff, L. G. Abele and A. B. Thistle (eds). *Ecological Communities. Conceptual Issues and the Evidence*. Princeton University Press, Princeton, NJ.

1989. Spatial scaling in ecology. *Functional Ecology* 3:385–97.

1990. Habitat fragmentation and wildlife populations: the importance of autecology, time, and landscape structure. *Congress Transactions of the International Union of Game Biology* 19:381–91.

1995. Habitat fragmentation: island v landscape perspective on bird conservation. *Ibis* 137:S97–S104.

Wiens, J. A., and R. T. Rotenberry. 1981. Censusing and the evaluation of avian habitat occupancy. *Studies in Avian Biology* 6:522–32.

Wilcove, D. S., and S. K. Robinson. 1990. The impact of forest fragmentation on bird communities in Eastern North America. Pp. 319–31 in A. Keast (ed.). *Biogeography and Evolution of Forest Bird Communities*. SPB Academic Publ., The Hague.

Wilcove, D. S., C. H. McLellan, and A. P. Dobson. 1986. Habitat fragmentation
    in the temperate zone. Pp. 237–56 in M. E. Soulé (ed.). *Conservation
    Biology. The Science of Scarcity and Diversity.* Sinauer, Sunderland, Ma.
Williams, G. C. 1992. *Natural Selection. Domains, Levels and Challenges.* Oxford
    University Press, Oxford.
Williamson, M. 1981. *Island Populations.* Oxford University Press, Oxford.
    1989. The MacArthur and Wilson theory today: true but trivial. *Journal of
    Biogeography* **16**:3–4.
    1996. *Biological Invasions.* Chapman and Hall, London.

8 Riparian forests

MARK M. BRINSON AND JOS VERHOEVEN

Only a small portion of most landscapes are occupied by riparian forests. While the contribution of these ecosystems to sustaining aquatic organisms is profound (Gregory et al. 1991), they also have a central role in sustaining a variety of terrestrial organisms, ranging from microbes to vertebrates. In most parts of the world, floodplain or riparian zones are dominated by trees. Particularly in arid regions, they may be the only sites supporting forested conditions. In such climates, the structure and species composition of vegetation are not only distinct from surrounding uplands, but species assemblages change over short distances making riparian forests diverse if only because of the steep environmental gradients that they contain. This chapter examines the reasons for this diversity, describes common threats, makes suggestions on how impacts to them may be minimized, and offers suggestions for their restoration.

What are riparian forests?

Riparian forests are located on river floodplains, and are part of a highly integrated system that includes the stream channel. Overlapping terms are riverine wetlands (Brinson 1990) and riparian corridors (Naiman et al. 1993). Riparian forest is the vegetated portion of the riparian corridor that Naiman et al. (1993) describe as '. . . that portion of the terrestrial landscape from the high water mark towards the uplands where vegetation may be influenced by elevated water tables or flooding, and by the ability of soils to hold water.' An analogous term for riparian zone is 'river marginal', particularly in the European literature (Maltby et al. 1996). Not all riparian zones or river marginal areas are forested in their natural condition, however. Even predominately forested areas may have inclusions of marshes dominated by emergent herbs, open water dominated by submersed plants or plankton, and unvegetated sand bars devoid of trees.

Modification of forests for grazing and agriculture may also displace the forested condition. In this chapter, we use the terms riparian forests, riparian zones, and riparian ecosystems somewhat interchangeably. The forested portion of this resource would normally extend from a stream bank through the base of hillslopes. In many situations, the bases of hillslopes receive lateral groundwater discharge and surface inflows from upslope, and thus their inclusion in riparian forests is crucial to effectively managing the integrity of the riparian zone as a whole.

Riparian forests play manifold roles in contributing toward diversity. As long, linear features in the landscape, riparian ecosystems share extensive boundaries with neighboring ecosystem types. From the upland side, these ecosystems meet some of the critical life history requirements of larger terrestrial animals. When uplands undergo land use changes to silviculture, agriculture, and more intensive activities (e.g., housing development and urbanization), riparian forests serve as buffers which potentially reduce impacts to streams. From the aquatic side, riparian forests supply organic matter for food webs, maintain microclimatic conditions of the stream, and stabilize stream banks. But riparian forests are not simply 'neighbors' of terrestrial and aquatic environments; they also represent unique conditions regardless of their proximity to adjacent lands and stream channels. The position of upland, riparian, and aquatic ecosystems, and some of the relationships among them, are shown in Figure 8.1. Wetlands would be considered the portion of the riparian forest that is saturated or inundated frequently enough to maintain hydric soil and hydrophytic vegetation (NRC 1995).

While most riparian forests are quite narrow and linear, others are wide enough that they no longer appear as ecotones, but as landscape entities in their own right. The wide riparian forests along the lower Mississippi River and much of the lowland Amazon River are extreme cases of this condition. Such broad differences in scale make it difficult to generalize about ecosystem functions and habitat conditions without conditional statements about their size. Whether a riparian forest is in a mountainous, piedmont, or relatively flat environment will influence its valley gradient and, therefore, the character of the hydroperiod and particle size distribution of sediments. For example, in mountainous regions where erosional processes dominate, riparian forests alternate between narrow bands where bedrock may control channel morphology and more gentle reaches where sediment deposition is taking place and floodplains are broader (Harris *et al.* 1987). At the other extreme are low-gradient rivers where depositional processes dominate. They generally have very broad floodplains,

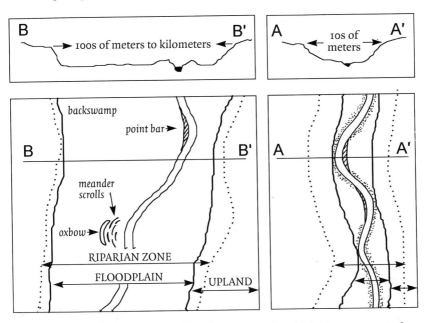

Fig. 8.1. Landscape position of riparian forest between aquatic and upland ecosystems. Left panels: the large alluvial floodplain has a broad riparian zone which includes a band of upland and all of the floodplain, the latter of which is dominated by wetlands. Right panels: a narrow, bedrock-controlled stream with a narrow riparian zone.

fine sediments, and a variety of aquatic environments ranging from ephemeral high flow channels to more permanent oxbow lakes.

Both abiotic forces and biotic control can greatly modify riparian forests. Floods are a common abiotic force which may remove large patches of forest and transport them downstream in a single event. While such physical power may often control the structure of riparian ecosystems, forest structure moderates the less disruptive physical forces. Plants are responsible for driving aquatic food webs, creating microclimatic conditions, and stabilizing channels. Animals play essential roles through herbivory, pollination, and seed dispersal as they do in other forests, but in river corridors large animals (e.g., hippopotamus [*Hippopotamus amphibius*], and warthog [*Phacochoerus aethiopicus*]) may also create wallows, trails, and canals (Naiman and Rogers 1997). Of all these species, however, beaver (*Castor* spp.) stands apart from others as one of the most effective (besides humans) in modifying riparian ecosystems to improve their own habitat.

In spite of the dynamic nature of many riparian forests, they are not immune to alteration from human activities. In fact, many human-induced alterations cause extreme changes in geomorphology and hydrology, the most fundamental properties of riparian forests. When such changes occur, such as constriction by levees and inundation by reservoirs, few management options are available that might conserve biotic integrity. Yet, even these modified sites may be among the last forested portions of some landscapes that have been otherwise converted to agriculture and other more intensive land uses. Even greatly modified floodplain sites often have high potential for restoration if agricultural use is abandoned, connections with the river are restored, and sedimentation–erosion processes return. With fluvial processes restored, chances for development of riparian forest are good because of the ample supply of propagules transported by the river, particularly in the lower reaches of the river.

Fluvial processes and hydroperiod

Riparian forests are among the most heterogenous ecosystems in a landscape. Fluvial processes and hydrologic regime combine to explain, at least in part, why riparian forests have diverse assemblages of species. Fluvial processes create heterogeneous conditions in riparian forests in many ways. For example, point bars and abandoned channels create new sites for colonization by shade-intolerant plants and the development of young successional forests (Kalliola *et al.* 1991). Although such new sites are ephemeral at a given location, their maintenance is assured as they shift locations through the landscape. Concurrently, portions of the migrating channel undercut mature stands of forest both within the floodplain and into adjacent upland portions of the riparian zone. Plant species composition and fluvial processes are profoundly interdependent in riparian areas at the foothills of the Andes leading to the Amazon basin. This situation has led Kalliola and Puhakka (1988) to state that 'All of the current floodplain vegetation has originated from riparian primary successions, and all riparian vegetation may be destroyed by further river erosion.'

Thus, river meandering is a driving force that maintains the spatial heterogeneity found on relic and current floodplains. Kalliola and coworkers (1991) claim that species richness is due in part to the high turnover (mortality and regeneration) of individuals in riparian forests, relative to surrounding areas (Figure 8.2). This phenomenon may contribute to the evolution of some plant species by providing a mechanism for more fre-

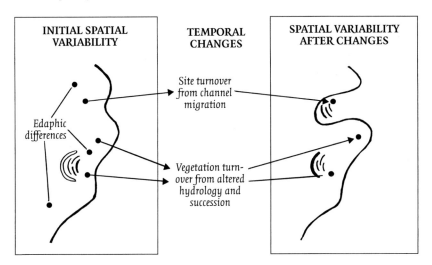

| INITIAL SPATIAL VARIABILITY | TEMPORAL CHANGES | SPATIAL VARIABILITY AFTER CHANGES |

Fig. 8.2. Spatial and temporal control over plant community heterogeneity by changes in fluvial landform and succession. In the left panel, reference points represent various site conditions of soil, inundation frequencies, species composition of vegetation, proximity to channel, etc. One of the sites undergoes turnover as the channel migrates through it. Other sites experience altered hydrology and undergo vegetation change. (Adapted from Kalliola and Puhakka 1988.)

quent sexual reproduction as seeds colonize newly created surfaces. On a larger scale, older surfaces interspersed with fluvial areas represent isolated patches that may have caused high endemism as a mechanism leading to speciation of plants (Räsänen et al. 1987). This is in contrast to mechanisms based on speciation arising from endemism created by climatic refugia.

Water flow through riparian forests is largely contained in stream channels. Flood events that inundate floodplains for days or weeks, however, provide the basis for several ecosystem functions (Junk et al. 1989, Bayley 1991). For example, flood waters typically import nutrients and sediments to the floodplain which generally lead to fertile soils. In fact, many floodplains, such as the lower Mississippi Alluvial Valley and the Nile Delta, are among the richest agricultural lands in the world. Floods create aquatic environments, albeit temporary, for fish and invertebrates to move from the stream channel, where they spend most of their life, to a floodplain rich in food resources and spawning habitat. It is common for fish to use floodplain forests for feeding and spawning during the relatively short periods of inundation, while spending most of their life cycle in the channel or one of the deeper aquatic environments within the floodplain.

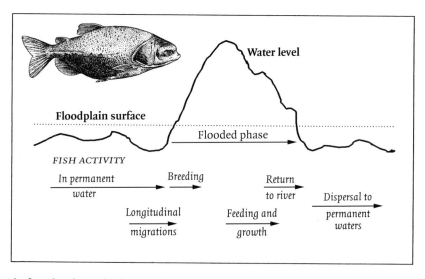

Fig. 8.3. The relationship between the annual flood cycle and fish utilization. Arrows encompass time intervals of activities by fish. (Adapted from Welcomme 1979.)

For example, Ross and Baker (1983) characterize 10 channel-dwelling fish species in Mississippi streams as 'flood exploitive' because they move quickly into the floodplains principally to feed but not to breed. The flood cycle is especially important to the fisheries in tropical streams (Figure 8.3). Amazonian (Goulding 1980) and African (Welcomme 1979) rivers are renowned for their capacity to support fish populations by means of feeding on fruits and seeds from trees in the floodplain forest. Finally, flooding events interact with floodplain topography to create a gradient of 'wetness' on the floodplain which influences species composition of vegetation and thus contributes directly to plant diversity and secondarily to the composition of animal communities.

Hydroperiod is the single most critical control over the species composition and functioning of wetlands (NRC 1995). This is also true for riparian forests because large portions of most riparian zones can be considered wetlands. Hydroperiod has been defined as the duration, frequency, depth, and seasonality of flooding. Each of these variables may influence the habitats of plants and animals. Duration and depth of flooding are responsible for allowing dominance by the more flood-tolerant tree species. In fact, most 'water-loving' riparian species do not dominate floodplains because they *require* long periods of deep flooding, but rather because they can *tolerate* and are more competitive than other species under these conditions.

Duration of flooding can be a strong selective force on species composition, and, under long hydroperiods, can be stressful enough to lower primary production (Megonigal et al. 1997). The relative abundance of water in riparian forests perpetuates plant species that are not drought tolerant, and thus are excluded from uplands (Keeley 1979). At the wetter end of the spectrum, relatively few woody plant species are capable of withstanding anoxic soil conditions for long periods of time, thus leading to lower species richness (Junk 1989, Wharton et al. 1982). Seasonal flooding, with water table drawdown occurring mainly during the growing season, leads to generally fast tree growth which makes floodplain sites attractive for timber production. While high productivity does not translate to high species richness or diversity, it potentially allows rapid recovery of ecosystem structure after timber harvests.

Frequency and seasonality of flooding can interact to select for species as well. On the River Waal floodplain in the lower Rhine basin, the Netherlands, germination of floodplain species (Salix viminalis, S. triandra, S. alba, and Populus nigra) occurs in narrow belts parallel to the river. The zonation of seedlings can be explained by the interaction between water level during the dissemination period and the timing of seed dispersal (Van Splunder et al. 1995). Peak flows create sand bars for seedling germination, but slow rates of recession from peak flows are required for seedlings to survive (Scott et al. 1996). Seasonal flooding is not a universal phenomenon, however. In the relatively aseasonal climate of the Andean foothills of eastern Ecuador, for example, floodplain forests may become flooded from overbank flow at any time of the year (Balslev et al. 1987).

Structural complexity of riparian forests

Spatial complexity is examined here at two scales: one that occurs within stands and one that occurs between stands and other landscape features. Within-stand structure refers to the three-dimensional arrangement of vegetative structural components as discussed in Chapter 11. By definition, a stand is relatively homogeneous in height, biomass distribution, and species composition. This contrasts with complexity that occurs between stands and between forests and adjacent, non-forested environments such as stream channels, oxbow lakes, and grasslands. These ecotone concepts were discussed in Chapter 6.

WITHIN-STAND STRUCTURE

There are wide ranges in stand structure across latitudinal gradients (Table 8.1). While there is a general trend for stem density and basal area to be higher in riparian forests of the humid tropics and lower temperate regions than in either arid regions or higher latitudes, patterns are quite weak. For example, stands can achieve basal areas well over 50 m² per hectare in the arid southwestern United States where a combination of high insolation and a supply of moisture from the river provide optimal conditions for growth. Riparian forests are not noted for high species diversity of trees. In fact, stressful conditions due to flooding often lead to nearly monotypic stands in the wettest portions of riparian forests.

Vertical stratification in forests is an important habitat feature for many species (Chapter 11). This is especially relevant to epiphytic plants and to arboreal animals that use branches and boles for foraging, perching, and denning (Wakeley and Roberts 1996). However, in many closed-canopy riparian forests, the shrub stratum tends to be limited in terms of both biomass and species richness, possibly due to the combination of light limitation and long hydroperiod (Brinson 1990).

While stand structure provides niches for animals and epiphytes in ways similar to other forest types, flooding contributes to aquatic ecosystem structure in a unique way. For example, when floodplain forests of the Amazon River become flooded, tree leaves provide a substrate on which periphyton (attached algae) colonize. Nitrogen fixation by cyanobacteria in the periphyton contribute to the nitrogen economy of lakes connected to the Amazon River (Doyle and Fisher 1994). Thus, it is the distinguishing combination of aquatic and terrestrial conditions rather than the forest structure itself that contributes to the complexity in riparian forests.

LANDSCAPE HETEROGENEITY

A highly intercorrelated group of physical features is found in riparian forests because of the physical relationships between stream channels and their floodplains (Leopold *et al.* 1964, Rosgen 1995). These include relationships between stream valley gradient, meander length, grain size of sediments, and metrics of channel morphology. Stream channel movement is one of the most important physical factors in creating and maintaining between-stand heterogeneity of riparian forests. Fluvial geomorphic features are controlled by large scale physiographic variables which differ between steep mountainous areas and flat coastal regions as

Table 8.1. *Structural characteristics of selected riparian forest stands*

Approximate location	Latitude	Strand basal area (m²/ha)	Number of tree species	Density (stems/ha)	Average tree diameter (cm)	Source
South Moravia, Slovakia	49	33–38	–	590–850	–	Penka et al. 1991
Montana, USA	49	34.6	3	715	25	Lee 1983
Washington, USA	48	38.8	3	793	25	Fonda 1974
Czechoslovakia	48	27.9	–	1104	18	Vyskot 1976
North Dakota, USA	47	28.8	9	574	25	Johnson et al. 1976
New Jersey, USA	41	28.6	12	670	23	Buell and Wistendahl 1955
Colorado, USA	40	18.0	2	126	43	Lindauer 1983
Illinois, USA	40	32.1	6	423	31	Brown and Peterson 1983
Virginia, USA	39	27.1	8	–	–	Hupp 1982
New Jersey, USA	39	33.4	5	910	22	Ehrenfeld and Gulick 1981
North Carolina, USA	36	69.0	4	2730	18	Brinson et al. 1980
North Carolina, USA	35	47.8	16	705	29	Mulholland 1979
New Mexico, USA	33	66.4	7	–	–	Freeman and Dick-Peddie 1970
Alabama, USA	32	77.1	2	1802	23	Hall and Penfound 1943
Florida, USA	30	32.5	–	1644	16	Brown 1981
Louisiana, USA	30	56.2	9	1235	24	Conner and Day 1976
Louisiana, USA	30	77.7	4	746	36	Hall and Penfound 1939
Florida, USA	26	80.2	7	856	35	Duever et al. 1984
Florida, USA	26	42.9	8	2032	16	Duever et al. 1984
Puerto Rico	18	55.0	13	1080	25	Alvarez-Lopez 1990
Puerto Rico	18	27.7	2	950	19	Alvarez-Lopez 1990
Costa Rica	11	54.9	4	290	49	Holdridge et al. 1971
Costa Rica	10	70.5	4	335	52	Holdridge et al. 1971
Panama	9	51.5	7	297	47	Mayo Melendez 1965

Notes:
Although the stands were chosen for comparison because they were relatively mature, stand age is an unknown source of variation in the data set. Average tree diameter is shown to provide a sense of stand structure because basal area alone does not provide information on density.
Source: Modified from Brinson (1990).

previously discussed. Because of these large differences, it is difficult to generalize about riparian forests, except to recognize that there is a common set of fluvial controls over structure and composition.

If most riparian forests are not particularly diverse in tree species at any given site, how do they gain notoriety in contributing to biodiversity at larger scales? There are two elements of this phenomenon. The first is that riparian forests make unique contributions of biota within landscapes that are normally dominated by drier terrestrial ecosystems. The other is that the cumulative diversity of riparian forests is principally a consequence of between-stand heterogeneity rather than the diversity within any one stand. There are three components to this diversity: between-stand heterogeneity, proximity to water, and proximity to uplands. Here we offer some specific examples.

Between-stand heterogeneity

Riparian forests can contribute disproportionately to the flora of some regions. At least 260 species (or 13%) of the total Swedish vascular plants occur along the Vindel River which holds the country's record of 131 species per 200 m length (Nilsson 1992). In spite of this contribution to a region, when one compares a given forest stand, the number of tree species is not particularly high at any given site. This goes back to the importance of fluvial processes in initiating and maintaining a variety of soil and moisture conditions within riparian forests. Because of the sensitivity of plant species to soil moisture and inundation, the high variety of microhabitats within a single floodplain can support a broad array of plant communities (Wharton et al. 1982).

This concept is illustrated by vegetation patterns in the Saskatchewan River delta in Canada (Dirschl and Coupland 1972). None of the plant communities at this latitude (54° N) is particularly species-rich, yet the delta vegetation was classified into 11 broad types according to species composition and physiognomy, with 6 of these consisting of woody vegetation (white spruce–hardwood forest, black spruce–tamarack forest, tall willow–alder shrub, medium willow shrub, low willow shrub, and bog birch shrub). Four of the woody vegetation classes are dominated by shrubs, while the remaining five types are dominated by herbaceous wetland vegetation. Consequently, forest stands are but one component of structurally complex riparian zones.

Even in arid regions where riparian vegetation represents the only forest structure in the landscape, tree species diversity is low, but age class and structural diversity are typically high. Linear bands of spatially separ-

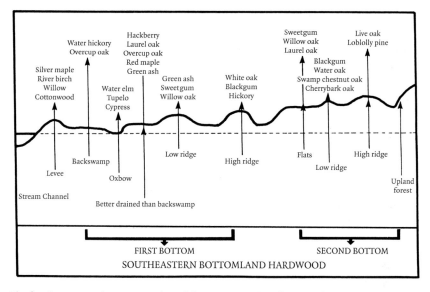

Fig. 8.4. Representative cross-section of plant communities of riparian forests of the south-eastern United States that illustrates between-stand heterogeneity. (After Wharton *et al.* 1982.)

ate age classes occur along streams of the southwestern U.S. where young-est cohorts are closest to the channel and older trees occupy floodplains as much as 200 m from the channel (Stromberg *et al.* 1991). Such linear bands of age classes may be caused by the germination and survival requirements of tree species with respect to water level. Owing to the dynamic nature of the water level fluctuations, suitable areas for germination, establish-ment, and seedling survival for floodplain tree species shift from year to year along the elevational ridge-swale gradients (Van Splunder *et al.* 1995). A representative cross-section of plant communities in a bottomland hardwood forest in the southeastern United States illustrates how between-stand heterogeneity contributes to overall diversity of a riparian forest (Figure 8.4).

Proximity to water

The contribution of riparian forests to the aquatic environment of channels is well known. For example, many of the in-stream habitat fea-tures such as coarse woody debris are derived from riparian forests (Beschta and Platts 1986). The structural integrity of streamside zones also contributes to water quality by reducing the input of nutrients and suspended sediments.

In addition to the floodplain-channel connection created for aquatic organisms during flooding, there is also a 'hidden' component of biodiversity that takes place in the hyporheic zone (the zone below the current bed of a stream). Relic channels of coarse-grained sediment within the hyporheic zone preferentially transport subsurface water to and from the modern channel. Diverse populations of aquatic insects (Stanford and Ward 1993) and intense biogeochemical processes (Pinay et al. 1992, Vervier et al. 1992, 1993) are concentrated within these flows. Insect communities not only maintain their own food web within the alluvium, but they also contribute to the better known food webs of stream channels.

Riparian forests are attractive to a number of birds, mammals, and amphibians, not because they are aquatic, but because they center their activities around aquatic ecosystems (Figure 8.5). While many birds and mammals are wide-ranging, such as the great blue heron (Ardea herodias) and the raccoon (Procyon lotor), they have strong riparian affinities because of feeding preferences afforded them by aquatic ecosystems.

Proximity to adjacent lands

Just as portions of riparian forest are exploited by aquatic animals during flood events, other species associated with drier habitats depend on riparian zones. Some amphibians spend most of their life in areas outside of riparian forests, but depend on wetter environments, such as those found in riparian zones, for reproduction. In areas with relatively moist climates, other wetland types (depressions, seeps, etc.; see Chapter 9) and water bodies (lakes, ponds) may satisfy this need. In arid regions, riparian forests may be the only sites in the landscape that maintain a relatively consistent source of water. Most wide-ranging upland species, such as ungulates and felines, depend on riparian forests in one way or another.

Role of biota in riparian ecosystem functioning

Even though riparian ecosystems tend to be dominated by the physical forces of water flow, the biotic portion plays an important role in modulating the physical environment and contributing to a host of ecosystem processes. Several processes exemplify the critical role that biota play in the functioning of physically dominated riparian forests: (a) providing a more physically stable riparian zone, (b) generating an energy source for aquatic and terrestrial food webs, and (c) intercepting nutrients and sediments that would otherwise be flushed downstream. While each of these

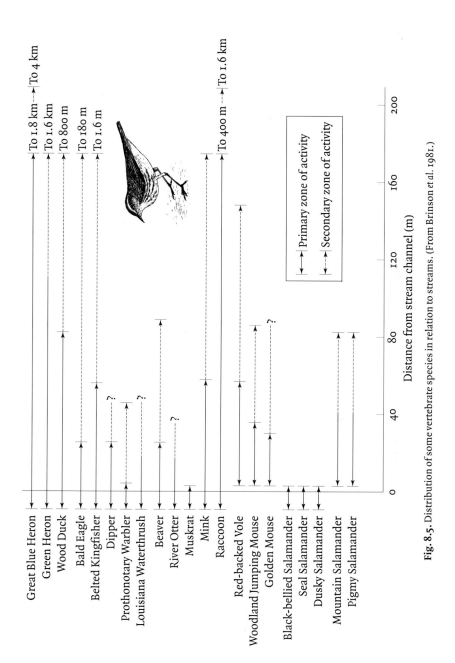

Fig. 8-5. Distribution of some vertebrate species in relation to streams. (From Brinson et al. 1981.)

processes has counterparts in adjacent lands, they have greater significance in riparian forests because of their stabilizing influence over strong
physical forces as discussed below.

From the physical perspective, shade and cover provided by trees and
shrubs have been widely recognized as having microclimatic significance
in modulating water temperature for aquatic and semiaquatic organisms.
Even more fundamental is the contribution of physical structure of roots
that stabilizes banks (Beschta and Platts 1986) and coarse woody debris
that influences local channel configuration and habitat, especially in steep
gradient streams (Fetherston et al. 1995).

Organic matter production in riparian forests not only supports food
webs in forests, but also within streams. Litterfall from the forest explains
the predominately heterotrophic bases for stream food webs (Webster et
al. 1995). Direct inputs of litter for floodplain streams averaged 588
g/m²/y in a survey of sites in the eastern United States with lateral inputs
(from rolls, slides, or blow-in) increasing this average to 685 g/m²/y
(Webster et al. 1995). Not only do assemblages of protozoans directly
graze bacteria attached to detrital particles, but separate assemblages of
particle feeders (mostly larval insects) depend on detritus as a primary
energy source.

The landscape position of riparian forests between uplands and rivers
makes them critical in protecting water quality through the removal or
retention of nutrients (Pinay et al. 1992, Brinson 1993). Surface and
groundwater movement in riparian forests has a distinct horizontal vector
in contrast to uplands. The cycling of nutrients is largely a process that
operates to counteract these downslope movements through uptake by
plants, return to the forest floor by litterfall and mortality, and release by
microbial mineralization for recycling by plants. The forest also stabilizes
soil and influences water balance, much as it does in adjacent lands.
Flood-prone portions of riparian forests generally provide areas for accumulation of sediment derived from overbank flow or transported from
adjacent slopes.

The importance of riparian forests as refugia and travel corridors for
animal communities is self-evident in most cases. However, the opposite
perspective is seldom taken on the contribution of animals in managing
riparian zones. Fish act as seed dispersal agents in Amazonian floodplains
(Goulding 1980, Smith 1981), crayfish aerate an otherwise anoxic waterlogged soil, and large animals create wallows that modify geomorphology
on a small scale (Naiman and Rogers 1997). One of the most effective ecosystem managers of all, beavers (*Castor* spp.), can fundamentally alter the

hydrology, species composition, and sediment balance of riparian forests (Naiman et al. 1994). Since beaver populations are no longer intensively trapped in eastern North America, their resurgence conflicts with management goals of forestry operations because of the capacity of this species to cause tree mortality and change species composition. This is not to suggest that beaver activity has had a negative influence on biodiversity of riparian environments. Rather, the opposite is likely true when one considers that their activity leads to interspersion of open-water environments and patches of canopy openings filled with shade-intolerant seedlings. This leads to the creation of different aged patches as beaver move their activities around the landscape.

Alteration of riparian forests

River systems are among the most fragmented and regulated portions of the landscapes of many countries. For example, 70% of the total water discharge of 139 of the world's largest river systems is affected by reservoir operation, interbasin transfer, and irrigation, primarily in industrialized nations (Dynesius and Nilsson 1994). This means that the interrelations between the river channel and its floodplain may be totally interrupted in many cases because of the regulation of discharge, either through withdrawals or from reservoir storage. These changes have altered or eliminated migration routes of anadromous fish, resulting in the collapse of many freshwater fisheries throughout the northern hemisphere (Dynesius and Nilsson 1994, Nilsson et al. 1997). Not only do parts of the integrated mosaic of channels, oxbows, islands, bars, and levees get displaced by conversion to other land uses, but their highly dynamic nature becomes stabilized.

Some of the most common alterations to riparian forests are stream channelization, channel constriction, and the upstream and downstream effects of altered flows due to impoundments and diversions (Table 8.2). All affect the fundamental character of the riparian forest by altering water delivery and geomorphology. In riparian forests, the water table is usually close to the surface, and for the stream channel and oxbow lakes, water is normally above the land surface. Many of the habitat features in riparian forests derive from this high soil moisture or the presence of free water. Consequently, permanent changes will alter habitat conditions. Such changes have obvious implications for community composition and species diversity. Other alterations can have significant effects on biota

Table 8.2. *Examples of riparian forest alteration listed in approximate order of decreasing geographic scale of influence*

Alteration	Structural change	Consequences
Impoundment: upstream effects	Loss of forest biomass and increase in water depth	Reduces primary productivity, nutrient cycling, and other forest processes. Restricts migrations through fragmentation.
Impoundment: downstream effects	Increase in channel capacity; reduction in supply of sediments; flows often moderated.	Reduces sediment supply; increases scour. Restricts migrations through fragmentation.
Channelization	Increase in channel capacity	Decreases overbank flow; reduces exchange of organisms, nutrients, and sediments between channel and floodplain
Channelization	Increase in channel gradient; decreased sinuosity	Increases pulses in flow and erosive power, resulting in loss of bank stability
Channel constriction by levees	Restricts floodplain access for water storage	Increases channel scour and sediment deposition on remaining narrow floodplain; reduces or eliminates surface area of floodplain for opportunistic channel-dwellers
Grazing by livestock	Changes age structure of forest; stream banks deteriorate.	Reduces primary productivity and sediment retention
Timber harvest followed by change to agriculture or intensive silviculture	Reduces standing stocks of biomass and nutrients	Alters trophic structure and forest structure

through changes in the biomass, age structure, species composition, and trophic structure.

In addition to fundamental changes in geomorphology and hydrology, riverine systems have suffered from loading by nutrients and toxins which have both direct and indirect effects on the biota of riparian ecosystems. In some cases, such degraded conditions can be reversed. For example, some of the rivers of western Europe became so polluted in the past that they no longer supported diverse populations of fish (Van Dijk *et al.* 1995). Recent reductions in pollution loads have allowed some of these populations to rebound.

The effects of agriculture, grazing, and timber harvesting can often be reversed through restoration if there have been no hydrologic alterations. A common problem with timber harvesting on wet soils is soil compaction. In a comparison of logging with skidders and log removal by helicopter in a water tupelo–bald cypress swamp in Alabama, USA, the effect of skidder traffic was significant on several soil properties (Aust and Lea 1992). For example, saturated hydraulic conductivity of the soil was decreased by the compaction, resulting in potentially stressful conditions from reduced oxygen content and lower redox potentials.

Species enhancement for game management, such as modifying plant species composition and canopy gaps, are some of the more benign alterations. An exception is the creation of green-tree reservoirs where the alteration is hydrologic. Shallow water is created in green-tree reservoirs to provide conditions in which waterfowl can feed on acorns and invertebrates (King 1995). Areas are impounded with low head dams or levees to inundate floodplains during the winter when vegetation is largely dormant. It was once argued that trees, in their dormant condition, would be unaffected by flooding; in fact early reports of enhanced growth provided confirmation of the lack of impacts from green-tree reservoirs. However, more recent studies have shown lack of regeneration and increased mortality of older trees which would inevitably lead to changes in both forest structure and species composition (King 1995).

Many floodplains along European rivers have long been used for hay-making and extensive livestock grazing and are still in use today. These land uses have resulted in species-rich grasslands on the ridges and swales. A good example of botanically rich floodplains are the 'callows' along the River Shannon in Ireland (personal observations).

Minimizing impacts and issues regarding restoration

Assuming that the alterations to riparian forests are not so severe that they completely eliminate the benefits of these zones for water quality maintenance and biomass production, what are some of the options for timber extraction that minimize impacts? Alternatively, if riparian zones have been so degraded that they can no longer support forests, what are the options for restoration? As with most land management issues, the options are driven not only by the original conditions and current ecological limitations of the sites, but they are influenced also by socioeconomic goals and constraints.

MINIMIZING IMPACTS BY MANAGING BUFFERS

We focus on the management of riparian forests for timber production and water quality maintenance because both are common practices, they are driven by important societal goals, and both influence biodiversity outcomes. Managing for timber production is less straightforward. For small streams, the entire riparian forest can represent a buffer, and the question is how to minimize harvesting impacts that might affect water quality. For large floodplains, however, the perspective can change with scale. Large floodplains managed primarily for timber production could benefit from some of the same precautions used to minimize impact in the harvesting of upland forests. Managing for water quality normally focuses on maintaining riparian forests as buffers for activities in uplands such as agriculture (Lowrance et al. 1985, Pinay and Decamps 1988) and urban land use (Ehrenfeld and Schneider 1993). Stream channels, ponds, lakes, seeps, and other aquatic environments would be the focus of protection using buffers located between the harvesting activities and the water.

The term 'buffer' commonly raises an image of a narrow strip of forest between a particular land use and the stream channel. This may be adequate for small streams for which a relatively narrow strip may be effective in protecting stream biota from the effects of adjacent land uses as illustrated in Figure 8.6b. The abundance and length of low-order streams makes them particularly important in establishing initial conditions for water quality in a watershed (Brinson 1993). With increasing stream order and corresponding increases in riparian forest width, it may not be practical to expand the riparian zone from one edge of the floodplain to another, especially ones that are a kilometer or more wide. Rather, some protection for stream biota may be afforded by leaving a forested buffer next to the channel as protection from agricultural and other activities within the floodplain (Figure 8.6a). Finer divisions of river and floodplain size are useful: Forman (1995) suggests five of them, each of which would have a minimum width of stream and river corridor based on ecological functioning (i.e., sponge effects, sediment trapping, wildlife corridors, etc.) ranging from seepages at the headwaters to 5th to 10th order rivers. Buffers for first order streams are particularly important in protecting areas downstream from flooding and pollution (Forman 1995). As it turns out, all five divisions include a portion of adjacent upland as part of the

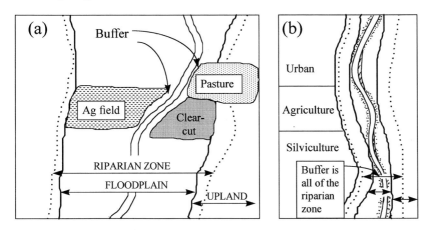

Fig. 8.6. Differing perspectives on riparian zones as buffers as a function of floodplain size and the location of activities causing alteration. (a) Large portions of the riparian forest are influenced by alternate land use practices within a broad floodplain. The buffer consists of a streamside zone only. (b) The entire riparian forest is the buffer with alterations limited to activities in upland.

buffer zone. This is consistent with the ecological functions that adjacent hillslopes provide to aquatic and wetland portions of the riparian zone.

How do certain animal populations in riparian forests respond to incrementally narrower forested buffer zones? One series of studies examined how width of buffer strips (commonly called streamside management zones) affected the population levels of vertebrates (Table 8.3). The adjacent, non-riparian activity was the harvesting of second-growth forests and converting them to pine plantations. For most vertebrates, the wider the buffer strip, the higher the population density (Table 8.3). Exceptions were the fulvous harvest mouse and the white-footed and cotton mouse which had higher densities in narrower strips. Presumably, these mice prefer the more open habitat provided by the adjacent young plantation. However, for all other species, wider strips clearly supported higher densities. In fact, some species such as Swainson's warbler (*Helmitheros swainsonii*) were never detected in riparian buffers less than 300 m in width, and had higher densities in buffers of greater than 1000 m width (Kilgo *et al.* 1996). In southern Ontario, Canada, herptile and mammal species richness increased with increasing forest cover on lands adjacent to wetland edges, out to at least 2 km distance (Findlay and Houlahan 1997). In fact, paved road density within this zone beyond the wetland edge diminished plant, bird, and herptile species richness within wetlands. Based on these observations, there is no 'best' recommendation for riparian buffer for

Table 8.3. *Comparison of densities of species observed and squirrel nests for stream-side management zones of hardwoods in a landscape of recently cut second growth*

Species/taxon	Relative number of individuals or occurrences (streamside management zone width, m)		
	Narrow (0–25 m)	Medium (30–40 m)	Wide (50–95 m)
Lizards[a]	73	247	265
Snakes[a]	9	32	35
Amphibians[a]	70	203	293
Reptiles[a]	82	282	302
Fulvous harvest mouse*[b]	73	4	3
White footed and cotton mouse**[c]	76	67	50
Squirrel observations***[c]	0	1	24
Squirrel nests***[c]	1	7	55

Notes:
[a] Rudolph and Dickson (1990); sampling effort equal across zones.
[b] Dickson and Williamson (1988); numbers per 832 trap nights per treatment.
[c] Dickson and Huntley (1987); sampling effort equal across zones.
* *Reithrodonyornys fulvascens*
** *Peromyscus leucopus* and *P. gossypinus*
*** Both gray (*Sciurus carolinensis*) and fox (*S. niger*)
Units vary among studies but number of sample sites was the same for each zone for individual species.

assemblages of vertebrates. In fact, the presence of forest cover well beyond wetland edges augments species richness. From a practical standpoint, goals should be established to determine the level of protection that is possible based on prevailing socioeconomic forces. Presumably those forces include society's recognition that biotic diversity is valuable. From this information, widths of buffers and activities within them could be negotiated.

Forested strips are effective in both sediment and nutrient (nitrogen and phosphorus) removal and retention (Daniels and Gilliam 1996). Studies along the Garonne River (France) have shown that riparian forest and shrub zones remove almost all nitrate in runoff and seepage from the adjacent upland (Pinay et al. 1994). Peterjohn and Correll (1984) suggested a 19-m zone width between the stream and agricultural fields for maintaining low levels of nutrient inputs to streams in an agricultural landscape. As a result of their study and several others, the Chesapeake Bay program has recommended that buffers consist of three specific management zones: (1) a grassed zone next to fields to disperse overland flow and reduce gullying; (2) a zone with trees that can be harvested; and (3) a zone without any tree harvesting or other disturbance (Nutrient Subcommittee of the Chesapeake Bay Program 1995). Where logging activities are the principal reason for buffer establishment, a two-tier approach may suffice (Hunter 1990). Beginning at the channel bank, there would be no cutting in a 10–25 m zone. Limited harvesting would be practiced in a somewhat wider zone adjacent to this.

While water quality and habitat conditions for fish and invertebrates tend to overlap, issues dealing with fish habitat focus more on shading for temperature control, cover for fish, organic matter inputs for trophic support, and coarse woody debris as structure for habitat (Gregory et al. 1991). The importance of large wood for habitat maintenance control in steep gradient streams is now widely recognized. Large wood maintains riffles and pools, creates in-stream islands, and contributes to 'dead water zones' important to maintaining spawning habitat and reducing energy requirements of fish (Fetherston et al. 1995). Given the fundamental importance of fluvial processes, and specifically geomorphic control by large wood, the source of this material should be kept intact for recruitment to stream channels. Generally, streamside zones should be maintained with mature forest such that the minimum buffer width equals the height of the tallest trees. This criterion recognizes that snags and trees within this zone have the potential of contributing large wood to the channel should they fall in that direction (Fetherston et al. 1995).

Biotic diversity issues for riparian forests in urban landscapes are particularly challenging. In urban landscapes, impervious surfaces make flows more flashy and often cause scouring rather than deposition. If riparian zones are to be kept relatively intact, considerable restoration and continuing maintenance may be necessary. While buffers in urban settings may contribute to water quality maintenance and flood-damage amelioration, high priority must be oriented toward stabilizing stream channels so the riparian forest can maintain itself. Regardless, expectations for maintaining biodiversity cannot be set as high as for less intensive land uses. Suburban watersheds in the New Jersey Pine Barrens showed a correlation between numbers of invading plant species and the number of altered hydrologic and chemical parameters (Ehrenfeld and Schneider 1993). Mechanisms to restore streams and corresponding riparian forests are available (Boon et al. 1992), but their success and application are highly contingent on original condition of the resource and the goals of society.

Some general principles emerge from the many studies on riparian forests as buffers: (a) wider is almost always better for maintaining biodiversity in the broad sense, but societal goals often make exceptionally wide options impractical; (b) the more intensive the activity being buffered, the wider the buffer required for achieving equivalent protection; (c) open water environments (streams, ponds, etc.) require forested buffers whether the adjacent land is floodplain or upland hillslope; and (d) headwater portions of streams are critical in maintaining water quality and flood control, yet are among the most vulnerable to upland and wetland alteration.

RESTORATION OPTIONS

Restoration options in riparian forests must take into account unique challenges due to the overriding importance of hydrology and geomorphology in maintaining these ecosystems. Because hydrologic and geomorphic alterations to riparian forests are common and have a profound effect on their condition, it may be impractical to restore them to their relatively unaltered condition. This is especially true if alterations are considered 'irreversible' due to socioeconomic considerations such as investments in costly infrastructure (big dams and levee projects) and if land use patterns are considered to be permanent (cities). In some regions, for example, riparian forests have been almost completely erased from the landscape they once occupied and from the memories of society. The ancient Greeks and Romans caused widespread degradation of the Mediterranean region. The almost total removal by Egyptians of timber and wild game from the Nile River valley is emblematic of the large impact on riparian zones by ancient civilizations (Hughes 1994). More recent activities in the river valleys of the Sacramento Valley in California have left the region now largely devoid of woody vegetation. At one time strips of woodland, sometimes several kilometers wide, occupied river margins (Thompson 1961). In such cases it is difficult to imagine the extent of reduction in biotic diversity because the original condition is so remote and vaguely characterized.

The effects of timber harvesting are not necessarily permanent, however, so long as harvesting does not change the hydrology or geomorphology of the riparian zone. Even so, more than a century may be required for a forest to recover to the reference condition (sensu Brinson and Rheinhardt 1996), particularly in those ecosystems that are dependent on inputs of a large woody component. This assumes that there is merit in restoring altered forests to a minimally altered community type, a condition which is consistent with using reference as a basis for setting restoration goals (Rheinhardt et al. 1997).

Such long-term objectives are seldom foremost in restoration efforts, however. In contrast to the long-term recovery suggested above, Hupp (1992) describes a six-stage recovery of the riparian forest (within about 50 m of the stream channel) after channelization in western Tennessee. Without human intervention, he estimates that an average of 65 years is required for recovery of the channel, bank stability, and the vegetation. This estimate may not differ substantially for restoration that includes planting, grading, etc. because decades are still required to establish forest structure (i.e., large trees and coarse woody debris). However, species composition can be controlled with planting and thinning in order to increase the probability of achieving reference conditions.

Restoration is particularly successful where cattle grazing has prevented tree reproduction (Dahlem 1979). The exclusion of cattle results in remarkable rates of recovery, not only in vegetation but also in hydrologic and geomorphic conditions (Elmore and Beschta 1987). In other cases, the earlier presence of livestock may facilitate restoration efforts. In floodplains of Kenya, *Acacia tortilis* establishment was better inside abandoned livestock corrals than outside, apparently in response to higher levels of nutrients and moisture provided by pastoralists and livestock (Reid and Ellis 1995).

The techniques of restoration to a particular reference forested condition use silvicultural practices common in forests elsewhere (Chapter 15). Restoration of hydrologic and geomorphic conditions, as discussed in Rosgen (1995), is beyond the scope of this chapter. However, if appropriate physical conditions are not in place prior to restoring vegetation, there is little likelihood of achieving a sustainable restoration endpoint. Planting of selected species, thinning of species overrepresented relative to the reference condition, and exclusion of exotics are all options available for meeting restoration goals. Riparian forests seem to have a preponderance of exotics that may be undesirable from a biodiversity perspective. Saltcedar (*Tamarix pentandra*) has displaced native riparian vegetation in many areas of the southwestern United States (Everitt 1980). Because such invasions generally are facilitated by hydrologic alterations, efforts to suppress further invasions should be preceded by restoration of the physical regime.

Although the floodplains along European rivers have been severely altered through the centuries, and many have lost their riparian forests, recently there is an enormous interest in restoring ecosystem functions

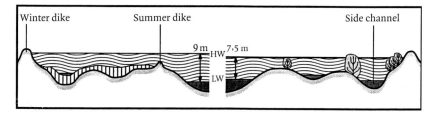

Fig. 8.7. Cross-section of the Waal River, The Netherlands, showing the present situation (left) and the situation after restoration of the floodplain (right). In the present situation, the river channel is protected by a summer dike which leads to low flooding frequency (<1 per year). The restoration will involve the removal of the clay layers and the summer dike so that flooding frequency will increase. HW, high water level; LW, low water level; vertical hatching, clay layer. (After WWF 1993.)

and biodiversity of at least part of the original floodplain. Along the Rhine River, which has been 'tamed' by the construction of dikes and the cut-off of meanders, the natural processes of erosion, sedimentation, and meander formation have been severely altered. In the lower Rhine basin in Germany and the Netherlands, narrow floodplains (1–3 km wide) still exist between winter dikes (Figure 8.7). These floodplains are protected from flooding during the growing season by lower summer dikes along the river bed, and have been used increasingly for intensive livestock raising. Initiatives are under way to restore these floodplains to a more natural state, although more complete restoration is still limited by the existence of the winter dikes (WWF 1993). In addition to removing the summer dikes, thick clay layers, which have formed through enhanced sedimentation in the last 100 years, must be removed. Seeds of more than a thousand plant species will be brought in by the river, and riparian forests are expected to return quickly in most of the floodplain area. The first restoration projects have so far been quite successful in terms of seedling establishment and return of invertebrate fauna (WWF 1993).

One of the most difficult issues to deal with in restoration is the dynamic and seemingly unpredictable nature of some riparian forests, particularly because of periodic erosion and deposition. From this perspective, some of the most 'stable' riparian forests should be considered highly degraded because they have replaced the braided mosaic of sandbars, shrub islands, and dense stands of large trees such as cottonwood (*Populus* spp.) and willow (*Salix* spp.). This has happened in some riparian forests of the American West where flows have been stabilized by reduced peak discharges maintained by upstream impoundments and by supplemented low flows due to additional groundwater from irrigation. For these reasons, the Platte River and its two major tributaries in Colorado and Nebraska have undergone a reduction by 80–95% in width in the past 100 years with the amount of forest vegetation increasing at the expense of aquatic surface area and vegetated islands (Nadler 1978, Johnson 1994). Due to the infrastructure built around impoundments for supplying water to cities and crop irrigation, this may be a good example in which management options may have rendered these systems 'beyond restoration' from a socioeconomic perspective.

In the final analysis, vegetation re-establishment is one of the simpler phases of restoration, and is unlikely to differ greatly from that for non-riparian forests, except for hazards of flooding that may be unique to riparian zones. More difficult, however, is restoration of geomorphic and hydrologic processes which are the fundamental underpinnings of the unique biota of riparian forests discussed earlier in the chapter. Most difficult is restoration to reference conditions in large rivers where societal commitment to an altered state is strong (Gore and Shields 1995).

Case study: the role of riparian buffers for steep, low order streams in the humid subtropics

The maintenance of riparian buffers is a recognized management option which can mitigate impacts to streams when upland forests are harvested. Riparian buffers are particularly critical in steep, unstable landscapes prone to erosion and slope failure. The mountainous, high rainfall environment of the Luquillo Experimental Forest in Puerto Rico epitomizes some of the challenges of management in a highly unstable landscape consisting of ephemeral aquatic environments, torrential flows from hurricanes, and steep slopes. On one hand, riparian buffers offer protection to aquatic communities that are already species-poor. On the other hand, there are economic considerations for timber extraction. This section seeks to illustrate how an understanding of physical factors and forest biodiversity can aid in assessing tradeoffs between riparian protection and access to valued timber species.

ENVIRONMENTAL SETTING

In the Luquillo Experimental Forest, the riparian forests occur along channels that drain amphitheater-shaped watersheds that range in area from 5 to 50 hectares. Fifty percent of some of the watersheds have slopes of greater than 45% (Scatena and Lugo 1995). Stream channels in this highly dissected landscape can be divided into three types: perennial main channels, intermittent channels, and leaf-lined swales (Scatena 1990). The main channels are third and fourth order streams with very limited floodplain development. Intermittent channels are first and second order, lined with clay and boulders covered with moss. Water flows in them several times a month, and during intervening rainless periods aquatic environments are maintained in numerous isolated pools of varying sizes and depths. Swales are depressions leading from upland to channels; they contain moist leaves and occasional saplings.

This landscape is sculptured by a hierarchy of forces beginning with the tectonic activity associated with mountain building. These geologic and mountain building forces combine with heavy rainfalls of the maritime climate to create the steep, highly dissected terrain that is subject to high rates of erosion and slope failure. Hurricanes that pass directly over the area about once every 60 years are the dominant agent in controlling the structure of the upland forests (Scatena and Lugo 1995). Within the riparian forests, tree-fall gaps and hurricanes have similar importance in structuring the forests. Slope failures are also common and provide the channels with large boulders (Ahmad *et al.* 1993). Downslope processes contribute sediments not only to the forested riparian zone, but also to the suspended load and bed load of the stream channel itself. As a result of these extremes in flows and contribution of sediment, the stream channel environment fluctuates between periods of torrential stream discharge capable of transporting whole trees and meter-diameter boulders and complete loss of the aquatic environment during dry-seasons without rainfall. Both aquatic and terrestrial life within riparian forests are exposed to these extremes in physical variation.

ASPECTS OF BIODIVERSITY

The upland forest in this area is dominated by tabonuco (*Dacryodes excelsa*), *Sloanea berteriana*, and the palm, *Prestoea montana*. Valley floors adjacent to these streams are dominated by *P. montana*, and a nearly continuous layer of relatively shade-intolerant herbs (Scatena 1990). Plant species distributions can be used to characterize the riparian ecosystem. Tree species richness, for example, is lower than in upland forests (Scatena and Lugo 1995). Ground cover in riparian forests is much richer and more abundant than it is under closed forests on slopes and ridges. The extent of herb cover also serves as a good indicator for the lateral extent of the riparian zones. Biomass, basal area, stem density, and species richness of both adults and seedlings decrease from ridges to valleys.

Aquatic primary productivity is quite low in the pools of small streams because of shading by trees. Litter and leaf packs accumulate in stream beds during non-flow or minimal-flow periods and serve as both habitat and food sources for the aquatic animal community. Coarse woody debris is uncommon apparently because it is swept out during peak discharges and decays rapidly. Invertebrate species include detritivorous shrimp (*Atya lanipes* and *Xiphocaris elongata*) which serve as prey for fish and larger shrimp, primarily *Macrobrachium carcinus*, at mid-elevational reaches (Covich et al. 1996). Fish are represented by predaceous eels (at low elevations), omnivorous mullets, and four species of gobiid fish. Also present are two species of grazing gastropods, eleven species of decapod crustaceans, and more than 60 species of aquatic insects.

Components of a food web are missing that might be expected in continental settings (e.g., otter and large fish). The oceanic barrier also eliminates major invertebrate groups such as predatory stoneflies, several herbivorous and detritivorous mayflies, and caddisflies. However, there are interactions between aquatic and terrestrial food webs including amphibious travel by decapod crustaceans that are able to exploit terrestrial food webs in humid streamside environments (Covich and McDowell 1996). Terrestrial species, such as small lizards (*Anolis* spp.), feed from their boulder perches on a wide range of emerging adult insects.

RECOMMENDATIONS FOR FORESTED BUFFERS

A major issue in selecting buffer widths is the relative cost of protecting these areas given their vulnerability to degradation by erosion. Storm-generated flows from direct rainfall on the channel and adjacent saturated soils yield approximately one-third of the annual discharge from only 9% of the area in the watersheds studied. This disproportionate contribution to hydrology is good reason to protect these zones for maintenance of stream hydrology and chemistry. Justification for protection is provided also by the already low species richness of aquatic food webs of this island environment and their dependence on detrital food supplies. Further alterations in this simple system could have relatively large effects. Questions arise as to how much land should be protected from logging, in terms of distance from streams, and the nature of the tradeoffs in level of protection versus access to timber products in the surrounding slopes.

To answer some of these questions, Scatena (1990) conducted an assessment of the effects of using differing buffer widths on the amount of commercial basal area for the riparian–slope–ridge complex. At one extreme, if buffers of 35 m were maintained on each side of all perennial and intermittent channels, the entire watershed would be excluded from logging. The model illustrates several less restrictive scenarios, and settles on an optimum of 22 m for perennial channels and 10 m for intermittent channels. This corresponds to the areas containing the dense herbaceous understory which characterizes the riparian vegetation in the area. Using this scenario, approximately 25% of the watershed is included within the buffers. However, because the young riparian forests have relatively low commercial value, only 20% or less of the commercial basal area is excluded from harvesting. Buffers wider than this result in a geometric increase in the amount of commercial basal area excluded from harvest. For less dissected landscapes, the area allocated to buffers would be proportionately lower.

Scatena (1990) further points out the importance of protecting saturated areas that contribute to runoff and unstable areas subject to landslides, whether or not they are located next to stream channels. Thus watershed protection should have not only a riparian focus, but should be more broadly centered around the stability of landforms in this dynamic, high-rainfall environment. This is a perspective that is often lost in less critical assessments of buffer zones that focus only on the riparian forest rather than on the nature of the landscape itself.

Summary

Riparian forests contain a combination of environmental features found nowhere else on the landscape. Their position between upland and aquatic ecosystems makes them essential to a number of species in those environments that use riparian forests only intermittently as well as to those species that reside within the riparian forest. Riparian forests are particularly critical to biodiversity in arid regions where no other forest vegetation exists. Species richness is principally a consequence of between-stand heterogeneity rather than the diversity within any one stand. The dynamic nature of these fluvial environments is responsible for creating and maintaining a variety of soil-moisture regimes along the river-upland gradient. Even though the physical forces of water flow tend to dominate these systems, there are important biotic feedbacks that modulate the transport and storage of water (e.g., beaver), nutrients (e.g., microbes and plants), and the flow of energy (e.g., food webs). The same landscape position that contributes to the amenities of biodiversity also makes riparian forests vulnerable to activities from upstream, from adjacent lands, and within the stream channel itself. This points out the need for constraints on certain land uses within riparian zones, and specifically for extractive uses of forests. These constraints and options are due largely to dominance by hydrologic processes that maintain structure and functioning of these ecosystems. Management of riparian forests not only must be responsive to these natural forces, but also to historical alterations, including stream channelization, flow diversions, and impoundments. Riparian forests are highly degraded worldwide, and thus present many opportunities for restoration. Forest management is a critical component of both the maintenance and restoration of riparian zones. Relatively unaltered examples of riparian forests provide templates for restoration goals and management objectives.

Further readings

For a general overview and synthesis of the literature on forested riparian zones, Malanson (1993) provides a very readable treatment on topics ranging from fluvial geomorphology to ecology. Naiman and Decamps (1990) emphasize water quality and biodiversity aspects of riparian management in a series of papers with worldwide coverage. Brinson (1990) provides a synthesis on the functioning of riparian forests, but with emphasis on bottomland hardwood forested wetlands of the southeastern United States.

Literature cited

Ahmad, R., F. N. Scatena, and A. Gupta. 1993. Morphology and sedimentation in Caribbean montane streams: examples from Jamaica and Puerto Rico. *Sedimentary Geology* **85**:157–69.

Alvarez-Lopez, M. 1990. Ecology of *Pterocarpus officinalis* forested wetlands in Puerto Rico. Pp. 251–65 in A. E. Lugo, M. M. Brinson, and S. Brown (eds). *Forested Wetlands*. Elsevier, Amsterdam.

Aust, W. M. and R. Lea. 1992. Comparative effects of aerial and ground logging on soil properties in a tupelo-cypress wetland. *Forest Ecology and Management* **50**:57–73.

Balslev, H., J. Luteyn, B. Ollgaard, and L. B. Holm-Nielsen. 1987. Composition and structure of adjacent unflooded and floodplain forest in Amazonian Ecuador. *Opera Botanica* **92**:37–57.

Bayley, P. B. 1991. The flood pulse advantage and the restoration of river-floodplain systems. *Regulated Rivers: Research and Management* **6**:75–86.

Beschta, R. L. and W. S. Platts. 1986. Morphological features of small streams: significance and function. *Water Resources Bulletin* **22**:369–79.

Boon, P. J., P. Calow, and G. E. Petts. 1992. *River Conservation and Management*. John Wiley and Sons, Chichester.

Brinson, M. M. 1990. Riverine forests. Pp. 87–141 in A. E. Lugo, M. M. Brinson, and S. Brown (eds). *Forested Wetlands*. Elsevier, Amsterdam.

1993. Gradients in the functioning of wetlands along environmental gradients. *Wetlands* **13**:65–74.

Brinson, M. M. and R. Rheinhardt. 1996. The role of reference wetlands in functional assessment and mitigation. *Ecological Applications* **6**:69–76.

Brinson, M. M., H. D. Bradshaw, R. N. Holmes, and J. B. Elkins, Jr. 1980. Litterfall, stemflow, and throughfall nutrient fluxes in an alluvial swamp forest. *Ecology* **61**:827–35.

Brinson, M. M., B. L. Swift, R. C. Plantico and J. S. Barclay. 1981. *Riparian ecosystems: their ecology and status*. FWS/OBS/-81/17. U.S. Fish and Wildlife Service, Washington, D.C. 155 pp.

Brown, S., 1981. A comparison of the structure, primary productivity, and transpiration of cypress ecosystems in Florida. *Ecological Monographs* **51**:403–27.

Brown, S. and D. L. Peterson. 1983. Structural characteristics and biomass productivity of two Illinois bottomland forests. *American Midland Naturalist* **110**:107–17.

Buell, M. F. and W. A. Wistendahl. 1955. Flood plain forests of the Raritan River. *Bulletin of the Torrey Botanical Club* **82**:463–72.

Conner, W. H. and J. W. Day, Jr. 1976. Productivity and composition of a baldcypress-water tupelo site and bottomland hardwood site in a Louisiana swamp. *American Journal of Botany* **63**:1354–64.

Covich, A. P. and W. H. McDowell. 1996. The stream community. Pp. 433–59 in D. P. Reagan and R. B. Waide (eds). *The Food Web of a Tropical Rain Forest*. University of Chicago Press, Chicago, Illinois.

Covich, A. P., T. A. Crowl, S. L. Johnson, and M. Pyron. 1996. Distribution and abundance of tropical freshwater shrimp along a stream corridor: response to disturbance. *Biotropica* **28**:484–92.

Dahlem, E. A. 1979. The Mahogany Creek watershed – with and without grazing. Pp. 31–4 in O. B. Cope (ed.). *Grazing and Riparian/Stream Ecosystems*. Trout Unlimited, Denver, Colorado.

Daniels, R. B. and J. W. Gilliam. 1996. Sediment and chemical load reduction by grass and riparian filters. *Soil Science Society of America Journal* **60**:246–51.

Dickson, J. G. and J. C. Huntley. 1987. Riparian zones and wildlife in southern forests: the problem and squirrel relationships. Pp. 37–9 in J. C. Dickson and O. E. Maughan (eds). *Managing southern forests for wildlife and fish – a* proceedings. Gen. Tech. Rep. SO-65, U.S. Department of Agriculture, Forest Service, Southern Forest Experimental Station, New Orleans, LA.

Dickson, J. G. and J. H. Williamson. 1988. Small mammals in streamside management zones in pine plantations. Pp. 375–8 in R. C. Szaro, K. E. Severson and D. R. Paton (tech. coords.). *Management of amphibians, reptiles, and small mammals in North America*. Gen. Tech. Rep. RM-166, U.S. Department of Agriculture, Forest Service, Rocky Mountain Station, Fort Collins, CO.

Dirschl, H. J. and R. T. Coupland. 1972. Vegetation patterns and site relationships in the Saskatchewan River delta. *Canadian Journal of Botany* 50:647–75.

Doyle, R. D. and T. R. Fisher. 1994. Nitrogen fixation by periphyton and plankton of the Amazon floodplain at Lake Calado. *Biogeochemistry* 26:41–66.

Duever, M. J., J. E. Carlson, and L. A. Riopelle. 1984. Corkscrew Swamp: a virgin cypress strand. Pp. 334–48 in K. C. Ewel and H. T. Odum (eds), *Cypress Swamps*. University Presses of Florida, Gainesville, Fla.

Dynesius, M. and C. Nilsson. 1994. Fragmentation and flow regulation of river systems in the northern third of the world. *Science* 266:753–62.

Ehrenfeld, J. G. and M. Gulick. 1981. Structure and dynamics of hardwood swamps in the New Jersey Pine Barrens: contrasting patterns in trees and shrubs. *American Journal of Botany* 68:471–81.

Ehrenfeld, J. G. and J. P. Schneider. 1993. Responses of forested wetland vegetation to perturbations of water chemistry and hydrology. *Wetlands* 13:122–9.

Elmore, W. and R. L. Beschta. 1987. Riparian areas: Perceptions and management. *Rangelands* 9:260–5.

Everitt, B. L. 1980. Ecology of saltcedar – a plea for research. *Environmental Geology* 3:77–84.

Fetherston, K. L., R. J. Naiman, and R. E. Bilby. 1995. Large woody debris, physical process, and riparian forest development in montaine river networks of the Pacific Northwest. *Geomorphology* 13:133–44.

Findlay, C. S. and J. Houlahan. 1997. Anthropogenic correlates of species richness in southeastern Ontario, Canada. *Conservation Biology* 11:1000–9.

Fonda, R. W. 1974. Forest succession in relation to river terrace development in Olympic National Park, Washington. *Ecology* 55:927–42.

Forman, R. T. T. 1995. *Land Mosaics: The Ecology of Landscapes and Regions*. Cambridge University Press, New York.

Freeman, C. E. and W. A. Dick-Peddie. 1970. Woody riparian vegetation in the Black and Sacramento Mountain Ranges, Southern New Mexico. *Southwestern Naturalist* 15:145–64.

Gore, J. A. and F. D. Shields, Jr. 1995. Can large rivers be restored? *BioScience* 45:142–52.

Goulding, M. 1980. *The Fishes and the Forest*. University of California Press, Berkeley, California.

Gregory, S. V., F. J. Swanson, W. A. McKee, and K. W. Cummins. 1991. An ecosystem perspective of riparian zones. *BioScience* 41:540–51.

Hall. T. F. and W. T. Penfound. 1939. A phytosociological study of *Nyssa biflora* consocies in southeastern Louisiana. *American Midland Naturalist* 22:369–75.

1943. Cypress-gum communities in the Blue Girth swamp near Selma, Alabama. *Ecology* 24:208–17.

Harris, R. R., C. A. Fox and R. Risser. 1987. Impacts of hydroelectric development on riparian vegetation in the Sierra Nevada region, California, USA. *Environmental Management* 11:519–27.

Holdridge, L. R., W. C. Grenke, W. H. Hatheway, T. Liang, T. and J. A. Tosi, Jr. 1971. *Forest Environments in Tropical Life Zones*. Pergamon Press, New York.

Hughes, J. D. 1994. *Pan's Travail: Environmental Problems of the Ancient Greeks and Romans*. The Johns Hopkins University Press, Baltimore, Maryland.

Hunter, M. L., Jr. 1990. *Wildlife, Forests, and Forestry*. Prentice Hall, Englewood Cliffs, New Jersey.

Hupp, C. R. 1982. Stream-grade variation and riparian-forest ecology along Passage Creek, Virginia. *Bulletin of the Torrey Botanical Club* 109:488–99.

Hupp, C. R. 1992. Riparian vegetation recovery patterns following stream channelization: a geomorphic perspective. *Ecology* 73:1209–26.

Johnson, W. C. 1994. Woodland expansion in the Platte River, Nebraska: patterns and causes. *Ecological Monographs* 64:45–85.

Johnson, W. C., Burgess, R. L. and Keammerer, W. R. 1976. Forest overstory vegetation on the Missouri River floodplain in North Dakota. *Ecological Monographs* 46: 59–84.

Junk, W. 1989. Flood tolerance and tree distribution in central Amazonian floodplains. Pp. 47–64 in L. B. Holm-Nielsen, I. C. Nielsen, and H. Balsley (eds). *Tropical Forests: Botanical Dynamics, Speciation, and Diversity*. Academic Press, Orlando, Florida.

Junk, W. J., P. B. Bayley, and R. E. Sparks. 1989. The flood-pulse concept in river-floodplain systems. *Canadian Special Publication of Fisheries and Aquatic Sciences* 106:110–27.

Kalliola, R. and M. Puhakka. 1988. River dynamics and vegetation mosaicism: a case study of the River Kamajohka, northernmost Finland. *Journal of Biogeography* 15:703–19.

Kalliola, R. J. Salo, M. Puhakka, and M. Rajasilta. 1991. New site formation and colonizing vegetation in primary succession on the western Amazon floodplains. *Journal of Ecology* 79:877–901.

Keeley, J. E. 1979. Population differentiation along a flood frequency gradient: physiological adaptations to flooding in *Nyssa sylvatica*. *Ecological Monographs* 49:89–108.

Kilgo, J. C., R. A. Sargent, K. V. Miller, and B. R. Chapman. 1996. Effect of riparian zone width on Swainson's Warbler abundance. Pp. 177–80 in K. M. Flynn (ed.), *Proceedings of the Southern Forested Wetlands Ecology and Management Conference*. Clemson University, Clemson, SC.

King, S. L. 1995. Effects of flooding regimes on two impounded bottomland hardwood stands. *Wetlands* 15:272–84.

Lee, L. C. 1983. The floodplain and wetland vegetation of two Pacific Northwest river ecosystems. Ph.D. Dissertation, University of Washington, Seattle, Washington.

Leopold, L. B., M. G. Wolman, and J. P. Miller. 1964. Fluvial processes in geomorphology. Freeman, San Francisco, California.

Lindauer, I. E. 1983. A comparison of the plant communities of the South Platte and Arkansas River drainages in eastern Colorado. Southwestern Naturalist 28:249–59.

Lowrance, R., R. A. Leonard, L. E. Asmussen, and R. L. Todd. 1985. Nutrient budgets for agricultural watersheds in the southeastern coastal plain. Ecology 66:287–96.

Malanson, G. P. 1993. Riparian Landscapes. Cambridge University Press, Cambridge.

Maltby, E., D. V. Hogan, and R. J. McInnes (eds). 1996. Functional Analysis of European Wetland Ecosystems, Phase 1: The Function of River Marginal Wetland Ecosystems. European Commission, Directorate-General XII, Science Research and Development, Luxembourg.

Mayo Melendez, E. 1965. Algunas características ecológicas de los bosques inundables de Darien, Panamá, con miras a su posible utilización. Turrialba 15:336–47.

Megonigal, J. P., W. H. Conner, S. Kroeger, and R. R. Sharitz. 1997. Aboveground production in Southeastern floodplain forests. Ecology 78:370–84.

Mulholland, P. J., 1979. Organic carbon cycling in a swamp-stream ecosystem and export by streams in eastern North Carolina. Ph.D. Dissertation, Univ. of North Carolina, Chapel Hill, North Carolina.

Nadler, C. T., Jr. 1978. River metamorphosis of the South Platte and Arkansas rivers, Colorado. M.S. Thesis, Colorado State University, Fort Collins, Colorado.

Naiman, R. J. and H. Decamps (eds). 1990. The Ecology and Management of Aquatic-Terrestrial Ecotones. Man and the Biosphere Series, Volume 4. UNESCO, Paris.

Naiman, R. J. and K. H. Rogers. 1997. Large animals and system-level characteristics in river corridors. BioScience 47:521–9.

Naiman, R. J., H. Decamps, and M. Pollock. 1993. The role of riparian corridors in maintaining regional biodiversity. Ecological Applications 3:209–12.

Naiman, R. J., G. Pinay, C. A. Johnston, and J. Pastor. 1994. Beaver influences on the long-term biogeochemical characteristics of boreal forest drainage networks. Ecology 75:905–21.

Nilsson, C. 1992. Conservation management of riparian communities. Pp. 352–72 in L. Hansson (ed.). Ecological Principles of Nature Conservation. Elsevier Applied Science, London.

Nilsson, C., R. Jansson, and U. Zinko. 1997. Long-term responses of river-margin vegetation to water-level regulation. Science 276:798–800.

NRC (National Research Council). 1995. *Wetlands: Characteristics and Boundaries.* National Academy Press, Washington, DC.

Nutrient Subcommittee of the Chesapeake Bay Program. 1995. *Water quality functions of Riparian Forest buffer systems in the Chesapeake Bay watershed.* EPA 903–R-95–004 CBP/TRS 134/95, Annapolis, Maryland.

Penka, M., M. Vyskot, E. Klimo, and F. Vasicek. 1991. *Floodplain Forest Ecosystem. II. After Water Management Measures.* Elsevier, Amsterdam.

Peterjohn, W. T. and D. L. Correll. 1984. Nutrient dynamics in an agricultural watershed: observations on the role of a riparian forest. *Ecology* **65**:1466–75.

Pinay, G. and H. Decamps. 1988. The role of riparian woods in regulating nitrogen fluxes between the alluvial aquifer and surface water: a conceptual model. *Regulated Rivers* **2**:507–16.

Pinay, G., A. Fabre, P. Vervier, and F. Gazelle. 1992. Control of C, N and P distribution in soils of riparian forests. *Landscape Ecology* **6**:121–32.

Pinay, G., N. E. Haycock, C. Ruffinoni, and R. M. Holmes. 1994. The role of denitrification in nitrogen removal in river corridoers. Pp. 107–16 in W. J. Mitsch (ed.). *Global Wetlands: Old World and New.* Elsevier, Amsterdam.

Räsänen, M. E., J. S. Salo, and R. J. Kalliola. 1987. Fluvial perturbance in the western Amazon basin: regulation by long-term sub-Andean tectonics. *Science* **238**:1398–401.

Reid, R. S. and J. E. Ellis. 1995. Impacts of pastoralists on woodlands in South Turkana, Kenya: livestock-mediated tree recruitment. *Ecological Applications* **5**:978–92.

Rheinhardt, R. D., M. M. Brinson, and P. M. Farley. 1997. Applying wetland reference data to functional assessment, mitigation, and restoration. *Wetlands* **17**:195–215.

Rosgen, D. 1995. *Applied River Morphology.* Wildland Hydrology, Pagosa Springs, Colorado.

Ross, S. T. and J. A. Baker 1983. The response of fishes to periodic spring floods in a southeastern stream. *American Midland Naturalist* **109**:1–14.

Rudolph, D. C. and J. G. Dickson. 1990. Streamside zone width and amphibian and reptile abundance. *Southwestern Naturalist* **35**:472–6.

Scatena, F. N. 1990. Selection of riparian buffer zones in humid tropical steeplands. Pp. 328–37 in *Research Needs and Applications to Reduce Erosion and Sedimentation in Tropical Steeplands.* IAHS-AISH Publication Number 192, Fiji.

Scatena, F. N. and A. E. Lugo. 1995. Geomorphology, disturbance, and the soil and vegetation of two subtropical wet steepland watersheds of Puerto Rico. *Geomorphology* **13**:199–213.

Scott, M. L., J. M. Friedman, and G. T. Auble. 1996. Fluvial process and the establishment of bottomland trees. *Geomorphology* **14**:327–39.

Smith, N. J. H. 1981. *Man, Fishes, and the Amazon.* Columbia University Press, New York.

Stanford, J. A. and J. V. Ward. 1993. An ecosystem perspective of alluvial rivers:

connectivity and the hyporheic corridor. *Journal of the North American Benthological Society* **12**:48–60.

Stromberg, J. C., D. T. Patten, and B. D. Richter. 1991. Flood flows and dynamics of Sonoran riparian forests. *Rivers* **2**:221–35.

Thompson, K. 1961. Riparian forests of the Sacramento Valley, California. *Annals of the Association of American Geographers.* **51**:294–315.

Van Dijk, G. M., E. C. L. Marteijn, and A. Schulte-Wulwer-Leidig. 1995. Ecological rehabilitation of the river Rhine: plans, progress, and perspectives. *Regulated Rivers: Research and Management* **11**:377–88.

Van Splunder, I., H. Coops, L. A. C. J. Voesenek, and C. W. P. M. Blom. 1995. Establishment of alluvial forest species in floodplains: the role of dispersal timing, germination characteristics and water level fluctuations. *Acta Botanica Neerlandica* **44**: 269–78.

Vervier, P., J. Gibert, P. Marmonier, and M.-L. Dole-Olivier. 1992. A perspective on the permeability of the surface freshwater-groundwater ecotone. *Journal of the North American Benthological Society* **11**:93–102.

Vervier, P., M. Dobson, and G. Pinay. 1993. Role of interaction zone between surface and ground waters in DOC transport and processing: considerations for river restoration. *Freshwater Biology* **29**:275–84.

Vyskot, M. 1976. Biomass production of the tree layer in a floodplain forest near Lednice. Pp. 175–202 in H. E. Young (ed.), *Oslo Biomass Studies*. University of Maine, Orono, Maine.

Wakeley, J. S. and T. H. Roberts. 1996. Bird distributions and forest zonation in a bottomland hardwood wetland. *Wetlands* **16**:296–308.

Webster, J. R., J. B. Wallace, and E. F. Benfield. 1995. Organic processes in streams of the eastern United States. Pp. 117–87 in C. E. Cushing, K. W. Cummins, and G. W. Minshall (eds). *River and Stream Ecosystems*. Elsevier, Amsterdam.

Welcomme, R. L. 1979. *Fisheries Ecology of Floodplain Rivers*. Longman, London.

Wharton, C. H., W. M. Kitchens, E. C. Pendleton, and T. W. Sipe. 1982. *The ecology of bottomland hardwood swamps of the southeast: a community profile.* FWS/OBS-81/37. U.S. Fish and Wildlife Service, Biological Services Program, Washington, D.C.

WWF. 1993. *Living Rivers*. WorldWide Fund for Nature, Zeist, The Netherlands. 28 pp.

9   Forested wetlands

ARAM J.K. CALHOUN

Quaking ground underfoot, cycles of flooding and drying – neither terrestrial nor aquatic, wetlands seem to occupy a category by themselves. In general terms, wetlands are defined by the presence of water within the rooting zone during the growing season such that it affects soil processes and plant growth. It follows that wetlands develop in the landscape where drainage is impeded, where water collects in topographic lows such as valleys or depressions, where the water table is high, or where there is significant flooding from rivers, lakes, or ocean tides. Forested wetlands occur in all these landscape settings.

Forested wetlands, more commonly known as swamps, flatwoods, mangals (mangroves), or inundated forests, have a wide distribution, occurring on every continent except Antarctica. They are extensive in equatorial areas, e.g., the Amazon, and the most abundant wetland type in temperate and boreal regions. Approximately 3% of the global land area is wetland and of this, it is estimated that 60% is forested (Matthews and Fung 1987). More exact areal estimates of forested wetland are unavailable because wetland statistics generally do not differentiate between forested and non-forested ecosystems, and forest statistics do not separate wetland from upland. Furthermore, compared with boreal and temperate upland forests, forested wetlands are a relatively understudied ecosystem worldwide (Lugo 1990). Descriptive literature on the most widely studied forested wetland ecosystem, mangrove swamps, can be traced back to 325 BC (Chapman 1976), yet research on ecosystem functions was not conducted until the 1930s (Walter and Steiner 1936). Studies in other forested wetland communities pale in contrast to the work on mangroves.

Food, fuel, and fiber have been provided by forested wetlands for thousands of years. However, as the human population increases, so does the demand for natural resources, agricultural land, housing, hydroelectric dams, and aquaculture. By the early 1990s, almost 40% of the earth's land surface had been converted to cropland and pasture, largely at the expense of grasslands and forests. All of these pressures have led to an alarming overall decrease in global wetland resources. However, rates of loss of forested wetlands are unknown because of a lack of baseline data on forested wetlands. One might, however, extrapolate from losses of the global forest resource (Figure 9.1). It is estimated that global forest cover has been reduced by one-third (Myers 1995). Looking at the distribution of forested wetlands worldwide (Figure 9.2) and comparing it with areas of general forest loss, one can see that forested wetland conversion is potentially significant. Loss of boreal forests is on the rise (Myers 1995) and extensive wetland areas of forested peatlands occur in this region. An inventory of coastal mangroves is lacking but data from individual countries suggest losses of 85–90% as typical. In the United States, although the rate of loss of wetlands overall has decreased, the proportional loss of forested wetland has increased from 54% of all freshwater wetlands between the 1950s and 1970s to 95% from the mid-1970s to 1980s (Dahl and Johnson 1991).

The World Conservation Monitoring Centre and World Wide Fund for Nature have estimated that 94% of the planet's forest cover has no official protection (Sugal 1997). Given the current trend of a 1% per year loss of forest land (Bryant et al. 1997), recognizing and understanding the value of forested wetlands becomes critical if conservation is an objective.

Forested wetlands, making up less than 2% of the earth's land area, contribute to global biodiversity by virtue of their relative rareness and uniqueness. In other words, they are an uncommon landscape feature which supports biota that do not occur in other ecosystems. Recognition of the whole suite of values of forested wetlands is reflected in the recent spate of publications specifically on forested wetland ecosytems (Ewel and Odum 1984, Hutchings and Saenger 1987, Hook et al. 1988, Lugo et al. 1990; Trettin et al. 1997, Rieley and Page 1997). The purpose of this chapter is to examine how forested wetlands contribute to biodiversity and to evaluate the strengths and weaknesses of current management strategies from a biodiversity perspective. First, I will define some terms and provide some insight into forested wetland ecosystem functions.

An overview of forested wetlands

SOME DEFINITIONS

'Wetlands are quirks and local aberrations of the hydrological cycle which differ from their surroundings by the persistent presence of free

Fig. 9.1 Threatened frontier forests of the world. Frontier forests (large, intact natural forest ecosystems that are relatively undisturbed) appear in dark grey; non-frontier forests (secondary forests, plantations, and otherwise degraded forest) appear in light grey. (Modified from *Threatened Frontier Forests of the World*, World Resources Institute, 1997.)

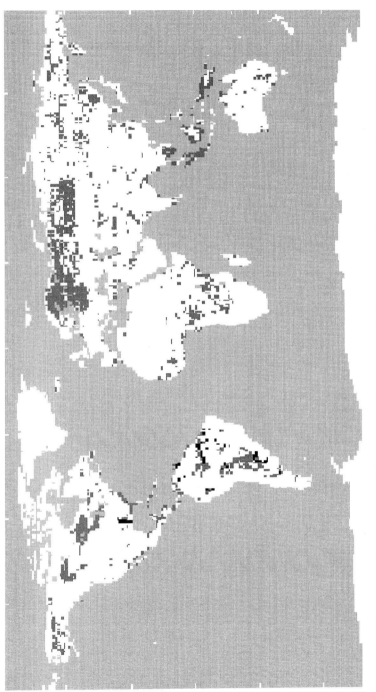

Fig. 9.2. Global distribution of forested wetlands. Black represents alluvial wetlands. Dark grey represents forested swamps and bogs. (Modified from Matthews and Fung, 1987).

water' (Paijmans *et al.* 1985). The words 'quirk' and 'local aberration' suggest an unusual ecosystem – something deviating from the norm – indeed, something deserving of our study and, possibly, conservation. But before pursuing this, my working definitions of both 'wetland' and 'forested wetland' need to be explicit.

The definition of 'wetland' differs depending on whether you are a biologist, a regulator, a developer, or a manager. For this chapter, I have adopted the most internationally recognized definition, developed by the Convention on Wetlands of International Importance (popularly known as the Ramsar Convention): 'Wetlands are areas of marsh, fen, peatland or water, whether natural or artificial, permanent or temporary, with water that is static or flowing, fresh, brackish, or salt, including areas of marine water the depth of which at low tide does not exceed six metres.' (Scott and Jones 1995).

Forested wetlands are broadly defined as a subset of wetlands (as defined above), characterized by a significant component of trees, regardless of their stature (Lugo *et al.* 1990). From a biodiversity perspective, forested wetlands are forested ecosystems in which an abundance of water plays a key role in shaping plant community structure and dynamics, animal life histories or morphological features, and biogeochemical processes.

The Ramsar Convention recognizes three types of forested wetlands which are separated by landscape setting rather than vegetation community type: peatlands, inland freshwater swamps, and tidal and estuarine forested wetlands (Figure 9.3). These are reviewed in Box 9.1.

Key features

Wetland forests are distinguished from upland forests by degree of wetness. Although this concept seems simple enough, there is a continuum of wetness that usually changes with season. Where along this continuum a non-wetland forested ecosystem becomes a wetland is often debated. For example, in arid regions of the world, lands subject to inundation that support distinctive vegetation are often called wetlands even though they may be dry for two or three consecutive years. Precipitation events can be severe and unpredictable and as a result, forests may appear to be upland in some years and wetland in others. In the United States, official governmental definitions would not recognize some of these areas as wetland (Environmental Laboratories 1987). In this section, an over-

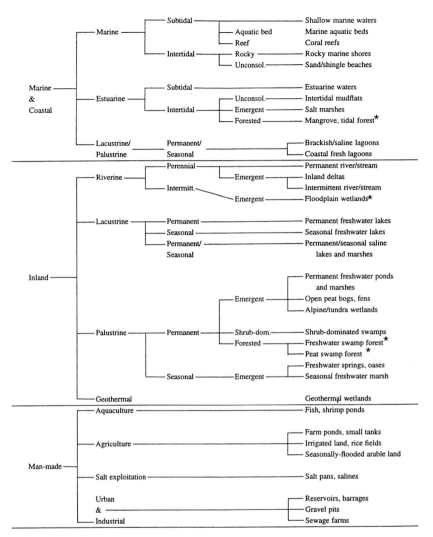

Fig. 9.3. Wetland classification used by the Ramsar Convention Bureau. Forested wetland classes are marked (*). (From Scott and Jones, 1995.)

view of forested wetlands will be given to lay the conceptual framework for how forested wetlands are distinct from upland forests.

Water is the most important regulator of forested wetlands and variation in its chemistry, inputs and outputs, and hydroperiod is responsible for the diversity of forested wetland types. Factors such as topography, soils, geology, catchment area, landscape position, and climate dictate the relationship between water and a forested wetland (Lugo *et al.* 1990). For

BOX 9.1 **Major types**

Freshwater swamp forests
Freshwater swamp forests are a diverse group of ecosystems compared with peatlands and estuarine forested wetlands. Swamp woodlands, sumplands, palusplains, damplands, and basin forests are all terms referring to palustrine, freshwater forested swamps (Figure 9.4). Although some of these swamps may have extensive muck or organic soils, they are traditionally separated from peatland forests where mosses, sedges, and ericaceous shrubs are the dominant peat builders. Freshwater forested wetlands form where drainage is impeded by soil characteristics or by a confining layer, where water collects in topographic lows (valleys or depressions), or where the groundwater is close to, or intercepts, the land surface. Hydrologic characteristics such as frequency and duration of flooding or saturation, major sources of water (groundwater, precipitation, overland flow), and hydrologic connections to other wetlands or deepwater habitats vary depending on landscape setting and climate. These differences, together with climate and geography, account for the diversity of floral and faunal communities associated with freshwater forested wetlands. Examples of freshwater forested swamps include the baldcypress (*Taxodium distichum*) and red maple (*Acer rubrum*) forested wetlands of the eastern United States, the low inundated forests of Mexico, and palm forests of the tropics.

Peatlands
Peat swamp forests, a subset of the freshwater swamp forests, are also known as pocosins, spruce mires, kerapah forests, wooded fens, and treed bogs (Figure 9.5). Peatlands are wetland ecosystems characterized by organic soils, or peat, which has been produced and deposited faster than it has decomposed because of saturated (and anaerobic) soil conditions. These conditions result from cool temperature and/or a humid climate, or some combination of the two, the result being an excess of precipitation over evapotranspiration. In the broadest definition, peatlands are those portions of the earth's landscape that are (a) wetland, (b) have organic soils, (c) and include all waters and organisms on top of or within the organic matter (Worley 1980). Peatlands are often associated with sphagnum mosses, sedges, and ericaceous shrubs. Often peatlands are nutrient poor, acidic environments characterized by low oxygen levels in the rooting zone. They develop in a variety of hydrogeomorphic settings (landscape positions in relation to hydrology, geology, and surficial features) including old lake basins, valleys, kettle holes and other isolated surface depressions, wet slopes, and waterlogged flats. Distinguishing peatlands from other wetlands is often based on peat depth (e.g., in Canada, the United States, and Sweden the minimum depth requirement ranges from 25 to 40 cm), but not

Fig. 9.4. Cypress swamp, South Carolina, USA. (Aram Calhoun photo)

Fig. 9.5. Spruce forested peatland, Isle of Haut, Maine, USA. (Aram Calhoun photo)

exclusively. In Finland, for example, there is no minimum peat depth criterion (Paavilainen and Paivanen 1995).

Global peatland area is estimated to be 550 million hectares (Heathwaite 1993, Paavilainen and Paivanen 1995). However, estimates are greatly compromised by incomplete inventory data and variable criteria for peatland classification. Extensive peatlands occur between 50° and 70° north latitude in Russia, Fennoscandia (Norway, Finland, and Sweden), Canada, and the United States (Alaska). Tropical peatlands are most extensive in Indonesia and are largely concentrated in coastal lowlands, with some occurring in mountainous regions and valleys (Paavilainen and Paivanen 1995). Forested peatlands in temperate and boreal zones support a variety of tree species with spruce (*Picea* spp.), larch (*Larix* spp.) and birch (*Betula* spp.) dominant (Van Hees 1990). Tree species diversity in tropical peatlands is much greater; for example, in Borneo alone, 242 peatland tree species have been recorded (Bruenig 1990).

Tidal and estuarine forested wetlands
Estuarine forested wetlands, variously called mangals, tidal forests, coastal forests, and mangrove forests, are a characteristic feature of sheltered shorelines of the tropics and subtropics (most commonly deltaic coasts, lagoons, and along estuarine shorelines) of Africa, Asia, Australia, New Zealand, and North, South and Central America (Figure 9.6). Mangrove ecosystems include woody plants from many different families and genera. These species are collectively called mangroves because they possess a

Fig 9.6. Mangrove swamp, Sarawak, Malaysia. (Aram Calhoun photo)

variety of morphological, physiological, and reproductive adaptations that allow them to grow in an estuarine tidal setting. Hence, the term 'mangrove' swamp is not restricted to the true mangrove family, .

Tidal regimes and variable salinity shape coastal wetland forest development. Geography, freshwater input, wave energy, sedimentation, shore slope, tidal range, and climate, among others, dictate mangrove community development (Hutchings and Saenger 1987). There is no typical mangrove community as they, like other forested wetlands, occur in a variety of landscape settings (Hutchings and Saenger [1987] recognized six). The most extensive mangrove forest complex in the world is the Sundarbans in India and Bangladesh (Dugan 1993).

example, in the palm swamps (common genera include *Mauritia, Raphia,* and *Metroxylon*) of Central and South America, structural and compositional complexity increases from basin settings to montane riverine settings; that is, from a stagnant to a flowing water situation (Klinge *et al.* 1990). Conversely, in coastal settings, complexity is greater in basin wetlands as compared with the riverine wetlands subject to inundation with salt water (Alvarez-Lopez 1990). Variable disturbance regimes (fire, drought, freezing, windthrows, hurricanes) or environmental gradients such as salinity will further enhance differences in ecosystem functions among forested wetlands (Lugo *et al.* 1990).

Saturated or flooded soil conditions that last for as little as two weeks during the growing season can profoundly influence soil conditions and affect plant species composition and structure (Environmental Laboratories 1987). Flooded soils may be anoxic as little as a few millimeters below the soil surface (King 1990) resulting in a unique set of plant strategies for oxygenating the rhizosphere, maintaining root functions with limited oxygen, and dealing with toxic compounds associated with anaerobic metabolism (Hook and Crawford 1978, Kozlowski 1983, Armstrong 1991). Wetland plant morphological adaptations include aerenchymous tissue (tissue with large, air-filled intercellular spaces) and lenticels (large pores in the tree bark) to facilitate oxygen transfer from the atmosphere to the roots, special root structures like pneumatophores purported both to provide support and possibly improve root aeration, and xeromorphic characteristics such as pubescence, waxy cuticles, and rolled leaf edges in response to water and/or nutrient stress (Kozlowski 1983, Lugo et al. 1990). Physiological adaptations may include altered root metabolic pathways, inhibited translocation of nutrients, and leaf abscission. For example, trees in the varzea white water forests subjected to flooding (as much as 10 meters of water for 280 days) adapt by shedding leaves and limiting growth during that time (Junk 1993). Reproductive strategies are often distinct from upland mechanisms. Many flooded forest trees have water- and fish-dispersed seeds. Waterlogging and its effects on tree growth have been examined in detail in the southeastern United States bottomland hardwood forests (Wharton et al. 1982).

Similarly, animals associated with forested wetlands often exhibit special adaptations for being successful in the wetland environment. Reproductive strategies, feeding strategies, physiological traits, or anatomical structures may reflect habitat specialization that may have evolved from time scales of decades to millennia. This is examined in more detail below.

Forested wetlands support biogeochemical processes distinct from upland ecosystems. Because of fluctuating water regimes, there is a dynamic interface between anaerobic and aerobic conditions that supports the microbially driven anaerobic/aerobic processes of methanogenesis and methanotrophy, denitrification and nitrification, and sulfate reduction and sulfate oxidation, to name a few. Transformation of inorganic nutrients to organic species which support aquatic food webs is a key function of riparian wetlands. Wetland environments may support a diverse array of specialized microorganisms that mediate these and other transformations (Westermann 1993).

Contribution to biodiversity

As noted earlier, forested wetlands are a special component of bio-diversity on a global scale because they are unique and relatively rare. The purpose of this section is to look beyond this role to ways in which forested wetlands contribute to the variety of life at all levels – ecosystem, species, and genetic.

ECOSYSTEM DIVERSITY

Forested wetlands as distinct landscape features

Large expanses of open grassland punctuated by linear floodplain forests: this is one dramatic image of how forested wetlands contribute to biodiversity at the landscape level. Riparian forests are perhaps the most distinctive landscape features in arid environments such as the western United States, Australia, and southern and western Africa. These flood-plain forests, often associated with marshes characteristic of inland deltas, stand out as highly productive ecosystems with water drawing an impressive array, in both numbers and diversity, of birds and other animals during the dry season (Dugan 1993).

In other parts of the world, including Europe, the Americas, and India, where riparian forests are a common forested wetland type, they contrib-ute to landscape biodiversity in more subtle ways. Often the forests them-selves have very low species diversity; in fact, plant diversity typically decreases with increased duration of flooding (Lugo *et al.* 1990). Yet the monotypic stands of palm, bald cypress (*Taxodium distichum*), or silver maple (*Acer saccharinum*) commonly associated with wetter riparian habi-tats create distinct communities. For example, riparian palm forests in the upland valleys of Peruvian Amazonia are rather homogeneous, yet they differ in floristic composition and community structure from the sur-rounding terra firma palm forests (Kahn and Mejia 1990). The situation is reversed in the southeastern United States where bottomland hardwood forests commonly support a diverse assemblage of tree species compared with the surrounding upland pinelands (Harriss 1984). In either case, landscape diversity is enhanced.

Forested wetland ecosystems may have structural attributes that differ from adjacent ecosystems thereby providing different habitat features. For example, the microclimate within forested wetlands may be more humid and have a more stable temperature regime than in the surrounding forest. Plant community structure may vary dramatically from that of adjacent upland forests. Depending on the hydroperiod, forested wetlands may support denser, smaller stemmed trees, have only a tree canopy, a tree and herb layer (dynamic floodplains) or three well-developed layers. Because forested wetlands are typically more difficult to log than dry forests, the probability of wetland forest supporting old growth is potentially greater than for the surrounding uplands. This is certainly true in the northern United States where forested wetlands make up a significant proportion of old-growth forests (Frelich and Graumlich 1994).

Forested wetlands with extensive areal coverage become distinct landscape features and contribute to overall landscape complexity. Boreal forested wetlands are expansive throughout the northern latitudes and may be largely monotypic stands of spruce, larch, or birch. Both plant and animal species diversity may be low in these ecosystems, but by virtue of their size they are an important component of the overall landscape.

Forested wetlands that are naturally rare, such as high-altitude swamps and bogs in tropical landscapes, tidal palm (*Mauritia flexuosa*) forests in South America, and depressional forested wetlands in India, or forested wetlands made up of species at their range limits, contribute to the richness of a landscape.

The number of forested wetlands threatened or endangered by human encroachment grows with world population. For example, extensive drainage of forested peatlands in Finland has greatly compromised landscape-scale biodiversity with fern-rich spruce mires, paludified herb-rich hardwood spruce forests, rich birch fens, and spring-influenced spruce mires becoming extremely threatened (Pakarinen 1995). Riparian forests in Europe and the western United States are similarly at risk, increasing the ecological value of these remnant forest types.

Interface between aquatic and terrestrial ecosystems

In contrast to isolated freshwater swamps, riparian and estuarine forested wetlands form an interface between terrestrial and aquatic environments. Just the term 'interface' connotes richness, evoking an image of unlike things coming together and intermingling. The Sundarbans of India and Bangladesh, one of the most productive ecosystems in the world, is exemplary of this intermingling: here riparian, estuarine, marine, and terrestrial ecosystems come together in a vast wetland complex (Dugan 1993). Such structural and physicochemical diversity encourages a rich assemblage of biota drawn from both the terrestrial and aquatic realms.

The following description of a mangrove swamp captures the value of

these forested wetlands as interfaces between aquatic and terrestrial ecosystems:

> The beaches on the coast I had come to visit are treacherous and the tides
> are always shifting things about among the mangrove roots . . . A world
> like that is not really natural . . . Parts of it are neither land nor sea and so
> everything is moving from one element to another, wearing uneasily the
> queer transitional bodies that life adopts in such places . . . Nothing stays
> put where it began because everything is constantly climbing in, or climb-
> ing out, of its unstable environment.   (Eiseley 1971)

Two major functions of these forested wetlands, each contributing to biodiversity, are alluded to in Eiseley's description and are discussed below.

Everything is moving from one element to another. Many wetland forests,
particularly estuarine and riverine forests where water from the adjacent
aquatic system defines the wetland, are characterized by their open biogeochemical cycles, that is, characterized by 'everything moving from one
element to another'. High rates of carbon export and transformation of
inorganic elements such as phosphorus and nitrogen to organic compounds are critical to consumer metabolism (food chain support) in
coupled systems. Twilley *et al.* (1987) showed not only that organisms in
aquatic systems utilize the foods exported from forested wetlands, but that
they are adapted to the timing and periodicity of such inputs. Conversely,
floodplains and mangrove swamps are enriched in oxygen and nutrients
by the waters flooding them.

Wetlands have been called the kidneys of the landscape (Meyer 1990) as
they often serve as a biofilter between terrestrial and aquatic ecosystems.
Such an organismal image underscores the importance of wetlands as
landscape features (as opposed to plant and animal habitat), often hydrologically connected to other ecosystems. Riparian coastal forests worldwide and the pocosin peatlands of the mid-Atlantic coast of the United
States, for example, have a direct impact on the water quality of estuaries
(Sharitz and Gibbons 1982). These inland wetlands decrease sediment
loads to estuaries, regulate freshwater flow, and provide organic matter
for food chain support. Loss of inland wetlands and the resulting interrup-
tion of flows of elements among hydrologically connected systems both
jeopardizes ecosystems and compromises biodiversity at a variety of
levels.

Nothing stays put . . . everything is constantly climbing in, or climbing out.
This observation aptly describes the role of forested wetlands in supporting species associated with both terrestrial and aquatic habitats. The vertical zonation associated with tropical mangrove forests is a good example

of the convergence of marine intertidal fauna with terrestrial forest denizens. Juvenile soldier crabs (Mictyris spp.) forage in the substrate and lower canopy of the mangroves while adults reside in the adjacent seagrass beds or mudflats. A few meters away, the upper canopy may provide roosting sites for herons or foraging sites for terrestrial vertebrates such as proboscis monkeys (Nasalis larvatus). Many temperate amphibian species, including ambystomid salamanders (Ambystoma spp.) and many ranids (Rana spp.), use wetlands for breeding and adjacent upland habitats outside of the breeding season (Semlitsch 1998).

Plant community structure and plant phenology in forested wetlands may be quite different from those in adjacent upland forests and thus provide opportunities for animal species not strictly associated with wetlands. For example, forested wetlands in the Amazon basin support 75% of the riverine fishery by providing fruits, seeds, leaves, and insects (Goulding 1985). Over 50 species of riverine fish feed or spawn in the bald cypress riparian wetlands in the southeastern United States (Dugan 1993). Similarly, terrestrial fauna are supported in bald cypress wetlands. Mast produced in winter (and insufficient in the adjacent upland forests) supports turkeys and other birds, wild hogs, deer, and squirrels while summer mast is provided in surrounding upland habitats. Even hydrologically isolated forested wetlands provide an important interface with the surrounding upland ecosystem. In the northeastern United States, evergreen forested wetlands are critical habitat for whitetail deer (Odocoileus virginianus) in winter as they provide food, cover from predators, and shelter from the severe, winter winds and snows. Skunk cabbage (Symplocarpus foetides), the first herbaceous species to emerge from the snow in northeastern forested wetlands, is a primary energy source for black bears (Ursus americanus) emerging from hibernation (Newton 1988).

Diversity among forested wetlands. Forested wetlands range from eutrophic to oligotrophic, large-statured to stunted, seasonally flooded to permanently flooded, species-rich to species-depauperate, freshwater to saline, and structurally complex to simple stands. These differences, driven by latitude, altitude, hydroperiod, hydrogeomorphic setting, and geography, among others, are highlighted in classification schemes for forested wetlands. These classification schemes systematically bring out the differences between wetlands; differences which reflect diversity in environmental characteristics and ecological functions. For example, Indonesia recognizes six types of mangrove forest and eight types of freshwater forests (Scott and Jones 1995). Some classification systems focus on vegetation type as in needle-leaved evergreen forest (e.g., black spruce

[*Picea mariana*] bog) or broad-leaved, deciduous forest (e.g., red maple [*Acer rubrum*] swamp) (Cowardin *et al.* 1979) while others categorize wetlands by hydrogeomorphic characteristics as reflected in the terms playa (intermittently flooded flat), wadi (intermittently inundated channel), barlkarra (intermittently flooded flat), and palusplain (seasonally waterlogged flats) (Semeniuk and Semeniuk 1995) or riverine, depressional, or slope (Brinson *et al.* 1995). Still others combine vegetation type and landscape setting, e.g., overwash mangrove, fringe mangrove, basin mangrove and so on (Hutchings and Saenger 1987).

The wide range of conditions under which forested wetlands develop results in a variety of ecosystems with diverse functions, plant and animal communities, and habitat value. Geographic location, for example, may shape diversity patterns. Faunal diversity among different mangrove swamps is dictated by variation in adjacent terrestrial ecosystems which may be lowland tropical forest, sedgelands, or melaleuca or eucalypt forest (Ford 1982). Palm swamps are often monotypic but genera of dominant palms vary geographically as well as among palm swamps in the same region. Variation in just one physicochemical parameter, such as water quality, can spawn diversity, as seen in the varzea and igapo floodplain forests of South America. In varzea forests, white water rivers (rich in nutrients from fertile sediments) flood the forests and support a fertile, deciduous community; in contrast, the nutrient-poor, acidic black water rivers are associated with the igapo forests, low fertility, evergreen forested wetlands (Junk 1993). Decapod crustaceans living in the nutrient-rich forest produce large numbers of small eggs which undergo a planktonic larval stage; decapod crustaceans in the nutrient-poor forest are k-selected and produce a few, large eggs and there is no planktonic larval stage (Magalhaes and Walter 1984). Unique assemblages of plants also contribute to ecosystem diversity as is the case for some swamp peatland communities in southeast Asia (Rieley and Page 1996), low inundated forest communities in the Yucatan Peninsula (Olmsted 1993), and bald cypress or Atlantic white cedar swamps (*Chamaecyparis thyoides*) in the eastern United States (Laderman 1989).

SPECIES DIVERSITY

Facultative species

Although not many animals are strictly confined to forested wetlands, there are many that make extensive use of wetlands, at least for certain purposes. More commonly, animals develop breeding or foraging strategies which follow the cycles of the wetland. For instance, breeding salamanders of the eastern United States (e.g., ambystomid salamanders) and wood frogs (*Rana sylvatica*) return to temporary pools in forested wetlands in early spring while Amazonian fish and invertebrates adapt foraging behavior to the cycles of fruit and seed production in the forest (Goulding 1985). Still other animals make adjustments to utilizing a habitat that may be flooded at some times of the year and not others. For example, proboscis monkeys living in mangrove forests are adept swimmers; the Virginia opossum (*Didelphis virginiana*) of the eastern United States forages on the ground in swamps during the dry season and is largely arboreal when the forest floods.

Forested wetlands have become increasingly important world wide as refugia for facultative fauna endangered by loss of habitat including the Florida panther (*Felis concolor coryi*), Bachman's warbler (*Vermivora bachmannii*; bottomland hardwoods, United States), wood bison (*Bison bison*; Canadian peatlands) (Rubec 1997), Bengal tiger (*Panthera tigris*; the Sundarbans, India) and black stork (*Ciconia nigra*; floodplain oak forests of Sava and Danube rivers). In Sweden, wet forests and forested bogs are habitat for 200 threatened species of flora and fauna (Dugan 1993). Forested peat swamps in southeast Asia play a key role in maintaining regional biodiversity and in the conservation of rare, threatened, and endangered facultative species including the Bornean orang utan (*Pongo pygmaeus*) (Meijaard 1997), the sun bear (*Helarctos malayanus*), and the clouded leopard (*Neofelis nebulosa*). Several mammal species found in peat swamp forests occur outside their previously known ranges (e.g., marbled cat [*Felis marmorata*] and slender tree shrew [*Tupaia gracilis*]) highlighting the importance of these wetlands in regional biodiversity (Stoneman 1997).

Obligate species

At the simplest level, forested wetlands contribute to biodiversity by supporting obligate flora and fauna that are largely restricted to their watery realm. Strategies evolved by wetland biota to make extreme habitats habitable point to the role of wetlands in enhancing the species richness of the overall landscape. 'Fish, some of them come out and breathe air and sit about watching you. Plants take to eating insects, mammals go back to the water and grow elongate like fish, crabs climb trees' (Eiseley 1977).

Forested wetlands may support individual plant species that are not found in upland habitats. For example, of the 81 species of mangroves recognized worldwide, 59 are exclusive to the mangrove ecosystem (estuarine forested wetland) (Saenger *et al.* 1983). Some plant species are restricted to other wetland plant species: certain ant plants (e.g., *Myrmecodia beccarrii*) and mistletoe (*Amyema* spp.) are confined to mangrove trees (Hutchings and Saenger 1987).

Obligate fauna include both resident species such as mudskippers (*Periophthalmus* and *Periophthalmodon* spp.), the air-breathing fish of the mangroves, or the Red Book listed Storm's stork (*Ciconia stormi*) and obligate breeders such as wood frogs (*Rana sylvatica*) which may spend the majority of their time in adjacent terrestrial habitats. Rare tropical peat swamp forest specialists include the hook-bill bulbul (*Setornis criniger*) and grey breasted babbler (*Malacopteran albogulare*) (Stoneman 1997). Others have developed tight relationships with a particular wetland plant species. For example, Hessel's hairstreak (*Mitoura hesseli*) larvae feed exclusively on Atlantic white cedar (Cryan 1985). Such tight associations can lead to local extinctions due to habitat loss. For example, two species of birds, the red grouse (*Lagopus lagopus*) and the ruff (*Philomachus pugnax*), restricted in Finland to southern mires, are regionally endangered due to habitat loss (personal communication, Kaisu Aapala, Finnish Environment Institute). Some scientists aver that the close relationship of North America's largest woodpecker, the ivory-billed woodpecker (*Campephilus principalis*), with old-growth cypress, led to its extinction following the extensive logging of cypress wetlands (Howell 1932).

Although less studied, microflora have also adapted to the stresses associated with certain wetland ecosystems. The microfloral assemblage associated with Atlantic white cedar swamps in the eastern United States is as distinctive as the canopy and shrub associations; the species have developed symbiotic relationships, along with a range of metabolic, morphologic and temporal adaptations to the acidic, nutrient-poor conditions of the wetland (Laderman 1989).

Speciation/endemism

Speciation, driven by the special demands of a wet environment occurring in disjunct wetland ecosystems, enhances biodiversity at the species level. In northeastern Australia and New Guinea, subspecies of the little shrike thrush (*Colluricincla megarhyncha aelptes*) and black butcher bird (*Cracticus quoyi*) living in mangroves have longer bills than those living in the rainforest, while the mangrove robin (*Eopsaltria pulverulenta*) has a rounded tail and wings, ostensibly for enhancing maneuverability in the dense mangroves (Hutchings and Saenger 1987).

Endemism may be quite high in some forested wetlands, particularly mangroves and tropical peatlands. A classic example comes from the mangrove systems of northwestern Australia. As areas of rainforest and monsoonal forests shrank during the arid conditions in the Pleistocene, birds became increasingly dependent on mangroves (Kemp 1978). These areas became isolated over time, and a high degree of endemism developed with the mangrove heron (*Butorides striatus*), mangrove warbler (*Gerygone magnirostris*), and mangrove kingfisher (*Halcyon chloris*) being exemplary (Ford 1982, Schodde *et al.* 1982). In comparison with temperate peatlands, ecological studies of tropical peatlands have been few. As more information becomes available, the value of these systems becomes increasingly apparent. In a study of peat swamps of peninsular Malaysia, for example, 100 endemic tree species were documented (Ng and Low 1982; Ibrahim 1997). Endemic fauna include the pygmy chimpanzee (*Pan panicus*) in Zaire and many endemic fish species, yet to be classified, in blackwater rivers and pools of Malaysia (Rieley and Page 1996).

Plant species growing in wetlands that also occur in terrestrial ecosystems may develop characteristics different from their upland counterparts (although they may or may not be based on genetic differences). Trees of the Amazonian inundation forest produce fruits and seeds that float while related species in the terra firma forests do not (Ducke 1948). Production of propagules that can float and the adaptation of fish to feed on and distribute such are apparently long-term processes of a co-evolutionary nature (Kubitzki 1985).

Management issues

Worldwide, there are several hundred million hectares of forested wetlands (Lugo *et al.* 1990). However, burgeoning human population, concomitant with increased demands for natural resources, may result in major losses from this forested wetland resource. A dramatic example of this phenomenon comes from Indonesia, a country with the majority of the world's tropical peatlands. Threats to the extensive peat swamp forests in central Kalimantan from farmer transmigration projects (World Bank 1994, from Internet information) and a proposed mega-rice development project (International Fund for Animal Welfare 1997, from Internet information) underscore the competition for space that forested wetlands face. Development of a suite of conservation tools with which to balance economic exigencies with conservation concerns may prevent a crisis situation. A discussion of potential management goals for maintaining biodiversity, some inherent problems in developing effective management strategies, and common management approaches used, including strengths and weaknesses associated with each, follows.

Ideally, forested wetlands managed for timber and other commodities would also be managed for maintenance of biodiversity. Emphasis should be on maintaining the basic ecological structure and functions of the wetland (e.g., hydrology, water quality, habitat for biota including rare and endangered species, maintaining gene pools, biogeochemical processes) rather than on increasing the number of species per unit area. Managers should recognize the contribution to landscape biodiversity of relatively species-poor ecosystems. The loss of the Carolina parakeet (*Conuropsis carolinensis*) following the degradation of cypress wetlands underscores the danger of mismanagement. Developing effective management strategies for extracting renewable resources while conserving biodiversity is often hindered by the following:

1. Inventory gaps. Many countries, particularly in the Middle East, Eastern Europe, and South Asia, have insufficient information on their forested wetlands. It is difficult to manage a resource without information on its extent and distribution. However, inventory efforts worldwide have increased and gaps in forested wetland inventory and research are being identified through the work and financial support of such organizations as the Food and Agriculture Organization (FAO), the United Nations Environment Programme (UNEP), the World Bank, the European Community (EC), and the International Waterfowl and Wetlands Research Bureau (IWWRB) (Scott and Jones 1995).

2. Lack of information. There is a dearth of information on forested wetland functions even in the most studied wetland ecosystems. For example, thousands of studies have been published on mangrove ecosystems, yet little or no published data are available on the minimum area required to maintain viable populations of key animals or how small patches of mangrove compare functionally with extensive areas. The bottomland hardwoods of the southeastern United States have been harvested for over 200 years and yet it is only within the last 10 years that information about the effects of harvesting on ecological functions has become available (Lockaby *et al.* 1997). Often management strategies developed for either upland forested ecosystems or different forested wetlands are applied to the ecosystems that are understudied, further contributing to mismanagement.

3. Negative perceptions. Historically, forested wetlands have been viewed as wastelands. Only an appreciation of them as valuable resources will drive development of management strategies keyed to conservation

rather than exploitation. It is still common practice to refer to draining of wetlands for silviculture as 'forest amelioration', forest improvement', or 'reclamation'. However, recognition of the ecological value of these systems is increasing. This trend is reflected in global conservation efforts. Currently, there are 881 Ramsar sites recognizing wetlands of international importance with 25% (221) of the designated sites including areas of forested wetland (20 sites have both inland and coastal forests, 50 have only coastal forest) (Edith Hubert, 1997, Wetlands International, personal communication). Still, as of 1996, less than 5% of the total number of designated sites were dominated by forested wetland (Frazier 1996). Given that an estimated 60% of all wetlands are forested, the proportion receiving international recognition is still very low. Clearly, recognizing the role of forested wetlands in enhancing biodiversity is an important first step to conservation.

4. Political considerations. Much of the resource is privately owned and rarely is there a single authority reviewing resource conditions, distribution, and management.

Recognizing these constraints, one can evaluate current management strategies with the understanding that management based on what is known is preferable to complacency. No single management strategy is being advocated. Indeed, in many cases a combination of strategies will be the most effective conservation tool (Hunter and Calhoun 1996).

PRODUCTION FORESTRY: THE AGRICULTURAL PARADIGM

Production forestry (see Chapters 2 and 12) is a reality borne from a history of changing 'wasteland' into 'productive' land. Wetlands have been sources of fiber, fuel, and food for millennia. Currently, over 50% of the world population depends on moderately to intensively managed wetlands for rice and fish (Whigham *et al.* 1993). Roughly 15 million hectares of peatlands and wetlands have been drained for timber production in boreal and temperate zones (Paivanen 1997). Greater than 90% of this drainage has occurred in Fennoscandia and the former Soviet Union. 'Forest amelioration', or draining, is still a common forestry practice in Fennoscandia, the British Isles, and the Baltic states (Paivanen and Paavilainen 1996).

In general, intensive use of wetlands for timber results in loss or degradation of wetland functions, and in the case of drainage, conversion of wetland to upland. From a conservation standpoint, production forestry is the least desirable practice. In Finland, landscape biodiversity has been severely compromised owing to such intensive forestry practices. At least four peatland forest types are endangered despite a relative abundance of forested peatlands (Pakarinen 1995). However, loss of rare wetland types is not the only concern. Long-term drainage practices lead to overall homogenization of plant species with upland species (Laine et al. 1995). Similar effects on birds (Vaisanen and Rauhala 1983), spiders, and soil fauna have been shown on drained peatlands in Finland (Koponen 1985, Markkula 1986). Intensive forestry in the southeastern United States has led to the extensive drainage of peatlands including pocosins, Carolina bays, and flatwoods, compromising the integrity of hydrologically con-nected estuaries which depend on such peatland functions as flood storage, organic matter production, and silt detention (Richardson 1991).

Production forestry does not necessarily involve long-term drainage. Site specific water management systems for bedding and fertilization treatments (Duncan and Terry 1983) or remedial ditches for site prepara-tion (Hanell 1991) involve partial drainage. Often changes in forest struc-ture and species composition are associated with these practices. Conversion of wet pine flatwoods dominated by longleaf pine (Pinus palus-tris) and pond pine (P. serotina) to loblolly (P. elliottii) and slash pine (P. taeda) plantations in the southeastern United States has produced gains in growth and stand quality, but also has caused a decline in habitat for the endangered red-cockaded woodpecker (Picoides borealis) and many other species (Allen and Campbell 1988).

Production forestry in forested wetlands may be an acceptable manage-ment practice from a biodiversity perspective under the following scen-arios:

1. The resource is abundant and can be managed intensively while main-taining critical ecosystem functions. An example would be black spruce peatland silviculture in Canada. In Canada, draining peatlands for timber production is relatively uncommon; less than 25 000 ha of peat-lands have been drained to date (Jeglum 1990). Silviculture in peatlands focuses on maintaining soil structure through harvesting practices (winter harvest, slash removal) and managing for advanced regeneration (preservation of layers, seed tree groups, clearcut strips) (Haavisto and Jeglum 1991, Jeglum and Kennington 1993). If the soil is compacted, 'watering up' occurs and the forest comes back as cattail or sedges (Dube and Plamondon 1995). However, silviculture on undrained peatlands may not be economically feasible on a large scale. To date, intensive management on a local scale has had little ecological impact.

2. Production forestry makes sense when a resource has been severely impacted and the only way to save remaining, relatively unaltered sites is to continue the intensive management of impacted sites. For example,

losses of mangrove ecosystems to rice paddies, aquaculture ponds, and timber harvest have been extensive. It has been suggested that the remaining tracts of mangrove could be better protected if future emphasis were put on improving existing aquaculture ponds, intensively managing low-yield mangrove areas at the landward edge where hydrological impacts to surrounding ecosystems would be minimal (McVey 1988), and discouraging extensive management, thereby limiting overall habitat destruction. This is also the case in Finland where emphasis has shifted from draining new peatlands to maintaining the productivity of the drained sites (Paivanen and Paavilainen 1996). Indeed, in developing countries where much of the population's survival is directly wed to subsistence use of natural resources, such compromises may prevail.

ECOLOGICAL FORESTRY AND MULTIPLE-USE FORESTRY: THE ECOSYSTEM-BASED PARADIGM

Ecological forestry and multiple-use forestry both differ from production forestry in that a key management goal is to maintain ecosystem functions. These functions often include providing habitat for endangered biota, hydrological functions, and biogeochemical processes involved in food chain support and water quality.

The advantages of ecosystem-based management are many. The protection of wetland functions and biological diversity is made more palatable to all as the interest base is expanded. That is, by not focusing strictly on the agricultural paradigm which focuses on maximizing timber production, a broader management goal will draw in people involved in fisheries, hunting, recreation, or who depend on the hydrological functions of the wetland. Economic exigencies can be met while maintaining the integrity of the wetland. This is especially critical in developing countries where the choice may be between preservation or livelihood. Management of wetlands for sustainable development is practical in this case.

Multiple-use forestry in wetlands probably is not a universal solution. One risks impacting the entire natural resource base, at some level, and being left without some relatively pristine, benchmark ecosystems. For example, in the black water palm and low terrace palm forests in Peru, forests are used for timber, fish production, and food. However, unfettered collection of the fruits of the palm *Mauritia flexuosa* has unexpectedly diminished the capacity of the forest to regenerate following timber extraction. This in turn could affect fish production (Parodi and Freitas 1990). Another disadvantage of multiple- use management is the flip side of 'everyone wins with multiple-use', i.e., everyone loses too.

Increased recognition of the importance of wetlands has led to the development of best management practices, or recommendations for ecologically sensitive forestry practices, which address site preparation, harvesting methods, road construction, timber extraction methods, and regeneration strategies. The challenge now is to develop these practices for the variety of forested wetland resources in the world. It has been successful in the bottomland hardwood forests of the southeastern United States where a growing amount of forested wetland is being managed for timber, fisheries, shellfishing, and wildlife. Technological developments, including specialized harvesting equipment designed for operation on wet soils (Stokes and Schilling 1997) and initiation of long-term studies on the effect of timber management practices on floral and faunal community dynamics, reflect a growing desire to meld conservation needs with production goals (Lockaby *et al.* 1997, Perison *et al.* 1997, Wigley and Roberts 1997). Management of mangrove systems for multiple-use is being explored as well. A mangrove cooperative in Costa Rica, Coopemangle, has provided the institutional framework for community management of the Tierra-Siepe Delta (Dugan 1993). Canada has embraced the Federal Policy on Wetland Conservation which focuses on the sustainable, wise use of wetlands consistent with the 'Wise Use' principles developed by at the Ramsar Convention. For example, this non-regulatory, cooperative approach encourages sustainable forestry on undrained forested peatlands by restricting harvest to winter-only, bole-only silvicultural prescriptions (Rubec 1997).

RESERVES: THE PRESERVATIONIST PARADIGM

From a biodiversity perspective, this is the most attractive option although it is not always realistic. Given that all wetlands make up less than 3% of the land area in the world, one could argue that all should be preserved. However, wetlands are not evenly distributed around the world. It is unrealistic to expect Canada, with 25% of the world's wetlands (Dahl and Zoltai 1997), to preserve this land area while Australia and South Africa share much less of this global resource. Hence, it is not economically or politically tractable to expect preservation as a rule; in fact, in some instances (e.g., in areas of high wetland density) conservation dollars would be better spent in protecting surrounding terrestrial ecosystems.

In cases where an ecosystem is so fragile as to obviate sustainable resource extraction, such as certain peat swamp communities, or in naturally rare, or endangered wetlands, preservation is warranted. Reserves can also serve as benchmarks for natural changes over time, increasing our understanding of the ecology of older forest communities, and may serve as back-up systems in case management strategies in similar ecosystems fail.

Successful reserve design requires long-range, proactive planning, not reactionary, crisis management. For example, the designation of reserves in areas where the forested wetland is embedded in a mosaic of incompatible land-uses will generally fail to meet conservation goals. One should question the value of a fern spruce mire reserve embedded in a sea of development that may alter the hydrology and ultimately change the nature of the protected area. Rather, choosing reserve areas before particular ecosystems are endangered is a better strategy. Canada, with almost 70% of its wetlands forested, may provide the testing ground for this strategy. Canadian foresters are considering implementing, at some level, the drainage paradigm of Fennoscandia (Sundstrom 1992). Now would be the time to take stock of peatland resources and diversity and select the optimal reserve plan thereby obviating the need for crisis management. It is indeed sobering to think that many of the wetland forests and associated biota that are rare or endangered now were once abundant.

REGULATION: THE BUREAUCRATIC PARADIGM

Regulation makes sense as a management tool in countries with a precedent for natural resource protection and the infrastructure to implement it. It would be inappropriate, or more to the point, ineffective, in countries with no single authority or enforcement arm. Finland has the dubious distinction of being showcased as an example of the negative impacts of intensive forestry in forested wetlands: one-third of Finland is mire; of that less than one-third remains in a natural state. Yet Finland should be lauded for seeking to redress the environmental shortcomings of past land-use policies. A proposed New Forest Act would protect key endangered forested wetland types including herb-rich spruce mires, fern spruce mires, and alluvial forested mires (Aapala et al. 1996). Similar efforts are being made in the United States where total wetland loss in the conterminous United States is estimated to be 50%. Federal and state agencies regulate activities in wetlands, although silvicultural activities are often exempt. Clearly, in a crisis situation, regulation may be an effective tool.

Summary

Forested wetlands have a wide distribution, occurring on every continent except Antarctica. Approximately 3% of the global land area is wetland and of this, an estimated 60% is forested. Rates of loss of forested wetland are not available on a global basis due to a lack of inventory information. However, forested wetlands accounted for 95% of the wetland losses suffered in the United States between the mid-1970s through the 1980s and similar trends probably occur elsewhere.

Forested peatlands, freshwater inland forested wetlands, and estuarine forested wetlands are distinguished from upland forests by hydroperiod: the duration, frequency, and timing of saturated or inundated conditions. As a result of this wetness, wetland ecosystems generally support a unique suite of biogeochemical processes and often have specialized plant and animal species adapted to these conditions.

Forested wetlands are valued for their flood control, water quality, and timber production. Less recognized is their contribution to biodiversity at a number of different scales. Forested wetlands contribute to ecosystem diversity as distinct landscape features, as interfaces between aquatic and terrestrial habitats, and in the diversity among different types of forested wetland ecosystems. Speciation, driven by the special demands of a wet environment, enhances biodiversity at the species level. Forested wetlands also support obligate flora and fauna not found in upland forests. Endemism is reportedly high in some forested wetlands such as mangrove swamps and tropical peat swamps. Finally, species growing in wetlands that also occur in terrestrial ecosystems may develop characterisitics, expressed at the genetic level, different from their upland counterparts.

Ideally, forested wetlands managed for timber and other commodities would also be managed for maintenance of biodiversity. Intensive management, extensive or multiple-use management, management as reserves, and regulation are all management tools currently implemented. Each has strengths and weaknesses. In an ideal world, one would want to preserve the remaining intact forested wetlands as they are a naturally rare landscape feature. However, political, social, and economic realities will dictate a variety of approaches in the management of forested wetlands. The key now is to figure out the proper balance of management approaches for meeting conservation and production goals of a diverse array of forested wetland ecosystems.

Further readings

For a general overview of the world's forested wetlands, Lugo *et al.* (1990) and Whigham *et al.* (1993) should be consulted. Of note are two recent edited publications dealing with concepts in ecology, management, and conservation of forested wetlands within specific geographical regions: Trettin *et al.* (1997) focuses on management of northern forested peatlands and drained peatlands and Rieley and Page (1997) provide a comprehensive look at functions, values, ecology, conservation, and sustainability of tropical forested peatlands. The most recent compilation of information on inventory and classification of global wetlands, including forested wetlands, is found in *Vegetatio* Volume 118 (1). More specific information on management practices in forested wetlands can be found in Hook *et al.* (1988) and Whigham *et al.* (1993).

Literature Cited

Aapala, K., R. Heikkila, and T. Lindholm. 1996. Protecting the diversity of Finnish mires. Pp. 45–57 in H. Vasander (ed.). *Peatlands in Finland.* Finnish Peatland Society, Helsinki.

Allen, H. L., and R. G. Campbell. 1988. Wet site pine management in the southeastern United States. In D. D. Hook, W. H. McKee, Jr., H. K. Smith, J. Gregory, V. G. Burrell, Jr., M. R. DeVoe, R. E. Sojka, S. Gilbert, R. Banks, L. H. Stolzy, C. Brooks, T. D. Matthews, and T. H. Shear (eds). *The Ecology and Management of Wetlands.* Volume 2: *Management, Use and Value of Wetlands.* Timber Press, Portland, Oregon.

Alvarez-Lopez, M. 1990. Ecology of *Pterocarpus officinalis* forested wetlands in Puerto Rico. Pp. 251–66 in A. E. Lugo, M. M. Brinson, and S. Brown (eds). *Ecosystems of the World: Forested Wetlands.* Elsevier, New York.

Armstrong, W., S. H. Justin, P. M. Beckett, and S. Lythe. 1991. Root adaptation to soil waterlogging. *Aquatic Botany* 39:57–73.

Brinson, M. M., F. R. Hauer, L. C. Lee, W. L. Nutter, R. D. Rheinhardt, R. D. Smith, and D. Whigham. 1995. *A guidebook for application of hydrogeomorphic assessments to riverine wetlands,* Technical Report WRP-DE-11, U.S. Army Engineer Waterways Experiment Station, Vicksburg, Mississippi.

Bruenig, E. F. 1990. Oligotrophic forested wetlands in Borneo. Pp. 299–334 in A. E. Lugo, M. M. Brinson, and S. Brown (eds). *Ecosystems of the World: Forested Wetlands.* Elsevier, New York.

Bryant, D., D. Nielsen, and L. Tangley. 1997. *The Last Frontier Forests: Ecosystems and Economies on the Edge.* World Resources Institute, Washington, D.C.

Chapman, V. J. 1976. *Mangrove Vegetation.* J. Cramer, Leutershausen, Amsterdam.

Cowardin, L. M., V. Carter, F. C. Golet, and E. T. Laroe. 1979. *Classification of wet-*

lands and deepwater habitats of the United States. US Fish and Wildlife Service FWS/OBS 79/31.

Cryan, J. F. 1985. Hessel's hairstreak: endangered cedar swamp butterfly. *Heath Hen* **2**:22–5.

Dahl, T. E., and C. E. Johnson. 1991. *Wetlands status and trends in the conterminous United States, mid-1970's to mid-1980's*. U.S. Fish and Wildlife Service, National Wetlands Inventory Project, Washington, D.C.

Dahl, T. E. and S. C. Zoltai. 1997. Forested northern wetlands of North America. Pp. 3–18 in C. C. Trettin, M. F. Jurgensen, D. F. Grigal, M. R. Gale, and J. K. Jeglum (eds). *Northern Forested Wetlands: Ecology and Management*. CRC Press, New York.

Dube, S., and A. P. Plamondon. 1995. Watering up after clear-cutting on forested wetlands of the St. Lawrence lowland. *Water Resources Research* **31**:1741–50.

Ducke, A. 1948. Arvores amazonicas e sua propagacao. *Boletim Museu Paraense Emilio Goeldi* **10**:81–92.

Dugan, P. (ed.). 1993. *Wetlands in Danger: a World Conservation Atlas*. Oxford University Press, New York.

Duncan, D. V., and T. A. Terry. 1983. Water management. Pp. 91–111 in E. L. Stone (ed.). *The Managed Slash Pine Ecosystem*. School of Forest Resource Conservation, University of Florida, Gainsville, Florida.

Eiseley, L. 1971. *The Night Country*. Scribners, New York.

Environmental Laboratories. 1987. *Corps of Engineers wetlands delineation manual*. Technical Report Y-87-1. U.S. Army Engineers Waterways Experiment Station, Vicksburg, Mississippi.

Ewel, K. C., and O. T. Odum (eds). 1984. *Cypress Swamps*. University Presses of Florida, Gainesville, Florida.

Ford, J. 1982. Origin, evolution and speciation of birds specialized to mangroves in Australia. *Emu* **82**:12–23.

Frazier, S. 1996. *An Overview of the World's Ramsar Sites*. Wetlands International Publication 39, 6th Conference of Contracting Parties to the Ramsar Convention, Brisbane, Australia.

Frelich, L. E., and L. J. Graumlich. 1994. Age-class distribution and spatial patterns in an old-growth hemlock-hardwood forest. *Canadian Journal of Forest Research* **24**:1939–47.

Goulding, M. 1985. Forest fishes of the Amazon. Pp. 267–76 in G. T. Prance, and T. E. Lovejoy (eds). *Amazonia*. Pergamon Press, Oxford.

Haavisto, V. F., and J. K. Jeglum. 1991. Peatlands potentially available for forestry in Canada. Pp. 30–7 in J. K. Jeglum, and R. P. Overend (eds). *Peat and Peatlands – Diversification and Innovation*, Volume 1, Canadian Society of Peat and Peatlands.

Hanell, B. 1991. Peatland forestry in Sweden. Pp. 19–25 in J. K. Jeglum, and R. P. Overend (eds). *Peat and Peatlands – Diversification and Innovation*, Volume 1, Canadian Society of Peat and Peatlands.

Harriss, L. D. 1984. *Bottomland Hardwoods: Valuable, Vanishing, Vulnerable*. School of Forest Resources and Conservation, University of Florida, Gainesville, Florida.

Heathwaite, A. L. (ed.). 1993. *Mires: Process, Exploitation and Conservation.* John Wiley and Sons, Chichester.

Hook, D. D. and R. M. M. Crawford (eds). 1978. *Plant Life in Anaerobic Environments.* Ann Arbor Science, Ann Arbor, Michigan.

Hook, D. D., W. H. McKee, Jr., H. K. Smith, J. Gregory, V. G. Burrell, Jr., M. R. DeVoe, R. E. Sojka, S. Gilbert, R. Banks, L. H. Stolzy, C. Brooks, T. D. Matthews, and T. H. Shear (eds). 1988. *The Ecology and Management of Wetlands. Volume 2: Management, Use and Value of Wetlands.* Timber Press, Portland, Oregon.

Howell, A. A. 1932. *Florida Bird Life.* Coward-McCann, New York.

Hunter, M. L. Jr. and A. J. K. Calhoun. 1996. A triad approach to landuse allocation. Pp. 477–91 in R. Szaro and D. Johnston (eds). *Biodiversity in Managed Landscapes.* Oxford University Press, Oxford.

Hutchings, P. and P. Saenger. 1987. *Ecology of Mangroves.* University of Queensland Press, New York.

Ibrahim, S. 1997. Diversity of tree species in peat swamp forest in peninsular Malaysia. Pp. 211–20 in J. O. Rieley and S. E. Page (eds). *Biodiversity and Sustainability of Tropical Peatlands.* Samara Publishing Limited, Cardigan, UK.

Jeglum, J. K. 1990. Peatland forestry in Canada: an overview. Pp. 19–28 in B. Hanell (ed.). *Biomass Production and Element Fluxes in Forested Peatland Ecosystems.* Swedish University of Agricultural Science, Department of Forestry Site Research, Umea.

Jeglum, J. K. and D. J. Kennington. 1993. *Strip Clearcutting in Black Spruce: a Guide for the Practicing Forester.* Forestry Canada, Ontario Region, Great Lakes Forestry Centre.

Junk, W. J. 1993. Wetlands of tropical South America. Pp. 679–739 in D. F. Whigham, D. Dykyjova, and S. Hefny (eds). *Wetlands of the World I: Inventory, Ecology and Management.* Kluwer Academic Publishers, Boston.

Kahn, F., and K. Mejia. 1990. Palm communities in wetland forest ecosystems of Peruvian Amazonia. *Forest Ecology and Management* **33/34**:169–79.

Kemp, E. M. 1978. Tertiary climatic evolution and vegetation history in the southeast Indian Ocean region. *Palaeogeography and Palaeoclimatology* **24**:169–208.

King, G. M. 1990. Dynamics and controls of methane oxidation in a Danish wetland sediment. FEMS *Microbiology and Ecology.* **74**:309–24.

Klinge, H., W. J. Junk, and C. J. Revilla. 1990. Status and distribution of forested wetlands in tropical South America. *Forest Ecology and Management* **33/34**:81–101.

Koponen, S. 1985. On changes in the spider fauna of bogs. *Memo.Soc. Fauna Flora Fenn.* **61**:19–22.

Kozlowski, T. T. 1983. Plant responses to flooding of soil. *BioScience* **34**:162–6.

Kubitzki, K. 1985. The dispersal of forest plants. Pp. 192–206 in G. T. Prance and T. E. Lovejoy (eds). *Amazonia.* Pergamon Press, Oxford.

Laderman, A. D. 1989. *The ecology of the Atlantic white cedar wetlands: a community* profile. U.S. Fish and Wildlife Service Biological Report 85 (7.21). Nation Wetlands Research Center, Washington, D.C.

Laine, J., H. Vasander, and R. Laiho. (1995). Long-term effects of water level drawdown on the vegetation of drained pine mires in southern Finland. *Journal of Applied Ecology* **32**:785–802.

Lockaby, B. G., R. H. Jones, R. G. Clawson, J. S. Meadows, J. A. Stanturf, and F. C. Thornton. 1997. Influences of harvesting on functions of floodplain forests associated with low-order, blackwater streams. *Forest Ecology and Management* **90**:217–24.

Lugo, A. E. 1990. Introduction. Pp. 1–10 in A. E. Lugo, M. Brinson, and S. Brown (eds). *Ecosystems of the World: Forested Wetlands*. Elsevier, New York.

Lugo, A. E., S. Brown, and M. M. Brinson 1990. Concepts in wetland ecology. Pp. 53–79 in A. E. Lugo, M. M. Brinson, and S. Brown (eds). *Ecosystems of the World: Forested Wetlands*. Elsevier, New York.

Magalhaes, C. and J. Walter. 1984. Desenvolvimento larval e distribuicao ecologica de seis especies de camaroes (Decapoda, Palaemonidae) da regiao amazonica. Pp. 92–3 in *Resumos do 11 Congresso brasileiro de zoologia*, Belem.

Markkula, I. 1986. Comparison of the communities of the oribatids (Acari: Cryptostigmata) of virgin and forest-ameliorated pine bogs. *Annales Zoologici Fennici:* **23**:33–8.

Matthews, E. and I. Fung. 1987. Methane emission from natural wetlands: global distribution, area, and environmental characteristics of sources. *Global Biogeochemical Cycles* **1**:61–86.

McVey, J. P. 1988. Aquaculture in mangrove wetlands: a perspective from southeast Asia. Pp. 303–15 in D. D. Hook, W. H. McKee, Jr., H. K. Smith, J. Gregory, V. G. Burrell, Jr., M. R. DeVoe, R. E. Sojka, S. Gilbert, R. Banks, L. H. Stolzy, C. Brooks, T. D. Matthews, and T. H. Shear (eds). *The Ecology and Management of Wetlands*. Volume 2: *Management, Use and Value of Wetlands*. Timber Press, Portland, Oregon.

Meijaard, E. 1997. The importance of swamp forest for the conservation of the Orang Utan (*Pongo pygmaeus*) in Kalimantan, Indonesia. Pp. 243–54 in J. O. Rieley and S. E. Page (eds). *Biodiversity and Sustainability of Tropical Peatlands*. Samara Publishing Limited, Cardigan, UK.

Meyer, J. L. 1990. A blackwater perspective on riverine ecosystems. *BioScience* **40**:643–51.

Myers, N. 1995. The world's forests: need for a policy appraisal. *Science* **268**:823–4.

Newton, R. B. 1988. *Forested Wetlands of the Northeast*. Environmental Institute Publication No. 88–1, University of Massachusetts at Amherst, Massachusetts.

Ng, F. S. P., and C. M. Low. 1982. *Check list of trees of the Malay Peninsula*. Malaysia Forestry Department, Research Pamphlet 88.

Olmsted, I. 1993. Wetlands of Mexico. Pp. 637–78 in D. F. Whigham, D. Dykyjova, and S. Hefny (eds). *Wetlands of the World I: Inventory, ecology and management*. Kluwer, Boston.

Paavilainen, E., and J. Paivanen. 1995. *Peatland Forestry: Ecology and Principles.* Springer-Verlag, New York.

Page, S. E., J. O. Rieley, K. Doody, S. Hodgson, S. Husson, P. Jenkins, H. Morrough-Bernard, S. Otway, and S. Wilshaw. 1997. Biodiversity of tropical peat swamp forest: a case study of animal diversity in the Sungai Sebangau Catchment of Central Kalimantan, Indonesia. Pp. 231–42 in J. O. Rieley and S. E. Page (eds). *Biodiversity and Sustainability of Tropical Peatlands.* Samara Publishing Limited, Cardigan, UK.

Paijmans, K., R. W. Galloway, D. P. Faith, P. M. Fleming, H. A. Haantjens, P. C. Heyligers, J. D. Kalma, and E. Loffler. 1985. *Aspects of Australian wetlands.* CSIRO Division of Water and Land Resources Technical Paper No. 44.

Paivanen, J. 1997. Forested mires as a renewable resource – toward a sustainable forestry practice. Pp. 27–44 in C. C. Trettin, M. F. Jurgensen, D. F. Grigal, M. R. Gale, and J. K. Jeglum (eds). *Northern Forested Wetlands: Ecology and Management.* CRC Press, New York.

Paivanen, J., and E. Paavilainen. 1996. Forestry on peatlands. Pages 72–83 in H. Vasander (ed.). *Peatlands in Finland.* Finnish Peatland Society, Helsinki.

Paivanen, J., and H. Vasander. 1994. Carbon balance in mire ecosystems. *World Resource Review* **6**:102–111.

Pakarinen, P. 1995. Classification of boreal mires in Finland and Scandinavia: a review. *Vegetatio* **118**:29–38.

Parodi, J. L., and D. Freitas. 1990. Geographical aspects of forested wetlands in the Lower Ucayali, Peruvian Amazonia. *Forest Ecology and Management* **33/34**:157–68.

Perison, D., J. Phelps, C. Pavel, and R. Kellison. 1997. The effects of timber harvest in a South Carolina blackwater bottomland. *Forest Ecology and Management* **90**:171–85.

Richardson, C. J. 1991. Pocosins: an ecological perspective. *Wetlands* **11**:335–54.

Rieley, J., and S. Page. 1996. The biodiversity, environmental importance, and sustainability of tropical peat and peatlands. *Environmental Conservation* **23**:94–5

Rieley, J. O., and S. Page (eds). 1997. *Biodiversity and Sustainability of Tropical Peatlands.* Samara Publishing Limited, Cardigan, UK.

Rubec, C. D. A. 1997. Policy for conservation of the functions and values of forested wetlands. Pp. 45–60 in C. C. Trettin, M. F. Jurgensen, D. F. Grigal, M. R. Gale, and J. K. Jeglum (eds). *Northern Forested Wetlands: Ecology and Management.* CRC Press, New York.

Saenger, P., E. J. Hegerl, and J. D. S. Davie. 1983. Global status of mangrove ecosystems. *Environmentalist* **3**:1–88.

Schodde, R., I. J. Mason, and H. B. Gill. 1982. The avifauna of the Australian mangroves. A brief review of composition, structure, and origin. Pp. 141–50 in B. F. Clough (ed.). *Structure, Function and Management of Mangrove Ecosystems in Australia,* AIMS with ANU Press, Australia.

Scott, D. A., and T. A. Jones. 1995. Classification and inventory of wetlands: a global overview. *Vegetatio* **118**:3–16.

Semeniuk, C. A., and V. Semeniuk. 1995. A geomorphic approach to global classification for inland wetlands. *Vegetatio* **118**:103–24.

Sharitz, R. R., and J. W. Gibbons. 1982. *The ecology of southeastern shrub bogs (pocosins) and Carolina Bays: a community profile.* U.S. Fish and Wildlife Service, Division of Biological Services, FWS/OBS-82/04, Washington, D.C.

Stokes, B. J., and A. Schilling. 1997. Improved harvesting systems for wet sites. *Forest Ecology and Management* **90**:155–60.

Stoneman, R. 1997. Ecological studies in the Badas Peat Swamps, Brunei Darussalam. Pp. 221–42 in J. O. Rieley and S. E. Page (eds). *Biodiversity and Sustainability of Tropical Peatlands.* Samara Publishing Limited, Cardigan, UK.

Sugal, C. 1997. Most forests have no protection. *World Watch* **10**:9.

Sundstrom, E. 1992. *Five year growth response in drained and fertilized black spruce peatlands. I. Permanent growth plot analysis.* Forestry Canada, Great Lakes Forestry Centre, Informational Report o–X-417.

Trettin, C. C., M. F. Jurgensen, D. F. Grigal, M. R. Gale, and J. K. Jeglum (eds). 1997. *Northern Forested Wetlands: Ecology and Management.* CRC Press, New York.

Twilley, R. R., A. E. Lugo, and C. Patterson-Zucca. 1987. Litter production and turnover in basin mangrove forests in southwest Florida. *Ecology* **67**:670–83.

Vaisanen, R. A. and P. Rauhala. 1983. Succession of land bird communities on large areas of peatland drained for forestry. *Annales Zoologici Fennici* **20**:115–27.

Van Hees, W. W. S. 1990. Boreal forested wetlands – what and where in Alaska. *Forest Ecology and Management* **33/34**:425–38.

Walter, H. and M. Steiner. 1936. Die Okologie der Ost-Afrikanishcen Mangroven. *Zeitschrift fur Botanik* **30**:65–193.

Westermann, P. 1993. Wetland and swamp microbiology. Pp. 215–38 in T. E. Ford (ed.). *Aquatic Microbiology.* Blackwell Scientific, Boston.

Wharton, C. H., W. M. Kitchens, E. C. Pendleton, and T. W. Sipe. 1982. *The ecology of bottomland hardwood swamps of the Southeast: a community profile.* FWS/OBS-81/37, U.S. Fish and Wildlife Service, Biological Service Program, Washington, D.C.

Whigham, D. F., D. Dykyjova, and S. Hefny (eds). 1993. *Wetlands of the World I: Inventory, Ecology and Management.* Kluwer Academic Publishers, Boston.

Wigley, T. B. and T. H. Roberts. 1997. Landscape-level effects of forest management on faunal diversity in bottomland hardwoods. *Forest Ecology and Management* **90**:141–54.

Worley, I. A. 1980. *Maine peatlands: their abundance, ecology, and relevance to the Critical Areas Program of the State Planning Office.* Planning Report No. 76, Vermont Agricultural Experiment Station Bulletin 687.

Part III
The micro approach, managing forest stands

10 Dying, dead, and down trees

WILLIAM McCOMB AND DAVID LINDENMAYER

Dying, dead, and down trees are products of the dynamics of forests and they have critical functions in forests around the world. These trees – long considered by timber interests to be a waste of wood fiber and a fire hazard – provide habitat for animals, serve as nursery sites for germination and subsequent growth of plants, and provide a store of nutrients that can be cycled through forest ecosystems (Davis *et al.* 1983, Harmon *et al.* 1986). These values have led managers to more carefully consider management of dead wood in forest stands and landscapes. In this chapter we outline: (a) patterns of dead, dying and down trees over space and time; (b) the importance of dead and dying trees and logs as key habitat components for forest wildlife; and (c) aspects of their management in forests managed for timber and other forest values. Although most of our examples come from North American and Australian forests, we focus on general concepts and trends that will have applicability to other forests such as intensively managed systems in Europe (Van Balen *et al.* 1982) and relatively unmanaged forests in the tropics (Paatanavibool and Edge 1996, Gibbs *et al.* 1993).

Patterns of dead and dying trees over space and time

Dying, dead, and down wood is produced by forest disturbances and the structure and function of the wood changes over time following the disturbances. Dead wood changes over time in two successional patterns. First, the seral stage of the stand surrounding the tree, snag (standing dead tree) or log (fallen tree or snag) can have a significant effect on its function in the stand (Table 10.1). Change in the function of the dead wood occurs as the stand progresses through ecological succession. Second, the structure and function of the dying and dead tree changes over time during the decay process.

Table 10.1. *Examples of animal species that would use four types of dead or dying trees in four stages of stand development in North American forests*

	Tree decay stage			
Seral stage	Live cavity tree	Hard snag	Soft snag	Log
Stand reinitiation	House wren	American kestrel	Western bluebird	Fence lizard
Stem exclusion	Carolina wren	Hairy woodpecker	Carolina chickadee	Ensatina salamander
Transition	Red-breasted nuthatch	Red-bellied woodpecker	Red-breasted sapsucker	Clouded salamander
Shifting-gap phase	Spotted owl	Pileated woodpecker	Northern flying squirrel	American marten

Notes:
See Appendix 10.1 for scientific names.

DEAD WOOD PRODUCTION AND ECOLOGICAL SUCCESSION

Dead wood is a product of forest disturbances. Disturbance frequency, intensity, and pattern influence the availability of dead wood in forest stands (McComb *et al.* 1993). Large additions of dead wood tend to be caused by stochastic events, such as insect attacks, wind, and fire. For instance, low frequency, high intensity disturbances such as forest fires can leave much dead wood within the stand-reinitiation stage of forest development (Spies *et al.* 1988). High levels of dead wood produced following a fire also may represent a significant fuel source for subsequent ignitions in fire-prone systems (Spies *et al.* 1988). Fear of recurring fire led to salvage logging and snag removal several decades ago in the Pacific Northwest of the United States (McWilliams 1940).

Following intense disturbances, dead wood volume declines through time as the wood decays. During natural stand development, suppression mortality which occurs in a stem exclusion stage of succession can lead to modest additions of dead wood (Spies *et al.* 1988). Dead wood volume then accumulates during late seral stages of stand succession as small-scale disturbances recruit large trees to the dead wood pool (Spies *et al.* 1988). Natural old forests contain high volumes of large pieces of dead wood, but not to the level found following intense disturbances such as fire. Under management that leads to harvest of dead trees or trees likely to die from suppression mortality, dead wood biomass may continue to decline in the stand over time.

CHANGES IN DEAD WOOD OVER TIME

Successional patterns also are evident within dying and dead trees (Mackowski 1984, Miller and Miller 1980). Trees that sustain physical damage from wind or fire often become infected with fungal decay (Shigo 1965). The death of branches by self-pruning, incomplete branch shedding and wound occlusion, or mechanical damage usually provide avenues for decay microbes to enter live trees, a situation common in eucalypt (*Eucalyptus* spp.) and other hardwood forests (Gibbons and Lindenmayer 1997). Compartmentalization of decay can lead to isolated columns of decay, commonly producing a cavity (Shigo 1984). If the tree remains alive, then compartmentalization of the wound and subsequent healing may preclude development of a cavity (Sedgwick and Knopf 1991). However, if the tree dies, decay processes proliferate. Fungal decay is often combined with the activities of invertebrates, such as termites (Mackowski 1984, 1987; Atkinson *et al.* 1992). Bole fragmentation, or the physical decomposition of the wood, creates a range of tree, snag, and log conditions (e.g., Cline *et al.* 1980, Lindenmayer *et al.* 1991a) that are colonized by a wide range of organisms (Scott *et al.* 1977, Bartels *et al.* 1985). For example, in western North America, species such as carpenter ants (*Camponotus* spp.) colonize dead trees, enhancing decay while also providing food for pileated woodpeckers (*Dryocopus pileatus*). In eastern North America, colonization of decaying logs by microinvertebrates can provide food and cover for forest floor amphibians such as red-backed salamanders (*Plethodon cinereus*). In Tasmania, wet logs provide critical habitat for invertebrates such as velvet worms (*Peripatus* spp.).

The size of the dead wood influences the rate of decomposition and its value to organisms. Large pieces of dead wood provide habitat for a large number of species in various seral stages (Ruggiero *et al.* 1991). These large remnant snags and logs can last for centuries before becoming an unrecognizable part of the forest humus (Tyrrell and Crow 1994).

Fall rates of live trees and snags vary among tree species (Keen 1955, Schmid *et al.* 1985, Morrison and Raphel 1993, Lindenmayer *et al.* 1997). Ten-year fall rates (the proportion of trees expected to fall in a 10-year period) for pine and fir snags (*Pinus ponderosa*, *P. contorta*, and *Abies* spp.) in the western United States and many hardwoods in the eastern United States exceed 50% (Keen 1955, McComb and Rumsey 1983, Schmid *et al.*

1985, Morrison and Raphael 1993). Fall rates of large-diameter Douglas-fir (*Pseudotsuga menziesii*) snags may be less than 20% per decade (Cline et al. 1980).

Decay rates also vary among tree species (e.g., Clark 1957, Embry 1963, Harmon and Sexton 1996). The combination of a tree's size and variability among species in their resistance to decay leads to considerable variation among trees in rate of decay and fragmentation (Bennett et al. 1994, Harmon et al. 1986). As fragmentation of the tree bole advances, the diameter and height (or length of logs) decreases (Tyrrell and Crow 1994). Tree species and size also influence other characteristics of dead and dying trees. For instance, snag longevity and the probability of a tree containing a cavity increases with increasing tree size in a wide range of tree species: eucalyptus (*E. regnans*, *E. delegatensis*, *E. cypellocarpa*, and *E. marginata*), oaks (*Quercus* spp.), hickories (*Carya* spp.), and Douglas-fir (Allen and Corn 1990, Gumtow-Farrior 1991, Lindenmayer et al. 1993).

The importance of dead and dying trees

Ecological functions of dead wood include nutrient cycling, a mechanism for detritus-based energy flow through various trophic levels, and structural habitat features for a wide variety of plants and animals. These functions will be described briefly in this section.

Photosynthesis leads to allocation of energy to leaves, fruits, boles and roots. In later stages of forest succession, most forest energy is stored in cellulose, and cellulose must be broken down into simpler molecules to allow the stored energy to become available to other organisms. This process is the primary mechanism allowing energy flow through trophic levels in detrital-based systems. Cellulose also is the primary source of stored carbon in forest systems. Carbon is slowly released as CO_2 during decomposition (Harmon et al. 1986). The decaying substrate also is associated with nitrogen-fixing bacteria that may contribute to the soil nitrogen, thereby influencing soil fertility in some forest types (Sollins et al. 1987).

The fungi and invertebrates responsible for decomposing and fragmenting the wood become the basis for energy flow into other organisms. The organisms responsible for decomposition can differ markedly between aquatic and terrestrial systems, often leading to slower rates of decay in submerged wood versus wood exposed to air. Further, dead wood can affect the function of terrestrial and aquatic systems. Dead wood adds complexity to forest floors, increasing ground-surface and below-ground heterogeneity. Trees and snags that fall into streams can have significant impacts on sediment deposition and scouring within the channel, leading to more complex channel structure than would be present without these logs (Bisson *et al.* 1987).

In some systems the decaying wood can be an important seedbed for regenerating trees, shrubs, and bryophytes, thus influencing the trajectory of stand succession. For instance, nurse logs in red alder (*Alnus rubra*) and salmonberry (*Rubus spectabilis*) stands in western Oregon and Washington can become important seedbeds for western hemlock (*Tsuga heterophylla*) establishment. Eastern hemlock (*Tsuga canadensis*) and yellow birch (*Betula allegehniensis*) also germinate on nurse logs in eastern North American forests. Logs also may be nursery sites for ferns and mosses in mountain ash (*E. regnans*) forests (Ashton 1986, Ough and Ross 1992) and for rainforest plants such as myrtle beech (*Nothofagus cunninghamii*) in Victoria, southeastern Australia (Howard 1973).

As trees die and decay the species that can use the tree change as well (Figure 10.1). Further, changes in the structure of forest stands through ecological succession influence the function of the dead and dying trees (Table 10.1). Animal species that use a given stage of tree decay in one seral stage may differ from those that can use the same type of tree in another seral stage. In Australia, over 400 species of vertebrates and many more species of invertebrates are dependent on tree cavities (Gibbons and Lindenmayer 1996). Scott *et al.* (1977) listed 85 species of cavity-nesting birds that occur in North American forests. In New England Forests, 41 species of birds and mammals use standing trees with decay present (DeGraaf and Shigo 1985). There are many more species of mammals, amphibians, reptiles, and invertebrates that use cavities or snags in North America (McComb and Noble 1981a, McComb and Noble 1982, Healy *et al.* 1989). During the past 20 years, land management decisions have become increasingly based on habitat relationships of animals dependent on dead wood in forests around the world. Often these relationships are summarized for large functional groups of species, such as primary and secondary cavity users, and log users.

PRIMARY CAVITY EXCAVATORS

Up to 40% of the bird species in North American forests are cavity nesters (Scott *et al.* 1977, Evans and Conner 1979). In many forest systems, primary cavity-nesting birds (species such as woodpeckers that excavate

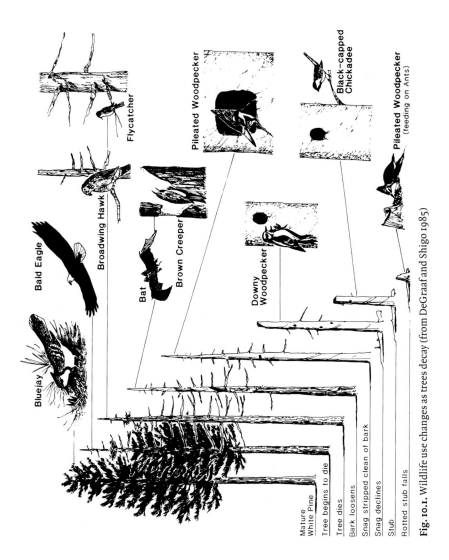

Fig. 10.1. Wildlife use changes as trees decay (from DeGraaf and Shigo 1985)

Bluejay

Bald Eagle

Broadwing Hawk

Flycatcher

Pileated Woodpecker

Bat

Brown Creeper

Black-capped Chickadee

Downy Woodpecker

Pileated Woodpecker
(feeding on Ants)

Mature
White Pine

Tree begins to die

Tree dies

Bark loosens

Snag stripped clean of bark

Snag declines

Stub

Rotted stub falls

their own cavities), play a key role by providing cavities that are used by secondary cavity nesters (species that use cavities excavated by primary cavity nesters or natural cavities created by decay). Much attention has been given to management of primary cavity nesters based on the assumption that if they are present and excavating cavities then secondary cavity nesters will have the habitat that they need to survive (Neitro *et al.* 1985). However, there are some forests, such as those in Australia and New Zealand, where woodpeckers do not occur. Fungal decay, insects, and fire play key roles in development of cavities for secondary cavity nesters in these forests (Mackowski 1984, 1987; Inions *et al.* 1989).

Although some species of primary cavity nesters can excavate cavities in living wood, most excavate cavities in either dead wood or through live wood into decaying heart wood (Conner *et al.* 1976). Trees or limbs that die from injury following disturbance, root rots, or through suppression mortality must be of sufficient diameter to allow a bird to create a cavity of adequate size within the decayed substrate (Miller and Miller 1980). Because most hardwoods and some conifers compartmentalize heart rot (Shigo 1984), excavation through sapwood into a softened heartwood may allow organisms to create cavities in tree sections that are only 2–3 times the diameter of a bird's body. However, in many conifers and some hardwoods, decay of sapwood must occur to a sufficient depth toward the heartwood to allow excavation of the sapwood alone (Miller and Miller 1980). For instance, pileated woodpeckers (*Dryocopus pileatus*) may excavate a cavity in a tree of only 55 cm in eastern hardwood forests of the United States (Evans and Conner 1979), but often select much larger conifer snags for nesting in the Pacific northwest of the United States (Nelson 1988). Generally, snags or dead limbs less than 10 cm in diameter are of little or no value as nest sites for primary cavity-nesting vertebrates (Scott *et al.* 1977). Small pieces of dead wood may become important feeding substrates for some species, but foraging probably is more energy efficient on larger stems than on smaller ones, leading to selection of large stems for foraging by most species (Brawn *et al.* 1982, Weikel 1997).

Most species of primary cavity-nesting birds use only one nest cavity per year, although a few species may use different cavities if they raise more that one brood of young in a year (Bent 1939). The excavation of a cavity is a required part of the nesting ritual for most primary cavity-nesting species (Nilsson 1984). Consequently, these species are continually producing cavities in available substrates within the pair's nesting territory over time. Additional cavities often are created and used by cavity-nesting birds as roost and rest sites (Bent 1939). A pair of cavity-nesting birds may use 1–10 or more cavities within a territory for nesting and roosting each year. For instance, species such as acorn woodpeckers (*Melanerpes formicivorus*) and red-cockaded woodpeckers (*Picoides borealis*) have nesting clans that include helpers to help raise the young (Lennartz and Harlow 1979, Neitro et al. 1985). Consequently, roost sites must be available for the breeding pair as well as the helpers.

Many species of primary cavity-nesting birds (e.g., hairy woodpeckers, *Picoides villosus*) feed on wood-boring insect larvae (e.g., Buprestidae) and so require dead wood as a foraging substrate within a territory (Otvos and Stark 1985, Petit et al. 1988). Consequently, there must be a continual replacement of feeding sites as well as nest sites within territories to allow them to remain occupied. Other species, such as common flickers, feed primarily on insects found on the ground or in understory vegetation; dead substrates are not as important as foraging sites for these species (Brawn et al. 1982). In summary, the need for dead trees or limbs varies considerably among different species of primary cavity-nesting birds occupying any given tract of forest. To effectively manage habitats for this group of species, the nesting and roosting requirements for each species must be carefully considered. The distribution and dynamics of habitat features are key to understanding if these organisms are likely to persist over time in a forest.

The distribution of key habitat features must be related to the territory or home range size of the organism. Generally, body mass is related to territory size for most species of primary cavity-nesting birds. For instance, pileated woodpecker (250 g) territories range from 60 to 300 ha depending on geographic location and forest type (Evans and Conner 1979, Mellen et al. 1992), while downy woodpeckers (*Picoides pubescens*) (12 g) have territories of 1–3 ha) (Evans and Conner 1979). The nest, roost, and foraging structures required by a breeding pair of each species must occur within a unit of space that represents a territory for the pair. Management for several species will require a multi-scale approach that carefully considers the spatial distribution of dead wood of various sizes across units of space representing potential territory sizes for each species being managed.

SECONDARY CAVITY NESTERS

Secondary cavity nesters can be conveniently placed into one of two groups: (1) those species that must have a cavity for nesting or breeding and (2) those that use cavities or dead wood opportunistically. We focus our discussion on the first group, but there are many species in the second group ranging from invertebrates (McComb and Noble 1982) to black bears (*Ursus americanus*) (Hellgren and Vaughan 1989) that opportunistically use dead or dying trees as cover. Also, the number of cavities used by an individual varies widely among species. Some cavity-nesting birds change nest sites between broods presumably to avoid parasite burdens (Mason 1944); some mammals also move among den sites in response to high ectoparasite loads (Muul 1968). For example, house wrens (*Troglodytes aedon*) and bluebirds (*Sialia* spp.) may use 1–3 nest cavities each year and defend each from other species (personal observations). Cavity-using mammals tend to use many den sites. For instance, in North America, northern flying squirrels (*Glaucomys sabrinus*) use multiple cavities as well as external nests within their home range (Martin 1994). More than 110 different living and dead trees with cavities were used by 16 mountain brushtail possums (*Trichosurus acninus*) during a two-year period in Australia (Lindenmayer *et al.* 1996).

Swifts and bats may roost communally, with hundreds of individuals occupying one site. There are many more species of secondary cavity nesters than of primary cavity nesters, and each species has its own requirements for the type of cavity or roost site used (Balda 1973). Long-legged bats (*Myotis volans*) and brown creepers (*Certhia americana*) use spaces behind loose bark on snags (Barbour and Davis 1969, Scott *et al.* 1977, Ormsbee and McComb 1998). House wrens use a wide range of cavity types and conditions, while species such as wood ducks (*Aix sponsa*) have more specific requirements and occupy large cavities usually near water (Prince 1968, Lowney and Hill 1989).

Cavities may be particularly important roost sites during the winter for resident species in temperate climates (Haftorn 1988). Feen (1997) found that northern flying squirrels select snags as winter den sites in high elevation sites in Oregon. Energy savings of cavity-roosting species can be significant where ambient temperatures drop below freezing over long winter nights (Weigl and Osgood 1974).

INVERTEBRATES

The above discussion has focused primarily on vertebrate use of dead wood, but there are many more species of invertebrates than vertebrates that use dead wood. Entire invertebrate communities may be dependent on water-filled tree cavities in some forests (Jenkins and Kitching 1990, Kitching and Callaghan 1982). One group of insects, bark beetles

(*Dendroctonus* spp.), play a significant role in the dynamics of some conifer forests (e.g., lodgepole pine, *Pinus contorta*) while also providing a food source for vertebrate cavity nesters, especially hairy and three-toed woodpeckers (*Picoides* spp.) (Koplin 1969, Otvos and Stark 1985). Humans tend to view bark beetle outbreaks as catastrophes, but these irruptions often occur because some other form of natural disturbance (e.g., fire) has been suppressed (Fischer and Bradley 1987). Carpenter ants require dead and dying wood and can contribute to control of defoliating insects in forests of the western United States and in turn they provide food for pileated woodpeckers (Torgersen and Bull 1995).

Although identification of habitat requirements of invertebrates is a daunting task, these species are being considered in forest management plans (e.g., USDA and USDI 1994). Current approaches place invertebrate taxa into functional groups (USDA *et al.* 1993), each having management guidelines. For invertebrates, natural history information is still rudimentary, and best guesses will need to be made with regard to how much, what tree species, and what spatial distribution of dead wood is required to meet their needs in managed forests. However, there is precedence for considering the individual needs of dead wood-dependent invertebrates. Torgersen and Bull (1995) have suggested that dead wood levels in forests of the western United States are sufficient to maintain carpenter ant colonies. Tasmanian forest managers have developed strategies for maintaining wet-log habitat for velvet worms (Mesibov 1990, Taylor 1990). Invertebrates such as worms from Tasmania or mollusks from the Pacific northwest of the United States (USDA and USDI 1994) may have small population sizes, limited ranges, poor dispersal capabilities, and specific habitat requirements, and face increased risk of localized or wide-scale extinction if prescribed burning, wood chipping, or ground disturbance are not carefully planned (New 1995).

LOGS AND LOG-USERS

When a tree dies it may: (a) remain standing, in some cases for decades, (b) be uprooted by wind, or (c) progressively break into pieces from damage or decay (Putz *et al.* 1983, Tyrrell and Crow 1994). Over time, however, the tree falls to the ground in one or more pieces. The function of a log is influenced by the characteristics of the wood before it fell to the ground (Maser *et al.* 1988). For instance, a green tree which is windthrown will progress through various stages of sapwood and heartwood decay (Figure 10.2). On the other hand, should a 'soft' snag (e.g., decay class 6,

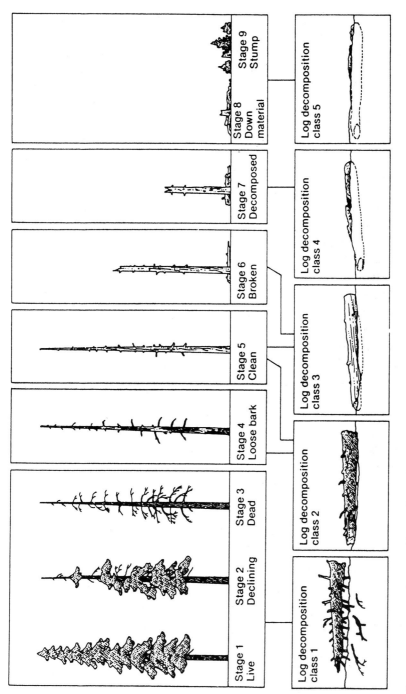

Fig. 10.2. Decay stages of snags and logs in the Pacific Northwest of the United States (From Maser et al. 1979).

see Figure 10.2) fall to the ground, it will likely fragment on impact and the pieces will already be in an advanced stage of decay. Similarly, a hollow log will only be present if the tree or snag was hollow prior to dying. Decay proceeds slowly from the outside to the inside, but decay rates are highly dependent on the tree species (Harmon *et al.* 1986).

Logs are used by many species of vertebrates and invertebrates as cover (e.g., salamanders [deMaynadier and Hunter 1995] and bears [Hellgren and Vaughan 1989]), foraging sites (e.g., termites [Mackowski 1984] and fungivorous voles [Maser and Trappe 1984]), and sites for attracting mates (e.g., ruffed grouse, *Bonasa umbellus* [Hammill and Moran 1984]). Logs in streams provide cover for fish and influence the scouring and deposition of sediments in streams, thereby increasing fish habitat complexity (Bisson *et al.* 1987). The interior of hollow logs, or the spaces beneath a log, provide a stable and often moist micro-environment that is especially important to the survival of some species of amphibians and reptiles (deMaynadier and Hunter 1995). Some species use the space between the bark and the wood (e.g., scarlet kingsnakes, *Lampropeltis triangulum* [Nussbaum *et al.* 1983]), some use the interior of well-decayed logs (e.g., clouded salamanders, *Aneides ferreus* [Stelmock and Harestad 1979]), and others also can occur in the spaces beneath logs (e.g., western red-backed salamanders, *Plethodon vehiculum* ([Nussbaum *et al.* 1983]). Log size dictates the area or volume of space available to be occupied (Maser *et al.* 1979). Logs smaller than 10 cm in diameter are probably of little value to most vertebrates; large logs seem to be used by more species than small ones. Moreover, large logs persist longer than small logs. Decay status also affects log use by organisms. Few species are capable of using undecayed logs (e.g., ruffed grouse); most use well-decayed logs (e.g., clouded salamanders and California red-backed voles, *Clethrionomys californicus*). Obviously, with species representing a range of organism sizes from microbes, mites, and tardigrades to salamanders, fishers (*Martes pennanti*) and bears, managing the spatial distribution of logs must consider a wide range of home range sizes. Ideally, the habitat requirements of each species must be considered when deciding where logs should be retained and what log characteristics are sufficient to meet their needs. Realistically, the needs of most species will probably best be met if large logs are retained in clumps of various sizes ranging from a few to many logs per hectare.

OTHER HABITAT CHARACTERISTICS

Dying, dead and fallen trees are only one component of forest stands and landscapes, and most organisms that use them require additional resources within their territory or home range. It is the combination of food and cover resources distributed over space and time that allow organisms to persist on certain sites and to disperse among sites (Lacy 1993). To be effective, management of dead wood resources must consider the spatial arrangement and dynamics of all components of habitat for each species of concern.

Management of tree cavities and snags

There are few data from which to derive accurate estimates of organism response to cavity or dead wood availability (e.g., Schrieber and deCalesta 1992, Dickson *et al.* 1983, Healy *et al.* 1989). Models such as Marcot's (1991, based on Neitro *et al.*, 1985) and management guides such as that provided by DeGraaf and Shigo (1985) are attempts to synthesize relationships between the amount of dead wood and animal abundance. Unfortunately, these models are based on limited data, most of which were collected from correlative rather than cause and effect studies. Monitoring programs that measure animal abundance and dynamics of cavities and dead wood are needed in many forest types to begin to understand the functional relationships between dead wood availability and animal abundance. As a first step, however, information synthesized among past studies can provide managers with guidance in forest planning.

MANAGING CAVITIES IN LIVE TREES – THE LEADBEATER'S
POSSUM EXAMPLE

Arboreal marsupials in montane ash forests of southeastern Australia are unable to survive without access to nest and den sites in large living and dead trees. Past studies in these forests have investigated the functional relationships between large living and dead trees with cavities and the distribution and abundance of arboreal marsupials, including the endangered Leadbeater's possum (*Gymnobelideus leadbeateri*) (Lindenmayer 1994). Several habitat relationships seemed to influence the abundance and distribution of the arboreal marsupials in the area: (a) a combination of large trees and other features of forest structure (e.g., understory characteristics) were associated with the abundance of each species of arboreal marsupial (Lindenmayer *et al.* 1990, 1991b); (b) arboreal marsupials were typically rare or absent from stands that lacked cavities; and (c) selection of specific den characteristics varied among the different species of arboreal marsupials sampled. For instance, greater gliders (*Petauroides volans*) tended to select large diameter trees, while Leadbeater's possums selected short, highly decayed trees (Lindenmayer *et al.* 1991c).

Two key factors are likely to underpin the highly significant relationships that allowed Lindenmayer (1994) to predict presence or absence of species based on the availability of large living and dead trees with cavities. First, each species selected trees with cavities that had specific characteristics, which probably reflect preference for different stages of stem senescence (Lindenmayer *et al.* 1991a). These results are consistent with cavity selection by secondary cavity-nesting vertebrates in North American forests (Neitro *et al.* 1985). Given the partitioning of cavity resources, forests with more and a greater variety of cavity-bearing stems are likely to support a greater abundance and variety of arboreal marsupials (Lindenmayer *et al.* 1991a). Second, individual animals use den sites in many trees and move regularly among them. Such behavioral patterns are more likely to be satisfied on sites with a greater abundance of potential nest sites (Lindenmayer *et al.* 1996). This example is one approach taken to develop the data necessary to make management recommendations to forest managers that could lead to population persistence for these species.

MANAGING HABITAT FOR SPECIES THAT USE CAVITIES, SNAGS, AND LOGS

Management of cavities in living trees has received attention in the United States (DeGraaf and Shigo 1985, McComb *et al.* 1986, Lowney and Hill 1989), and is reflected in the comparative success of species using this resource compared with those using dead trees. Few vertebrate species, if any, are threatened by lack of cavities in live trees in North America (although northern spotted owls, *Strix occidentalis caurina*, will use large natural cavities as nest sites). On the other hand, several species which excavate dead or living trees have been extirpated or endangered in the United States (e.g., red-cockaded woodpeckers, *Picoides borealis*; ivory-billed woodpeckers, *Campephelis principalis*). Secondary cavity nesters in the United States and Europe have received attention primarily through nest box programs (e.g., wood ducks, bluebirds, bats). Only recently has active snag management been incorporated into forest planning (USDA and USDI 1994).

Managing snag abundance is the approach most often taken to provide cavities for cavity-dependent species in North American conifer stands (Land *et al.* 1989, Zarnowitz and Manuwal 1985). This is because most live conifers are not prone to formation of decay cavities (McComb *et al.* 1986, but see Parks *et al.* 1995). Snag management may not be as essential in many hardwood forests. Hardwoods tend to be more prone to formation of decay cavities than conifers, and hardwoods often produce large dead limbs on live trees so snags become less important as cavity excavation sites than live trees in many hardwood forests (Sedgwick and Knopf 1986, Waters *et al.* 1990). Providing nest or den habitat for cavity-using vertebrates in hardwood stands generally involves identifying cavity-prone tree species and retaining those trees as live trees in the stands (DeGraaf and Shigo 1985). Hardwood trees vary in their propensity to support cavities. For instance, Oregon oak (*Quercus garryana*), bigleaf maple (*Acer macrophyllum*), red maple (*Acer rubrum*), and tupeloes (*Nyssa* spp.) seem to be more prone to decay and cavity formation than species such as cherries (*Prunus* spp.), black locust (*Robinea pseudoacacia*), and sassafras (*Sassafras albidum*) (McComb *et al.* 1986, Gumtow-Farrior 1991, Harmon and Sexton 1996).

There are four key steps to managing habitat for species that depend on cavities, snags, or logs. First, goals for stand or forest prescriptions must be developed based on a knowledge of the cavities, snags or logs used and needed for reproduction and shelter by each species being considered for management. If biodiversity is the goal, then the prescription may reflect conditions within the natural range of variability under dominant disturbance regimes for that specific forest type. Second, logs, trees, and/or snags need to be identified for retention during harvest or, if harvest has already occurred, then the cavity and dead wood resources currently existing on the management area must be estimated. Third, cavity and dead wood availability must be estimated over time while considering predicted losses and gains. Finally, dead wood resources need to be monitored during stand development. If resources are insufficient to meet the needs of those species being managed, then remedial measures need to be considered in an adaptive management approach (Ball *et al.* 1996). The management process is:

1. Establish dead wood or tree cavity goals

The first step is to estimate the number of cavity-bearing trees, snags, and/or logs that would meet goals for assemblages of species that could use the stands (Neitro *et al.* 1985, Thomas *et al.* 1979) over time (Tables 10.2 and 10.3). Of course, other ecosystem processes (e.g., stand

Table 10.2. *Species of native vertebrates that use snags and tree cavities in the stand reinitiation stage of forest development, Watcom County, Washington, USA*

Species	Territory/Home range (ha)	Min. dbh (cm)[a]	Snag type			Live	Number needed per year
			Hard	Soft	Hollow		
Wood duck	1	50	x	x		x	1
Barrow's goldeneye	1	60	x	x		x	1
Common merganser	10	65	x	x		x	1
Hooded merganser	1	45	x	x		x	1
American kestrel	110	45	x	x		x	1
Northern saw-whet owl	30	45	x	x		x	1
Common barn owl	80	65			x	x	1
Vaux's swift	1	65			x	x	1
Northern flicker	15	45		x			3
Red-breasted sapsucker	8	40	x			x	3
Downy woodpecker	2	25		x			3
Hairy woodpecker	10	30		x			3
Black-backed woodpecker	45	30	x				3
Tree swallow	1	35	x	x		x	1
Violet-green swallow	1	35	x	x		x	1
Purple martin	1	35	x	x		x	1
House wren	1	35	x	x		x	2
Bewick's wren	2	30	x	x		x	2
Western bluebird	4	40	x	x		x	2

Species		dbh[a]					
Mountain bluebird	4	40		x	x	x	2
Yuma myotis	1	45			x	x	2
Long-eared myotis	1	45	x		x	x	2
Little brown myotis	1	45	x		x	x	2
Long-legged myotis	1	45	x		x	x	2
California myotis	1	45	x		x	x	2
Silver-haired bat	1	45	x		x	x	2
Big brown bat	1	45	x		x	x	2
Black bear	400	80	x				1
Raccoon	15	65	x		x	x	1

Notes:
See Appendix 10.1 for scientific names.
[a] Estimates for dbh from various sources listed in Literature Cited section and personal observations.
Source: Brown (1985).

Table 10.3. *Species of native vertebrates that use logs for reproduction in the stand reinitiation stage of forest development, Watcom County, Washington, USA*

Species	Territory (ha)/ Home range	Min. diam (cm)[a]	Log type Hard	Log type Soft	Log type Hollow	No. used per year
Long-toed salamander	1	35	x	x		1
Northern alligator lizard	1	35	x	x		1
Rubber boa	1	35	x	x		1
Gopher snake	4	45	x	x		1
Western terrestrial garter snake	1	35	x	x		1
Common garter snake	1	35	x	x		1
Virginia opossum	8	50			x	3
Townsend's chipmunk	1	35	x	x		3
Black bear	400	80			x	1
Ermine	10	35			x	3
Long-tailed weasel	280	45			x	3

Notes:

Additional logs may be needed to meet foraging needs. See Appendix 10.1 for scientific names.

[a] Estimates for diameter from various sources listed in Literature Cited section and from personal observations.

nutrient availability) also need to be considered when developing management guidelines. Attempts to estimate required numbers of habitat features often rely on summing estimates developed for each species that could occur at the site (Neitro et al. 1985, DeGraaf and Shigo 1985). Setting goals for log-using species is particularly problematic. There are virtually no studies that quantify the relationship between log size, density or biomass and animal abundance. Because dead wood is necessary to meet only a part of the life history needs of most cavity nesters, the associations between animal abundance and cavity availability over a range of stand conditions (e.g., tree density, crown cover, etc.) that are likely to develop over time also must be considered (Table 10.1). Given the species listed in Tables 10.2 and 10.3, we predicted the number of snags, cavity trees and logs that would be needed to meet the needs of the entire assemblage of species in managed stands in the stand reinitiation stage of development by summing the number of snags and logs needed to meet each species needs (Table 10.4). It is unreasonable to expect all species to have their needs met in every stand, however, and some resources may actually be shared among species, so values presented in Table 10.4 may be overestimates for vertebrates in that area in that seral stage. Similar estimates would have to be developed for other stages of stand development. Estimates from stand growth models can provide insight into stand structural characteristics (Hester et al. 1989), especially if stand visualization tools are used, although these models may not project stand development long enough to adequately consider natural cavity formation (Ball et al. 1996).

2. Estimate the availability of existing cavities, snags and/or logs

Even intensively managed forest lands contain snags and logs, but the amount retained is highly variable among stands (Ohmann et al. 1994). Consequently, an estimate of the existing dead wood resource is necessary before predicting dead wood availability over time within a stand. Ideally, cavity trees, snags, and logs should be selected for retention prior to harvest. The Washington Department of Natural Resources et al. (1992) have developed guidelines for retention of trees and snags to increase compatibility with timber harvest operations on state and private lands. DeGraaf and Shigo (1985) provided similar guidelines for eastern United States forests. In the United States, harvest operations must be coordinated with retention of snags to avoid interference with harvest systems (e.g., skid trails and cable corridors) and to ensure worker safety during the operations (Hope and McComb 1994). For example, hard snags and

Table 10.4. *Predicted snag densities per hectare and log densities per hectare to provide optimum potential habitat for all species of vertebrates that could use snags, cavity trees or logs in the stand reinitiation stage of forest development, Watcom County, Washington, USA[a]*

Type	Diameter class (cm)									Total
	>25	>30	>35	>40	>45	>50	>60	>65	>80	
Snags										
Hard or soft or live cavity-tree	0	1	5	0.9	15	1	1	0.1	0	24.0
Hard or soft	1.5	0	0	0	0.2	0	0	0	0	1.7
Hard	0	0.1	0	0	0	0	0	0	0	0.1
Soft	0	0.3	0	0	0	0	0	0	0	0.3
Hollow tree or snag	0	0	0	0	0	0	0	1	0.1	1.1
Live cavity-tree	0	0	0	0	0	0	0	0.1	0	0.1
Total	1.5	1.4	5	0.9	15.2	1	1	1.2	0.1	27.3
Logs										
Hard or soft	0	0	6.1	0	0.3	0	0	0	0	6.1
Hard	0	0	0	0	0	0	0	0	0	0
Soft	0	0	0	0	0	0	0	0	0	0
Hollow	0	0	0	0	0.1	0	0	0	0.2	0.3
Total	0	0	6.1	0	0.4	0	0	0	0.2	6.4

Notes:
[a] The number of snags or logs needed per hectare by each species by each decay class was summed from Tables 10.2 and 10.3 to estimate values needed only for reproduction. Additional dead wood may be needed for foraging sites or for future seral stages.

replacement green trees often are left in clumps between cable corridors or between skid trails, and soft snags are left opportunistically between the clumps. U.S. federal agencies have proposed general guidelines for dead wood levels (USDA and USDI 1994). It is possible, indeed likely in intensively managed stands, that insufficient resources are currently available to meet habitat goals for the stand.

The number of cavities, cavity-bearing trees, snags and/or logs of different size and decay classes must be estimated in stands for which prescriptions are to be developed. The sizes and decay classes of dead and dying wood that should be marked and measured will be dependent on the needs of each species and each ecological process considered important in the area being managed.

Sampling trees for cavities often is complicated by inadequate access to or visibility of cavities in standing trees. Cavities judged to be suitable from the ground may not be useable by a given species (Mackowski 1984, Healy *et al.* 1989). Typically, sampling for cavities is conducted during the leafless period in temperate climates if hardwoods are present in the stand. The size and number of plots used to sample for cavities will be largely a function of the density and among-plot variability in cavity density. To adequately predict the prevalence of trees with cavities, a very large number of plots may be required to sample the variation within the array of variables associated with cavity occurrence (Healy *et al.* 1989, Gumtow-Farrior 1991, Lindenmayer *et al.* 1991b). Sampling strategies for dead wood in stands often is hierarchical in design with small plots nested within large ones to sample different sizes of dead wood. Alternatively, line transect sampling has proven very effective for assessing amounts of logs in stands (Harmon and Sexton 1996). Very large snags and logs often require a complete census within the stand to obtain a reliable estimate of abundance (Bull *et al.* 1990b).

3. Estimate cavity and dead wood recruitment

An estimate of tree densities by diameter classes must be developed for each stand if a forest stand growth model is to be used to predict stand development and tree mortality (Hester *et al.* 1989). A random sample of plots should be established within a stand, and the tree diameters by species, site index (height of the dominant and co-dominant trees at a specified age), tree height, live crown ratio, and tree growth rates should be estimated for each plot (Hester *et al.* 1989). Once the live tree resource is estimated, the addition of dead wood through suppression mortality can be predicted (Neitro *et al.* 1985, Figure 10.3). Although most current models of snag dynamics assume that when a tree dies it becomes a snag (e.g., Marcot 1991), many trees do not remain standing after or during death (Putz *et al.* 1983, Lindenmayer *et al.* 1997). Ten-year remeasurement surveys indicate that up to half of the trees that die from suppression mortality in Douglas-fir stands are likely to fall within the first 10 years after death in western Washington (W. C. McComb and J. L. Ohmann, unpublished data). Also, trees that die from suppression mortality tend to be less than half the diameter of the dominant and co-dominant trees in a stand, so it is not until some trees have grown for a considerable time that large snags and logs will be recruited into the stand through suppression mortality alone. The time that it takes to produce snags and logs of a given size is highly dependent on site index and tree stocking. Stands with high

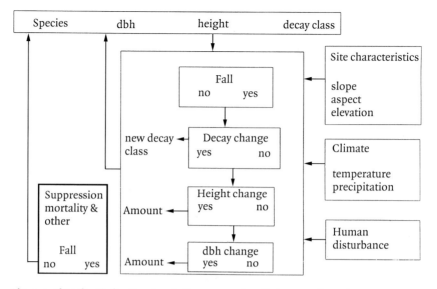

Fig. 10.3. Flow chart indicating steps in the process of predicting snag dynamics.

stocking on low quality sites may take many decades to produce snags of a size usable by cavity nesters. In contrast, stands on high quality sites that are lightly stocked at stand initiation allows trees to grow quickly and produce large snags once relative densities exceed 0.55 (Drew and Flewelling 1977), at which time competition among trees is likely to cause intermediate and suppressed trees to die.

Predicting cavity availability in a stand from tree size and species information is more problematic. Cavity occurrence in a tree is a function of tree size and tree age, as well as the often highly stochastic disturbance factors that initiate cavity formation. Nonetheless, it seems that there are relationships that can be developed for some hardwood species in North America (McComb et al. 1986, Allen and Corn 1990), Australia (Lindenmayer et al. 1993), and Thailand (Paatanavibool and Edge 1996). In general, large diameter trees with some past injury are more cavity prone than small diameter trees that lack obvious signs of past injury. Assumptions made regarding the processes of cavity formation, such as the continued role of insects and fire, must be monitored carefully throughout prescription development and implementation.

4. Manage recruitment of dead and dying trees

The quantitative goals for dead wood in a stand should be compared with the levels of dead and dying trees predicted to occur in the stand

Table 10.5. *Predicted average stand characteristics of a 5-year-old plantation planted to 740 trees per hectare on a site index 120 (50-year) using DF-SIM, Coos County, Oregon*

Prescription	Age with 100-cm dbh trees (years)	Age with 50-cm dbh snags (years)
No treatment	220	112
Thinning to 25 sq. m./ha		
basal area every 20 years	115	67
Thinning to 100 trees/ha	105	51

Source: Curtis *et al.* (1981).

over time. The forest manager can then estimate the amounts of dead wood that may have to be added to the stand during development of stand prescriptions. The process for deciding which trees to retain during management activities have largely been driven by tree species, tree size, and costs associated with forgoing timber value (Washington DNR *et al.* 1992, Gibbons and Lindenmayer 1996). Generally, large trees with some timber defect have the potential to provide tree cavities and dead and dying wood (Healy *et al.* 1989). In intensively managed stands, defective or diseased trees may be thinned early in stand development. In these stands, dominant and co-dominant trees may provide habitat for cavity-using species early in the rotation if some of these large trees are retained and killed (McComb and Rumsey 1983, Bull and Partridge 1986) or injected with fungal spores (Parks *et al.* 1995). Indeed, thinning can accelerate tree diameter growth tremendously in some forest types, providing an opportunity to kill some large trees much sooner than would occur in the absence of management (Table 10.5).

There are a range of methods available for killing trees to produce snags or cavity trees for vertebrates (Bull and Partridge 1986). Topping the trees with a chain saw or explosives is effective for both Douglas-fir and ponderosa pine (*Pinus ponderosa*) (Bull and Partridge 1986, Chambers *et al.* 1997). Herbicides also have been shown to be an effective method for killing trees that are then used by primary cavity nesters (Conner *et al.* 1981, McComb and Rumsey 1983). Girdling, although potentially effective (Hennon and Loopstra 1991), may be less cost effective than other techniques simply because trees often break at the point of girdling, creating short snags of limited value to some species. Hardwoods have been killed to increase invertebrate food resources for woodpeckers in Europe (Aulen 1991), but live hardwoods may be used by more species for a longer period of time than dead hardwoods. Indeed, killing trees may not be appropriate in all managed forests, such as Australian eucalypt forests, because primary excavators are not present there. Furthermore, even in Thailand where primary excavators occur, 92% of cavity-bearing trees were alive (Paatanavibool and Edge 1996). Killing trees as habitat management for wildlife must be done based on needs for primary cavity excavators and the potential for subsequent use of these cavities by secondary users. Generally, killing trees as a remedial measure is most appropriate in managed conifer forests.

Wood decaying fungi has been experimentally injected into live trees to create a pocket of rot that then can be excavated by cavity nesters at some later date (Parks *et al.* 1995). Artificial cavities have been created by excavating holes in live trees in eastern hardwood forests (Carey and Sanderson 1981), and cavity inserts have been used to create artificial nest sites for red-cockaded woodpeckers in pine trees without heart rot. Nest boxes are widely used to increase nesting and roosting site availability for a number of species, and the proportion of nest boxes used by animals can be higher than use of natural cavities for a number of species (McComb and Noble 1981a). However, maintenance costs for nest boxes are high, microclimates are less stable (McComb and Noble 1981b), and primary cavity nesters rarely use them unless they are filled with a substance that can be excavated. Nest boxes should only be considered a temporary solution to a problem (McKenney and Lindenmayer 1994) and one that can only be used in a relatively small area (Lindenmayer *et al.* 1991c) for a small number of species.

MONITORING CAVITY-TREE, SNAG, AND LOG USE AND DYNAMICS

Most goals for dead wood management in managed forests are based on a number of assumptions. These include, but are not limited to: estimates of the number of snags required by each individual or breeding pair; distribution of trees, snags and logs within territories; estimates of fall rates and decay rates of snags; and persistence of populations that may become isolated over time. Given the uncertainty in (a) the requirements for each species, (b) stand projection estimates and (c) estimates of snag decay and fall rates, monitoring of management effectiveness is a key part of the management process. Effective management of dead wood habitat will require consideration of not only the primary cavity nesters (Neitro *et al.* 1985, Morrison *et al.* 1986), but also foraging and nesting sites for those secondary cavity nesters that do not use nest sites abandoned by the primary cavity nesters (e.g., bats, wood ducks, and invertebrates). Secondary cavity nesters are generally dependent on the activities of primary cavity nesters and on cavities formed by wood decay processes. Consequently, secondary cavity nesters may be better candidates to monitor the effects of forest management on dead-wood dependent species.

Monitoring has been separated into three phases when conducting adaptive management: implementation, effectiveness, and validation monitoring (USDA *et al.* 1993). Implementation monitoring collects information that allows the manager to ask if the prescriptions developed for a stand are being implemented correctly. Are trees being marked for retention? Are marked trees actually retained? Are they surviving prescribed burns or other site preparation activities? Are marked trees of the correct size and species? Are snags of the correct decay class? These are all questions that should be asked to ensure that the management plan is being implemented correctly.

Often it is necessary to measure snags and logs only in a random sample of stands, making inferences to other unsampled stands. Snags, logs, and cavity trees should be measured at three stages: (1) after marking but prior to harvest, (2) immediately following harvest, and (3) following establishment of regeneration. Some National Forest Ranger Districts in the U.S. have found less than half of the stand prescriptions implemented correctly once monitoring commenced (Morrison *et al.* 1986). Both wildlife biologists and timber workers in the Pacific Northwest of the U.S. have raised concerns regarding snag management (e.g., safety and effectiveness) that could and should be addressed by a monitoring program (Hope and McComb 1994).

Data collected during effectiveness monitoring allow the manager to answer the question, 'Are my management approaches producing the goals that I established?' Usually a stratified random sampling system can be used to monitor the longevity and decay of dead and dying trees and to assess changes in the abundance of the organisms that rely on them. It is important that sampling of organisms be conducted at spatial scales that are biologically meaningful (Corn and Bury 1990, Bull *et al.* 1990a). Often prescriptions are established for stands of 10–20 ha (20–40 acres). However, the abundance of cavity-nesting birds may need to be monitored over much larger areas so that multiple territories can be sampled and the spatial requirements of wide-ranging species can adequately be considered.

Validation monitoring allows managers and researchers to address the validity of the assumptions on which management decisions are made. A linear relationship between bird abundance and snag abundance (Marcot 1991) has been assumed in some conifer forests. However, there is some evidence that the relationship may be nonlinear for some species (Raphael and White 1984). Replicated monitoring of bird abundance and snag abundance, over a range of snag densities, could allow managers to more accurately define this relationship for each species.

To understand how snag numbers will change over time, snag decay and fall rates must be estimated. Current estimates are from restricted areas. These estimates need refinement and testing at local sites to validate or refine estimates that are currently being used. Further, there are several research questions that should be addressed, ideally using manipulative studies, where appropriate.

- What is the relationship between cavity or dead wood abundance and animal abundance across a range of seral stages, taxonomic groups, and forest types?
- How does the distribution of dead and dying tree resources affect the abundance or persistence of associated species?
- Do current models of snag or tree dynamics (e.g., Ball *et al.* 1996) accurately reflect snag decay and fall rates over spatial scales that are biologically meaningful to the species that rely on these resources?
- Can we develop decision support models that find spatially explicit solutions for integrating management of dead wood and cavities with forest harvest systems.

Summary

Forest management activities that influence the frequency, intensity, and pattern of disturbances in forest systems can have marked effects on the abundance of cavities and dead and dying trees in the system. Dead and dying trees function differently in each stage of forest succession and the trees themselves progress though a succession of decay stages. Dead and dying trees provide seedbeds for other plants, habitat for animals, and storage sites for carbon and nitrogen. Forest managers must actively manage the dead wood resource if they wish to maintain these functions in managed forests.

Management of dead and dying wood usually focuses on habitat for vertebrates, but there are many invertebrate species that rely on dead wood as well. Live trees with decay are especially important to animals in hardwood forests. Standing and fallen dead trees are particularly important in conifer forests. Integration of management of dead, dying and decayed trees in forest management will be key in any management prescription. Delay in initiating active management can have long-term implications because of the time needed to both recruit large trees and for the large wood to decay to a stage suitable for certain organisms.

There are four key steps to managing habitat for species that depend on cavities, snags, or logs. First, goals for stand or forest prescriptions must be developed. Second, logs, trees, and/or snags need to be identified for retention during harvest. Third, cavity and dead wood availability must be estimated over time while considering predicted losses and gains. Finally, because of uncertainty in relationships between the quantity of dead wood and ecosystem functions, managers need to monitor the effectiveness of their management plans and adjust prescriptions using an adaptive management approach.

Further readings

Spies *et al.* (1988) provide an excellent documentation of the role of forest disturbance in driving the dynamics of dead wood in forest systems. To understand the ecology of tree decay and dead wood ecology, Maser and Trappe (1984), Harmon *et al.* (1986), and Maser *et al.* (1988) provide excellent overviews of dead wood function in forest systems.

Snag and cavity-tree management has been summarized by Evans and Conner (1979), Thomas *et al.* (1979), Neitro *et al.* (1985), and Lindenmayer (1994). Decision support tools are perhaps best exemplified by the Snag Recruitment Simulator model of Marcot (1991). Information on cavity-nesting birds in the United States can be found in a variety of sources, including Scott *et al.* (1977) who provide a brief overview of each of 85 species of cavity-nesting birds in the United States, DeGraaf and Shigo (1985) who provide guidelines for managing cavity-nester habitat in New England, and Lindenmayer *et al.* (1991b) who provide an overview of the cavity-dependent marsupials of Victoria.

Appendix 10.1. Scientific names of species listed in tables and text

Common name	Scientific name
Plants	
bigleaf maple	*Acer macrophyllum*
red maple	*Acer rubrum*
tupeloes	*Nyssa* spp.
red alder	*Alnus rubra*
salmonberry	*Rubus spectabilis*
western hemlock	*Tsuga heterophylla*
myrtle beech	*Nothofagus cunninghamii*
blackbutt	*Eucalyptus piularis*
mountain ash	*E. regnans*
eucalyptus	*E. elegatensis*
eucalyptus	*E. cypellocarpa*
jarrah	*E. marginata*
Oregon oak	*Quercus garryana*
oaks	*Quercus* spp.
hickories	*Carya* spp.
Douglas-fir	*Pseudotsuga menziesii*
ponderosa pine	*Pinus ponderosa*
lodgepole pine	*P. contorta*
firs	*Abies* spp.
sassafras	*Sassafras albidum*
black locust	*Robinea pseudoacacia*
cherries	*Prunus* spp.
Invertebrates	
carpenter ants	*Camponotus* spp.
velvet worms	*Peripatus* spp.
Amphibians	
clouded salamander	*Aneides ferreus*
ensatina salamander	*Ensatina eschschlotzii*
red-backed salamander	*Plethodon cinereus*
western red-backed salamander	*Plethodon vehiculum*
long-toed salamander	*Ambystoma macrodactylum*
Reptiles	
northern alligator lizard	*Elgaria coerulea*
rubber boa	*Charina bottae*
gopher snake	*Pituophis melanoleucus*
western terrestrial garter snake	*Thamnophis elegans*
common garter snake	*Thamnophis sirtalis*
scarlet kingsnake	*Lampropeltis triangulum*
fence lizard	*Sceloporus occidentalis*

Appendix 10.1. (cont.)

Common name	Scientific name
Birds	
wood duck	*Aix sponsa*
Barrow's goldeneye	*Bucephala islandica*
common merganser	*Mergus merganser*
hooded merganser	*Lophodytes cucullatus*
hairy woodpecker	*Picoides villosus*
northern flicker	*Colaptes auratus*
downy woodpecker	*Picoides pubescens*
red-cockaded woodpecker	*Picoides borealis*
black-backed woodpecker	*Picoides arcticus*
pileated woodpecker	*Dryocopus pileatus*
ivory-billed woodpecker	*Campephelis principalis*
red-bellied woodpecker	*Melanerpes carolinus*
acorn woodpecker	*Melanerpes formicivorus*
red-breasted sapsucker	*Sphyrapicus ruber*
northern saw-whet owl	*Aegolius acadicus*
common barn owl	*Tyto alba*
spotted owl	*Strix occidentalis*
American kestrel	*Falco sparverius*
brown creeper	*Certhia americana*
Carolina chickadee	*Parus carolina*
black-capped chickadee	*Parus atricapillus*
red-breasted nuthatch	*Sitta canadensis*
house wren	*Troglodytes aedon*
Carolina wren	*Thryothorus ludovicianus*
Bewick's wren	*Thryomanes bewickii*
ruffed grouse	*Bonasa umbellus*
Vaux's swift	*Chaetura vauxi*
tree swallow	*Tachycineta bicolor*
violet-green swallow	*Tachycineta cyaneoviridis*
purple martin	*Progne subis*
mountain bluebird	*Sialia mexicana*
western bluebird	*Sialia currucoides*
Mammals	
Virginia opossum	*Didelphis virginiana*
Leadbeater's possum	*Gymnobelideus leadbeateri*
mountain brushtail possum	*Trichosurus acninus*
greater gliders	*Petauroides volans*
Yuma myotis	*Myotis yumanensis*
long-eared myotis	*Myotis evotis*
little brown myotis	*Myotis lucifugus*

Appendix 10.1. (cont.)

Common name	Scientific name
long-legged myotis	Myotis volans
California myotis	Myotis californicus
silver-haired bat	Lasionycteris noctivigans
big brown bat	Eptesicus fuscus
vagrant shrew	Sorex vagrans
Townsend's chipmunk	Tamias townsendii
northern flying squirrel	Glaucomys sabrinus
California red-backed vole	Clethrionomys californicus
American marten	Martes americana
fisher	Martes pennanti
ermine	Mustela erminea
long-tailed weasel	Mustela frenata
raccoon	Procyon lotor
black bear	Ursus americana

Literature cited

Allen, A. W., and J. G. Corn. 1990. Relationships between live tree diameter and cavity abundance in a Missouri oak hickory forest. *Northern Journal of Applied Forestry* 7:179–83.

Ashton, D. H. 1986. Ecology of bryophytic communities in mature *Eucalyptus regnans* F. Muell. Forest at Wallaby Creek, Victoria. *Australian Journal of Botany* **34**:107–29.

Atkinson, P. R., K. M. Nixon, and M. J. P. Shaw. 1992. On the susceptibility of Eucalyptus species and clones to attack by *Macrotermes natalensis* Haviland (Isoptera: Termitidae). *Forest Ecology and Management* **48**:15–30.

Aulen, G. 1991. Increasing insect abundance by killing deciduous trees: a method of improving the food situation for endangered woodpeckers. *Holarctic Ecology* **14**:68–80.

Balda, R. P. 1973. *The relationship of secondary cavity nesters to snag densities in western coniferous forests.* Wildlife Habitat Technical Bulletin No. 1. Albuquerque, New Mexico, USA; USDA Forest Service, Southwestern Region. 37 pp.

Ball, I. R., H. P. Possingham, and D. B. Lindenmayer. 1996. *Modeling of retained trees in logged forests.* Major Report to the Australian Nature Conservation Agency. September 1996. 118 pp.

Barbour, R. W. and W. H. Davis. 1969. *Bats of America.* University Press of Kentucky, Lexington. 286 pp.

Bartels, R., J. D. Dell., R. L. Knight, and G. Schaefer. 1985. Dead and down woody material. Pp. 171–86 in E. R. Brown (Tech. ed.) *Management of wild-life and fish habitats in forests of western Oregon and Washington.* USDA Forest Service Publication R6–F&WL-192–1985.

Bennett, A. F., L. F. Lumsden, and A. O. Nichols. 1994. Tree hollows in remnant woodlands: spatial and temporal patterns across the northern plains of Victoria, Australia. *Pacific Conservation Biology* 1:222–35.

Bent, A. C. 1939. *Life histories of North American woodpeckers*. U.S. National Museum Bulletin 174. Smithsonian Institution, Washington, D.C. 334 pp. + 39 plates.

Bisson, P. A., R. E. Bilby, M. D. Bryant, C. A. Dolloff, G. B. Grette, R. A. House, M. L. Murphy, K. V. Koski, and J. R. Sedell. 1987. Large woody debris in forested streams in the Pacific Northwest: past, present, and future. Pp. 143–90 in E. O. Salo and T. W. Cundy (eds). *Streamside Management: Forestry and Fishery Interactions*. University of Washington, Institute of Forest Resources, Seattle, WA. Contribution No. 57.

Brawn, J. D., W. H. Elder, and K. E. Evans. 1982. Winter foraging by cavity nesting birds in an oakhickory forest. *Wildlife Society Bulletin* 10:271–5.

Brown, E. R. (tech. ed.) 1985. *Management of wildlife and fish habitats in forests of western Oregon and Washington*. USDA Forest Service Publication No. R6–F&WL-192–1985.

Bull, E. L. and A. D. Partridge. 1986. Methods of killing trees for use by cavity nesters. *Wildlife Society Bulletin* 14: 142–6.

Bull, E. L., R. S. Holthausen, and M. G. Henjum. 1990a. *Techniques for monitoring pileated woodpeckers*. General Technical Report PNW-GTR-269. Portland, OR: USDA Forest Service, Pacific Northwest Research Station. 13 pp.

Bull, E.L., R. S. Holthausen, and D. B. Marx. 1990b. How to determine snag density. *Western Journal of Applied Forestry* 5:56–8.

Carey, A. B., and H. R. Sanderson. 1981. Routine to accelerate treecavity formation. *Wildlife Society Bulletin* 9:14–21.

Clark, J. W. 1957. Comparative decay resistance of some common pines, hemlock, spruce, and true fir. *Forest Science* 3:314–20.

Cline, S. P., A. B. Berg, and H. M. Wight. 1980. Snag characteristics and dynamics in Douglas-fir forests, western Oregon. *Journal of Wildlife Management* 44:773–86.

Chambers, C. L., T. Carrigan, T. Sabin, J. Tappeiner III, and W. C. McComb. 1997. Use of artificially created Douglas-fir snags by cavity-nesting birds. *Western Journal of Applied Forestry* 12: 93–7.

Conner, R. N.., O. K. Miller, Jr., and C. S. Adkisson. 1976. Woodpecker dependence on trees infected by fungal heart rots. *Wilson Bulletin* 88: 575–81.

Conner, R. N., J. G. Dickson, and B. A. Locke. 1981. Herbicide killed trees infected by fungi: potential cavity sites for woodpeckers. *Wildlife Society Bulletin* 9:308–310.

Corn, P. S., and R. B. Bury. 1990. *Sampling methods for terrestrial amphibians and reptiles*. USDA Forest Service General Technical Report PNW-GTR-256. 34 pp.

Curtis R. O., G. W. Clenenden, and D. J. DeMars. 1981. A new stand simulator for coastal Douglas-fir; DF-SIM: a users guide. USDA Forest Service General Technical Report PNW-128.

Davis, J. W., G. A. Goodwin, and R. A. Ockenfels (tech. coordin.) 1983. *Snag habitat management: Proceedings of the Symposium*. USDA Forest Service General Technical Report RM-99.

DeGraaf, R. M., and A. L. Shigo. 1985. *Managing cavity trees for wildlife in the northeast*. USDA Forest Service General Technical Report. NE-101. 21pp.

DeMaynadier, P. G., and K. L. Hunter, Jr. 1995. The relationship between forest management and amphibian ecology: a review of the North American literature. *Environmental Reviews* 3: 230–61.

Dickson, J. G., R. N. Conner, and J. H. Williamson. 1983. Snag retention increases bird use of a clearcut. *Journal of Wildlife Management* **47**:799–804.

Drew, T. J., and J. W. Flewelling. 1977. Some Japanese theories of yield-density relationships and their application to Monterey pine plantations. *Forest Science* **23**:517–34.

Embry, R. S. 1963. *Estimating how long western hemlock and western redcedar trees have been dead*. USDA Forest Service Research Note NOR-2. 2 pp.

Evans, K.E. and R. N. Conner. 1979. Snag management. Pp. 214–25 in *Proceedings of the workshop, Management of north central and northeastern forests for nongame birds*. USDA Forest Service General Technical Report NC-51.

Feen, J. S. 1997. Winter den sites of northern flying squirrels in Douglas-fir forests of the south-central Oregon Cascades. M.S. Thesis, Oregon State Univ., Corvallis. 45 pp.

Fischer, W. C. and A. F. Bradley. 1987. *Fire ecology of western Montana forest habitat types*. USDA Forest Service General Technical Report INT-223. 95pp.

Gibbons, P. and D. B. Lindenmayer. 1996. A review of issues associated with the retention of trees with hollows in wood production forests. *Forest Ecology and Management* **83**:245–79.

1997. *Conserving hollow-dependent fauna in timber-production forests*. New South Wales National Parks and Wildlife Service Environmental Heritage Monograph Series No. 3. 110 pp.

Gibbs, J. P., M. L. Hunter, Jr., and S. M. Melvin. 1993. Snag availability and communities of cavity-nesting birds in tropical versus temperate forests. *Biotropica* **25**:236–41.

Gumtow-Farrior, D. L. 1991. Cavity resources in Oregon white oak and Douglas-fir stands in the mid-Willamette valley, Oregon. M.S. Thesis, Oreg. State Univ., Corvallis. 89 pp.

Haftorn, S. 1988. Survival strategies of small birds during winter. Pp. 1973–80 in H. Oullet (ed.). *Acta XIX Congressus Internationalis Ornithologica*. Vol. II. Ottawa, Canada.

Hammill, J. H., and R. J. Moran. 1984. A habitat model for ruffed grouse in Michigan. Pp. 15–18 in J. Verner, M. L. Morrison, and C. J. Ralph (eds). *Wildlife 2000: Modeling Habitat Relationships of Terrestrial Vertebrates*. The Univ. of Wisconsin Press, Madison.

Harmon, M. E., and J. Sexton. 1996. *Guidelines for measurements of woody detritus in forest ecosystems*. U.S. LTER Publication No. 20. 73 pp.

Harmon, M. E., J. F. Franklin, F. J. Swanson, P. Sollins, S. V. Gregory, J. D. Lattin, N. H. Anderson, S. P. Cline, N. G. Aumen, J. R. Sedell, G. W. Lienkaemper, K. Cromack, Jr., K. W. Cummins. 1986. Ecology of coarse woody debris in temperate ecosystems. *Advances in Ecological Research* Vol. 15. 302 pp.

Healy, W. M., R. T. Brooks, and R. M. DeGraaf. 1989. Cavity trees in sawtimber-size oak stands in central Massachusetts. *Northern Journal of Applied Forestry* 6:61–5.

Hellgren, E. C., and M. R. Vaughan. 1989. Denning ecology of black bears in a southeastern wetland. *Journal of Wildlife Management* 53:347–53.

Hennon, P. E. and E. M. Loopstra. 1991. *Persistence of western hemlock and western redcedar trees 38 years after girdling at Cat Island in Southeast Alaska.* USDA Forest Service Research Note PNW-RN-507. 4 pp.

Hester, A. S., D. W. Hann, and D. R. Larsen. 1989. *ORGANON: Southwest Oregon growth and yield model user manual.* Oregon State University Forest Research Laboratory, Corvallis. 59 pp.

Hope, S. and W. C. McComb. 1994. Perceptions of implementation and monitoring of wildlife tree prescriptions on National Forests in western Washington and Oregon. *Wildlife Society Bulletin* 22:383–92.

Howard, T. M. 1973. Studies in the ecology of *Nothofagus cunninghamii* Oerst. I. Natural regeneration on the Mt. Donna Buang massif, Victoria. *Australian Journal of Botany* 21:67–78.

Inions, G. B., M. T. Tanton, and S. M. Davey. 1989. Effect of fire on the availability of hollows in trees used by the common brush-tailed possum, *Trichosurus vulpecula* Kerr, 1792, and the ringtail possum, *Pseudocherius peregrinus* Boddaerts, 1785. *Australian Wildlife Research* 16:449–58.

Jenkins, B. and R. L. Kitching. 1990. The ecology of water-filled tree holes in Australian rainforests: food web reassembly as a measure of community recovery after disturbance. *Australian Journal of Ecology* 15:199–205.

Keen, F.P. 1955. The rate of natural failing of beetle-killed ponderosa pine snags. *Journal of Forestry* 53: 720–3.

Kitching, R. l., and C. Callaghan. 1982. The fauna of water-filled tree holes in box forest in south-east Queensland. *Australian Entomological Magazine* 8:61–70.

Koplin, James R. 1969. The numerical response of woodpeckers to insect prey in a subalpine forest in Colorado. *Condor* 71(4):436–8.

Lacy, R. C. 1993. VORTEX: a computer simulation model for population viability analysis. *Wildlife Research* 20:45–65.

Land, D. W., R. Marion, and T. E. O'Meara. 1989. Snag availability and cavity nesting birds in slash pine plantations. *Journal of Wildlife Management* 53:1165–71.

Lennartz, M. R., and R. F. Harlow. 1979. The role of parent and helper red-cockaded woodpeckers at the nest. *Wilson Bulletin* 91:331–5.

Lindenmayer, D. B. 1994. The impacts of timber harvesting on arboreal marsupials at different spatial scales and its implications for ecologically sustainable forest use and nature conservation. *Australian Journal of Environmental Management* **1**:56–68.

Lindenmayer, D. B., R. B. Cunningham, M. T. Tanton, A. P. Smith, and H. A. Nix. 1990. The habitat requirements of the Mountain Brushtail Possum and the Greater glider in the montane ash-type eucalypt forests of the Central Highlands of Victoria. *Australian Wildlife Research* **17**: 467–78.

———. 1991a. Characteristics of hollow-bearing trees occupied by arboreal marsupials in the montane ash forests of the Central Highlands of Victoria, south-east Australia. *Forest Ecology and Management* **40**:289–308.

———. 1991b. The conservation of arboreal marsupials in the montane ash forests of the Central Highlands of Victoria, south-east Australia. III. The habitat requirements of Leadbeater's possum, *Gymnobelideus leadbeateri*, McCoy and models of the diversity and abundance of arboreal marsupials. *Biological Conservation* **56**:295–315.

Lindenmayer, D. B., M. T. Tanton, and R. B. Cunningham. 1991c. A critique of the use of nest boxes required for the conservation of the Leadbeater's possum, *Gymnobelideus leadbeateri*. *Wildlife Research* **18**:619–24.

Lindenmayer, D. B., R. B. Cunningham, C. F. Donnelly, M. T. Tanton, and H. A. Nix. 1993. The abundance and development of cavities in montane ash-type eucalypt trees in the montane forests of the Central Highlands of Victoria, south-eastern Australia. *Forest Ecology and Management* **60**:77–104.

Lindenmayer, D. B., A. Welsh, C. F. Donnelly, R. B. Cunningham, and R. A. Meggs. 1996. The use of nest trees by the Mountain Brushtail possum (*Trichosurus caninus*) (Phalangeridae: Marsupalia). 1. Number of occupied trees and frequency of tree use. *Wildlife Research* **23**: 343–61.

Lindenmayer, D. B., R. B. Cunningham, and C. F. Donnelly. 1997. The collapse of hollow trees in contiguous forest and wildlife corridors in forests of Central Victoria, southeastern Australia. *Ecological Applications* **7**:625–41.

Lowney, M. S., and E. P. Hill. 1989. Wood duck nest sites in bottomland hardwood forests of Mississippi. *Journal of Wildlife Management* **53**:378–82.

Mackowski, C. M. 1984. The ontogeny of hollows in Blackbutt, *Eucalyptus piularis* and its relevance to the management of forests for possums, gliders and timber. Pp. 517–25 in A. P. Smith and I. D. Hume (eds). *Possums and Gliders*. Surrey Beatty and Sons, Sydney.

———. 1987. *Wildlife hollows and timber management in the blackbutt forest*. M. Nat. Res., University of New England, Armidale. 155 pp.

Marcot, B. G. 1991. *Snag Recruitment Simulator (computer model)*. USDA Reg. 6, Portland, OR.

Martin, K. 1994. Movements and habitat associations of northern flying squirrels in the central Oregon Cascades. M.S. Thesis, Oregon State Univ., Corvallis. 44 pp.

Maser, C., and J. M. Trappe (tech. eds). 1984. *The seen and unseen world of the fallen tree*. USDA Forest Service General Technical Report PNW-164. 56 pp.

Maser, C., R. G. Anderson, and K. Cromack, Jr. 1979. Dead and down woody material, pages 78–95 in J. W. Thomas (Tech. Ed.). *Wildlife Habitats in Managed Forests: the Blue Mountains of Oregon and Washington*. USDA Forest Service Agriculture Handbook No. 553.

Maser, C., R. F. Tarrant, J. M. Trappe and J. F. Franklin (eds). 1988. *From the forest to the sea: a story of fallen trees*. USDA Forest Service General Technical Report PNW-GTR-229. Pacific Northwest Research Station. Portland, OR: 153 pp.

Mason, E. A. 1944. Parasitism by Protocalliphora and management of cavity-nesting birds. *Journal of Wildlife Management* **8**:232–47.

McComb, W. C., and R. E. Noble. 1981a. Nest box and natural cavity use in three mid-South forest habitats. *Journal of Wildlife Management* 45:92101.

1981b. Microclimates of nest boxes and natural cavities in bottomland hardwoods. *Journal of Wildlife Management* 45:284–9.

McComb, W. C., and R. E. Noble. 1982. Invertebrate use of natural tree cavities and nest boxes. *American Midland Naturalist* **107**:163–72.

McComb, W. C., and R. L. Rumsey. 1983. Characteristics and cavitynesting bird use of picloramcreated snags in the central Appalachians. *Southern Journal of Application Forestry* 7:34–7.

McComb, W. C., S. A. Bonney, R. M. Sheffield, and N. D. Cost. 1986. Den tree characteristics and abundances in Florida and South Carolina. *Journal of Wildlife Management* **50**:584–91.

McComb, W. C., T. A. Spies, and W. H. Emmingham. 1993. Stand management for timber and mature-forest wildlife in Douglas-fir forests. *Journal of Forestry* **91**(12):31–42.

McKenney, D. W., and D. B. Lindenmayer. 1994. An economic assessment of a nest box strategy for the conservation of an endangered species. *Canadian Journal of Forest Research* **24**: 2012–19.

McWilliams, H. G. 1940. *Cost of snag falling on reforested areas*. Research Note. B.C. Forest Service No. 7. 3 pp.

Mellen, T. K., E. C. Meslow and R. W. Mannan. 1992. Summertime home range and habitat use of pileated woodpeckers in western Oregon. *Journal of Wildlife Management* **56**(1):96–103.

Mesibov, R. 1990. Velvet worms: a special case of invertebrate fauna conservation. *Tasforests* **2**: 53–6.

Miller, E. and D. R. Miller. 1980. Snag use by birds. Pp. 337–56 in R. M. DeGraaf, (Tech. Ed.). *Management of western forests and grasslands for nongame birds*. USDA Forest Service Gen. Tech. Rep. INT-86.

Morrison, M. L. and R. G. Raphael. 1993. Modeling the dynamics of snags. *Ecological Applications* **3**:322–30.

Morrison, M. L., M. F. Dedon, M. G. Raphael, and M. P. Yoder-Williams. 1986. Snag requirements of cavitynesting birds: are USDA Forest Service guidelines being met? *Western Journal of Applied Forestry* **1**: 3840.

Muul, I. 1968. *Behavioural and physiological influences on the flying squirrel Glaucomys volans*. University of Michigan Museum of Zoology Miscellaneous Publication No. 134.

Neitro, W. A., V. W. Binkley, S. P. Cline, R. W. Mannan, B. G. Marcot, D. Taylor, F. F. Wagner. 1985. Snags. Pp. 129–69 in E. R. Brown (tech. ed). *Management of wildlife and fish habitats in forests of western Oregon and Washington.* USDA Forest Service Publication No. R6–F&WL-192–1985.

Nelson, S. K. 1988. Habitat use and densities of cavity nesting birds in the Oregon Coast Range. M.S. Thesis, Oregon State University, Corvallis. 157 pp.

New, T. R. 1995. Onychophora in invertebrate conservation: priorities, practice and prospects. In: *Onychophora: past and present.* M. H. Walker and D. B. Norman (eds). *Zoological Journal of the Linnean Society* **14**: 77–89.

Nilsson, S. G. 1984. The evolution of nest-site selection among hole-nesting birds: the importance of nest predation and competition. *Ornis Scandinavica* **15**:167–75.

Nussbaum, R. A., E. D. Brodie, Jr., and R. M. Storm. 1983. *Amphibians and Reptiles of the Pacific Northwest.* Univ. Press of Idaho, Moscow. 332 pp.

Ohmann, J. L., W. C. McComb, and A. A. Zumrawi. 1994. Snag abundance for primary cavity-nesting birds on nonfederal forest lands in Oregon and Washington. *Wildlife Society Bulletin* **22**:607–19.

Ormsbee, P. C., and W. C. McComb. 1998. Selection of day roosts by female long-legged myotis in the central Oregon Cascade Range. *Journal of Wildlife Management* **62**:596–603.

Otvos, I. S. and R. W. Stark. 1985. Arthropod food of some forest-inhabiting birds. *Canadian Entomologist* **117**:971–90.

Ough, K. And J. Ross. 1992. *Floristics, fire and clearfelling in wet forests of the Central Highlands of Victoria.* Silvicultural Systems Project Technical Report No. 11. Dep. Of Conservation and Environment, Melbourne.

Paatanavibool, A. and W. D. Edge. 1996. Single-tree selection silviculture affects cavity resources in mixed deciduous forests of Thailand. *Journal of Wildlife Management* **60**:67–73.

Parks, C. G., E. L. Bull, and G. M. Filip. 1995. Using artificial inoculated decay fungi to create wildlife habitat. Pp. 175–7 in C. Aguirre-Bravo, L. Eskew, A. B. Vilal-Salas, and C. E. Gonzalez-Vicente (eds). *Partnerships for sustainable forest ecosystem management.* USDA Forest Service General Technical Report RM-GTR-266. 201 pp.

Petit, D. R., T. C. Grubb, Jr., K. H. Petit, and L. J. Petit. 1988. Predation of over-wintering woodborers by woodpeckers in clearcut forests. *Wilson Bulletin* **100**:306–9.

Prince, H. H. 1968. Nest sites used by wood ducks and common goldeneyes in New Brunswick. *Journal of Wildlife Management* **32**:489–500.

Putz, F. E., P. D. Coley, A. Montalvo, and A. Aiello. 1983. Snapping and uprooting of trees: structural determinants and ecological consequences. *Canadian Journal of Forest Research* **13**:1011–20.

Raphael, M. G. and M. White. 1984. Use of snags by cavity-nesting birds in the Sierra Nevada. *Wildlife Monographs* **86**:1–66.

Ruggiero, L. F., K. B. Aubry, A. B. Carey, and M. H. Huff. (Tech. Coords). 1991.

Wildlife and vegetation of unmanaged Douglas-fir forests. USDA Forest Service General Technical Report PNW-GTR-285. 533 pp.

Schmid, J. M., S. A. Mata, and W. F. McCambridge. 1985. *Natural falling of beetle-killed ponderosa pine.* USDA Forest Service Research Note RM-454.

Schrieber, B. and D. S. deCalesta. 1992. The relationship between cavity-nesting birds and snags on clearcuts in western Oregon. *Forest Ecology and Management* 50:299–316.

Scott, V. E. 1979. Bird response to snag removal in ponderosa pine. *Journal of Forestry.* 77:26–8.

Scott, V. E., K. E. Evans, D. R. Patton, and C. P. Stone. 1977. *Cavity-nesting birds of North American Forests.* USDA Forest Service Agriculture Handbook 511. 112 pp.

Sedgwick, J. A. and F. L. Knopf. 1991. The loss of avian cavities by injury compartmentalization. *Condor* 93:781–3.

1986. Cavity-nesting birds and the cavity-tree resource in plains cottonwood bottomlands. *Journal of Wildlife Management* 50:247–52.

Shigo, A. L. 1965. *Pattern of defect associated with stem stubs on northern hardwoods.* USDA Forest Service Research Note Northeastern Forest Experimental Station No. NE34. 4 pp.

1984. Compartmentalization: a conceptual framework for understanding how trees defend themselves. *Annual Review of Phytopathology* 22: 189–214.

Sollins, P., S. P. Cline, Verhoeven, D. Sachs and G. Spycher. 1987. Patterns of log decay in old-growth Douglas-fir forests. *Canadian Journal of Forest Research* 17:1585–95.

Spies, T. A., J. F. Franklin, and T. B. Thomas. 1988. Coarse woody debris in Douglas-fir forests of western Oregon and Washington. *Ecology* 69:1689–702.

Stelmock, J. J., and A. S. Harestad. 1979. Food habits and life history of the clouded salamander (*Aneides ferreus*) on northern Vancouver Island, British Columbia. *Syesis* 12:71–5.

Taylor, R. J. 1990. *Fauna Manual.* Forest Commission, Hobart, Tasmania.

Thomas J. W., R. G. Anderson, C. Maser, and E. L. Bull. 1979. Snags. Chapter 5 in J. W. Thomas (Tech. Ed.). *Wildlife habitats in managed forests: the Blue Mountains of Oregon and Washington.* USDA Forest Service Agriculture Handbook No. 553.

Torgersen, T. R. and E. L. Bull. 1995. Down logs as habitat for forest-dwelling ants – the primary prey of pileated woodpeckers in northeastern Oregon. *Northwest Science* 69:294–303.

Tyrrell, L. E., and T. R. Crow. 1994. Dynamics of dead wood in old-growth hemlock-hardwood forests of northern Wisconsin and northern Michigan. *Canadian Journal of Forest Research* 24:1672–83.

USDA, USDI, USDC and EPA. 1993. *Forest ecosystem management: and ecological, economic and social assessment.* U.S. Government Printing Office 1993 794–478.

USDA and USDI. 1994. *Record of decision for amendments to Forest Service and Bureau of Land Management planning documents within the range of the northern spotted owl.* U.S. Government Printing Office. 1994 – 589–111 / 00003 Region 10. 74 pp.

Van Balen, J. H., C. J. H. Booy, J. A Van Franeker, and E. R. Osieck. 1982. Studies on hole-nesting birds in natural nest sites. 1. Availability and occupation of natural nest sites. *Ardea* **70**: 1–24.

Washington DNR, USDA Forest Service, WFPA, Washington Department of Wildlife, Washington contract loggers Association, and State of Washington Department of labor and industries. 1992. *Guidelines for Selecting Reserve Trees.* Allied Printers, Olympia, WA. 24 pp.

Waters, J. R., B. R. Noon, and J. Verner. 1990. Lack of nest site limitation in a cavity-nesting bird community. *Journal of Wildlife Management* **54**:239–45.

Weigl, P. D. And D. W. Osgood. 1974. Study of the northern flying squirrel, *Glaucomys sabrinus*, by temperature telemetry. *American Midland Naturalist* **92**:482–6.

Weikel, J. M. 1997. Habitat use by cavity-nesting birds in young thinned and unthinned Douglas-fir forests of western Oregon. M.S. Thesis, Oregon State University, Corvallis. 102 pp.

Zarnowitz, J. E., and D. A. Manuwal. 1985. The effects of forest management on cavity-nesting birds in Washington. *Journal of Wildlife Management* 49:255–263.

11 Vertical structure

NICHOLAS V. L. BROKAW AND RICHARD A. LENT

Looking up at a 50 meter tall *Ceiba pentandra* in Panama, or a 60 meter dip-
terocarp in Borneo, or a 70 meter Douglas-fir (*Pseudotsuga menziesii*) in
Oregon, you know that forests are, above all, vertical. Even in short forests
the dimension from ground to canopy includes layers of foliage, gradients
of microclimate, and a diversity of plants and animals that respond to that
vertical structure. Human use of forests alters those layers, those gradients, and those arrays of plants and animals. In a world where more and
more forest is disturbed, our goal in this chapter is to develop an understanding of vertical structure and its relation to biodiversity, and to suggest
ways that forest management can maintain the vertical structure that supports biodiversity.

The study of animals and vertical structure has at least an 80 year
history. Early in this century ecologists visualized strata in forests and recognized that different animals frequented different strata (Shelford 1912).
At mid-century ecologists took another step, showing that differences in
the complexity of vertical structure could explain differences among
forests in diversity of birds (MacArthur and MacArthur 1961). While later
studies showed that more than vertical structure is needed to explain
diversity (James and Wamer 1982), no one disputes that a vertically
complex forest generally supports more species than a simple forest.
Meanwhile, foresters have increased their knowledge of how forest development and management determine vertical structure (Oliver and Larson
1996), and at century's end ecologists and foresters are applying these
accumulated insights to conservation (DeGraaf *et al.* 1992, Franklin *et al.*
1997).

In this chapter we: (a) define vertical structure in forests, (b) discuss
factors that determine vertical structure, (c) describe how particular plants
and animals are influenced by vertical structure, (d) present examples of
the connection between vertical structure and species richness, and (e)
discuss how forest management affects vertical structure and therefore
species richness, illustrating this with a case study.

What vertical structure is

Vertical structure is the bottom to top configuration of above-ground vegetation within a forest stand (a relatively homogeneous area of forest with a common history of development). One can think of vertical structure as vegetation complexity, and horizontal variation among stands as vegetation heterogeneity (August 1983, McCoy and Bell 1991).

Of course it is often difficult to separate vertical and horizontal components. For instance, variation in vertical structure produces horizontal patchiness: in a grassland–shrubland–forest mosaic, addition of a vegetation layer makes a new kind of patch (Roth 1976). Furthermore, the degree of horizontal patchiness can change with vertical position in a stand. In some well-developed tropical forests the understory is comparatively homogeneous and the canopy is heterogeneous. At 2 m above ground there may be about 1000 small tree crowns in a hectare, each about 2 m² in area; at 40 m there may be 12 tree crowns, each about 500 m²; and at middle levels, between these extremes, there will be intermediate numbers of trees and crown sizes (Terborgh 1992).

Among stands vertical structure varies in terms of canopy and tree height, branching patterns, abundance of different plant life forms (trees, shrubs, herbs, vines, epiphytes), arrangement of leaves on branches, and the amount and distribution of twigs, branches, and leaves (Parker 1995; Figure 11.1). There is a controversy about whether defined vegetation strata exist (Smith 1973), but we will use 'strata' for convenience; what is important is that vertical structure varies and can be measured. Some researchers draw profiles of forests based on measurements in particular areas; others use quantitative data to draw statistically representative profiles or graphs showing the distribution of foliage, basal area, or stem density within different height intervals (Knight 1963, Popma *et al.* 1988; Figure 11.2). European foresters have developed methods for obtaining profile data (Blondel and Cuvillier 1977, Kruijt 1989).

To compare foliage profiles among forests, MacArthur and MacArthur (1961) rendered the density and height distribution of foliage into a single statistic, 'foliage height diversity' (FHD). The density of foliage was measured within various height intervals above ground (MacArthur and Horn 1969), and these data were used to calculate FHD with the Shannon-Weiner Diversity Index (H'), to take into account both the total density of foliage and its distribution along the height gradient. Thus $FHD = -\Sigma f_i \log f_i$, where $f_i = d_i/D$, $d_i =$ the density of foliage in layer i, and D = the total density of foliage over all layers in the vertical profile. The most diverse ver-

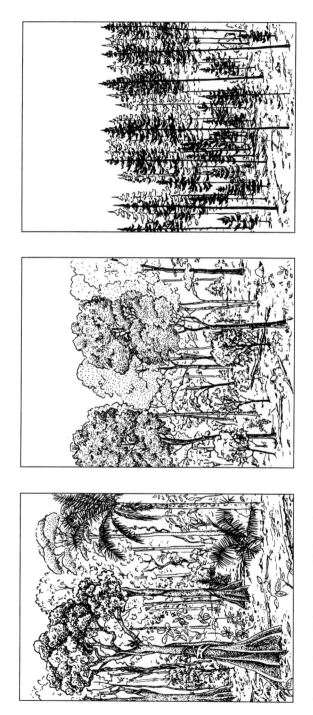

Fig. 11.1. The vertical structure of different forest types (greatly generalized): (left) tropical, (middle) temperate deciduous, and (right) boreal conifer forests.

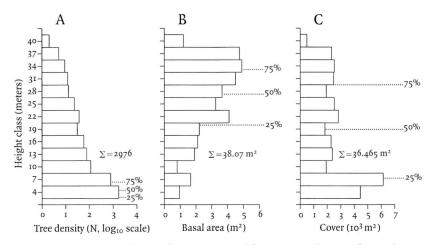

Fig. 11.2. The vertical distribution of various structural features in one hectare of tropical forest in Veracruz, Mexico (for all trees ≥ 1 cm DBH): (a) tree density (number of trees whose top height reaches particular height intervals), (b) basal area (amount contributed by trees whose top height reaches particular height intervals), and (c) foliage cover. (Adapted from Popma *et al.* 1988, with permission from Kluwer Academic Publishers.) Cumulative percentages for each parameter are shown: 75% of all individuals were ≤6 m tall; 50% of total basal area was contributed by trees > 26 m tall; there was a distinct layer of foliage contributed by dense understory palms, while overstory foliage was evenly distributed. The upper limit of each height class interval is included in that class.

tical structure (highest FHD) has foliage evenly distributed among many layers. As we shall see, FHD often explains variation in bird species diversity, but the exceptions highlight other correlates of diversity.

Forests are also compared on the basis of leaf area index (LAI), the mean area of leaves stacked up above a unit of ground area. We do not discuss LAI further. LAI tends to reflect site productivity (Hedman and Binkley 1988), which may correlate with species richness, but productivity versus species richness is not our subject. Moreover, LAI is poorly related to forest height and FHD (Aber 1979), important parts of our subject.

Variation in vertical structure

FOREST TYPE AND SITE CONDITIONS

Every forest type has a different vertical structure, almost by definition, due to the particular climate, soil, tree species, and plant life forms that produce a definable type. Boreal forests composed of pagoda-form conifers have different profiles from temperate zone forests of laterally branching trees, or tropical forests with umbrella-crowned emergents (Figure 11.1). Structure can get exceptionally complex near the equator. To the many tree growth forms in tropical forests (Hallé et al. 1978) are added the complexity of vines, epiphytes, stranglers, and palms. However, even at one latitude the variety of vertical structures is wide.

The taller a forest is, generally the more complex will be its structure (Brown 1991), simply because there are more possible vertical positions for foliage. The vertical availability of light, however, can organize the vertical distribution of foliage in different ways, depending on forest height and angle of the sun. For example, in forests in the southeastern United States understory trees tend to grow up to, and form a stable layer at, the height where rays of light passing at generally low angles through holes in the upper canopy converge to form a spatially uniform light field (Figure 11.3; Terborgh 1985). This mechanism tends to limit complexity compared with profiles in taller tropical forests, where light passing through canopy holes at higher angles can pass farther down the longer vertical gradient, producing a more complex light environment and vertical distribution of foliage.

Site conditions can also affect vertical structure. In southern Wisconsin forests foliage profiles (and species) shift, on a mesic-xeric gradient, from nearly a monolayer foliage distribution on the most mesic sites, to increasingly uniform distribution at medium sites, to a distinctly two-layer distribution, of upper canopy and dense shrub layer, at the most xeric sites (Aber et al. 1982). Site fertility, however, did not clearly affect vertical structure in Piedmont hardwood forests in North Carolina (Hedman and Binkley 1988). Instead, vertical profiles in these stands reflected stand composition, age structure, and history.

SUCCESSION AND STAND DEVELOPMENT

Vertical structure changes markedly during forest succession. Early successional stands have simple structure, but as succession proceeds, inherent differences in height growth between regenerating tree species produce strata and more complex vertical structure. At Hubbard Brook, New Hampshire, for example, stratification results from differential growth rates during succession by species cohorts of pin cherry (*Prunus pensylvanica*), sugar maple (*Acer saccharum*), and beech (*Fagus grandifolia*), in descending order (Bicknell 1982). Similarly, black ash (*Fraxinus nigra*) outgrows elm (*Ulmus americana*) in Great Lakes forests (Guldin and Lorimer

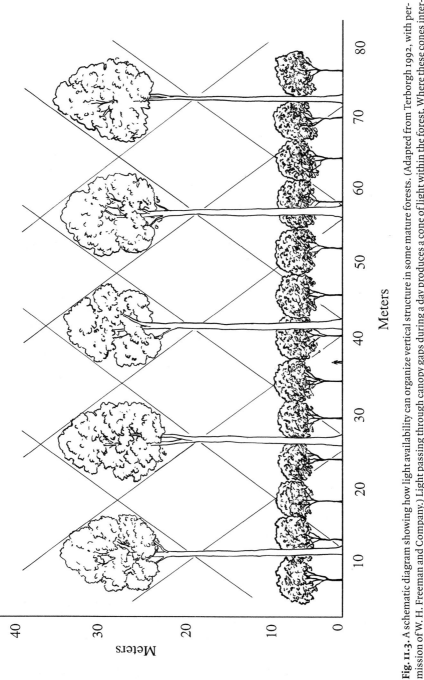

Fig. 11.3. A schematic diagram showing how light availability can organize vertical structure in some mature forests. (Adapted from Terborgh 1992, with permission of W. H. Freeman and Company.) Light passing through canopy gaps during a day produces a cone of light within the forest. Where these cones intersect in the understory there is a spatially uniform light field. Understory trees tend to grow up to, and form a stable layer at, this height. Between the canopy and this layer, light is more variable and vegetation sparser.

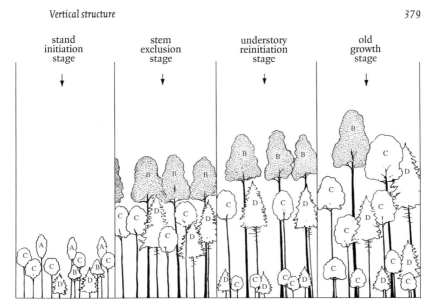

Fig. 11.4. Schematic diagram showing how vertical structure develops during succession in some forests. After stand initiation, differentiation of crown height and form results from variable height growth and mortality among individual trees and from contrasting species-specific architectures that are increasingly apparent as trees mature. Differentiation of canopy trees permits increased light below and the initiation of an understory stratum. There are multiple cohorts and maximum vertical complexity in old growth. In central New England, USA, typical tree species in this sequence would be, as designated by letters in the diagram: A, black birch (*Betula lenta*), B, red oak (*Quercus rubra*), C, sugar or red maple (*Acer sacharrum, A. rubrum*), D, hemlock (*Tsuga canadensis*). (Adapted from Oliver 1981, with permission from Elsevier Science.)

1985), and secondary species top primary species during succession in Ghana (Swaine and Hall 1983), thereby differentiating strata during regrowth.

As the overstory layer matures, it becomes more horizontally heterogeneous and vertically complex due to thinning and to differential height growth and shaping of crowns (Figure 11.4). This permits more light to penetrate lower levels, and in response an understory layer develops, further complicating vertical structure (Oliver 1980). Yet when complexity increases with forest age it is not necessarily manifested by more and distinct foliage layers. In 12 New Hampshire stands ranging from three to 57 years old, plus one at 200 years, foliage did concentrate into strata through year 30, but later became more evenly distributed from forest floor to canopy (Aber 1979). In older forest stands, big trees die, leaving large gaps where vertical structure redevelops through a process similar to the stand-scale succession just described. The staggered timing and horizontal patterning of this gap-phase regeneration produces variation in vertical structure within a stand (Oliver and Larson 1996) (also see Chapter 4).

Some forests become less vertically complex with time. The giant, emergent figs (*Ficus insipida*) and spanish cedar (*Cedrela odorata*) that colonize early in succession along the Río Manu, Peru, eventually die and are replaced by shorter, more shade-tolerant species (Foster *et al.* 1986). On a longer time scale (100 000 years), soil weathering and leaching in tall Queensland rainforest eventually stunted the vegetation (Walker *et al.* 1981), and some forests become sphagnum bogs (Oliver and Larson 1996).

Having discussed what vertical structure is and how and why it varies among forests, we next consider how vertical structure affects plants and animals. Understanding those mechanisms will help us manage forests for biodiversity. In a later section we will relate these mechanisms to patterns of species richness.

Effects of vertical structure: mechanisms

The vertical organization of forest vegetation has various direct effects on animals and plants. The vertical arrangement of flowers, fruits, and foliage is the vertical arrangement of food for some animals, as well as the arrangement of sites for nesting, resting, perching, basking, and mating (Bell *et al.* 1991). For stranglers, vines, and epiphytes it is the vertical arrangement of substrate for attachment.

The vertical organization of forest vegetation also has indirect effects on animals and plants, because it affects internal stand microclimates and the distribution of animal prey (Bell *et al.* 1991, Robinson and Holmes 1982). From canopy top to forest floor there are gradients of decreasing light and wind, increasing humidity, and increasing (night) or decreasing (day) temperature (Chiarello 1984). The slopes of these gradients are usually not smooth but change markedly at heights of foliage concentrations that intercept light and interrupt air movement. Thus profile complexity produces complexity in internal stand microclimate, and profile differences among stands produce different arrays of microclimates. The range of microclimatic values in tall forests may be greater than in short forests, while the gradient may be less steep.

During stand development, changes in vertical profiles alter the vertical array of microclimates. In a chronosequence of tulip-poplar (*Liriodendron tulipifera*) forests, light transmittance to the ground was lowest through the dense regeneration in young stands. It increased at about 50 years as the regeneration grew taller, permitting growth of an understory, then decreased in stands of 65–340 years, as the understory formed a dense layer (Brown and Parker 1994).

EXAMPLES: DIRECT EFFECTS

The distribution of animals that eat plants is directly influenced by the vertical location of plant food. The most productive layer is the upper canopy, exposed to light that stimulates leaf, flower, and fruit production (Terborgh 1992) and attracting numerous insects (Sutton 1983) and birds (Stiles 1983). This active surface is better visualized not as a level, upper-canopy stratum but as a foliage–light interface (cf. Stiles 1983) that follows the outer contours of the canopy trees and descends into the gaps between them (Chapter 4). Also, a more detailed look at the distribution of insect herbivores reveals that many are more attracted to lower strata with softer, more edible, shade leaves (Lowman 1995) than to upper canopy leaves that may be leathery to resist desiccation.

Large arboreal herbivores are directly affected by vertical structure because they require adequate support for their bodies and appropriate configurations of vegetation for their movements (Pounds 1991). For instance, in tropical forests monkeys tend to be found well above ground level, where there are thicker branches, rather than in the more continuous, but thin and weak, branches of lower levels (Terborgh 1992). In Surinam, body sizes and locomotion of different monkey species are related to the forest strata they use (Fleagle and Mittermeier 1991), and in India the giant squirrel (*Ratufa indica*) requires a certain amount of canopy continuity for travel through the forest (Datta and Goyal 1996).

Foraging of insectivorous birds is also directly affected by vertical structure. In West Virginia, a forest that had regrown after logging in the early 1900s was taller and had a larger vertical span of relatively foliage-free area beneath the main canopy than did a forest regrown since clearcutting in 1958 (Maurer and Whitmore 1981). In the older forest Acadian flycatchers (*Empidonax virescens*) preferentially sallied for flying insects in the sub-canopy open space, whereas in the young forest they were more broadly distributed vertically and used other foraging techniques to cope with the lack of open area. In Belize, some forest birds seem to adjust their foraging height depending on overall forest height (Mallory and Brokaw in press), and different European warbler species prefer different vegetation structures to which their particular leg morphologies are adapted (Winkler and Leisler 1985).

EXAMPLES: DIRECT/INDIRECT EFFECTS

Plants create the vertical structure in forests, but they are also influenced by it. Epiphytes are plants that grow on other plants but are not otherwise parasitic. They include many dicot species, especially orchids and bromeliads, as well as mosses and lichens. Epiphyte distribution is influenced directly and indirectly by vertical structure. For example, in Connecticut (Hale 1965) and Jamaica (Kelly 1985), particular epiphyte species are found in characteristically different vertical locations on trees and at different places on branches, presumably because they are confined to certain substrates that are suitable both for attachment (direct effect) and for light and humidity (indirect effect). In turn, the vertical distribution of certain bromeliad species determines the vertical distribution of particular mosquito species that breed in them (Pittendrigh 1948).

Insects and other invertebrates are finely tuned to the variation in physical and biological factors associated with vertical complexity (Speight and Wainhouse 1989). Species of *Anopheles* mosquitoes in Panama frequent different levels in the forest corresponding to differences in humidity (Bates 1944), and there is pronounced vertical stratification of arthropods, correlated with architectural and microclimatic variables in Missouri oak–hickory (*Quercus–Carya*) forest (Dowdy 1947) and other temperate forests (Davidson 1930, Fichter 1939, Adams 1941)

We have seen how the height of understory trees is limited by the angle of light passing through the upper layer of some forests (Figure 11.3). This indirect effect would also select for plant species adapted to reach maturity in the light climate at that level, such as dogwoods (*Cornus* spp.) and redbud (*Cercis canadensis*) in North American forests (Terborgh 1985). Similarly, in a developing stand, the continuous canopy of the early phase may allow only shade-tolerant plant species below it. However, the heterogeneous canopy of later phases permits more light penetration, ranging in area from sunflecks that sustain forest floor herbs (Anderson *et al.* 1969) to large gaps where light-demanding tree species establish (Denslow 1987). Although gaps are productive spots for some species, damage to the upper canopy can decrease abundances of animals adapted to shaded understory. Hurricane Hugo in Puerto Rico destroyed much forest canopy, raising temperatures, reducing humidity, and consequently depressing the abundances or changing distributions of understory snails, walking-sticks, a frog (*Eleutherodactylus portoricensis*), and *Anolis* lizards (Reagan 1991, Willig and Camilo 1991, Woolbright 1991).

We have now reviewed some mechanisms by which particular features of vertical structure in forests affect the distribution of particular plant and animal species. That enables us to understand the next topic: how vertical structure affects the number of species that coexists in forests.

Effects of vertical structure: species richness

In general, the more vertically diverse a forest is the more diverse will be its biota, for two main reasons. First, a more complex habitat contains more kinds of microclimates and microhabitats for more species. For instance, we have seen how different epiphytes and lizards prefer different kinds of substrates, at different vertical locations, for attachment or perching; the more kinds of those substrates included in a forest, the more kinds of epiphytes and lizards there can be. Second, it follows that a more complex vertical structure, supporting more kinds of plants and animals, provides more diverse food resources for more diverse consumers (Malcolm 1995). Yet there are exceptions to this relationship between vertical complexity and species richness, because other factors, such as biogeographic patterns and differential response to habitat structure among taxonomic groups, also influence richness.

Whereas relatively many studies describe the vertical distributions of species in forests, fewer take the next step and show that forests differing in vertical complexity also differ in species richness. However, the examples below illustrate the generally positive correlation of complexity with richness in all forest types and for all taxonomic groups that have been studied, but also illustrate some exceptions.

PLANTS

For plants vertical complexity is in itself an expression of species richness, because complexity is in part an expression of the variety of plant life forms and species-specific morphologies (Terborgh 1992, Aiba and Kohyama 1996). In tall tropical forests the variability of light conditions in middle layers (Figure 11.3) contributes to a higher species richness of trees in the middle strata as compared with other strata, and as compared with temperate forests with more uniform light conditions beneath the canopy (Terborgh 1992). The species-specific preferences of epiphytes for vertical positions and substrates probably contributes to such high diversity as the 77 species in 17 families found on three neighboring, 45–50 m tall trees in French Guiana (Freiberg 1996). Epiphytes contribute a large part of the plant species richness of tropical and temperate forests (Rose 1974, Gentry and Dodson 1987) and, in turn, support a rich fauna (Gerson and Seward 1977, Nadkarni and Matelson 1989).

MAMMALS AND REPTILES

Mammal and reptile species richness in tropical forest often reflects vertical complexity. For example, seven co-occurring squirrels in Africa differ in their use of the vertical vegetation column (Emmons 1980). In Venezuela the richness of mammal species is correlated with the increasing vertical complexity from savanna to tall forest, related to increasing potential food resources (August 1983). Surprisingly, the increased richness was in mainly terrestrial species, not arboreal species. Small mammal species richness and abundance in Brazil were correlated with density of understory vegetation (Malcolm 1995). In this case understory density was higher in disturbed forests. Intercontinental differences in the richness of gliding mammals and reptiles may be attributed to intercontinental differences in vertical structure. In taller Indo-Malaysian forests there are more gliding species than in Africa or America, perhaps because this mode of travel is more rewarding where launching from taller trees permits longer glide distances (Dudley and DeVries 1990). As a final example, species of *Anolis* lizards in Puerto Rico coexist partly by choosing different perch types that are stratified by height in the forest (Reagan 1992).

BIRDS

Birds are the best studied group in relation to vertical structure in forests. The association between bird species diversity (BSD) and foliage height diversity (FHD, see above) has been demonstrated in many places. BSD, like FHD, is calculated using H', to take into account both the total number of species present and the evenness of their abundances. The most diverse bird community (highest BSD) has birds evenly distributed among many species, and this community is frequently found in forests with the most diverse vertical structure (highest FHD), in which foliage is evenly distributed among many layers.

BSD was positively correlated with FHD in, for example, the northeastern United States (MacArthur and MacArthur 1961), Illinois (Karr 1968), Australia (Recher 1969), Scandinavia (Røv 1975), and Scotland (Moss 1978). The Scottish study showed that the more complex forests were used by small numbers of many bird species, rather than large numbers of few species, explaining why BSD was better correlated with FHD than were simply the numbers of species or of individual birds. The intercontinental consistency of these results suggests that the relationship is not due merely to the kinds of birds in these forests but to the universal process of diversification to fill niches in complex habitats (Recher 1969). Moreover, BSD is correlated with FHD because FHD is not only an index of the vertical complexity of foliage layers, but because it tends to be correlated with other components of habitat diversity important to birds, such as the greater variety of bark and leaf types that generally occur in older, more vertically complex forests (Holmes *et al.* 1979).

FHD is not always a good predictor of BSD, because other factors contribute to diversity. In various British studies on the correlation of BSD with FHD, it was sometimes not clear if it was vertical structure itself that affected diversity, as opposed to something else correlated with FHD, such as tree species composition, site, or altitude (Avery and Leslie 1990). The importance of additional factors is obvious from the fact that there are more birds in Amazonian forests than in Panamanian, Puerto Rican, and North American forests of similar FHD (Terborgh and Weske 1969). Furthermore, within a region the correlation between FHD and BSD may be misleading. On a gradient from 500 to 3500 m elevation in eastern Peru both BSD and FHD declined, but this was due mostly to a decline in the richness of insectivorous birds; nectarivores did not decline and frugivores declined only slightly, because foods of these two groups are less related to FHD than is the food of insectivores (Terborgh 1977). A more dramatic exception to the expected correlation between BSD and FHD is the greater number of Argentine bird species in scrub-cedar (*Austrocedrus chilensis*) vegetation than in adjacent, more vertically complex southern beech (*Nothofagus* spp.) forest (Ralph 1985). It appears that scrub-cedar habitat, although vertically simpler, draws birds from a wider area of similar habitat, to which more species may have adapted, than does the more complex beech forest (see Engstrom *et al.*, 1984, for a similar example).

SUCCESSION, VERTICAL STRUCTURE, AND SPECIES RICHNESS

Because more vertically complex forests usually contain more species than simpler forests do, and because vertical complexity generally increases with forest age, it follows that species richness usually increases with succession (Chapter 4). The species richness of beetles and bugs increased with succession from old field to forest in Britain; even as plant species diversity declined in later stages, beetle and bug richness increased as vertical complexity increased (Southwood *et al.* 1979). Similarly, the density and, presumably, species richness of arthropods increases with forest age and vertical complexity in Douglas-fir forests in Oregon (Schowalter 1995). Species richness of birds increases during succession in various European forests (Glowacinski and Järvinen 1975, Turcek 1957).

However, when richness increases with succession, it is not necessarily monotonic, partly because the increase in vertical complexity with succession may not be monotonic. For example, in northern hardwoods and spruce–fir (*Picea–Abies*) forests in the United States, the number of animal species is high in regenerating stands, drops in the pole stage, when the canopy is fairly uniform and the understory is suppressed, then increases to a maximum in mature and overmature stands, as canopy structure diversifies and the understory develops (DeGraaf *et al.* 1992). It is important to understand the connections between succession, vertical complexity, and species richness in forests, because forest management usually maintains much forest area in early- and mid-successional stages. In the next section we discuss the impacts of logging on vertical structure and, briefly, the value of agroforestry for biodiversity.

Forest management, vertical structure, and biodiversity

FORESTRY

Our review of the literature suggests, as a generalization with exceptions, that tall, mature forests contain the most vertical complexity and that vertical complexity is positively correlated with species richness. Thus ideal management to conserve species richness within a stand is probably to let it attain maturity and not disturb it. Still, the most species-rich stand will lack some species characteristic of vertically simpler stands. For example, in northern hardwoods forest some bird species prefer recently logged stands (Lent and Capen 1995), and in this forest type no single stand structure is preferred by all species (DeGraaf *et al.* 1992). Therefore, to conserve biodiversity across landscapes it is best to maintain a collection of stands of different vertical structures, as produced by natural disturbances (wind, fire, flood, etc.) that create a mosaic of

different-aged successional stands. This suggests that the best management for biodiversity over a landscape would mimic the natural disturbance regime to which the local biota are adapted, including creation of
early successional stands with simple vertical structure. It will not,
however, be possible to exactly mimic natural disturbance and regeneration in forests managed for timber. After all, the very idea of silviculture is
to alter nature, to promote the abundance and growth of preferred tree
species and harvest some of them before their natural deaths (Putz and
Viana 1996). With care, however, native plants and animals can be maintained in logged landscapes.

Forestry systems are of three basic types that differ in their effects on
vertical structure at the stand and landscape levels (Chapter 2). In single-
cohort systems all trees are harvested over a certain area, in the practice
known as clearcutting. In two-cohort systems most or many trees are cut
in a stand but individuals or patches of trees are retained uncut. In multi-
cohort systems single, or small groups of, trees are selectively felled at
scattered locations in a stand. What are the impacts of these various
systems on vertical structure?

In single-cohort systems, clearcutting trees in patches initiates secondary succession, during which vertical structure develops as described
earlier. At the stand level clearcutting initially simplifies vertical structure.
Post-harvest planting or thinning may further simplify vertical structure
by limiting species composition and therefore tree form, or by creating a
cohort of same-sized trees. Alternatively, thinning can accelerate stand
differentiation and development of vertical structure (DeBell et al. 1997).
The biggest potential problem in single-cohort systems is that stands with
vertical structure typical of old growth may never be allowed to develop, if
harvest rotation period is too short (Curtis 1997), or will be too small or
isolated to support viable populations of dependent organisms. Yet if there
is a range of stand ages (vertical structures), including old growth, and
treatments do not overly homogenize seral stages, species richness might
be maintained over the landscape, although the relative abundances of
organisms will differ from what they would be in a pristine system. The
impact on biodiversity of single-cohort systems that create a landscape
mosaic of different-aged stands is treated in Chapter 4, but keep in mind
that a differentiating feature of the stands, and one significant for biodiversity, is vertical structure.

In two-cohort systems, retention of scattered single trees or patches of
trees diversifies the vertical structure of subsequent regenerating stands
(Franklin et al. 1997), as typically occurs with natural disturbances, which

destroy stands but leave scattered old trees or tree patches. This legacy of vertical structure has direct, positive effects on biodiversity; for example, in New England oak–pine (*Quercus–Pinus*) forests, leaving 'bull pines' provides hawks and herons with perches and nest sites (DeGraaf *et al.* 1992). Retention has indirect effects also, because retained vertical structure ameliorates microclimatic extremes in harvested areas and hastens reestablishment of later-successional conditions. Studies in Oregon and Tasmania suggest that retained trees enhance species richness in regenerating forests (Hansen *et al.* 1991, Taylor and Haesler 1995). A strength of the two-cohort system is how flexibly it can be adjusted in terms of amount, location, and dispersion of retained vertical structure, according to forest type and management goals (Franklin *et al.* 1997). For instance, retention well suits the goals of shelterwood systems, in which understory and lower canopy trees are removed and replaced by seedlings of desirable species under the shelter of canopy trees, and of seedtree systems, in which scattered trees are left to provide seed for a new stand.

In multi-cohort systems selection cutting of single trees produces a finer-grained mosaic of vertical structures than single- or two-cohort systems do. Instead of initiating secondary succession in whole stands, single tree selection initiates gap-phase regeneration. The resulting stand mimics unlogged forest with natural treefall gaps, except that gaps and regenerating patches are more frequent. Group selection generally creates more large gaps than in a natural forest but not on the scale of clearcutting. Thus the impact on vertical structure of multi-cohort systems varies according to how many trees are taken per unit area and time (Whitman *et al.* 1997), yet the range in vertical structures among stands will not be so great as in single- or two-cohort systems.

At the stand level in a multi-cohort system, vertical complexity and species richness may be higher than in any seral stage in other systems. Nevertheless, species richness may be less than in old growth, especially due to impacts of felling and removal of canopy trees on the vertical structure in lower strata. Compared with the patchy environment created by the crowns of large, diversely shaped canopy trees, the understory is structurally and climatically uniform (Terborgh 1992). The felling of a large tree disrupts that uniformity by direct physical damage and by raising light levels, increasing temperature variation, reducing humidity, and encouraging dense growth near the ground. This, and log removal along the ground, alter the understory habitat and can reduce numbers of some understory species (Lambert 1992, and see Case Study below). However, as with clearcutting, some species benefit, for example, frugivores that take advantage of increased fruiting stimulated by light penetrating the broken canopy (Johns 1988).

Canopy biota are certainly also affected by selection cutting. In Brazil, cutting of only eight trees per ha reduced canopy cover from 80% to 43% (Uhl and Viera 1989). Such damage disrupts arboreal pathways of upper strata animals (Datta and Goyal 1996). Liana cutting to reduce felling damage (Putz 1991) would moderate this disruption, but would also eliminate the pathways and vertical complexity contributed by those lianas. Perhaps more serious is that selection cutting often removes the largest trees, valuable for epiphytes and some animals. For example, selection cutting of large Norway spruce (*Picea abies*) significantly alters relative abundances of lichen species in northern Sweden (Essen and Renhorn 1996). To mitigate negative impacts in multi-cohort management, tree felling should not greatly exceed natural treefall rates, some large trees should be retained, and loggers should practice reduced impact methods for felling and skidding (Pinard and Putz 1996). The best animal indicators of logging impacts may be arthropods, due to their fine-scale associations with vertical structure and rapid response to disturbance (Kremen *et al.* 1993, Niemela 1997).

AGROFORESTRY

Agroforestry is a production system that yields crops from both canopy trees and other plant life forms growing in the same site, or at least retains trees to benefit an understory crop. Though less vertically complex than most natural forests, agroforests are usually far more complex and rich in plants and animals than is conventional agriculture of annual crops. In one region of Brazil at least 60 plant species are used in different agroforestry systems. Some of these systems combine commercial timber trees, fruit trees, palms, shrubs, vines, and herbs (Subler and Uhl 1990).

A widespread agroforestry system is the cultivation of coffee (*Coffea* spp.), an understory tree, under a canopy of taller trees, but this system is threatened by new techniques that simplify its vertical structure (Perfecto *et al.* 1996). Coffee is traditionally grown either in natural forest cleared of its understory or where canopy trees are planted, along with other plants such as bananas (*Musa* spp.). Both systems provide a vertically complex vegetation that supports a high diversity of other plants and many groups of animals. Given the large area in the world devoted to coffee, these traditional, vertically complex plantations conserve many species. However, new, high-yield strains of coffee, grown in full sun in vertically simple plantations of coffee monoculture, have already replaced half the area of coffee planted in northern Latin America. Not only are all upper strata and dependent organisms eliminated in 'sun coffee' plantations, but the remaining coffee stratum itself is much poorer in species due, in part, to its harsher microclimate without a buffering upper canopy.

Case study: Effects of silvicultural treatments on vertical structure and birds in Venezuela

Three different silvicultural treatments were applied to a forest in southern Venezuela, each with different impacts on vertical structure and the species richness of birds (Mason 1996). The first treatment was selection cutting, in which about 2.3 trees/ha (7.3 m³ wood/ha) were removed, with no further treatment. The second was selection felling followed by bulldozing of 'enrichment strips', 3 m wide and 1000 m long, separated by about 50 m of logged forest, and planted with seedlings of commercial species. The bulldozed trees were shoved beyond the 3 m width into the forest. The third treatment was low intensity selection cutting, followed by cutting of all woody vines at ground level.

Working in replicate 200 × 200 m plots following each treatment, and in primary forest, Mason mist-netted birds in two long sessions within a period of 1.75 years. Mist-nets were set in the understory of the unlogged forest matrix of each treatment, not in the directly affected sites. He also measured canopy height, canopy openness, and understory stem density in each treatment and the primary forest.

Over the 1.75 years Mason mist netted 3783 birds of 117 species, and discovered that birds were strongly affected by two of the silvicultural treatments. Compared with primary forest, bird assemblages were significantly different in selectively logged forests, even more different in the forest with enrichment strips, but not different in very selectively logged forest where vines were cut. The logged forests generally had lower, more open canopies and denser understories than did the primary forest. Differences in mist-netted bird assemblages were best correlated with understory stem density: as stem density increased, bird assemblages increasingly diverged from the assemblage in primary forest. Percent canopy openness was also, but less strongly, correlated with changes in bird assemblages.

We can understand the differences in these bird assemblages by looking at impacts on different feeding guilds and how the foraging habits and preferred foods of those guilds may have been affected by changes in vertical structure. Hummingbirds benefited from logging, presumably because upper canopy openings increased light in the understory, stimulating flowering that provides nectar and attracts insects, both eaten by hummingbirds. The response of frugivores to logging was mixed: some increased and others decreased. Fruit is a patchy resource even in primary forest, thus changes in vertical structure due to logging may not have significantly changed the distribution or abundance of this resource. In fact, as with nectar, logging may increase fruit abundance by permitting more light to penetrate the forest and stimulate reproductive activity in the understory.

The biggest impact was on insectivorous birds, whose foraging mode is often closely tied to vegetation structure. For example, of 22 antbird species found in primary forest, 12 species were less abundant in the selectively logged area, four were absent, two were equal in numbers, and four were more common. Differences between primary and logged forest with enrichment strips were greater: six species were less abundant, nine were absent, and seven were more abundant. The response of sally-feeding flycatchers was similar to that of antbirds: of 22 species present in primary forest, 14 were less abundant or absent in selectively logged forest or in logged forest with enrichment strips.

In this Venezuelan forest a significant portion of the understory bird community was less abundant or even absent, while a few species increased, after selective logging and silvicultural treatments that affect vertical structure. Opening the canopy changed the understory microclimate and promoted increased plant density and perhaps plant reproduction. The degrees of change in canopy openness and understory density were correlated with changes in the avifauna. Logging followed by clearing of enrichment strips had the most impact on vertical structure and birds. Because the strips were only 50 m apart this treatment affected both the immediate impact zones and the intervening forest understory. Low intensity logging followed by vine cutting had little effect on understory birds, perhaps because vine cutting altered vertical structure little.

Summary

Vertical structure is the bottom to top spatial configuration of above-ground vegetation within a forest stand. Vertical structure is depicted in profile diagrams and sometimes quantified as 'foliage height diversity', a measure based on the Shannon-Weiner Diversity Index. Each forest type has a different vertical structure due to differences in height and shape of trees and other plant life forms composing a forest. Within a forest type, vertical structure and complexity vary with successional stage and site conditions. Generally, forests become more vertically complex with age, because they become taller, trees differentiate in height and crown form, and large trees die, initiating gap-phase regeneration.

Vertical structure directly affects biota because it constitutes the arrangement of attachment sites for epiphytes and foraging, perching, and nesting sites for animals. Vertical structure indirectly affects biota because it controls internal stand microclimates to which animals and plants respond, and it influences the distribution of prey for carnivores and insectivores.

In general, the more vertically complex a forest is the more species-rich it is, and both parameters usually increase with succession. Vertical complexity is in part an expression of plant species richness, and it further creates variation in microclimate, substrate, and food resources that support other biota. The best known example is the frequently observed positive correlation between foliage height diversity and bird species diversity in forests, to which, however, there are exceptions.

Clearcutting in single-cohort forest management systems creates a landscape mosaic of stands of different ages and vertical structures. Overall, this system may support a diversity of species adapted to the different successional stages. However, single-cohort systems may reduce species richness if the complex vertical structure of old growth becomes too rare in the landscape. Long rotations can permit development of old-growth vertical structure, while thinning can hasten its development. Retention of scattered old trees or tree patches in two-cohort systems enriches the regenerating stand with vertical structure typical of later successional stages and can accelerate its development. Selection felling of single or grouped trees in multi-cohort systems may diversify vertical structure within a stand and therefore benefit some species, just as natural treefall gaps do. However, the frequency of felled tree gaps and cutting of large trees may exceed the frequency of natural gaps and death of large trees and have negative impacts on animals and plants that depend on relatively continuous canopy pathways, uniform understory conditions, or large trees. Agroforestry in the tropics maintains vertically and biologically diverse stands of overstory trees and other plant life forms.

Acknowledgments

We thank Alan White, Richard DeGraaf, Douglas Reagan, and anonymous reviewers for comments on the manuscript, and Phillip deMaynadier, Tim Schowalter, and Elizabeth Mallory for help with the literature. This chapter is a joint product of the Luquillo and the Harvard Forest Long-Term Ecological Research Programs, supported by grants from the U.S. National Science Foundation. The U.S. Forest Service (Department of Agriculture) and the University of Puerto Rico provided additional support.

Further readings

Further reading on vertical structure, biodiversity, and forest management should start with Hunter (1990), who wrote on these same subjects. For a discussion of various ways vertical structure can be defined and quantified, a good article is Popma *et al.* (1988). The variety of vertical structures among different forest types, how structure changes during forest development, and effects of management are shown in detail by Oliver and Larson (1996). Terborgh (1992) describes vertical structure in temperate and tropical forests and its relationship to species diversity. Suggestions on how partial retention harvesting (Franklin *et al.* 1997), rotation length (Curtis 1997), and thinning (DeBell *et al.* 1997) can maintain vertical structure and biodiversity in managed forests are presented in Kohm and Franklin (1997).

Literature cited

Aber, J. D. 1979. Foliage height profiles and succession in northern hardwood forest. *Ecology* **60**:18–23.

Aber, J., J. Pastor, and J. M. Melillo. 1982. Changes in forest canopy structure along a site quality gradient in southern Wisconsin. *American Midland Naturalist* **198**:256–65.

Adams, R. H. 1941. Stratification, diurnal and seasonal migration of the animals in a deciduous forest. *Ecological Monographs* **11**:190–227.

Aiba, S.-I., and T. Kohyama. 1996. Tree species stratification in relation to allometry and demography in a warm-temperate rain forest. *Journal of Ecology* **84**:207–18.

Anderson, R. C., O. L. Loucks, and A. M. Swain. 1969. Herbaceous response to canopy cover, light intensity, and throughfall precipitation in coniferous forests. *Ecology* **50**:255–63.

August, P. V. 1983. The role of habitat complexity and heterogeneity in structuring tropical mammal communities. *Ecology* **64**:1465–513.

Avery, M., and R. Leslie. 1990. *Birds and Forestry*. T & A D Poyser, London.

Bates, M. 1944. Observations of the distribution of diurnal mosquitoes in a tropical forest. *Ecology* **25**:159–70.

Bell, S. S., E. D. McCoy, and H. R. Mushinsky. 1991. *Habitat Structure: the Physical Arrangement of Objects in Space*. Chapman and Hall, London.

Bicknell, S. H. 1982. Development of canopy stratification during early succession in northern hardwoods. *Forest Ecology and Management* **4**:42–51.

Blondel, J., and R. Cuvillier. 1977. Une méthode simple et rapide pour décrire les habitats d'oiseaux: le stratiscope. *Oikos* **29**:326–31.

Brown, M. J., and G. G. Parker. 1994. Transmission of photosynthetically active radiation in relation to stand age and canopy structure. *Canadian Journal of Forest Research* **24**:1694–703.

Brown, V. K. 1991. The effects of changes in habitat structure during succession in terrestrial communities. Pp. 141–68 in S. S. Bell, E. D. McCoy, and H. R. Mushinsky (eds). *Habitat Structure: the Physical Arrangement of Objects in Space*. Chapman and Hall, London.

Chiarello, N. 1984. Leaf energy balance in the wet lowland tropics. Pp. 85–98 in E. Medina, H. A. Mooney, and C. Vázquez-Yanes (eds). *Physiological Ecology of Plants of the Wet Tropics*. Dr W. Junk Publishers, The Hague, Netherlands.

Curtis, R. O. 1997. The role of extended rotations. Pp. 165–70 in K. A. Kohm and J. F. Franklin (eds). *Creating a Forestry for the 21st Century: The Science of Ecosystem Management*. Island Press, Washington, D.C.

Datta, A., and S. P. Goyal. 1996. Comparison of forest structure and use by the Indian Giant Squirrel (*Ratufa indica*) in two riverine forests of central India. *Biotropica* **28**:394–9.

Davidson, V. S. 1930. The tree layer society of maple-red oak climax forest. *Ecology* **11**:601–6.

DeBell, D. S, R. O. Curtis, C. A. Harrington, and J. C. Tappenheimer. 1997. Shaping stand development through silvicultural practices. Pp. 141–9 in K. A. Kohm and J. F. Franklin (eds). *Creating a Forestry for the 21st Century: The Science of Ecosystem Management*. Island Press, Washington, D.C.

DeGraaf, R. M., M. Yamasaki, W. B. Leak, and J. W. Lanier. 1992. *New England wildlife: management of forested habitats*. General Technical Report NE-144, Radnor, PA: USDA Forest Service, Northeastern Forest Experiment Station, 271 pp.

Denslow, J. S. 1987. Tropical rainforest gaps and tree species diversity. *Annual Review of Ecology and Systematics* **18**:431–51.

Dowdy, W. W. 1947. An ecological study of the arthropods of an oak-hickory forest, with reference to stratification. *Ecology* **28**:418–39.

Dudley, R., and P. DeVries. 1990. Tropical rain forest structure and the geographical distribution of gliding vertebrates. *Biotropica* **22**:432–4.

Emmons, L. H. 1980. Ecology and resource partitioning among nine species of African rain forest squirrels. *Ecological Monographs* **50**:31–54.

Engstrom, R. T., R. L. Crawford, and W. W. Baker. 1984. Breeding bird populations in relation to changing forest structure following fire exclusion. *Wilson Bulletin* **96**:437–50.

Essen, P.-E., and K.-E. Renhorn. 1996. Epiphytic lichen biomass in managed and old-growth boreal forests: effect of branch quality. *Ecological Applications* **6**:228–38.

Fichter, E. 1939. An ecological study of Wyoming spruce-fir forest arthropods with special reference to stratification. *Ecological Monographs* **9**:184–215.

Fleagle, J. G., and R. A. Mittermeier. 1991. Locomotor behavior, body size, and comparative ecology of seven Surinam monkeys. *American Journal of Physical Anthropology* **52**:301–14.

Foster, R. B., J. Arce B., and T. S. Wachter. 1986. Dispersal and sequential plant communities in Amazonian Peru floodplain. Pp. 357–70 in T. H. Fleming and A. Estrada (eds). *Frugivores and Seed Dispersal*. Dr. W. Junk Publishers, Dordrecht.

Franklin, J. F., D. A. Berg, D. A. Thornburgh, and J. C. Tappenheimer. 1997. Alternative silvicultural approaches to timber harvesting: variable retention harvesting systems. Pp. 111–39 in K. A. Kohm and J. F. Franklin (eds). *Creating a Forestry for the 21st Century: The Science of Ecosystem Management*. Island Press, Washington, D.C.

Freiberg, M. 1996. Spatial distribution of vascular epiphytes on three emergent canopy trees in French Guiana. *Biotropica* **28**:345–55.

Gentry, A. H., and Dodson, C. H. 1987. Contribution of non-trees to species richness of a tropical rain forest. *Biotropica* **19**:149–56.

Gerson, U., and M. R. D. Seward. 1977. Lichen-invertebrate associations. Pp. 69–119 in M. R. D. Seward (ed.). *Lichen Ecology*. Academic Press, London. 550 pp.

Glowacinski, Z., and O. Järvinen. 1975. Rate of secondary succession in forest bird communities. *Ornis Scandinavica* **6**:33–40.

Guldin, J. M., and C. G. Lorimer. 1985. Crown differentiation in even-aged northern hardwood forests of the Great Lakes region, U.S.A. *Forest Ecology and Management* **10**:65–86.

Hale, M. E. 1965. Vertical distributions of cryptograms in a red maple swamp in Connecticut. *Bryologist* **69**:193–7.

Hallé, F., R. A. A. Oldeman, and P. B. Tomlinson. 1978. *Tropical Trees and Forests: an Architectural Analysis*. Springer-Verlag, Berlin.

Hansen, A. J., T. A. Spies, F. J. Swanson, and J. L. Ohmann. 1991. Conserving biodiversity in managed forests. *BioScience* **41**:382–92.

Hedman, C. W., and D. Binkley. 1988. Canopy profiles of some Piedmont hardwood forests. *Canadian Journal of Forest Research* **18**:1090–3.

Holmes, R. T., R. E. Bonney, Jr., and S. W. Pacala. 1979. Guild structure of the Hubbard Brook bird community: a multivariate approach. *Ecology* **60**:512–20.

Hunter, M. L., Jr. 1990. *Wildlife, Forests, and Forestry: Principles of Managing Forests for Biodiversity*. Prentice Hall, Englewood Cliffs, New Jersey.

James, F. C., and N. O. Wamer. 1982. Relationships between temperate forest bird communities and vegetation structure. *Ecology* **63**:159–71.

Johns, A. 1988. Effects of 'selective' timber extraction on rain forest structure and composition and some consequences for frugivores and folivores. *Biotropica* **20**:31–7.

Karr, J. R. 1968. Habitat and avian diversity on strip-mined land in east central Illinois. *Condor* **70**:348–57.

Kelly, D. L. 1985. Epiphytes and climbers of a Jamaican rain forest: vertical distribution, life forms and life histories. *Journal of Biogeography* **12**:223–41.

Knight, D. H. 1963. A distance method for constructing forest profile diagrams and obtaining structural data. *Tropical Ecology* **4**:89–94.

Kohm, K. A., and J. F. Franklin (eds). 1997. *Creating a Forestry for the 21st Century: The Science of Ecosystem Management*. Island Press, Washington, D.C.

Kremen, C., R. K. Colwell, T. L. Erwin, D. D. Murphy, R. F. Noss, and M. A. Sanjayan. 1993. Terrestrial arthropod assemblages: their use in conservation planning. *Conservation Biology* **7**:796–808.

Kruijt, B. 1989. Estimating canopy structure of an oak forest at several scales. *Forestry* **62**:269–84.

Lambert, F. R. 1992. The consequence of selective logging for Bornean lowland forest birds. *Philosophical Transactions of the Linnean Society London, Series B* **335**:443–57.

Lent, R. A., and D. E. Capen. 1995. Effects of small-scale habitat disturbance on the ecology of breeding birds in a Vermont (USA) hardwood forest. *Ecography* **18**:97–108.

Lowman, M. D. 1995. Herbivory as a canopy process in rain forest trees. Pp. 431–55 in M. D. Lowman and N. M. Nadkarni (eds). *Forest Canopies*. Academic Press, San Diego, California.

MacArthur, R. H., and H. S. Horn. 1969. Foliage profiles by vertical measurements. *Ecology* **50**:802–4.

MacArthur, R. H., and J. W. MacArthur. 1961. On bird species diversity. *Ecology* **42**:594–8.

Malcolm, J. R. 1995. Forest structure and the abundance and diversity of neotropical small mammals. Pp. 179–97 in M. D. Lowman and N. M. Nadkarni (eds). *Forest Canopies*. Academic Press, San Diego, California.

Mallory, E. P., and N. V. L. Brokaw. (in press). Mist-netting in subtropical habitats in Belize: effects of season, rain, time of day, and site on capture rates. C. J. Ralph (ed.). *In Monitoring Bird Populations by Mist Nets*.

Mason, D. 1996. Responses of Venezuelan understory birds to selective logging, enrichment strips, and vine cutting. *Biotropica* **28**:296–309.

Maurer, B. A., and R. C. Whitmore. 1981. Foraging of five bird species in two forests with different vegetation structure. *Wilson Bulletin* **93**:478–90.

McCoy, E. D., and S. S. Bell. 1991. Habitat structure: the evolution and diversification of a complex topic. Pp. 3–27 in S. S. Bell, E. D. McCoy, and H. R.

Mushinsky (eds). *Habitat Structure: the Physical Arrangement of Objects in Space.* Chapman and Hall, London.

Moss, D. 1978. Diversity of woodland song-bird populations. *Journal of Animal Ecology* **47**:521–7.

Nadkarni, N. M., and T. J. Matelson. 1989. Bird use of epiphyte resources in neotropical trees. *Condor* **91**:891–907.

Niemela, J. 1997. Invertebrates and boreal forest management. *Conservation Biology* **11**:601–10.

Oliver, C. D. 1980. Forest development in North America following major disturbances. *Forest Ecology and Management* **3**:153–68.

Oliver, C. D., and B. C. Larson. 1996. *Forest Stand Dynamics* (second edition). McGraw-Hill, Inc., New York.

Parker, G. G. 1995. Structure and microclimate of forest canopies. Pp. 73–106 in M. D. Lowman and N. M. Nadkarni (eds). *Forest Canopies.* Academic Press, San Diego, California.

Perfecto, I., R. A. Rice, R. Greenberg, and M. E. Van der Voort. 1996. Shade coffee: a disappearing refuge for biodiversity. *BioScience* **46**:598–608.

Pinard, M. A., and F. E. Putz. 1996. Retaining forest biomass by reducing logging damage. *Biotropica* **28**:278–95.

Pittendrigh, C. S. 1948. The bromeliad-*Anopheles* complex in Trinidad. I. The bromeliad flora. *Evolution* **2**:58–81.

Popma, J, F. Bongers, and J. Meave del Castillo. 1988. Patterns in the vertical structure of the tropical lowland rain forest of Los Tuxtlas, Mexico. *Vegetatio* **74**:81–91.

Pounds, J. A. 1991. Habitat structure and morphological patterns in arboreal vertebrates. Pp. 107–19 in S. S. Bell, E. D. McCoy, and H. R. Mushinsky (eds). *Habitat Structure: the Physical Arrangement of Objects in Space.* Chapman and Hall, London.

Putz, F. E. 1991. Silvicultural effects of lianas. Pp. 493–501 in F. E. Putz and H. A. Mooney (eds). *The Biology of Vines.* Cambridge University Press, Cambridge.

Putz, F. E., and V. Viana. 1996. Biological challenges for certification of tropical timber. *Biotropica* **28**:323–30.

Ralph, C. J. 1985. Habitat association patterns of forest and steppe birds of northern Patagonia, Argentina. *Condor* **87**:471–83.

Reagan, D. P. 1991. The response of *Anolis* lizards to hurricane-induced habitat changes in a Puerto Rican rain forest. *Biotropica* **23**(Suppl.):468–74.

Reagan, D. P. 1992. Congeneric species distribution and abundance in a three-dimensional habitat: the rain forest anoles of Puerto Rico. *Copeia* **1992**:392–403.

Recher, H. F. 1969. Bird species diversity and habitat diversity in Australia and North America. *American Naturalist* **96**:167–74.

Robinson, S. K., and R. T. Holmes. 1982. Foraging behavior of forest birds: the relationships among search tactics, diet, and habitat structure. *Ecology* **63**:1918–31.

Rose, F. 1974. The epiphytes of oak. Pp. 250–73 in M. G. Morris, and F. H. Perring (eds). *The British Oak*. Classey, Faringdon. 376 pp.

Roth, R. R. 1976. Spatial heterogeneity and bird species diversity. *Ecology* **57**:773–82.

Røv, N. 1975. Breeding bird community structure and species diversity along an ecological gradient in deciduous forest in western Norway. *Ornis Scandinavica* **6**:1–14.

Schowalter, T. D. 1995. Canopy invertebrate community response to disturbance and consequences of herbivory in temperate and tropical forests. *Selbyana* **16**:41–8.

Shelford, V. E. 1912. Ecological succession IV: Vegetation and the control of land animal communities. *Biological Bulletin* **23**:59–99.

Smith, A. P. 1973. Stratification of temperate and tropical forests. *American Naturalist* **107**:671–83.

Southwood, T. R. E., V. K. Brown, and P. M. Reader. 1979. The relationships of plant and insect diversities in succession. *Biological Journal of the Linnean Society* **12**:327–48.

Speight, M. R., and D. Wainhouse. 1989. *Ecology and Management of Forest Insects*. Clarendon Press, Oxford. 374 pp.

Stiles, F. G. 1983. Birds. Pp. 502–43 in D. H. Janzen (ed.). *Costa Rican Natural History*. University of Chicago Press, Chicago, Illinois.

Subler, S., and C. Uhl. 1990. Japanese agroforestry in Amazonia: a case study in Tomé-Açu, Brazil. Pp. 152–66 in A. B. Anderson (ed.). *Alternatives to Deforestation: Steps Toward Sustainable Use of the Amazonian Rain Forest*. Columbia University Press, New York.

Sutton, S. L. 1983. The spatial distribution of flying insects in tropical rain forests. Pp. 77–91 in S. L. Sutton, T. C. Whitmore, and A. C. Chadwick (eds). *Tropical Rain Forest: Ecology and Management*. Blackwell Scientific Publications, Oxford.

Swaine, M. D., and J. B. Hall. 1983. Early succession on cleared forest land in Ghana. *Journal of Ecology* **71**:601–27.

Taylor, R. J., and M. E. Haesler. 1995. Effects of partial logging systems in Tasmania. *Forest Ecology and Management* **72**:131–49.

Terborgh, J. 1977. Bird species diversity on an Andean elevational gradient. *Ecology* **58**:1007–19.

1985. The vertical component of plant species diversity in temperate and tropical forests. *American Naturalist* **126**:760–76.

1992. *Diversity and the Tropical Rain Forest*. Scientific American Library, W. H. Freeman and Co., New York.

Terborgh, J., and J. Weske. 1969. Colonization of secondary habitats by Peruvian birds. *Ecology* **50**:765–82.

Turcek, F. J. 1957. The bird succession in the conifer plantation on mat-grass land in Slovakia. *Ibis* **99**:587–93.

Uhl, C., and I. C. G. Viera. 1989. Ecological impacts of selective logging in the Brazilian Amazon: a case study from the Paragominas region of the State of Pará. *Biotropica* **21**:98–106.

Walker, J., C. H. Thompson, I. F. Fergus, and B. R. Tunstall. 1981. Plant succession and soil development in coastal sand dunes of subtropical eastern Australia. Pp. 107–31 in D. C. West, H. H. Shugart, and D. B. Botkin (eds). *Forest Succession: Concepts and Application*. Springer-Verlag, New York.

Whitman, A. A., N. V. L. Brokaw, and J. Hagan. 1997. Forest damage caused by selection logging of mahogany (*Swietenia macrophylla*) in northern Belize. *Forest Ecology and Management* **92**:87–96.

Willig, M. R., and G. R. Camilo. 1991. The effect of Hurricane Hugo on six invertebrate species in the Luquillo Experimental Forest of Puerto Rico. *Biotropica* **23**:455–61.

Winkler, H., and B. Leisler. 1985. Morphological aspects of habitat selection in birds. Pp. 415–34 in M. L. Cody (ed.). *Habitat Selection in Birds*. Academic Press, New York.

Woolbright, L. 1991. The impact of Hurricane Hugo on forest frogs in Puerto Rico. *Biotropica* **23**(Suppl.):462–7.

12 Plantation forestry

SUSAN E. MOORE AND H. LEE ALLEN

With worldwide population growth, there are increasing demands on forests to provide an array of benefits. Growing demand for wood for energy, fiber, and wood products requires that more forests be intensively managed. As silvicultural activities are intensified to meet these demands, all forest organisms will be increasingly affected. The key question is: is intensive forest management compatible with maintenance of biodiversity? In this chapter we will cover how intensive silvicultural activities such as harvesting, site preparation, vegetation control, and fertilization may impact biodiversity. Plantation management is a dominant and growing form of intensive management. Because pine plantations of the southern United States are currently one of the most studied intensively managed forest systems, many of the examples and references cited refer to these systems. Implications, however, are more globally applicable as plantation forestry continues to expand throughout the world (Shepherd 1993, Cubbage *et al.* 1996).

The relationship between sustainable productivity and biodiversity in intensively managed forests is uncertain. Clearly, the components of biodiversity that are important for tree growth should be identified and maintained. Without knowing which components these are, the 'wise tinkerer's rule' (Leopold 1966) says that all biodiversity should be maintained. But do we need to maintain a complete array on every hectare? Or should the concurrent objective be to minimize off-site impacts of intensive forest management? And is it possible to conserve more biodiversity in plantations with little cost to fiber production? By intensively managing some land for wood production, the total amount of land needed to meet the demand for wood products can be reduced and the pressure for harvesting indigenous forests can be relieved (Shepherd 1993, Angelstam *et al.* 1997). This also makes more land available for other uses, including conserving the entire array of biodiversity, not just the components directly related to tree growth (Hunter and Calhoun 1996).

The growing world human population creates an ever-increasing

400

demand for wood products (Shepherd 1993). Human population levels are projected to increase from the current 5.7 billion to 8.3 billion by 2025 and to 10 billion by 2050 (World Resources Institute 1996, chapter 8). There is a direct correlation between the number of people and the amount of solid wood and paper products used, and many developing countries which currently have a low use rate per capita of wood products are likely to increase that rate as they become more developed (Shepherd 1993, Cubbage *et al.* 1996). Intensive plantation silviculture is a tool to satisfy this demand on a smaller land base (Shepherd 1993, Angelstam *et al.* 1997, Kimmins 1997).

An estimate of world forest plantation levels reveals that there are currently over 130 million ha, with about half this land area in Asia, and a quarter of it in Europe (Cubbage *et al.* 1996). The United States, India, Japan and Indonesia also have large plantation areas. These numbers represent both industrial wood plantations and fuelwood production. In Europe, management of both timber and pulpwood is intensive, production is high, and there is increasing pressure to intensify forest production to help local and national economies in Eastern Europe and Russia (Angelstam *et al.* 1997). Most of this intensive production is in new plantation forests on formerly agricultural land. It is easy to understand the importance of forest plantations in a global sense when one considers their potential to both slow deforestation and degradation of natural forests, and to satisfy the growing demand for forest products, particularly in developing countries (Shepherd 1993).

The challenge for forest managers today is to manage in ways which prevent site degradation and undesired off-site effects while generating cost-effective and adequate production to meet the increasing demand for forest products. To prescribe a silvicultural system that will minimize negative impacts on biodiversity, it is important to understand the impacts of various practices on site resources and species composition. Silviculture activities must be coordinated both spatially and temporally at the stand, forest, and landscape scales (Primack and Hall 1992, Banerjee and Banerjee 1994, Larsen 1995). Managed stands interspersed with natural stands of all age classes within a forest, as well as across the broader landscape, will provide for greater plant and animal diversity (Strelke and Dickson 1980, Enge and Marion 1986, Hansen *et al.* 1991, Lautenschlager 1993, Attiwill 1994, Banerjee and Banerjee 1994, Roth *et al.* 1994, Wilcox 1995) (Figure 12.1). On a stand basis, while there may be things forest managers can do to improve the conditions for conserving biodiversity, intensive wood production and complete maintenance of biodiversity may be conflicting objectives; however both goals may be met on a landscape

Fig. 12.1. Loblolly pine plantations interspersed with natural forest in the southeastern United States coastal plain. (R. G. Campbell, Weyerhaeuser Co. photo)

scale. So, to answer the original question posed above, as pointed out in Chapter 2, when evaluating the effects of management on biodiversity we must not limit ourselves solely to plantations at the stand level, but expand our focus to a larger scale as well.

What is intensive silviculture?

Traditionally, silviculture has been defined as the art and science of controlling the establishment, growth, composition, health, and quality of forests (SAF 1971) with the focus being on the manipulation of vegetation. In the United States, as in Europe, the practice of silviculture has always been explicitly based on meeting landowner objectives on a sustainable basis (Smith *et al.* 1997). Over time, both the profession's and society's concept of sustainability has evolved from one of regulated timber outputs to maintaining functioning ecosystems for all species and outputs (Ministry of Agriculture and Forestry 1994, Wallace *et al.* 1994). We believe the practice of silviculture now recognizes the need to manage forest land such that the diverse needs and values of both the landowner and society are met. As silviculture on certain lands has intensified, the sole focus on vegetation manipulation has also been replaced with the rec-

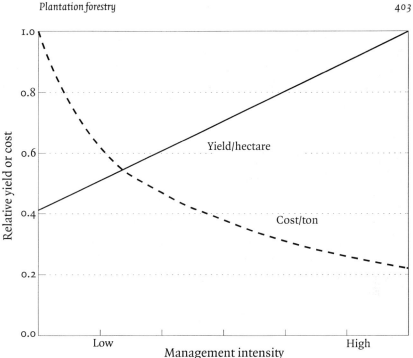

Fig. 12.2. Intensive forest management decreases per unit production costs as productivity increases.

ognition that silviculture includes manipulation of the soil as well as vegetation. Stone (1975) recognized the important role of soil manipulation in plantation forests and noted the obvious parallels with agriculture. In fact, the practice of agronomy has always included the manipulation of both plants and soils. It is this purposeful manipulation of both the vegetation and the soil that differentiates intensive silviculture and domesticated forests from traditional silviculture and regulated forests.

The principal objectives of intensive plantation silviculture are to increase usable wood fiber production per unit area per unit time and simultaneously maintain or reduce the per unit production costs. Intensive soil preparation, planting of selected genotypes, vegetation control, and nutrient additions are silvicultural treatments that have been used successfully throughout the world to increase productivity and reduce production costs (Allen *et al.* 1990) (Figure 12.2). Investments in such treatments can easily exceed US$1000 per hectare over a rotation.

Unlike some of the earlier agronomic approaches that viewed natural processes as something to ignore or purposely subvert, sustainable agriculture and sustainable management of forest crops will always require careful attention to the natural system. In domesticated forests, natural processes such as nitrogen mineralization still provide the basis for much of the productive capacity of plantations. Natural processes also cannot be ignored because tree crops are perennial crops and forest managers must live with their mistakes for many years.

Why is biodiversity important to forests managed for production?

In Chapter 1 and elsewhere we have seen many reasons why scientists, conservationists, and the public value biodiversity. The importance of maintaining biodiversity is frequently justified by the genetic resources it engenders, the potential medicinal uses of as yet unclassified species, the sheer aesthetic beauty of it, and perhaps most importantly, a lack of knowledge of the consequences of altering it. Less widely discussed, but recently recognized as important, is the potential value of biodiversity to the sustainability of intensively managed forests.

We define forest sustainability as the long-term ability of a forest ecosystem to retain its function within the larger landscape at a high level of productivity. If, as some studies have shown (Naeem *et al.* 1994, Larsen 1995, Tilman *et al.* 1996), biodiversity contributes to system stability, structure, and productivity, then it must be important to sustainability as well. Can sustainability be achieved if stability, structure, and productivity are purposefully altered by intensive silviculture, or more simply, by plantation management where the objective is to produce an even-aged, even-sized crop of a single species, and to produce it regularly on a short rotation?

STABILITY

Ecosystem stability, characterized by the system's ability to resist perturbations or recover from them, may be impacted by changes in biodiversity. Ecosystems are evolutionarily adapted to particular natural disturbances such as fire, wind storms, hurricanes, or pest outbreaks. In fact, maximum diversity and productivity in the forest are maintained by random periodic disturbance (Loucks 1970, Haggstrom and Kelleyhouse 1996). Managed disturbances, such as harvesting, prescribed fire, and herbicide use can, in some cases, mimic natural disturbance patterns (Greenberg 1993, Haggstrom and Kelleyhouse 1996, Smith *et al.* 1997) which are a central force in forest development (Attiwill 1994).

An ecosystem is a complex web of interacting organisms and their physical environment, and it has been hypothesized that ecosystem stability increases with the degree of interrelationships in the food web. While this remains a debatable point among ecologists (Lawton and Brown 1993, Tilman and Downing 1994, Wilcox 1995, Kimmins 1997) if it were the case, then increased trophic complexity would in turn lead to increased community stability (Larsen 1995). A decrease in biodiversity would likely decrease trophic complexity, which may in turn eliminate various ecosystem interactions, thus affecting many ecosystem processes which support the stability of the system. Both spatial and temporal effects of intensive silviculture systems and their impact on ecosystem stability must be considered, as silvicultural manipulations may modify ecosystem processes critical to stability.

The stability of a site following a disturbance is related in part to the system's ability to recycle nutrients. Forest floor vegetation plays an important part in these processes (Borman and Likens 1979), as 'the quantity and quality of the ground vegetation may significantly contribute to biogeochemical stability' (Larsen 1995) due to the role it plays in promoting diversity and activity of heterotrophic organisms (including decomposers) leading to a balance between production and mineralization.

Single species crops are more likely to be affected by pest or disease problems and other natural disturbances due to their low genetic and structural diversity. Mixed stands, on the other hand, may have greater resistance (Larsen 1995) due to the presence of diverse genetics, structure, and function. These system attributes are difficult to measure and are really indirect benefits of biodiversity that may not be realized until they are lost. Brown (1987) states that 'a strong argument can be made for the importance of maintaining plant-eating insects as well as invertebrates in general, to ensure the continued evolution and diversification of plant species, including the maintenance of genetic resources.' Interdependence of organisms in ecosystems implies that varied organisms at all trophic levels contribute to the viability and functioning of an ecosystem.

STRUCTURE

Several attributes of forest structure are generally positively associated with forest age, including abundance of large trees, variation in tree size, abundance of understory plants, and presence of snags and fallen

Fig. 12.3. Leaving snags standing in a plantation adds structural diversity.

logs. Plantation forestry typically produces forests that are relatively uniform in tree species, size, and distribution, and thus structural features such as a multi-layered canopy, varied tree sizes, and abundant snags and fallen logs are generally missing. If, for these reasons, forest plantations support fewer species than natural forests, the key questions are: are the species critical to crop tree production being supported on the site? And, is there adequate habitat for the missing species elsewhere in the landscape?

There is concern that managed forests, particularly managed plantations, may not provide this habitat variety, thus supporting a more depauperate plant and animal community. Forests with more habitat options, such as a multi-layer canopy, forest floor variation, dead and live trees, will support a more diverse biotic community (Figure 12.3). This is why landscape-scale forest management is critical to maintenance of biodiversity (Strelke and Dickson 1980, Enge and Marion 1986, Hansen *et al.* 1991, Lautenschlager 1993, Attiwill 1994, Banerjee and Banerjee 1994, Roth *et al.* 1994, Wilcox 1995.)

PRODUCTIVITY

Enhancing the productivity of the desired crop species is clearly the primary objective of intensive timber management. In the short run, controlling all 'unwanted vegetation' and focusing site resources on crop trees may maximize their productivity (Cain and Mann 1980, Nelson et al. 1981, Pehl and Bailey 1983, Creighton et al. 1987, Zobel et al. 1987, Clason 1993). In the longer term, this may not be the case.

Recent evidence from a well-replicated grassland experiment indicated that ecosystem productivity increased significantly with increased plant diversity (Tilman et al. 1996). Specifically, more diverse systems were found to more fully utilize soil mineral nitrogen, the main limiting nutrient in these systems. More diverse communities have also been shown to have higher primary productivity than less diverse communities, because they have more structurally and spatially variable canopies which are able to intercept more light (Naeem et al. 1994). Since all ecosystem functions are affected by energy input (Naeem et al. 1994), this has implications for ecosystem stability and sustainability as well.

While numerous studies have shown that soil fertility influenced biodiversity (Grime 1973, Tilman and Pacala 1993), the grassland study in initially homogeneous soils showed that the converse was also true – that increasing plant diversity had significant positive effects on productivity, nutrient use, and nutrient retention (Tilman et al. 1996). There may be further implications for system sustainability as well as productivity, if soil nutrient cycles are affected by biodiversity. One question regarding intensive silviculture that demands further study is: which aspects of biodiversity contribute to crop tree productivity, in other words, the production of more usable wood fiber?

Intensive silviculture practices

The cycle of management begins with initiation of a regeneration cut, typically a clearcut in plantation management. Most plantation management requires no provision for natural regeneration, except perhaps to exclude it, and a rotation is typically started with the preparation of a pasture, agricultural field, or previously clearcut stand for planting. One of the major benefits of planting seedlings or cuttings is the ability to select the species, genotype, or clone. Selections made based on growth potential, wood quality, and insect and disease resistance may result in substantial gains in yield and value. In addition, spacing is controlled and considerable time may be saved as compared with natural regeneration systems. The quality of the clearcutting job will have considerable impact on the amount of slash; the number, species, and size of residual trees; and the condition of the soil. These factors largely influence the selection and cost of subsequent site preparation and cultural treatments which serve to reduce slash, ameliorate soil limitations, and control unwanted vegetation.

Slash disposal is accomplished with various treatments (e.g., roller drum chopping, shearing, raking, piling, and burning), that can have considerable impact on both vegetation and soil properties. Depending on soil conditions, tillage may be used to improve soil aeration, reduce soil strength, incorporate organic matter, and reduce growth of non-crop tree vegetation (Morris and Lowery 1988). Treatments such as bedding, disking, or subsoiling can be very effective at ameliorating the physical limitations of soil whether they occur naturally or from equipment trafficking. Bedding on wet sites, subsoiling on well-drained clays, and disking of skid trails have also provided substantial improvements in survival and growth of planted seedlings (Allen et al. 1990).

Control of non-crop tree vegetation using mechanical or chemical methods is becoming common because vegetation control can be very effective at reallocating site resources to crop trees (Allen et al. 1990). With appropriate timing, many of the treatments used for slash disposal and tillage can be quite effective at controlling unwanted woody vegetation. Herbicides are now available that can be used at site preparation for hardwood and brush control, before or after planting for grass and herbaceous weed control, and during the life of a stand to release crop trees, particularly conifers, from competition with less desirable woody vegetation (Lowery and Gjerstad 1991, NCSFNC 1996). Thinning (removal of the same species as the crop trees), and prescribed burning are also used in intermediate-age stands to allocate site resources to crop trees.

In addition to amelioration of soil physical limitations and control of competing vegetation, nutrient limitations, particularly of phosphorus and nitrogen are very widespread in both the United States, the tropics and Europe (Allen 1987, Taylor 1991, Binkley et al. 1995). These deficiencies are typically ameliorated with fertilization at or near the time of planting (Jokela et al. 1991, Binkley et al. 1995). Additions of potassium and boron are also becoming more common throughout the rotation because rapid growth rates in intensively managed plantations place greater nutrient demands on soil resources (NCSFNC 1996), and the resulting average annual growth increases are significant (Binkley et al. 1995).

Fertilization is routine for pine plantations in the southeastern United States (Allen 1987). Nitrogen and potassium fertilization are of great significance for tropical tree plantations as well (Chew and Pushparajah 1995, Binkley et al. 1995). Essentially all 30 000–45 000 ha of forest plantations in Australia and New Zealand (primarily Pinus radiata) receive fertilization (Boomsma and Hunter 1990), about a third of all plantations in Japan (Kawana and Haibara 1983), and most of the Eucalyptus plantations in Brazil (Barros et al. 1990).

Potential impacts on biodiversity from intensive silviculture

Many of today's plantations are second or third generation planted forests. Furthermore, many new plantations are being established on abandoned agricultural crop or pasture land, or land which was previously in agriculture and reverted to forest. In these cases, the diversity of the planted forests, and the variety of available habitat niches is certainly greater than it was under the previous agricultural land use, and these plantations have the potential to contribute to maintenance of the world's biodiversity (Mathur 1993, Shepherd 1993, Chey et al. 1997). This still begs the question, what is natural diversity on these lands? And what level of diversity should forest managers strive to maintain or restore? This greatly complicates the issue and adds to the uncertainties and lack of universal pronouncements that can be made concerning the effects of intensive forest management on biodiversity, and the goals of intensive management with respect to biodiversity. It is unreasonable and too simplistic to try to manage for 'biodiversity' when any management action will benefit some species and hinder others (Hansen et al. 1995b). Given that the overall objective of intensive management is to enhance the productivity of the crop tree, the goal with respect to biodiversity must be to ensure that the diversity which enhances, or is benign to, productivity is maintained at the stand level, and that undesired off-site impacts on biodiversity are minimized.

FLORA

The natural flora present in a plantation can be an important contributor to site productivity as it serves to sequester and recycle nutrients. The impacts of intensive forest management on the flora have been extensively studied. One common observation is that intensive management results in repeated returns to the early seral stage of the forest, providing extensive habitat for this community type (Swindel et al. 1982, Swindel et al. 1986). Secondly, intensive management apparently causes no decline in species richness, although the species composition and evenness may vary from that of an old-growth or unmanaged forest (Mellin 1995). And thirdly, while certain species may never gain dominance under intensive silviculture, species are rarely lost (Blake et al. 1987, Zutter et al. 1987, Freedman et al. 1993, Boyd et al. 1995, Mellin 1995). Floral analyses show that the pine plantations of the southeastern United States are not absolute monocultures (Mellin 1995). There is a single species overstory, but there is usually a diverse understory community, particularly prior to crown closure. This observation must be interpreted with caution, however, as many plantations tend to support a community of weedy, widespread plant species, quite different from that of a natural stand (Michelsen et al. 1996).

Established vegetation on an intensively managed site is considered competition for the site resources, with the potential to limit the growth of the planted seedlings. To minimize this potential, site preparation activities are designed to substantially reduce existing woody and herbaceous vegetation. As a result, established plant community composition and structure may be reduced or altered, at least in the short-term. The duration of this impact will depend on the intensity of the practices, and the use, if any, of specific vegetation-control practices later in the rotation.

Complete canopy removal generally results in increased vegetative biomass and more diverse floral composition than that of undisturbed forests. The increase in solar radiation, due to the opening of the canopy, results in higher temperatures, and higher rates of photosynthesis and nutrient mineralization. But clearcutting alone does not constitute intensive forest management. When clearcutting is combined with treatments such as disking, bedding, and herbicide use, the plant community is usually altered substantially.

In the southeastern United States and elsewhere, the use of intensive forest practices such as these has not resulted in a loss of species richness in these stands. Species richness on intensively managed sites has increased, or stayed the same, up to twenty years following treatment (Swindel et al. 1982, Swindel et al. 1986, Swindel and Grosenbaugh 1988, Clason 1993, Greenberg 1993, Mellin 1995). Of course, species richness can be a misleading concept because it does not address the relative abundance of different species or the presence of rare or specialized species (Chapter 1). Initially, following intensive management, the floral composition shifts from a woody plant-dominated community to an herb-dominated one. However, over time, the community shifts to one similar to the antecedent second growth. The use of more intensive practices, which creates more soil and litter disturbance, slows this plant community transition.

Even with the use of herbicides, total species richness generally does not decline, particularly when a single, banded (applied in a narrow strip directly along a row of seedlings) herbicide application is used at the time of planting. The herbicide treatment allows the planted seedlings greater access to site resources such as light, water, and nutrients; however, it does not eliminate all vegetation, even when broadcast applications are used. Certain floral species may be favored over others, depending on the herbicide used (Miller et al. 1995), especially immediately following application. In the first growing season, species richness and diversity may decrease (Brockway and Outcalt 1994), and the plants which dominate the composition may differ (Wilkins 1992). However, over time, as the planted seedlings exert dominance, the plant community which was present on the pretreated site will return (Blake et al. 1987, Zutter et al. 1987, Freedman et al. 1993, Boyd et al. 1995, Mellin 1995). Even where repeated herbicide applications are made, this extreme treatment makes very minor alterations to the successional pattern; for example, where woody vegetation was controlled there was a slight increase in forb cover over the control; where herbaceous control was applied, the proportions of trees increased with a decrease in shrubs (Miller et al. 1995).

The temporary shift in species resulting from intensive management can be characterized as an earlier seral stage of the forest (Swindel et al. 1982, Swindel et al. 1986, Frederickson et al. 1991, Mellin 1995), and a change in species composition is a natural consequence of succession (Miller et al. 1995). The species that were present in the prior stand do not disappear (Conde et al. 1986, Newton et al. 1989, Freedman et al. 1993), however they may be less abundant in the stand. Following any natural or managed disturbance which opens the canopy, floral composition will shift to species which are shade-intolerant and opportunistic. As the planted trees exert dominance and the canopy begins to close, many of these early successional species cannot thrive and the floral community begins a shift to the more shade-tolerant species commonly associated with more mature forests. With shorter rotations and the single species focus of many plantations, the stand will repeatedly return to this early seral stage. This will inevitably lead to a shift in the relative abundance of coexisting species (Hunter 1990, Westman 1990). The extended duration of the early seral stage has structural implications as well.

Fig. 12.4. Planting at wider spacing allows for greater floral diversity. (R. G. Campbell, Weyerhaeuser Co. photo)

Evidence that species richness does not decline with intensive forest management practices does not address the abundance of keystone, rare, or endemic species, which are important in their own right and may provide critical habitat for specialized organisms. It is also possible that species may be lost after multiple rotations of plantation management. Reductions in particular plant species on intensively managed hectares may be compensated for by managing all hectares on a landscape basis, thus providing all seral stages. However, even on a stand level, one way forest managers may be able to conserve more biodiversity is by leaving small areas of native understory brush untreated by herbicides or other site preparation activities, or even unplanted (Morrison and Meslow 1984a, Santillo *et al.* 1989, Buse and Good 1993, Santillo 1994). Planting trees at wider spacing or performing thinning operations years before the final harvest may also help increase floral diversity (Figure 12.4). Both will allow more light to reach the soil surface, thus providing microclimatic variation in terms of temperature and moisture (Waters *et al.* 1994) and providing enough light to ensure continuous cover of ground flora (Larsen 1995). And thinning with variable spacing between trees may be even more beneficial than with even spacing, because it provides the spatial heterogeneity characteristic of mature natural forests (Carey *et al.* 1991, Carey and Johnson 1995).

FAUNA

The impacts of intensive silviculture on the forest fauna tend to be more indirect than the impacts on the flora. As described in earlier chapters, clearcutting, along with other intensive management practices, can greatly alter the local environment if there is a loss of old-growth stands which are repeatedly replaced with early successional stands. Of all the forest fauna, the response of both birds and herpetiles to intensive forest management has been most extensively studied.

Avifauna

Forest birds play important roles in seed dispersal, as well as in insect pest dispersal and control, which may contribute to timber productivity. The distribution and abundance of bird species often depends on the vegetation structure. The types and amounts of available food resources influence bird foraging patterns, behaviors closely associated with vegetation structure (Cruz 1988). Compared with natural forests, plantations with a single species overstory may provide relatively less foraging and nesting habitat.

Bird species richness is positively correlated with increasing vertical and horizontal vegetation structure (MacArthur and MacArthur 1961, Shugart and James 1973). Many studies have shown that pine forests support lower avian abundance than deciduous or mixed hardwood–conifer forests (Suckling et al. 1976, Winternitz 1976, Winkler and Dana 1977) and that the conversion of natural forests to plantations alters the structure by reducing both horizontal and vertical diversity (Harris et al. 1979). Changes in habitat structure between different forest age-classes can result in successional replacement of bird species (Greenberg 1993, Westworth and Telfer 1993). Intensive management precipitates earlier canopy closure, thus shading out more vigorous understory growth (White et al. 1975) and reducing forest structure and niche options. In fact, in a study in Texas pine plantations, bird species diversity and abundance both increased after thinning which allowed abundant regeneration of understory vegetation (Chritton 1988). Leaving areas of natural vegetation in the understory untreated by herbicide can also be beneficial to birds. In Oregon, the bird community found in small patches of untreated brush within herbicide-treated clearcuts was similar to that found in untreated clearcuts (Morrison and Meslow 1984b).

Studies of the impacts of intensive forest management practices on birds have shown that, reflecting the importance of stand structure, there is a correlation between stand age and bird abundance and diversity

(Reppenning and Labinsky 1985, Parker *et al.* 1994). Older pine plantations are particularly important for cavity-nesting birds which avoid young stands (Land *et al.* 1989). While creating early-successional forest stages may not precipitate a decline in floral richness and diversity, the opposite effect has often been found with birds. In fact, more mature natural forest stands generally support a more diverse bird community than plantations at any age (Reppenning and Labinsky 1985). Longer plantation rotations would enhance diversity by providing mature forested habitat and structural complexity; however this is not considered cost effective with intensive management except where the end product is high value and large sized, such as specialty hardwoods.

In certain cases where a managed disturbance can mimic natural disturbance patterns in the ecosystem, there may be little effect on the species mix. In a sand pine scrub ecosystem in Florida, for example, in which high-intensity wildfires are a naturally and regularly occurring disturbance, no differences were observed in bird populations between a 55-year-old sand pine (*Pinus clausa*) forest and three 5- to 7-year-old disturbance treatments (Greenberg 1993). The characteristic bird community responded similarly to both natural and high-intensity treatments. The longer term effects of several rotations of intensive management on these sites remains unclear; however, it appears the potential exists to minimize negative impacts on biodiversity with well-designed silvicultural systems specific to the ecosystem type, and with carefully designed strategies which benefit the species or community attributes managers are most concerned with (Hansen *et al.* 1995b). Because all diversity cannot be protected on every acre or in every stand, sound landscape-scale management is also critical.

Bird density and diversity may be enhanced by the juxtaposition of mature forest and intensively managed plantations, resulting in considerable edge habitat which is hospitable to many bird species (Strelke and Dickson 1980, Thompson *et al.* 1992), although a different species mix may be present. Indeed even some forest-interior birds make substantial use of young, regenerating stands and their abundance will not decline with intensive forest management (Thompson *et al.* 1992). MacKinnon and Freedman (1993) found relatively small and short-term effects of the silvicultural use of the herbicide glyphosate in a Canadian study of prominent bird species of regenerating clearcuts.

However, intensive management practices such as clearcutting, herbicide use, and site preparation which keep the forest in an early seral stage may result in a loss of some forest-interior or cavity-nesting bird species.

On a stand level, bird diversity can be enhanced by leaving snags and a few large live trees in plantations (Hansen *et al.* 1995b, Taylor and Haseler 1995, Haggstrom and Kelleyhouse 1996, Pattanavibool and Edge 1996). Many studies (Vega 1993, Hansen and Hounihan 1995, and Hansen *et al.* 1995a) in the Pacific Northwest suggest that leaving canopy trees in managed forests enhances structural complexity and provides habitat for many native bird species. Leaving only five mature trees per hectare resulted in substantial increases in bird species richness compared with clearcuts (Hansen *et al.* 1995a). In southern United States pine stands, regressions on stand and snag characteristics explained nearly all of the variation in cavity-nesting bird density and diversity (Land *et al.* 1989). It is also necessary to maintain a mosaic of age classes/forest structures across the landscape to ensure maintenance of avian biodiversity.

Herpetofauna

Herpetofauna are considered a good indicator of habitat impacts because of their position in the food chain, usually as predators, and their use of both terrestrial and aquatic habitats. In addition, in parts of the world where much intensive silviculture is practised, amphibian and reptile biomass and species density can exceed that of breeding birds and mammals (Pough *et al.* 1987, Enge and Marion 1986, Vickers *et al.* 1985), and a significant perturbation in the amphibian community would affect a broad range of species (Blaustein and Wake 1990). Consequently, there has been considerable recent research into the dynamics of herpetofaunal communities in managed forest systems. Furthermore, much concern has arisen in scientific communities about an apparent worldwide decline in many amphibian species (Barinaga 1990, Phillips 1990, Pechmann *et al.* 1991, Wake 1991) although the major likely causes (e.g., acid precipitation, depletion of the ozone layer, and wetland loss) are not directly tied to forestry. However, the fact that clearcutting and intensive site preparation can alter the structure and composition of the native flora and the forest floor, as well as alter the water table, has implications for the herpetofaunal community.

Studies in many ecosystems have documented the importance of vegetation structure on herpetofaunal communities (Pianka 1973, Fuentes 1976, Lillywhite 1977, Cody and Mooney 1978, Braithewaite 1987, Mushinsky and Gibson 1991, Greenberg *et al.* 1994). Processes such as thermoregulation, locomotion, burrowing, and egg-laying, which differ by species, are all impacted by cover availability, microclimate, productivity and prey availability, which structure influences (Greenberg *et al.* 1994).

In particular, coarse woody debris is usually important for herpetofaunal communities and is cleared from the forest floor with intensive site preparation.

Comparisons between mature pine stands and 3- to 4-year-old pine plantations in the southeastern United States have shown that total herpetofaunal biomass did not differ, but that its distribution across taxonomic groups was altered (Enge and Marion 1986). More intensive treatment (harvesting with feller-buncher; followed by stump removal, burning, windrowing with a K-G blade, harrowing, bedding, and planting) resulted in lowered reptile abundance and species richness, and species richness for reptiles and amphibians combined was higher in both the mature forest and the minimum treatment (chain saw harvesting followed by roller drum chopping, bedding and planting) than in the more intensive treatment (Enge and Marion 1986). Amphibian species richness was not reduced by clearcutting in this flatwoods community, but certain species were less abundant in the clearcuts than in the forest. On wet sites, a rise in water table following harvest generally results in an immediate, short-term extension of the hydroperiod and an increase in surface water (O'Neill 1995). Because the ecology of amphibians is closely tied to water, increased presence of water is likely to result in increased amphibian abundance and decreased reptile abundance. This effect, however, lasts only 2 to 3 years until vegetation regrowth increases transpiration and returns surface water to pre-cut levels (Troendle 1970, Abrahamson and Hartnett 1990, Brown et al. 1990).

Salamander numbers in a deciduous forest in the northeastern United States were lower in 7- and 25-year-old clearcuts than in an adjacent old-growth forest (Pough et al. 1987). However, there was no difference in numbers between a 60-year-old second growth stand and an old-growth stand. Perhaps short-term depression in herpetofaunal population densities following intensive forest management may correct themselves over the longer term.

Some researchers have speculated that perhaps conifer plantations are inhospitable to salamanders based on the observation that higher amphibian populations have been documented in natural forests (Pough et al. 1987, Bennett et al. 1980). Important variables affecting amphibian abundance, such as soil acidity, leaf litter depth and type, hardwood shrub abundance, and coarse woody debris are generally substantially reduced in forest plantations, presumably leading to a reduction in the overall abundance and diversity of amphibians (deMaynadier and Hunter 1995). Leaving some coarse woody debris or logging slash in place following a harvest can help conserve amphibian communities in plantations, as would excluding some forest patches from chopping, disking and other site preparation activities.

In particular ecosystems, intensive practices such as clearcutting may mimic natural processes well enough that species evolutionarily adapted to those natural disturbances will not be negatively impacted. For example, in a fire-adapted, open sand pine scrub system in northern Florida, reptile species diversity, richness, and evenness did not differ in response to clearcutting followed by site preparation as compared with high-intensity wildfire followed by salvage logging (Greenberg et al. 1994). In this case, although reptile diversity was not reduced by intensive management, species composition differed markedly between the mature forest and the disturbance treatments. Many other fire-adapted ecosystems may depend on high intensity disturbance, whatever the means, to maintain their biological integrity (Greenberg et al. 1994). In evaluating the impacts of a particular forest management system, it is important to take into account the natural evolutionary adaptations of the system. There are some communities which are adapted to open conditions such as those created by a well-managed clearcut, yet there are also many species dependent on more mature forest structure and composition. On a landscape scale, both types of habitat should be provided.

Mammals

Studies investigating the impacts of intensive forest management practices on forest mammals have most often focused on vegetation control. Vegetation control is an integral part of intensive management, and may affect the cover, nesting, or foraging habitat of various mammals. Clear statements on mammal diversity have not emerged.

Much of the relevant research has focused on small mammals, such as mice and voles, probably because they are generally abundant, highly active, have a small home range, and are relatively easy to survey. Their small size probably also makes them more sensitive to environmental change, as their ability to relocate is more limited than that of larger mammals (Stoddart 1979). Lautenschlager (1993) reviewed 14 studies of the effects of herbicides on small mammals in northern coniferous forests and found the responses were species-specific. Some species selected herbicide-treated areas, and others avoided them, while in general the residents of the treated areas were unaffected (see Lautenschlager 1993). Several studies of the effect of herbicide use on deer and moose forage and habitat showed no change in mammal activity in the treated areas

although browse was reduced for 1–3 growing seasons following herbicide application (Sullivan and Sullivan 1979, Sullivan 1985, Eschholz *et al.*
1992). Other studies showed a decline in moose use of herbicide-treated
areas for up to three years following treatment, with the degree of decline
varying with the herbicide and the rate used (Hjeljord and Gronvold 1988,
Lloyd 1989, 1990a, 1990b). As evident from these results, it is impossible to
generalize on the effects of herbicide use on mammals, particularly community level impacts.

The reduced structural complexity and lack of coarse woody debris in
plantations can also impact mammals. Fallen trees are particularly important to small mammals inhabiting the forest floor, although this dependence has not been well documented (Carey and Johnson 1995). Small
mammal species abundance has been shown to vary with the amount of
coarse woody debris on the ground (Seagle 1985), although Carey and
Johnson (1995) found no difference in small mammal community composition between managed young forests and old growth in the Pacific northwest. A study in the Yukon, Canada of the effects of forest fertilization on
herbivory showed that snowshoe hares were attracted to the nitrogen-fer-
tilized plots and grazed more heavily there (Nams *et al.* 1996). Snowshoe
hares are an important prey base for a variety of northern predators
(Lautenschlager 1993). Additional well-replicated studies with appropriate controls and consistent data collection including pretreatment data are
necessary to determine long-term impacts on mammal diversity
(Lautenschlager 1993) and to elucidate the factors governing mammal
biomass and community composition which are conducive to management (Carey and Johnson 1995).

Invertebrates

Invertebrates are less visible than many vertebrates; however, they
contribute greatly to ecosystem function. The response of invertebrates to
intensive forestry practices may have implications for understanding the
responses of higher trophic levels (Atlegrim and Sjöberg 1996).
Insectivorous birds, for example, may be greatly affected by changes in the
available food supply (Atlegrim and Sjöberg 1996).

There have been few studies of the impacts of intensive forest management on invertebrates, and the work in this area has generally focused on
invertebrate response to disturbance. However, because the increased use
of intensive forest management practices has generated more attention
concerning impacts on vegetation, soil, and the health of surrounding
aquatic systems, some effects on the habitats of invertebrates are being

addressed. In certain landscapes such as Florida and the Georgia coastal plain, this is particularly relevant as cypress (*Taxodium distichum*) domes and strands – wetlands which support large benthic invertebrate communities – are frequently intermingled with intensively managed pine plantations.

Benthic invertebrates, which play a central role in stream function and structure (Vannote *et al.* 1980) can be a reliable indicator of stream health by virtue of their abundance and sensitivity to habitat changes (Adams *et al.* 1995, Vuori and Joensuu 1996). Consequences of careless application of intensive silviculture treatments such as nutrient loading from excess fertilization, toxin runoff from pesticide use and sedimentation resulting from harvesting may result in detrimental impacts on benthic invertebrates. Direct application of pesticide to coldwater forest streams in Canada resulted in catastrophic invertebrate drift and measurable benthos depletion (Kreutzweiser and Kingsbury 1987). However, Helson *et al.* (1993) found in a follow-up study that an unsprayed buffer zone of 150 m around sensitive and productive water bodies would effectively eliminate the impact of pesticide spray drift on aquatic organisms in water 25 cm or greater in depth.

A recent study in a Florida cypress swamp showed that benthic invertebrate species composition differed markedly between a mature forest and disturbance treatments (Ewel *et al.* 1995). Where both cypress ponds and surrounding pine flatwoods were clearcut, the dominant benthic invertebrate communities were distinctly different from those of both unharvested sites and the pretreatment community. Santillo *et al.* (1989) and Morrison and Meslow (1984b) both found decreased abundance of invertebrates, particularly herbivores, in herbicide-treated clearcuts compared with untreated areas. In their study in Sweden, Atlegrim and Sjöberg (1996) found that the abundance of herbivorous larvae was affected by harvest practices, and the degree of response was closely related to the amount of tree layer removed. In Malaysia, moth diversity in various exotic forest plantations was 'unexpectedly high', in particular in the *Eucalyptus delgupta* plantation, as high as that of natural second growth forest (Chey *et al.* 1997). In a UK study, Buse and Good (1993) found that much greater beetle diversity was achieved by designing conifer forests to contain more habitat types, including leaving small areas of different vegetation types unplanted. Greenberg and Thomas (1995) found no differences in terrestrial coleopteran assemblages species diversity, evenness or richness between mature forested sand pine scrub and three younger disturbance treatments, a finding attributed to possibly similar plant communities or structural features across treatments.

Arthropods, particularly ants, may serve as good indicators of treatment impacts, due to their abundance and wide distribution throughout the world in diverse habitats (Roth et al. 1994). Ecologically, arthropods also have great functional significance, are a major component of most ecosystems, and are known for their overall success at proliferating into available niches (Gorham et al. 1996). Their key role in food webs makes arthropod assemblages important indicators of the impacts of forest management practices on ecosystem function (Kremen et al. 1993).

Given that ant activity increases with increasing surface temperature (Lynch et al. 1988), ant diversity may not be adversely impacted by intensive clearcut harvesting which opens the forest floor to direct insolation (Brian 1983). Roth et al. (1994) found that the diversity of ground foraging ants in Costa Rica was not significantly reduced with increased disturbance (a disturbance gradient that ranged from primary rain forest to abandoned cacao plantations, productive cacao plantations and banana plantations), although species evenness was highest in the least disturbed habitat and some species were restricted to these sites. Greenberg and McGrane (1996) found similar results in a xeric sand pine scrub habitat in Florida: biomass and abundance of surface-active ground-dwelling arthropods were similar across both silviculturally disturbed and mature sand pine scrub. In general, invertebrate studies suggest that leaving small untreated areas within a plantation will attract many insectivorous animals due to the increased invertebrate abundance.

Important research needs

Many impacts from intensive silviculture and plantation management are evident in the early years post-treatment, but may not be critical in the long term. Therefore, the importance of long-term studies is clear. In designing forest management systems to maintain biodiversity, we must focus our efforts on long-term, broad-scale effects. Replicated experiments which compare long-term post-treatment effects on floral and faunal abundance and composition with the pre-treatment conditions of the site, as well as with replicated control plots, are necessary. It is important to collect baseline data on all treatment plots as well as controls, rather than just assuming that an adjacent control is fundamentally the same as an area that is to be treated experimentally. In addition to the traditional focus on birds, herpetiles, and flora, future research should include the impacts on fungi and invertebrates, as well as mammals. An examination of the effectiveness of forestry Best Management Practices in protecting habitat characteristics is also needed. Additional Best Management Practices may be necessary as intensive management becomes more widespread.

Not only should future research encompass a longer temporal scale, it should also focus on a larger spatial scale. Because worldwide demand for forest products is increasing, and more forest land will be managed in plantations, future research should focus on the ability of plants and animals to adapt to plantations or thrive elsewhere in the landscape. Studies which help predict the outcome of management practices on a large portion of the biota should be undertaken rather than individual species-oriented studies and management. This involves landscape-scale studies which examine the dynamics of biodiversity in a mosaic pattern of clearcut, intensively managed hectares interspersed with extensively managed forests and reserve forests. This will require coordination and cooperation between various universities, land management agencies, industry and other landowners, and is no small task.

Another area where more research is needed involves the question of what impacts certain activities which better conserve biological diversity in plantations (such as leaving a few large live trees per hectare, leaving small areas untreated by herbicides, etc.) may have on fiber production or per unit costs. It may be that conserving more biodiversity in plantations is possible without a significant reduction in production. This will depend in part on the site and species characteristics, as well as the market conditions, but should be investigated.

Summary

Plantation forests which are started on land previously in agricultural use are likely to have a greater variety of habitat niches than were available under the previous land use. This is not the case, however, when natural forests are converted to plantations.

Forest managers of the future will have to manage some land with short-rotation intensive silviculture systems to meet increasing demand for wood products on a shrinking forested land base. The question posed at the beginning of this chapter was: is intensive forest management compatible with maintenance of biodiversity? Many studies showed that intensive forestry greatly alters the habitat for all biota, eliminating some key habitat components. Clearly, this will reduce biological diversity especially if one considers the rare and endemic species which may be eliminated over successive rotations. However, it is not possible or necessary to maintain the same level of biodiversity on every hectare, and intensively managed forests on some lands will free up other lands for conservation uses. Yet that assumes that these other lands will indeed be converted to biological reserves, and current forest policy does not actively encourage this (Hunter 1996). Consequently, it is necessary for forest managers to try to minimize impacts at the stand level as well.

The clearcut, as a standard component of a plantation forestry system, may be described as a disturbance that repeatedly moves the site back to an earlier successional stage. There are many species which are highly adapted to early seral stages, and clearcuts may provide for a tremendous diversity of early successional plants, animals and invertebrates. Given the fact that much of the land in the United States and elsewhere which is now in plantation was formerly agricultural or pasture land, it is generally accepted that biodiversity has often been enhanced on these sites, as compared with the immediately prior land use.

However, this still does not address the value and function of the species dependent on late successional stands. It is not enough for silvicultural treatments to maintain a desired level of species richness, but it is also critical that the entire suite of native species be maintained across the landscape. On sites where short-rotation plantation silviculture is practised, a mature forest seral stage will not occur and thus critical habitat for mature forest species will not be provided. Given that there appears to be a negative correlation between intensity of treatment and impact on biodiversity, it would be wise for forest managers to intersperse intensively managed short-rotation forests with longer-rotation stands and preserved late successional natural forests, thus providing a myriad habitat types.

However, even within a stand, there are some things that forest managers can do to enhance conservation of biodiversity in plantations. Some of these activities, such as leaving snags and a few live mature trees, should cost little in fiber production. Other activities, such as leaving coarse woody debris on the site or leaving small areas of natural understory vegetation within herbicide-treated plantations, are also very unlikely to have a significant impact on fiber production or per unit costs. Wider spacing of plantation trees or thinning stands can also promote biodiversity. Early thinnings can hasten the development of forest stature and structure and provide for understory diversity (Carey and Johnson 1995) and microclimatic forest floor heterogeneity. Thinnings also provide intermediate financial yields which should prove attractive to forest managers (Carey and Johnson 1995). Adopting some or all of these practices will improve the ability of forest plantations to conserve biodiversity at the stand-level. In addition, forest managers must be aware of controlling off-site impacts of plantation management, such as erosion and chemical runoff, and new and more Forestry Best Management Practices may need to be developed as intensive plantation forestry expands.

Studies of forest biodiversity have concluded that the most important way to minimize negative impacts is to provide the entire array of age classes of forest. Clearly, it is not possible to accomplish this on intensively managed hectares alone. On a larger scale, while some land is devoted to intensive fiber production, and continually provides early successional habitat, elsewhere in the landscape more land can be left as old forest reserves, or less intensively managed in longer rotations (Shepherd 1993, Hunter and Calhoun 1996, Angelstam et al. 1997). In the interest of maintaining overall biodiversity, forest managers must think on a landscape scale, as well as endeavor to minimize detrimental impacts within the stand to the greatest extent feasible.

Management recommendations

Forest managers who practice intensive silviculture can take steps to enhance biodiversity within plantations. Both floral and bird species diversity can be enhanced by wider spacing and thinning, which allow for abundant regeneration of understory vegetation, and by leaving areas of natural vegetation untreated by herbicides in the understory. This will also lead to increased invertebrate abundance, attracting many various species of higher trophic levels. Cavity-nesting birds will particularly benefit from leaving mature live trees and snags within the plantation, or by implementing a longer plantation rotation where possible. It would be particularly helpful to leave large trees of *varying species*. Amphibian diversity can be enhanced by leaving areas with coarse woody debris or logging slash following harvesting. When conducting site preparation activities such as disking or chopping, managers should leave select strips or patches untreated to enhance surface micro-habitat variation.

Studies show that the potential apparently exists to minimize negative impacts on biodiversity in plantations by applying well-designed silvicultural systems specific to the ecosystem type, setting specific biodiversity goals, and by practising this sound management on a landscape level, including juxtaposing mature forest and intensively managed plantations.

Further readings

One theme in this chapter was that of managing forests on a landscape scale. Forman's (1995) classic text on landscape ecology covers this topic extensively, and Boyce (1995) is a good choice for more detail on landscape forestry. For a more general treatment on biodiversity as discussed here, readers might choose Szaro and Johnston (1996) or Naeem *et al.* (1994). Good publications specifically addressing pine plantations in more detail include Allen *et al.* (1996), Conde *et al.* (1986), and Swindel *et al.* (1986). For more detail on specific silvicultural practices, consult Kimball and Hunter's chapter 'Intensive silviculture', pp. 200–34 in Hunter (1990).

Literature cited

Abrahamson, W. G. and D. C. Hartnett. 1990. Pine flatwoods and dry prairies. Pp. 103–49 in R. L. Meyers and J. J. Ewel (eds). *Ecosystems of Florida*. University of Central Florida Press, Orlando, Florida.

Adams, T. O., D. D. Hook, and M. A. Floyd. 1995. Effectiveness monitoring of silvicultural best management practices in South Carolina. *Southern Journal of Applied Forestry* 19(4):170–6.

Allen, A. W., Y. K. Bernal, and R. J. Mouton. 1996. *Pine Plantations and Wildlife in the Southeastern United States: An Assessment of Impacts and Opportunities*. USDI National Biological Service Information and Technology Report 3.

Allen, H. L. 1987. Fertilizers: adding nutrients for enhanced forest productivity. *Journal of Forestry* 85:37–46.

Allen, H. L., P. M. Dougherty, and R. G. Campbell. 1990. Manipulation of water and nutrients – practice and opportunity in southern US pine forests. *Forest Ecology and Management* 30:437–53.

Angelstam, P. K., V. M. Anufriev, L. Balciauskas, A. K. Blagovidov, S. Borgegård, S. J. Hodge, P. Majewski, S. V. Ponomarenko, E. V. Shvarts, A. A. Tishkov, L. Tomialojc, and T. Wesolowski. 1997. Biodiversity and sustainable forestry in European forests: how East and West can learn from each other. *Wildlife Society Bulletin* 25(1):38–48.

Atlegrim, O. and K. Sjöberg. 1996. Effects of clear-cutting and single-tree selection harvests on herbivorous insect larvae feeding on bilberry (*Vaccinium myrtillus*) in uneven-aged boreal *Picea abies* forests. *Forest Ecology and Management* 87:139–48.

Attiwill, P. M. 1994. Ecological disturbance and the conservative management of eucalypt forests in Australia. *Forest Ecology and Management* 63:301–46.

Banerjee, U. K. and S. Banerjee. 1994. Forest management and biodiversity. *Indian Forester* Sept.:786–90.

Barinaga, M. 1990. Where have all the froggies gone? *Science* 247:1033–4.

Barros, N. F., R. F. Novais, and L. C. L. Neves. 1990. Fertilição e correção do solo para plantio de Eucalipto. Pp. 127–86 in N. F. Barros and R. F. Novais (eds). *Releção Solo-Eucalipto*. Department of Soils, Federal University of Viçosa, MG Brazil.

Bennett, S. H., Gibbons, J. W., and Glanville, J. 1980. Terrestrial activity, abundance and diversity of amphibians in differently managed forest types. *American Midland Naturalist* **103**:412–16.

Binkley, D., R. Carter, and H. L. Allen. 1995. Nitrogen fertilization practices in forestry. Pp. 421–41 in P.E. Bacon (ed.). *Nitrogen Fertilization in the Environment*. Marcel Dekker, Inc., New York.

Blake, P. M., G. A. Hurst, and T. A. Terry. 1987. Responses of vegetation and deer forage following application of hexazinone. *Southern Journal of Applied Forestry* **11**:176–80.

Blaustein, A. R., and D. B. Wake. 1990. Declining amphibian populations: A global phenomenon? *Tree* **5**(7):203–4.

Boomsma, D. B. and I. R. Hunter. 1990. Effects of water, nutrients, and their interactions on tree growth, and plantation forest management practices in Australasia: a review. *Forest Ecology and Management* **30**:455–76.

Borman, F. H., and G. E. Likens. 1979. *Pattern and Processes in a Forested Ecosystem*. Springer, New York.

Boyce, S. G. 1995. *Landscape Forestry*. Wiley, New York.

Boyd, R. S., J. D. Freeman, J. H. Miller, and M. B. Edwards. 1995. Forest herbicide influences on floristic diversity seven years after broadcast pine release treatments in central Georgia, USA. *New Forests* **10**:17–37.

Braithewaite, R. W. 1987. Effects of fire regimes on lizards in the wet-dry tropics of Australia. *Journal of Tropical Ecology* **3**:265–75.

Brian, M. V. 1983. *Social Insects*. Chapman & Hall, New York.

Brockway, D. G., and K. W. Outcalt. 1994. Plant cover, diversity and biomass in longleaf pine wiregrass sandhills ecosystems following hexazinone application. *Ecological Society of America Bulletin* Supplement **75**(2):24.

Brown, K. S. Jr. 1987. O paper dos consumidores na conservacao e no manejo do recursos geneticos florestais in situ. *IPEF* **35**:61–9.

Brown, R. B., E. L. Stone, and V. W. Carlisle. 1990. Soils. Pp. 35–69 in R. L. Meyers and J. J. Ewel (eds). *Ecosystems of Florida*. University of Central Florida Press, Orlando, Florida.

Buse, A. and J. E. G. Good. 1993. The effects of conifer forest design and management on abundance and diversity of rove beetles (Coleoptera: Staphylinidae): implications for conservation. *Biological Conservation* **64**:67–76.

Cain, M. D. and W. F. Mann. 1980. Annual brush control increases early growth of loblolly pine. *Southern Journal of Applied Forestry* **4**:67–70.

Carey, A. B. and M. L. Johnson. 1995. Small mammals in managed, naturally young and old-growth forests. *Ecological Applications* **5**(2):336–52.

Carey, A. B., M. M. Hardt, S. P. Horton, and B. L. Biswell. 1991. Spring bird communities in the Oregon coast ranges. Pp. 123–44 in L. F. Ruggerio, K. B.

Aubry, A. B. Carey, and M. H. Huff (Technical Coordinators). *Wildlife and vegetation of unmanaged Douglas-fir forests*. USDA Forest Service General Technical Report PNW-285.

Chew, P. S. and E. Pushparajah. 1995. Nitrogen management and fertilization of tropical plantation tree crops. Pp. 225–93 in P. E. Bacon (ed.). *Nitrogen Fertilization in the Environment*. Marcel Dekker, Inc., New York.

Chey, V. K., J. D. Holloway, and M. R. Speight. 1997. Diversity of moths in forest plantations and natural forests in Sabah. *Bulletin of Entomological Research* **87**:371–85.

Chritton, C.A. 1988. Effects of thinning a loblolly pine plantation on nongame bird populations in East Texas. M.S.F. Thesis, Stephen F. Austin State University. Nacogdoches, TX. 103 p.

Clason, T. R. 1993. Hardwood competition reduces loblolly pine plantation productivity. *Canadian Journal of Forest Research* **23**:2133–40.

Cody, M. L., and H. A. Mooney. 1978. Convergence versus non-convergence in Mediterranean-climate ecosystems. *Annual Review of Ecology and Systematics* **9**:265–321.

Conde, L. F., B. F. Swindel, and J. E. Smith. 1986. Five years of vegetation changes following conversion of pine flatwoods to *Pinus elliottii* plantations. *Forest Ecology and Management* **15**:295–300.

Creighton, J. L., B. R. Zutter, G. R. Glover, and D. H. Gjerstad. 1987. Planted pine growth and survival response to herbaceous vegetation control, treatment duration, and herbicide application technique. *Southern Journal of Applied Forestry* **11**:223–7.

Cruz, A. 1988. Avian resource use in a Caribbean pine plantation. *Journal of Wildlife Management* **52**(2):274–9.

Cubbage, F. W., W. S. Dvorak, R. C. Abt, and G. Pacheco. 1996. *World timber supply and prospects: models, projections, plantations and implications*. Central America and Mexico Coniferous Resource (CAMCORE) Annual Meeting, Bali, Indonesia.

deMaynadier, P. G., and M. L. Hunter, Jr. 1995. The relationship between forest management and amphibian ecology: a review of the North American literature. *Environmental Reviews* **3**: 230–61.

Enge, K. M., and W. R. Marion. 1986. Effects of clearcutting and site preparation on herpetofauna of a north Florida flatwoods. *Forest Ecology and Management* **14**:177–92.

Eschholz, W., K. Raymond, and F. Servello. 1992. *Herbicide effects on habitat and nutritional ecology of moose and deer in Maine*. Cooperative Forestry Research Unit Report 31. Maine Agricultural Experiment Station Miscellaneous Report 376:31–34.

Ewel, K. C., W. P. Casey, A. Leslie, J. Prenger, S. W. Vince, T. Workman, and J. Leverette. 1995. Impacts of clearcutting on important animal populations in cypress ponds. Pp. 66–121 in *NCASI Wetland Study 1995 Annual Report*, University of Florida, Gainesville, FL.

Forman, R. T. T. 1995. *Land Mosaics: the Ecology of Landscapes and Regions*. Cambridge University Press, Cambridge.

Frederickson, T. S., H. L. Allen, and T. R. Wentworth. 1991. Competing vegetation and pine growth response to silvicultural treatments in a six-year-old Piedmont loblolly pine plantation. *Southern Journal of Applied Forestry* 15(3):138–44.

Freedman, B., R. Morash, and D. MacKinnon. 1993. Short-term changes in vegetation after the silvicultural spraying of glyphosate herbicide onto regenerating clearcuts in Nova Scotia, Canada. *Canadian Journal of Forest Research* 23:2300–11.

Fuentes, E. R. 1976. Ecological convergence of lizard communities in Chile and California. *Ecology* 57:3–17.

Gorham, L. E., B. D. Keeland, S. Mopper, S. L. King and D. J. Johnson. 1996. Effects of canopy gap dynamics on arthropod abundance in a bottom-land forest in northeast Arkansas. Pp. 165–9 in K. M. Flynn (ed.). *Proceedings of the Southern Forested Wetlands Ecology and Management Conference*, Clemson University, Clemson, South Carolina.

Greenberg, C. H. 1993. Effect of high-intensity wildfire and silvicultural treatments on biotic communities of sand-pine scrub. Ph.D. Dissertation. University of Florida, Gainesville, FL.

Greenberg, C. H. and A. McGrane. 1996. A comparison of relative abundance and biomass of ground-dwelling arthropods under different forest management practices. *Forest Ecology and Management* 89:31–41.

Greenberg, C. H. and M. C. Thomas. 1995. Effects of forest management practices on terrestrial coleopteran assemblages in sand pine scrub. *Florida Entomologist* 78(2):271–85.

Greenberg, C. H., D. G. Neary, and L. D. Harris. 1994. Effect of high-intensity wildfire and silvicultural treatments on reptile communities in sand-pine scrub. *Conservation Biology* 8(4):1047–57.

Grime, J. P. 1973. Competitive exclusion in herbaceous vegetation. *Nature* 242:344–7.

Haggstrom, D. A. and D. G. Kelleyhouse. 1996. Silviculture and wildlife relationships in the boreal forest of interior Alaska. *The Forestry Chronicle* 72(1):59–62.

Hansen, A. J. and P. Hounihan. 1995. A test of ecological forestry: canopy retention and avian diversity in the Oregon Cascades. In R. Szaro (ed.). *Biodiversity in Managed Landscapesa: Theory and Practice.* Oxford University Press, London.

Hansen, A .J., T. A. Spies, F. J. Swanson, and J. L. Ohmann. 1991. Conserving biodiversity in managed forests. *BioScience* 41(6):382–92.

Hansen, A. J., S. L. Garman, J. F. Weigand, D. L. Urban, W. C. McComb and M. G. Raphael. 1995a. Alternative silviculture regimes in the Pacific northwest: simulations of ecological and economic effects. *Ecological Applications* 5:525–54.

Hansen, A. J., W. C. McComb, R. Vega, M. Raphael, and M. Hunter. 1995b. Bird habitat relationships in natural and managed forests in the west Cascades of Oregon. *Ecological Applications* 5:555–69.

Harris, L. D., D. H. Hirth, and W. R. Marion. 1979. *The development of silvicultural systems for wildlife*. Report 4(5), Intensive Management Practices Assessment Center, University of Florida School of Forest Resources And Conservation, Gainesville, Florida.

Helson, B. V., N. J. Payne and K. M. S. Sundaram. 1993. Impact assessment of spray drift from silvicultural aerial applications of permethrin on aquatic invertebrates using mosquito bioassays. *Environmental Toxicology and Chemistry* 12:1635–42.

Hjeljord, O., and S. Gronvold. 1988. Glyphosate application in forest-ecological aspects. VI. Browsing by moose (*Alces alces*) in relation to chemical and mechanical brush control. *Scandinavian Journal of Forest Research* 3:115–21.

Hunter, M. L. 1990. *Wildlife, Forests, and Forestry: Principles of Managing Forests for Biological Diversity*. Prentice-Hall, Englewood, New Jersey.

1996. *Fundamentals of Conservation Biology*. Blackwell Science, Inc. New York. 482 pp.

Hunter, M. L., and A. Calhoun. 1996. A triad approach to land use allocation. Pp. 477–91 in R. C. Szaro and D. W. Johnston (eds). *Biodiversity in Managed Landscapes*. Oxford University Press, New York.

Jokela, E. J., H. L. Allen, and W. W. McFee. 1991. Fertilization of southern pines at establishment. Pp. 263–77 in M. L. Duryea and P. M. Dougherty (eds). *Forest Regeneration Manual*. Kluwer Academic Publishers, The Netherlands.

Kawana, A. and H. Haibara. 1983. Fertilization programs in Japan. Pp. 357–64 in R. Ballard and S. Gessel (eds). *IUFRO Symposium on Forest Site and Continuous Productivity*. USDA Forest Service General Technical Report PNW-163, Portland, Oregon.

Kimmins, J. P. 1997. *Forest Ecology*. Prentice Hall, Upper Saddle River, New Jersey.

Kremen, C., R. K. Colwell, T. L. Erwin, D. D. Murphy, R. F. Noss, and M. A. Sanjayan. 1993. Terrestrial arthropod assemblages: their use in conservation planning. *Conservation Biology* 7:796–808.

Kreutzweiser, D. P. and P. D. Kingsbury. 1987. Permethrin treatments in Canadian forests. 2. Impact on stream invertebrates. *Pesticide Science* 19:49–60.

Land, D., W. R. Marion, and T. E. O'Meara. 1989. Snag availability and cavity nesting birds in slash pine plantations. *Journal of Wildlife Management* 53: 1165–71.

Larsen, J. B. 1995. Ecological stability of forests and sustainable silviculture. *Forest Ecology and Management* 73:85–96.

Lautenschlager, R. A. 1993. Response of wildlife to forest herbicide applications in northern coniferous ecosystems. *Canadian Journal of Forest Research* 23:2286–99.

Lawton, J. H. and V .K. Brown. 1993. Pp. 255–70 in E. D. Schulze and H. A. Mooney (eds). *Biodiversity and Ecosystem Function*. Springer, Berlin.

Leopold, A. 1966. *A Sand County Almanac*. Oxford University Press, New York.

Lillywhite, H. B. 1977. Effects of chaparral conversion on small vertebrates in southern California. *Biological Conservation* 11:171–84.

Lloyd, R. A. 1989. *Assessing the impact of glyphosate and liquid hexazinone on moose browse species in the Skeena region.* Fish and Wildlife Branch, British Columbia Ministry of the Environment, Victoria, Canada.

1990a. *Assessing the impact of glyphosate and liquid hexazinone on moose browse species in the Skeena region. Addendum.* Fish and Wildlife Branch, British Columbia Ministry of the Environment, Victoria, Canada.

1990b. *Impact on vegetation after operational vision treatment at varying rates in the Skeena region.* Fish and Wildlife Branch, British Columbia Ministry of the Environment, Victoria, Canada.

Loucks, O. L. 1970. Evolution of diversity, efficiency, and community stability. *American Zoology* **10**:17–25.

Lowery, R. F., and D. H. Gjerstad. 1991. Chemical and mechanical site preparation. Pp. 251–61 in M. L. Duryea and P. M. Dougherty (eds). *Forest Regeneration Manual.* Kluwer Academic Publishers, The Netherlands.

Lynch, J. F., A. K. Johnson, and E. C. Balinsky. 1988. Spatial and temporal variation in the abundance and diversity of ants (Hymenoptera: Formicidae) in the soil and litter layers of a Maryland forest. *American Midland Naturalist* **119**(1):31–44.

MacArthur, R. H., and J. W. MacArthur. 1961. On bird species diversity. *Ecology* **42**:594–8.

MacKinnon, D. S. and B. Freedman. 1993. Effects of silvicultural use of the herbicide glyphosate on breeding birds of regenerating clearcuts in Nova Scotia, Canada. *Journal of Applied Ecology* **30**:395–406.

Mathur, A. 1993. Review. In A. Mathur (ed.). *Afforestation Policies, Planning and Progress.* Belhaven Press, London.

Mellin, T. C. 1995. *The effects of intensive forest management practices on the natural vegetative communities of loblolly pine plantations in North Carolina.* Thesis. North Carolina State University, Raleigh, North Carolina.

Michelsen, A., N. Lisanework, I. Friis, and N. Holst. 1996. Comparisons of understorey vegetation and soil fertility in plantations and adjacent natural forests in the Ethiopian highlands. *Journal of Applied Ecology* **33**: 627–42.

Miller, J. H., B. R. Zutter, S. M. Zedaker, M. B. Edwards, and R. A. Newbold. 1995. Early plant succession in loblolly pine plantations as affected by vegetation management. *Southern Journal of Applied Forestry* **19**(3):109–26.

Ministry of Agriculture and Forestry. 1994. *Ministerial conference of the protection of forests in Europe, 16–17 June 1993.* Helsinki, Finland.

Morris, L. A., and R. F. Lowery. 1988. Influence of site preparation on soil conditions affecting stand establishment and tree growth. *Southern Journal of Applied Forestry* **12**: 170–8.

Morrison, M. L., and E. C. Meslow. 1984a. Effects of the herbicide glyphosate on bird community structure, western Oregon. *Forest Science* **30**:95–106.

1984b. Response of avian communities to herbicide-induced vegetation changes. *Journal of Wildlife Management* **48**: 14–22.

Mushinsky, H. R., and D. J. Gibson. 1991. The influence of fire periodicity on habitat structure. Pp. 237–59 in S. S. Bell, E. D. McCoy, and H. R. Mushinsky (eds). *Habitat Structure: The Physical Arrangement of Objects in Space.* Chapman and Hall, London.

Naeem, S., L. J. Thompson, S. P. Lawler, J. H. Lawton, and R. M. Woodfin. 1994. Declining biodiversity can alter the performance of ecosystems. *Nature* **368**:734–6.

Nams, V. O., N. F. G. Folkard, and J. N. M. Smith. 1996. Nitrogen fertilization stimulates herbivory by snowshoe hares in the boreal forest. *Canadian Journal of Zoology* **74**:196–9.

Nelson, L. R., *et al.* 1981. Impacts of herbaceous weeds in young loblolly pine plantations. *Southern Journal of Applied Forestry* **5**:153–8.

Newton, M., E.C. Cole, R. A. Lautenschlager, D. E. White and M. L. McCormack. 1989. Browse availability after conifer release in Maine's spruce-fir forests. *Journal of Wildlife Management* **53**:643–9.

NCSFNC. 1996. *North Carolina State Forest Nutrition Cooperative. 25th Annual Report.* Department of Forestry. North Carolina State University, Raleigh, NC. 22 pp.

O'Neill, E. D. 1995. Amphibian and reptile communities of temporary ponds in a managed pine flatwoods. Pp. 179–82 in *NCASI Wetlands Study 1995 Annual Report.* University of Florida, Gainesville, Florida.

Parker, G. R., D. G. Kimball, and B. Dalzell. 1994. Bird communities breeding in selected spruce and pine plantations in New Brunswick. *Canadian Field-Naturalist* **108**:1–9.

Pattanavibool, A. and W. D. Edge. 1996. Single-tree selection silviculture affects cavity resources in mixed deciduous forests in Thailand. *Journal of Wildlife Management* **60**(1):67–73.

Pechmann, J. H. K., D. E. Scott, R. D. Semlitsch, J. P. Caldwell, L. J. Vitt, and J. W. Gibbons. 1991. Declining amphibian populations: the problem of separating human impacts from natural fluctuations. *Science* **253**:892–5.

Pehl, C. E., and R. L. Bailey. 1983. Performance to age ten of a loblolly pine plantation on an intensively prepared site in the Georgia Piedmont. *Forest Science* **29**:96–102.

Phillips, K. 1990. Where have all the frogs and toads gone? *BioScience* **40**:422–4.

Pianka, E. R. 1973. The structure of lizard communities. *Annual Review of Ecological Systems* **4**:53–74.

Pough, F. H., E. M. Smith, D. H. Rhodes, and A. Collazo. 1987. The abundance of salamanders in forest stands with different histories of disturbance. *Forest Ecology and Management* **20**:1–9.

Primack, R. B. and P. Hall. 1992. Biodiversity and forest change in Malaysian Borneo. *BioScience* **42**(11):829–37.

Repenning, R. W., and R. F. Labinsky. 1985. Effects of even-age timber management on bird communities of the longleaf pine forest in northern Florida. *Journal of Wildlife Management* **49**(4):1088–98.

Roth, D. S., I. Perfecto and B. Rathcke. 1994. The effects of management systems on ground-foraging ant diversity in Costa Rica. *Ecological Applications* **4**(3):423–36.

SAF. 1971. *Terminology of forest science, technology, practice and products.* (F.C. Ford-Roberston, editor.) Society of American Foresters, Washington, D.C.

Santillo, D. J. 1994. Observations on moose, *Alces alces,* habitat and use on herbicide-treated clearcuts in Maine. *Canadian Field-Naturalist* **108**(1):22–5.

Santillo, D. J., P. W. Brown, and D. M. Leslie, Jr. 1989. Response of songbirds to glyphosate-induced habitat changes on clearcuts. *Journal of Wildlife Management* **53**:64–71.

Seagle, S. W. 1985. Competition and coexistence of small mammals in an East Tennessee pine plantation. *American Midland Naturalist* **114**:272–82.

Shepherd, K. R. 1993. Significance of plantations in a global forestry strategy. *Australian Forestry* **56**(4):237–335.

Shugart, H. H. Jr., and D. James. 1973. Ecological succession of breeding bird populations in northwestern Arkansas. *Auk* **90**:62–77.

Smith, D. M., B. C. Larson, M. Kelty, and P. M. S. Ashton. 1997. *The Practice of Silviculture: Applied Forest Ecology.* John Wiley & Sons, New York.

Stoddart, D. M. 1979. *Ecology of Small Mammals.* Chapman & Hall, London.

Stone, E. L. 1975. Soil and man's use of forest land. Pp. 1–9 in B. Bernier and C. H. Winget (eds). *Forest Soils and Forest Land Management.* Les Presses de L'Universite Laval, Quebec. 675 pp.

Strelke, W. K., and J. G. Dickson. 1980. Effect of forest clear-cut edge on breeding birds in east Texas. *Journal of Wildlife Management* **44**(3):559–67.

Suckling, G. C., E. Backen, A. Heisler, and F. G. Neumann. 1976. *The flora and fauna of Pinus radiata plantations in north-eastern Victoria.* Bulletin 24, Forestry Commission of Victoria, British Columbia.

Sullivan, T. P. 1985. Effects of glyphosate on selected species of wildlife. Pp. 186–99 in E. Grossbard and D. Atkinson (eds). *The Herbicide Glyphosate.* Butterworths, London.

Sullivan, T. P., and D. S. Sullivan. 1979. The effects of glyphosate herbicide on food preference and consumption in black-tailed deer. *Canadian Journal of Zoology* **57**:1406–12.

Swindel, B. F., and L. R. Grosenbaugh. 1988. Species diversity in young Douglas-fir plantations compared to old growth. *Forest Ecology and Management* **23**:227–31.

Swindel, B. F., L. F. Conde, and J. E. Smith. 1982. Effects of forest regeneration practices on plant diversity and succession in Florida ecosystems. in S. Coleman, A. Mace and B. Swindel (eds). *Impacts of Intensive Forest Management Practices.* Symposium Proceedings, IMPAC Report, vol. 7, University of Florida, Gainesville, FL.

1986. Successional changes in *Pinus elliottii* plantations following two regeneration treatments. *Canadian Journal of Forest Research* **16**:630–6.

Szaro, R. C., and D. W. Johnston (eds). 1996. *Biodiversity in Managed Landscapes: Theory and Practice.* Oxford University Press, New York.

Taylor, C. M. A. 1991. *Forest Fertilization in Britain.* Bulletin 95, Forestry Commission, Her Majesty's Stationery Office, London.

Taylor, R. J. and M. E. Haseler. 1995. Effects of partial logging systems on bird assemblages in Tasmania. *Forest Ecology and Management* 72:131–49.

Thompson, F. R., W. D. Dikak, T. G. Kulowiec, and D. A. Hamilton. 1992. Breeding bird populations in Missouri Ozark forests with and without clearcutting. *Journal of Wildlife Management* 56: 23–30.

Tilman, D. and J. A. Downing. 1994. Biodiversity and stability in grasslands. *Nature* 367:363–5.

Tilman, D., and S. Pacala. 1993. Pp. 13–25. in R. Ricklefs and D. Schluter (eds). *Species Diversity in Ecological Communities*. Univ. of Chicago Press, Chicago, Illinois.

Tilman, D., D. Wedlin, and J. Knops. 1996. Productivity and sustainability influenced by biodiversity in grassland ecosystems. *Nature* 379:718–20.

Troendle, C. A. 1970. *A comparison of soil-moisture loss from forested and clearcut areas in West Virginia*. U.S.D.A. Forest Service Note NE-120. Northeastern Forest Experiment Station, Upper Darby, Pennsylvania.

Vannotte, R. L., G. W. Minshaw, K. W. Cummins, J. R. Sedell, and C. E. Cushing. 1980. The river continuum concept. *Canadian Journal of Fisheries and Aquatic Sciences* 37:130–7.

Vega, R. 1993. Bird communities in managed conifer stands in the Oregon Cascades: habitat associations and nest predation. Thesis. Oregon State University, Corvallis, Oregon.

Vickers, C. R., L. D. Harris, and B. F. Swindel. 1985. Changes in herpetofauna resulting from ditching of cypress ponds in coastal plains flatwoods. *Forest Ecology and Management* 11:17–29.

Vuori, K. M. and I. Joensuu. 1996. Impact of forest drainage on the macroinvertebrates of a small boreal headwater stream: do buffer zones protect lotic diversity? *Biological Conservation* 77:87–95.

Wake, D. 1991. Declining amphibian populations. *Science* 153:860.

Wallace, M. G., H. J. Cortner, S. Burke, and M. A. Moote. 1994. Moving towards ecosystem management: examining a change in philosophy for resource management. Prepared for presentation at the Fifth International Symposium on Society and Natural Resources, June 7–10, Fort Collins, Colorado.

Waters, J. R., K. S. McKelvey, C. J. Zabel, and W. W. Oliver. 1994. The effects of thinning and broadcast burning on sporocarp production of hypogeous fungi. *Canadian Journal of Forest Research* 24:1516–22.

Westman, W. E. 1990. Managing for biodiversity. *BioScience* 40:26–33.

Westworth, D. A., and E. S. Telfer. 1993. Summer and winter bird populations associated with five age classes of aspen forest in Alberta. *Canadian Journal of Forest Research* 23:1830–6.

White, L. D., L. D. Harris, J. E. Johnston, and D. G. Milchunas. 1975. Impact of site preparation on flatwoods wildlife habitat. *Proceedings of the Southeast Associated Game and Fisheries Commission* 13:288–91.

Wilcox, B. A. 1995. Tropical forest resources and biodiversity: the risks of forest lost and degradation. *Unasylva* 181 46:43–9.

Wilkins, R. N. 1992. Changes in vegetation following site preparation and understory restoration with the forest herbicide hexazinone. Ph.D. Dissertation. University of Florida, Gainesville, Florida.

Winkler, D. W., and G. Dana. 1977. Summer birds of a lodgepole-aspen forest in southern Warner Mountains, California. *Western Birds* 8:45–62.

Winternitz, B. L. 1976. Temporal change and habitat preference of some montane breeding birds. *Condor* 78:383–93.

World Resources Institute. 1996. *World Resources 1996–1997*. Oxford University Press, New York.

Zobel, B. J., G. VanWyk and P. Stahl. 1987. *Growing Exotic Forests*. John Wiley & Sons, New York.

Zutter, B. R., G. R. Glover, and D. H. Gjerstad. 1987. Vegetation response to intensity of herbaceous weed control in a newly planted loblolly pine plantation. *New Forests* 4:257–71.

13   Special species

IAN D. THOMPSON AND PER ANGELSTAM

By now you have read a considerable amount in this book about the importance of a holistic, or integrative approach to the conservation of biodiversity in sustainable forest management. These approaches to forestry are advanced under the assumption that if a complete array of functioning ecosystems is maintained, then all species will be present on the landscape. However, forest and wildlife managers must frequently make decisions based on individual species. The two approaches, holistic and species-oriented, are not mutually exclusive and actually complement one another by focusing efforts at multiple scales. Regardless of how a 'biodiversity management program' is designed, the end result must be assessed primarily in terms of the conservation of species.

Within any political jurisdiction (at all scales, from country to local municipality) certain species will receive more attention from managers than others, for a variety of reasons. Some species may have attracted the interest of the public because they are rare, attractive, or culturally or economically important. Many species have value as indicators of a particular condition (such as old-growth forests) and are monitored by managers because they are good barometers of ecosystem health. Species selected for monitoring and study as indicator species are chosen with a view to indicating functioning of forest ecosystems, and because they themselves may play critical roles in forested systems (i.e., keystone species). As an example, a breeding population of a particular woodpecker species may indicate sufficient dead or dying trees in a forest type or age class to support many of the species that use these structures (Angelstam and Mikusinski 1994). Species can also serve as pedagogical 'tools' to illustrate success or failure of forest management interventions. Human perceptions bias the relative importance of species, and each species is accorded status based on human values. To a significant extent, forest management programs are driven by public interests and the values attached to individual species.

Historically, wildlife managers concentrated their efforts on game species, in particular large ungulates, upland game birds, and waterfowl, in response to demands of hunters who actively promote their sport. Over the past decade, the issue of biological diversity has captured the minds of many people on a global scale. Concern by the public that managers consider all species and not just game animals, has led to a change in the species now forming the cornerstones of management programs of government agencies. Of course, not all species constitute special concerns, but it is now the rule rather than the exception that species like greater gliders (*Petauroides volans*) in Australia, tigers (*Panthera tigris altaica*) in Russia, white-backed woodpeckers (*Dendrocopus leucotos*) in Scandinavia, sable (*Martes zibellina*) in China, spotted owls (*Strix occidentalis*) in the northwestern United States, and small-whorled pogonias (*Isotria medeoloides*) in eastern North America receive individual attention as special species in forest management.

Management of individual species represents a tractable problem to forest managers, unlike the difficulties of attempting to comprehend the myriad linkages within ecosystems and all of the species that these represent. Further, the inclusion of a number of special species in forest management plans forces managers to examine the forests they produce for more than simply the tree component at the stand level. Species are easy to visualize and study, relatively simple to manage (compared with more nebulous concepts like 'ecosystem management'), and species management programs are readily explicable to the public. However, a number of criticisms have been leveled at a 'species approach' to forest management, including that it fails to recognize ecological communities or the functioning of ecosystems. Such an approach may ignore disturbance regimes in time and space, and assigns some preference to certain species over others, while failing to account for diversity. While these critiques may be valid in some situations, the management of forests requires both the species and holistic approaches together, because some species are indeed 'special' and require greater attention than an ecosystem approach would afford. The inclusion of special species in forest management programs is an appropriate part of an enlightened, pluralistic approach to the problem of sustainable forestry. In this chapter, we will look at why some species are considered special, how various management agencies are attempting to reconcile holistic and special species management concerns, and how special species are managed.

We have organized the chapter by grouping species that merit individual consideration into four main classifications: species that are ecologically important based on their functional role within forests, species that are sensitive to change in forest habitats such as endangered species or those existing in fragmented habitats, species of economic importance, and finally species that are used to monitor forest condition. These groups form an initial or first-order categorization for the selection of species for individual management attention. Although non-endemic species that have been introduced into forest ecosystems constitute individual management problems, we do not discuss these issues in this chapter.

Ecologically important species

Some species play prominent roles in forest ecosystems by affecting other species either by their presence or by their absence. Carnivores may influence the populations of some prey; ectomycorrhizal fungi facilitate more rapid tree growth than if they were absent; periodic elevated levels of certain parasites or diseases may cause die-offs to occur in host species; and dominance hierarchies exist among some species (for example among small forest rodents). Ecosystems function through numerous cycles that convert energy into biomass and through trophic linkages (food webs) among species that live in the ecosystem. Some research has indicated that certain species affect the linkages in food webs so strongly that their removal results in a reorganization within the food web. Such species are referred to as 'keystone species' (Figure 13.1).

Paine's (1966) original definition of keystone species (although he did not call them keystones) referred to the trophic links between a predator and its prey. He showed that removal of a predator from a system could result in large changes in the absolute and relative abundances of prey species and their competitors. More recently, there has been an acceptance of a broader definition of keystone species, beyond food web effects, to refer to any species that if removed from a system would have a disproportionately large impact on that system (Power *et al.* 1996). Plants too can be keystone species. In Peru, 12 species of figs and palms maintain all frugivores for three months each year (Terbourgh 1986), and some frugivorous species have declined in association with their food trees in logged tropical forests (Frumhoff 1995). Thus it is the amount of interaction or linkage among a particular species and other species within the system that is important; keystone species are exceptional in this regard.

The effects of the loss of a predator from a system may cascade to trophic levels below consumers, for example through the effects of increased herbivory on plant community structure. A good example of this

Fig. 13.1. Keystone species play important roles in providing and maintaining habitats and structures used by numerous other species for breeding, shelter, and feeding.

has occurred in some boreal forest areas, where wolves (*Canis lupus*) have been mostly or completely eliminated, including Norway, Sweden, and the Canadian province of Newfoundland. In each of these areas, lack of predation has resulted in elevated moose (*Alces alces*) populations with consequent effects on the composition of forest vegetation. In Newfoundland, excessive browsing by high densities of moose ($3–5/km^2$) has resulted in abnormal forest tree and herbaceous plant communities, thereby altering ecosystem diversity on large portions of the island (Bergerud and Manuel 1968, Thompson *et al.* 1992, Thompson and Curran 1993). In particular, forest stands dominated by white spruce (*Picea glauca*), a species that is rarely co-dominant, instead of balsam fir (*Abies balsamea*) can now be found. Similarly, browsing on Scots pine (*Pinus sylvestris*) by moose is of great concern to foresters in Sweden, and has resulted in research on how to balance the interests of foresters, hunters, and the general public. Consumption of Scots pine has increased dramatically with increasing

moose densities (Hultkranz and Wibe 1989, Hörnberg 1995) and the damage can be locally severe (Lavsund 1987). The high browsing pressure on Scots pine has occurred as more preferred deciduous species were depleted through the combined effects of intensive forest management that selectively removed these species, and high browsing pressure by moose. Because of increased concern for conservation of ecosystems, the presence of deciduous trees is now actively promoted in Sweden. Success of these biodiversity recovery programs will depend in part on the management of moose to maintain populations at reasonable levels.

Keystone species do not always occupy an elevated trophic status (Power et al. 1996). Jones et al. (1994) used the term 'ecosystem engineers' (or keystone modifiers, after Mills et al., 1993) to refer to species that create, modify, or maintain certain environments. These species are keystones because they play important functional roles in ecosystems by creating habitats required by other species. Therefore, the removal of the engineering species from an environment results in species impoverishment beyond loss of the species itself. Some readily identifiable ecosystem engineers are beavers (Naiman et al. 1986), ants (Elmes 1991, Puntilla et al. 1994), and earthworms (Thompson et al. 1993). In the case of the latter two groups of species, much of the activity is invisible to humans, but extremely important to energy and nutrient flows within ecosystems. Ants are responsible for seed and spore dispersal for certain plants (including many fungi), soil mixing and aeration, and decomposition of wood. Ants have specific competitive effects on the distribution of other ant species and ground-dwelling arthropods, certain canopy arthropods, and some vertebrates including pileated woodpeckers (*Dendrocopus pileatus*) and ant-eaters in tropical forest systems (Puntilla *et al.* 1994, Elmes 1991, and Holldobler and Wilson 1990). Beavers (*Castor canadensis*) are common throughout North America, and a similar species (*C. fiber*) is re-establishing itself in Europe and Asia. Their damming of streams to flood small tracts of timber creates habitat for numerous aquatic and semi-aquatic species, while abandoned, previously flooded areas succeed to meadows providing habitat for a host of species. Current management of riparian areas by leaving buffer strips of old forest, to protect waterways from siltation and to provide skyline vistas to conceal logged areas, may eventually reduce beaver populations because this species requires young deciduous trees as food. Some woodpecker species may be considered keystone modifiers because they excavate cavities in large old trees that are subsequently essential for successful reproduction by other species. If habitat needs of the woodpeckers are fulfilled through careful planning, then habitat will be created for secondary cavity-using species including forest bats, cavity-nesting passerines, cavity-nesting owls, certain wasp species, and tree squirrels.

It is likely that most keystone species have not been identified as such because many are soil invertebrates, pollinators, mutualists, and pathogenic organisms (Krebs 1985, Power *et al.* 1996). Consequently, it makes sense to err on the side of caution by attempting to maintain ecosystem components likely to be important to these species. Management can be directed at maintaining a certain density of snags for woodpeckers, and 'normal' amounts of fallen wood for microorganisms, particularly in shelterwood and selective forest harvesting systems. In clearcut systems, maintaining uncut areas within cuts will ensure that sources for small keystone species exist from which to repopulate regenerating areas. Finally, protection of soils through the use of low pressure tires, reduced skidding, and less use of scarification will enhance the maintenance of functioning soil communities.

Species sensitive to disturbance

Certain species are more sensitive to disturbance than others, usually because they have narrow habitat requirements, exist in low numbers, or because they migrate or over-winter in large groups making them vulnerable to disease, habitat destruction, or stochastic events.

Regardless of the mechanism that makes such species sensitive to disturbance, they require particular attention to ensure survival if sustainable development is to proceed.

AREA-SENSITIVE SPECIES

Forest fragmentation (discussed in Chapters 6 and 7) can alter processes such as predator/prey relations, mutualisms, primary production, and succession. Furthermore, these processes may be altered over some distance into a forest stand away from the edges, effectively removing the habitat for species that require forest interior. In some forest types, such as boreal forests, fragmentation is an ephemeral event and therefore of little consequence over temporal scales of several hundred years. However, in other forest types that are longer lived, or that regenerate through the development of small gaps, fragmentation is an important problem for species management. Lovejoy et al. (1986) studied the effects of fragmentation in Brazilian rainforest and found edge effects on birds up to 50 m into small patch reserves, whereas Temple (1986) suggested that 100 m was a more likely distance. The actual distance likely varies with the effect and species in question (see Laurance and Yensen 1991). For example, although an isolated square forest patch may be 100 ha, functionally there may be only 60 ha of available habitat because of edge effects. As a result, some small passerine birds could continue to exist in the patch, but an owl species that requires 70 ha of forest interior for its home range could not be sustained in the stand. Species that have a lower limit for habitat patch size are termed 'area sensitive' (or 'core sensitive'; Leopold 1933). Many bird species are 'forest-interior' species (Terbourgh 1989), and in tropical forests for example, it appears that avian insectivores are disproportionately affected by small patch size (Frumhoff 1995). Forest-interior species cannot successfully breed near forest edges, usually because they or their nests become subject to high levels of predation at ecotones. Several studies suggest that forest bird species depending on, or benefiting from, old forest have shown strongly negative population trends in fragmented habitats (e.g., Angelstam and Mikusinski 1994, Virkkala et al. 1994). Capercaillie (Tetrao urogallus) is often a symbol of these changes (see Sjöberg 1996). The main factor explaining variations in capercaillie density is the proportion of the landscape covered by old forest, defined as forests with a well-developed ground cover with Vaccinium myrtillus and pines of sufficient size in order to carry the weight of foraging capercaillie (Rolstad and Wegge 1987). Most species that have narrow habitat tolerances are area-sensitive.

Thresholds exist in the ecological requirements of animal populations that make responses to habitat change nonlinear (Boyce 1992, Tilman et al. 1994, Bascompte and Solé 1996). Declines (or increases) in animal numbers, once a threshold is passed, are much more rapid than would be expected based on the initially observed linear population response to available habitat. Knowledge of where thresholds occur, and how these may be influenced by patch geometry, is important in management, particularly for rare species. Andrén (1994) suggested that there were cascading effects of habitat change and habitat loss on animal species when about 30% of the original, formerly continuous, habitat remained. This level of habitat loss thus appears critical, and the consequences for many species support these models (for example: spotted owl [Thomas et al. 1990], capercaillie [Rolstad and Wegge 1987], hazel grouse Bonasa bonasia [Åberg et al. 1995], white-backed woodpecker Dendrocopos leucotos [Carlson and Stenberg 1994], and the small passerines Parus palustris, Sitta europea, Aegithalus caudatus [Enoksson et al. 1995]). For all these species, population levels were lower than would be expected based on the amount of available habitat alone, when about 30% of the original amount of habitat remained, and they were usually extinct locally when only 5–10% remained.

The area-dependence concept could also be applied to populations of larger-bodied mammals. In particular, if patch sizes created by forest management are different from those created by natural disturbance, then species that have body sizes matching the scale of disturbance will be most affected. For example, observations of wintering woodland caribou (Rangifer tarandus) herds suggested that they require a minimum patch size of several hundred square kilometers of old forest (Cumming and Beange 1987, Darby and Duquette 1986, Chubbs et al. 1993). If forest harvesting creates patches much smaller than this, say on the order of tens of square kilometers, the result may be the fracturing of overwintering herds into small bands that may be more susceptible to predation than they would normally be in huge tracts of forest, and well away from edges (Bergerud 1974). Moreover, an increase in predation on caribou can be expected if numbers of early-successional ungulates increase in response to habitat change from logging, and consequently result in an increase in local wolf populations (Seip 1992).

Because logging of forests can isolate portions of populations, and reduce effective forest area for some species, area-sensitive species must be given special consideration in forest planning. Forest management requires that close attention be paid to contiguity, connectivity, size, and geometry of habitat patches of various types and age classes in time and in space (see also, Chapters 6 and 7).

(see also, Chapters 6 and 7)

SPECIES THAT CONCENTRATE DURING SOME TIME OF THE YEAR

An important aspect of the life history of many animal species is their movement to restricted areas that meet their needs for some portion of the year. During periods when a species congregates at high density in localized areas, a large proportion of local populations or even of the entire population is particularly susceptible to disturbance or habitat loss. In forest ecosystems, there are many examples of species that move into localized high-density areas, often in winter: moose in some parts of Sweden and Norway (Sweanor 1987), certain species of bats (roosting, breeding, hibernating), monarch butterflies (*Danaus plexippus*), and woodland caribou. Many species of amphibians congregate to breed in vernal pools in forests or forests margins. These species require special attention to ensure that adequate habitat is available where they can concentrate, and that they are not disturbed enough to alter an often precarious energy balance. For example, hibernating bats in temperate climates will die if they are disturbed too frequently in winter, and excessively disturbed deer can die of exhaustion if they are harassed in deep snow. A component of ecosystem management is to safeguard the special habitats associated with species that concentrate. In some situations, such as caves that are used by bats to hibernate, identifying and maintaining buffer areas is sufficient. For other species that use old forests, however, considerable planning is needed to ensure long-term habitat maintenance.

Among the most interesting of the migratory species that concentrate is the monarch butterfly of North America (Malcolm and Zalucki 1993). This species exists in two distinct wintering populations, one in Mexico and the other in California. The over-wintered butterflies migrate to lay eggs on the breeding grounds throughout Canada and the United States each summer, and the adult generation born latest in summer then migrates south to one of the two wintering areas. There, they over-winter in a state of torpor. The Mexican wintering areas, about 80 km west of Mexico City, are particularly small

and it would be possible to eliminate the species through logging of the extremely restricted wintering habitat. The Mexican government has declared the wintering grounds ecological preserves, but there is considerable local pressure to allow logging to continue (Malcolm and Zalucki 1993). Salvation for the monarchs continues to depend on money from tourists who travel to the area to see this spectacular gathering of the butterflies.

In areas where snow accumulates in winter making movements difficult and forage hard to obtain, many species of ungulates are forced to migrate to areas where the forest canopy reduces the snow depth on the ground and allows some access to food near the sheltering conifers. In montane habitats, animals move down from alpine meadows and forests to winter in valleys where shelter and food is available. Such behavior is common to elk (*Cervus elaphus*), mountain sheep (*Ovis* spp.), mule deer (*Odocoileus hemionus*), and white-tailed deer (*O. virginianus*) in North America, red deer and ibex (*Capra ibex*) in central Europe, and tahr (*Hemitragus jemlahicus*) in Asia, among many other species globally. In central North America, white-tailed deer tend to move to traditional wintering areas in response to accumulating snow, and the northern range of white-tailed deer is limited by mean annual snow depth plus minimum temperature as modified by available winter habitat (Voigt *et al.* 1992). In northern Sweden, pitfall traps built by hunters thousands of years ago in sandy pine forests of river valleys, coincide with current seasonal migration pathways of moose. Sweanor (1987) studied the seasonal migration of these moose in a 1400 km² area in central Sweden. During late autumn, moose move to lower altitudes at varying dates, but consistently about one month after the first snowfall and when approximately 40 cm of snow has accumulated on their upland summer range. Migratory moose then join resident moose in lowland pine forests. About 70% of the population in the study area was migratory and individual moose averaged movements of 37 km (range: 5–98 km).

The important consideration for most over-wintering ungulates is that they traditionally reuse the same habitats, and these may often represent all that is now available to them following forest harvesting or human developments. Timber managers must plan for the long-term presence of these seasonal winter habitats by using selection harvests in traditional wintering areas to allow new food to grow, and by ensuring an adequate amount of mature forest cover is always present. Loss of available suitable winter habitat results either in extirpation of local populations, or the need for expensive management programs to maintain the animals over winter by supplementary feeding.

RARE, THREATENED, AND ENDANGERED SPECIES

Rarity is a common feature of many species in natural biological systems, and rarity in itself does not necessarily mean that a species is endangered. Rabinowitz et al. (1986) described six forms of rarity based on three variables, geographical distribution that is broad or restricted, habitat specificity that is either specific or general, and local population size that is large or small (they termed this 'somewhere large or somewhere small'). The rarest species then, are those that are endemic to a small area, require a relatively scarce habitat type, and occur only at low density within that habitat. There are many examples of highly specialized endemic plant and animal species occuring at low densities in tropical forest systems, particularly on islands. Body size and life history are often correlates to degree of rarity, particularly in carnivores where larger carnivores usually occur at low density, regardless of geographical distribution or habitat specificity. For example, this is particularly the case for a solitary territorial forest species, such as wolverine (*Gulo gulo*) and grizzly bear (*Ursus arctos*).

All forest species, including the rare ones, can suffer from poor forest management practices through habitat loss and degradation. However, rare species require specific attention because individual populations can readily be eliminated through anthropogenic disturbance and/or environmental or stochastic demographic processes whose effects are accentuated because of small populations. Careful planning beyond simple habitat preservation is required to deal with the question of how to maintain rare species in forest ecosystems. Changes to ecosystem functioning in areas surrounding preserved areas can result in negative effects on rare species through invasion by non-native species that may be competitors of the rare species, increased pollution, disturbance as a result of increased access, altered microclimate, or increased predation. Further, within preserved forest areas, succession may ultimately eliminate the rare habitat they were established to maintain. Active management is often required to reduce impacts of forestry within the habitats of rare species and the habitats that surround the preserved areas, and to ensure temporal availability of the habitats needed by rare species.

The rarity of individual species is an important criterion for designation of a species as special, and the loss of a species is the ultimate sign of environmental degradation and mismanagement. We distinguish between rare species whose populations are never abundant, or have limited geographic range, and threatened species whose populations have declined, almost invariably because of anthropogenic causes. Rare species are often also threatened and threatened species are often rare, but there are exceptions; i.e., some rapidly declining species are considered threatened even though their populations are still large, while many naturally rare species are not considered threatened. Those species whose populations have declined sufficiently to cause concern over their future viability are perhaps the most special of the 'special species' that are the subjects of this chapter. Species become threatened for several reasons, most of which are related to human population growth and misuse of natural resources such as habitat loss and degradation, overhunting (including poaching), poor management of economically important species, pollution, invasion by non-native species, and climate change. It is important to distinguish between ultimate and proximate causes of species decline. The latter only begin to drive the population once it becomes small but may not have been responsible for most of a given decline.

Causal factors operate at a range of temporal and spatial scales and will differentially affect plants and animals, and animal species of differing body sizes. The smaller the population the greater the likelihood of extinction, but what constitutes 'small' for a species depends to some extent on body size. A small and threatened population of carabid beetles may be several tens of thousands of animals, but this would hardly be considered small for a large-bodied species. Although small populations are at great risk of extinction, they do not always go extinct. Stochasticity, both demographic and environmental, play key roles in the long-term persistence or extinction of small populations, as do social structure, genetics, individual longevity, temporal habitat structure, and the interaction among these factors (Pimm 1991). Extinction is a common event in evolutionary history; however, the current rate of loss of species because of anthropogenic-related habitat change is unprecedented.

Political jurisdictions have various categories to describe the risk of possible extinction associated with threatened species and many maintain lists of such species. The International Union for the Conservation of Nature (IUCN) recently revised its 'Red List Categories' (IUCN 1994) as follows: critically endangered (risk of immediate extinction), endangered (very high risk of extinction), and vulnerable (high risk of extinction in the medium-term future) – all these categories are 'threatened'; and a second group of categories that includes: conservation dependent (species that are the foci of continuing habitat conservation programs), near threatened (close to being vulnerable), and least concern (not conservation-dependent nor close to near-threatened) – all of these categories are 'lower risk'. Each of the threatened categories has an associated series of criteria relating population size and viability, rate of decline, amount of remaining habitat or its occupancy, indicating potential for survivorship of the species.

In many parts of Europe where humans have actively altered landscapes for many centuries, certain forest types only exist in discrete patches. Remnants of such forests host a large number of red-listed species that are extremely rare as a consequence of agricultural development and amelioration of forest wetlands (Hansson 1997). Some endangered lichens (e.g., *Usnea longissima* and *Ramalina thrausta*) and endangered fungi (e.g., *Fomitopsis rosea*, *Fellinus ferruginofuscus*), are being used as indicators of such conditions (Karström 1992). Long-term studies of the population trends of species specializing in this type of habitat show that such stands are often very sensitive to changes in the local microclimate due to removal of adjacent stands. Sjöberg and Ericson (1992) reported that 16 years after the removal of the borders of a forest surrounding trees with the red-listed lichen *Evernia divaricata*, the species had gone locally extinct. A particularly high diversity occurs in forests that are 50–100 years or more older than the age at which trees are usually harvested in boreal forests (80–120 years, depending on the local climate and species). The lichen *Alectoria sarmentosa* and its associated fauna (Esseen *et al.* 1996) are good examples of species only found in remnant old-growth forests. In Scandinavia, management for conifers at the expense of aspen (*Populus tremula*) and willow (*Salix caprea*) has also produced a decline in lichen species found only with these trees (Kuusinen 1996).

A fundamental strategy in the protection of threatened species is to adopt a policy of 'spreading the risk' by attempting to foster the growth of two or more distinct populations. Separate populations are unlikely to be simultaneously affected by catastrophe. However, individual populations must be sufficiently large to avoid the genetic bottleneck than can result from inbreeding, the consequences of which may include low sperm counts, poor sperm viability and increased susceptibility to disease or change in living conditions. There has been considerable debate over the role of genetics in species declines, and some cases of population decline, previously thought to have resulted from a loss of heterozygosity, may have been the result of other factors (e.g., cheetahs in Africa) (Caro and Laurenson 1994). Certainly inbreeding can be a proximate cause of decline, and in very small populations the genetic consequences of inbreeding can become a paramount problem. Florida panthers (*Felis concolor coryi*) provide a particularly illustrative example of the genetic effects of small population size. Fewer than 50 breeding Florida panthers exist in southern Florida, USA. Random fixation has resulted in poor sperm viability, low sperm motility, probably low juvenile survivorship (Hedrick 1995), and an apparently high susceptibility to disease. Despite protection of the remaining habitat (representing an extremely small portion of its former range) the population has continued to decline. Recent recommendations are to attempt to increase viability of the Florida subspecies by importing new genes into the population by releasing female panthers of another subspecies from Texas (*Felis concolor stanleyana*) (Seal 1994). The ultimate causes of decline of this species were anthropogenic influences on habitat availability, and the proximate cause of problems for recovery of the species are genetic.

Many management agencies have adopted a planning approach to try to 'recover' threatened or endangered species. Recovery planning is a formal strategy that establishes objectives and sets a time period over which to accomplish the plan. Although there is no universal format for recovery planning, it represents an attempt by governments and private agencies to work together to prevent extinctions, often before a severe decline becomes imminent. Basic steps in recovery planning involve: determining the status of the species (is the species declining?), identifying habitat requirements (does the species require a specific habitat type that is declining?), identifying the factors that underlie a decline (why is the species declining?), determining which of these factors can be significantly influenced through management (can any of the important sources of mortality or decline be mitigated?), and establishing and implementing a recovery plan (how can the decline be reversed and what will it cost?). Although a population decline may be obvious, the underlying causes for a decline are often not simple and there are numerous cases where assumed causes appeared obvious but were in fact incorrect (e.g., see Simberloff 1995). The proper approach to discovering the causes for a population decline is through research that tests hypotheses under the appropriate theory. A recovery plan may suggest a wide variety of rescue techniques, such as captive breeding/release, habitat protection, habitat enhancement, reduction of mortality factors (e.g., predator control), and public education. There have been a few wonderful successes in recovering endangered species through intensive and careful management and through the investment of considerable funds and effort. However, it is noteworthy that once in place, a recovery plan neither ensures that the plan will be implemented, nor that the species will be recovered, and Belovsky *et al.* (1994) pointed out that only 1% of active recovery programs for endangered species have been successful in North America.

Economically important species

Economically important species are those species that are used to generate revenue. In this chapter we are excluding the logging of trees from this category, as this is dealt with elsewhere. Economic uses of wild organisms that immediately spring to mind are viewing of wildlife in association with tourism, industrial or medicinal uses of species, and sport hunting. Traditional wildlife biology has primarily involved the management of game species and although the main focus of many wildlife agencies has now turned to implementing 'biodiversity management programs', game management remains an important consideration. Considerable revenue in North America and Europe is also generated from bird-watching when one considers travel costs, equipment purchases and the associated tax dollars. In some parts of Asia, Africa, Central and South America there is a burgeoning industry associated with wildlife-viewing and 'ecotourism'. In tropical forests, some estimates of the potential revenue from the use of forests for fruits, nuts, rubber production, and tourism exceed the value from more consumptive uses. In these latter two examples of the economic importance of species, wildlife-viewing and various uses of plants, it is often the presence of one or just a few species that has resulted in the protection of entire forests and landscapes.

In many tropical forest nations, forest reserves created primarily for tourism have resulted in the preservation of areas that otherwise would have been converted to farms or plantations. Prime examples of this are the Bwindi Forest Reserve in Uganda, and National Volcano Park in Rwanda, that were established to protect mountain gorillas (*Gorilla gorilla* beringei). Revenue for these reserves is derived almost entirely from tourism. Considerable funds in the latter countries and in Zaire are gained from tourism and directed to protection of the gorillas from poachers and to public education programs aimed at conservation of the forest reserves. Elsewhere in Africa, tourism and big-game hunting provide funds for reserves for large animals, for example in Zimbabwe and Kenya. Without this direct revenue from wild species, much habitat would have been converted to croplands. Zimbabwe, for example, has adopted a cost/benefit approach to maintaining large wild species. Similarly in Costa Rica, reserves such as the Monteverde Cloud Forest and Carrera National Park were established, in large part, because of ecotourism to see flagship species such as scarlet macaw (*Ara macao*), quetzal (*Paromachrus mocinno*) or howler monkey (*Alouatta caraya*).

Among the best-known species afforded some special status are game animals that are managed for sport hunting. The management of game animals forms an important part of the culture and history of most countries; for example much of the early exploration of North America and of Russia was solely to obtain the furs of animals for European trade. Management practices for game species have the goal of maximizing recreational use of the resource over the long-term. Techniques often involve two main courses of action: manipulations to create and maintain habitat, and direct population management. Habitat management is planned at two scales: site and landscape. Habitat management at the large scale involves maintaining certain amounts of habitat in age-classes preferred by a species over time across a landscape. In the case of moose or deer (*Cervidae*) species, managers sustain younger forest stages through logging. For capercaillie, large tracts of old forests are required and so stands may be withdrawn from harvest for a longer than normal rotation, or not harvested at all. At a finer scale, small cuts of a few hundred square meters to supply browse for ungulates may be an appropriate technique to improve the carrying capacity of traditional winter habitats. Other site-level techniques include selection logging and the use of herbicides to manage for long-term availability of cover species, maintaining buffer zones around areas known to be used for birth sites, and planning individual cuts to intersperse shelter and food.

Population management for game species employs modeling techniques to understand how age-specific mortality, altered sex ratios, and levels of predation may influence population growth or the production of certain age-classes, such as trophy males or breeding-aged females. Obtaining adequate data for accurate modeling requires substantial research, but for many game species a wealth of information exists and so models are reasonably accurate. Management of game populations is organized by management areas of several thousand square kilometers, where regulations are applied across the entire management unit, because game species are capable of considerable movement. High mortality in one portion of the management area is often compensated for by high net production elsewhere on the area. The management of game species has generally proven to be highly successful in meeting population objectives as a result of its long history of adaptive management based on research and modeling.

Game management and management for biodiversity need not be mutually exclusive, as long as the former is planned within the context of the latter. Many game species have large home ranges, and so it can be argued that maintaining populations of these species benefits a large array of other species simultaneously. This is a featured species approach that implicitly suggests if one species is present, then so too must other species that require the same general types of habitat. In Ontario, Canada, for example, the management agency argued that 70% of the vertebrate species of the province's boreal forest might benefit from management directed at enhancing moose populations (Ontario Environmental Assessment Board 1994). Moose then become an indicator for a large number of other species that use young forests. The benefits and drawbacks of using indicator species as an approach to forest management are considered next.

Indicator species

As agencies move to deal with the myriad species under their mandate to maintain biodiversity, attempts are being made to simplify the problem. A plausible simplification is to assume that if species A or ecosystem B changes in abundance, then so too do other species normally found in the same habitat as species A or associated with ecosystem B. In this context, species A and ecosystem B are indicators of some condition that is equally important to several species (Figure 13.2). The indicator concept has been used for more than 30 years, originally in aquatic systems to suggest levels of contamination. Use of indicators has now evolved to the international political level, as part of an effort by nations that export forest products to assure their clients that the wood was harvested sustainably. Under 'green labeling', a series of criteria and indicators are being developed independently by these countries or by auditing agencies, that if met, would supposedly indicate forest ecosystem replenishment, and would enable the 'certification' of forest products as having been produced sustainably. Although such indicators may be abiotic, here we consider the use of individual species.

At local levels, management of forests using indicator species to assess ecosystem function has great appeal because the concept bridges the natural tendency of managers to focus on species within the broader question of sustainable forestry. However, biologists are particularly adept at finding fault with suggested management techniques, and the use of indicators in terrestrial systems has been criticized rather extensively (Van Horne 1983, Verner 1984, Landres et al. 1988, Walker 1992, and see numerous papers in Verner et al. 1986). The major criticisms of management by indicator species are: species occupy different niches and so change in one species cannot directly indicate change in another; population regulatory mechanisms differ among species; demographic stochasticity; cascading effects of changes in populations of keystone species; and presence in a habitat type may not indicate optimality. Nonetheless, forests will continue to be logged, and so managers must continue to assess effects and mitigate change to the best extent possible. What better indicator species is there of an old-growth Douglas-fir (Pseudotsuga menziesii) forest than a certain density of large, old Douglas-fir trees? Animal species integrate structure and process within ecosystems at various scales depending on their body size, and so by their presence indicate the status of those structures and processes. Armed with a strong knowledge of natural history and population biology, and with an appreciation of the limitations of

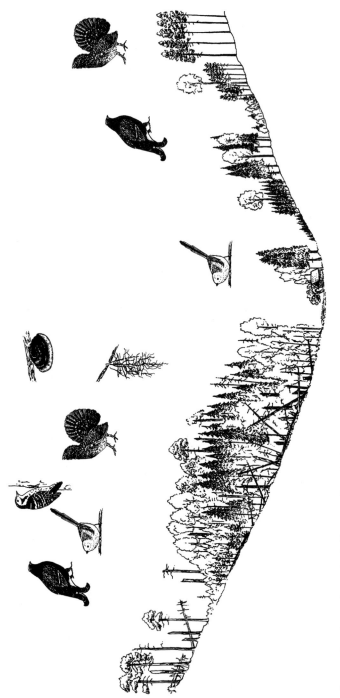

Fig. 13.2. Certain species can be 'indicators' of specific forest types, structures, and/or age classes. The left side of this figure depicts relationships between six species (black grouse, long-tailed tit, lesser spotted woodpecker, capercaillie, *Fomitopsis rosea*, *Usnea longissima*) and various conditions in an unmanaged landscape; three of these species find analogous conditions in the harvested landscape on the right.

management by indicator species, well-informed biologists can use indicator species as an integral part of a comprehensive approach to sustainable forest use and the conservation of biodiversity. Using species as indicators, as opposed to abiotic or integrative indicators such as ecosystems, also has considerable heuristic value in the education of the public and forest managers, because people can identify, visualize, and thus understand the effects of change on species.

Indicators may be used to suggest the effects of change within a system at particular scales, or to indicate population trends that result from altered ecological processes. Properties of dependable indicators have been suggested by Noss (1990) and Noss and Cooperrider (1994): the indicator must be a good surrogate for the objective (the objective should be explicit and well-understood); changes in the indicator should suggest a problem before it is too late to rectify (i.e., the species should be sensitive to forest management activities and dependent on forests for some stage of its life cycle); whenever possible a control should exist against which to measure change; there should be an accepted sampling protocol; the data collection should be cost effective; within bounds, detection of the indicator should be independent of sample size (except for a rare species); and whenever possible the species should be readily identifiable by the public. To that list we would add that species should reflect different trophic levels and a range of life histories. Choice of indicator species must reflect the scale of the objective, and so body size and migratory status should also be considered. We recommend among the suite of indicator species selected for a management area that few migratory animals be chosen. Populations of these species may be affected during migration and by habitat changes on the wintering grounds, making changes in numbers observed in the breeding habitats difficult to attribute to local conditions. Although endangered species may be, by definition, fine-filter indicators, we recommend that they not be chosen as indicators because of sampling problems related to small populations.

The choice of indicator species, and the number of indicators to choose is a difficult task for forest managers. Ideally, a suite of species would be chosen as indicators of forest change for each of the spatial scales important in forest management: tree or site, stand, forest, landscape, or region. Large-bodied indicator species that select habitat at large spatial scales may be indicative of change of coarse-grained features, such as at the forest and landscape levels; for example, moose, wolves, and mountain gorillas. Fine-grained indicator species are those species that are either of small body size and thus select habitat at small scales, or larger bodied species that either have narrow niches overall or require some special habitat feature. A good example is owls that nest in tree cavities. Use of species as fine-grained indicators requires detailed information about the particular species. Monitoring programs are a necessity to examine effects of management actions on indicator species relative to controls, and an adaptive management approach must be taken to the responses of indicators to perturbations. The use of indicator species in forest management is not a replacement for ecosystem management, but rather they form an integral component of such a program.

Integrating concerns for special species

We started this chapter by suggesting that the conservation of biological diversity, and managing for special species, are not mutually exclusive. We return now to that theme by suggesting that it is important from both a biological and heuristic perspective to manage for many species individually, but for different reasons. Species-based management has been criticized on the basis that biological diversity cannot be safeguarded by managing for each species because there are too many species to make this approach practical. We agree with that perspective, but suggest that many species must be managed individually, and ultimately, that a holistic approach to forest management can only be successful if species as well as ecosystems survive. The choice of which species become 'special' in a management context depends on many factors, including: whether or not the species plays a key role in an ecosystem, rarity, vulnerability to change, capability to indicate change, or economic importance. The major decision is which species to select, because using too many species in management planning will result in overly complex programs. We want to re-emphasize the point that for the task of species selection, there can be no substitute for people with strong backgrounds in natural history, who have considerable field experience, and an understanding of population biology.

The development of spatially explicit population models, through the application of geographic information systems, can substantially improve the strength of a combined species and ecosystems approach to forest management. These models may help to solve a problem that has long plagued forest management: the lack of experimental data on which to base management (Murphy and Noon 1991). Application of hypothesis testing, first through modeled spatial and temporal comparisons, and ultimately through controlled forest management programs, can enable pro-active adaptive management. One approach is based on attempts to reconstruct the history of forest tracts (e.g., Heinselman 1973), and then mapping past forest interventions through time. Using these maps as experimental treatments allows models to be constructed to test hypotheses of response by individual species. A second approach is to plan forest harvesting as an experiment, based on well-formed hypotheses (Walters and Holling 1990), and to follow how species react in time and space relative to expected results. Use of these modeling techniques will improve our capability to manage forests. Effects on individual species can be used to illustrate and communicate forest management techniques, and ultimately improved communication between researchers and managers will lead to better forest management.

Summary

Special species refers to those species that are either managed individually or monitored as indicators of some feature, as part of a holistic approach to maintaining biological diversity. Choice of species is guided by values attached by society, whether they play a key role in an ecosystem, or by their usefulness within a management strategy. Management for a species requires detailed information on habitat requirements so that active management can ensure sufficient habitat in space and time to ensure long-term survival. A major task facing forest managers lies in the selection of an appropriate suite of species to manage and monitor individually for their area. Each species chosen adds a degree of complexity and effort required in management planning. On the other hand, insufficient choices can lead to the potential for population endangerment. The loss of species is the ultimate of failures in the use of resources by humans.

Further readings

There is no shortage of reading materials available dealing with individual species that may be of interest. Journals such as *Conservation Biology*, *Biological Conservation*, *Journal of Wildlife Management*, and *BioScience* are replete with articles about the conservation of species. Ideas about the modeling of species and their habitats can be gained from Verner *et al.* (1986), and Morrison *et al.* (1992).

Literature cited

Åberg, J., G. Jansson, J. Swenson, and P. Angelstam. 1995. The effect of matrix on the occurrence of hazel grouse (*Bonasa bonasia*) in isolated habitat fragments. *Oecologia* **103**:265–9.

Andrén, H. 1994. Effects of habitat fragmentation on birds and mammals in landscapes with different proportions of suitable habitat: a review. *Oikos* **71**:355–66.

Angelstam, P., and G. Mikusinski. 1994. Woodpecker assemblages in natural and managed boreal and hemiboreal forest – a review. *Annales Zoologici Fennici* **31**:157–72.

Bascompte, J., and R. V. Solé. 1996. Habitat fragmentation and extinction thresholds in spatially explicit models. *Journal of Animal Ecology* **65**:465–73.

Belovsky, G. E., J. A. Bissonette, R. D. Dueser, T. C. Edwards, C. M. Luecke, M. E. Ritchie, J. B. Slade, and F. H. Wagner. 1994. Management of small populations: concepts affecting the recovery of endangered species. *Wildlife Society Bulletin* **22**:307–16.

Bergerud, A. T. 1974. Decline of caribou in North America following settlement. *Journal of Wildlife Management* **38**:757–70.

Bergerud, A. T., and F. Manuel. 1968. Moose damage to balsam fir-white birch forests in central Newfoundland. *Journal of Wildlife Management* **32**:729–46.

Boyce, M. S. 1992. Population viability analysis. *Annual Review of Ecology and Systematics* **23**:481–506.

Carlson, A., and I. Stenberg. 1995. *Vitryggig hackspett (Dendrocopos leucotos) – biotopval och sårbarhetsanalys*. Department of Wildlife Ecology Report 27, Swedish University of Agricultural Sciences, Uppsala. (In Swedish)

Caro, T. M., and M. K. Laurenson. 1994. Ecological and genetic factors in conservation: a cautionary tale. *Science* **263**:485–6.

Chubbs, T. E., L. B. Keith, S. P. Mahoney, and M. J. McGrath. 1993. Responses of woodland caribou to clearcutting in east-central Newfoundland. *Canadian Journal of Zoology* **71**:487–493.

Cumming, H. G., and D. B. Beange. 1987. Dispersion and movements of woodland caribou near Lake Nipigon, Ontario. *Journal of Wildlife Management* **51**:69–79.

Darby, W. R., and L. S. Duquette. 1986. Woodland caribou and forestry in northern Ontario, Canada. *Rangifer*, Special Issue **1**:87–93.

Elmes, G. W. 1991. Ant colonies and environmental disturbance. *Symposium Zoological Society London* **63**:1–13.

Enoksson, B., P. Angelstam, and K. Larsson. 1995. Deciduous trees and resident birds – the problem of fragmentation within a coniferous landscape. *Landscape Ecology* **10**:257–75.

Esseen, P.-A., K.-E, Renhorn, and R. B. Pettersson. 1996. Epiphytic lichen biomass in managed and old-growth boreal forests: effect of branch quality. *Ecological Applications* **6**:228–38.

Frumhoff, P. C. 1995. Conserving wildlife in tropical forests managed for timber. *BioScience* **45**:456–64.

Hansson, L. (ed.) 1997. Boreal ecosystems and landscapes – structures, functions and conservation of biodiversity. *Ecological Bulletins* **46**.

Hedrick, P. W. 1995. Gene flow and genetic restoration: the Florida panther as a case study. *Conservation Biology* **9**:996–1007.

Heinselman, M. L. 1973. Fire in the virgin forests of the Boundary Waters Canoe Area, Minnesota. *Quarternary Research* **3**:329–82.

Holldobler, B., and E. O. Wilson. 1990. *The Ants*. Belknap Press, Cambridge University Press, Cambridge. 736 pp.

Hörnberg, S. 1995. *Moose density related to occurrence and consumption of different forage species in Sweden*. Department of Forest Survey, Swedish University of Agricultural Sciences. Report 58.

Hultkrantz L., and S. Wibe. 1989. *Skogsnäringen: Miljöfrågor, avreglering, framtidsutsikter*. Bilaga 8 till Långtidsutredningen, 1990. SOU. Finansdepartementet, Stockholm.

IUCN. 1994. *IUCN Red List Categories*. IUCN Species Survival Commission, 40th Meeting, Gland, Switzerland. 21 pp.

Jones, C. G., J. H. Lawton, and M. Shachak. 1994. Organisms as ecosystems engineers. *Oikos* **69**:373–86.

Karström, M. 1992. Steget före i det glömda landet. *Svensk Botanisk Tidskrift* **86**:115–46.

Krebs, C. J. 1985. *Ecology: the Experimental Analysis of Distribution and Abundance*. Harper and Row, New York.

Kuusinen, M. 1996. *Epiphytic lichen flora and diversity in old-growth boreal forests of Finland*. Ph.D. thesis, Publications in Botany from the University of Helsinki 23.

Landres, P .B., J. Verner, and J. W. Thomas. 1988. Ecological uses of vertebrate indicator species: a critique. *Conservation Biology* **2**:316–28.

Laurance, W. F., and E. Yensen. 1991. Predicting impacts of edge effects of fragmented habitats. *Biological Conservation* **55**:77–92.

Lavsund S. 1987. Moose relationships to forestry in Finland, Norway and Sweden. *Swedish Wildlife Research*, Supplement **1**:229–44.

Leopold, A. 1933. *Game Management*. Charles Scribners Sons, New York. 481 pp.

Levins, R. 1969. Some demographic consequences of environmental heterogeneity for biological control. *Bulletin of the Entomological Society of America* **15**:237–40.

Lovejoy, T. E., R. O Bierregaard, A. B. Rylands, J. R. Malcolm, C. E. Quintela, L. H. Harper, K. S. Brown, A. H. Powell, G. V. N. Powell, H. O. R. Schubart, and M. B. Hays. 1986. Edge and other effects of isolation on Amazon forest fragments. Pp. 257–85 in M. Soulé (ed.). *Conservation Biology: the Science of Scarcity and Diversity*. Sinauer Press, Sunderland Massachusetts.

Malcolm, S. B., and M. P. Zalucki. 1993. *Biology and Conservation of the Monarch Butterfly*. Natural History Museum of Los Angeles County. Los Angeles, California.

Mills, L. S., M. E. Soulé, and D. F. Doak. 1993. The keystone-species concept in ecology and conservation. *BioScience* **43**:219–24.

Morrison, M. L., B. G. Marcot, and R. W. Mannan. 1992. *Wildlife–habitat Relationships: Concepts and Applications*. University of Wisconsin Press, Madison, WI. 343pp.

Murphy, D. D., and B. D. Noon. 1991. Coping with uncertainty in wildlife biology. *Journal of Wildlife Management* **55**:773–82.

Naiman, R. J., J. M. Melillo, and J. M. Hobbie. 1986. Ecosystem alteration of boreal forest streams by beaver. *Ecology* **67**:1254–69.

Noss, R. F. 1990. Indicators for monitoring biodiversity: a hierarchical approach. *Conservation Biology* **4**:355–64.

Noss, R. F. and A. Y. Cooperrider. 1994. *Saving Nature's Legacy: Protecting and Restoring Biodiversity*. Island Press, Washington, DC. 416 pp.

Ontario Environmental Assessment Board. 1994. *Class environmental assessment by the Ministry of Natural Resources for timber management on Crown lands in Ontario*. Toronto, Ontario, Canada. EA-87–02.

Paine, R. T. 1966. Food web complexity and species diversity. *American Naturalist* **100**:65–75.

Pimm, S. L. 1991. *The Balance of Nature?* University of Chicago Press, Chicago, IL. 434 pp.

Power, M. E., D. Tilman, J. A. Estes, B. A. Menge, W. J. Bond, L. S. Mills, G. Daily, J. C. Castilla, J. Lubchenco, and R. T. Paine. 1996. Challenges in the quest for keystones. *BioScience* **46**:609–20.

Puntilla, P., Y. Haila, J. Niemela, and T. Pajunen. 1994. Ant communities in fragments of old-growth taiga and managed surroundings. *Annales Zoologici Fennici* **31**:131–44.

Rabinowitz, D., S. Cairns and T. Dillon. 1986. Seven forms of rarity and their frequency in the flora of the British Isles. Pp. 182–201 in M. Soulé (ed.). *Conservation Biology: the Science of Scarcity and Diversity*. Sinauer Press, Sunderland Massachusetts.

Rolstad, J., and P. Wegge. 1987. Distribution and size of capercaillie leks in relation to old forest fragmentation. *Oecologia* **72**:389–94.

Seal, U. S. 1994. *A plan for genetic restoration and management of the Florida panther*. Report to the US Fish and Wildlife Service. Conservation Breeding Specialist Group. SSC/IUCN, Apple Valley, Minnesota.

Seip, D. R. 1992. Factors limiting woodland caribou populations and their interrelationships with wolves and moose in southeastern British Columbia. *Canadian Journal of Zoology* **70**:1494–503.

Simberloff, D. 1995. Habitat fragmentation and population extinction of birds. *Ibis* **137**:S105–S111.

Sjöberg, K. 1996. Modern forestry and the capercaillie. Pp. 111–35 in R. DeGraaf and R. I. Miller (eds). *Conservation of Faunal Diversity in Forested Landscapes*. Chapman and Hall, London.

Sjöberg, K., and L. Ericson. 1992. Forested and open wetlands. Pp. 326–51 in L. Hansson (ed.). *Ecological Principles of Nature Conservation*. Elsevier, London.

Sweanor, P. 1987. *Winter ecology of a Swedish moose population: social behavior, migration and dispersal.* Department of Wildlife Ecology, Swedish University of Agricultural Sciences, Report 13.

Temple, S. A. 1986. Predicting impacts of habitat fragmentation on forest birds: a comparison of two models. Pp. 301–4 in J. Verner, M. L. Morrison, and C. J. Ralph (eds). *Wildlife 2000: Modeling Habitat Relationships of Terrestrial Vertebrates.* University of Wisconsin Press, Madison, WI.

Terbourgh, J. 1986. Community aspects of frugivory in tropical forests. Pp. 371–84 in A. Estrada and T. H. Fleming (eds). *Frugivores and Seed Dispersal.* Dr. W. Junk, Dordrecht.

1989. *Where have All the Birds Gone?* Princeton University Press, Princeton, NJ. 207 pp.

Thomas, J. W., E. D. Forsman, J. B. Lint, E. C. Meslow, B. R. Noon, and J. Verner. 1990. *A conservation strategy for the northern spotted owl.* US Department of Interior Bureau of Land Management, Fish and Wildlife Service, and National Park Service, Portland, Oregon.

Thompson, I. D., and W. J. Curran. 1993. A reexamination of moose damage to balsam fir–white birch forests in central Newfoundland: 27 years later. *Canadian Journal of Zoology* **23**:1388–95.

Thompson, I. D., W. J. Curran, J. A. Hancock, and C. E. Butler. 1992. Influence of moose browsing on succesional forest growth on black spruce sites in Newfoundland. *Forest Ecology and Management* **47**:29–37.

Thompson, L., C. D. Thomas, J. M. A. Radley, S. Williamson, and J. H. Lawton. 1993. The effect of earthworms and snails in a simple plant community. *Oecologia* **95**:171–8.

Tilman, D., R. M. May, C. L. Lehman, and M. Nowak. 1994. Habitat destruction and the extinction debt. *Nature* **371**:65–6.

Van Horne, B. 1983. Density as a misleading indicator of habitat quality. *Journal of Wildlife Management* **47**:893–901.

Verner, J. 1984. The guild concept applied to management of bird populations. *Environmental Management* **8**:1–14.

Verner, J., M. L. Morrison, and C. J. Ralph (eds). 1986. *Wildlife 2000: Modeling Habitat Relationships of Terrestrial Vertebrates.* University of Wisconsin Press, Madison, WI. 470 pp.

Virkkala, R., A. Rajasärkkä, R. A. Väisänen, M. Vickholm, and E. Virolainen. 1994. Conservation value of nature reserves: do hole-nesting birds prefer protected forests in southern Finland. *Annales Zoologici Fennici* **31**:173–86.

Voigt, D. R., G. Deyne, M. Malhoit, B. Snider, R. Stefanski, and M. Strickland. 1992. *White-tailed deer in Ontario: background to a policy.* Ontario Ministry Natural Resources, Wildlife Policy Branch, Toronto. 83 pp.

Walker, B. H. 1992. Biodiversity and ecological redundancy. *Conservation Biology* **6**:18–23.

Walters, C. J., and C. S. Holling. 1990. Large-scale management experiments and learning by doing. *Ecology* **71**:2060–8.

14 Genetic diversity

CONSTANCE I. MILLAR

Genetic diversity rarely makes headline news. Whereas species extinctions, loss of old-growth forests, and catastrophic forest fires are readily grasped public issues, genetic diversity is often perceived as arcane and academic. Yet genes are the fundamental unit of biodiversity, the raw material for evolution, and the ultimate source of all variation among plants and animals on earth (Dobzhansky 1970, Soulé and Wilcox 1980). Why then have they escaped central attention in conservation? Although genes are pervasive, controlling individual fates and determining offspring destinies, they are minuscule molecules, unyielding to meaningful direct observation even through a microscope: their direct structures and functions are essentially invisible. Over the decades we have learned about their existence and significance indirectly by studying the effects that genes have on individuals, populations, and species. Because genes are passed among generations in mathematically predictable ways, we have developed a towering theoretical understanding of the way genes ought to work in nature (Wright 1978). Increasingly we are able to penetrate the nature of genes directly, through biochemical and molecular analysis (Figure 14.1; Nei 1987, Neale and Harry 1994). We are beginning, dimly, to perceive empirical connections between changes in gene pool diversity and species declines, changes in forest health, and loss of ecosystem productivity. This cumulative knowledge teaches us that attention to genetic diversity will pay off in achieving the goals of forest conservation.

With an emphasis on North American conifers, this chapter presents general approaches to conserving forest gene pools and provides examples illustrating how genetic management can be integrated within other conservation efforts.

Genes as the foundation of biodiversity

Genetic diversity may be mostly hidden to the naked eye, but when illuminated through genetic study, its variation and structure are complex.

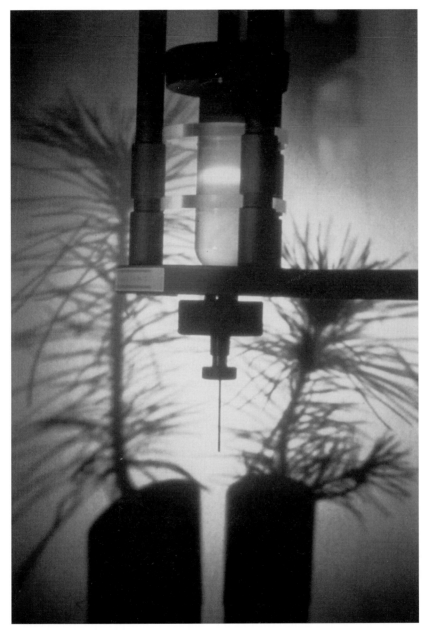

Fig. 14.1. DNA, the basic molecule of inheritance, extracted from sugar pine (*Pinus lambertiana*) and visible with ethidium-bromide staining. (From Conkle 1986.) (P. Hodgskiss photo)

Genetic differences exist at many levels. Most obvious are the myriad differences that exist among individuals. Because of the way groups of individuals tend to become isolated and interbreed, genetic differences evolve that distinguish groups of individuals at many scales: for instance, among populations, among ecotypes or local strains, among geographic races or subspecies, and among species, genera, taxonomic families, and so on. Whereas mutation and recombination (primarily events occurring at cell division and in sexual reproduction) are the main sources of new genetic diversity among individuals, ecological effects, such as natural selection, gene flow, and genetic drift are the major architects of genetic patterns among groups. These forces are described in more detail below.

Although genetic differences distinguish species and higher taxonomic levels, genetic diversity usually refers to the genetic variation that exists within species (the *gene pool*). From the conservation standpoint, efforts to maintain biodiversity ideally blend seamlessly from the gene to the species to community levels. In practice, these are often separated and too often uncoordinated. In this chapter, I focus on genetic diversity within species, yet try to show the connection of genetic conservation to other biodiversity management levels. Natural diversity of genes within and among populations, ecotypes, and subspecies, movements of genes between them, and changes in gene pool compositions over time are the focus of forest genetic conservation efforts.

INFLUENCES ON GENETIC DIVERSITY

Many forces influence the dynamics of composition and structure in gene pools. When these are natural forces and natural changes, we call the process evolution. Mutations, or mistakes in DNA replications, occur as changes to the structure of DNA. Mutations occur with low but consistent frequency, from about 1 in 1000 to 1 in 1 000 000 cell divisions. Ultimately mutations are the source of all new genetic variation in nature, both detrimental and beneficial. Once new alleles arise by mutation, they are assorted and distributed among individuals by recombination, which leads to the remarkable diversity among individuals that exists even within families.

How individuals mate strongly influences the fate of genetic variation, both within and among populations. For instance, regular inbreeding (which some species do) or mating among individuals within a local population, leads to individuals within populations being genetically similar, but isolated groups becoming different. By contrast, regularly outbreeding species, especially those like conifers whose genes travel far and wide, have high variation within populations, but the populations remain rather similar due to the mixing effects of gene flow (long-distance dispersal of genes).

Natural selection is, of course, the grand architect. Individuals either survive or die, pass on many offspring or few, based on their ability to survive and function in their particular local habitats. Those individuals whose suite of genetic characteristics provides them with advantages, such as surviving extreme weather, attracting mates, or avoiding predation, produce more offspring on average than those more unlucky (Hartl 1988). The reason that these genetically endowed individuals only win 'on average' rather than always is because of chance. Many chance events, collectively called genetic drift, occur within natural populations and affect genetic compositions, from the roll-of-the-dice probabilities of recombination during sexual reproduction to events such as wildfires randomly burning some populations and not others (Patton and Feder 1981). These are much more likely to have large effects in small populations (including rare species) than where population sizes are large (Hudson 1991). Chance events aside, the advantages accumulating over generations, however, that result from natural selection translate into tremendous adaptations of individuals to local environments. They also result in adaptations of groups of populations to regionally distinct environments. When gene flow among groups is diminished, for example by groups being geographically isolated (e.g., by mountain ranges, or just enough distance), natural selection over time leads to the evolution of ecotypes, geographic races, and subspecies (e.g., Clausen et al. 1940, Antonovics et al. 1971, Daly and Patton 1990). Genetic conservation seeks to maintain both the widest set of adaptations that have evolved within species as well as the continuing potential of populations to adapt to ever-changing new environments.

Human actions almost always have some consequence on gene pools and evolution (Stern and Roche 1974, Schonewald-Cox et al. 1983, Ledig 1991, Hedrick and Miller 1992, Baradat et al. 1995). They may mimic natural influences, exceed them in rate of change or strength of selection, or show novel effects. Some consequences are minor compared with background genetic changes; some far overwhelm the path of evolution.

In general, activities of greatest concern to management are those that change the direction and rate of natural selection and gene flow significantly. Some affect gene pools directly, others indirectly. Some activities are likely to have significant genetic effects. These include activities that:

- add or remove a significant number of individuals from natural populations (e.g., tree, grass, or forb planting, fish stocking, timber harvest, fishing and hunting);
- significantly change population sizes (especially decrease) of native species (e.g., livestock grazing, land clearing and habitat type conversions, biological control);
- eliminate populations, especially systematically from portions of a species range (e.g., by urban development, dam construction);
- move individuals among ecologically distinct locations (e.g., ecological restoration, fish stocking);
- significantly alter sex ratios, number of breeding individuals, reproductive capacity, fecundity, viability of individuals, or survival and mortality of certain age classes (e.g., grazing, timber harvest, fire suppression);
- introduce disease vectors or insect pests, especially those that are non-native (made worse by roads, trails and other access points into native populations);
- significantly increase the potential for hybridization over what would occur naturally (e.g., tree planting or introducing non-local germplasm);
- fragment populations such that gene flow is drastically reduced; conversely, alter population structure such that formerly isolated populations regularly interbreed (e.g., road and dam construction);
- disrupt or significantly alter meta-population structure and other geographic patterns and related processes (timber harvest, fish stocking, dam construction).

By and large we lack data on actual genetic effects of these activities and our predictions about their significance come from population-genetic theory (Ledig 1988, 1991, Hedrick and Miller 1992). In the few cases where we have data, we find that the actual genetic consequences depend on how each activity is conducted. With timber harvest, for example, the type of cutting and intensity, the phenotype and ages of trees cut and the season of harvest, may have different genetic effects. Where ecologically appropriate silvicultural procedures have been applied, no significant changes in genetic frequencies have been found (Savolainen and Karkkainen 1991). Similarly, studies have shown no significant changes in gene frequencies have occurred due to normal nursery and outplanting practices for forest trees (Campbell and Sorenson 1984, Kitzmiller 1990). In the case of air pollution's effect on genetic diversity, however, there is some evidence that human-caused atmospheric effects cause changes in allelic proportions within populations, although the ecological or evolutionary significance of these changes has not been easily interpreted (Hertel and Ewald 1995).

Genetic conservation

Forest genetic conservation focuses on managing the current and future condition of genes in forest species for the purpose of influencing the health and adaptability of individuals, populations, and species. Although genetic conservation is usually associated with maintaining biodiversity and restoring ecosystems (the context of this book), there are other equally important goals. Maintenance of genetic diversity has been advocated in contexts of crop breeding and animal husbandry (Frankel and Soulé 1981), experimental research (e.g., *Drosophila*, Dobzhansky 1970), maintaining indigenous cultivars and wild relatives of crop plants for agriculture (Oldfield 1984), and for medicinal (e.g., Pacific yew, *Taxus brevifolia*, for cancer drugs; Wheeler 1996) and horticultural uses (Oldfield 1984). Key early work in wildland genetic conservation was done to benefit breeding and production programs for commercial forest trees and fish. In these cases, maintenance of genetic diversity was paramount to success of these programs (e.g., for trees, Zobel 1977, Libby, 1973, Ledig 1988), and provided early insights into the importance of local origins and genetic-adaptation zones, maintenance of diversity, potential problems of inbreeding, and contamination from poorly adapted stocks. The information that developed in these breeding and production contexts provided an important foundation of knowledge, which has proved valuable for developing genetic conservation goals within biodiversity protection contexts.

GOALS FOR GENETIC CONSERVATION WITHIN A BIODIVERSITY CONTEXT

Environmental challenge comes to individuals and groups of native species in many forms. These range from 'expected' events, such as predation, disturbance, and succession (fire, disease), to chance events or long-term changes such as volcanic eruptions, climate change, or human impacts. In forest genetic conservation we attempt to maintain genetic diversity and evolutionary processes so that individuals and populations of native species retain their resiliences to changes in the short- and long-term. There is no single approach or one right way to practice genetic conservation, because there are so many different management objectives of forested lands. Specific applications require that genetic goals be integrated with local and regional management objectives to determine appropriate actions (Ingram 1996).

Genetic conservation optimally involves a combination of *ex situ* and *in* situ practices. In *ex situ* conservation, germplasm (seeds, pollen, whole plants and animals, sperm, and other genetic propagules) is removed from native habitats and preserved in storage, such as refrigeration, dehydration, cryopreservation, or as whole plants in nursery plantations (Oldfield 1984, National Resource Council 1991, Millar 1993). Although these tissues prove useful for genetic analysis, the main purpose is to store genes in a safe environment and make them available as needed for reintroduction or augmentation of natural populations. For example, in the late 1980s, the rare Torrey pine (*Pinus torreyana*) was threatened by a bark beetle epidemic, which caused many drought-weakened trees to die. Germplasm was needed to restore the greatly diminished population. Seeds collected years earlier from a large number of healthy trees in the same population were used for restoration (Ledig 1991). Approaches to gene sampling and maintenance of genes *ex situ* have been designed to meet such conservation goals (Bonner 1990, Brown and Briggs 1991, Center for Plant Conservation 1991, Eriksson 1995).

A drawback to *ex situ* methods is that genes are preserved in a static condition with no opportunity for continuing adaptation to dynamic environments (Soule and Wilcox 1980, Oldfield 1984). The environments for reintroduction change (due to climate, pathogen or insect, or anthropogenic pressures) while the germplasm is in storage, causing samples to 'slip behind' evolutionarily. Further, potential losses to germplasm while in storage, such as seed or sperm death, reduce the value of the collections for restoration. Practical concerns that collections might be lost accidentally due to fire or technological breakdown cannot be underestimated. For instance, fires burned the seed storage facility not once but twice at the Centro de Genetica Forestal in Chapingo, Mexico, devastating irreplaceable germplasm collections and burning research labs and storage buildings. Despite the limitations and risks, however, storage of germplasm in various ways is a critical element in integrated gene conservation programs (Falk and Holsinger 1991).

Genetic conservation for maintenance of biodiversity is usually practiced through many *in situ* approaches, that is, where natural populations are managed to achieve genetic conservation goals (Ledig 1988, Holsinger and Gottlieb 1991, Adams *et al.* 1992, Baradat *et al.* 1995). This can range from establishing single-purpose genetic conservation areas to developing genetic management prescriptions for lands that are actively managed for other purposes, such as production forestry or recreation. *In situ* gene conservation comes into consideration in designing nature reserves (e.g., biosphere reserves, natural areas), protecting populations of rare or endangered species, restoring species, habitats, and communities, planning or mitigating activities that manipulate native populations of plants and animals (e.g., harvesting, grazing, fish stocking), or in restoring populations after natural disturbances such as flood and fire. Discussions that follow emphasize *in situ* conservation.

MEASURING GENETIC DIVERSITY

Any decision to develop genetic conservation or genetic management plans implies there is a known or suspected concern for impacts to gene pools, and a desire to protect species from assumed detrimental genetic effects. Because species vary widely in their genetic attributes and in susceptibility to management actions and situations (e.g., prescribed fire, tree harvest, ecological restoration), this decision presupposes that knowledge about the genetic structure of species and its potential vulnerability is available or can be measured or inferred.

By and large, genetic variation is hidden to the eye of the general observer, and is effectively revealed only through expensive and time-consuming methods (see reviews in Adams *et al*. 1992, Boyle and Boontawee 1995, Baradat *et al*. 1995, Hunter 1996). It is tempting to consider counting the frequency of individuals in a sample having readily observed morphological variants (e.g., specific flower or fur color) and assume this represents genetic variation. If counts are made on individuals in wild populations, however, the resulting frequencies combine both genetic and environmental influences, and only those few traits unaffected by environmental variation will yield genetic information.

To detect heritable variation in these traits (i.e., genetic diversity) requires much more work. 'Common garden' tests or captive rearing projects must be done subject to experimental controls (such as replication and randomization), with the age of individuals and the environment in which they are raised kept uniform among all individuals (Figure 14.2). Common-garden studies to determine genetically based variation in plants are relatively straight-forward but take many years (decades, in some cases) to yield useful information. Pedigree analysis in animals also takes many years, requiring several generations in captivity with controlled breeding. Further, although these tests reveal general and indirect information about genetic variance, they do not yield direct information about gene or genotype frequencies.

Genetic diversity can also be measured at the molecular and biochemical levels, which involves detecting variants in, for instance, DNA, RNA,

Fig. 14.2. Variation in height among equal-aged white fir (*Abies concolor*) plants growing in a common plantation in California, USA. Seedlings collected from throughout white fir's range in western North America were planted together, and over the years the differences that were observed reflect genetic differences both among individuals and among groups of individuals adapted to different parts of the species range. Seedlings from two populations shown here come from populations at 2380 m (left) and 975 m (right) in the Sierra Nevada (Libby *et al.* 1980). (C. I. Millar photo)

isoenzymes, terpenes, and flavonoids (Clegg 1990, Neale and Harry 1994). Some of these are under strong genetic control, allowing genetic diversity to be directly measured. For example, DNA and isozymes do not appear to be modified by the environment in which organisms are living, and samples from an organism of any age and any site can be taken directly from the field and reliably yield a genetic interpretation (i.e., a common-garden test or captive rearing is unnecessary) (Figure 14.3). Although they require sophisticated laboratory equipment and experienced geneticists for interpretation, these methods do give genetic information about specific genes, are relatively rapid, and can often be consistently applied across taxa.

Unfortunately the relationships among the various kinds of genetic data (morphological, biochemical, and molecular) are difficult to interpret (Asins and Carbonell 1987, Adams *et al.* 1992, Baradat *et al.* 1995). Different genetic traits (and different approaches to measuring them) regularly yield different patterns of genetic architecture. This is likely due to differing evolutionary and ecological influences on different genes. For

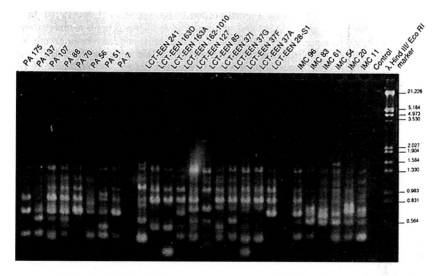

Fig. 14.3. Molecular (DNA) variation among 25 accessions of *Theobroma cacao* as determined by polymerase chain reaction (PCR) techniques, whereby differences in low-copy genes can be assessed. (From Russell *et al.* 1995.)

genetic conservation, genes actually or potentially affecting survival and fitness are most important. Some morphological or physiological traits (e.g., body or foliar weight, drought or frost resistance) seem to reflect adaptive variation, and thus reveal important information for conservation.

By contrast, the adaptive or ecological significance of many sequences of DNA or isoenzyme variants is unknown. For this reason, the latter are referred to as marker genes, meaning that, to a certain degree, they indicate (or mark) the nature of genes that may be of greater interest but are intractable to analysis. For many of these genes, although we may know the specific function of a gene we are measuring (e.g., an enzyme in the Kreb's Cycle), we have little idea of the physiological role played by the variants that we can measure. Variants in marker genes generally seem to have relatively neutral or minor adaptive values, and tend to reflect events in a species' evolutionary history, such as colonizing events, bottlenecks, and other chance effects rather than natural selection. Our ability to evaluate the condition and vulnerability of a gene pool is thus compromised by our inability to understand the specific physiological importance of the genetic variants we are most able to detect.

Because of these limitations, direct analyses have been undertaken for only a small number of taxa, especially those species of special interest, such as commercial forest trees or rare and endangered species of high conservation visibility. Because measuring genetic diversity is expensive and time-consuming, indirect approaches have been sought as alternatives to direct analysis. In plants, such studies have indicated that weak but significant correlations exist between genetic architecture and some life-history traits. For instance, Hamrick and his associates (see Hamrick and Godt 1990, Hamrick 1983, Hamrick et al. 1979) reviewed statistical correlations in 400 plant species between isozyme diversity and features such as geographic range, longevity, seed-dispersal mechanisms, and mating system (Table 14.1). Although these correlations are useful at a general level, they provide little help when evaluating individual populations or species because of the many exceptions that exist (i.e., the weak regression among genetic diversity and life-history traits).

Clearly we are still learning about the relationships among the questions we ask, the genetic data we collect, and the adaptive, evolutionary, and conservation implications of these data. It is important for natural resource managers to be aware of the biases of different types of genetic variation, and the difficulties in interpreting their significance before assessing vulnerability or making management prescriptions. Significantly, information is lacking about current and historic genetic structure for most forest species (except a few of high significance), and will likely remain this way in the future. In regard to wildland taxa, we are in the position where genetic assessments, vulnerabilities, and priority setting must, for the time being, be based primarily on inferred consequences rather than on empirical measurements.

SETTING PRIORITIES FOR GENETIC CONSERVATION

Sometimes priorities are obvious. For instance, a species listed as endangered must be evaluated for genetic vulnerability prior to a project approval. Or, a set of species is targeted for ecological restoration, and genetic guidelines for these taxa at specific sites must be determined. In other cases, priorities are not targeted nor obvious. Rather, conservation planners are faced with the daunting challenge of how to address genetic conservation at a bioregional scale, where thousands of taxa (i.e., natural ecosystems filled with abundant native plants and animals, including invertebrates, fungi, etc.) must be considered. Allocating priorities among the conservation needs let alone genetic issues, and winnowing the list of many taxa and their genetic subunits (ecotypes, races, important populations) down to a manageable number, becomes an essential task.

Setting priorities for genetic management begins by identifying those

Table 14.1. *Correlations of genetic variation with life history characteristics as an indirect approach to measuring genetic variation. Upper figure: within species; middle figure: among populations, and lower figure: within populations*

| Correlates with genetic variation within plant species[a] | | |
Trait[b]	Highest level	Lowest level
Geographic range	Widespread	Endemic
Life form	Long-lived, woody perennials	Short-lived perennials
Breeding system	Mixed mating, wind pollinated	Mixed maint, animal pollinated
Seed-dispersal mechanism	Attached	Explosive
Taxonomic status	Gymnosperms	Dicots
Regional distribution	Boreal-temperate	Tropical or temperate
Mode of reproduction	Sexual	Sexual and asexual
Successional status	Late successional	Mid successional

| Correlates with genetic variation among populations within plant species[a] | | |
Trait[b]	Highest level	Lowest level
Breeding system	Self-pollinated	Outcrossing, wind pollinated
Life form	Annuals	Long-lived, woody perennials
Seed-dispersal mechanism	Gravity dispersed	Gravity attached
Successional status	Early successional	Late successional
Taxonomic status	Dicots	Gymnosperms
Regional distribution	Temperate	Boreal-temperate

| Correlates with genetic variation within populations of plant species[a] | | |
Trait[b]	Highest level	Lowest level
Breeding system	Mixed mating, wind pollinated	Self-pollinated
Geographic range	Widespread	Endemic
Life form	Long-lived, woody perennials	All others
Taxonomic status	Gymnosperms	Dicots
Seed-dispersal mechanisms	Attached	Explosive
Regional distribution	Boreal-temperatures	Temperate or tropical
Successional status	Late successional	Early successional

Notes:
[a] Derived from Hamrick and Godt 1990; Hamrick *et al.* 1979.
[b] Traits are arranged in approximate order of their strength of correlation with genetic variation. Thus, breeding systems and geographic range are very strongly correlated with genetic variation within populations, but successional status is only mildly related.

taxa which, by virtue of inherent or evolutionary condition, specific social value, or conservation vulnerability, deserve special attention (Millar and Libby 1991). In the former category, taxa would be targeted for specific genetic conservation evaluation if there are:

- evolutionarily distinct taxa, such as the sole representative of a genus or family in an area, marginal populations, populations at extremes of distribution limits or outside the primary range, unusual ecotypes, or populations containing individuals with unusual attributes (distinct morphologies);
- ecologically distinct situations, such as species or populations outside the expected ecological conditions, unusually diverse communities, extremely rare taxa, unusual hybrid populations.

Species may also be considered separately for genetic conservation when they have unique value to humans, such as:

- species or populations of actual or potential medicinal, horticultural, agricultural, or agronomic importance, including wild relatives of domesticated species;
- taxa of value to indigenous cultures;
- taxa of value to production industries, such as commercial forest trees and sport fisheries;
- taxa of value to wildland reclamation, such as grasses and soil stabilizers.

Sometimes genetic risk comes to a species by management context rather than inherent in its evolutionary or ecological conditions. Candidates for special attention include those populations and species with urgent conservation liabilities, specifically those species or populations whose existence is threatened or endangered by some human activities. In addition, there are many management situations or activities which, because of their potential to detrimentally affect gene pools, act as a red flag signaling a need to evaluate genetic effects and plan mitigative management. In general, these include actions that could lead to significant:

- changes in genetic diversity (losses are likely most risky, but increases in diversity can also lead to loss of adaptability);
- changes in populations sizes;
- changes in mating structure (e.g., reductions in population sizes can lead to increased inbreeding, which for many species is detrimental);
- disruption of natural patterns of gene exchange among populations (fragmentation on one hand, merging formerly isolated populations on the other);
- systematic losses of populations in particular habitat zones (e.g., at low elevations, on distinct soils, at extremes of range distribution);
- at the landscape and regional levels losses of ecotypic, racial, or subspecies diversity;

- gene contamination, that is, non-local genes being incorporated into native, local populations;
- intraspecific or interspecific hybridization and introgression that would not occur naturally.

Management practices or land uses that could lead to these effects include actions noted earlier that significantly add individuals to, or remove individuals of native species from, natural populations; introduce exotic species; add individuals of native species adjacent to natural populations; move individuals from place to place; and activities that significantly change number of breeding individuals, demography, reproductive behavior, or natural mortality. Specific examples of practices include:

> timber harvest; tree, shrub, or grass breeding; wildlife habitat improvement; land development; fire suppression, prescribed fire, ecological restoration and reclamation; fish planting and other wildlife introductions; forest tree planting; livestock grazing; forest health control; road and dam construction.

None of these practices or methods in and of itself leads to detrimental genetic effects. When applied prudently, many may have no significant effect, although this depends on the species targeted. However, if management is poorly thought out, or if genetic effects are ignored during planning for these activities, undesired consequences are more likely.

GENERAL GENETIC CONSERVATION GUIDELINES

Given the goal of maintaining genetic diversity for short- and long-term adaptability, the primary objective for genetic conservation is to maintain natural levels of genetic diversity and genetic processes (gene flow, natural selection, etc.) at the individual, population, race, and species level. For species of concern or management situations identified as high risk, specific attention may be needed. Developing genetic conservation plans for these situations requires an approach tailored to the species and the context. The potential for risk depends on the genetic profile of the populations, including the amount of information known about its genetic structure and function, its general reproductive fitness and ecological conditions relative to other native taxa, nature of environmental challenges, and specific details of the proposed action. Because of unique circumstances in these cases, management takes different forms. One approach is outlined below for sugar pine (Pinus lambertiana).

In situations where otherwise non-vulnerable taxa are at risk due to specific management or land-use circumstances, general guidelines have been developed to aid management (Box 14.1). These focus on the goals of

BOX 14.1 **General management guidelines for maintaining genetic diversity in situations where it may be threatened or at risk.**

I.   When introducing individuals into natural habitats:, (e.g., tree or grass planting, species reintroductions, biological control):

– Use germplasm from local donor populations that are geographically close and ecologically similar to those of the introduction site. Determining what is local depends on the species and context, but is related to the size of genetic neighborhoods, selection gradients, and historic events.
– Collect donor germplasm from local populations that are large, viable, uncontaminated (by non-local genotypes of the same species or interspecific hybridizations).
– Do not use germplasm of unknown origin.
– Maintain natural sex ratios and demographically appropriate age-class structure.
– Maintain high effective population sizes when collecting and propagating germplasm for reintroduction. Maximize the number and diversity of distinct founding genotypes, and maintain equal contributions from each donor individual through to the outplanting or introduction phase.
– Introduce healthy founders; avoid introducing disease with founders.
– Favor rapid early population growth.
– Choose introduction sites that match the optimal habitat requirements of the species (both physical and ecological, e.g., metapopulation structure).
– Avoid sites near (i.e., within significant gene flow distance of) populations of non-local genotypes or races of the same species capable of contaminating the introduced populations.
– Choose sites that are geographically large enough to accommodate large effective populations sizes, unless metapopulation structure suggests otherwise.
– Minimize inbreeding (in species that naturally outbreed) by maintaining large population sizes, minimizing relatedness in founders (avoid using clones), equalizing sex ratios, maintaining representative age-classes, and maximizing diversity (within above standards).
– Promote reproduction and dispersal by favoring natural pollinators, seed dispersers, connectivity, disturbance regimes, and habitat availability (safe sites) for sexually reproducing species.
– For asexually reproducing species, maintain high numbers of clones, as they will determine the amount and distribution of resident genetic diversity.

BOX 14.1 (cont.)

II.   When removing individuals from natural populations (e.g., timber harvest, hunting and fishing):

- Avoid significant reductions in effective population size (e.g., significant reductions in census number of individuals, unequal sex ratios, unequal contributions from parents, unequal numbers of offspring, drastically fluctuating population sizes).
- Avoid unnatural changes in mating systems (e.g., isolated seed trees or clumps of retention trees may promote inbreeding).
- Avoid increases in undesired intraspecific or interspecific hybridizations (e.g., changes in gene-flow corridors, fragmentation).
- Mimic natural structural patterns (spatial distributions, age-class distributions, patterns and intervals of mortality) and processes, especially disturbance regimes.
- Maintain or restore natural selection regimes (e.g., native pathogens and insects, pollinator relationships, nature fire regimes).

maintaining local germplasm and promoting natural genetic processes in the range of management situations met in wildlands, from minimally disturbed areas (e.g., wilderness) to multiple-use or manipulative situations. Sometimes these guidelines specifically emphasize genetic conservation within ecological restoration (Millar and Libby 1990, Knapp and Rice 1994), rare and endangered species conservation (Falk and Holsinger 1991, Falk et al. 1996), or production forestry (Kitzmiller 1990) contexts. Such 'best genetic management practices' help guide development of specific genetic prescriptions, as the examples later in the chapter illustrate.

Principles of ecosystem management remind us that our attention should be focused on a broader array of species and environments than individual taxa targeted as high risk. Genetic conservation under ecosystem management ideally brings the best genetic management to all native species. Because of the enormous number of species this entails, the lack of genetic information for all but a minute fraction of these, and the expense and sophistication needed to gain that information, a general approach is needed for these remaining species. Under many circumstances, genetic diversity may be adequately maintained by focusing on species and habitat conservation, without further modification for genetic concerns. This is because natural genetic structure and function (i.e., evolutionary processes) occur when populations are functioning with minimum human disturbance and in generally natural habitats. Thus, in many cases, species and ecosystem conservation serve as adequate surrogates for genetic conservation for the vast multitude of forest species.

Genetic conservation for specific management situations

As described above, emphasis in genetic conservation is on protecting single species identified as high risk, mitigating certain management practices, and providing general protection to all species in an ecosystem management context. Examples of some approaches are described below.

GENETIC CONSERVATION IN PRODUCTION FORESTRY

Production forestry is one situation where genetic conservation goals are combined with others in a multiple-use landscape. Several silvicultural practices in the early days of forestry were potentially detrimental to tree gene pools. High-grading, or harvesting trees with superior growth and form traits and leaving poor quality trees to regenerate stands, was regularly practiced, and likely led to declines in growth and productivity in subsequent generations. In the early decades of planting, the genetic source of seedling stock was not considered, which contributed to plantation failure or poor performance, tree mortality, and decline in forest productivity. The ill effects of such early activities, seen in the light of modern information on genecology in forest trees, catalyzed the establishment of genetic practices to maintain productivity. For example, in 1934 a forest seed law was passed in Germany that called for the destruction of certain low productivity stands and forbade seed collection from 50% of the stands. Similar problems accumulated in the United States and many older plantations still exist on public and private lands where trees of unknown, but offsite, source essentially downgrade the sites due to poor performance. By 1939, the U.S. Department of Agriculture established policy on seed transfers for federal forests with the goal of maintaining local germplasm and representative diversity.

The California region of the U.S. Forest Service provides a more specific example (Kitzmiller 1976, 1990). A long-term objective is to maintain and promote broad adaptability of tree populations of all species, but the primary focus is on conifer species of highest commercial value, namely ponderosa and sugar pines (*Pinus ponderosa*, *P. lambertiana*), Douglas-fir (*Pseudotsuga menziesii*), incense-cedar (*Calocedrus decurrens*), and white fir

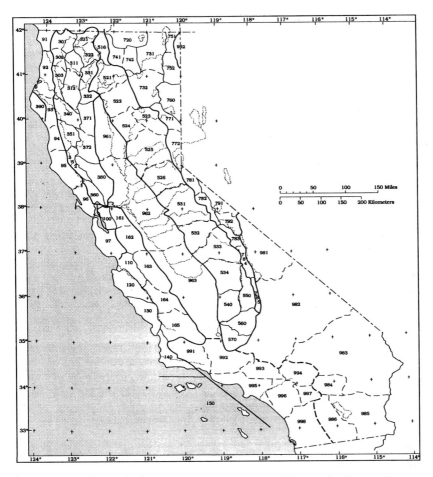

Fig. 14.4. Tree seed zones for forest genetic conservation in California. When harvested areas are planned for reforestation, seeds are collected within 150 m elevation of the planting site and within the same major zone. (From Buck *et al.* 1970, Kitzmiller 1990.)

(*Abies concolor*). The approach emphasizes *in situ* maintenance of genetic architecture by maintaining genetic standards (as described earlier in this chapter and Box 14.1) throughout harvest and planting regions. Scattered set-asides (reserve areas), designated for other conservation purposes, also contribute to maintaining population and ecotypic genetic diversity. Three elements compose the core of the program:

1. Tree seed zones. Forested ecosystems are divided into zones of general similarity in selection pressure (i.e., similarity in climate, forest types and species, soils, elevation, aspect) (Figures 14.2, 14.4). Movement of germplasm is restricted both within and among these zones. That is,

seed to be used for planting harvested sites is collected within the same zone and within the same 150 m elevation band as the planting site.

Zones for this map were first developed by a group of forest geneticists and foresters who based their estimates on general and anecdotal knowledge of land forms, elevation, and climatic zones (Buck et al. 1970). Little direct genetic information was available to inform those who drew the zone boundaries, although some elevation and latitudinal transect studies provided information. Subsequent analyses of genetic variation in these species (Figure 14.5), and ecological mapping of species and habitats, have shown that these early estimates of genecological provinces were surprisingly good.

2. Seed collection and nursery practices. Once locations for seed collecting are determined, seed is collected from a minimum of 20 forest stands per zone, with one to many trees per stand serving as seed parents (Kitzmiller 1976, 1990). Equal contributions of seeds from each donor are sought to create bulked (combined) seedlots from each stand. Similarly, attempts are made to keep numbers of seeds and seedlings per tree and per stand equal throughout the nursery phases to maintain effective population sizes and thus favor high genetic diversity. During seed collection and culling operations in the nursery, slight selection is exerted toward traits of interest to production forestry (e.g., rapid height growth, stem straightness, flat branch angles). This latter practice integrates the objective for gains in productivity, whereas the other recommendations assure the retention of adequate adaptive genetic diversity.

3. Harvest practices. The main genetic conservation goal for tree harvest is to avoid systematic alterations in the gene pool, or high-grading. Thus, when partial-harvest methods are used, a mix of tree phenotypes is left rather than the best trees repeatedly being harvested and poor phenotypes being left as parents of natural regenerants. Federal laws (National Forest Management Act 1976) require that harvested sites be planted with the same mix and abundance of native species that existed on the site prior to harvest.

No formal monitoring exists within the California program, although research studies have shown that genetic diversity is similar in production seedlots and the native stands where seeds were collected.

GENETIC CONSERVATION AREAS

Sometimes genetic conservation goals are the primary emphasis in land management. Where activities occur that might significantly affect genetic diversity (such as those described earlier in this chapter), parcels of land may be chosen to conserve representative genetic diversity. Such *genetic conservation areas* (GCAs) have the goal of conserving allelic,

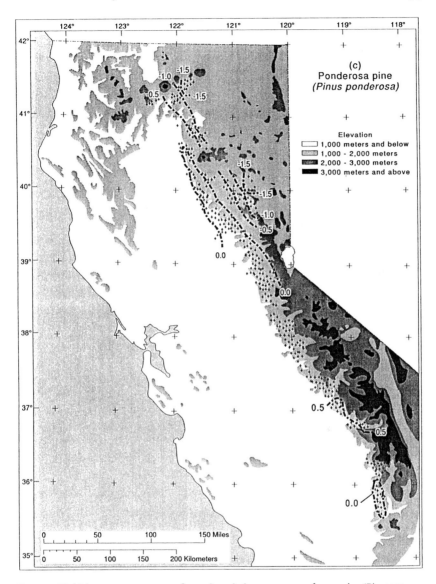

Fig. 14.5. Multi-locus contour maps of genetic variation among ponderosa pine (*Pinus ponderosa*) populations in the Sierra Nevada of California. Contours are derived from canonical trend surface analyses of many isozyme loci. Contour intervals are based on 0.50 standard deviation units from the analysis. Highly resolved genetic studies such as these provided refinement of original tree seed-zone boundaries. (From Westfall and Conkle 1992.)

genotypic, population, and species genetic variation through designation and genetic management of natural habitat distributed over the native range of target species. In addition to conserving *in situ* genetic diversity and genetic function, these GCAs can be used for genetic monitoring, serving as baselines against which manipulative treatments can be compared. Wilderness areas, national parks, nature reserves and natural areas, and other specific conservation areas (such as for rare or endangered species) often function effectively as GCAs. For rare species, there may be as few as one to several GCAs (Nabhan and Norman 1992), whereas for widespread species, networks of many GCAs are developed, ideally with individual units being carefully selected to represent important parts of genetic architecture (Wilson 1990, Arbez 1995). Whereas GCAs are usually managed similarly to strict nature reserves (with no manipulative activities allowed), they can be developed from areas where certain kinds of manipulation occur, as long as native species are maintained and land management priorities allow genetic standards to be maintained.

Although forest GCAs have long been discussed, they have been slow to be implemented. Several pilot networks are planned or developed for Norway spruce (*Picea abies*), cork oak (*Quercus suber*), and a few hardwood species in western Europe (Arbez 1995). In Malaysia, a network for hardwood species is being developed (Tsai and Yuan 1995). The Turkish government has established a national genetic conservation area program that provides a model for other countries (see case study below).

Determining the size and locations of individual units within GCA networks has been approached in several different ways. In the state of Washington, USA, over 100 GCAs (there called gene pool reserves) for Douglas-fir were designated in each 152 m elevation band within every seed zone. Reserves were selected to be 10 ha and containing at least 400 dominant or co-dominant trees (Wilson 1990). These reserves are withdrawn from timber harvest and managed strictly for genetic-conservation purposes.

In Europe, 31 countries, the European Community, and four international organizations approved six resolutions in 1990 pertinent to forest genetic conservation (Arbez 1995). One emphasized the development of *in situ* methods, including the development of pilot GCA programs and eventual comprehensive networks. For European silver fir (*Abies alba*) in France, available genetic information was used to select 20 populations considered to be representative of the important genetic variation in the region. The total area of this network covers about 200 ha, less than 1% of the species distribution in France. Each stand is about 10–15 ha, ensuring at least 600 trees. An additional 90 ha isolation zone protects the stands from gene contamination. Genetic management guidelines are integrated with the general management plans for each area, and do not significantly constrain wood production goals for these areas.

In California, USA, a research GCA project for key conifers was initiated in the Sierra Nevada which demonstrated a quantitative approach to using genetic information in designing GCA size and placement (Millar and Libby 1991). The focus of this GCA project was the five commercial conifer species of the Sierra Nevada (ponderosa pine, sugar pine, incense-cedar, Douglas-fir, and white fir). Throughout most of their ranges, these species are subject to timber harvest, and also conserved under the genetic conservation practices of the U.S. Forest Service described for production forestry above. The development of a GCA network was proposed as a back-up and insurance to the operational gene conservation practices, and also as baseline for assessing the efficacy of those operational guidelines.

Siting and size decisions about the individual units demonstrate how genetic data can be used to improve the efficiency of designing a GCA network. Areas were selected according to four generalized steps: (1) compile genetic data for multiple traits; (2) develop multivariate statistical models and analyses to locate alternative network designs for GCAs that combine all five species and represent genetic diversity gradients at regular intervals across the landscape; (3) survey on-the-ground to find areas where all species represented are in appropriate conditions and age classes, and where natural processes have been least disrupted by human activities (e.g., minimal history of timber harvest, road building, fire suppression or catastrophic fire); (4) develop and implement management plans that prescribe goals, restricted and permitted activities, monitoring, and restrictions on adjacent land use.

Recommended size of each GCA in this project was calculated by considering the size of an area that would maintain stable effective population sizes into the future (i.e., no decline in genetic diversity). Areas must be large enough to avoid inbreeding, retard loss of diversity due to drift, and buffer against pollen contamination from neighboring stands. The recommended sizes ranged from 500 ha to 3000 ha, depending on stand conditions of the sites and management of adjacent areas.

Management plans for this GCA network would emphasize natural structure and process, including ecologically appropriate mixes of species, age classes, and densities, as well as appropriate fire and natural insect/pathogen regimes. Carefully controlled harvest, artificial regeneration, and other manipulative practices could occur if genetic considerations were given highest priority. This arguably diminishes or obviates their usefulness as baseline areas for comparison with harvested areas. In most parts of the world, however, undisturbed (by human influence) forest doesn't exist. In light of this, the best approach is to choose areas with least historic disturbance, greatest record of past effect, and highest likelihood of achieving genetic standards and practices in future management.

ENDANGERED SPECIES MANAGEMENT

Much conservation activity is focused on endangered species. Protection of these species can be both preventative, in minimizing or halting the activities that eroded or contaminated genetic diversity, and restorative, in reintroducing allelic, genotypic, and ecotypic diversity. Often a management decision hinges on determining how much genetic diversity is enough; that is, whether a rare population or species' gene pool would be 'significantly impaired' by a proposed management project (e.g., timber harvest, trail-building, grazing allocations, fire). Significant genetic change is difficult to interpret even with monitoring, and thus it is difficult to determine what constitutes a threat, especially to small or weakened populations.

One way to evaluate the significance of proposed actions involving endangered species is to model or predict the implications on short- and long-term genetic diversity and population viability. An example comes from sugar pine, an ecologically and commercially important species of western North America. Sugar pine, along with other white pines native to North America, is threatened by an exotic pathogen, *Cronartium ribicola*, which causes the fatal white pine blister-rust disease (Smith 1996). White pine blister rust was introduced into North America in 1910 on a shipment of infested eastern white pine (*Pinus strobus*) from France, and has spread with variable speed through sugar pine and other white pine forests in western and eastern parts of the continent.

Sugar pine is highly susceptible to blister rust. Seedlings and young trees are killed outright, while old trees die more slowly, losing portions of their crowns over many years. A major gene for resistance, which appears to be widely distributed in sugar pine populations at very low levels, was found almost 30 years ago (Figure 14.6, Kinloch et al. 1970, Kinloch 1992). Threat of population or species extinction from blister rust is attenuated by sugar pine's naturally low stand densities, which were further reduced as a result of heavy harvest during the settlement period in California (late nineteenth century).

Fig. 14.6. A single dominant gene in sugar pine (*Pinus lambertiana*) confers
resistance from white pine blister-rust disease to individuals that carry the gene (right).
Individuals carrying the normal allele die when exposed to the pathogen (left). Frequencies of
the resistant gene vary in sugar pine forests from absent to about 10%. (From Kinloch *et al.*
1970, Kinloch 1992.) (B.B. Kinloch photo)

Models have been developed to predict changes in genetic diversity and to assess long-term population viability in sugar pine (Millar *et al.* 1996). The assessment focused on the rate and geographic extent of the spread of the rust, the effects on sugar pine populations as the epidemic reached all parts of the species' range, and the consequences to the species at populations, ecotypic, and species levels. In modeling, effective population size was tracked as the key marker of genetic diversity during the predicted rust epidemic. Effective population size (N_e) is similar to the census size of a population (the actual count of individuals) but is adjusted to represent the number of genetically effective individuals. N_e is equal to the actual census only when mating is random, all parents contribute offspring equally, where sex ratios are equal, and population sizes remain unchanging over time.

Following effective population size in sugar pine shows some surprising results (Figure 14.7). As blister rust becomes epidemic, sugar pine populations decline rapidly in size. A few individuals in most populations are likely to survive due to the resistance gene. These individuals produce resistant progeny. In subsequent generations, populations increase rapidly in size due to strong selection for the resistance gene (Figure 14.7). An important outcome from modeling, however, is the significant and long-lasting decline in N_e. This suggests that a large portion of genetic diversity in sugar pine populations will be lost even though the populations recover in size. Without its complement of genetic diversity, however, the long-term stability of sugar pine is hampered since the species would lose resilience to meet future environmental changes.

Comprehensive management programs have tackled the blister-rust problem in sugar pine for several decades (Kitzmiller 1976). Most recently, a breeding program is developing resistant sugar pine seedlings to outplant after timber harvest (Samman and Kitzmiller 1996). Seeds are collected from known resistant trees in wild stands, and resistant seedlings are returned to reforestation sites within the same adaptive zone. This augmentation of resistant stock should significantly improve sugar pine's chances for successfully passing through the epidemic and maintaining genetic diversity as well.

A less obvious implication from the modeling is the effect that harvesting genetically susceptible old-growth sugar pine individuals would have on long-term loss of genetic diversity. Although it might seem that these genotypes are extraneous to the population since they will likely be killed by the rust, in fact as long as trees with susceptible genotypes are alive (and many may take years to die), they contribute genes through pollen to

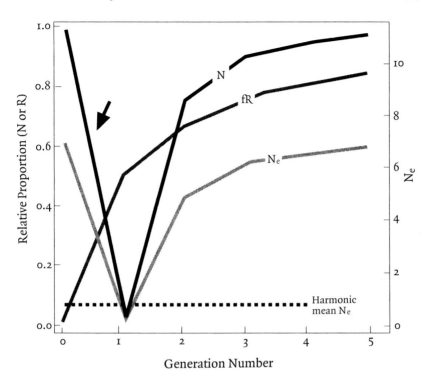

Fig. 14.7. Evaluating impacts to genetic diversity in sugar pine from white pine blister rust with predictive models. The model shows the effect of five generations of blister rust on population size (N) of sugar pines, frequency of the sugar pine resistant allele (fR), effective population size in sugar pine (N_e) over five generations, and harmonic mean N_e. Harmonic mean N_e is the average effective population size over the five generations and is used to evaluate effect on genetic diversity. With a mean N_e of 0.2, in five generations approximately 95% of sugar pine's genetic diversity could be lost. (From Millar *et al.* 1996.)

resistant mother trees. They also can bear resistant seeds themselves through pollination from resistant father trees. The genetic diversity they contribute at genes other than the blister rust gene is significant, and emphasizes why it is so important that these trees be kept alive during the epidemic.

This example demonstrates how projections that focus only on population numbers can be misleading: although a population may appear to be stable or recovering in census size, significant undesired impacts may be accruing, as in the case of sugar pine, to long-term genetic diversity, which could impair long-term resilience and adaptability in the species. Preventative and proactive management approaches that 'load the dice' genetically can be chosen where practical.

GENETIC MONITORING

Although the importance of ecological monitoring extends to the genetic level, genetic diversity is difficult to assess, requiring costly laboratory methods or time-consuming field studies for detection. The genetic structure of several forest tree and fish species have been studied in many places, but few if any studies have been repeated, and time trends are unavailable. With no long-term studies, we have little understanding of natural fluctuations or response to ecological disturbances, and thus no patterns of temporal or spatial variability to use as a baseline. A related barrier to genetic monitoring is the difficulty in interpreting changes in diversity relative to adaptability, resilience, and vigor. With current techniques, by the time we could detect significant changes in genetic diversity, populations and species may already be irretrievably in demographic decline. New approaches combining molecular with physiological techniques, such as quantitative trait locus (QTL) monitoring, are encouraging (Neale and Harry 1994), but these techniques are not yet available for conservation use. In sum, although genetic theory provides expectations about changes in diversity, we have not yet developed a meaningful approach to genetic monitoring because we do not know whether increases, decreases, or other changes we may measure are significant for a particular species or population. For now we can advance the objectives of genetic monitoring by understanding ecological contexts within which genetic trend data are collected, integrating genetic diversity measurements with other ecological monitoring data, and using ecological surrogates for genetic inference (Bawa and Menon 1995, Boyle and Boontawee 1995).

Case study: preserving a priceless legacy of genes in Turkey

An ambitious and comprehensive project is under way to conserve the rich genetic resources of native plants and wild relatives of important crop, medicinal, and ornamental plants of Turkey (Global Environment Facility 1995, Adams et al. in press). The program is jointly administered by the Turkish Ministry of Agriculture and Rural Affairs, Ministry of Forestry, and Ministry for the Environment and funded by the Global Environment Facility of the World Bank. Turkey is one of the richest countries in plant genetic resources. Over 30% of its 9000 species are endemic. Turkey has a unique biogeographical setting located at the junction of the Euro-

Siberian, Mediterranean, and Irano-Turanian floristic regions. Diverse environmental and climatic conditions contribute to making Turkey a major center of origin for globally important plant genetic resources and the native home of widely used domesticated plants.

This project is the first of its kind in the world to protect both woody and non-woody wild crop relatives through the development of *in situ* multi-species genetic conservation areas. Whereas many nations have undertaken some form of *ex situ* genetic conservation (seed storage, primarily), Turkey is the first to integrate *ex situ* with *in situ* methods in a national program for the management of genetic resources. In addition to identifying and establishing gene conservation areas, a project goal is to strengthen the institutional capacity in Turkey for implementing an ongoing national program for genetic conservation and integrating with other current conservation efforts in the country.

The project includes five major components: surveys and inventories, gene conservation areas (called gene management zones in this project), data management, a national plan for a larger network of *in situ* conservation areas, and institutional strengthening for gene conservation. This pioneering program began in March 1993 with a three-year pilot phase that emphasized development of eco-geographic surveys and inventories of species and genetic diversity (isozyme and common garden studies) of tree and crop relative species across the country to determine appropriate locations for genetic conservation areas. These areas would be located to preserve unique genetic resources as well as conserve areas of high species diversity. The number of areas and their size would vary with site and species richness. Areas will be selected that contain more than one population of target species, and that contain core areas (center of the zone) and buffer zones. The pilot program focused on areas within Kazdagi National Park, Ceylanpinar State Farm, and the Anatolian Diagonal.

Each GCA designated in the Turkish network will have a separate management plan, and a scientific and technical team from several government agencies will implement and review conservation activities of each site. Management will emphasize non-manipulative uses initially, especially in core areas. Cessation of grazing will be the most important management action. For areas that have endangered species, recovery plans will be written and implemented but the focus emphasizes restoring ecosystem function not just species representation. Removal of invasive plants and feral animals and fertilization of some parts of the GCA may be needed. Permanent sampling and monitoring plots will be established to monitor baseline biotic and physical environmental changes. Plots will be resampled every 3–5 years, and ecological research will be encouraged in these areas. These GCAs of forest and crop species are intended to serve as the core of a much larger network of conservation areas that will comprehensively cover all plant species in Turkey.

Summary

Genetic variation is the fundamental source of all biological diversity. Without genetic variation, adaptation to changing environments would not occur. Because species are subject to natural selection, gene flow, chance events of genetic drift, and other evolutionary forces that shape their genetic composition, they have evolved highly structured patterns among individuals, populations, and widely separated portions of native ranges. No two species are alike in their genetic architecture, although some species that are similar in mating systems (e.g., inbreeders vs. outbreeders), geographic distribution (e.g., widespread vs. rare), or longevity (e.g., annual vs. perennial) may share similar general patterns in genetic diversity. Much of this variation has evolved as a consequence of natural selection fine-tuning populations for adaptation to local environments, although many ecosystem forces alter the genetic structure of species in random ways as well. Human actions also influence genetic diversity, in both beneficial and detrimental ways.

Genetic conservation is a component of land management that aims to maintain the ecological and evolutionary potential of species' gene pools. Traditionally genetic considerations have been limited to a very few taxa (commercial forest species) and a few aspects of forest management (tree improvement or reforestation). General guidelines and strategic genetic plans that aim to maintain and restore genetic diversity need to be more widely integrated across suites of taxa in forest planning. Where the management goal is to maintain biodiversity, genetic objectives can be aided by actions that maintain native genetic diversity and function, and avoid genetic contamination. These include using local germplasm of native species (in projects like tree planting, fish stocking, ecological restoration, or rare species reintroduction); maintaining natural population sizes, distributions, and connectivity; ensuring that parents of future generations are genetically representative of current generations when individuals are removed (e.g., in tree harvest, hunting and fishing); providing sources of back-up genes in storage in case of emergency needs (e.g., seeds in a seedbank, frozen sperm); and promoting natural disturbance agents that act as selection agents (e.g., fire and native insects/pathogens). Specific genetic conservation prescriptions may be needed when genetic diversity seems at risk; these include germplasm collection and transfer rules, minimum population size guidelines, genetic conservation areas, and guidelines on selection of individuals for removal or introduction.

Further readings

Hartl (1988), Hartl & Clark (1989) and Hedrick (1983) develop the basic population-genetic theory that underlies conservation genetics. Early conservation biology treatments, such as Soule and Wilcox (1980) and Frankel and Soulé (1981), set the stage for important conservation genetic precepts. These are further developed generally in Oldfield (1984) and Soulé (1987), while Ledig (1988), Schoenewald-Cox *et al.* (1983), Falk & Holsinger (1991) and National Research Council (1991) take up genetic conservation within specific management contexts. More recent treatments include Hedrick and Miller (1992), Rogers and Ledig (1996), and Friedman (1997).

Literature cited

Adams, W. T., S. H. Strauss, D. L. Copes, and A. R. Griffin (eds). 1992. *Population Genetics of Forest Trees*. Kluwer Academic Publishers. Boston.

Adams, W. T., Y. Anikster, Z. Keya, N. Zencirci (eds). (In press). In situ genetic conservation in Turkey: National programs and scientific bases. *Proceedings from the Symposium on In Situ Conservation of Genetic Resources in Turkey. November 1996.* Antalya, Turkey.

Antonovics, J., A. D. Bradshaw, and J. Turner. 1971. Heavy metal tolerance in plants. *Advances in Ecological Research* 7:1–85.

Arbez, M. 1995. A federative plan for the conservation of forest genetic resources in Europe. Pp. 465–72 in Ph. Baradat, W. T. Adams, and G. Mueller-Starck (eds). *Population Genetics and Genetic Conservation of Forest Trees*. SPB Academic Publishing, Amsterdam.

Asins, M. J. and E. A. Carbonell. 1987. Concepts involved in measuring genetic variability and its importance in conservation of plant genetic resources. *Evolutionary Trends in Plants* 1(1):51–62.

Baradat, Ph., W. T. Adams, and G. Mueller-Starck (eds). 1995. *Population Genetics and Genetic Conservation of Forest Trees*. SPB Academic Publishing, Amsterdam.

Barrett, S. C. and J. R. Kohn. 1991. Genetic and evolutionary consequences of small population size in plants: Implications for conservation. Pp. 3–30 in Falk, D. and K. Holsinger (eds). *Genetics and Conservation of Rare Plants.* Oxford University Press, New York.

Bawa, K. S. and S. Menon. 1995. Biodiversity monitoring: the missing element. *Trends in Ecology and Evolution* 12(1):42.

Bonner, F. 1990. Storage of seeds: potential and limitations for germplasm conservation. *Forest Ecology and Management* 35(1,2):35–44.

Boyle, T. J. and B. Boontawee (eds). 1995. Measuring and monitoring biodiversity in tropical and temperate forests. *Proceedings of a IUFRO Symposium held at Chiang Mai, Thailand, August 27–September 2, 1994.* Center for International Forestry Research, Bogor, Indonesia.

Brown, A. H. D. and J. D. Briggs. 1991. Sampling strategies for genetic variation in ex situ collections of endangered plant species. Pp. 99–122 in Falk, D. and K. Holsinger (eds). *Genetics and Conservation of Rare Plants.* Oxford University Press, New York.

Buck, J. M., et al. 1970. *California tree seed zones.* Miscellaneous Publication. USDA Forest Service.

Campbell, R. K. and F. C. Sorenson. 1984. Genetic implications of nursery practices. Pp. 183–91 in M. L. Duryea and T. D. Landis (eds). *Forest Nursery Manual: Production of Bareroot Seedlings.* Martinus Nijhoff/Dr W. Junk Publishers, Boston.

Center for Plant Conservation. 1991. Genetic sampling guidelines for conservation collections of endangered plants. Pp. 225–38 in Falk, D. and K. Holsinger (eds). *Genetics and Conservation of Rare Plants.* Oxford University Press, New York.

Clausen, J., D. D. Keck, and W. M. Heisey. 1940. *Experimental studies on the nature of species. I. Effect of varied environments on western North American plants.* Carnegie Institution of Washington Publication No. 520.

Clegg, M. T. 1990. Molecular evaluation of plant genetic resources. Pp. 13–17 in B. Fraleigh (ed.). *Proceedings of a workshop on the genetic evaluation of plant genetic resources, 1988,* Ottawa, Ontario.

Conkle, M. T. 1986. Tree genetics and improvement. *Journal of Forestry* 84(1):34–6.

Daly, J. C. and J. L. Patton. 1990. Dispersal, gene flow, and allelic diversity between local populations of Thomomys bottae picket gophers in the coastal ranges of California. *Evolution* 44(5):1283–94.

Dobzhansky, T. 1970. *Genetics of the Evolutionary Process.* Columbia University Press. New York.

Eriksson, G. 1995. Which traits should be used to guide sampling for gene resources? Pp. 349–59 in Ph. Baradat, W. T. Adams, and G. Mueller-Starck (eds). *Population Genetics and Genetic Conservation of Forest Trees.* SPB Academic Publishing, Amsterdam.

Falk, D. and K. Holsinger (eds). 1991. *Genetics and Conservation of Rare Plants.* Oxford University Press, New York.

Falk, D., C. I. Millar, and P. O. Olwell (eds). 1996. *Restoring Diversity: Reintroduction of Rare and Endangered Plants.* Island Press, Washington D.C.

Frankel, O. H. and M. E. Soule 1981. *Conservation and Evolution*. Cambridge University Press, Cambridge.

Friedman, S. 1997. Forest genetics for ecosystem management. Pp. 203–212 in K. Kohm and J. F. Franklin (eds). *Creating a Forestry for the 21st Century, The Science of Ecosystem Management*. Island Press, Washington D.C.

Global Environment Facility. 1995. In-situ conservation of genetic diversity in Turkey. Agricultural Research, Turkish Ministry of Agriculture and Rural Affairs. *Global Environment Facility Newsletter* 1:1–4.

Hamrick, J. L. 1983. The distribution of genetic variation within and among natural plant populations. Pp. 335–48 in C. M. Schonewald-Cox, S. M. Chambers, B. MacBryde, and W. L. Thomas (eds). *Genetics and Conservation*. Benjamin/Cummings Co. Inc. Menlo Park, California.

Hamrick, J. L. and M. J. W. Godt. 1990. Allozyme diversity in plant species. Pp. 43–63 in A. H .D. Brown, M. T. Clegg, A. L. Kahler, and B. S. Weir (eds). *Plant Population Genetics, Breeding, and Genetic Resources*. Sinauer Associates Inc., Massachusetts.

Hamrick, J. L., Y. B. Linhart, and J. B. Mitton. 1979. Relationships between life history characteristics and electrophoretically-detectable genetic variation in plants. *Annual Review of Ecology and Systematics* 10:173–200.

Hartl, D. L. 1988. *A primer of Population Genetics*. Sinauer, Sunderland, Massachusetts.

Hartl, D. L. and A. G. Clark 1989. *Principles of Population Genetics*, 2nd edition. Sinauer, Sunderland, Massachusetts.

Hedrick, P. 1983. *Genetics of Populations*. Science Books International, Boston.

Hedrick, P. and P. Miller. 1992. Conservation genetics: techniques and fundamentals. *Ecological Applications* 2(1):30–46.

Hertel, H. and C. Ewald. 1995. Conservation of genetic diversity in SO_2–polluted stands of Norway spruce (*Picea abies*). Pp. 413–20 in Ph. Baradat, W. T. Adams, and G. Mueller-Starck (eds). *Population Genetics and Genetic Conservation of Forest Trees*. SPB Academic Publishing, Amsterdam.

Holsinger, K. E. and L. D. Gottlieb. 1991. Conservation of rare and endangered plants: principles and prospects. Pp. 195–208 in Falk, D. and K. Holsinger (eds). *Genetics and Conservation of Rare Plants*. Oxford University Press, New York.

Hudson, W. E. 1991. *Landscape Linkages and Biodiversity*. Defenders of Wildlife, Washington DC.

Hunter, M. L. 1996. *Fundamentals of Conservation Biology*. Blackwell Science, Cambridge, Massachusetts.

Ingram, 1996. Integration of in-situ conservation of plant genetic resources into landscape and regional planning. Pp. 454–76 in R. C. Szaro and D. W. Johnston (eds). *Biodiversity in Managed Landscapes*. Oxford University Press, New York.

Kinloch, B. B. 1992. Distribution and frequency of a gene for resistance to white pine blister rust in natural populations of sugar pine. *Canadian Journal of Botany* 70(7):1319–23.

Kinloch, B. B., G. K. Parks, and C. W. Fowler. 1970. White pine blister rust: simply inherited resistance in sugar pine. *Science* **167**:193–95.

Kitzmiller, J. H. 1976. *Tree Improvement Master Plan for the California Region*. USDA Forest Service, San Francisco.

——— 1990. Managing genetic diversity in a tree improvement program. *Forest Ecology & Management* **35**(1–2):131–49.

Knapp, E. and K. Rice. 1994. Starting from seed: Genetic issues in using native grasses for restoration. *Restoration Management & Notes* **12**(1):40–5.

Ledig, F. T. 1986. Heterozygosity, heterosis, and fitness in outcrossing plants. Pp. 77–104 in M. E. Soulé (ed.). *Conservation Biology: the Science of Scarcity and Diversity*. Sinauer Associates, Sunderland, Massachusetts.

——— 1988. Conservation of diversity in forest trees: Why and how should genes be conserved? *BioScience* **38**:471–9.

——— 1991. Human impacts on genetic diversity in forest ecosystems. *Oikos* **63**:87–108.

Libby, W. J. 1973. Domestication strategies for forest trees. *Canadian Journal of Forest Research* **3**:265–76.

Libby, W .J., K. Isik, and J. P. King. 1980. Variation in flushing time among white fir population samples. *Annales Forestales* **8**(6):123–38.

Millar, C. I. 1993. Conservation of germplasm in forest trees. Pp. 42–65 in W. J. Libby and R. Ahuja (eds). *Clonal Forestry II. Conservation and Application. 2.* Springer-Verlag, Berlin.

Millar, C. I. and W. J. Libby. 1990. Disneyland or native ecosystem: The genetic purity question. *Restoration Management* **7**(1):18–23.

Millar, C. I. and W. J. Libby. 1991. Strategies for conserving clinal, ecotypic and disjunct population diversity in widespread species. Pp. 149–70 in D. Falk and K. Holsinger (eds). *Genetics and Conservation of Rare Plants*. Oxford University Press, New York.

Millar, C. I., B. B. Kinloch, and R. D. Westfall. 1996. Conservation of biodiversity in sugar pine: Effects of the blister rust epidemic on genetic diversity. Pp. 190–99 in B. B. Kinloch, M. Marosy, and M. Huddleston (eds). *Sugar pine; status, values, and roles in ecosystems*. Proceedings of a symposium presented by the California Sugar Pine Management Committee, March 30–April 1, 1992, University of California, Davis, CA. University of California, Division of Agriculture and Natural Resources, Publication 3362.

Nabhan, G. and D. Norman. 1992. *A proposal for natural area designation in the Tumacacori Mountains of the Coronado National Forest as a genetic reserve to protect plants of economic importance*. Miscellaneous publication of Native Seeds/SEARCH. Tucson AZ. 42 pp.

National Research Council. 1991. *Forest Trees*. Committee on managing global genetic resources: agricultural imperatives. National Academy Press, Washington D.C.

Neale, D. G. and D. E. Harry. 1994. Genetic mapping in forest trees: RFLPs, RAPDs, and beyond. *AgBiotech News and Information* **6**(5):107N–114N.

Nei, M. 1987. *Molecular Evolutionary Genetics*. Colombia University Press. New York. Oldfield, M. L. 1984. *The value of conserving genetic resources*. USDI National Park Service Washington D.C.

Patton, J. L. and J. H. Feder. 1981. Microspatial genetic heterogeneity in pocket gophers: Non-random breeding and drift. *Evolution* **35**(5):912–20.

Rogers, D. L. and F. T. Ledig (eds). 1996. *The status of North American temperate forest genetic resources*. Report No. 15. Genetic Resources Conservation Program, University of California, Davis, California.

Russell, J. R., F. Hosein, E. Johnson, W. T. G. Van Der Ven, R. Waugh, and W. Powell. 1995. The use of RAPD markers to genetically differentiate between Cocoa (*Theobroma cacao*) populations. Pp.s 135–8 in Ph. Baradat, W. T. Adams, and G. Mueller-Starck (eds). *Population Genetics and Genetic Conservation of Forest Trees*. SPB Academic Publishing, Amsterdam.

Samman, S. and J. Kitzmiller. 1996. The sugar pine program for development of resistance to blister rust in the Pacific Southwest Region. Pp. 162–70 in B. B. Kinloch, M. Marosy, and M. Huddleston (eds). *Sugar pine; status, values, and roles in ecosystems*. Proceedings of a symposium presented by the California Sugar Pine Management Committee, March 30–April 1, 1992, University of California, Davis, CA. University of California, Division of Agriculture and Natural Resources, Publication 3362.

Savolainen, O. and K. Karkkainen. 1991. Effect of forest management on gene pools. Pp. 329–46 in W. T. Adams, S. H. Strauss, D. L. Copes, and A. R. Griffin (eds). *Population Genetics of Forest Trees*. Kluwer Academic Publishers. Boston, Massachusetts.

Schonewald-Cox, C. M., S. M. Chambers, B. MacBryde, and W. L. Thomas (eds). 1983. *Genetics and Conservation: A Reference for Managing Wild Animal and Plant Populations*. Benjamin/Cummings Co. Inc. Menlo Park, California.

Smith, R. S. 1996. Spread and intensification of blister rust in the range of sugar pine. Pp. 112–24 in B. B. Kinloch, M. Marosy, and M. Huddleston (eds). *Sugar pine; status, values, and roles in ecosystems*. Proceedings of a symposium presented by the California Sugar Pine Management Committee, March 30–April 1, 1992, University of California, Davis, CA. University of California, Division of Agriculture and Natural Resources, Publication 3362.

Soulé, M. E. (ed.). 1987. *Viable Populations for Conservation*. Cambridge University Press, New York.

Soulé, M.E. and B. A. Wilcox (eds). 1980. *Conservation Biology, An Evolutionary-Ecological Perspective*. Sinauer Associates, Sunderland, Massachusetts.

Stern, K. and L. Roche. 1974. *Genetics of Forest Ecosystems*. Springer-Verlag, Berlin.

Tsai, L. M. and C. T. Yuan. 1995. A practical approach to conservation of genetic diversity in Malaysia: genetic resource areas. Pp.s 207–18 in T. J. Boyle, and B. Boontawee (eds). *Measuring and monitoring biodiversity in tropical and temperate forests*. Proceedings of a IUFRO Symposium held at Chiang Mai, Thailand, August 27–September 2, 1994. Center for International Forestry Research, Bogor, Indonesia.

Westfall, R. D. and M. T. Conkle. 1992. Allozyme makers in breeding zone desig-
  nation. *New Forests* **6**:279–309.
Wheeler, N. C. 1996. The Pacific yew: minor species or cancer remedy? Pp. 23–4
  in D. L. Rogers and F. T. Ledig (eds). *The status of North American temperate
  forest genetic resources*. Report No. 15. Genetic Resources Conservation
  Program, University of California, Davis, California.
Wilson, B. C. 1990. Gene pool reserves of Douglas-fir. *Forest Ecology and
  Management* **35**(1– 2):121–30.
Wright, S. 1978. *Evolution and the Genetics of Populations*. University of Chicago
  Press, Chicago.
Zobel, B. 1977. Gene conservation – as viewed by a tree breeder. *Forest Ecology and
  Management* **1**:339–44.

Part IV
Synthesis and implementation

15 Restoration ecology

LEE E. FRELICH AND KLAUS J. PUETTMANN

Restoration has the goal of returning an ecosystem to a desired, more natural state after human disturbance. Setting this goal is different from restoration science itself. Scientists rarely choose the goals for restorations, which are generally determined in some political process, hopefully with the input of scientists who can advise which goals are feasible. The restoration scientist is then asked: how do we achieve this goal? The design and implementation of a plan for attaining the goal is the actual science of restoration ecology. Often experiments will be necessary to determine whether components of a proposed plan will work. For example, will creating gaps in a forest allow coexistence of a large number of native tree species? Will the gaps help keep non-native species in check, or help them further their invasion? Restoration ecology is fundamentally an interdisciplinary field and restoration ecologists draw knowledge from disturbance ecology, population biology of plant and animals, and soil science among others.

Restoration of forests also brings interactions with silviculturalists and timber harvesters. This has two implications for a forest restorationist. First, the science of restoration ecology bridges the boundary between basic and applied science. The restorationist has to know basic biology, which must be applied to direct ecosystem development towards a specific outcome. Second, forest restoration also bridges the boundary between preservation of natural areas and production forestry. In most forests of the world, only a small portion of the landscape is reserved from timber harvest. Therefore, maintenance of biodiversity may require the restoration of natural processes and species outside of nature reserves, while allowing for a flow of forest products.

Why forest restoration is necessary: factors that degrade forest ecosystems

Humans have transformed one-third to one-half of the ice-free surface of the earth, a land use change that at this time is the largest component of global change (Vitousek 1994). This includes clearing of land for settlement, farming, urbanization, mining, and timber ultilization. For example, in the Great Lakes region of the United States, only 1.1% of all forests extant at the time of European settlement have not been logged at least once and 40% of all former forest lands have been converted to other uses (Frelich 1995). Land use change is the overarching change in vegetation that either directly influences or inadvertently precipitates all of the other factors that degrade forests from their natural state.

Deforested land may be subject to erosion in upper parts of a watershed and the corresponding flooding of the lower parts. Biological invasions also are a major factor impacting forests (Vitousek *et al.* 1996). Species from other continents are often introduced to a region and their invasion into native vegetation is facilitated by disturbance to the soil occurring during land use changes. Land use changes usually also precipitate changes in the fire regime, often by interrupting the contiguity of fuel, thereby disrupting the movement of fires across the landscape. Finally, land use change may be accompanied by increased intensity of browsing on woody stems and grazing of herbaceous plants by cattle and native animals.

Importance of the blueprint – a goal for restoration

There is a gradient in the degree to which the factors discussed above have shifted individual sites from their natural condition, and many restoration possibilities exist for stands anywhere along this gradient (Figure 15.1). Therefore, one must establish a goal for restoration. Common goals include: single-species goals, e.g., bringing back a formerly abundant tree species; multiple-species goals, e.g., re-establishing formerly abundant plant communities; and process-oriented goals, e.g., bringing back fire as a force on the landscape or improving water quality in a watershed. Time and money available for a given restoration project are generally limited, and it must be decided how far to attempt to move along this gradient of naturalness. On those sites furthest removed from the natural condition, such as mine tailings and areas where soil has been

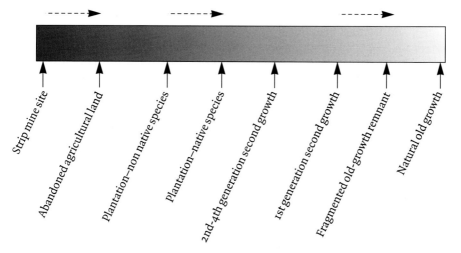

Fig. 15.1. Gradient of naturalness in forest stands. Darker shading indicates further removal from natural condition. Dotted arrows show that most restoration efforts within a human planning horizon can only move a stand part way across the gradient. In this hypothetical example, moving a site from the condition of a strip mine to that of a field; moving from non-native plantation to native plantation; and moving from first generation second growth to nearly natural old growth all require about the same investment of time and resources.

stripped, it is necessary to restore soil and plants to the site – a process known as reclamation. Abandoned agricultural lands that were formerly forested require reforestation, or the return of trees and forest plants. Restoration in an existing second-growth forest may require only adjustments in the tree-species mixture and return of structural features such as coarse woody debris to achieve a nearly natural forest ecosystem.

NATURAL VERSUS HUMAN DESIGNED BLUEPRINTS

When the goal is to restore a natural ecosystem, three sources of information for designing a blueprint are commonly used: remnant natural areas, paleoecological data, and historical records. Many 'natural area systems' have been established with the goal of preserving examples of native vegetation types. Many of these have been affected by land use changes in the surrounding areas, a major drawback in using them as a blueprint. For example, the successional trajectories in a natural area may have been changed by elimination of fire and edge effects. Thus, the natural area itself may need restoration, and the goal of restoration may need to be chosen from the other two major sources of information for designing a blueprint: paleoecological and historical records.

Paleoecological records from fossil pollen and vegetation parts such as cones and needles preserved in wetland sediments may help determine which species were dominant in the vegetation before widespread conversion of the landscape to other uses. Fossil charcoal may also help determine former fire frequencies. Many types of historical records of former vegetation occur around the world. In the United States, the General Land Office Surveys, conducted by the federal government during the ninteenth century, provide a record of the presettlement forest, via witness trees that were recorded at township and section corners, as well as notes on the vegetation that were taken as surveyors walked along the section lines (Galatowitsch 1990). Certain features of the natural disturbance regimes such as fire and windthrow rotations can sometimes also be calculated from these records (Whitney 1986). Accounts of vegetation by ancient travelers, for example, Tacitus' travel through Germany (Tacitus 98), or by settlers, and paintings or photographs have also been used to reconstruct the history of vegetation.

Detailed studies are usually needed to construct a blueprint from a remnant natural area and historical data. Knowledge obtained includes structure and composition of the vegetation, and timing, severity and spatial patterns of disturbances. Some stands undergo succession in species composition after natural disturbances, but others do not. For example, in North American hemlock (*Tsuga canadensis*)–sugar maple (*Acer saccharum*) forests and boreal jack pine (*Pinus banksiana*) forests, the disturbance regime favors regeneration of the same tree species over and over again (Frelich and Reich 1995). Nevertheless, even in these cases, understory plant species composition may be changing through succession. Also, many natural disturbances do not totally kill the canopy or the propagules over large areas. For example, although the Yellowstone fires of 1988 burned over 250 000 ha, 75% of the severely burned land was within 200 m of unburned or lightly burned forest within the overall fire perimeter (Turner *et al.* 1994). These are the sorts of data one should have in hand to determine how to modify forest management to emulate natural patterns.

In the absence of a natural blueprint, a number of different goals may be selected. In long-settled regions of Europe and Asia, nature reserves may represent human-made agricultural landscapes rather than natural vegetation. In these situations the goal may be to restore functional attributes. For example, one may decide that a forest of any sort is better than no forest – because forests reduce erosion and slow the rate of runoff in a watershed – and proceed to restore forest vegetation without regard to details of the presettlement or natural forest attributes.

Some restoration projects may attempt to establish and maintain representative examples of all known vegetation types and/or successional stages in a given region. Large-scale processes are often involved in formation of a pattern of different types or stages across the landscape. An example is a system with large, wide-ranging herbivores, such as elephants in Africa. Because elephant movements are greatly restricted in settled parts of Africa, overbrowsing and destruction of woodland within nature reserves occurs. Simulations have been used to see how various frequencies of burning may help maintain both the elephant herd and woodland at the same time within a limited area (Starfield et al. 1993). The main goal of this example, to bring the various components of the landscape into some sort of balance, could be implemented simply because people want each of the components for economic, aesthetic, or other reasons.

RESTORATION IN NATURAL AREAS VERSUS PRODUCTION FORESTS

Within remnant natural areas, restoration projects always raise the issue of what is natural. The regional changes in fire frequency, fragmentation, and browsing by large herbivores that often accompany land use changes have large effects within so-called 'natural areas'. There may be no way to know what the vegetation would be like now if people had never settled the area. Due to successional or climatic change, it could be that a natural area is not like it was prior to settlement, but that it is no different from how it would have been without settlement. Thus, the 'museum approach' of trying to reconstruct the vegetation exactly as it was prior to extensive settlement of an area, does not necessarily yield the 'natural state' of the vegetation. There is nothing wrong with the museum approach, especially if the goal is to have an example of a natural area to show visitors what the landscape was like at the time their ancestors first inhabited the area. This makes the function similar to 'period rooms' in art museums or old villages in historical museums. Such a restoration may meet other goals, such as providing habitat for species that are uncommon in the region, and providing the various services of natural vegetation, such as steady flow of water and climate stabilization. The alternative to the museum approach is called 'aiming for a moving target'. This involves discovering what the presettlement condition was, and then extrapolating how the forest would have changed due to natural forces such as climate change, since the time of settlement. The predicted forest condition at the current time then becomes the restoration goal.

In production forests, the goal of restoration is to simultaneously maintain biodiversity while producing commodities. Governmental programs
may offer a chance to do this if restorationists have input in their development. A policy such as 'Big Tree Silviculture' (see section on 'Large trees'
below) may allow certain old-growth forest characteristics to develop over
an entire landscape. Another option is Best Management Practices
(BMPs), which are guidelines for timber owners and harvesters on such
issues as rotation periods, harvest methods (e.g., clearcut versus selection
cut), gap size, leaving snags and seed trees, and riparian zone practices.
BMPs have so far mainly been designed to improve water, soil, and visual
quality (Ellefson et al. 1995), but can include methods for restoring forests
across the landscape insofar as restoration blueprints are codified in
them. A BMP may specify that a certain number of trees with cavities be left
standing on each hectare within a harvest. In a sense, this is restoration
ecology for a particular component of the ecosystem, in this case cavity-
nesting birds. In Bavaria, Germany, monetary incentives reward private
landowners who successfully regenerate mixed-species stands. Thus,
various elements of forest restoration can be incorporated into normal
forestry operations, and this offers restoration ecologists an opportunity
to bridge the gap between natural area management and production
forestry.

IMPORTANCE OF EXPERIMENTS AND MONITORING

Experiments may be necessary to ensure that a given blueprint is
feasible, and to work out a plan to get to the condition specified in the blueprint. For example, upland white cedar (Thuja occidentalis) forests on the
north shore of Lake Superior in Minnesota, USA, have not had significant
regeneration for the last 80 years. Many managers believed that browsing
by white-tailed deer (Odocoileus virginianus) prevented the spread of white
cedar from small patches embedded in a landscape matrix of second-
growth paper birch (Betula papyrifera) forest. Deer exclosures were built
and proved that indeed deer browsing is a limitation. However, seed distribution studies and seedling surveys under both the cedar and birch canopies showed that other problems exist as well (Cornett 1997). Cedar seeds
are not dispersed very far into the surrounding paper birch forests, most
cedar seedlings die when germinating on birch duff, and the most
common microsites for white cedar germination – rotten conifer logs –
are not common in birch forests. A restoration plan under preparation,
backed up by experimental data, will show to what extent cedar can invade

the surrounding birch forest, given the limitations discovered during the experimental research. Once this plan is in place, monitoring will be necessary to ensure that unforseen factors are not interfering with progress towards the goal.

Stand level restoration

SPECIES COMPOSITION

Monoculture vs. mixed species

In many parts of the world, forest management has promoted monocultural stands by regenerating one species and eliminating competing species through site preparation or release treatments. Converting multi-species stands into monocultures has a variety of impacts on soils (Perry 1994), understory vegetation (Simmons and Buckley 1992), animal populations (Smith 1992), and ecosystem functions. Thus many restoration efforts will aim to establish native species mixtures (Bayerisches Staatsministerium 1987, Otto 1993). However, alteration of soil characteristics or hydrologic regime might prevent some of the native species from successfully reestablishing (Shear *et al.* 1996).

Regeneration of mixed species can be enhanced by using site preparations that create diverse seedbed conditions, such as band spraying of herbicides, or mechanical treatments that limit the disturbance to rows or small patches within the forest. Diverse seedbed conditions, the seedbank, and the presence of sprouting or suckering species can provide a patchy mixture of tree regeneration even under fairly homogeneous overstory conditions (Cornett 1997). Alternatively, if seed sources for one or more of the desired species are lacking, these species can be seeded or planted in an arrangement that takes advantage of microsite variability by placing species on mounds or in depressions to better fit their germination and growing requirements.

Site preparation and planting arrangements, along with patchiness of natural seedfall and the soil, determine the spatial layout of mixed species stands. The most common arrangements are the single tree, row, or group mixtures. The single tree mixtures allow for the most interaction between tree species, a desirable situation when one species benefits the other. For example, single red alder (*Alnus oregoni*) trees mixed into a Douglas-fir (*Pseudotsuga menziesii*) stand provide the most benefits through nitrogen fixation (Miller and Murray 1986). Row plantings have the advantage of being easier to implement on a larger scale. In both single-tree and row mixtures any tree will have trees of other species as direct neighbors. In these arrangements the growth patterns of the desired species should be fairly compatible to minimize suppression and mortality of the slower growing species. Alternatively, patches of the slow-growing species can be made larger, so that neighbors within groups can buffer competition with other species, allowing a few individuals of the slower growing species to survive and reach upper canopy status (Hibbs 1982). Varying the size of patches dominated by each species throughout a stand will probably sim-ulate natural conditions. For example, patches dominated by either sugar maple or hemlock in unlogged forest remnants in Upper Michigan range from 0.01 ha to 20 ha (Frelich *et al.* 1993). During a harvest, gaps of different sizes can be interspersed throughout a stand, favoring a patchy mixture of species with differing levels of shade tolerance (Poulson and Platt 1989).

Managing exotic species

Exotic species are those growing outside their native range. In many instances exotic trees have been introduced because they can provide more benefits (e.g., faster growth rates) than the local species. Large acreages of native tropical and temperate hardwoods have been replaced by exotic conifers that can be regenerated more easily and managed in plantations. It is not always possible to separate the effects of high-inten-sity plantation management from the effects of introducing an exotic (vs. a native) species. However, the likelihood of maintaining native understory biota and soil properties in managed forests is higher when planting indigenous overstory species. Restoration efforts reflect this by emphasiz-ing the use of native plant material and natural regeneration (Otto 1993), although there are cases where severe site conditions will not allow native trees to grow, and reforestation with exotic tree species may be better than no forest at all.

A second kind of exotics are invading weedy species, either herbaceous plants or shrubs with high seed production that can colonize disturbed or undisturbed areas quickly. Invading species can impact ecosystems through competition with natives, prevention of tree regeneration, altera-tion of food and cover for animals, and alteration of disturbance (espe-cially fire) regimes.

It would be ideal if we could prevent invasion or eliminate exotics once they invade. However, experience shows that this is often impractical, and learning to live with a component of exotic species within the forest may be necessary. Thus, the restoration ecologist is often faced with the task of maintaining a balance between exotic and native species. This can be accomplished by direct removal of aggressive exotic species through cutting or pulling out, by applications of a specific herbicide, and by use of fire or grazing. Keeping in mind that undisturbed systems, like dense forests, are most resistant to invaders, restoration efforts should be applied very carefully if seed sources of exotic species are still present in the area (Berger 1993). This is especially critical in areas where the native seed-bank has been lost. Thus, strategies to remove exotic plants should include measures to ensure the establishment of native vegetation.

Understory trees, shrubs, herbs

Understory composition and density change throughout succession and stand development, and within a single growing season. Compared with monocultures, forests with mixed species in the canopy often have a relatively high understory plant cover and species diversity (Simmons and Buckley 1992). On the other hand, the overall level of competition between trees in mixed-species forest might be higher than in monocultures, leaving fewer resources available for the understory. In these cases the restoration of understory vegetation will be slower, or limited to shade-tolerant species (Guariguata et al. 1995).

In established forests, efforts to restore understory vegetation can be applied at various stages of stand development. Preparation of a planting or seeding site can facilitate survival and growth of understory herbs and shrubs by excluding portions of the stands from intensive disturbance, such as mechanical site preparation. Areas within a prescribed burn can be wetted down to reduce fire impacts. A lower planting density will delay time to crown closure (stem exclusion) and ensure longer presence of understory herbs and shrubs. In addition, thinning can move a stand through the stem exclusion phase more quickly by allowing enough light and other resources to support dense and diverse understory vegetation (Simmons and Buckley 1992). Thinning operations or other intermediate stand treatments should avoid disturbing existing understory vegetation by using designated skid trails or accessing stands during winter. Slash from thinning operations should be distributed to minimize interference with understory vegetation.

In restoration programs, it is often assumed that understory vegetation will establish over time ('plant trees and the rest will come'), but natural invasion may not automatically bring back all species desired (Matlack 1994). Instead, species with good dispersal mechanisms and high competitive abilities are favored. Many herbs, mosses, and other small components of forests do not disperse widely and they often require special microhabitats such as rotten wood. If restoration is taking place in a remnant natural area, native species already present cannot be guaranteed to persist, given the possibility of local extinctions caused by predation, disease, disturbance, or inbreeding. Therefore, these species need to be taken into account in the blueprint, so that they can be actively restored and monitored along with the larger components, such as trees. Structural features that provide microhabitats for many smaller species, such as tip-up mounds and large coarse woody debris, will eventually form through stand development processes, but big trees must be present first. The processes that create structural complexity can be sped up by thinning to get larger trees faster, or by creating artificial microhabitats.

Where seed sources are lacking or species are slow invaders, plants can be introduced through seeding or planting. Fire, herbicide treatments, or mechanical removal of current understory vegetation might be necessary to prepare adequate seedbeds and growing conditions for desired species. For restoration purposes, native understory species can be separated into groups that (a) establish and mature quickly, usually more light-demanding forest edge species, (b) require a long establishment phase, usually shade-tolerant forest understory species and (c) have limited seed supply (Francis and Morton 1995). Moderate (3 kg/ha) and high (10 kg/ha) density seeding is recommended for the first two groups, respectively. Seeds from the third group should be germinated under controlled conditions and the seedlings be allowed to slowly acclimate to forest conditions before outplanting. Introducing seeds or seedlings in clumps improves establishment and mimics the mosaic spatial pattern of natural vegetation. Patch layout should take advantage of overstory conditions that favor the desired species. Obviously, large-scale establishment of understory vegetation through these measures is quite costly. However, small transplanted patches of native forest floor species can act as inoculation centers and initiate a process that allows native understory vegetation to spread.

In some ecosystems, for example the ponderosa pine (*Pinus ponderosa*) region in the western United States, the natural understory is characterized by low-density vegetation. Elimination of fire during the last several decades has allowed development of dense understory vegetation. In these areas restoration efforts may employ frequent understory disturbances (e.g., prescribed underburning or manual or chemical removal of understory shrubs) to move understory conditions closer to the natural densities. Other measures like mowing, cutting and removing trees, or introducing native seedbank may prepare a site before re-establishment of the natural disturbance regime is attempted (Covington 1996).

Mycorrhizae and other microbes

Mycorrhizae and other fungi and microbial organisms are greatly impacted by forest management through alteration of soil structures, lack of host species, and microclimate changes (Perry 1994). However, if these changes do not persist, populations might be able to recover. For example, mycorrhizal populations are lowered through prescribed fire, but recover quickly as vegetation cover returns to the site (Lavender et al. 1990). Land use changes that alter soil structure, hydrologic regime, nutrient status, or microclimate will have a greater and longer-lasting effect than fires.

In restoration sites where quick establishment of trees is critical, inoculation of seeds or seedlings with mycorrhizae and other organisms, like nitrogen-fixing Frankia spp., might be beneficial (Molina et al. 1993). Large-scale mycorrhizal inoculations in the United States on southern pines and inoculations of Rhizopogon on ponderosa pine and Douglas-fir container seedlings in the Pacific Northwest have focused on fast tree establishment and growth, rather than restoring native fungal communities. As with any inoculations, concerns exist about the interaction between the inoculum and native fungal communities. Some studies have indicated that some mycorrhizae species are very widespread and not specific to individual sites or conditions, and other studies have shown that the benefits of inocula are limited and the inoculation material will most likely be replaced by native fungi already present in the forest floor (Molina et al. 1993).

Animals

Most reforestation efforts are limited to plants, and land managers rely on the natural ability of animals to colonize restored forest land. Although higher animals are quite mobile, soil invertebrates may not be very mobile, and can be strongly affected by forest management activities. It is estimated that half of the soil fauna species and 90% of the individuals disappear after clearcutting old-growth Douglas-fir forests (Perry 1994). Analysis of arthropods in a restored wetland indicated rapid establishment of a diverse fauna, although the overall abundance of arthropods, especially predators and parasites, was lower on the restored site than on a nearby reference site (Williams 1993). To accelerate the invasion of soil microfauna, soil from nearby forests can be brought in and spread through the restored forest as inoculation centers. This might also benefit the forest by introducing a native seedbank.

Restoring natural vegetation patterns and dynamics might require reducing populations of animals that negatively impact vegetation. For example, white-tailed deer populations in North America and red deer (Cervus elephus) or roe deer (Capreolus capreolus) populations in central Europe have increased over the last several decades. At extremely high levels, deer browsing can significantly affect regeneration of tree, shrub, and herb species. Browsers such as deer usually prefer certain woody species in a given region, and prolonged browsing can lead to successional replacement of the preferred species (Watson 1983). Grazing of herbaceous plant species can dramatically alter community composition. Plants with multiple-leaved stems and recurrent flushes of growth throughout the growing season are less sensitive to grazing pressure than plants with a single flush and one set of leaves (e.g., many geophytes, such as Trillium spp.). Throughout the season, grazers adjust their diet according to which species are near the flowering stage, so that a whole suite of species may be affected (Augustine 1997). Common methods used to deal with browsing and grazing are protection of the terminal leader of conifers with bud caps, fencing, or reduction of deer numbers.

STRUCTURAL COMPONENTS

Single canopy vs. multiple canopy layers

Most production forests that are single-cohort monocultures also have a single canopy layer. During the stem exclusion phase of development, the stand structure of monocultures is usually relatively simple as stands lack significant amounts of midstory or understory vegetation (Oliver and Larson 1996). The trend to simplified canopy structures is further emphasized through thinning practices (Smith et al. 1997). For example, low thinnings that take out trees in the lower portion of the canopy will homogenize the canopy structure even further. However, considerable experience exists in managing stand structure and natural structural attributes (e.g., size distribution, canopy layers) can be mimicked in both planted and naturally regenerated forests (Shear et al. 1996).

Thinning or other cutting practices and prescribed fire can be designed to restore a natural canopy structure. Removal of trees by cuttings has the advantage that specific trees or groups of trees in all canopy layers can be targeted, and can also diversify stand structure by leaving patches with different densities of trees. Size of patches and densities can be patterned to achieve the desired range of tree and crown sizes. This kind of variable density thinning can also prepare a stand for conversion from single-cohort to multi-cohort, multi-structured canopy conditions. Prescribed fires are efficient in thinning out high-density patches of trees, retarding shrub growth, and removing invading seedlings of shade-tolerant tree species in cases where the desired goal is to restore an early-successional forest type.

Silvicultural guidelines developed for timber production purposes have to be modified if restoration goals are to be accommodated. For example, if the aim of restoration is to simulate a landscape shaped by frequent surface fires, i.e., a high proportion of large trees, the q-factor that determines the ratio of small to large diameter trees in multi-cohort stands needs to be lower than that used in standard prescriptions. Alternatively, a certain number of large diameter trees might be set aside, i.e., not included in the diameter distribution used to develop management guidelines. This would allow maintaining large diameter trees in the stand, while managing for commodity production.

Large trees

'Big trees' are an important characteristic of many mature and old-growth stands. Also, in managed stands big trees can provide important habitat components, like nesting sites for raptors, and special recreational and aesthetic values. Because of interest in these special values, the state of Wisconsin, USA, has developed management guidelines known as 'big tree silviculture', aimed specifically at restoring a landscape dominated by large diameter trees on state-owned lands. The state of Minnesota, USA, has approached the same problem with a policy of extended rotation forestry on state forest lands, under which some stands (ranging from 10% to 70% of all stands in a given state forest) are allowed to grow 50–100% longer than standard rotations. Either policy may restore some old-growth features like large trees and coarse woody debris over part of the landscape.

The contrast between the approaches of these two adjacent states is interesting. In Wisconsin, big tree silviculture is aimed at producing trees greater than a certain diameter. Species that are selected as 'big trees' should have longevity, wind firmness, resistance to rot and other diseases, and should be present in various stages of successional development. In contrast, the Minnesota policy of extended rotation recognizes that older forests on poor sites, where a few trees reach old ages but not necessarily large size, have intrinsic value. Some stands composed of early successional species such as aspen (*Populus tremuloides*) also are allowed to go into extended rotation, and such stands may develop an understory of late-successional species that is not common in aspen stands under the standard rotation.

Coarse woody debris

Dead limbs, boles, and roots on the forest floor with a minimum diameter from 2.5 cm to 15 cm have been defined as coarse woody debris (Harmon *et al.* 1986). Coarse woody debris (CWD) exists in all forests in various amounts and stages of decomposition. Benefits for long-term sustainability of forest ecosystems include storage and slow release of water and nutrients, and serving as an important microsite for tree regeneration and many species of mosses, fungi and microfauna (Harmon *et al.* 1986; Chapter 10). Harvesting, slash disposal, and site preparation has reduced the amounts of CWD found in most managed forests.

Efforts to restore natural amounts and dynamics of CWD should recognize that amounts, size distributions, and longevity of CWD vary between ecosystems and with stand development stage (Graham *et al.* 1994). Establishing natural fire cycles will be helpful in restoring natural rates of accumulation and decomposition of CWD. Slash left after stand restoration treatment should be composed of different species because decomposition patterns, longevity, and species that use the CWD as habitat, vary (Harmon *et al.* 1986). During harvest and site preparation operations the slash should be distributed across the site, rather than in piles. Chopping or chipping of slash will also alter the decomposition dynamics and should be avoided.

Timing to maximize effectiveness of restoration efforts

There are certain stages of stand development and succession during which relatively small efforts will yield relatively large changes in the future condition of a stand. Two key times to influence future species composition are the beginning of stand initiation, and the beginning of understory reinitiation (Figure 15.2). At these points, the stand may be open to invasion by new species. If the new species is a desired part of the blueprint, then action could be taken to amplify its establishment. If not, then it is easiest to eliminate it at the point of early invasion. For example, in eastern North America, succession in paper birch stands on soils of medium quality could go to either sugar maple or white pine (*Pinus strobus*). There are several avenues for conversion of the birch stand to white pine (Figure 15.2). The more inroads sugar maple makes into the birch stand, the higher the amount of intervention and cost of conversion

Spatial layout of stands:

Current status   Desired blueprint

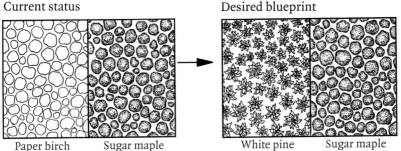

Paper birch   Sugar maple   White pine   Sugar maple

Probable course of stand development and succession in birch stand:

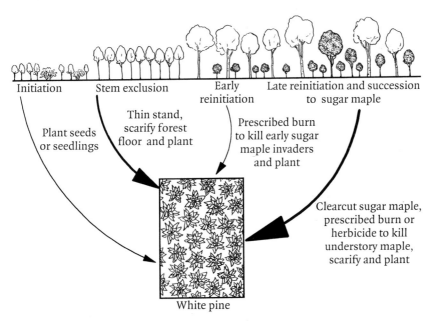

Initiation   Stem exclusion   Early   Late reinitiation and succession
                                    reinitiation   to sugar maple

            Thin stand,
            scarify forest   Prescribed burn
Plant seeds floor and plant   to kill early sugar
or seedlings   maple invaders
                                    and plant

                                                    Clearcut sugar maple,
                                                    prescribed burn or
                                                    herbicide to kill
                                                    understory maple,
                                                    scarify and plant

                    White pine

Fig. 15.2. Stand development and time windows during which alteration of the
successional trajectory is most effective. To get to the desired blueprint, the successional
trajectory of the birch stand must be altered so that maple from the adjacent stand does not
become dominant. This is most easily accomplished in the initiation or reinitiation stages of
stand development. During the stem exclusion stage or in the latter part of reinitiation when
maple has become abundant, much more effort would be required to establish pine. Arrow
thickness is proportional to difficulty of establishing the desired white pine forest.

to white pine. The proper timing of treatments (i.e., prescribed burning when sugar maple is first invading) provides the best opportunity to achieve the desired blueprint. A good restoration ecologist should always be aware of the present and future desired condition of the stand so that no such opportunity ever slips away.

As a general rule, once shade-tolerant or sprouting species are established, it is hard to eliminate them. The same is true for shrubs in fire-dependent ecosystems. Changing the disturbance regime from fire to logging can often lead to an increase of shrub abundance, especially if late-successional tree species are removed by logging operations before they dominate the stand and shade out the shrubs. If logging maintains early successional tree species that cast relatively light shade, shrubs can become a problem that gets progressively worse.

Reforestation of agricultural land

Changing ownership patterns and lower profitability of agricultural operations can lead landowners to abandon farming and consider alternative land uses including forest management. Natural successional processes usually allow forest to return on sites that were forested before farming. In many cases, however, an active restoration program can accelarate the transition from field to forest, and may lead to a more complete forest community. Before restoring native forests to fields, site conditions should be evaluated carefully, because soil structure, hydrologic regime, and nutrient status might have been so altered that site conditions are no longer suitable for native vegetation (Luedemann 1993). Plow layers and grazing on abandoned farm fields in the temperate zone often favor certain species for decades or centuries after abandonment of an agricultural field (Peterken and Game 1984). For example, the native species white cedar often dominates on sites in southern Quebec, Canada, that were dominated by sugar maple at the time of settlement, used as pasture, and then abandoned (deBlois and Bouchard 1995). Thus, substantial effort may be necessary to counteract the legacy of farming and restore the balance among native tree species on abandoned farmland. In addition, reforestation of agricultural land has focused on establishing trees with very little attention paid to understory plants (Ferris-Kaan 1995). Active restoration of native understory vegetation is especially critical in areas that had long-term agricultural use, where woodland species are absent from the seedbank, and current seed sources of native plants are too

Table 15.1. *Problems and some solutions in restoring forest to abandoned agricultural land*

Problem	Potential solutions
High nutrient content of soil causes excessive weed competition	Let field lay fallow or harvest without fertilization for several years prior to restoration; kill weeds with herbicides or use mats to keep weeds away around tree seedlings
Soil structure (plow layer)	Harrowing to break up plow layer and addition of organic matter
Harsh initial conditions (high sunlight, wind, dry soil)	Plant a 'cover crop' of pioneer species (e.g., birch or aspen); plant sensitive tree species with soil ball rather than bareroot
Lack of mycorrhizae	Inoculate seedlings before planting; transplantation of soil plugs from nearby forest into the field
Lack of propagules for herbs, mosses and fungi	Direct seeding; transplantation of mature plants; transplantation of existing forest floor plugs containing seedbank and sporebank
Lack of soil microfauna	Transplantation of existing forest floor plugs
Lack of microsites	Move large logs onto site; make 'tip-up mounds' with shovel
Deer grazing	High-density initial plantings so that some survive; fence deer out of the restoration area; special hunts to keep deer numbers low
Lack of small mammal community	Reintroduction from other forests in the region

distant for natural dispersal to be effective. Harsh initial conditions and deer grazing may lead to high mortality, so that high-density plantings may be necessary to ensure survival of enough plants to establish a permanent viable population.

Clearly, successful restoration efforts must address these problems (Table 15.1). Merely identifying a list of problems and their potential solutions, however, will not bring back the forest. The order in which components of restoration are carried out is just as important. For example, introduction of forest rodents may require pre-existing understory plants, which in turn require a pre-existing overstory, which may require prior removal of agricultural weed communities and simultaneous introduction of mycorrhizae for establishment.

Despite the complexity of reforesting agricultural land, it is currently the major land use change in many European countries (Baur 1993,

Erlbeck 1993). In fact, concern has been raised that regions like the Black Forest in Germany will lose their picturesque appeal for tourists through encroachment of forests.

Landscape level restoration

THE LANDSCAPE AS A COLLECTION OF STANDS

The juxtaposition of stands with different stages of succession and/or different forest types with unique endpoints to succession is an important consideration in restoration of a forested landscape. There are two fundamental reasons why a mosaic of different communities forms over the landscape. First, different ecosystem types exist, as defined by physiography, soil, climate, and species composition in the absence of severe disturbance (Arbeitsgemeinschaft Standortskartierung 1980). Second, disturbances overlay a mosaic of successional stages within a given ecosystem type, on top of the base mosaic. Severe disturbances such as crown fires tend to override the effects of different ecosystem types and homogenize the landscape, while low-severity disturbances such as individual treefall or selection cutting tend to advance successional development, allowing different successional pathways.

Consequently, the mosaic of ecosystem types and the disturbance mosaic must be blended to create the landscape closest to a given blueprint goal. If the goal is to restore late-successional forest types in a region where they are rare, then divergent succession to several different forest types should be facilitated when one stand of early successional species (e.g., aspen originating after fire or farm abandonment), spans several ecosystem types (Figure 15.3). If the goal of restoration is to create a natural disturbance mosaic, then some severe disturbances will be necessary to create young stands of pioneer species, while in other places, similar young stands are undergoing succession to other stand types (Figure 15.3). In any case, delineating the stands based on current composition and using that information as a static representation of the landscape will not maintain diversity for the long term.

SCALE OF RESTORATION

The scale of most restoration efforts is strongly influenced by the ownership size. Ownerships that cover vast contiguous areas, like

Aspen-dominated landscape after land clearing and burning

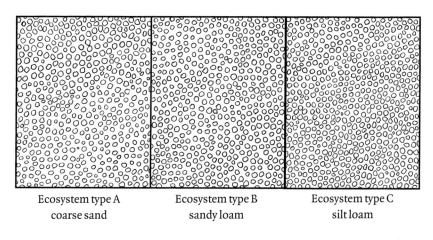

| Ecosystem type A | Ecosystem type B | Ecosystem type C |
| coarse sand | sandy loam | silt loam |

Blueprint allowing divergent succession

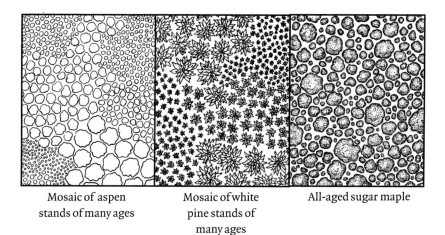

Mosaic of aspen	Mosaic of white	All-aged sugar maple
stands of many ages	pine stands of	
	many ages	

Fig. 15.3. Landscape mosaic as a blend of ecosystem type units (A–C) and disturbances. This blueprint shows how divergent succession from aspen could occur, based on the probable climax vegetation in each ecosystem type. Within a given ecosystem type, natural or harvest disturbances could lead to a mosaic of stands of many ages.

national forests in the United States, can develop restoration plans for entire watersheds or regions. A second scenario includes ownerships that are large but not contiguous, for example, U.S. Forest Service land that is intermixed with Bureau of Land Management and private land.

Restoration efforts in these areas should integrate across public and private landholdings. In many cases, management of private land will be driven by economic incentives, and regional restoration plans have to accommodate private property rights and objectives. A third scenario involves small tracts of forest scattered throughout an agricultural landscape. For example 83% of all woodlands in farm-dominated areas in Great Britain are 20 acres or less (Ferris-Kaan 1995). In these cases, strategies to minimize edge effect may be necessary to retain area-sensitive species such as certain song birds (Chapters 6 and 7). Edge effects might be minimized by attempting to acquire and reforest an adjacent parcel, or to link a network of woodlots with forested corridors (Noss and Harris 1986).

Within some ownerships restoration efforts can focus only on small portions like riparian areas or forest edges. If restoration includes taking land out of production, starting restoration efforts with a limited, well-defined scope might provide an opportunity to convince landowners of the benefits of restoration. Landowners are more prone to accept production losses on areas that have management problems, like meandering borders (rivers) or slopes. Restoration efforts could stay contained to these areas or eventually spread across broader parts of ownerships.

EMULATING DISTURBANCE AND SPATIAL PATTERNS FOUND IN NATURE

Disturbance regimes are very variable in timing, severity and size, and this variability is responsible in part for maintaining biodiversity (Chapter 4). Some stands are hit twice by major disturbances within a few years, favoring species with short generation times. Other areas are not disturbed for a long time and succeed to late-successional species. Severity also varies tremendously, from individual treefalls to complete canopy kill accompanied by removal of the duff layer and seedbank. The overall result is a tremendously complex mosaic of species that have responded to variable intervals and severities of disturbances (Johnson 1992).

In contrast, harvesting regimes tend to be much more uniform than natural disturbances. For management purposes most forested landscapes are delineated into stands. Stand layouts in many regions have not been determined by analyzing natural disturbance patterns, but have been arranged to accommodate harvesting equipment, resulting in fairly homogeneous stand sizes. In addition, harvests tend to apply similar rotation periods to all stands across the landscape, as well as between harvests within one stand, using techniques that reproduce similar disturbance severity.

Restoring the landscape structure to reflect a more natural pattern will likely result in many small and few large stands. Restoration efforts may include varying treatments within stands. This concept was implemented in recent experiments in British Columbia, Canada. Harvesting units were laid out to mimic the natural gap size distribution, i.e., single tree, group selection, and small clearcut type openings were created within one harvesting unit (D. Coates, personal communication). Alternatively, to increase patch size without rearranging stand delineations, several stands could be managed together as a 'superstand', i.e., the same management prescriptions will apply to adjacent stands. Harvesting operations can also be made more variable with regard to length of time between harvests and severity of harvests. For example, a given stand could be harvested at a short rotation (e.g., 40 years) and the next harvest could be after a much longer interval (e.g., 100 years). The principles of varying size and timing of disturbance applies both across the landscape (variation among stands) and within stand (variation among gaps).

Case study

RESTORATION OF NATIVE FORESTS IN THE LUENEBURGER HEIDE, GERMANY

During the middle ages extensive areas in northern Germany, specifically in what is now known as Lueneberger Heide, were deforested and used for sheep grazing. The grazing areas were characterized by Heide or heather (*Calluna vulgaris*). The area presented in this case study covers the Forest District (Forstamt) Sprakensehl, in the southeastern part of the Lueneburger Heide (Ebeling 1992). The inventory of 1777 indicated that 43% of the 6600 ha area was forested, 2% was farmed, and over half (55%) was covered by heather. Ninety percent of the forested area was occupied by oak (*Quercus robur*) with European beech (*Fagus sylvatica*) mixed in. The rest of the forest land was in conifers, mainly Scots pine (*Pinus sylvestris*). The case study presents a two-stage restoration program. First the heather areas were reforested with a conifer; the second step is the conversion from conifer monoculture to mixed, more natural forest structures.

Restoration efforts started in the mid 1800s. Initial efforts centered on filling in open areas in the oak forests by planting Scots pine and planting oak seedlings on only 20% of the oak sites. During 1860 to 1890, heather areas adjacent to forest land were purchased and extensive areas were planted with Scots pine. Current forest composition consists of Scots pine (66%), Norway spruce (*Picea abies*, 14%), oak (11%), Douglas-fir (4%), larch (*Larix decidua*, 3%) and European beech (2%). The majority of the stands (64%) are younger than 40 years, and very few (8%) are older than 120 years. In general the stands are loosely stocked and average volume is 50% of the yield table estimates.

Currently, restoration efforts strive to restore natural species composition and stand structures. A series of ecological analyses were conducted to construct a blueprint describing the natural vegetation for the area. A soil survey indicated that the apparently homogeneous heather sites are an intricate mosaic of loams, sand, loess, clay, and bogs. The soil survey information, climate conditions, and pollen analyses, suggested that 60% of the area was originally occupied by acidic beech forests, and 40% by oak communities. Scots pine would have been a pioneer species that occurred in stands near bogs and swamps. Spruce would mainly have been limited to low abundance in mixed-species stands.

The current restoration efforts are attempting reforestation of the better quality sites with the 'natural species combination' of beech and oaks. Scots pine will stay prominent on lower quality sites, but will be mixed with a variety of other species. Scots pine is regenerated naturally while other species like beech will be underplanted and, if necessary, fenced to prevent browsing losses. Thus, the existing mature forest conditions will be maintained during the conversion period.

Summary

Restoration ecology usually involves returning an ecosystem to a natural state after disturbance by humans. Forests may need restoration after being converted to farmland, and subjected to erosion, alteration of disturbance regimes, invasions of exotic species, and high levels of grazing. An important role of a restoration ecologist is to work with the political process to select a feasible goal or blueprint for restoration, and then design and implement a restoration plan including technical details for species, spatial patterns, types of harvesting or other physical manipulations to carry out on the ground. Establishment of restoration plans will often require examination of paleoecological and historical records to determine what the natural state of the forest should be, and experiments to determine how the biota will respond to proposed treatments.

Restoration may take place in both natural areas and production forests. Natural area restorations generally have the goal of creating an example of presettlement forest. In production forests, the goal of restoration is to maintain species and structural diversity and natural processes while simultaneously producing commodities. Maintenance of mixed tree species, eliminating exotic species, recreating original understory vegetation, fauna, and structural components such as coarse woody debris, are the usual tasks to accomplish in forest restoration. Developing silvicultural techniques that mimic natural disturbances, which are extremely variable in size, shape, severity and timing, is one method that usually helps restore natural components of a forest. Restoration at the landscape scale requires blending a mosaic of ecosystem types, as defined by soils and physiography, with a mosaic of stands at different stages of succession after disturbance.

Further readings

Restoration ecology and its relationship with other aspects of ecological sciences are discussed in Jordan *et al.* (1987) and Hobbs and Norton (1996). For discussion of the role of restoration ecology in maintaining ecosystem diversity and endangered species see Cairns (1988), Falk *et al.* (1996), and Noss and Cooperrider (1996). Whelan (1995) provides an overview of the difficulties of re-establishing natural fire regimes in natural areas.

Literature cited

Arbeitsgemeinschaft Standortskartierung. 1980. *Forstliche Standortsaufnahme.* Muenster-Hiltrup.

Augustine, D. W. 1997. White-tailed deer grazing and conservation of native plant communities in a fragmented maple-basswood forest ecosystem. M.S. Thesis. University of Minnesota, St. Paul, MN.

Baur, F. 1993. Walderneuerung auf Island. *Allgemeine Forstzeitschrift* **48**:241–6.

Bayerische Staatsministerium. 1987. *Grundsaetze fuer einen naturnahen Waldbau.* Bayerisches Staatsministerium fuer Ernaehrung, Landwirtschaft, und Forsten. Muenchen, Germany.

Berger. J. J. 1993. Ecological restoration and nonindigenous plant species: a review. *Ecological Restoration* **1**:74–82.

Cairns, J., Jr. 1988. Increasing diversity by restoring damaged ecosystems. Pp.
    333–43 in E. O. Wilson and F. M. Peter (eds). *Biodiversity*. National
    Academy Press, Washington, DC.
Cornett, M. W. 1997. Conifer regeneration in mixed deciduous–evergreen
    forests. M.S. Thesis. University of Minnesota, St. Paul, MN.
Covington, W. 1996. Implementing adaptive ecosystem restoration in western
    long-needled pine forests. Pp. 44–8 in W. Covington and P. K. Wagner
    (coordinators). *Conference on adaptive ecosystem restoration and management:
    restoration of Cordilleran conifer landscapes of North America*. General Technical
    Report RM-GTR-278. Fort Collins Colorado: U.S. Department of
    Agriculture, Forest Service, Rocky Mountain Forest and Range
    Experiment Station.
deBlois, S., and A. Bouchard. 1995. Dynamics of Thuja occidentalis in an agricultu-
    ral landscape of southern Quebec. *Journal of Vegetation Science* 6:531–42.
Ebeling, K. 1992. Entwicklung im Forstamt Sprakensehl: Vom Pionierwald zum
    gemischten Wald. *Allgemeine Forstzeitschrift* 47:608–11.
Ellefson, P. V., A. S. Cheng, and R. J. Moulton. 1995. *Regulation of private forestry
    practices by state governments*. Minnesota Agricultural Experiment Station
    Bulletin 605. Minnesota Agricultural Experiment Station, St. Paul, MN.
Erlbeck, R. 1993. Erstaufforstung in Groszbritannien. *Allgemeine Forstzeitschrift*
    48:239–40.
Falk, D. A., C. I. Millar, and M. Olwell. 1996. *Restoring Diversity: Strategies for
    Reintroduction of Endangered Plants*. Island Press, Washington, DC.
Ferris-Kaan, R. (ed.). 1995. *The Ecology of Woodland Creation*. J. Wiley and Sons,
    New York.
Francis, J. L. and A. J. Morton. 1995. Restoring the woodland field layer in young
    plantations and new woodlands. Pp. 1–14 in K. M. Urbanska, and K.
    Grodzinska (eds). *Restoration Ecology in Europe*. Geobotanical Institute
    SFIT, Zurich.
Frelich, L. E. 1995. Old forest in the Lake States today and before European set-
    tlement. *Natural Areas Journal* 15:157–67.
Frelich, L. E. and P. B. Reich. 1995. Neighborhood effects, disturbance, and suc-
    cession in forests of the western Great Lakes Region. *Ecoscience* 2:148–58.
Frelich, L. E., R. R. Calcote, M. B. Davis, and J. Pastor. 1993. Patch formation and
    maintenance in an old-growth hemlock–hardwood forest. *Ecology*
    74:513–27.
Galatowitsch, S.M. 1990. Using the original landsurvey notes to reconstruct pre-
    settlement landscapes in the American west. *Great Basin Naturalist*
    50:181–95.
Graham, R. T., Harvey, A. E., Jurgensen, M. F., Jain, T. B., Tonn, J. R., and D. S.
    Page-Dumroese. 1994. *Managing coarse woody debris in forests of the Rocky
    Mountains*. USDA Forest Service Intermountain Research Station
    Research Paper INT-RP-477.
Guariguarta, M. R., Rheingans, R. and F. Monatagnini. 1995. Early woody inva-
    sion under tree plantation in Costa Rica: implications for forest restora-
    tion. *Restoration Ecology* 3:252–60.

Harmon, M. E., Franklin, J. F., and F. J. Swanson. 1986. Ecology of coarse woody debris in temperate ecosystems. *Advances in Ecological Research.* **15**:133–302. Academic Press, New York.

Hibbs, D. E. 1982. White pine in the transition hardwood forest. *Canadian Journal of Botany* **60**:2046–53.

Hobbs, R. J. and D. A. Norton. 1996. Towards a conceptual framework for restoration ecology. *Restoration Ecology* **4**:93–110.

Johnson, E. A. 1992. *Fire and Vegetation Dynamics. Studies from the North American Boreal Forest.* Cambridge University Press, Cambridge .

Jordan, W. R. III, M. E. Gilpin, and J. D. Aber (eds). 1987. *Restoration Ecology.* Cambridge University Press, Cambridge.

Lavender, D. P., R.Parish, C. M. Johnson, G. Montgomery, A. Vyre, R. A. Willis, and D. Winston (eds). 1990. *Regenerating British Columbia's Forest.* University of British Columbia Press, Vancouver, BC.

Luedemann, G. 1993. Anlage und Pflege von Erstaufforstungen. *Allgemeine Forstzeitschrift* **48**:210–14.

Matlack, G. R. 1994. Plant species migration in a mixed-history forest landscape in eastern North America. *Ecology* **75**:1491–502.

Miller, R. E. and M. D. Murray. 1986. *Early survival and growth of planted Douglas-fir with red alder in four mixture regimes.* USDA Forest Service, Pacific Northwest Forest and Range Experiment Station Research Paper PNW-366.

Molina, R., D. Myrold, and C. Y. Li. 1993. Root symbioses of red alder: technological opportunities of enhanced regeneration and soil improvement. Pp. 23–46 in D. E. Hibbs, D. S. DeBell, and R. F. Tarrant (eds). *The Biology and Management of Red Alder.* Oregon State University Press, Corvallis, ORA.

Noss, R. F. and A. Y. Cooperrider. 1996. *Saving Nature's legacy: protecting and restoring biodiversity.* Island Press, Washington, DC.

Noss, R. F. and L. D. Harris. 1986. Nodes, networks and MUMs: preserving diversity at all scales. *Environmental Management* **10**:299–309.

Oliver, C. D. and B. C. Larson. 1996. *Forest Stand Dynamics.* John Wiley and Sons, New York.

Otto, H-J. 1993. Waldbau in Europa – seine Schwaechen und Vorzuege – in historischer Perspektive. *Forst und Holz* **48**:235–7.

Perry, D. A. 1994. *Forest Ecosystems.* The Johns Hopkins University Press, Baltimore, MD.

Peterken, G. F. and M. Game. 1984. Historical factors affecting the number and distribution of vascular plant species in the woodlands of central Lincolnshire. *Journal of Ecology* **72**:155–82.

Poulson, T. L. and W. J. Platt. 1989. Gap light regimes influence canopy tree diversity. *Ecology* **70**: 553–5.

Shear, T. H., T. J. Lent, and S. Fraver. 1996. Comparison of restored and mature bottomland hardwood forest of southwestern Kentucky. *Ecological Restoration* **4**:111–23.

Simmons, E. A. and G. P. Buckley. 1992. Ground vegetation and planted mixtures of trees. In M. G. R., Cannell, Malcolm, D. C., and P. A. Robertson (eds). *The Ecology of Mixed-species Stands of Trees*. Blackwell Scientific Publications, Oxford.

Smith, D. M. 1992. Ideas about mixed species stands. In M. J. Kelty, B. C. Larson, and C. D. Oliver (eds). *The Ecology and Silviculture of Mixed-species Forests*. Kluwer Academic Publishers, Dordrecht.

Smith, D. M., B.C. Larson, M. J. Kelty, and P. M. S. Ashton. 1997. *The Practice of Silviculture: Applied Forest Ecology*. 9th edn. John Wiley and Sons, New York.

Starfield, A. M., D. H. M. Cumming, R. D. Taylor, and M. S. Quadling. 1993. A frame-based paradigm for dynamic ecosystem models. *AI Applications* 7:1–13.

Tacitus, C. 98. *De origine et situ Germanorum liber*. Holder A. (ed.) 1882. Mohr, Freiburg.

Turner, M. G., W. W. Hargrove, R. H. Gardner, and W. H. Romme. 1994. Effects of fire on landscape heterogeneity in Yellowstone National Park, Wyoming. *Journal of Vegetation Science* 5: 731–42.

Vitousek, P. M. 1994. Beyond global warming: ecology and global change. *Ecology* 75:1861–76.

Vitousek, P. M., C. M. D'Antonio, L. L. Loope, and R. Westbrooks. 1996. Biological invasions as global environmental change. *American Scientist* 84:468–78.

Watson, A. 1983. Eighteenth century deer numbers and pine regeneration near Braemar, Scotland. *Biological Conservation* 25:289–305.

Whitney, G. G. 1986. Relation of Michigan's presettlement pine forests to substrate and disturbance history. *Ecology* 67:1548–59.

Whelan, R. J. 1995. *The Ecology of Fire*. Cambridge University Press, Cambridge.

Williams, K. S. 1993. Use of terrestrial arthropods to evaluate restored riparian woodlands. *Ecological Restoration* 1:107–16.

16 Forest reserves

DAVID A. NORTON

Historically, the design of forest reserves and forest reserve systems (including national parks, wilderness areas, ecological areas, etc.) has been largely determined by non-scientific considerations such as economic or social factors, with most reserves being located in areas that contained low economic values, such as mountainous regions with little timber or potential for agricultural development. However, in the last 30 years there has been a strong scientific interest in reserve design arising from both a growing concern about biodiversity conservation in general (Myers 1988) and from the development of island biogeography theory (MacArthur and Wilson 1965, 1967). Island biogeography theory has been applied to mainland habitat 'islands' such as forest remnants and used to develop guidelines for reserve design (e.g., Diamond 1975). Since MacArthur and Wilson's work, several aspects of island biogeography theory and its subsequent application have been questioned, while other issues equally relevant to reserve design have been highlighted (e.g., representativeness, metapopulation dynamics, and the importance of considering natural disturbance regimes) which have contributed towards our current understanding of reserve design.

In this chapter I initially discuss why we need forest reserves. I then highlight some of the inadequacies in past approaches to reserve design before focusing on the importance of representativeness in reserve systems, as well as some other considerations in designing reserves and reserve systems. I then review some numerical approaches that have been proposed for developing optimal reserve systems, and finally briefly discuss reserve implementation and management.

Why do we need forest reserves?

While strong arguments for the total protection of some forest areas for biodiversity conservation purposes are regularly made in both the popular and technical media, forests managed for timber can enhance biodiversity conservation compared with many other productive land uses such as agriculture and urban development. In particular, properly managed forests can contribute significantly to soil and water conservation, and provide habitat for a range of indigenous plant and animal species. Furthermore, these forests have many aesthetic values and provide varied opportunities for recreation. So why is it necessary to establish reserves that are set aside from all production activities in forested areas? On scientific grounds, reserves are important because they contribute to protecting the full range of biodiversity, including ecosystem processes, that characterizes the forest and because they act as reference sites against which to assess the impact of management actions. Reserves are also important because they provide for different aesthetic opportunities from those that occur in forests managed for timber.

It is clear that if we are to protect the tremendous diversity of life that occurs on this planet, then there must be some areas set aside from all productive use where natural ecological processes are allowed to proceed largely unhindered by human activities (Noss and Cooperrider 1994). Thus a primary reason for reserves is to ensure that representative examples of biodiversity indigenous to an area are protected. While many indigenous species can persist in forests managed for timber, changes in the composition and age structure of forest stands resulting from forest management alter habitat availability for many species (Norton 1996a). The dependence of species as diverse as marsupials, birds and invertebrates on mature and old-growth forest stands has been extensively documented (e.g., Bart and Forsman 1992, Lindenmayer and Norton 1993, Benkman 1993, Niemelä 1997) and highlights the value of having some areas free from all production management. The continuance of ecosystem processes such as pollination and dispersal in forests managed for timber is also likely to be dependent on the presence of reserves of unmodified forest habitat. For example, successful production of Amazonian Brazil nut (*Bertholletia excelsa*) is dependent on pollination by Euglossine bees which are in turn dependent on epiphytic orchid flowers for reproduction (Prance 1991). Successful production of Brazil nuts requires protection of adjacent areas of unmodified rainforest with appropriate epiphytic orchids in order to sustain Euglossine bee habitat.

Reserves are particularly important in forests managed for timber as the spatial distribution of these forests is usually biased towards lower altitude and more fertile areas (see next section). Conservation of all biodiversity within a region requires the setting aside of reserves that are representative of the full range of ecosystems and landforms that occur in the area. Confining reserves to areas with little or no productive value will result in protection being biased towards ecosystems and species that occur in these areas only.

Reserves also provide important benchmarks against which to compare changes in managed ecosystems (e.g., for assessing the long-term effects of sustained-yield timber harvesting on biodiversity). Without such reference sites, it is difficult to make, for example, objective assessments on the sustainability of forest management. This is particularly important in the face of climate change where baseline conditions are continuing to change. Reserves set aside from timber production also have important aesthetic, spiritual and recreational values that do not occur in managed forests (e.g., as related to the presence of very large trees).

While it has been argued by some that 'limited' low-impact use of reserves may be acceptable, even small impacts can have substantial effects on ecosystem processes and hence on biodiversity within the reserve. While it is possible, for example, to extract trees using helicopters from conservation forests with minimum direct impacts, the long-term consequences of these actions will compromise the very values for which these forests were protected through small changes in a variety of ecosystem processes (e.g., soil turnover and provision of raised seedling establishment sites; Norton 1996a). If our overriding goal for managing a reserve is to protect the full range of biodiversity within it, then the changes that result from sustainable management, no matter how subtle, are not compatible with this goal.

It is important, however, to recognize that reliance on reserves alone is unlikely to be sufficient for effective forest conservation as most forest land lies outside reserves (Franklin 1993). Strategies that facilitate the conservation of forest-dependent species outside reserves must be of equal value to reserves in forest planning (Hunter 1996, Lindenmayer and Franklin 1997). Furthermore, the survival of many species within reserves is going to be dependent on the nature of the surrounding matrix as most reserves will not be large enough to protect all species or to allow for migration to replace populations that become locally extinct. Therefore matrix management must be given the same priority as reserve management in forested ecosystems.

Inadequacies with past approaches to forest reserve design and management

By the 1960s and early 1970s many, mainly developed, countries had apparently well-developed national park and other reserve systems. As a teenager with a growing interest in the outdoors, I recall reading about New Zealand's national parks and being impressed that some 10% of the total New Zealand land area was protected in perpetuity in this way. Similar books on North American national parks (Banff, Yellowstone, Yosemite), the great icons of that period of nature conservation, also impressed me with the wonders of nature they protected. It was only later as a student and especially as a teacher and researcher of conservation biology that I began to appreciate the many weaknesses that lay in the reserve systems of that time. In many ways, the books and articles about these national parks reinforced a world view dominated by the need for development. Here the majority of parks were simply places that didn't warrant development, rather than being places that we consciously chose not to develop because of their ecological values. These early reserve systems were highly deficient from a biodiversity conservation perspective and these deficiencies provide a useful contrast for considering approaches to reserve design today.

Many forest reserve systems have historically been unrepresentative with respect to the ecosystems they protect, usually being biased towards mountainous ecosystems. This discrepancy has arisen because of conflicts between economic and ecological values, with mountainous areas having lower merchantable timber volumes or being less suitable for agricultural and urban development (Mark 1985). The paucity of protected areas in lowland forests of New Zealand's South Island west coast in the late 1970s compared with the almost total protection of mountainous forests highlights this imbalance (Figure 16.1). Similar imbalances have been documented in other forested areas, with the lower elevation sites which tend to harbour the highest levels of biodiversity being least well represented in reserve systems (e.g., Harris 1984, Saunders and Hobbs 1992, Pressey and Tully 1994, Chatelain et al. 1996). Only rarely have ecological values taken precedence and even when they have, the areas protected have often been small. Although there is a growing awareness of the importance of truly representative reserve systems, this economic/ecological conflict continues to the present (Pressey and Tully 1994).

Apart from large primarily mountainous national parks and related areas, many reserve systems, especially in more intensively developed

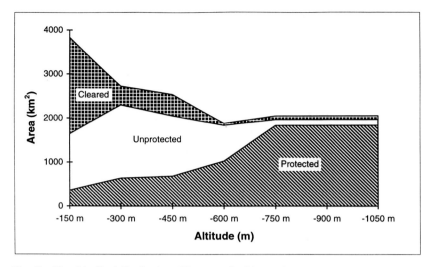

Fig. 16.1. The altitudinal distribution of forest north of the Cook River, west coast, South Island, New Zealand, prior to European settlement (1840) showing the proportion protected, unprotected and cleared in 1978. (Redrawn from Mark 1985.)

regions, have been dominated by a multitude of small reserves. Their protection has occurred because of a diversity of factors including local community interest, presence of 'waste' land and scenic qualities (e.g., roadside corridors), rather than ecological considerations. The result has been systems of small, often very isolated reserves (Figure 16.2). For example, the area of old-growth Douglas-fir (*Pseudotsuga menziesii*) forest in Siuslaw National Forest, Oregon, was reduced to 3.3% of its former extent by 1981, with 61% of remaining old-growth remnants being less than 16 ha in size (Harris 1984). In most countries, the regions with the smallest reserves are those that have been most developed, while regions with the largest reserves have only limited development (e.g., Norton 1988, Vogelmann 1995, Chatelain *et al.* 1996). The small size of many reserves leads to a diversity of problems associated with size, edges, external influences, and isolation (Saunders *et al.* 1991, Bierragaard *et al.* 1992, Hobbs 1993) making the long-term future of these reserves and especially their contribution to overall biodiversity conservation uncertain (but see Shafer 1995).

Historically, there has often been limited recognition of ecological values in reserve management, with management focusing on facilitating human visitation (e.g., Sax 1980). This has often been confounded by a lack of awareness of the key ecological factors that affect natural

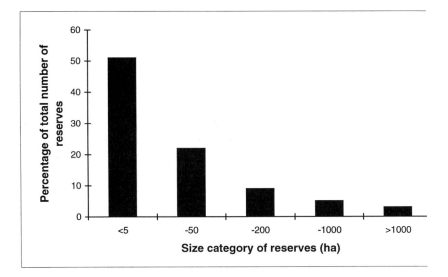

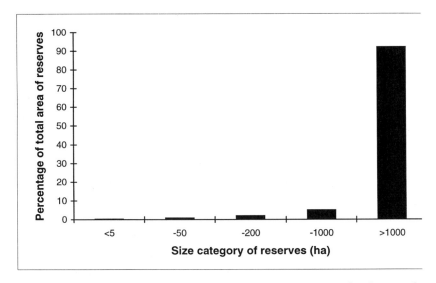

Fig. 16.2. Percentage of reserves in different size classes and the percentage of total protected lands in different sized reserves for all lands administered by the New Zealand Department of Conservation. (Redrawn from Simpson 1997.)

ecosystems. For example, inappropriate equilibrium views of forested North American ecosystems, including fire-suppression policies, have led to major changes in ecosystem composition and condition (e.g., Shinneman and Baker 1997). Furthermore, consideration of interactions between a reserve and its surrounding environment has usually focused on the effects the reserve may have on the surrounding environment (e.g., livestock predation by wolves in North America and northern Europe) rather than on the effects the surrounding environment has on the reserve (cf. Hobbs 1993). The effects of this lack of awareness of ecological values in reserves has often been confounded by a lack of resources to undertake key management actions such as pest control required to meet biodiversity goals.

While there has been a long history of reserve implementation and management, especially in more developed countries, there are also a number of significant weaknesses associated with these systems. However, over the last few years there has been a growing shift in how we view reserve design that addresses many of these weaknesses and in the rest of this chapter I will explore some of these key issues.

Representativeness

Representativeness is increasingly considered the most important criterion in selecting land for nature conservation (Usher 1986, O'Connor et al. 1990). The concept of representativeness is based on the notion that a reserve system should contain the full range of natural variation characteristic of a region (Austin and Margules 1986, Kelly and Park 1986). Representativeness is based on comparisons with the natural character of the landscape (i.e., prior to recent human impacts), but is not a directly measurable parameter although there are several measures associated with it (O'Connor et al. 1990). A commonly used measure of representativeness is to compare elements of natural diversity such as species or community diversity in the present landscape with those that existed at some time in the past (e.g., prior to recent human impacts associated with European settlement). This comparative approach provides an evaluation of how much of the landscape character has remained unmodified.

Two steps are involved in assessing representativeness in an area. The first is to develop a biogeographical framework within which to assess representativeness. Such a framework can be based on global classification schemes (Dasmann 1973, Pielou 1979) or on local schemes (Kelly and Park

1986, Belbin 1993). Local ecological classification schemes, usually based on topographic, climatic, soil and biological features, have been developed in many countries including Australia, Canada, New Zealand and the USA.

The second step involves undertaking ecological surveys to assess the past and current extents of those natural ecosystems that occurred in the area prior to recent human impacts. Assessing past extents can be difficult, but is necessary to estimate how representative current patterns are of past patterns. Evaluation of past extent can be based on broad landscape and bioclimatic units, and knowledge from historical and paleoecological information (Küchler 1964, Foster 1992, Strittholt and Boerner 1995). Current extents can be assessed from satellite imagery, aerial photography, and ecological survey (Caicco et al. 1995, Awimbo et al. 1996). Once past and current extents of natural ecosystems have been calculated it is then possible to quantitatively assess how representative current reserves are, and hence to identify where further protection might be needed.

An example of the application of representativeness comes from the Hokitika Ecological District, New Zealand (Awimbo et al. 1996), an area that was predominantly forested when first settled by people of European descent 130 years ago. Within this district (102 300 ha) only 35% of the land area has remained relatively unmodified (vegetation patterns similar to those present prior to European settlement). Of the nine major landform--vegetation units recognized (Table 16.1), only mountainous ecosystems were adequately represented in the remaining unmodified areas. Lowland ecosystems were poorly represented. For example, lowland alluvial landform–vegetation units (mainly alluvial floodplain forests) covered 19.2% of the pre-European land area, but made up <0.1% of the 1990 total land area and 0.2% of the 1990 unmodified lands. Coastal sandplain forests and shrublands covered 2% of the pre-European land area, but accounted for 0.2% of the 1990 total land area and 0.5% of the 1990 unmodified lands. Clearly, any future additions to the Hokitika Ecological District reserve system should aim to redress the underrepresentation of lowland landform–vegetation systems.

These problems of imbalance are not unique to New Zealand. For example, in the Western Australian wheatbelt, woodlands on heavier soils were cleared and utilized preferentially and are now poorly represented in the remaining areas of natural vegetation (Saunders and Hobbs 1992). In contrast, lands with low commercial value are usually least modified and often well represented in reserve systems (e.g., with shallow soils or in

Table 16.1. *Representativeness of 1860 landform-vegetation classes in the present-day landscape, Hokitika Ecological District, New Zealand*

Landform-vegetation class	% 1860 total area	% 1990 total area	1990 area as % unmodified area	1990 area as % 1860 area
Coastal	2.0	0.2	0.5	8.2
Wetland	2.4	1.0	2.8	39.4
Lowland alluvial	19.2	<0.1	0.2	0.3
Lowland outwash terrace and moraine	35.5	3.7	11.0	10.5
Lowland hill and fan	21.0	10.9	32.0	52.0
Mid-elevation hill	11.9	10.3	30.3	86.4
Montane	5.7	5.7	16.6	100.0
Subalpine	2.0	2.0	5.8	100.0
Alpine	0.3	0.3	0.8	100.0

Source: From Awimbo *et al.* (1996).

mountainous areas). For example, in Nepal there is a disproportionate number of reserves at higher elevations (>3500 m) coincident with low human population densities (Hunter and Yonzon 1993). Unfortunately, most of Nepal's faunal diversity occurs at lower elevations (<3500 m) and so is underrepresented in these reserves.

These examples highlight a significant universal scale problem for the design of reserves. While it is often politically expedient for an agency or government to set targets to protect natural areas for conservation (e.g., IUCN, 1980, suggest 10% as a target for a representative reserve system), such targets are of little value unless the issue of representativeness is addressed. Representativeness needs to be addressed at the scale of local ecological patterns (Belbin 1993, Awimbo *et al.* 1996), rather than simply through protecting a certain percentage of all lands in a state or country. Ideally a reserve system should aim to protect a certain portion of each eco-system type within an ecological district or similar biogeographical unit. The challenge for individuals and agencies involved in reserve design is to ensure that representativeness is assessed at a realistic biogeographical scale in improving current reserve systems.

Gap analysis (Scott *et al.* 1987, 1993) is a technique for the rapid assessment of biodiversity conservation over large spatial areas (hundreds to thousands of square kilometers) based on comparison of spatial information on biodiversity with spatial information on land tenure and management. Gaps in the representation of particular biodiversity elements in existing reserve systems are identified and form the focus for future con-servation advocacy. Geographical information systems are an important component of gap analysis and have been increasingly applied in both North and South America (eg., Caicco et al. 1995, Stritdholt and Boerner 1995, Fearnside and Ferraz 1995). Gap analysis has the potential to provide a relatively rapid overview of the degree of representation of major ecosys-tem types within reserve systems over a large spatial area and the identifi-cation of ecosystem types that require further protection.

Area and forest reserve design

Much of the recent interest in reserve design has arisen from the work of MacArthur and Wilson (1963, 1967) who suggested that the number of species that occur on an island is the balance between the number of species arriving (immigration) versus the number of species going extinct, and that immigration and extinction are area dependent (called the equilibrium theory of island biogeography). Although numer-ous studies have validated the basic observation that small islands have fewer species than large islands (see references in Connor and McCoy 1979), there has been considerable debate about the validity of the equilib-rium model (see Rosenzweig 1995 for a recent review), and especially its application to nature conservation (Simberloff 1974, 1976, Connor and McCoy 1979, Gilbert 1980, Boecklen and Gotelli 1984, Harris 1984, Shafer 1990). Despite this, it has had a major influence on conservation thinking with respect to reserve design. The isolation of an area of forest has been likened to the isolation of an island by rising sea levels and it has been argued that factors that control species number in forest remnants are similar to those that affect species number on real islands. Because of this, it has been suggested that island biogeographic principles can be applied in nature conservation, especially in the design of forest reserves (Diamond 1975, Wilson and Willis 1975).

Diamond has been a major proponent in applying island biogeograph-ical ideas to reserve design and has suggested four implications of island biogeography theory for reserve design (Diamond 1975) that have formed the basis of much subsequent debate and conservation policy: (1) the ulti-mate number of species that a reserve will protect is likely to increase with increasing reserve area; (2) the rate at which species go extinct from a reserve is likely to decrease with increasing reserve area; (3) the relation between reserve area and the probability of a species survival is character-

istically different for different species; and (4) explicit suggestions can be
made for optimizing the design of reserves.

SPECIES–AREA RELATIONSHIPS

Numerous studies have shown that there is a relationship between
species number and area in forest remnants (e.g., Blake and Karr 1987,
Ogle 1987), but this relationship is usually not as strong as it is for islands
for at least three reasons. First, remnants have often been created recently
and the biota present may not necessarily be at equilibrium with current
conditions, especially species with long-lived individuals such as forest
trees. The time period taken for biota to return to some form of equilibrium may be considerable and current biotas may not truly reflect the
potential biota of the remnant. Second, the degree of isolation of remnants
is usually not as complete as it is for islands, with remnant biotas being
able to utilize surrounding areas. For example, in a study of bird faunas in
Illinois woodlots it was found that the faunas of small woodlots were dominated by generalist species capable of using both woodland and agricultural habitat, while specialist forest species occurred only in the larger
woodlots (Blake and Karr 1987). Third, remnant biotas are often augmented by invasive species from surrounding land that can sometimes
result in larger rather than smaller species numbers, especially in small
remnants with large edge areas. For example, butterfly faunas of small
forest remnants in Brazil are frequently augmented through invasion at
the edges by species typical of more open habitats (Lovejoy et al. 1986).

SPECIES EXTINCTION

As the area of a reserve becomes smaller, population sizes usually
decrease, especially for larger organisms, and these populations become
increasingly vulnerable to local extinction (Shaffer 1981, Gilpin and Soulé
1986, Soulé 1987). Local extinctions can occur because of chance disturbances such as fire or drought, or because of chance variations in demographic factors (e.g., a failure to breed in a particular year). Extinctions can
also occur because of deterministic processes such as the introduction of a
predator or climatic change. Several studies have shown that small populations also have less genetic variation than large populations (e.g.,
Billington 1991), making them less able to deal with changing environmental conditions and more vulnerable to a number of deleterious genetic
effects, again making them more vulnerable to extinction. However, the

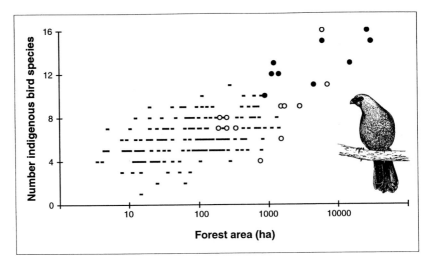

Fig. 16.3. Number of native bird species in different sized forest patches, central North Island, New Zealand (1982–83). ● patches with kokako (*Callaeas cinerea wilsonii*); ○ patches which had kokako within the past 20 years; ■ patches that are not known to have had kokako. (Redrawn from Ogle 1987.)

amount of change in genetic variation is likely to be dependent on both the time since fragmentation and on the size of the remnant population (Young *et al.* 1993). In unmodified natural systems, demographic, genetic and chance processes can result in local extinction, but are usually followed by recolonization from adjacent populations, but in small isolated reserves they can result in the local extinction of the species with subsequent recolonization being dependent on the nature of the surrounding matrix and the proximity of other populations (cf. metapopulation dynamics).

ORGANISM SPECIFICITY IN RESPONSE

Different organisms operate at different spatial scales (Wiens 1989, Lord and Norton 1990), and as a result their area requirements differ (Chapter 7). The different requirements of insects and birds are obvious, but even within one group, clear differences occur. For example, in New Zealand some bird species persist in very small forest remnants, while others require forest remnants larger than 1000 ha to survive (Ogle 1987; Figure 16.3). For some species, even the largest reserves will not be sufficient to sustain them and networks of reserves with adequate linkages between them will be required for the conservation of these species (e.g.,

Table 16.2. *Principles of reserve design proposed by Diamond (1975) based on island biogeographical theory*

Better	Worse
large	small
one large	several small (same total area)
close together	far apart
arranged equidistantly	arranged linearly
corridors present	corridors absent
compact shape (e.g., round)	not compact shape (e.g., elongated)

for large carnivores in the Rocky Mountains; Noss *et al.* 1996). Clearly when considering reserve size and especially species–area relationships, it is essential to take into account the scale at which the organism operates and to consider the nature of the surrounding matrix and its influence on species survival.

RESERVE DESIGN PRINCIPLES

Diamond (1975) proposed six better/worse geometric principles for reserve design (Table 16.2) that have been widely, although often uncritically, taken up by conservation managers. These ideas have come under increasing scrutiny and debate in the scientific literature and their validity has been widely questioned (see Shafer 1990 for a review), especially the suggestion that a single large reserve is better than several small reserves (the 'SLOSS' debate; Diamond 1975, Simberloff and Abele 1976, 1982, Simberloff and Gotelli 1984). Proponents for single large reserves argued that only these could provide sufficient habitat to sustain the full range of diversity, especially of larger species and of ecosystem functions. In contrast, the proponents for several small reserves argued that well-placed small reserves are likely to include more habitat diversity and support more populations of uncommon species than a single large reserve. It seems clear now that the approach taken to reserve design should be dependent on the particular situation and species being considered rather than specific rules about size. While it is generally accepted that large reserves are better than small reserves because of greater habitat diversity and because they contain larger populations, it is also recognized that in many instances small reserves can form key components of reserve systems because they protect particular combinations of biodiversity not present elsewhere and because they increase the total number of populations for some species. However, the reality is that in many areas there is little choice about what size reserves will be because of the pervasive influence of land clearance.

It is clear that while island biogeographical theory has contributed much towards our understanding about reserve design, the validity of many of island biogeography's underlying assumptions have been seriously questioned (see above references). At the same time several other factors have been increasingly emphasized as equally as important in reserve design. Rather than repeating much of the last twenty years of debate on island biogeographical theory and reserve design, the rest of this chapter emphasizes these other factors that are increasingly regarded as critical for reserve design.

Other considerations in forest reserve design

METAPOPULATION DYNAMICS

Perhaps one of the most fundamental shifts in conservation thinking in the last ten years has been the changing emphasis from island biogeography to metapopulation dynamics as a basis to understanding how populations and communities are affected by processes such as habitat fragmentation (Hanski and Simberloff 1997). Island biogeography is an equilibrium-based concept that focuses on species richness in single habitat islands. In contrast, metapopulation dynamics is a dynamic non-equilibrium based concept that recognizes that populations are spatially structured into assemblages of local breeding populations and that migration between local populations is important for processes such as re-establishment after local extinction.

While metapopulation theory focuses on the interaction between spatially discrete populations, it is important to recognize that migration is strongly influenced by the matrix within which the metapopulation is located (Wiens 1997). Migration between patches is the key process that links a metapopulation and hence the nature of the matrix can have an important effect on the viability of the metapopulation. For example, in a New Zealand agricultural landscape with scattered forest remnants, brown kiwi (*Apteryx australis mantelli*) used all forest remnants up to 80 m from other remnants, with the maximum distance of pasture crossed between remnants being 330 m (Potter 1990). However, longer movements (up to 1200 m) were made only when small forest remnants could be used as stepping stones. Thus the nature of the matrix has an important influence on the survival of the metapopulation.

Metapopulation theory has much to offer reserve design, especially because it highlights the importance of not considering populations in isolation. Migration between populations is critical for long-term population persistence and suggests that in reserve design much consideration needs to be given to the nature of the surrounding matrix through which species can move. In forested ecosystems this is particularly important as there is the opportunity to manage the matrix in a manner that will facilitate species migration. For example, the use of long-rotation islands (Harris 1984) in the management of Pacific Northwest forests will both increase the total area of habitat available to many old-growth species and increase the connectivity between old-growth remnants without increasing the total reserve area. This occurs because the core area of old-growth forest is surrounded by segments of forest that are managed on long rotations, with the core area always having at least one mature long-rotation forest area adjacent to it. Peterken *et al.* (1992) outline a similar approach to the management of Britain's upland conifer plantations.

While metapopulation theory has been hailed by some as a new paradigm for conservation biology replacing island biogeography as the way we think about fragmented landscapes (Hanski and Simberloff 1997), it is important that we do not focus on metapopulation dynamics to the exclusion of other issues in reserve design. The importance of the matrix in particular (Hobbs 1993, Forman 1995, Wiens 1997) is critical for understanding the way fragmentation affects indigenous biota and hence for designing optimum reserve networks for nature conservation.

LANDSCAPE POSITION

Reserves do not occur in isolation, they are part of a wider landscape and interact with other landscape components in many ways. Two key aspects of landscape position relevant to reserve design are edges and connectivity.

Edges are the contact zone between a reserve and its surrounding environment and are particularly well developed in forest remnants (Murcia 1995). Edge zones are typically warmer, windier, and drier than the forest interior, and edge communities are commonly dominated by plants and animals typical of disturbed sites, rather than of the forest interior. The extent to which edge effects penetrate into forest remnants varies depending on forest type, edge age, and aspect, and the variable being considered. Several studies have documented microclimate changes extending 50–60 m into forest remnants, with edge effects extending further into forest at edges facing towards the equator (e.g., Matlack 1993). Edge effects are most pronounced at recently created edges, although there is good evidence for edge effects even at very old edges.

One approach to dealing with edges in reserve design is to minimize the extent of edge by minimizing the edge/interior ratio. Another approach is through buffer zone management. Buffer zones minimize unwanted interactions between the reserve and its surrounding environment. The need for buffers has been emphasized in agricultural landscapes where small reserves can be strongly influenced by a variety of processes resulting from adjacent agricultural activities (e.g., changing hydrology, nutrient levels and weed invasion; Hobbs 1993) but are equally important in forested landscapes. The development of buffer zones, either through restoration plantings or through appropriate management of adjacent areas (e.g., single tree extraction rather than clearcutting) can be a major factor in minimizing edge effects, especially in small reserves. Harris (1984) and Noss and Harris (1986) outlined an approach to buffer zone management involving a core conservation area surrounded by concentric zones (or buffers) of increasing human use (which together are called multiple-use modules) that has considerable potential for forest management especially if linked with the ideas of long-rotation islands discussed earlier.

Connectivity is also an important aspect of reserve design; long-term viability of fragmented natural systems may often be dependent on maintaining links with other remnants. Such links can range from narrow linear strips or corridors connecting two reserves to large areas of land that permit seasonal movement of migratory animals (see papers in Saunders and Hobbs, 1991, for examples). Connectivity can also occur without the presence of specific corridors, as organisms are able to utilize different components of the intervening matrix (cf. Potter 1990). Connectivity and corridors have received considerable attention and debate in the conservation literature (Simberloff and Cox 1987, Noss 1987, Hobbs 1992, Simberloff et al. 1992). One recommendation made by Diamond (1975) for reserve design was that linked reserves are better than isolated ones, because links or corridors would allow organisms to move between reserves.

Increased connectivity has been predicted to have several benefits (Table 16.3) that will increase colonization rates and decrease extinction rates in the connected reserves (Noss 1987, Thomas 1991). However, corri-

Table 16.3. *Predicted benefits and costs associated with increased connectivity between reserves*

Benefits
Increased reserve area by combining several small reserves together.
Increased chance of recolonization of one reserve from others following local extinction.
Facilitation of seasonal movement of animals between temporarily available resources.
Enhanced gene flow between populations in different reserves.
Costs
Loss of local adaptations due to gene flow to previously isolated populations.
Facilitation of the spread of diseases and unwanted species into reserves.
Facilitation of the spread of abiotic disasters like fire.
Increased exposure of species using corridors to poachers and other predators.

Source: Noss (1987) and Thomas (1991).

dors may also have negative effects on the connected reserves (Table 16.3). One aspect of corridors that has been emphasized very strongly by Simberloff and Cox (1987) and Simberloff et al. (1992) is that for corridors to be of value, animals must use them for movement. They suggest that there is little evidence to support such movement and suggest that we would be better off to spend our limited conservation funds on protecting more large reserves than creating new corridors. Hobbs (1992) has taken a more pragmatic approach, and while acknowledging that the number of studies showing movement is limited, he suggested that there is a growing body of data showing that movement does occur, and where possible we should retain corridors in conservation networks. While the value of corridors for movement may still be debated, they have other values including aesthetic ones and as nuclei for restoration and future expansion of the reserve system. I would argue that we should not abandon existing corridors and that we should look at potential options for improving connectivity on a case-by-case basis.

While corridors can provide continuous habitat between forest reserves, appropriate management of the intervening matrix can also provide considerable opportunities for species movement between reserves. Planning of harvesting operations, for example to ensure that there is always continuous forest habitat between reserves, will enhance the ability of many old-growth forest species to use the matrix for movement. However, for some old-growth forest species, even small changes in forest composition and structure may still form a barrier to movement.

DISTURBANCE REGIMES

While much of the debate about reserve design has focused on species–area relationships, species richness is not the only factor affected by area. Natural vegetation is dynamic, with disturbance being essential for the maintenance of many species and processes (Connell 1978, Pickett and White 1985). Fragmentation can modify existing disturbance regimes as well as introduce new forms of disturbance (Pickett and Thomson 1978, Hobbs 1987, Hobbs and Huenneke 1992). In designing reserve systems, we need to minimize modifications to existing disturbance regimes and the introduction of new disturbances.

Disturbance and vegetation change are ubiquitous landscape features and result in the natural landscape comprising a mosaic of different sized and aged patches (White 1979). Because regeneration of many plants and the survival of their associated animals is dependent on disturbance, allowance must be made for patch dynamics in designing reserves (Pickett and Thomson 1978). The use of patch dynamics to design forest reserves requires knowledge of the disturbance regime and associated patterns of vegetation change. This should include infrequent disturbance events (e.g., irregular fire) as well as regular disturbances (e.g., windthrow) as both play an integral part in the overall ecology of natural ecosystems.

Five guidelines for reserve design taking into account patch size have been proposed by Pickett and Thomson (1978). The reserve should: (1) be considerably larger than the largest disturbance patch size, allowing, if at all possible, for infrequent disturbance events; (2) include multiple examples of each ecosystem type to allow for recolonization after disturbance; (3) include different ages of disturbance-generated patches; (4) be large enough to allow viable populations to persist when parts of the reserve have been disturbed; and (5) be sufficiently large so that points 1–4 are applicable to each ecosystem type included.

The importance in taking into account different scales of disturbance in designing forest reserves has been highlighted in numerous studies of forest dynamics. For example, in the northern hardwoods–hemlock–white pine forests of southwestern New Hampshire the natural disturbance regimes are characterized by frequent small-scale disturbances such as windstorms, lightning, pathogens and fire, and by occasional large-scale disturbances associated with hurricane winds (Foster

1988). Overall forest structure and composition is therefore a product of disturbances occurring at a range of spatial and temporal scales, and reserve design that ignores the infrequent large-scale disturbances is unlikely to sustain the full diversity of these forests.

CLIMATE CHANGE

Even if we could design the 'best' reserve system today, there are still changes occurring that will affect their long-term viability. Climate change is perhaps the most widely recognized of these and presents some very real problems for reserve design (Peters and Darling 1985, Hunter *et al.* 1988, Graham 1988). As a result of human landscape modifications, especially fragmentation, it is much more difficult now for most species to adjust their ranges to changing climatic conditions (cf. at the end of the last glaciation; Huntley and Webb 1989) because of the widespread occurrence of unsuitable habitat (e.g., agricultural or urban land). Reserve design should therefore try to encompass as wide a climate range as possible within the reserve (Weiss and Murphy 1993) to allow for species movement in response to human-induced climate changes. For example, a forest reserve could include a valley floor to alpine timberline sequence, with both north and south facing aspects to ensure species movement in response to climate change.

Maintaining connectivity for species movement in response to climate change has been suggested, although the usefulness of such connections is uncertain (Hobbs and Hopkins 1991). Connections may facilitate movement of more mobile species, but are likely to be of less value for species with poor dispersal abilities. Unfortunately there is most often insufficient suitable land to develop such connections, while the speed with which climate change is likely to occur may well be much greater than that to which many organisms can respond.

The individuality of species response to climate change will compound the problems associated with allowing for species movement. Modern plant and animal communities are the product of current environmental and biotic conditions and often include unique combinations of species that have not occurred in the past and may be unlikely to occur in the future (Hunter *et al.* 1988, Graham 1988, Huntley and Webb 1989). For example, in North America beech (*Fagus*) and hemlock (*Tsuga*) occur together today, but their ranges did not overlap 12 000 years ago (Jacobson *et al.* 1987) and so we should not expect their ranges to be the same in the future.

A further consideration is the interdependence that occurs between species (e.g., a plant and its mycorrhizal fungi). Even if it were possible for a tree, for example, to migrate 1000 km to a suitable new site, there is no guarantee that its associated microflora will do the same in the time available (Perry *et al.* 1990). Loranthaceae mistletoes face even more complex problems, being dependent on both specific birds for dispersal and specific host trees for establishment (Norton and Reid 1997). Persistence of such species, especially in the face of rapid climate change, may be difficult unless essential mutualists and hosts are able to migrate together.

RESTORATION ECOLOGY

While we tend to think of reserve design involving only 'natural' areas, this need not be the case. Because human impacts have been so dramatic, especially in fertile ecosystems, there are often very few natural areas left that could be protected. While degraded sites may appear unattractive and of little value to conservation they may provide the opportunity for restoration (Chapter 15; Hobbs and Norton 1996) and can in the long term add considerably to a reserve system (Awimbo *et al.* 1996). The concept of reintegrating fragmented landscapes (Hobbs and Saunders 1992) has received increasing attention and suggests that in designing reserve systems we should be considering future potential as well as current condition. For example, small restoration areas may connect or complete topographical or other gradients within existing reserves, providing increased opportunities for species to migrate in response to seasonal or longer-term climate variations (Weiss and Murphy 1993). By taking an integrated approach to landscape management involving a combination of activities such as strict protection, low-impact use (e.g., sustainable tree harvesting) and higher-impact use (e.g., clearcutting), and restoring key linkages, we are more likely to achieve biodiversity conservation than by simply dividing the landscape into protection and use areas.

Choosing reserves

While earlier approaches to reserve design have been largely *ad hoc* and driven by economic considerations, there has been growing interest in systematic and objective approaches to choosing reserves. A large literature has developed on the different ways to evaluate and choose areas for protection and good reviews can be found in Usher (1986), O'Connor *et al.* (1990), Margules and Austin (1991) and Forey *et al.* (1994). Evaluation is not easy because of the many factors involved and most approaches to choosing reserves have been based on evaluation systems that combine information from several criteria (e.g., representativeness, species richness, area, rarity and condition) in order to obtain a score for each site.

Because of the large amounts of data that can be generated in an evaluation exercise, it has been common to add the scores together to produce a single value for a site. This approach has a number of problems including comparability of scores (e.g., is a score of 4 for diversity the same as a score of 4 for rarity?), the potential for sites to receive similar scores for different reasons, and the lack of independence between the different criteria used (Smith and Theberge 1987). The assessment of scores can also be subjective, especially for criteria such as condition. For these reasons there has been a shift away from using single derived scores for evaluation.

Alternative approaches to evaluation have included gap analysis and the application of selection algorithms. Gap analysis, discussed earlier, provides a method for identifying gaps within reserve systems, for example, from the perspective of areas of high vertebrate diversity, rather than being a method for selecting individual reserves. Selection algorithms have been proposed as an important tool for decision-making in reserve design in the face of limited conservation resources and competing land uses (Margules et al. 1988, Pressey et al. 1993). This approach is based on mathematical models that identify the minimum number of sites to ensure protection of the full range of biological diversity in a given region.

While selection algorithms have not yet been applied to forest reserves, an application to wetlands illustrates their use. A study of 432 Australian wetlands containing 98 indigenous plant species sought to select the optimum minimal set of wetlands that ensured plant diversity protection (Margules et al. 1988). This was done by applying a series of rules in selecting wetlands so that all 98 plant species would be protected: (1) select all wetlands with any species which occurs only once; (2) starting with the rarest unrepresented species (i.e., the least frequent species in the data matrix), select from all wetlands in which it occurs the wetland containing the maximum number of additional unrepresented species (this is continued until all species are represented); (3) where two or more wetlands contribute equal numbers of additional species, select the wetland with the least frequent group of species (i.e., with those species that occur least often in the overall data matrix); and (4) where two or more wetlands contribute an equal number of infrequent species, select the first wetland encountered. The model can be modified to select all wetlands that would include two populations (i.e., wetlands) of each species and so on. It can also be modified to emphasize other values (e.g., rarity). The results show that of the 432 wetlands in the area, 20 are enough to encompass all plant species at least once, and 65 each species at least five times.

It is commonly assumed that by protecting a representative series of ecosystems the maximum number of species are also protected. This approach can also be tested by modifying the rules, based on different ecosystem types. Margules *et al.* (1988) recognized nine ecosystem types in their Australian study area based on plant species composition. The steps that were used to ensure that all nine ecosystem types were protected as well as all 98 plant species were: (1) select the wetland from each ecosystem type which has the greatest number of plant species; if all species are included then stop analysis; (2) select a second wetland from each ecosystem type which adds the most new species (an ecosystem type will be missed if there are no wetlands from this type that add any new species); if all species are included, then stop; and (3) continue to select a third, fourth, etc. up to ninth, wetland from each ecosystem type until all plant species are protected.

The results showed that eight steps were required to protect all ecosystem types and all plant species, involving 29 wetlands (cf. 20 wetlands using the other set of rules). Of the 20 wetlands required to represent each plant species once, 18 are included in the list of 29 required to represent each species and each ecosystem type once. However, these 18 wetlands only represent four of the nine habitat types, suggesting that simply protecting species will not result in protection of all habitat types.

This modeling approach to selecting reserves has been increasingly applied in several countries in recent years (e.g., Margules *et al.* 1988, Pressey *et al.* 1994, Freitag *et al.* 1996) and provides an explicit approach for objectively selecting reserves. Unfortunately, in many parts of the world there is simply insufficient baseline data on which to base such evaluations, limiting the more general application of these techniques.

Forest reserve implementation and management

Designing representative forest reserve systems can only achieve positive outcomes for nature conservation if there is a genuine commitment to recognize and manage the individual reserves once they have been formally protected. Unfortunately in many parts of the world, reserve systems exist only on paper and continue to be exploited on the ground (e.g., Peres and Terborgh 1995). While these problems are often most acute in developing countries, many reserves in developed countries also suffer because of insufficient resources for adequate management, a lack of clear management objectives, a lack of monitoring, and through inappropriate use. A further problem in both developed and developing countries is inappropriate activities in surrounding lands and the lack of buffer zones to protect reserves from these activities. Appropriate management of the matrix surrounding reserves has the potential to considerably enhance biodiversity conservation within reserves (e.g., the long-rotation islands approach to forest management discussed earlier).

Reserve design and implementation are only part of a conservation effort (Norton 1988) and even the 'best' designed forest reserve system will not necessarily protect all the values for which it was selected without appropriate management. This is especially true in the face of the pervasive influence of invasive species (including humans), fragmentation, global change and pollution. In most cases the primary objective of reserve management is to maintain ecological processes in order to sustain indigenous ecosystems and species. Management should aim to allow ecological processes to proceed as free as possible from non-local influences. Factors that might perturb these processes can be external or internal to the reserve (cf. Saunders et al. 1991). External factors include disturbances (e.g., fire spreading in from adjacent areas), inappropriate management of adjacent areas (e.g., altered water tables or fertilizer application) and the activities of non-local species (including humans) that invade the reserve. Internal factors might be a consequence of small population sizes of resident species, changes in species interactions because of past changes in species abundances (e.g., loss of a key fruit disperser), changes to disturbance regimes resulting from fragmentation or past management (e.g., fire suppression), and impacts of inappropriate use of the reserve (e.g., by recreationists).

The options for reserve management are many and have been well documented elsewhere (e.g., Spellerberg et al. 1991, Willison et al. 1992, Caughley and Sinclair 1994, Sutherland and Hill 1995). However, it is important for successful management to be based on a good understanding of the ecology of the ecosystems being managed, clearly formulated and ecologically appropriate goals for the area, regular monitoring of ecosystem condition and management actions that feeds back into future management (Norton 1996b), and management goals and practices supported by interest groups, including local communities.

Summary

Earlier approaches to forest reserve design have been largely *ad hoc*, reflecting the dominance of economic over conservation interests. Arising from MacArthur and Wilson's island biogeography theory, a more objective approach has been developed, focusing in particular on the area and arrangement of reserves. Many of the ideas about what makes a 'good' reserve arising from island biogeographical theory (e.g., single large versus several small) have been a source of debate, and there is a growing recognition that area is only one of a number of considerations important in reserve design. Representativeness is a key concept and is based on the notion that a reserve system should contain the full range of natural variation characteristic of a region. Other important considerations in reserve design include metapopulation dynamics, landscape position (especially with respect to edges and connectivity), disturbance regimes, climate change and restoration potential. Two increasingly used numerical approaches to reserve design are gap analysis and the application of selection algorithms. Both approaches have considerable potential, but are limited by the need for good data sets on which to base analyses. Designing representative reserve systems for forested ecosystems can only achieve positive outcomes for nature conservation if there is a genuine commitment to recognize and manage the individual reserves once they have been formally protected. Unfortunately this often does not happen. Even the 'best' designed forest reserve system will not necessarily protect all the values for which it was selected without appropriate management, especially in the face of the pervasive influence of invasive species, fragmentation, global change and pollution, and it is essential in forest reserve management that as much emphasis is given to management of the matrix as to management of the reserve itself. If appropriately managed, the matrix can considerably enhance the overall conservation values of a forested landscape.

Further readings

Other recent treatments of issues relating to the design of reserves are given in Harris (1984), Usher (1986), O'Connor *et al.* (1990), Shafer (1990), and Hunter (1996). The theory of island biogeography is elegantly explained by MacArthur and Wilson (1967) and a recent review of species–area relationships is given by Rosenzweig (1995). A good overview of metapopulation dynamics is given in Hanski and Gilpin (1997) while Forman (1995) provides an excellent discussion on issues relating to the relationship between remnant patches and the rest of the landscape.

Literature cited

Austin, M. P. and C. R. Margules. 1986. Assessing representativeness. Pp. 45–67 in M. B. Usher (ed.). *Wildlife Conservation Evaluation*. Chapman and Hall, London.

Awimbo, J. A., D. A. Norton and F.B. Overmars. 1996. An evaluation of representativeness for nature conservation, Hokitika Ecological District, New Zealand. *Biological Conservation* **75**:177–86.

Bart, J. and E. D. Forsman. 1992. Dependence of northern spotted owl Strix occidentalis caurina on old growth forests in western USA. *Biological Conservation* **62**:95–100.

Belbin, L. 1993. Environmental representativeness: regional partitioning and reserve selection. *Biological Conservation* **66**:223–30.

Benkman, C. W. 1993. Logging, conifers, and the conservation of crossbills. *Conservation Biology* **7**:473–9.

Bierregaard, R. O., T. E. Lovejoy, V. Kapos, A. A. dos Santos and R. W. Hutchings. 1992. The biological dynamics of tropical rainforest fragments. *BioScience* **42**:859–66.

Billington, H. L. 1991. Effect of population size on genetic variation in a dioecious conifer. *Conservation Biology* **5**:115–19.

Blake, J. G. and J. R. Karr 1987. Breeding birds of isolated woodlots: area and habitat relationships. *Ecology* **68**:1724–34.

Boecklen, W. J. and N. J. Gotelli. 1984. Island biogeographic theory and conservation practice: species-area or specious area relationships? *Biological Conservation* **29**:63–80.

Caicco, S. L., J. M. Scott, B. Butterfield and B. Csuti. 1995. A gap analysis of the management status of the vegetation of Idaho (U.S.A.). *Conservation Biology* **9**:498–511.

Caughley, G. and A. R. E. Sinclair. (1994). *Wildlife ecology and management*. Blackwell Scientific Publications, Oxford.

Chatelain, C., L. Gautier, and R. Spichiger. 1996. A recent history of forest fragmentation in southwestern Ivory Coast. *Biodiversity and Conservation* **5**:37–53.

Connell, J .H. 1978. Diversity in tropical rain forests and coral reefs. *Science* **199**:1302–10.

Connor, E. F. and E. D. McCoy. 1979. The statistics and biology of the species-area relationship. *American Naturalist* **113**:791–833.

Dasmann, R. F. 1973. *A system for defining and classifying natural regions for purposes of conservation*. Occasional paper 7, pp 1–47, IUCN, Gland, Switzerland.

Diamond, J. M. 1975. The island dilemma: lessons of modern biogeographic studies for the design of nature reserves. *Biological Conservation* 7:129–45.

Fearnside, P. M. and J. Ferraz. 1995. A conservation gap analysis of Brazil's Amazonian vegetation. *Conservation Biology* 9:1134–47.

Forey, P. L., C. J. Humphries and R. I. Vane-Wright. 1994. *Systematics and conservation evaluation.* Systematics Association and Clarendon Press, Oxford.

Forman, R. T. T. 1995. *Land Mosaics: the Ecology of Landscapes and Regions.* Cambridge University Press, Cambridge.

Foster, D. R. 1988. Disturbance history, community organization and vegetation dynamics of the old-growth Pisgah forest, south-western New Hampshire, U.S.A. *Journal of Ecology* 76:105–34.

    1992. Land-use history (1730–1990) and vegetation dynamics in central New England, USA. *Journal of Ecology* 80:753–72.

Franklin, J. F. 1993. Preserving biodiversity, species, ecosystems, or landscapes? *Ecological Applications* 3:202–5.

Freitag, S., A. O. Nicholls and A. S. van Jaarsveld. 1996. Nature reserve selection in the Transvaal, South Africa: what data should we be using? *Biodiversity and Conservation* 5:685–98.

Gilbert, F. S. 1980. The equilibrium theory of island biogeography: fact or fiction? *Journal of Biogeography* 7:209–35.

Gilpin, M. E. and M. E. Soulé 1986. Minimum viable populations: processes of species extinction. Pp. 19–34 in M. E. Soulé (ed.). *Conservation Biology: the Science of Scarcity and Diversity.* Sinauer Associates, Sunderland, USA.

Graham, R. W. 1988. The role of climatic change in the design of biological reserves: the paleoecological perspective for conservation biology. *Conservation Biology* 2:391–4.

Hanski, I. A. and M. E. Gilpin (eds). (1997). *Metapopulation Biology, Ecology, Genetics, and Evolution.* Academic Press, San Diego.

Hanski, I. and D. Simberloff. 1997. The metapopulation approach, its history, conceptual domain, and application to conservation. Pp. 5–26 in I. A. Hanski and M. E. Gilpin (eds). *Metapopulation Biology, Ecology, Genetics, and Evolution.* Academic Press, San Diego.

Harris, L. D. 1984. *The Fragmented Forest.* University of Chicago Press, Chicago.

Hobbs, R. J. 1987. Disturbance regimes in remnants of natural vegetation. Pp. 233–40 in D. A. Saunders, G. W. Arnold, A. A. Burbidge and A. J. M. Hopkins (eds). *Nature Conservation: the Role of Remnants of Native Vegetation.* Surrey Beatty, Chipping Norton, Australia.

    1992. The role of corridors in conservation: solution or bandwagon? *Trends in Ecology and Evolution* 7:389–92.

    1993. Effects of landscape fragmentation on ecosystem processes in the Western Australian wheatbelt. *Biological Conservation* 64:193–201.

Hobbs, R. J. and A. J. M. Hopkins. 1991. The role of conservation corridors in a changing climate. Pp. 281–90 in D. A. Saunders and R. J. Hobbs (eds). *Nature Conservation 2: The Role of Corridors.* Surrey Beatty, Chipping Norton, Australia.

Hobbs, R. J. and L. F. Huenneke. 1992. Disturbance, diversity, and invasion: implications for conservation. *Conservation Biology* 6:324–37.

Hobbs, R. J. and D. A. Norton. 1996. Towards a conceptual framework for restoration ecology. *Restoration Ecology* 4:93–110.

Hobbs, R. J. and D. A. Saunders (eds). 1992. *Reintegrating Fragmented Landscapes. Towards Sustainable Production and Nature Conservation.* Springer-Verlag, New York.

Hunter, M. L., Jr. 1996. *Fundamentals of Conservation Biology.* Blackwell Science, Oxford.

Hunter, M. L. and P. Yonzon. 1993. Altitudinal distributions of birds, mammals, people, forests, and parks in Nepal. *Conservation Biology* 7:420–3.

Hunter, M. L., Jr., G. L. Jacobson Jr. and T. Webb III. 1988. Paleoecology and the coarse-filter approach to maintaining biological diversity. *Conservation Biology* 2:375–85.

Huntley, B. and T. Webb III. 1989. Migration: species' response to climatic variations caused by changes in the earth's orbit. *Journal of Biogeography* 16:5–19.

International Union for Conservation of Nature and natural Resources (IUCN) 1980. *World conservation strategy: living resource conservation for sustainable development.* IUCN-UNEP-WWF, Gland, Switzerland.

Jacobson, G. L., Jr., T. Webb III and E. C. Grimm. 1987. Patterns and rates of vegetation change during the deglaciation of eastern North America. Pp. 277–88 in W. F. Ruddiman and H. E. Wright Jr. (eds). *North America and Adjacent Oceans during the Deglaciation. The Geology of North America,* volume K-3. Geological Society of America, Boulder.

Kelly, G. C. and, G. N. Park (eds). 1986. *The New Zealand protected natural areas programme: a scientific focus.* Biological Resources Centre publication no. 4, Department of Lands and Survey, Wellington, New Zealand.

Küchler, A. W. 1964. *Potential natural vegetation of the conterminous United States.* Special publication no. 36, American Geographical Society, New York.

Lindenmayer, D. B. and J. F. Franklin. 1997. Managing stand structure as part of ecologically sustainable forest management in Australian mountain ash forests. *Conservation Biology* 11:1053–68.

Lindenmayer, D. B. and T. W. Norton. 1993. The conservation of leadbeater's possum in southeastern Australia and the northern spotted owl in the pacific north-west of the USA; management issues, strategies and lessons. *Pacific Conservation Biology* 1:13–18.

Lord, J. M. and D. A. Norton. 1990. Scale and the spatial concept of fragmentation. *Conservation Biology* 4:197–202.

Lovejoy, T. E., R. O. Bierregaard, A. B. Rylands, J. R. Malcolm, C. E. Quintela, L. H. Harper, K. S. Brown, A. H. Powell, G. V. N. Powell, H. O. R. Schubart and M. B. Hays. 1986. Edge and other effects of isolation on Amazon forest fragments. Pp. 257–85 in M.E. Soulé (ed.). *Conservation Biology: the Science of Scarcity and Diversity.* Sinauer Associates, Sunderland, USA.

MacArthur, R. H. and Wilson, E. O. 1965. An equilibrium theory of insular zoogeography. *Evolution* 17:373–87.

1967. *The Theory of Island Biogeography*. Princeton University Press, Princeton.

Margules, C. R. and M. P. Austin (eds). 1991. *Nature Conservation: Cost Effective Biological Surveys and Data Analysis*. CSIRO, Melbourne, Australia.

Margules, C. R., A. O. Nicholls and R. L. Pressey. 1988. Selecting networks of reserves to maximise biological diversity. *Biological Conservation* **43**:63–76.

Mark, A. F. 1985. The botanical component of conservation in New Zealand. *New Zealand Journal of Botany* **23**:789–810.

Matlack, G. R. 1993. Microenvironment variation within and among forest edge sites in the eastern United States. *Biological Conservation* **66**:185–94.

Murcia, C. 1995. Edge effects in fragmented forests; implications for conservation. *Trends in Ecology and Evolution* **10**:58–62.

Myers, N. 1988. Threatened biota's: 'hotspots' in tropical forests. *Environmentalist* **8**:1–20.

Niemelä, J. 1997. Invertebrates and boreal forest management. *Conservation Biology* **11**:601–10.

Norton, D. A. 1988. Managing for the long term. *Forest and Bird* **19**(2):32–4.

1996a. Ecological realism and the sustainable management of indigenous forests for timber production. Pp. 70–7 in D. A. Norton and J. C. Allen (eds), *Professional Forestry – Evolving Issues in Forest Management*. School of Forestry, University of Canterbury, Christchurch.

1996b. Monitoring biodiversity in New Zealand's terrestrial ecosystems. Pp. 19–41 in B. McFadgen and P. Simpson (compilers). *Biodiversity*. Department of Conservation, Wellington.

Norton, D. A. and N. Reid. 1997. Lessons in ecosystem management from management of threatened and pest loranthaceous mistletoes in New Zealand and Australia. *Conservation Biology* **11**:759–69.

Noss, R. F. 1987. Corridors in real landscapes: a reply to Simberloff and Cox. *Conservation Biology* **1**:159–64.

Noss, R. F. and A. Y. Cooperrider. 1994. *Saving Nature's Legacy. Protecting and Restoring Biodiversity*. Island Press, Covelo, California.

Noss, R. F. and L. D. Harris. 1986. Nodes, networks, and MUMs: preserving diversity at all scales. *Environmental Management* **10**:299–309.

Noss, R. F., H. B. Quigley, M. G. Hornocker, T. Merrill and P. C. Paquet. 1996. Conservation biology and carnivore conservation in the Rocky Mountains. *Conservation Biology* **10**:949–63.

O'Connor, K. F., F. B. Overmars and M. M. Ralston. 1990. *Land evaluation for nature conservation. a scientific review compiled for application in New Zealand*. Conservation Science publication no. 3, Department of Conservation, Wellington.

Ogle, C. C. 1987. The incidence and conservation of animals and plant species in remnants of native vegetation within New Zealand. Pp. 79–87 in D. A. Saunders, G. W. Arnold, A. A. Burbidge and A. J. M. Hopkins (eds). *Nature Conservation: the Role of Remnants of Native Vegetation*. Surrey Beatty, Chipping Norton, Australia.

Peres, C. A. and J. W. Terborgh. 1995. Amazonian nature reserves: an analysis of the defendibility status of existing conservation units and design criteria for the future. *Conservation Biology* **9**:34–46.

Perry, D. A., J. G. Borchers, S. L. Borchers and M. P. Amaranthus. 1990. Species migrations and ecosystem stability during climate change: the below ground connection. *Conservation Biology* **4**:266–74.

Peterken, G. F., D. Ausherman, M. Buchenau and R. T. T. Forman. 1992. Old-growth conservation within British upland conifer plantations. *Forestry* **65**:127–44.

Peters, R. L. and J. D. S. Darling. 1985. The greenhouse effect and nature reserves. *BioScience* **35**:707–17.

Pickett, S. T. A. and J. N. Thompson. 1978. Patch dynamics and the design of nature reserves. *Biological Conservation* **13**:27–37.

Pickett, S. T. A. and P. S. White (eds). 1985. *The Ecology of Natural Disturbance and Patch Dynamics.* Academic Press, Orlando.

Pielou, E. C. 1979. *Biogeography.* John Wiley, New York.

Potter, M. A. 1990. Movement of North Island brown kiwi (*Apteryx australis mantelli*) between forest remnants. *New Zealand Journal of Ecology* **14**:17–24.

Prance, G. T. 1991. Rates of loss of biological diversity: a global view. Pp. 27–44 in R. J. Spellerberg, F. B. Goldsmith and M. G. Morris (eds). *The Scientific Management of Temperate Communities for Conservation.* Blackwell Scientific Publications, Oxford.

Pressey, R. L. and S. L. Tully. 1994. The cost of *ad hoc* reservation: a case study in western New South Wales. *Australian Journal of Ecology* **19**:375–84.

Pressey, R. L., C. J. Humphries, C. R. Margules, R. I. Vane-Wright and P. H. Williams. 1993. Beyond opportunism: key principles for systematic reserve selection. *Trends in Ecology and Evolution* **8**:124–8.

Rosenzweig, M. L. 1995. *Species Diversity in Space and Time.* Cambridge University Press, Cambridge.

Saunders, D. A. and R. J. Hobbs. 1991. *Nature Conservation 2: The Role of Corridors.* Surrey Beatty, Chipping Norton, Australia.

Saunders, D. A. and R. J. Hobbs. 1992. Impact on biodiversity of changes in land-use and climate. Pp. 61–75 in R. J. Hobbs (ed.). *Biodiversity of Mediterranean ecosystems in Australia.* Surrey Beatty, Chipping Norton, Australia.

Saunders, D. A., R. J. Hobbs and C. R. Margules. 1991. Biological consequences of ecosystem fragmentation: a review. *Conservation Biology* **5**:18–29.

Sax, J. L. 1980. *Mountains without Handrails: Reflections on the National Parks.* University of Michigan Press, Ann Arbour.

Scott, M. J., B. Csuti, J. D. Jacobi and J. E. Estes 1987. Species richness: a geographical approach to protecting future biological diversity. *BioScience* **37**:782–8.

Scott, J. M., F. Davis, B. Csuti, R. Noss, B. Butterfield, C. Groves, H. Anderson, S. Caicco, F. D'Erchia, T. C. Edwards Jr., J. Ulliman and R. G. Wright. 1993. Gap analysis: a geographical approach to the protection of biological diversity. *Wildlife Monographs* **123**.

Shafer, C. L. 1990. *Nature Reserves: Island Theory and Conservation Practice*. Smithsonian Institute Press, Washington D.C.

—— 1995. Values and shortcomings of small reserves. *BioScience* **45**:80–8.

Shaffer, M. L. 1981. Minimum population sizes for species conservation. *BioScience* **31**:131–4.

Shinneman, D. J. and W. L. Baker. 1997. Nonequilibrium dynamics between catastrophic disturbances and old-growth forests in ponderosa pine landscapes of the Black Hills. *Conservation Biology* **11**:1276–88.

Simberloff, D. 1974. Equilibrium theory of island biogeography and ecology. *Annual Review of Ecology and Systematics* **5**:161–82.

Simberloff, D. 1976. Species turnover and equilibrium island biogeography. *Science* **194**:572–8.

Simberloff, D. A. and L. G. Abele. 1976. Island biogeography theory and conservation practice. *Science* **191**:285–6.

—— 1982. Refuge design and island biogeographic theory: effects of fragmentation. *American Naturalist* **120**:41–50.

Simberloff, D. and J. Cox. 1987. Consequences and costs of conservation corridors. *Conservation Biology* **1**:63–71.

Simberloff, D. and N. Gotelli. 1984. Effects of insularization on plant species richness in the prairie-forest ecotone. *Biological Conservation* **29**:27–46.

Simberloff, D., J. A. Farr, J. Cox and D. W. Mehlman. 1992. Movement corridors: conservation bargains or poor investments. *Conservation Biology* **6**:493–504.

Simpson, P. 1997. *Ecological restoration in the Wellington Conservancy*. Department of Conservation, Wellington, New Zealand.

Smith, P. G. R. and J. B. Theberge. 1987. Evaluating natural areas using multiple criteria: theory and practice. *Environmental Management* **11**:447–60.

Soulé, M. E. (ed.). 1987. *Viable Populations for Conservation*. Cambridge University Press, Cambridge.

Spellerberg, I. F., F. B. Goldsmith and M. G. Morris. 1991. *The Scientific Management of Temperate Communities for Conservation*. Blackwell Scientific Publications, Oxford.

Strittholt, J. R. and R. E. J. Boerner. 1995. Applying biodiversity gap analysis in a regional nature reserve design for the edge of Appalachia, Ohio (U.S.A.). *Conservation Biology* **9**:1492–505.

Sutherland, W. J. and D. A. Hill. 1995. *Managing Habitats for Conservation*. Cambridge University Press, Cambridge.

Thomas, C. D. 1991. *Ecological corridors: an assessment*. Department of Conservation, Wellington, New Zealand.

Usher, M. B. (ed.). 1986. *Wildlife Conservation Evaluation*. Chapman and Hall, London.

Vogelmann, J. E. 1995. Assessment of forest fragmentation in southern New England using remote sensing and geographic information systems technology. *Conservation Biology* **9**:439–49.

Weiss, S. B. and D. D. Murphy. 1993. Climatic considerations in reserve design and ecological restoration. Pp. 89–107 in D. A. Saunders, R. J. Hobbs and

P. Ehrlich (eds). *Nature Conservation 3: Reconstruction of Fragmented Ecosystems*. Surrey Beatty, Chipping Norton, Australia.

White, P. S. 1979. Pattern, process, and natural disturbance in vegetation. *Botanical Review* **45**:229–99.

Wiens, J. A. 1989. Spatial scaling in ecology. *Functional Ecology* **3**:385–97.

1997. Metapopulation dynamics and landscape ecology. Pp. 43–62 in I. A. Hanski and M. E. Gilpin (eds). *Metapopulation Biology, Ecology, Genetics, and Evolution*. Academic Press, San Diego.

Willison, J. H. M., S. Bondrup-Nielson, C. Drysdale, T. B. Herman, N. W. P. Munro and T. L. Pollock. 1992. *Science and the Management of Protected Areas*. Elsevier, Amsterdam.

Wilson, E. O. and E. O. Willis. 1975. Applied biogeography: the design of nature preserves. Pp. 522–34 in M. L. Cody and J. M. Diamond (eds). *Ecology and Evolution of Communities*. Harvard University Press, Cambridge.

Young, A. G., H. G. Merriam and S. I. Warwick. 1993. The effects of forest fragmentation on genetic variation in *Acer saccharum* Marsh. (sugar maple) populations. *Heredity* **71**:277–89.

17 Forest organization, management, and policy

CHADWICK D. OLIVER, MELIH BOYDAK, GERARDO SEGURA AND B. BRUCE BARE

Forest ecosystems provide many things which people value. Exactly what things are provided change as forests grow and are impacted by natural[1] disturbances and human activities. Each change provides some values, but precludes others (Oliver *et al.* 1997). For example, a large clearcut or fire provides timber as well as habitat for species needing large openings (Hunter 1990, Oliver *et al.* 1998) but precludes future timber and habitat for species needing closed forests until the forest regrows. Selective harvesting provides timber and habitat for species needing closed forests, but does not provide large openings for species which need this habitat. Manipulating one forest also affects activities and values in nearby or distant forests. Stopping harvest in one forest leads to more harvesting in other forests (Perez-Garcia 1993), resulting in too little habitat for open forest species in the first area and too much open habitat in the second. Forest activities can also affect non-forest values. For example, too little forest harvesting will lead to high timber prices and cause people to use steel, aluminum, concrete, and brick products instead. Because these non-wood products consume so much more fossil fuel in their manufacturing, they add much more carbon dioxide pollution to the atmosphere than if wood products had been used instead (Koch 1991, Kershaw *et al.* 1993).

An emerging challenge is to maintain biodiversity in the face of constantly changing 'natural' conditions, increasing human populations, conversion of some forests to other uses, extraction of commodity values from forests, and use of forests for other non-commodity values such as

---

1. 'Natural' is an arbitrary term since people can be considered part of nature and people have affected most forests in the world for thousands of years. 'Natural' is used in this chapter to describe processes generally free of immediate human participation.

recreation. Forest management is concerned with maintaining these values. The complexity of forests – from the individual organism to the global scale – makes the management task daunting; however, the alternative of not managing forests can lead to extremely wide fluctuations in the availability of habitats and commodities, and so be of little benefit either for biodiversity or for people's material needs.

People manage most of the world's forests using fire, domestic grazing, tree girdling, tree cutting, and other means to provide habitats, agricultural areas, grazing land, wood products, and other things. Concerns during the past few centuries of anticipated or existing wood shortages, poor water quality, erosion, and danger from forest fires have led to organization and management systems which have helped alleviate these problems (Olson 1971, Perlin 1989). These management systems are evolving and becoming increasingly successful. For example, forest management has helped prevent anticipated timber shortages and has reduced erosion in many developed countries. As these immediately life-threatening and material concerns are being alleviated, people are also wanting the forest to provide other values, such as biodiversity. These new values – objectives of management – share a common property with the more traditional management objectives: they all need coordination at many spatial and temporal scales – from individual organisms to the global scale. Management needs to become increasingly effective to provide the increasing objectives people are demanding from forests.

For forest management to satisfy the many objectives, there needs to be a smooth coordination of forest growth, natural disturbances, and the many human activities across many spatial scales. The challenge of coordinating many activities at many scales for many objectives is not unique to forestry. Many segments of society are meeting the challenge using a scientific approach (Reich 1983). This approach – 'management science' – emerged as a discipline about 100 years ago when people realized that management methods could be systematically tested to determine effective ways of achieving desired results (Taylor 1911). Like all sciences, these disciplines are evolving.

This chapter will describe a generalized system for coordinating forest management to provide biodiversity as well as other values. It is based on the principles of management science. Many elements of the system are being used to manage various forests (Bare *et al.* 1984, Davis and Johnson 1987); however, other elements are just being incorporated into forest management. Explicit recognition of the systematic, modular approach, as described in this chapter, can help make management more effective.

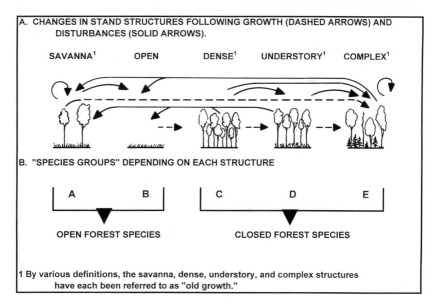

Fig. 17.1. Forests contained a variety of stand structures as disturbances and regrowth changed each area. Some species depend on each structure for habitat (e.g., A,B,C,D, and E). For this chapter, 'savanna' and 'open' structures are referred to as 'open' habitat; and 'dense', 'understory', and 'complex' structures are referred to as 'closed' habitat.

This chapter first describes an organizational hierarchy to address the complexity of forest management. It then shows how this organization can be viewed as a system – an ecosystem. Lastly, it describes how this ecosystem can be managed using decision analysis and adaptive management techniques.

A spatial hierarchy for forest management

Each organism and species contributes to the biodiversity of an ecosystem. However, a distribution of organisms – trees, shrubs, snags, etc. – provides a structure within an area (a stand) which may benefit certain species groups but not others (Figure 17.1). A landscape – a group of stands with different structures – may benefit many groups of species at a larger scale. A group of landscapes may provide habitats for other species, and even larger areas may provide several geographic areas which each contain their own group of species.

Other values such as timber products from forests also may be consid-

ered from several spatial scales. The individual tree can be considered for harvest to provide timber products. The occasional flow of timber from a stand, the more continuous flow of timber from a landscape, and the tradeoffs in timber flow among different geographic areas can also be considered.

Because many values can be provided at different spatial scales, it is convenient to group forests into several spatial scales to facilitate management. Such hierarchical arrangements are commonly used to facilitate management (Litterer 1965, Clegg et al. 1996). Forest management has conventionally been spatially organized as a nested hierarchy from the individual operation on a specific stand to national or international scales (Figures 17.2 and 17.3).

This chapter will use five spatial subdivisions to describe the forest management hierarchy. These subdivisions are: silvicultural operations, silvicultural regimes, landscape patterns, subforest and forest plans, and regional, national or global forest policies (Figure 17.3).

Such a management hierarchy is often referred to as a 'pyramid.' For this chapter, the 'policy' end of the hierarchy will be referred to as the 'diffuse' level and the 'operations' end will be referred to as the 'specific' level (Figure 17.4). The hierarchy is intended to provide a division of tasks, so people can focus on the objectives which can best be provided at each level. One level of the hierarchy can feed information immediately to more diffuse or specific levels, and so coordinate among the levels, as will be discussed. In addition, feedback mechanisms must be provided to link the various levels.

Although public and private forests in many countries have commonly been subdivided into spatial groups for implementing forest operations, most aspects of management have generally been more centralized. Increasing understanding of the behavior of each level of the hierarchy allows it to be managed more effectively. The five hierarchical levels listed above and shown in Figures 17.3 and 17.4 will be discussed in detail below.

OPERATIONS

This level focuses on individual plants and animals within a stand and is concerned with changing their abilities to survive and grow at a given time and place through various activities. These activities mimic, avoid, or help the plants and animals recover from such processes as disturbances and regeneration. In the process, various commodity and non-commodity values are provided. In various countries, this level has been a

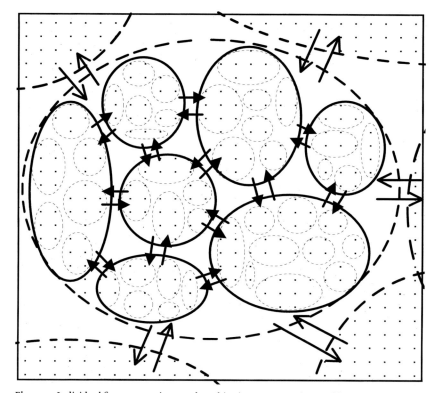

Fig. 17.2. Individual forest operations such as thinning, regenerating, and harvesting are shown as dots in this figure. Individual operations can each be treated as system; or they can be coordinated by grouping all operations to the same stand and treating each operation as a subsystem, and treating the stand as a system (shown as light dashed lines). These stands can be grouped into landscape systems (solid lines) and each stand treated as a subsystem. The landscapes can also be grouped into subforest or forest systems (dark, dashed lines) and each landscape treated as a subsystem. The result is a hierarchical grouping of systems into a 'pyramid'. Management of each system is done by using external inputs to the system to influence internal inputs and outputs among subsystems to provide the desired external outputs. Inputs among landscapes (solid arrowheads) and among subforests or forests (open arrowheads) are shown.

part of silviculture, wildlife management, silvicultural engineering, or logging engineering.

Specific operations include silvicultural and other activities which change the forest condition, such as harvesting all or some of the trees, creating snags, reforesting or afforesting, weeding, changing the nutrient status, controlled burning, pruning, hunting, trapping, introducing animals, road construction, and collecting non-timber forest products (e.g., mushrooms, floral greens, medicinal plants, and resins). There are a

TYPICAL FORESTRY SPATIAL SCALES	EQUIVALENT LEVELS USED IN THIS PAPER
LANDOWNER, STATE, PROVINCE COMPANY, NATIONAL, INTERNATIONAL	POLICIES
SUBCOMPARTMENT, COMPARTMENT, BLOCK, DISTRICT, FOREST, REGION	FOREST & SUBFOREST PLANS
	LANDSCAPE PATTERNS
STAND	SILVICULTURAL REGIMES
	SILVICULTURAL OPERATIONS

Fig. 17.3. Common classification of levels of spatial hierarchy in forest management (left) and abbreviated, equivalent classification used in this chapter (right).

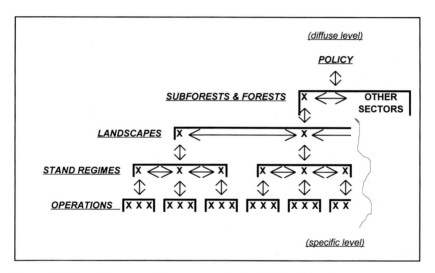

Fig. 17.4. The 'nested' systems of Figure 17.2 can be described as a 'hierarchy', or pyramid, of systems. Each system ('X') becomes one of the subsystems of another hierarchical level. For this chapter, the policy 'end' of the pyramid is referred to as the 'diffuse' end and the operations 'end' is referred to as the 'specific' end. Management is done by identifying, analyzing, making and implementing decisions and then monitoring and auditing specifics relative to the external inputs and outputs among systems. Methods have been developed to avoid inefficiencies and dysfunctionalities in managing the systems.

variety of techniques to accomplish each operation. For example, reforestation can be done by planting or seeding; and planting can be done by hand labor or with machines. Which technique is appropriate depends on area-specific conditions of the species of concern: climate, soil, accessibility, slope, and weed competition, as well as capital, labor and equipment infrastructure capabilities and availability.

The feasibility of any technique can only be determined for each specific case; consequently, decisions about which techniques can accomplish a given operation need to be made at this level of the hierarchy. Considerable expertise has been developed in implementing the various techniques in nearly all parts of the world (Daniel et al. 1979, Smith et al. 1997); and there are many scheduling, planning, and other engineering techniques which can be readily used for designing, planning, and improving techniques (Dieter 1991, Krick 1962).

The various operations are developed by studying 'natural' processes and mimicking them; consequently, nearly all operations mimic such processes to varying extents. For example, harvesting operations such as clearcutting mimic natural stand-replacement disturbances; and thinnings and selective harvesting mimic natural partial disturbances. The operations may concentrate on a narrower range of processes than occurred naturally; for example, clearcutting has been widely practiced as an effective operation for economically efficient timber production; but such complete stand-replacing disturbances are only a limited part of the range of natural disturbances which have impacted most areas. Rarely have silvicultural operations mimicked the extremes of natural processes such as glaciation and extreme erosion, which reduce tree growth potential for many centuries.

Just as no two natural disturbances are identical, no silvicultural operation will exactly duplicate any single natural disturbance. Species have evolved an ecological amplitude – the ability to survive and benefit from a range of disturbances or other influences. This ecological amplitude generally allows species to respond similarly to a range of natural disturbances and to human disturbances which resemble them. For example, Cedar of Lebanon (Cedrus libani A. Rich.) had regenerated following natural fires in parts of Turkey and Lebanon before people inhabited the area. Prescribed broadcast burning is now used as a silvicultural operation which mimics the natural fires and helps regenerate this species in Turkey (Boydak 1996a,b).

Silvicultural operations can help maintain the character of a previously natural condition when exotic insects, diseases, or aggressive plants and animals threaten to displace or kill native ones (Campbell and Schlarbaum 1994). Operations can selectively remove pests, keep them from spreading and restore populations of native species.

SILVICULTURAL REGIMES

This level focuses on the individual stand and is concerned with coordinating the various silvicultural and engineering operations to achieve the desired stand structures and other outputs over time. A 'silvicultural regime' is defined in this chapter as the series of operations applied to a specific stand at specific times to try to achieve the target changes in structures and flows of outputs, such as timber and such non-commodity outputs as habitats for certain species.

Stand management has been awkwardly described, prescribed, and analyzed using the terms 'silvicultural systems' and 'rotation ages'. Silvicultural systems are broad management approaches based on different methods of regenerating forests (Smith et al. 1997). Rotation ages are often determined as a generality for a given species, site, and ownership (Davis and Johnson 1987). In contrast, the term 'silvicultural regime' is used here to describe a stand-specific set of operations (e.g., regeneration, thinning, pruning, snag creation, harvesting) prescribed for specific times to a specific stand.

Stand structures change in two ways: (a) through growth and regular mortality and (b) through natural disturbances and human operations. The stand structure at a given time determines the stand's usefulness for providing many values. For example, each structure contributes to the habitat for some species (Figure 17.1). Some species in many North American forests are either extinct or threatened and endangered because of a lack of the savanna, open, or complex habitats (Oliver et al. 1997). The different structures also provide different aesthetic and recreational values and different levels of resistance to fires, windstorms, and insect and disease outbreaks (Oliver and Larson 1996). Stands in the dense, understory, complex, and savanna structures have an immediate potential to provide timber through various harvesting operations (e.g., clearcutting, thinnings, selection cuttings). Stands in the open structure do not. The operations which change the stand structures also provide other values, such as timber and non-timber forest products and income and employment from the operations.

Some structures can more rapidly be changed to others through silvicultural operations. For example, dense and understory stands can be changed to complex structures through selective cutting, but open or savanna stands take many more years to be changed to complex structures.

Each stand has certain times when various operations can be done effectively, referred to as 'windows' of opportunity (Oliver and Larson 1996). For example, a recently harvested or burned stand has a 'window' of one to several years when the species composition of the subsequent stand can be controlled by planting, seeding, or weeding. Once a new stand has regrown and occupied the growing space, it is much more difficult to change the species composition and the regeneration 'window' is lost. Similarly, a stand can be thinned during certain 'windows'. If the stand is not thinned during this window, the crowded trees continue to grow in height but not diameter and bend and break or become susceptible to insects and diseases (Oliver and Larson 1996). Attempts to thin after the window has passed will only exacerbate the bending and breaking.

At a given window, several different operations could be applied to the stand. Each different operation initiates a different regime, creating a different sequence of stand structures, and providing different values at different times (Figure 17.1). For example, a stand in the dense structure could be:

- allowed to grow without intervention and so remain in the dense structure for many years;
- subjected to a series of thinnings and so be changed to the understory structure;
- immediately selection harvested and so changed more rapidly to the complex structure;
- immediately 'shelterwood' harvested followed by planting with the same or another species, and so changed to the savanna structure; or,
- immediately clearcut and planted and so changed to the open structure.

Each of these regimes provides different commodity and stand structure values at different future times.

Both the feasibility of each regime and the values it provides at each future time are very stand specific. They depend on the present stand structure, the site's growth potential and risk of disturbances, and the feasibility of the different operations needed to implement the regime. Considerable expertise as well as various tools have been developed to help determine the feasibility and consequences of managing stands by alternative regimes. Such tools include silvicultural decision keys and diagrams (Oliver and Larson 1996), stand growth models, economic and valuation analysis (present net worth) techniques (Davis and Johnson 1987), and habitat suitability indexes, among others. (See also Oliver and Twery in press).

Most silvicultural regimes mimic natural processes and so create structures which occur naturally. As a general rule, however, most silvicultural regimes narrow the range of processes which naturally occur within a region as well as the range and distribution of structures. They generally do not allow stands to contain trees which grow to extremely old ages; they have generally reduced the time when the stand is in the open structure; and they have generally not developed the savanna structure. Within many regions, concentrating on a few regimes – such as where all stands are clearcut shortly after they reach the dense structure – has reduced the range of regimes even further. The significance of narrowing this range of regimes depends on the values and tradeoffs in values desired. For example, clearcutting and short rotation regimes provide high volumes of wood at low costs, but they do not provide high quality timber or the variety of habitats needed for high biodiversity.

LANDSCAPES

This level of the hierarchy focuses at a landscape area of approximately 400 to 1500 hectares (1000 to 6000 acres). The size can vary, but it may be useful to bound an area with watershed boundaries (or sub-boundaries) or to encompass animal home ranges. Management at the landscape level requires coordination of the spatial and temporal considerations of the silvicultural regimes for all stands included in the landscape. This coordination ensures that the proposed regimes are physically feasible within the access and spatial conditions of the landscape and that they will provide the commodity flows, distributions of stand structures, and other values across the landscape and through time.

Often ownership boundaries, present stand structures, access, soils, or other physical conditions limit the silvicultural regimes which are feasible for a stand. For example, if a stand is only accessible by traveling through another stand, it may be necessary to schedule operations in both stands at the same time, even if the operations are not identical (e.g., one stand may be thinned while the other is harvested; Hann and Bare 1979).

Some values are provided by the distribution of stands across the landscape, rather than at the individual stand level. For example, habitats of some animal species consist of 'edges' between openings and closed stand structures, while other species ('interior' species) require areas away from 'edges' – either large openings or large closed forests (Chapters 6 and 7 of this book; Hunter 1990, Oliver et al. 1998). Such habitats are often created by spatially and temporally coordinating structures among different stands. A landscape's suitability for habitat changes with time. For example, a new clearcut next to a complex forest will create an 'edge' and favor edge species for the first few decades and then regrow to form a large, contiguous area of closed forest. Other values such as aesthetics, recreation, and avoiding fire, insect, and windthrow catastrophes are partly based on a stand's topographic position and the condition of the surrounding stands. Consequently, they are better managed at the landscape level than at the individual stand level.

Managing from the landscape perspective is a recent addition to usual forest management approaches (Iverson and Alston 1986, Hunter 1990, Oliver 1992, Boyce 1995, McCarter et al. 1998). During the past two decades, landscape management has been proposed, and tools for applying it have been developed (Boyce 1985, 1995, Oliver 1992, Boyce and McNab 1994, McCarter et al. 1998). Prior to this addition, scheduling harvesting operations used simplistic silvicultural regimes and were done for a forest as a whole with little regard to the spatial feasibility of the operations or resulting changes in stand structures (Davis and Johnson 1987). Consequently, stand regimes planned at the forest or subforest level were often infeasible (Schuster et al. 1993). Where they were feasible, they often created landscapes which did not provide many of the values (Johnson 1992). Addition of the landscape hierarchical level allows spatial constraints to be taken into account. Dykstra (1984) and Weintraub and Bare (1996) discussed a variety of approaches suggested for handling spatial concerns. These approaches rely on linear programming, integer programming, combinatorial heuristics, or some combination of the preceding. Spatial components concern both the adjacency of operations over time as well as the ensuing patterns which result across the landscape.

A landscape can be managed to provide different components at various future times, and to provide different quantities, species, and qualities of timber and other commodity products. For example, a landscape where all stands are presently in the dense structure can be managed by preventing human activities and all stands would probably remain in the closed, crowded condition for many decades. Complex and open structures could occur after partial or stand-replacing disturbances. Alternatively, different stands can be thinned, selectively harvested, clearcut, and shelterwood harvested to achieve a variety of stands with understory, complex, open, and savanna structures, respectively. Or, all stands can be clearcut to create a landscape exclusively of the 'open' structure without edges; this landscape will, of course, regrow to a continuous closed structure within a few decades. Each of these and other possible silvicultural regimes provide different habitats and other values, as well as different flows of products.

Although a wide range of landscape components, habitats, other non-commodity values, and commodities can be provided, certain landscape components and values cannot be immediately provided from a given landscape pattern. For example, it may take many decades to provide old-growth interior habitats across the landscape if management is begun immediately following clearcutting of the entire landscape. Such a landscape will not initially provide timber commodities either, although it will probably provide many berries as well as habitats for species requiring openings.

In most forests, a variety of structures existed and fluctuated across the landscape, with some structures generally found more often in certain topographic positions than others (Romme and Knight 1981, Segura and Snook 1992, Camp et al. 1997, Oliver et al. 1998). For example, pinyon pine forests of Mexico were found to grow rapidly to dense structures in productive soils in gullies, while they grew slowly and remained in savanna and complex structures on surrounding ridges. The cyclic fires burned hotter in the dense stands in the gullies, returning them to the open condition and perpetuating the gully-forming process. On the surrounding hills, the fires burned less hot, killing only some trees, perpetuating the savanna and complex structures, and providing seed sources that regenerated the gullies (Segura and Snook 1992). Similarly, in the eastern Cascade Mountains of Washington, USA, complex structures are most commonly found on the north slopes near streams, where the cool microclimates protect the forests from fires for extended periods (Camp et al. 1997).

On a given landscape area, it may or may not be desirable to follow the natural pattern – and fluctuation – of stand structures. Even where the objective is to maintain habitats for all species, it may be appropriate to increase certain structures beyond their 'historical range' to compensate for shortages of habitats in other landscapes (Morgan et al. 1994). The natural distribution and fluctuation is helpful in indicating the risk of managing different stand structures in different topographic positions (Oliver 1998). For example, it may be inappropriate to apply silvicultural regimes which create complex structures in topographic positions where historically the stands have frequently blown over or burned up.

SUBFORESTS AND FORESTS

These spatial scales are usually divided into several hierarchical levels, covering areas of several stands (e.g., 40 000 hectares) to large regions (e.g., millions of hectares). These levels have commonly been designated as subcompartments, blocks, districts, forests and/or regions in traditional forest management. They have the common property of being too large to allow effective spatial coordination of the structures of individual stands. For this chapter, they will be collectively referred to as the 'forest' hierarchical level. Where hierarchical subdivisions within this level are discussed, they will be referred to as the 'forest' and 'subforest' levels.

The forest level provides commodity and non-commodity values by coordinating the changes in commodity and non-commodity values among the landscapes (or subforests) within its area. A forest can be delineated as an area having a relatively uniform range of soils, climate, vegetation, animal populations, human demographic conditions, and/or political or ownership conditions. Then, general values identified at more diffuse levels can be translated into more specific, measurable objectives which can be coordinated among the landscape or (subforest) levels within the forest (Figure 17.5). Management at the forest level does not become concerned with the spatial distributions or the feasibilities of stand regimes within the landscapes it is coordinating. Instead, it coordinates the changes in landscape patterns, timber flows, and other values among the landscapes to achieve the desired values of the forest as a whole. It also utilizes the economies of scale both to coordinate the investments in equipment, labor, and other pieces of infrastructure needed for performing the various operations and to target specific products to be marketed.

Managing across larger areas allows conditions in one landscape area to complement and compensate for conditions in another area, thus giving a greater ability for the forest as a whole to provide the desired values. For example, even if complex stand structures were identified as one of the objectives of management, some landscape areas within a forest may contain only very young stands and so be unable to provide complex structures for many decades. In this case, the forest plan would choose those alternative plans in other landscapes within the forest which maintain large amounts of complex structure – until this structure could be grown and provided elsewhere.

It may even be desirable to manage some landscape areas to fluctuate between predominantly open and closed structures, with other landscape areas behaving similarly, but countercyclically, if both large closed and large open habitat areas are target values. Other landscape areas may be managed to maintain a diversity of structures so that 'edges' and habitats for species needing several structures are provided. Similarly, one landscape area may be targeted for harvesting high amounts of timber until

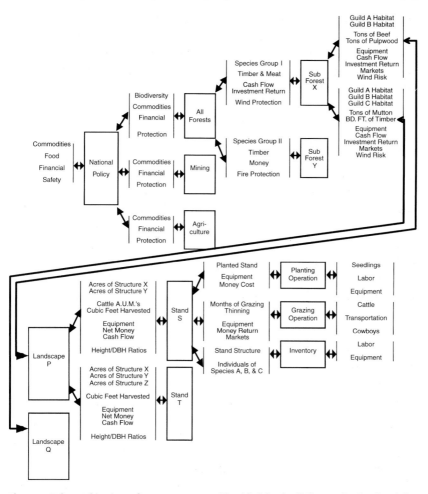

Fig. 17.5. Values (objectives of management) are identified for the diffuse, policy level (to left). These values become the inputs and outputs of the systems being managed, and expanded in terms which are measurable and have local interpretation and relevance to the more specific system (to the right). By keeping a consistent set of management values (inputs and outputs), management is coordinated from the operations to the policy levels. To keep management efficient, only a few key inputs and outputs are managed at each level.

trees in other landscape areas are old enough to contribute to the timber output from the forest as a whole.

As an example, an analysis of the Washington State Department of Natural Resources habitat conservation plan showed that the financial cost of meeting habitat targets was quite high when the target was required on individual subunits of the forest (Bare *et al.* 1997). When these habitat goals were targeted over a larger area so that excesses of a certain habitat in one subunit could compensate for too little of that habitat in another subunit, the financial costs decreased.

The forest level also determines what commodities can be provided in sufficient quantities so that markets can be developed. For example, if much of the forest area is suitable for grazing as well as timber production, it is appropriate to develop markets for livestock products (meat, leather, wool) as well as the timber species growing there. If, however, only a very small area of the forest is capable of supporting grazing, it may not be worthwhile to develop markets for the small amount of livestock potentially available. Similarly, silvicultural operations needed for many stands during a short period can be made more efficient by research which develops appropriate tools and techniques at the forest level; however, an operation which will only be performed occasionally may not benefit from the investment in making it more efficient.

A variety of landscape patterns have always existed within a forest area. For example, large fires, sometimes preceded by an insect outbreak or a windstorm, or volcanic eruptions could leave contiguous areas of hundreds of thousands of hectares in the open structure, to grow up uniformly to the closed structure (Oliver and Larson 1996). Populations of animals and plants fluctuated dramatically with these changes, with some species migrating or becoming extirpated as the habitat became unfavorable (Oliver and Larson 1996, Oliver et al. 1998). For a variety of values, it is often undesirable to have such large disturbances and their consequences; therefore, forest plans may attempt to maintain a diversity of landscape patterns on a smaller scale than would occur without human intervention.

POLICIES

This level of the management hierarchy attempts to coordinate the commodity and non-commodity values of a uniform political unit, such as a region, state, province, individual (or corporate) private forest landowner, on a national, or global scale. It may actually consist of several levels – one for each of these scales. Eventually, there may be global policies regarding forests – in which case another system at an even more diffuse hierarchical level would emerge.

Within its jurisdiction, the policy level coordinates the commodity and non-commodity values provided from different forests within its jurisdiction to provide a desired flow of values. A privately owned forest may be concerned with providing a consistent flow of timber from its forest, so it can maintain a market position relative to other forest landowners. Those making public policy may be concerned with coordinating its biodiversity among several forests (public and/or private) and coordinating the flow of timber, employment, and other values among both the forests and other sectors of society – agriculture, steel and concrete industries, fisheries, and military sectors, among others. This coordination is usually done by a combination of incentives and regulations. These incentives and regulations include taxes (or tax reductions), market incentives, education, research, direct monetary grants, and laws and procedural rules (Lippke and Oliver 1993, Bourland and Stroup 1996, Kennedy *et al.* 1996, Lippke and Fretwell 1997).

The national policy level coordinates the potential values provided by the various socioeconomic sectors of its country. It also works with other countries to coordinate the total flow of values to and from that country with values provided by other countries. For example, a country with excess forest growth relative to its potential for timber consumption may emphasize timber export as a source of income to obtain more food, education, defense, and other values. Another country may emphasize importing wood, but exporting commodities such as agricultural products if its agricultural potential were large but its forest area were small and contained unique species which were best protected by avoiding timber harvest.

The objectives considered at the policy level are necessarily expressed in general terms, since the climatic, soil, biological, and social variations among forests necessitate different interpretations of the values (Figure 17.5). For example, livestock and conifer timber production may be interpreted as target commodities in a dry pine subforest suitable for grazing, but a subforest of moist broadleaf species where grazing is not suitable may identify hardwood timber as the target commodity instead.

Much of the policy approach to forest management has been zonation – delineating different subforest areas to provide different values. Zonation has been used to protect land areas from more intensive land uses, or to provide objectives (externalities) which are not well incorporated into a free market economic system (Ierland 1993, Castro 1994). At different times, zonation has been used to protect forest animals from intensive hunting, to protect the forest from the intensive pressure to overharvest, deforest, or convert forest land to farmland; or to protect aesthetically pleasing areas from timber harvest, grazing, agricultural clearing, and urban development.

Rapid changes in transportation, communication, public health, mechanization, energy, and agriculture have led to dramatically changing rural land uses in many countries. The population is increasingly moving to cities; agricultural production is becoming increasingly *de facto* 'zoned' to the most productive non-urban lands; and less productive lands are regrowing to forests in many places. A very real concern of the past few hundred years has been an impending 'timber famine' – a lack of timber (Olson 1971, Perlin 1989). Where this has occurred, the consequences have been drastic for both the people and the sustainability of biodiversity and other forest values. The likelihood of an impending timber famine has declined in many countries because forests are regrowing in formerly agriculture and grazed areas; foresters have protected and reforested many areas; wood is transported over vast distances; and fossil fuel-based products have been substituted for wood energy and building materials. With decline of the concern of a 'timber famine', some people are emphasizing other values from the forest, including biodiversity, aesthetics, and recreation. Others are emphasizing that timber is still a financially dominant and ecologically valuable use of forests. As will be discussed, the best management approach will be one that can provide such values in the proper balance.

To provide this wider array of values, several policy approaches are emerging (Hunter 1990, Oliver *et al.* 1997). One approach is to allow timber production to continue to follow the agricultural model, in which the most productive (and accessible) lands not used for agriculture are used for timber production; and the other values are expected to be provided on even less productive lands. This approach is effective if earlier harvesting or zonation has eliminated a supply of 'free timber' growing on the less productive lands. It is questionable, but beyond the scope of this chapter, if the lands not used for timber production have the wildlife habitats or the economic ability to sustain the other values without active management both to maintain the habitats and to help pay for the other management. Intensive 'tree farms' differ from intensive agriculture. Areas outside 'tree farms' often still grow timber, which can compete with the tree farm timber and keep the price of the intensively grown timber low unless the tree farm timber is of a different species, different quality, or matures when there is a shortage of other timber – or the non-tree farm timber is artificially excluded from harvest by zonation. Timber also differs from agriculture because timber does not usually perish if not harvested at a certain time, but instead grows larger and to higher quality. Unless the timber outside of the tree farms burns, blows down, or otherwise perishes, there is increasing pressure to harvest this timber during times of economic or political strife.

Certain lands – often, but not always, the least productive – are excluded from timber production and are expected to provide other, non-commodity values. In some places these areas are stimulating a local recreation-based economy, which is supporting management of the area. In other places, the reserves are becoming increasingly difficult to manage since the costs of access into them is not being supported by commodity extraction; large disturbances are causing them to fluctuate in habitats (Christensen *et al.* 1989); local people are viewing the timber as attractive commodities to utilize – or a nuisance to be burned if they can not be used – and exotic pests are changing the original character of these forests (Campbell and Schlarbaum 1994). 'Biosphere Reserves' have been developed in many countries as part of UNESCO's 'Man and Biosphere' program. These reserves are zoned for different commodity and non-commodity uses.

A third, 'integrated' approach to forest management differs from both the agriculture approach of financially efficient management for a single commodity or the reserve approach which excludes commodity extraction. This third approach attempts to manage a large forest area jointly for many commodity and non-commodity products. Increasingly refined techniques to apply this approach have been developed in the past two decades, under such names as 'Landscape management' (Oliver 1992, Boyce and McNab 1994, Boyce 1995), and 'High Quality Forestry' (Weigand *et al.* 1994), and 'Integrated Management' (Oliver *et al.* 1997). Others refer to this approach as ecosystem management.

This integrated approach provides many of the forest's commodity and non-commodity values by maintaining a mixture of stand structures across the landscape and maintaining different patterns on different landscapes within a forest area. These structures, landscape patterns, and their arrangements within forests provide the habitats for most species, and so allow the 'coarse filter' approach of managing habitats instead of managing for individual species to provide biodiversity (Hunter 1990).

The different structures and patterns are maintained and/or created by silvicultural and harvesting operations, which provide employment and commodities in the process of maintaining or enhancing biodiversity. This approach has been refined by identifying habitats for animal guilds or stand structures for all vegetation types and maintaining these through management (e.g., Plum Creek Timber Company, Seattle, Washington, USA; Boise Cascade Corporation, Boise Idaho, USA; Potlatch Corporation, Lewiston, Idaho, USA). The key distinction between the agricultural model and an integrated approach is that the former focuses on commodities while the latter focuses on providing both non-commodity values such as biodiversity and commodity values such as timber.

Some countries have adopted these approaches and allocated some of their subforests to be managed under each approach. New Zealand, for example, has divided its land between reserves free of timber extraction and tree farms of very intensively managed, exotic tree species (Birchfield and Grant 1993). The United States and Mexico have zonations of some areas free of timber extraction; other, usually private, subforests where intensive timber management is practiced; and national forests and some private, non-industrial lands where integrated management is done. Recent public pressures have decreased the area of public forests managed almost exclusively for commodity extraction and encouraged many industrial forests to be managed by the 'integrated' approach. Turkey's forests are primarily publicly owned, and some areas are reserved for non-commodity values (Boydak 1996a, Muthoo 1997).

Avoiding complex, inefficient, centralized management

For forest management to be effective, there needs to be a smooth coordination from the diffuse to the specific levels of the spatial hierarchy. Without this coordination, apparently effective management at one spatial scale may prove counterproductive at another. As examples:

 − The operation of replanting with a given species may be so efficient that large areas are replanted to the same species and spacing. Within a few years there may be so many stands of the same age and spacing which need thinning that it may not be possible to thin some stands, whereas a wider spacing, or a variety of spacings for different stands, would have been better at the silvicultural regime level. At the landscape level, the regrowth of many stands of the same age, species, and spacing could create problems providing a diversity of habitats; while at the subforest or forest level, there could be problems marketing the large amount of uniform timber ready for harvest at one time.
 − A decision to follow a silvicultural regime which efficiently maximizes net present value by harvesting all stands over a given age (e.g., 60 years) may result in clearcutting large landscapes. As a consequence, at the landscape level the stands may not provide very diverse habitats; at the subforest or forest level there may not be enough cash flow and/or labor to replant, thin, and otherwise manage the uniformly regrowing stands.
 − A landscape-level decision to provide both timber flow and open habitats by harvesting part of a landscape which presently contains only closed habitats may not be appropriate at the forest level, if either the landscape

was the only one with enough closed forest to contain habitats for 'interior' species or there were so many salvage harvesting operations occurring in other areas that the timber market was temporarily flooded.

- A decision at the forest level to provide certain timber products and habitats by promoting a thinning infrastructure may not be effective if the policy decision is to manage the forests as 'reserves' which do not allow timber harvest.

- A decision at the policy level to import timber may be intended to create such a low price for domestic timber that people will stop harvesting native forests and preserve them instead. The actual consequence, however, may be that local people burn the forests (which they perceive as worthless) to provide more open area for grazing and agriculture.

THE FOREST AS AN ECOSYSTEM

A 'systems' perspective to managing complex entities has been developed to help avoid the unintended consequences described above (Shugart and O'Neill 1974, Patten 1971). Tansley (1935) first applied the systems perspective to ecological thinking when he developed the term and concept of an 'ecosystem'. The systems perspective is useful where so many different entities affect each other that it is impossible to account for each of them; this perspective groups common entities and focuses on the interactions among the groups. These groupings are called 'stations', 'modules', or 'subsystems'; and a 'cluster' of these 'subsystems' is regarded as a system.

Ecosystems – or any systems – can be grouped in different ways by different people (Kimmins 1987). For example, if the concern is how microbes, insects, small mammals, temperature, and water interact within a rotting log, the log and accompanying environment can be defined as an 'ecosystem' and the microbes, insects, temperature, log, etc. each defined as a 'subsystem'. If the concern is how different forests, different people, the oceans, and the atmosphere affect each other, the whole earth can be defined as an ecosystem and the different countries, the oceans, etc. defined as 'subsystems'. The organizational hierarchy described earlier in this chapter and in Figures 17.2 through 17.5 is a convenient way to define ecosystems for management and research. Each level – the stand, landscape, etc. – can be considered either as a 'subsystem' of a larger system or a 'system' by itself.

An action occurs in a subsystem to transform the inputs entering the subsystem to outputs coming out of the subsystem. For example, a stand can be considered a subsystem and how it changes during a finite period

(e.g., five years) may be described by growth, natural or human disturbances. Carbon dioxide and sunlight enter the 'subsystem' and more
oxygen may come out (if growth exceeds disturbances), as well as more
wood volume, a changed stand structure, and many other factors. These
actions, or changes, are referred to as 'activities', 'processes', or 'functions'.

The inputs and outputs entering and leaving each subsystem may be
referred to as 'events', 'patterns', or 'structures'. For example, the inputs
into a landscape subsystem may be open stand structures from several
stands and a large amount of harvested timber. The outputs of the same
landscape may be a lack of biodiversity because there are too few closed
and complex structures (Figure 17.1); a large amount of open structure;
and too much harvested timber for the local mills to process. Like subsystems, there are so many potential inputs and outputs that these, too are
grouped. For example, when each stand is considered as a subsystem, it
may be appropriate to describe the suitability of the stand's structure for
individual species; and these species could be some of the outputs.
Alternatively, when each landscape is considered a subsystem, it may be
appropriate to describe the suitability of the landscape for different guilds
– or groupings of species – and these guilds would become the outputs.
When the forest or policy levels are considered subsystems so that geographic areas with different species and guilds are coordinated, it may be
appropriate to group the viability of guilds native to each area into a single
name – such as 'biodiversity'.

A system is constructed by arranging the outputs of one subsystem as
the inputs of another (Figures 17.4 and 17.5). For example, the outputs of
each component stand 'subsystem' are 'stand structures', 'timber harvest
volumes', 'habitats', 'fire risk', etc. These become inputs to a landscape
subsystem which then provide the outputs of 'habitat distributions', 'biodiversity measures', 'timber flows', 'overall fire risk', etc. Similarly, the
inputs to a 'national policy' subsystem are the commodity (e.g., timber)
and non-commodity (e.g., biodiversity) values for each region, as well as
inputs from other segments of society – agriculture, mining, defense,
trade, etc.

An understanding of the system is needed to know what entities are to
be grouped into 'subsystems' and 'inputs/outputs' and what subsystems
are 'linked' by the outputs of one becoming the inputs of another. The
arrangement of subsystems and their inputs/outputs can vary with knowledge and schools of thought (Senge 1990). Knowledge, adaptive management, and research can help improve the system. A dramatic change in the

organization of a system caused by a large improvement in understanding is referred to as a 'paradigm shift' (Kuhn 1970).

Two paradigm shifts are presently occurring in ecosystem management:

1. There is a realization that forests were not 'closed systems' before people interfered with them (Botkin and Sobel 1975, Oliver and Larson 1996). The closed forest was believed to exist as a 'steady state' where all inputs to each subsystem are outputs from other subsystems within the system. Consequently, it was assumed that no net input or output existed for the forest system as a whole. Human interference in the forest was believed to be an external input which is so unusual that it would radically change the interactions of the forest. Research of the past few decades has shown that forests are not 'closed systems', but have always been impacted by such external inputs as climate changes, species migrations, and natural disturbances which create variations in inputs comparable to, if not greater than, those created by people.

2. There is a realization that there may not be an immediate threat that an increasing world human population and finite resources will soon cause massive starvation and decline of these resources, as has been predicted (Meadows 1972). Changing technologies and economics are both creating 'resources' from things previously thought useless and causing a reduction in human population growth (Simon 1996). In fact, the population may stabilize and resources may not prove to be as limiting as expected within the next few decades (Sedjo in press).

Such shifts in ways of thinking – and organizing systems – usually require several decades to be understood and accepted by all scientists, policymakers, the media, teachers, and the general public. During the shift, there is often considerable confusion since different people view the system with different assumptions, 'mental models' (Senge 1990), and paradigms (Kuhn 1970).

Some people define ecosystems to exclude humans and their actions or refer to 'natural' ecosystems as those which have no human influences. All forests contain inputs and outputs from people. Inputs include increases in carbon dioxide from fossil fuel combustion. Outputs are sometimes commodities, such as timber. Other forests are excluded from timber harvest and provide such non-commodity outputs as 'existence' to people who may never visit them. 'Existence' is the appreciation that some forests exist free from the 'obvious hands of people.' As will become apparent later, definitions of ecosystems which provide the most effective understanding and management include human components and processes. Management where human activities are excluded would measure the human inputs as zero.

MANAGING THE FOREST ECOSYSTEM

The objectives of forest management are varied. Usually, they involve the maximization of desired outputs that the system is capable of producing as efficiently as possible. The objectives can be expressed in terms of desired and undesired inputs and outputs. Biodiversity, clean water, wildlife, and timber volume may be desired outputs which people value; while wildfires, insect epidemics, and costs of management may be undesired outputs or inputs to be minimized. Management of ecosystems involves changing the inputs to influence the processes within the subsystems to provide the desired outputs while minimizing the undesirable outputs and inputs.

A common practice has been to try to manage ecosystems (and other systems) from increasingly more diffuse levels in the hierarchy, often resulting in 'central planning' where people try to control the inputs and outputs of even the most site-specific subsystems from a regional or national level. For example, at times the decision of whether to thin, harvest, or not enter an individual stand is made by those responsible for the policies of all of a nation's forests. This 'central control' approach to managing systems began many decades ago in various manufacturing and service organizations. Although efficient in managing simple systems, it removed decision-making from those closely associated with each subsystem (Reich 1983) and imposed undesirable uniform inputs on complex, varied subsystems. Such uniform inputs did not account for biological and socioeconomic differences among ecosystems at the more specific subforest, landscape, stand, and/or operational levels.

Forest management has conventionally been spatially organized as a nested hierarchy as described earlier (Figures 17.2 through 17.5). This hierarchy is sometimes separated into strategic, tactical, and operational levels. To coordinate this continuum, forestry is often divided into several subdisciplines:

- silviculture, which coordinates management activities within each stand –operational planning;
- forest management, which coordinates management among generally contiguous stands within an area – tactical planning; and,
- policy, which generally coordinates management within a political unit – strategic planning.

Sometimes these subdisciplines are further subdivided.

Even though forests have long been organized in a spatial hierarchy for implementing operations, decisions of which operations to implement have generally been done at the scale of the 'subforest' or 'forest.' These decisions have historically tried to coordinate the silvicultural regimes of individual stands within the forest using various optimization computer programs (Iverson and Alston 1986, Keeney and Raiffa 1993). Such programs have proved difficult to apply, since they do not analyze spatial and similar limitations, and therefore often prescribe infeasible or undesirable regimes to stands (Schuster *et al.* 1993). Management has partly tried to overcome the difficulties by allocating different forest areas (of many landscapes) to predominant uses, with different activities allowed within each of them.

The inefficiencies described above can be avoided by permitting each system's manager to manage only inputs and outputs among its constituent subsystems, but not those of another system, nor should a system manager become involved in management within its constituent subsystems. In this way, managers at each hierarchical level of the organization (Figure 17.5) are concerned with managing only the few inputs and outputs among subsystems within their system. Stand regime outputs are managed by changing the various operations; landscape patterns are managed by changing the various stand regimes; forest outputs are managed by changing the various landscape patterns; and strategic policies are managed by changing the various forest inputs and outputs. Management does not become concerned with processes *within* each of its subsystems as long as the decided-upon inputs to, and outputs from, it are provided. For example, a forest manager may designate a desired amount of beef, habitat for species A, and tons of pulpwood be provided by a specific landscape (e.g., Figure 17.5). However, the forest manager does not determine exactly which stands within the landscape provide each of these values at each time. Consequently, a landscape manager is able to adjust management within the landscape as better analyses or unforeseen catastrophes dictate, so long as the decided-upon inputs and outputs to the subforest level are maintained or improved.

Recent experience with National Forest planning in the United States has shown that the hierarchical approach is very promising. A single large-scale linear programming model which tried to coordinate all stands within a very large area did not work well because model size and complexity exceeded the managers' abilities to understand and assimilate the information. The advantage of the hierarchical approach is that it increases 'our understanding and predictive capabilities by pursuing the simplification inherent in the decomposition of the large system into its constituent subsystems' (Bare 1996). Not only does this approach save computational effort and allow spatial issues to be modeled, it also emphasizes the hierarchical nature of the decision-making process since, in reality, decisions are often made by many people at many different levels in a large forestry organization.

Several other, specific practices can also help ensure this tendency for central control is avoided:

1. Allowing each system (or subsystem) to coordinate with only a few sub-systems.
2. Within each system, focusing on the few, critical inputs and outputs among subsystems being managed.
3. Managing each input and output at the most specific subsystem possible.
4. Ensuring that the subsystem receiving input dictates the form, but not the quantity of input.

The management process

Even when a systems approach reduces each management task to the consideration of a relatively few inputs and outputs, making and implementing good management choices is difficult. This is especially evident at the more diffuse management levels where decisions seem somewhat abstract and, unless organized correctly, overwhelming. Historians have documented behaviors that led to many foolish decisions. Such behaviors include charisma, power, or panic (Tuchman 1984, Oliver and Twery in press, Janis 1967).

Management sciences have developed a systematic procedure to help ensure more effective management. This procedure can be divided into several components:

1. Analysis
2. Decision-making
3. Implementation

'Monitoring and feedback' is often considered a separate, fourth component, but is actually part of all three components.

ANALYSIS

Considerable research has been done on the analysis process (Morgan and Henrion 1990, Oliver and Twery in press). Very similar objective, systematic procedures for analysis have emerged in various management and engineering science fields to ensure that the various values are identified and treated fairly in the management process (Krick 1962,

Rowen 1976, Roberts 1979, Dieter 1991). These procedures are incorporated into National Forest planning under the United States National Environmental Policy Act (United States of America Federal Register 1962) and the United States National Forest Management Act (1976).

The procedures generally follow the steps listed below, although sometimes several steps are combined, subdivided, or repeated (Oliver and Twery in press):

1. Identify the decision-maker(s), and their authorities
2. Identify the values and express them as goals and objectives
3. Relate the objectives to the conditions of the area to be managed
4. Develop objectively measurable criteria to determine the degree to which each objective is reached.
5. Develop alternative actions to achieve the objectives.
6. Compare each alternative with each objective.
7. Select the best alternative (i.e., make a decision).
8. Implement the chosen alternative.

Steps three through six are the analytical roles of professionals and scientists, while steps one and two are developed iteratively between the analysts and the decision-makers. As discussed later, step 7 is the responsibility of the decision-maker(s); and step 8 is the role of those implementing the decision.

Theoretically, the analysis (and follow-up decision-making and implementation) steps occur as a rigid, sequential process among various levels in the hierarchy. In reality, the steps occur simultaneously at many levels, while responding to changes in inputs and desired outputs from more diffuse hierarchical levels by changing inputs and desired outputs of more specific levels.

It is useful to understand the theoretical, sequential process, which will be described below and shown schematically in Figure 17.6; however, it must then be realized that the processes occur simultaneously at many hierarchical levels.

Scope (part of steps 2 and 3)

The management objectives are determined by the landowners and policy-makers (who represent the public). Local ecological and social conditions and traditions largely determine what objectives (outputs of the system) are feasible; therefore, a 'scoping' process is usually done in which the array of possible outputs from each level (or subsystem) are communicated upward through the hierarchical pyramid (Figure 17.6) to the policy level. During the scoping process, the various outputs which serve as possible management objectives from each immediately more

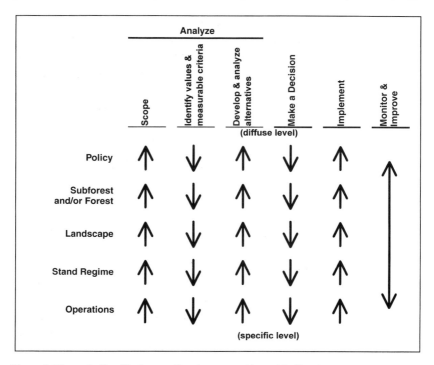

Fig. 17.6. Theoretically, effective coordination among hierarchical levels is done by different activities of analysis, decision, and implementation flowing separately as inputs and outputs in different directions in the hierarchy – to or from the more specific (and from and to the more diffuse). This theoretical flow is helpful in understanding coordination; however, in reality various activities occur simultaneously, iteratively, and continuously within and among hierarchical levels.

site-specific level are used as inputs to the next more diffuse level. The outputs of this level are based on these inputs, but are combined into a few, more generalized possible values. These more generalized outputs are sent as inputs to the next more diffuse level and combined until a robust, relatively small set of possible objectives reaches the policy level (Figures 17.5 and 17.6). The possible objectives received through this scoping are deliberated by policy-makers in relation to possible objectives for other forests and/or other, non-forestry objectives. The policy-makers then decide which of the possible objectives are worth adopting – the inputs and outputs to be provided or maintained.

> *Identify objectives and develop measurable criteria to ensure that each objective is reached (steps 2 through 4)*

The objectives and measurable criteria for expressing and monitoring each of them need to be identified and communicated by the policy-makers to managers of the next most specific subsystem – the forest.

Therefore, after the policy level has determined the broad objectives for management, there is a flow of information from the policy level to the forest level. The policy level describes to the forest level which objectives are to be managed for and how they are to be measured, although it does not dictate how much of each objective is to be provided. Managers at the forest level refine the objectives by developing measurable criteria that are appropriate for inputs to it from the subforest levels and describes these to the subforest level managers. The subforest level managers then continue the process of making the objectives and measurable criteria more explicit for managers of the progressively more site-specific levels that they manage (Figure 17.6), until specific objectives and measurable criteria are identified for each operation.

For example, United States National Forests in the east do not place meat production as a strong objective of forest management, since much of the meat is produced from privately managed agricultural lands. Consequently, most management objectives at each hierarchical level do not emphasize providing high-quality grazing land within the forests. As another example, forest policy-makers in many countries are beginning to realize that management will not be effective without the support of local communities living within the forests (Eleventh World Forestry Congress 1997). Consequently, enlightened managers are ensuring that 'providing local community values' is included as one of the national forest policy objectives. Exactly what these local values are is determined at more site-specific management levels for each local community.

Develop and analyze management alternatives to achieve the objectives (steps 5 and 6)

The manager of each subsystem then develops several alternative management approaches that will, through time, achieve the objectives to various degrees. Each subsystem's manager describes each alternative in terms of the amount of each objective that the alternative will provide over time and sends these alternatives with their descriptions to the manager of the next, more diffuse subsystem level. The manager of this more diffuse subsystem accumulates the alternatives from all the immediately more specific subsystems that it is coordinating and combines them to develop a few, robust alternatives for its subsystem, which it then sends to the manager of the next more diffuse system (Figures 17.6 and 17.7). This process continues until policy-makers (at the policy system) can examine and coordinate the alternatives from the forest and other sectors of concern.

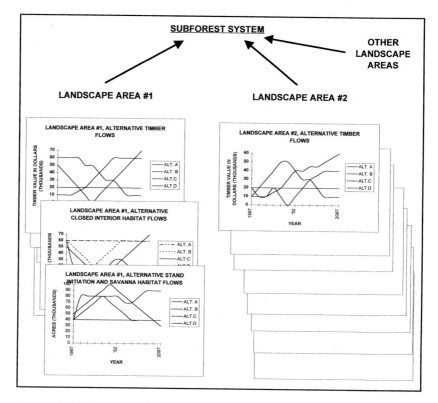

Fig. 17.7. Each subsystem would provide several management options to the next, more diffuse system, showing the effects of each option on the changes in pre-specified objectives over time. Above is an example of a subforest system integrating the flows of several landscape areas. Note landscape area #2 cannot provide much timber flow for the first few decades; the subforest system may decide to choose an alternative from landscape area #1 with a high timber flow for the first few decades to balance this, assuming other values could be similarly balanced.

Within the past decade, methods for coordination have been developed using an intermediate analysis-which fits the 'landscape system' of this chapter (Iverson and Alston 1986). This technique requires that several alternative landscape plans be developed for each landscape (Figure 17.7); each plan is known to be operationally feasible. The inputs and outputs of costs, habitats, timber, and other non-commodity and commodity values are projected over time for each landscape using each alternative. These alternatives are forwarded to managers of the subforest system, where the external inputs and outputs of values for the forest as a whole are 'optimized' by choosing the best fitting alternative for each landscape. A few such forest alternatives can be developed by optimizing different objectives, and these alternatives can be forwarded to the policy level, to be coordinated with other sectors of society. Methodologically, the alternative regimes for each landscape can be generated using simulation combinatorial heuristic techniques. However generated, this bottom-up approach ensures that spatially feasible schedules will be passed forward to the forest or policy system. At that level another combinatorial heuristic or linear programming model can be used to determine the best overall forest management solution. Since only spatially feasible alternatives are sent forward, the forest plan also is ensured of being spatially feasible.

An important key to effective management is to find an alternative which provides many of the objectives with the fewest negative tradeoffs (Mendoza *et al.* 1987, Rustagi and Bare 1987, Bare and Mendoza 1988, Liu and Davis 1995). Whereas no alternative is wrong or unscientific, those which provide only a few output values and sacrifice many others can be quite uncreative. Many people have assumed that providing biodiversity is incompatible with providing timber products because they have thought that excluding forests from management and managing them solely for timber were the only two management alternatives possible. Only when the integrated management alternative was presented did people realize that there is a way to manage forests to provide both more biodiversity and more commodities (Oliver 1992, Boyce and McNab 1994, Oliver and Lippke 1995, Bare *et al.* 1997).

MAKING A DECISION (STEP 7)

Theoretically, decision making proceeds after the analysis of alternatives described above is completed. The policy-makers (managing the policy system) select one of the alternatives presented from the forest system to be compatible with the values provided by other forests and other sectors of society. They communicate the chosen alternative to the manager of each forest system awaiting the decision. Once given an alternative to implement, each forest manager chooses one of the alternatives for each subforest from among those presented. The choices are expected to allow the forest's objectives to be met. The chosen alternative for each subforest is communicated to that subforest. Each subforest manager chooses the alternative for each landscape that, when combined with other landscapes, meet the subforest's objectives. Each landscape manager chooses the stand alternatives that allow each landscape to develop according to its chosen alternative. Operations for each stand are chosen from the alternatives presented by the operations subsystem.

The result should be that all operations decided upon by those coordinating management are feasible, since they were among the alternatives proposed by those 'on-the-ground' and most able to determine what is feasible. The alternative actions decided upon for each subsystem best achieve the objectives of the next most diffuse subsystem and, eventually, national policy – since they were chosen by this more integrative (diffuse) subsystem.

In reality, the decision-making is reiterative, since the policy-makers identify the values to be managed for after the scoping process, and so limit the range of management alternatives. The reiterative nature of the process is important, since values change with understanding, time, technology, and paradigm shifts.

Decision-making can be impeded by conflicting laws and regulations or indecision at the various hierarchical levels. Conflicting laws can result from policy-makers demanding two or more outputs from a forest which are mutually exclusive. For example, one law may require forest management to provide the maximum amount of a closed species' habitat, while another law may mandate providing the maximum amount of an open species' habitat. Since no management alternative can maximize both of these, the decision-maker must decide which law to break.

Such confusion, or the confusion resulting from shifts in paradigms, may cause the decision to be delayed under the pretext of needing more analysis. It is important to realize that operations are performed in stands at discrete 'windows', described earlier. As a 'window' is passed, the stand's response to an operation changes. The consequences of a delayed decision will often be dramatically different from a timely one; and delay can have the effect of nullifying previous analysis.

Less research has been directed at the decision-making process than at analysis. As a general rule, most decisions in forestry do not have irreversible consequences if made at the appropriate level in the hierarchy. This occurs because forest management and policy are carried out by site-specific implementation of many discrete, small operations. Only a small percentage of a forest's stands receive operational treatments each year because the 'windows' for operations usually occur in each stand only every few years or decades. Each stand is a very small portion of the subforest or forest; therefore, each operation does not have a significant effect on broader goals. It is the aggregate effects of many individual operations over time and space which affect most forest management objectives. Consequently, the effects of management and policy on such values as timber quality or stand structures for habitat and aesthetics occur slowly.

A decision made during a window which maintains a range of future options can be adjusted by decisions made later to other stands or during later decision windows.

Other decisions, however, can rapidly reduce the ability of the forest to provide future values. A decision to change the structure of a stand that is the only remaining habitat for an endangered species can eliminate the species. Such decisions may occur by harvesting the last remaining complex structure needed by a species or by not maintaining the last remaining open structure (e.g., in the case of the butterfly species; Young 1992, Fry and Money 1994). Avoiding an operation that would control a large wildfire can eliminate the landscape habitat diversity, people's homes, and future timber availability for many decades. A decision to avoid all forest harvesting for only a few years may eliminate the infrastructure of skilled labor for logging and processing timber, and so eliminate the future options of thinning or harvesting the stands to provide many values.

IMPLEMENTATION (STEP 8)

Implementation is a process used to accomplish the decided-upon best management alternative. It does not have any of the deliberate questioning of alternatives of the analysis process or the value judgments of the decision process. For implementation to be effective, there need to be explicit directions for each subsystem of when and what is expected, with clear contingencies and measurable expectations and safeguards.

Various engineering tools have been developed to help implement decisions. These tools include goal, task, and budgeting procedures; implementation plans; tree diagrams; 'force field analyses'; 'implementation road maps'; time lines; 'Gantt charts'; critical path analyses; optimization analyses; action plans; contingency analyses; risk management plans; and others (Dieter 1991, CH2MHill 1994).

MONITORING AND FEEDBACK

The analysis and implementation, of course, will never be perfect for many reasons. The measured inputs and outputs among systems are approximations for several reasons:
- the systems approach combines important influences and ignores others which appear unimportant;
- the understanding of the relations of various components and processes is imperfect;

- society's values and the ability to implement various operations change with demographic changes and technology;
- an unforeseen event can alter conditions dramatically. For example, the catastrophic volcanic eruption of Mt St Helens in Washington State, USA, converted 35 000 hectares of forest to the open structure in less than fifteen minutes. Such an occurrence would alter most intended silvicultural operations and regimes, landscape plans, and subforest and forest decisions.

To ensure that the results of management are those intended, the outputs from a forest system need to be monitored. This monitoring involves measuring the inputs and outputs resulting from the management of each system, comparing them with the predicted inputs and outputs from the preceding analyses, determining the causes of important discrepancies, and correcting them (Fiegenbaum 1951 and 1983, Holling 1978, Deming 1982, Ishikawa 1982, Baskerville 1985, Walters 1986, Nemoto 1987, Juran and Gryna 1988). Specific methodologies have been developed to make this 'on-line' research very effective under the names of 'continuous quality improvement' or 'adaptive management' (Feigenbaum 1951 and 1983, Walters 1986). With improvements using monitoring and feedback, the analysis, decision, and implementation processes can continuously provide better alternatives, analyses, and results.

Managing public, private, and multiple forest ownerships

Unlike the theoretically rigid sequence of steps described above, in practice, the scoping, analysis, decision-making, and implementation occur concurrently and continuously at all hierarchical levels. Efficient, continuous analyses at all hierarchical levels – and communication with the decision-makers – allow small, frequent adjustments to management decisions. These adjustments are less disruptive and more efficient than are large infrequent changes in management direction.

Management is most effective if the inputs and outputs from a system or subsystem are developed through mutual agreement, such as a contractual situation, rather than through 'command-and-control' from the diffuse levels of the hierarchy. Such agreement is often gained by the more diffuse levels providing a mixture of incentives – information, markets, equipment, research, and other factors – and regulations (Lippke and Oliver 1993, Bourland and Stroup 1996, Kennedy *et al.* 1996, Lippke and Fretwell 1997). Incentives encourage managers to provide values that are not otherwise produced (externalities), and regulations discourage managers from making and implementing decisions that destroy values. With slight modifications, the same process can be used whether the forest is under public ownership, single or multiple private ownerships, or mixtures of public and private ownerships.

Under a single ownership, the management process may proceed smoothly through all hierarchical levels, since the policy-makers presumably have authority over all forests and therefore can control all subsystems. Large forest areas in many countries are owned by the government or a single private landowner (e.g., a corporation). If managed properly, such ownerships allow analysis and new decisions to be implemented rapidly, thus enabling the forest to respond rapidly to changing values. Such single ownerships can become inefficient if they lead to a top-down management approach, whether in public or private ownership.

The organization and management described above can also be accomplished under multiple owners – even where each stand is separately and autonomously owned. The planning process is similar to that described above, with each subsystem being managed by one or more free market entrepreneurs. Whereas the danger of a single ownership is that management will be concentrated in an inefficient, top-down approach, the danger of a free market system is that concerns that are important to society will be ignored if they are not well incorporated into the free market system. Such concerns include intergenerational equity and non-commodity values such as biodiversity, aesthetics, and existence (Ierland 1993, Castro 1994). Government and non-governmental organizations (NGOs) may be important in providing market values for these non-commodity values (externalities); for ensuring that market and management information is available; and for ensuring that monopolistic practices do not occur.

Applications to specific cases

Different aspects of the management system described above are being applied to many forests throughout the world. Nearly all forests are divided into a spatial hierarchy for inventory and implementing operations. In many cases, however, the analysis and decision-making are frequently concentrated away from site-specific hierarchical levels. Management for stand structures across the landscape is beginning to be done by several public and private agencies (e.g., Plum Creek Timber

Company, Washington state, USA; Boise Cascade Corporation, Washington and Idaho states, USA; Potlatch Corporation, Idaho state, USA; Oregon Department of Forestry, Oregon state, USA). The analysis process is used in preparing U.S. Forest Service plans (United States Federal Register 1992). Some countries are dividing their forests into those to be managed by different approaches – no commodity extraction; management only for commodities; and integrated management. Some private companies are beginning to find advantage in managing their forests through integrated management by treating their forests as management portfolios instead of 'warehouses' (Oliver 1994). Some incentives are being offered by various public and private organizations. To date, no public or private organization appears to have incorporated all of the aspects of management described in this chapter; however, many are rapidly making adjustments in this direction.

Summary

Proper management can ensure that forests provide the values people want by coordinating operations among forests – so that one forest does not provide too much of a value while another provides too little. Forests can be organized as a hierarchy of systems – ecosystems – from the individual operations level to the policy level. Systems management can then be utilized to make management efficient and flexible – for whatever mix of values society desires.

The ecosystem hierarchy is managed by coordinating the analysis, decision making, and implementing of management activities at the different spatial scales to obtain the desired values. Systematic and scientific approaches to the analyses, decisions, and implementations have been developed which make the processes efficient, avoid the inefficiencies common in central planning, and minimize the negative effects of ignoring such newly emerging values as biodiversity.

Further readings

More information about the various topics is listed below:
The ecology of animals and forests: Hunter (1990) and Oliver and Larson (1996).
Silvicultural operations and regimes: Daniel et al. (1979) and Smith et al. (1997).

Landscape management: Boyce (1995) and Oliver (1992).

Forest management: Buongiorno and Gilless (1987) and Davis and Johnson (1987).

Systems design and management: Krick (1962) and Dieter (1991).

Decision support: Oliver and Twery (in press).

Analytical methods: Iverson and Alston (1986); Weintraub and Bare (1996) and Keeney and Raiffa (1993). Adaptive management and continuous quality improvement: Deming (1982), Walters (1986), Feigenbaum (1951 and 1983), Holling (1978), Ishikawa (1982), Nemoto (1987), and Juran and Gryna (1988).

Literature cited

Bare, B. B. and G. A. Mendoza. 1988. Multiple objective forest land management planning: an illustration. *European Journal of Operational Research* **34**(1):44–55.

Bare, B. B., D. G. Briggs, J. P. Roise and G. F. Schreuder. 1984. A survey of systems analysis models in forestry and the forest products industries. *European Journal of Operational Research* **18**(1):1–18.

Bare, B. B. 1996. Hierarchical forest planning: some general observations. Pp. 164–5 in *Proceedings of a Workshop on Hierarchical Approaches to Forest Management in Public and Private Organizations*. (University of Toronto, May 25–29, 1992). Information Report PI-X-124, Petawawa National Forestry Institute, Canadian Forestry Service.

Bare, B. B., B. R. Lippke, W. Xu, C. D. Oliver, J. Moffett and T. R. Waggener. 1997. *Demonstration of Trust Impacts from Management Alternatives to Achieve Habitat Conservation Goals on Washington Department of Natural Resources Managed Lands*. College of Forest Resources, University of Washington, Seattle, Washington. 60 pp. plus Appendices.

Baskerville, G. 1985. Adaptive management: wood availability and habitat availability. *Forestry Chronicle* **61**(2):171–5.

Birchfield, R. J., and I. F. Grant. 1993. *Out of the Woods: the Restructuring and Sale of New Zealand's State Forests*. GP Publications, Wellington, New Zealand. 250 pp.

Botkin, D. B., and M. T. Sobel. 1975. Stability in time-varying ecosystems. *American Naturalist* **109**(970):625–46.

Bourland, T. R., and R. L. Stroup. 1996. Rent payments as incentives: making endangered species welcome on private lands. *Journal of Forestry* **94**(4):18–21.

Boyce, S. G. 1985. *Forestry decisions*. USDA Forest Service General Technical Report SE-35.

1995. *Landscape Forestry*. John Wiley and Sons, New York. 239 pp.

Boyce, S. G., and W. S.McNab. 1994. Management of forested landscapes. *Journal of Forestry* **92**(1):27–32.

Boydak, M. 1996a. *Ecology and Silviculture of Cedar of Lebanon* (Cedrus libani A. Rich.) *and Conservation of its Natural Forests*. Ministry of Forestry Publication Department, Ankara, Turkey. 68 pp.

1996b. *Effects of Prescribed Fire and Some Other Factors on the Regeneration Success of Lebanon Cedar* (Cedrus libani A. Rich.) *at Elmali-Antalya Region*. Turkish Ministry of Forestry, South-West Anatolia Forest Research Institute, Antalya, Turkey. 42 pp. (In Turkish with English summary)

Buongiorno, J., and J. K.Gilless. 1987. *Forest Management and Economics*. Macmillan, New York. 285 pp.

CH2MHill. 1994. Decision and implementation: quality in environmental management. Workshop Notebook for CH2MHill Engineering Consultants, Portland, Oregon.

Camp, A., C. Oliver, P. Hessburg, and R. Everett. 1997. Predicting late-successional fire refugia pre-dating European settlement in the Wenatchee Mountains. *Forest Ecology and Management* **95**:63–77.

Campbell, F. T. and S. E. Schlarbaum. 1994. *Fading forests. North American trees and exotic pests*. Natural Resources Defense Council Report. 47 pp.

Castro, J. I. 1994. *The internationalization of external environmental casts and sustainable development*. UNCTAD/OSG/DP/81. 5 pp.

Christensen, N. L., J. K. Agee, P. F. Brussard, J. Hughes, D. H. Knight, G. W. Minshall, J. M. Peek, S. J. Pyne, F. J. Swanson, J. W. Thomas, S. Wells, S. E. Williams, and H. A. Wright. 1989. Interpreting the Yellowstone fires of 1988. *Bioscience* **39**:678–85.

Clegg, S. R., C. Hardy, and W. R. Nord (eds). 1996. *Handbook of Organization Studies*. Sage Publications, London. 730 pp.

Daniel, T. W., J. A.Helms, and F. S.Baker. 1979. *Principles of Silviculture*. Second edition. McGraw-Hill, New York. 500 pp.

Davis, L. S., and K. N. Johnson. 1987. *Forest Management*. McGraw-Hill, New York.

Deming, W. E. 1982. *Out of the Crisis*. Massachusetts Institute of Technology, Center for Advanced Engineering Study, Cambridge, Massachusetts. 507 pp.

Dieter, G. E. 1991. *Engineering Design*. Second Edition. McGraw-Hill, New York. 721 pp.

Dykstra, D. P. 1984. *Mathematical Programming for Natural Resource Management*. McGraw-Hill, New York.

Eleventh World Forestry Congress. 1997. *Antalya Declaration of the XI World Forestry Congress: Forestry for Sustainable Development: Towards the XXI Century*. Antalya, Turkey. 13 October, 1997. 3 pp.

Feigenbaum, A. V. 1951 and 1983. *Total Quality Control*. McGraw-Hill, New York. 851 pp.

Fry, M .E., and N. R.Money. 1994. Biodiversity conservation in the management of utility rights-of-way. Pp. 94–103 in *Proceedings of the 15th Annual Forest*

Vegetation Management Conference, January 25–27, 1994, Redding, California, USA.

Hann, D. W. and B. B. Bare. 1979. *Uneven-aged forest management: state of the art (or science?)*. USDA Forest Service, General Technical Report INT-50, Intermountain Forest and Range Experiment Station, Ogden, Utah. 18 pp.

Holling, C. S. (ed.). 1978. *Adaptive Environmental Assessment and Management*. John Wiley and Sons, New York.

Hunter, M. L., Jr. 1990. *Wildlife, Forests, and Forestry*. Regents/Prentice Hall, Englewood Cliffs, New Jersey. 370 pp.

Ierland, E. 1993. *Macroeconomic Analysis of Environmental Policy*. Elsevier, Amsterdam.

Ishikawa, K. 1982. *Guide to Quality Control*. Asian Productivity Organization. Quality Resources. White Plains, New York. 225 pp.

Iverson, D. C., and R. M.Alston. 1986. *The genesis of FORPLAN: a historical and analytical review of Forest Service planning models*. USDA Forest Service General Technical Report INT-214. 33 pp.

Janis, I. L. 1967. *Victims of Groupthink*. Houghton-Mifflin, Boston, Massachusetts. 276 pp.

Johnson, K. N. 1992. Consideration of watersheds in long-term planning models: the case for FORPLAN and its use on the national forests. Pp. 347–60 in R. J. Naiman (ed.). *Watershed management: balancing sustainability and environmental change*. Springer-Verlag, New York.

Juran, J. M., and F. M. Gryna (eds). 1988. *Juran's Quality Control Handbook*. Fourth Edition. McGraw-Hill, New York. 180 pp.

Keeney, R. L., and H. Raiffa. 1993. *Decisions with Multiple Objectives*. Cambridge University Press, Cambridge. 569 pp.

Kennedy, E. T., R.Costa, and W. M. Smathers, Jr. 1996. Economic incentives: new directions for red-cockaded woodpecker habitat conservation. *Journal of Forestry* 94(4):22–6.

Kershaw, J. A., Jr., C. D. Oliver, and T. M. Hinckley. 1993. Effect of harvest of old growth Douglas-fir stands and subsequent management on carbon dioxide levels in the atmosphere. *Journal of Sustainable Forestry* 1:61–77.

Kimmins, J. P. 1987. *Forest Ecology*. Macmillan, New York. 531 pp.

Koch, P. 1991. *Wood vs. non-wood materials in U.S. residential construction: some energy-related international implications*. CINTRAFOR Working Paper 36, Center for International Trade of Forest Products, College of Forest Resources, University of Washington, Seattle. 38 pp.

Krick, E. V. 1962. *Methods Engineering: Design and Measurement of Work Methods*. John Wiley and Sons, New York.: 530 pp.

Kuhn, T. S. 1970. *The Structure of Scientific Revolutions*. University of Chicago Press, Chicago. 210 pp.

Litterer, J. A. 1965. *The Analysis of Organizations*. John Wiley and Sons, New York. 471 pp.

Lippke, B., and Fretwell, H. L. 1997. The market incentive for biodiversity. *Journal of Forestry* 95, January: 4–7.

Lippke, B., and C. D. Oliver. 1993. Managing for multiple values: a proposal for the Pacific Northwest. *Journal of Forestry* **91**:14–18.

Liu, G. and L. S. Davis. 1995. Interactive resolution of multiobjective forest planning problems with shadow price and parametric analysis. *Forest Science* **21**(1):109–22.

McCarter, J. B., J. S. Wilson, P. J. Baker, J. L. Moffett, and C. D. Oliver. 1998. Landscape management through integration of existing tools and emerging technologies. *Journal of Forestry* **96**(6):17–23.

Meadows, D. H. 1972. *The Limits to Growth: a Report for the Club of Rome's Project on the Predicament of Mankind.* Universe Books, New York.

Mendoza, G. A., B. B. Bare and G. E. Campbell. 1987. Multiobjective Programming for Generating Alternatives: A Multiple-use Planning Example. *Forest Science* **33**(2):458–68.

Morgan, M. G., and M. Henrion. 1990. *Uncertainty: A Guide to Dealing with Uncertainty in Quantitative Risk and Policy Analysis.* Cambridge University Press, Cambridge 332 pp.

Morgan, P., G. H.Aplet, J. B.Haufler, H. C.Humphries, M. M.Moore, and W. D. Wilson. 1994. Historical range of variability: a useful tool for evaluating ecosystem change. *Journal of Sustainable Forestry* **2**(1/2):87–111.

Muthoo, M. K. 1997. *Forests and Forestry in Turkey.* The Government of Turkey, Ankara, Turkey. ISBN 975–6964–01–4. 81 pp.

Nemoto, M. 1987. *Total Quality Control for Management.* Prentice Hall, Englewood Cliffs, New Jersey. 238 pp.

Oliver, C. D. 1992. A landscape approach: achieving and maintaining biodiversity and economic productivity. *Journal of Forestry* **90**: 20–5.

　1994. A portfolio approach to landscape management: an economically, ecologically, and socially sustainable approach to forestry. Pp. 66–76 in *Proceedings: Innovative Silvicultural Systems in Boreal Forests.* A symposium held October 4–8, 1994. Mayfield, Inn, Edmonton, Alberta, Canada. Canadian Forest Service, International Union of Forest Research Organizations. Clear Lake Limited, Edmonton, Alberta.

　1998. Passive vs pro-active forest management approaches to achieve goals. In J. Calhoun (ed.) *Forest Policy: Ready for Renaissance?* Symposium sponsored by the Olympic Natural Resources Center, College of Forest Resources, University of Washington, Seattle.

Oliver, C. D., and B. R. Lippke. 1995. Wood supply and other values and ecosystem management in western Interior Forests. In *Ecosystem Management in Western Interior Forests. A Symposium held May 3–5, 1994, Spokane, Washington.* Washington State University, Pullman, Washington.

Oliver, C. D., and B. C. Larson. 1996. *Forest Stand Dynamics.* Update edition. John Wiley and Sons, New York. 521 pp.

Oliver, C. D., and M. Twery. In press. Decision support systems: models and analyses. In *Proceedings of the Ecological Stewardship Workshop, Tucson, Arizona, December 1995.* USDA Forest Service.

Oliver, C., D. Adams, T. Bonnicksen, J. Bowyer, F. Cubbage, N. Sampson, S.

Schlarbaum, R. Whaley, H. Wiant, and J. Sebelius. 1997. Report on Forest Health of the United States by the Forest Health Science Panel. A panel chartered by Charles Taylor, Member, United States Congress, 11th District, North Carolina. Summary: 72 pp. Main document: 334 pp. (Submitted April 7, 1997). (Available through internet through U.S. House of Representatives Resources Committee at: 'http://www.house.gov/resources/105cong/fullcomm/ apr09.97/taylor.rpt/taylor.htm') Also available as reprint through University of Washington College of Forest Resources CINTRAFOR RE43 (main document) and RE43A (summary).

Oliver, C. D., A. Camp, and A. Osawa. 1998. Forest dynamics and resulting animal and plant population changes at the stand and landscape levels. *Journal of Sustainable Forestry* 6(3/4):281–312.

Olson, S. H. 1971. *The Depletion Myth: a History of Railroad Use of Timber*. Harvard University Press, Cambridge, Massachusetts.

Patten, B. C. (ed.). 1971. *Systems Analysis and Simulation in Ecology*. Academic Press, New York.

Perez-Garcia, J. P. 1993. *Global forestry impacts of reducing softwood supplies from North America*. CINTRAFOR Working Paper 43, Center for International Trade of Forest Products, College of Forest Resources, University of Washington, Seattle. 35 pp.

Perlin, 1989. *A Forest Journey: the Role of Wood in the Development of Civilization*. Harvard University Press, Cambridge, Massachusetts. 445 pp.

Reich, R. B. 1983. *The Next American Frontier*. Penguin Books, New York. 324 pp.

Roberts, J. C. 1979. Principles of land use planning. Pp. 47–63 in *Planning the Uses and Management of Land*. American Society of Agronomy, Madison, Wisconsin.

Romme, W. H., and D. H. Knight. 1981. Fire frequency and subalpine forest succession along a topographic gradient in Wyoming. *Ecology* 62:319–26.

Rowen, H. S. 1976. Policy analysis as heuristic aid: the design of means, ends, and institutions. Pp. 217–31 in L. H. Tribe, C. S. Schelling, and J. Voss (eds). *When Values Conflict: Essays on Environmental Analysis, Discourse, and Decision*. Ballinger, Cambridge, Massachusetts. (Original not seen; cited from Morgan and Henrion 1990.)

Rustagi, K. P. and B. B. Bare. 1987. Resolving multiple goal conflicts with interactive goal programming. *Canadian Journal of Forest Research* 17:1401–7.

Schuster, E. G.; L. A. Leefers, and J. E. Thompson. 1993. *A guide to computer-based analytical tools for implementing national forest plans*. USDA Forest Service, General Technical Report INT-296, Ogden, Utah. 269 pp.

Sedjo, R. In press. Forests: supply and demand. In *Proceedings of the Annual Meeting of the United States Society of American Foresters, Washington, D.C.*

Segura, G., and L. Snook. 1992. Stand dynamics and regeneration patterns of a pinyon pine forest in east central Mexico. *Forest Ecology and Management* 47:175–94.

Senge, P. M. 1990. *The Fifth Discipline: the Art and Practice of The Learning Organization.* Currency Doubleday, New York. 423 pp.

Shugart, H. H., and R. V. O'Neill (eds). 1979. *Systems Ecology.* Dowden, Hutchinson & Ross, Stroudsburg, Pa.

Simon, J. L. 1996. *The Ultimate Resource 2.* Princeton University Press, Princeton, New Jersey. 734 pp.

Smith, D. M., B. C. Larson, M. J. Kelty, and P. M. S. Ashton. 1997. *The Practice of Silviculture: Applied Forest Ecology.* Ninth Edition. John Wiley & Sons, New York. 537 pp.

Tansley, A. G. 1935. The use and abuse of vegetational concepts and terms. *Ecology* **16**:284–307.

Taylor, F. W. 1911. *The Principles of Scientific Management.* Harper and Brothers, New York.

Tuchman, 1984. *The March of Folly: from Troy to Vietnam.* Alfred A. Knopf, New York. 448 pp.

United States Federal Register. 1992. *Forest Service: National Environmental Policy Act: Revised Policy and Procedures.* Volume 57, No. 182. Friday, September 18, 1992: 43180–213.

Walters, C. 1986. *Adaptive Management of Renewable Resources.* Macmillan, New York. 374 pp.

Weigand, J. F., R. W. Haynes, and J. L. Mikowski (compilers). 1994. *High Quality Forestry Workshop: the Idea of Long Rotations.* College of Forest Resources, University of Washington CINTRAFOR SP15:43–61.

Weintraub, A., and B. B. Bare. 1996. New issues in forest land management from an operations research perspective. *Interfaces* **26**(5):9–25.

Young, M. R. 1992. Conserving insect communities in mixed woodlands. Pp. 277–96 in M. G. R. Cannell, D. C. Malcolm, and P. A. Robertson (eds). *The Ecology of Mixed-species Stands of Trees.* Blackwell Scientific, Oxford.

18   The economic perspective

BRUCE R. LIPPKE AND JOSHUA T. BISHOP

Biological diversity provides important benefits – in some sense it is the basis of all economic value – yet the conservation of biodiversity also involves significant costs. Economics offers insight into the tradeoffs and complementarities involved, between the benefits of biodiversity conservation and the many other goods and services that people desire. Economics can also help us find ways to reduce the costs and maximize the benefits of biodiversity conservation by making use of market incentives that influence how people use natural resources.

The production and consumption of goods and services generally has a negative impact on the environment, either through depletion of natural resources or pollution. Markets often fail to account for the environmental costs of production and consumption, due to the fact that many resources and environmental inputs are provided free of charge by nature. However, both governments and business have made great strides in recent years in the difficult task of measuring and reducing the environmental impact of economic activity. Some of the most innovative policies and programs take advantage of market forces to minimize the costs of environmental protection.

Efforts to sustain or restore biodiversity should be assessed in terms of their social, economic and environmental impacts. Programs and policies intended to regenerate, conserve or manage biodiversity have costs, large or small. Some actions will affect the prices of other goods and services, or result in unintended market shifts that lead to loss of livelihoods or environmental damage to other regions or resources. Tradeoffs arise where values conflict. The difficulty is not that some people care only about the environment while others care only about jobs or profit, but that all of us want stable employment and a comfortable standard of living, as well as a clean and healthy environment.

Ensuring desirable environmental outcomes while avoiding unintended impacts requires that close attention be paid to the economic linkages between markets, resources and geographic regions. Equally, we should respect and wherever possible exploit the powerful creative forces of the market, so that it conserves important values such as biodiversity while also continuing to provide useful goods and services.

This chapter will review some basic concepts in economics, including how markets allocate scarce resources and why they often fail to protect or produce 'non-market' amenities such as biodiversity and other landscape values. The challenges of measuring and comparing such non-market values will be contrasted with more familiar indicators of economic value. Alternative strategies to maintain biodiversity are described and compared in terms of their respective costs. The distributional aspects of conservation policy are also discussed, showing how different groups are affected and how 'win/win' policies can be found even when there are conflicting goals. Examples of strategies for selected regions are provided, in order to anchor the discussion in the real world. The chapter concludes with a summary of policy options for making markets account for the benefits of biodiversity conservation in forested landscapes.

Economics and the environment

HOW MARKETS ALLOCATE SCARCE RESOURCES

Economics describes how inputs (labor, capital, natural resources) are used to produce outputs for consumption (goods and services), as well as the way that inputs are obtained and outputs are distributed. In principle, a competitive market economy will accurately assess the costs and adjust the prices of goods and services in such a way that, in the aggregate, consumers pay the lowest possible cost to satisfy their desires. In this way, the market system successfully produces wood, paper, and other agricultural commodities desired by consumers. (A brief introduction to the theory of market supply and demand is provided in Box 18.1.)

Many basic inputs to industrial or agricultural production are obtained from nature and, following consumption, the residues of most outputs are returned to it. For example, air, soil, and water contribute to the growth of trees which are harvested and processed into lumber and other products, which are in turn used to produce buildings, packaging, paper and other goods. The resulting products may be cherished for years or used only briefly and recycled, but all are eventually discarded to decompose,

BOX 18.1 **Market demand and supply**

Demand/consumption
All resources, whether natural or produced by humans, are limited in their availability to some degree. We express the demand for consumption of a traded resource (or product) as a relationship between price and quantity, which generally reflects a diminishing propensity to consume as market price increases. This reflects the fact that most consumers have a limited budget with which to purchase many different goods and services. The relationship between price and quantity may be expressed mathematically or depicted graphically as a demand curve (see Figure 18.1). The same basic relationship can be used to represent the demand of a single individual for a single good, or of an entire region for a basket of goods like wood and paper products.

Supply/production
The existence of demand creates the opportunity for producers to deliver goods and services to consumers. Producers' willingness to deliver products can equally be represented as a relationship between market price and quantity, or a supply curve. Typically, the cost of supplying additional units of a good will rise as the necessary inputs (resources) become more difficult to obtain. Higher prices are thus required to motivate increased supply.

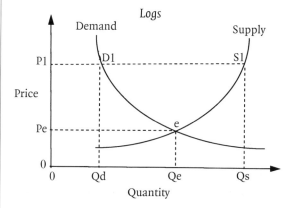

Fig. 18.1. Demand and supply for a marketed product (e.g., logs).
Demand: As price rises from Pe to P1, the quantity demanded declines from Qe to Qd.
Supply: As price rises from Pe to P1, production increases from Qe to Qs.
Equilibrium: At price Pe and quantity Qe there is no excess or shortage as production exactly equals consumption. On the other hand, at P1 the quantity supplied, Qs, exceeds the quantity demanded, Qd. Such a glut would not normally last, however, as producers would tend to cut their prices in order to reduce unsold inventory. Conversely, shortages would lead consumers to compete among each other by offering to pay higher prices in order to secure supplies. Thus over the long term, market price and quantity will tend to stabilize at Pe and Qe.

BOX 18.1 (cont.)

Market equilibrium
The intersection of supply and demand pinpoints a potential equilibrium, where consumers' willingness to pay (marginal benefit) is equal to suppliers' willingness to deliver (marginal cost). So long as the costs of all inputs are included in the supply curve and all benefits are included in the demand curve, the market equilibrium will result in the maximum net benefit to producers and consumers alike and the market price of the good will accurately reflect its value (Henderson and Quandt 1958). This is the concept of efficient market allocation.

While most markets are adequately described by this construct, prices are rarely in perfect equilibrium. Delays in the flow of information and investment, combined with the lumpiness of supply response as large factories open or close, may result in brief periods of over- or under-production and thus volatile prices. The failure of markets to reflect environmental costs and benefits is a more fundamental problem, resulting in market prices which do not reflect true value, and the possibility of over- or under-production and inefficient allocation of resources (see Box 18.2).

returning their constituent elements to the environment. In addition to inputs to production, natural resources also provide benefits that consumers enjoy directly (e.g., clean air and water, hunting, hiking, and other forest activities).

The fact that producers can use and consumers enjoy the benefits provided by the natural environment proves that they have value. However, many if not most of these environmental benefits do not belong to anyone, are not actively or directly traded in markets, and have no observable price. Indeed, many environmental goods and services cannot be produced profitably by private firms, while 'bads' (dis-benefits) such as pollution and waste can be released into the environment at little or no financial cost to the polluter.

Economists have identified several reasons why the market often fails to account fully for environmental costs and benefits, and hence why market prices may not fully reflect the value of protecting the environment or the true cost of using natural resources (Box 18.2 provides a description of non-market values and market failure). To the extent that environmental 'market failure' results in the inefficient allocation of resources, it is no different from other problems which commonly afflict markets and reduce social welfare, such as anti-competitive behavior, barriers to trade,

BOX 18.2 **Total economic value and market failure**
Markets will allocate resources efficiently only if prices reflect both the full
costs of production and the full benefits of consumption. Economists use
the term 'total economic value' to refer to the various benefits which may be
obtained from a natural resource. These include the *direct use value* of a
resource as it becomes an input to production or as a consumption good, its
indirect use value through protecting or sustaining economic activity, and its
non-use value to people who derive satisfaction from the mere existence of a
resource, even though they may never see it or consume any product
obtained from it (Pearce, *et al.* 1989; Munasinghe and Lutz 1993). The total
economic value of any given land use is simply the sum of the underlying
component values (provided these are separate and mutually compatible).

Examples of direct use values in forestry include timber and most non-
timber products, but also such intangible benefits as forest recreation.
Indirect use values include, for example, the role of forests in protecting
watersheds and fisheries. Non-use values in forestry include such intangible benefits as the continued existence of certain species of wildlife,
which the general public wishes to protect for posterity. In some cases
different values may conflict, e.g., forest recreation and timber production.

In general, direct use values are most likely to be reflected in market
prices. Indirect use values may be reflected in the prices of certain goods
and services which depend heavily on the underlying environmental
benefit, while non-use values are rarely reflected in market prices or decision-making. The main reason why market prices fail to reflect environmental costs and benefits fully (or at all, in some cases) is that no one 'owns'
the resources in question or, even if they do, they cannot make other people
pay for using them. For example, no one traveling on a public thoroughfare
can be charged for enjoying a pretty view, even if the land in question is privately owned. By the same token, however, if the land owner removes vegetation or puts up an ugly building, no charge is incurred for destroying the
view.

Societies have developed various ways to ensure that producers and consumers 'internalize' such environmental costs and benefits in their behavior. Direct regulation is the most well-known approach, e.g., restrictions on
land use in certain areas or at certain times, required production processes
or treatments of waste, etc. Another approach uses market incentives to
modify behavior, e.g., hunting license fees to regulate demand for particular species, pollution taxes to encourage firms to reduce emissions, etc.
Some of the most ambitious schemes involve the creation of property rights
and markets to improve efficiency, for instance the allocation of a fixed
quota of tradable rights to pollute among firms in a given area.

excessive regulation or other inappropriate economic policies. Unlike bad policy, however, the solution to environmental market failure often requires more government intervention, rather than less. Nevertheless, there is a big difference between good and bad environmental policy, with some types of regulation costing far more than others, for the same environmental benefit.

FORESTRY AND THE ENVIRONMENT

Industrial forestry takes many forms, ranging from opportunistic extraction of commercially valuable timber, to intensive cultivation of plantation trees for sustained yield production, and various intermediate management regimes. Whatever form it takes, industrial forestry typically involves significant disturbance of natural ecosystems. Rarely does it reproduce the disturbance regime and evolution of natural forests.

For example, in most parts of the world, industrial forest management involves rotations measured in decades, compared with natural disturbance cycles which may last centuries (Chapter 4). Harvesting timber on such relatively short rotations alters the character of forest stands, reducing the availability of certain structures associated with older forests, such as ancient trees, rotting logs and stumps, etc. This can lead in turn to a decline in populations of forest dwelling species dependent upon those structures, and/or an increase in populations of species which are better adapted to disturbed forests. To the extent that pristine (undisturbed) ecosystems are generally preferred for conservation purposes, disturbances serving commercial purposes may be considered unambiguously bad from a purely environmental perspective.

From an economic perspective, however, the case is not so clear. Some non-market values may increase as a result of timber extraction and/or a shift to more intensive management, while others will decline. The construction of logging roads, for example, can open up areas for hunting, fishing, and hiking, or extraction of other non-timber forest products by local populations. Disturbed or secondary forests are often preferred habitat for certain high-value 'charismatic' species such as deer, or elephants in the tropics. And of course the value of timber itself must be included in the equation. The net impact of forest disturbances on consumer welfare will thus depend on the relative importance of timber and non-timber values, and the magnitude of change in these values. As all of these values are changing over time, finding the right balance in land use policy and practice is a major challenge!

In some cases, of course, the question is moot. Many forest stands are simply not economic to manage intensively, while others are too remote or poorly stocked even to cover the cost of removing mature timber. Although growing demands for food and fiber or declining costs may eventually bring some of this land into production, many forested areas will be left undisturbed and continue to contribute to biodiversity values. However, forests that are not worth managing for timber may be atypical in other ways, including low levels of biodiversity and other non-market values.

Resource scarcity, supply response and market failure

Normally, when a valuable natural resource becomes scarce, its market price rises. Producers respond by finding ways to use less of the resource, while others may try to obtain more supplies or develop substitutes. Thus while global consumption of marketed goods has increased about 400% over the past 50 years, in real (inflation-adjusted) terms, we see relatively little increase in the prices of raw materials or resource-dependent products (CEA 1997, Moore 1995). Rising consumer demand, due to the increased productivity of labor and capital, has been matched by investments to increase the supply of goods and services. Shortages of raw materials have been avoided through continuous improvements in technical efficiency and substitution by other products and processes (such as steel and concrete for wood).

Because biodiversity and other non-market amenities are not traded, however, the market generally fails to respond to their declining availability. Thus although the implicit non-market price of biodiversity is clearly rising (as seen by mounting public concern and political activity to protect it), there is at present no way for biodiversity – as an object of consumer demand – to compete in markets for the resources (inputs) that it needs. At the same time, because the costs of biodiversity loss are not charged to the producers and consumers of forest products, prices of these products will tend to be lower and consumers will purchase more of them than if environmental costs were taken into account. Box 18.3 describes these linkages graphically, showing how growth in demand for timber and other commodities leads to tighter supply and an increase in the implicit 'price' of biodiversity.

Markets for amenity values

In a few cases, the demand for non-market amenities has been sufficient to stimulate market solutions with little or no government intervention. For example, hunting and fishing rights in some regions are bought and sold, spurring property owners to undertake management to

BOX 18.3 **Increased demand for timber and reduced supply of non-market amenities**

Changes in the supply and demand for a single product can have significant impacts on the availability and price of other goods and services which rely on the same natural resource inputs. Thus increased demand for industrial forest products results in greater use of inputs, including big trees that are important to biodiversity. In Figure 18.2, this is shown as a shift in the supply curve for other uses dependent upon the same resource.

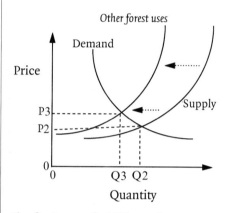

Fig. 18.2. Impact of a shift in supply.
Supply: As timber is harvested for the market, the supply of inputs to other uses such as biodiversity is reduced (leftward shift of supply curve); price rises from P2 to P3 as quantity falls from Q2 to Q3.
If consumer demand for biodiversity shares the same features as demand for market products (i.e., downward sloping from left to right), we would expect a leftward shift in the supply curve for biodiversity to result in a rising unit value (implicit price) for biodiversity. In reality, of course, there is no market for biodiversity and thus we cannot easily measure the reduction in quantity or the higher price that consumers should be willing to pay. Various methods of estimating non-market values in monetary terms have been developed in recent years, however, and these may be used to assess changes in consumer demand for biodiversity.

increase prey habitat, such as in grouse and deer stalking estates in Europe and salmon rivers in the United Kingdom (Willis and Garrod 1992).

While the goal of biodiversity conservation is presumably assisted by such initiatives, they are not likely to provide sufficient biodiversity to meet consumer demand. Market prices of traded environmental amenities such as hunting, fishing and camping rights will tend to understate the total economic value of wildlife habitat, as they reflect only direct use values but not the full non-use value of biodiversity conservation. (Note also that the management of natural areas for recreational purposes may be inconsistent with conservation objectives, to the extent that natural landscapes are modified to favor certain species over others.)

The reason is that many values associated with natural ecosystems cannot easily be captured by private land owners, and thus will not be reflected in the market price of such land. For example, some people derive pleasure (utility in economic terms) simply by virtue of living near an area known to harbor wildlife. Others may obtain satisfaction just from knowing that such areas exist, even if they are very remote. Such sentiments form the basis of fund-raising campaigns by many environmental organizations. Some, such as the Nature Conservancy in the United States, devote funds to the purchase of environmentally sensitive lands, although most prefer to seek environmental constraints on property owned by others through legal and political pressure.

One of the obstacles is the 'public good' nature of many environmental amenities. This refers to the fact that no one can be effectively excluded from enjoying certain environmental values (such as the existence of elephants) and that one person's enjoyment of such values does not generally diminish that of anyone else. Economic theory states that the market will systematically under-provide such public goods, and that collective action (e.g., by government) is required to ensure adequate provision.

This theoretical argument is consistent with the more general sentiment that biodiversity should not be bought and sold like other goods and services. The tradition of free access to natural resources is as old as human history and, when challenged, is readily defended by the public. Nevertheless, with growing populations and increased mobility it has become a luxury in many areas. Thus in some developed regions today consumers have become accustomed to paying for access to beaches, parks and forests which, in other regions, would be open to all free of charge (and probably unmanaged). This brings us to the key role of property rights in natural resource management.

The role of property rights

Property rights are central to market economies, influencing what and how much is produced, as well as where and how it is produced. Property rights also play an important role in environmental protection. For example, market economies are supported by legal systems that allow property owners to profit from the use of their assets and, to some extent, hold them liable for actions that impose losses on others. Thus if the production of a commodity such as timber injures others, damages may be assessed in a court of law. The resulting assessment or the cost to avoid injury to others may be considered part of the cost of production.

An interesting extension of the principle of environmental damages, with potentially wide-ranging implications, arose in the case of the *Exxon Valdez* oil spill. In this case, innovative economic methods were used to evaluate the loss of consumer welfare associated with damages to wildlife and natural habitat (Arrow *et al.* 1993, Loomis 1996). These estimates formed the basis of a damage assessment against Exxon which, while hotly contested, set an important precedent for compensation based on the loss of non-market values.

In practice, the standard of harm in damage cases is not always clear (see Ward and Duffield 1992 for a discussion of natural resource damages with many examples). Moreover, legal remedies are not always practical even when there is a clear public cost. When environmental damage results from the combined effects of many operations over time or multiple owners, for example, it may prove difficult to assess costs fairly. Similarly, when the harm involves the loss of benefits for which no individual was paying, it may be difficult to show the magnitude of loss incurred.

Another important feature of property rights is the protection of investors' claim on the proceeds of their investments. In the absence of such protection, investors will tend to seek other opportunities. Accordingly, where legal remedies or property rights are not strong, investment is often difficult to stimulate. In many developing countries, for example, forest resources are considered public property and local populations enjoy virtually free access to woodland areas for the extraction of fuel and other uses. Consequently, little wood remains in the vicinity of population centers, biodiversity is diminished and little private investment in forestry occurs.

Hyde *et al.*, (1996) point out that defending private (or indeed public) property is not without costs, e.g., the costs of the legal system and protection activity such as fencing and guards. These costs must be compared with the potential benefits that can be derived from different uses of the land before any firm conclusions can be drawn about whether the absence of property rights will result in inefficient use of resources. Property rights tend to be secure and acknowledged for relatively high-value land uses, e.g., modern agriculture, timber plantations and sedentary ranching, but not for low-value uses such as shifting cultivation, itinerant livestock production, or extensive timber management. Even where private rights to timber are secure, such as in concessions on public land, they may not be worth defending after the first cut, due to the long rotation and relatively low density of commercial species. The key factor here is the relatively low productivity of land uses, especially in many developing countries.

Regulatory approaches

Where property rights over natural resources cannot be defined or defended profitably, or when the public nature of an environmental amenity means that the market will under-provide it, then direct government intervention is usually called for. The usual approach involves direct intervention in the production process, by imposing constraints on the use of resource inputs or emission of pollutants. Examples in forestry include harvest area limits, minimum tree diameter restrictions, riparian buffer strips, land set-asides, and other measures.

One effect of conventional forest regulations is to increase the cost of supplying timber. Unfortunately, most regulations are simply punitive and do little or nothing to encourage positive changes in management practices to conserve biodiversity and other non-timber amenities. Moreover, because regulations often impose a uniform standard with no allowance for differences between sites, the costs and benefits of compliance can vary widely. While uniform standards have the advantage of administrative simplicity, they often lead to inefficiencies in how environmental objectives are achieved, with some producers incurring high costs for relatively little environmental benefit, and vice versa.

Alternatives to direct regulation and uniform standards do exist, including policies which motivate forest landowners and managers to 'produce' diversity, and which therefore achieve conservation objectives more efficiently. Various policy options to internalize non-market forest values in landowner or producer behavior are discussed later in this chapter. Before tackling this issue of incentives, however, we must first address a more fundamental problem in conservation policy, namely how to compare the costs and benefits of market forest goods and services with non-market amenities such as biodiversity. In short, on what basis can policy-makers set priorities for forest land management.

Moving biodiversity values into the market

THE MEASUREMENT PROBLEM

Forest management systems can be described in many different ways, in terms of their social, economic and physical attributes (e.g., species mix, timber volume and rotation period, wildlife habitat quality, water production, rural employment and labor productivity, tax receipts, etc.). Different approaches to maintaining or restoring biodiversity can likewise be characterized in terms of various biological and socioeconomic indicators. Conflicts and tradeoffs across different indicators will inevitably arise when comparing alternative approaches and management systems. This raises the difficult problem of how to weigh one set of indicators against another and, in particular, how to compare economic with physical indicators. The task is even harder when market and non-market values are perceived or incurred differently by different groups in society.

In principle, if environmental values can be expressed in monetary terms, then choosing the optimal land use or the preferred approach to conservation is a relatively straightforward application of Cost Benefit Analysis (CBA). The preferred land management regime is simply the one offering the highest total economic value, provided that benefits exceed costs, and with appropriate adjustments for risk and timing (see Tietenberg 1996 for a detailed treatment; CBA may not be so simple when costs and benefits are thought to be distributed inequitably). Monetary estimates of non-market values can also be used to design appropriate tax and subsidy instruments, so that producers and consumers internalize environmental costs and benefits in their behavior. In practice, the answer to how much non-market benefits are worth will vary with place and time, depending on local culture, the stage of economic development, the distribution of incomes, and differences in values held by rural and urban populations.

While economists have recently made progress in estimating non-market values in monetary terms, the methods are still evolving and valuation results are not yet widely accepted or adopted. Techniques such as contingent valuation (CV), dose-response, hedonic pricing, the travel cost method and others are all designed to estimate consumer willingness-to-pay for non-market benefits, or willingness-to-accept compensation for environmental damages (Kahn 1995, Jakobsson and Dragun 1996).

One of the most widely used techniques for estimating non-market benefits is contingent valuation (CV) surveys of public responses. Arrow *et al.* (1993) argue that CV methods can yield reliable estimates of non-market value, directly comparable with market prices, but they also propose such demanding criteria that most studies to date would probably be found deficient. Hanley and Milne (1996) highlight the frequency of protest bids in CV surveys, i.e., refusal to respond on the basis that certain environmental benefits are 'priceless'. Such responses are not normally included in the final estimated value which, of course, tends to bias the result. Others are more disparaging, such as Diamond and Hausmann

(1994), who argue that contingent valuation surveys do not measure preferences accurately and fail to provide useful information for policy.

In a recent survey of research on non-wood benefit estimation in forestry, mainly covering Europe and North America, Wibe (1995) found consistency in the level of estimates, although whether this reflects stability in the underlying value or simply consistency in the methods used is not clear. Pearce (1996) summarized global valuation studies, noting their crude procedures but also that the estimates obtained are not wildly divergent. Loomis (1996) concluded from a recent survey of contingent valuation studies that consumers' willingness-to-pay to protect old-growth forests is likely to be very high. These and other studies do suggest that people place relatively high values on non-market forest amenities, which thus deserve serious consideration.

Valuing biological diversity

The benefits of biodiversity are particularly difficult to assess in monetary terms, as it is not always clear exactly what is being valued. Genetic diversity (within species); species richness (the number of different species); habitat diversity (the variety of different ecosystems): each is associated with different types of value, including both instrumental or 'use values' as well as non-use values such as existence or bequest value.

One oft-cited justification for saving ecosystems is the potential value of natural genetic material or naturally occurring compounds (organic metabolites) for pharmaceutical research and the development of new prescription drugs. Studies of the commercial value of a future discovery that might be lost due to the extinction of a single species have produced estimates ranging from a few dollars per species to many millions. Simpson *et al.* (1996) and Barbier and Aylward (1996) reviewed the methodologies and results from several earlier studies and derived their own estimates of the value of the marginal species (or biotic sample) and the maximum value of preserving land in identified biodiversity 'hot spots.' Both studies find values of only a few dollars per hectare, insufficient on their own to justify changing current land uses but perhaps significant when added to other non-market values of conservation.

Other values of biodiversity include developing new chemicals for agricultural or industrial uses, as well as the value of wild genetic information as a storehouse of information for crop breeding and selection. Indeed the entire biochemistry industry, still very much in its infancy, is predicated on the existence of a vast unexplored natural 'library' of genetic and chemical information. Of course, genetic manipulation through biotechnology may ultimately reduce the future value of genetic material in the wild. Attempts to estimate the future value of biodiversity are speculative at best (see Box 18.4 for a discussion of time-dependent values).

BOX 18.4 **Time-dependent values**

Many of the benefits of biodiversity are thought to lie in the future, e.g., genetic information for the development of new drugs and biochemical compounds, amenity and recreational values for our children and grand-children. The costs of biodiversity conservation, on the other hand, are apparent today in the form of lower employment in the forest industry, declining exports and tax revenues, and higher prices for wood products. How can current costs and future benefits be compared?

Economists invoke the concept of discounting in order to compare present and future values. The procedure involves converting costs and benefits which arise in different periods to a 'present value'. Normally a single, constant discount rate is used: the higher the rate the faster the decline in the present value of future costs and benefits and hence the less weight that is attached to future outcomes. While the mathematics is straightforward, discounting is often controversial when applied to environmental values, which may only become apparent after many years and may involve irreversible changes.

Nevertheless, the rationale for discounting is firmly rooted in both human behavior and market practice. One fundamental reason for discounting is that most individuals prefer current over future consumption. This is an expression of 'pure' time preference, which arises from the fact that we exist in time, are conscious of our own mortality and uncertain as to what the future holds. On the other hand, because society as a whole does not die, and can pool risk across many individuals, economists generally admit that the social rate of time preference will be lower than private (individual) rates.

The tradeoff between present and future consumption of marketed goods and services is expressed in the market rate of interest. This is simply the price of investment capital and reflects the balance between demand (from borrowers) and supply (by savers), adjusted for the risk or likelihood that the saver will get his/her money back. Risk-free investments like long-term US government bonds have returned about 3% per year on average (in 'real' inflation-adjusted terms), over many decades, consistent with long-run economic growth. If an asset does not grow in value, returning something like 3% with little risk or 6% with typical investment risks, investors can be expected to sell it in favor of alternative assets.

In developed countries, timber is considered a less risky asset than most other securities and is therefore managed for about 5% (real before-tax)

BOX 18.4 (cont.)

returns. Average expected returns are higher in developing countries, reflecting higher levels of investment risk generally. Note that where the required rate of return exceeds the natural growth rate of the resource, investors may be tempted to liquidate timber stocks as quickly as possible, and will have little incentive to engage in reforestation or long-term management.

In principle, non-market values such as biodiversity may be discounted in similar fashion. In this case, however, there are added complications, due to the difficulty of expressing biodiversity values in monetary terms, as well as uncertainty about the likely magnitude of future biodiversity values, and the potential irreversibility of biodiversity loss. The usual approach of adjusting future returns to account for risk may not apply, to the extent that some future non-market values cannot be expressed in terms of discrete probabilities. In such cases, comparisons with other assets may be impossible.

No doubt the debate among economists on the reliability of contingent valuation and other non-market valuation methods will continue. In the meantime, however, forest managers and policy-makers need information for their decision-making. Fortunately, other methods to compare alternative land uses and management systems can be used.

Cost effectiveness of alternative measures

Even when non-market benefits cannot be measured directly in monetary terms, it is often possible to compare the relative costs of alternative means of producing them. Some means of providing environmental benefits can be shown to be more efficient than others, in terms of priced inputs or loss of market values. While such an approach may be of limited value when comparing different benefits across different sites, it can at least help to identify where the costs of provision are likely to be lowest.

Where the economic costs of producing a given level of non-market benefit can be measured, it is relatively easy to derive benefit-to-cost ratios (e.g., units of habitat conserved per dollar of cost). So long as costs and benefits are measured consistently, determining the best option is a simple matter of selecting the lowest-cost approach to achieve a desired level of benefit. Moreover, even if the target range of benefits is not well defined, benefit-to-cost ratios may be used to indicate potential efficiency gains (Arrow et al. 1996).

Stand structure as proxy for diversity

While it is not currently possible to define the habitat requirements of every species, a feasible alternative is to evaluate forests and management systems in terms of ecosystem characteristics and their suitability for broad classes of species. Specifically, if we can measure forest conditions supportive of a wide variety of species, we have a better chance of producing the necessary habitats for all species. Many studies have characterized forest structures (Oliver 1992, Boyce and McNab 1994). Hunter (1990) recommends maintaining a balance of stand structures as a 'coarse filter' means of sustaining conditions for multiple species, as contrasted with a species-by-species approach.

Although forests are constantly changing, the extent and spatial distribution of stand structures can be classified at any particular moment in time, in terms of the composition and size of different tree species and of understory vegetation, the presence of debris and the successional stage. Industrial forestry generally results in the reduction of 'late-seral' structures, i.e., older stands characterized by large trees and a partially open canopy, rich in snags, downed logs and other debris which support a diverse understory vegetation and wildlife habitat. Prevailing forest management systems tend to result in a large share of stands in the 'competitive exclusion' stage, in which the vigorous growth of young trees produces a tightly closed canopy with little understory vegetation. Relatively few species can thrive in such conditions. Using such indicators as proxies for biological diversity, forest conditions can be tracked over time and significant deviations from historic patterns can be quantified.

A key question is how to decide when there is 'enough' of a particular structure. One approach would be to consider the extent of each type of stand structure that existed before industrialization as an historic norm (keeping in mind possible changes in climate and the impact of aboriginal populations; see Chapter 2). Noting that there have been large variations in the extent of different stand structures over time, one could define a particular quantity, e.g., the mean extent or one standard deviation below the mean, as a 'safe' minimum.

Carey *et al.* (1996) correlate forest stand structure to several multi-species habitat indicators and develop alternative forest treatments (i.e., biodiversity management pathways or 'biopathways') which accelerate the development of diverse structures, compared with natural aging. Parviainen *et al.* (1994) describe similar biodiversity information systems for Europe. Although the plight of individual species may hold public attention, the distribution of forest stand structures may be a better guide to biodiversity status and conservation.

While it is clearly feasible to measure forest stands and the diversity within them, there is no ideal target or goal. The task is more difficult for tropical rainforests, where the number of species is greater and the nature of disturbances and recovery less well known. But if measurable indicators of biodiversity can be identified and management treatments are defined which produce corresponding forest structures, then the cost to produce them can also be determined. Such cost information may be enough to enable the public and their political representatives to decide how much and what kind of governmental support should be applied, at least until a market mechanism evolves to pay for more diverse forests.

Figure 18.3 illustrates the distribution of different stand structures (Lippke and Fretwell 1996) developed in Carey et al. (1996) under two alternative management regimes: one for commercial commodity production and the other a biopathway designed to ensure a minimum level of late-seral structures supporting biodiversity (see Box 18.5 for stand structure definitions and treatment descriptions). The distribution of 'natural' stand structures, based upon past disturbance rates and stand structure progressions (Moffett and Lippke 1994), is shown for comparative purposes.

The figure shows clearly that commodity market management with short (50 year) rotations increases *competitive exclusion* structures at the expense of *late-seral* structures; decrease in the latter structures has in turn resulted in the listing of several endangered species. The biopathway treatments include successive thinnings to develop more diverse structures with a complex understory, retention of snags and downed logs. A combination of commercial harvests with biopathways (i.e., a mixed management regime) could be used to avoid any shortage of *competitive exclusion* structures.

In short, broad indicators of structural diversity may be more immediately relevant to forest management decisions than separate indicators of habitat quality for individual species. While the latter are of clear scientific interest, they are impractical when the challenge is to protect a wide range of species in a single area. In contrast, forest structural diversity which provides support for all species can be measured and explicitly included in regulatory or incentive mechanisms. Hence the focus now turns to how best to create and maintain diverse structures, given that there are many different ways to produce a diverse forest.

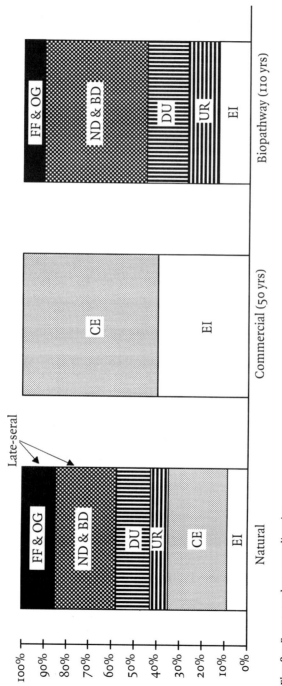

Fig. 18.3. Forest stand structure diversity.

BOX 18.5 **Stand structure stages under natural, commercial, and biopathway progressions**

Stand structure stages (summary of structural conditions for west slope of Cascades, USA, western Hemlock Site No. 105 land productivity):

1. Ecosystem initiation (EI): open stand initiated by a stand-clearing natural disturbance or a clearcut while retaining some debris and snags (lasting from 0 to 20 years).
2. Competitive exclusion (CE): vigorous growth produces a closed canopy with no understory (lasting from 20 to 80 years if not subject to a substantial natural disturbance, thinning or harvest. Returns to stage 1 upon harvest).
3. Understory re-initiation (UR): partially opened canopy from maturing trees supports understory growth (lasting from 80 to 100 years if not initiated sooner by a disturbance or thinning, but can be as soon as year 20 under a pre-commercial thinning. Canopy will close again in about 20 years returning to stage 2 without successive thinnings).
4. Developed understory (DU): maturing understory but lacking diversity (lasting from 100 to 150 years if not initiated sooner by a disturbance or thinning but can be as soon as year 30 with a first biopathway thinning).
5. Diverse (niche-diverse, ND, if biopathway; or botanically-diverse, BD, if natural aging): contains diverse understory, snags and debris but less variability and smaller trees than natural old-growth (lasting from 150 to 250 years if not initiated sooner by a thinning, but can be as early as year 50 with a second variable-density biopathway thinning providing additional debris, snags and some hardwood understory trees).
6. Old growth (fully functional to old growth from a biopathway, FF; or if natural, OG): forest functions comparable to old growth, including limb size, understory and canopy (starting about 250 years if not initiated by thinnings or disturbance, but could be reached by year 90 or 100, 4–5 decades after a heavy second or third biopathway thinning).

Note: Late-seral conditions (including diverse plus old-growth stages) would normally be achieved after about 150 years, compared with about 50 years with appropriate biodiversity management treatments. Naturally diverse structures may never evolve in areas subject to fire controls, however, due to the lower frequency of small fires and corresponding increase in fuel loads and risk of catastrophic fires.

Economics of strategies to maintain biodiversity

MANAGEMENT VS. NO MANAGEMENT

Reserves

There are many competing strategies to maintain or restore biodiversity, each with different biological and economic consequences. Some advocate heavy reliance on reserves or totally protected areas, especially for older forest structures thought to be in short supply. Where new reserves are created from forests that were previously available to produce timber or other commodities for the market, the economic loss is clear. However, even lands placed in reserve status long ago represent market opportunities foregone.

While the non-market amenity values of reserves may be difficult to measure, the market cost of maintaining them can be directly estimated in terms of reduced economic activity. The potential commodity value of standing timber is simply the difference between product prices in the market and the costs of harvesting, processing and distribution. Hence the opportunity cost of maintaining land and timber in reserves will vary with the productivity of the land for commodity production, the distance to market and other factors. Economic activity is also foregone in reduced harvesting, processing and distribution of commodities, but these losses are returns to labor and capital in facilities and equipment rather than returns to land, and are less directly relevant to efficient land allocation. Nevertheless, concerns about employment are often equally important to policy-makers, resulting in an emphasis on the value-added economic activity from processing timber.

Examples of the opportunity cost of reserves

Table 18.1 shows typical market values for standing timber in different regions, as well as the value-added that would be generated by converting the timber into marketable products. Highly-productive lands with mature timber close to cheap water transportation and markets result in very high timber values, as in the Pacific Northwest of the United States. Mature timber on low-productivity land distant from markets may have almost no timber value, as in the interior of Russia. In still other regions, the costs of management and removal may be so high that net timber values are negligible.

Because the economic opportunity cost of maintaining biodiversity through reserves varies so widely, we might expect the social value of biodiversity to exceed timber values in some regions but not in others. Where

Table 18.1. *Typical opportunity cost of reserve stands (US$)*

	$ timber /hectare to land owner	$ value-added /hectare to processors
USA PNW mature forest (over 80 years old)	76,000	63,000
USA PNW commercial forest at harvest (50 years old)	30,000	38,000
USA South commercial forest (30 years old)	10,000	17,000
Russia Far East interior	near 0	9,000
Malaysia (old forest)	5,000	9,000

Notes:
PNW, Pacific Northwest.
Source: Timber values and typical processing costs in the CINTRAFOR Global Trade Model (Perez-Garcia 1994).

net timber returns are near zero and there are large negative effects on bio-diversity from logging, total social welfare may be enhanced by retaining stands in reserve status (even if particular socioeconomic groups are dis-advantaged). Conversely, where timber values are very high the argument for commodity production is strengthened. The same logic applies within as well as across regions, given the considerable variation in timber values across different sites within a single region. Furthermore, it may be possible to ensure minimum levels of diversity within a given region at the least cost by moving different forest stands in and out of reserve status over time, as managed alternatives are developed. Hence we now turn to the role of managed stands in biodiversity conservation.

Management alternatives

Oliver (1992) argued that a diversity of forest structures can be maintained while still producing timber products. Natural disturbances such as fires and windstorms can be approximated by thinning treat-ments, so that forest structures more quickly acquire the characteristics of older stands. Moreover, with treatments the growth of wood is concen-trated on fewer stems, producing larger diameter trees and higher-quality wood, thereby earning higher prices which help to defray the cost of treat-ments. In such cases increased forest structural diversity and higher-quality wood may be complementary, i.e., it may be less costly to produce diversity and timber jointly than to manage some land for timber and other land for biodiversity. Unfortunately, in many cases the increased market value of larger trees available from longer rotations only partly compensates for the loss in present value due to discounting future harvests over a longer period.

Each region invites different management strategies with different economic consequences. Since it is usually possible to determine the economic costs (including foregone revenue) of achieving a given level of forest diversity, one might choose to define a target level of cost and then determine how best to manage the forest estate to produce the greatest restoration in diversity relative to an historic benchmark, within that target. Alternatively, by setting the level of restoration as the goal, one can determine the lowest cost strategy to achieve that goal (as well as who will pay!). For instance, in a region with low timber values one might rely on reserves to achieve biodiversity conservation. In another region with higher timber values, stands might be managed aggressively for production of diverse structures, so as to reduce the need for and high cost of reserves. In a third region, one might emphasize the development of short-rotation plantations to reduce pressure on natural forest areas.

No single prescription will do for every region, nor indeed for every site within any single region. In some places threatened species are associated with a lack of early successional stands, while elsewhere other species are limited by the extent of old-growth forests. Hence the importance of understanding the costs of alternative strategies, as even within a single region the most efficient approach will almost certainly include a mix of strategies.

Cost of management example

To illustrate these concepts we will examine the biopathways developed by Carey *et al.* (1996) for the west side of the Cascades in the United States Pacific Northwest (see description provided earlier in Box 18.5). Biopathways apply periodic thinnings with retention of woody debris and snags in order to achieve relatively quickly the diverse stand structure and functionality of late-seral forest development stages, which are considered to be in short supply due to decades of commodity production. The economic loss to the landowner from adopting biopathways provides the information needed to derive a cost schedule for various biodiversity goals over different time intervals.

Net present value

Each thinning generates revenue, as does the final harvest of large-diameter high-quality wood produced by the biopathway, along with the revenue from successive rotations. Figure 18.4 illustrates the landowner's

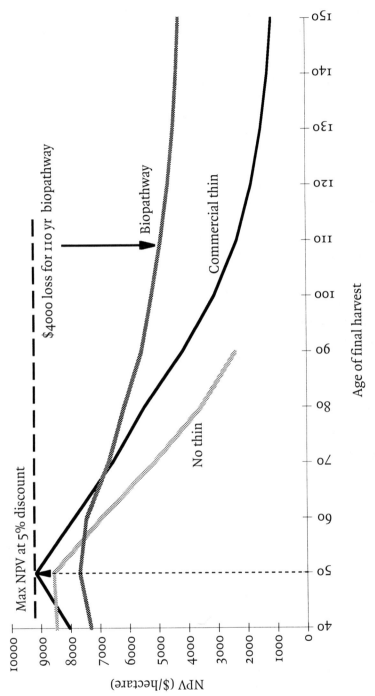

Fig. 18.4. NPV loss for biopathway and other treatments.

net present value (NPV) as a function of the age of final harvest for the bio-pathway in comparison with commercial thinning or no-thinning alternatives. The value of commercial rotations after the first rotation harvest has been included in the derived NPV so that the returns are comparable regardless of different harvest ages. The NPV loss for the biopathway relative to the optimal age commercial rotation represents the cost to the landowner of producing more diverse stand structures.

The NPV for the stand receiving the commercial thinning treatment peaks at age 50, the optimal commercial harvest age, beyond which the growth in revenue is less than the assumed 5% discount rate. Any other rotation age or harvest treatment results in a loss in NPV to the landowner. Extending the harvest age beyond the optimal rotation to improve biodiversity results in a reduction in NPV. However, the loss in NPV is lower under a biopathway than for a commercial thinning at the same age, as the latter does not produce high-quality wood as quickly.

In this example, the loss of $4000 per hectare identified with the bio-pathway at age 110, compared with the peak NPV for commercial thinning, represents the level of incentive (assuming payment in year 30 at the time of the first thinning decision) that would be required to make the land-owner indifferent between managing for an optimal commercial (50 year) rotation and a biopathway (110 year) rotation. Under the biopathway, *diverse* structures are reached at age 50 and structures fully functional to *old growth* by age 100, resulting in 46% of the stand in *diverse* structures and 9% *old growth* structures, or 54% *late-seral* structures (i.e., *diverse* and *old growth*). In contrast, neither the commercial thinning treatment nor a no-thin treatment would produce any *late-seral* structures through natural aging before 150 years. The biopathway restores biodiversity by accelerating the development of *late-seral* structures, albeit at a significant financial cost compared with the optimal commercial rotation. Nevertheless, the bio-pathway is far less costly than the $76 000 per hectare that was earlier estimated as the opportunity cost of placing a hectare of older forest in reserve (although of course the biopathway takes much longer to reach comparable functionality). The required incentive payment would be lower for faster-growing sites, where high-quality wood and *late-seral* forest conditions can be created more quickly with less economic loss.

Cost curves to produce late-seral structures

By considering a range of treatment alternatives to enhance biodiversity and selecting those with the lowest cost (i.e., lowest loss relative to commercial practices), cost curves to produce/restore *late-seral* structures

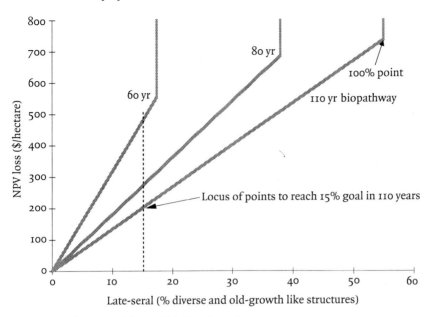

Fig. 18.5. NPV loss to reach *late-seral* biodiversity goals.

as a biodiversity goal over different time horizons can be developed (Figure 18.5). These are analogous to the cost curves used to describe the production of timber for markets.

To reach any production goal for *late-seral* structures, biopathways would be phased in such as treatment of 1 hectare each year up to the rotation age (e.g., 110 years), followed by the same requirement for the second rotation. The present value (PV) of the incentive payment for the first hectare under a 110 year rotation was $4000, but to purchase one hectare each year, the value of future years are discounted (at the 5% discount rate) and the present value of all 110 hectares under the rotation is used to derive the average PV cost per hectare, shown as $730 per hectare. The 110 year rotation produces 54% of the stand in *late-seral* structures anytime after 110 years, the phase in period. (The general formula for this conversion from treating a single hectare to phasing in a full rotation is: $ PV loss per hectare = [$ incentive per hectare treated]/[discount rate]/[rotation years]).

It is not possible to produce more than 54% *late-seral* stands with the 110 year biopathway; hence this point becomes a breakpoint on the cost curve with the cost rising to infinity for higher *late-seral* levels (costs in the figure rise vertically beyond the break point). Any lower level target can be

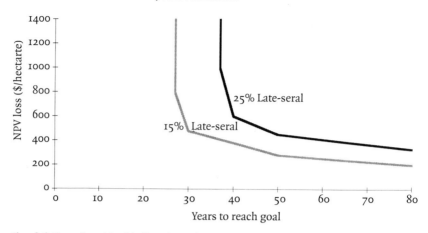

Fig. **18.6.** Cost of reaching biodiversity goals over time.

reached by allocating only a portion of the acres to the biopathway with the remainder managed commercially (at no loss). This is represented by the locus of points from the origin (100% commercial) to the breakpoint (100% biopathway). Thus the cost to produce any feasible percentage of *late-seral* structures for any given biopathway and rotation is derived. The *late-seral* targets can be achieved more quickly with short rotations, but at a higher cost, since a smaller portion of the land reaches the desired structure, thereby requiring more land to reach a given target. Reserving an old-growth stand was shown earlier to cost as much as $76 000 per hectare and hence, $15 600 per acre to reach a 20% *late-seral* target. The biopathway requires a little more than 60 year old stands or 30 years after the first thinning treatments to reach that target but at a cost of only $600 per hectare.

While this appears to offer a lower cost approach to achieve targets, albeit in a longer period of time, this same analysis applied to low-productivity land with high transport costs might generate so little revenue that the cost of the biopathway could exceed the cost of reserves.

A cost curve for any target level of diverse structures can then be developed for any feasible length of time by examining the locus of costs for that target along different treatments (such as the intersection of the vertical line at 15% *late-seral* with the cost curves for different treatments as shown in Figure 18.5). Figure 18.6 illustrates this cost to reach a particular goal as a function of time. It is impossible to reach a high level of diversity immediately, hence the curves will characteristically rise to infinite cost at the youngest age the target can be met. By initiating the biopathway on the first thinning treatment, i.e., age 30, the target is reached in 30 years less than the rotation age. The cost is lower for lower target levels of diverse structures or for taking longer to reach the target, as fewer hectares must be devoted to the more costly treatments.

Lowest cost to reach time-dependent biodiversity goals

Based on these management and no-management examples we have many alternatives for maintaining biodiversity. For the Pacific Northwest, if we have $11 400 to spend, under the no-management example we can purchase 0.15 hectares of old growth as a reserve, contributing to a 15% *late-seral* goal for one hectare. Instead we could achieve the same 15% goal on 22 hectares with a 60 year biopathway, but not until the stand reaches age 60, or 30 years after initiating the first thinning treatment. Similarly we could achieve the goal on 57 hectares with a 110 year biopathway but not until 80 years after the first thinning. If time is not a crucial factor and the functionality of managed structures sufficient, the longer biopathways are lower cost.

In order to minimize cost but to achieve a goal immediately, we could defer the harvest of an old forest just long enough for a lower cost biopathway to achieve the same goal at less cost. Other treatments that might reach *late-seral* structures more quickly than these biopathways might also have lower costs than deferring the harvest of old forests. A very heavy (50%) thinning treatment of a mature *competitive exclusion* stand, while retaining woody debris and snags, should be able to achieve the *late-seral* structure conditions in less than 10 years. Deferring the *old-growth* harvest for only 10 years costs $4574 instead of $11 400 for the reserve, a $6826 savings, reduced by about $1000 in cost to retain the heavily thinned substitute stand on a longer rotation. That cuts the $11 400 cost of a reserve roughly in half while still supporting the functionally equivalent 15% late-seral biodiversity goal immediately.

Of course, any of these strategies require that minimum levels of critical structures needed for biodiversity can be defined and agreed upon on a regional basis. Moreover, some high-value reserves may be desirable, given that managed late-seral forests may not be a perfect substitute for undisturbed reserves. But even unmanaged stands appear to be much more dense and of different structure than in earlier history, suggesting perhaps no greater predictability in supporting diversity goals over the long term than managed alternatives. As research produces more reliable predictors in terms of ecology, species richness and other environmental features, an emphasis on applying a narrower mix of strategies may become acceptable. Given less than precise predictors of the results of

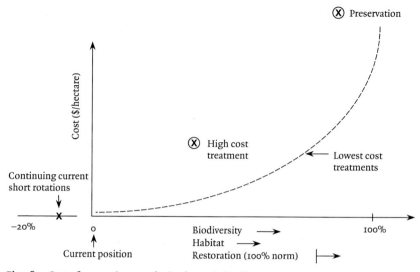

Fig. 18.7. Cost of restoration or reducing losses in biodiversity.

either management or no management alternatives a range of strategies will reduce the risk of a single strategy being inadequate.

Cost of restoring structures in short supply

In general, the combination of many treatment alternatives across a landscape makes up a rising cost curve to reach or restore higher levels of structures that have become in short supply as illustrated in Figure 18.7. Applying strictly commercial practices on the remaining stands that are older than the optimal economic rotation would result in the further reduction of biodiversity measures. Many alternatives will be inefficient and considerably more costly than the lowest cost alternatives. And the costs to reach prescribed goals quickly are much higher than slower strategies. To the degree that benefit values can be agreed upon, they provide guidance as to whether the treatments can be justified as cost effective. Innovative institutional arrangements are needed to internalize these values into the market decision-making process.

POLICY ALTERNATIVES

The examples described above demonstrate that cost-effective methods to maintain and restore forest biodiversity do exist. The main reason they are not more widely adopted is that commodity markets typically motivate management practices that produce products but degrade biodiversity. Timber producers and land owners have no financial incentive to adopt biodiversity management treatments. Appropriate policy can help to redress the balance, by encouraging a shift in management practices.

Existing forest policies range from simple 'command and control' measures, such as the designation of legally protected areas or minimum riparian reserves, to indirect market-based instruments designed to influence producer behavior in ways that favor non-market values. The latter include the use of taxes to favor environmentally benign behavior, as well as the creation of new markets for environmental services (e.g., recreational concessions). More commonly, existing forestry regulations have simply been recast (sometimes in name only) to support environmental goals. Thus, for example, minimum diameter cutting limits and long rotation periods on public lands are increasingly justified in environmental terms.

In general, economists prefer policy approaches which exploit market incentives in ways that reduce the costs of environmental protection. Likewise there is global recognition that the protection of environmental forest amenities will be facilitated if environmental costs and benefits are more fully reflected in markets. Forest Principle 13c, adopted at the United Nations Conference on Environment and Development in Rio de Janeiro, encourages this both domestically and internationally (Heissenbuttel et al. 1992). With our increased knowledge about the costs of attaining forest diversity goals, we can now compare various policy options for reaching them.

Reserve requirements

The dominant regulatory means of protecting wildlife habitat is generally to prevent the harvest of timber in the immediate vicinity, i.e., to create a reserve. This results in an upward shift in the cost curve for producing timber in wildlife-reach areas; in effect, a cost rather than a reward for saving habitat. This motivates commercial managers to shorten rotations and to utilize treatments that will eliminate potential or even existing habitat that is not already subject to regulation, so as to avoid future costs. Thus non-industrial private forest owners in Washington state (USA), for example, are liquidating their older stands and shortening their rotations with harvest rates above sustainable levels in contrast to their earlier pattern of relatively low harvest rates while retaining older stands. Surveys suggest that a major cause of the apparent change in behavior is a widespread perception among land owners that more stringent regulations will impact them (Elway Research 1995).

A more promising regulatory approach is to allow the land owner to develop a habitat conservation plan that is less costly than blanket harvest constraints. United States regulations to save endangered species provide for such an option. Owner-generated conservation plans must provide adequate levels of habitat acceptable to the regulator for the right to harvest high valued timber in the vicinity of existing habitat. By allowing the owner to substitute less costly habitat (i.e., land with less timber value) for existing habitat, the cost to produce habitat is reduced, while providing incentives for the land owner to increase habitat. Nevertheless, even this approach does not fully exploit market mechanisms to produce habitat in the most efficient way across different land owners, or even across different regions for the same owner. So long as the central regulator determines the distribution of habitat across regions, the outcome is unlikely to be cost efficient. The approach also invites unequal treatment, since each plan is developed through direct negotiations between government agencies and the landowner.

Regulations that restrict activity to save endangered species have been challenged in the United States on both economic and environmental grounds (Lambert 1995), with critics citing conflicts over land use, inequitable impacts, excessive cost, negligible environmental benefit, and more. Such challenges are generally directed at the unintended consequences of existing policy, rather than the goal of saving species or protecting diversity.

Global market links

One of the most significant unintended consequences of current forest policy is the redirection of timber production and environmental impact to other regions, reflecting the integration of global timber markets. Sedjo (1995) and Perez-Garcia (1995) show that reduced timber production in one region (for environmental or other reasons) will result in increased production in other regions, or increased reliance on non-wood substitutes which may also have significant adverse environmental impacts.

It can be shown that the marginal (highest-cost) log removed from a forest generates zero net financial return, while leaving it in the forest would almost certainly contribute positively to biodiversity values. Any increase in timber prices resulting from a supply constraint in one region will make it profitable to remove more logs from more remote stands in many areas around the world, with adverse impacts on diversity. Since these marginal suppliers are generally higher cost sources, i.e., less efficient, Perez-Garcia (1996) shows that more hectares are likely to be harvested than are protected, on a global basis. (Of course, if regions with increasing harvests have a surplus of the structures being lost, their loss may be considered less important than the diversity retained in the region where harvests are constrained.)

If the social cost of degrading biodiversity can be introduced simultaneously in all markets, producers will efficiently produce for markets while minimizing their impact on biodiversity. Imposing additional costs in only one region or only for one product simply makes that region or product less competitive and effectively 'exports' the environmental problem elsewhere. The linkages between trade policy and environmental impacts have been a major focus of much recent policy analysis (Barbier 1994, Smith and Espinosa 1996, Harrison 1994, Simula 1994, JSTEE, 1994).

Boycotts

Concerns about the exploitation of tropical rainforests in Southeast Asia led to boycotts of tropical timber in several European countries. Advocates hoped that reduced consumer demand for tropical timber would slow the destruction of the rainforest. Boycotts did lower demand for tropical timber, but they also lowered the value of tropical forests for timber production. This in turn discouraged investment in managing the resource and in some cases may have encouraged more rapid conversion of forest land to other uses such as plantation agriculture, thus accelerating rather than discouraging deforestation. In an analysis of the tropical timber trade, Barbier et al. (1994) concluded that 'In order for sustainable timber management to be a viable forest land use option it must yield net returns to developing countries that are greater than those derived from competing uses, such as conversion for frontier agriculture.' Regions where efforts were under way to manage tropical forests on a more sustainable basis were penalized by declining markets and prices rather than helped by the European ban (Eastin 1996). From a global perspective, these unintended negative consequences may have been partially offset by the increased attention producing countries gave to sustainability issues and policies, but the distributional impacts were far from balanced.

Certification systems

Certification labeling to distinguish forest products derived from well-managed forests (Upton and Bass 1996) offers a more sophisticated means of mobilizing consumer demand for environmentally friendly products. Producers submit to an independent environmental audit of their practices and, if the result is satisfactory, they are certified by the auditor to be producing according to the criteria of 'sustainable' forestry developed for that region. If certification is successful, the consumer buying certified products voluntarily pays for practices that maintain (if not restore) forest biodiversity. The product functionality is unchanged except for the value of the certification label.

One of the key assumptions underlying certification is that consumers who care will pay a premium for certified products (on the assumption that more sustainable forestry is also more expensive). Evidence to date, however, suggests that many consumers are unwilling to pay the higher price required to cover the cost of managing for certification. Barbier *et al.* (1994) surveyed UK firms selling wood products to ascertain how much they thought their customers were willing to pay for tropical wood certified as coming from sustainably managed forests. Seventy-five percent of respondents did not feel that their customers would pay any premium at all, while most of the rest thought they would pay only a 5–10% premium.

Since consumers generally buy finished products composed of component materials made from many sources, it becomes difficult to track the chain of custody from certified forests to finished products. Product producers have found it difficult to obtain the full range of components from certified forests with sufficient volume to support a line of certified products. Hence only a small portion of the harvest gains the benefit of reaching the consumer as certified, making it even more difficult to recover the cost of certification from environmental market premiums.

Forest certification systems have so far avoided conflict with international trade rules, because they are voluntary. Conflict would arise, however, if governments make certification mandatory. In any case, certified timber currently occupies a very small niche in global forest product markets; it is not at all clear how large the market for certified products will eventually become. It is also not yet evident which regions or types of producers are best placed to take advantage of certification systems, although there is concern that smaller producers in developing countries may find it somewhat harder to meet the standards required. Finally, while most certification systems promulgate different standards for different regions, they are not able to account for differences in the costs of meeting certifiable standards across different sites within a single region. In this regard certification is no more efficient than most existing environmental regulations.

Concession agreements

When a land owner leases property to another party to manage or harvest timber, it is often difficult to ensure that the owner's best interests are protected. A particularly undesirable impact on biodiversity has been the lack of accountability by loggers for the health of the residual stand. Loggers aim to minimize costs, hence they have little motivation to do more than what is required under their contract. Thus for example most logging in tropical forests results in the removal of only the highest grade trees, often with substantial damage to the remaining forest. Such damage reduces the economic return on subsequent harvests and adversely affects biodiversity, but the logger is not liable for these costs, and has no interest in limiting them. In contrast, owner-operators benefit from their own good practices. Attempts to stipulate good management practices in the terms of contracts often has the same effect as setting uniform minimum standards. Costs are simply increased rather than promoting more informed, site-specific decision-making.

Tradable permits or swaps

Developing countries are generally more interested in raising incomes than in environmental protection, and may be even less willing to adopt policies that are perceived to constrain job creation. If a global market for environmental benefits could be devised, however, developing countries (and others) could be compensated for their contributions to biodiversity. Environmental permit markets are in their infancy, however, and are rife with technical and political complexities (Hahn and Hester 1989). While the concept is attractive, there is little prospect of global markets for biodiversity arising in the near term.

Incentive systems for land managers

Economists generally argue that subsidies lead to inefficient allocation of resources, as consumers use more of a subsidized product than they would if prices reflected true marginal costs. However, if incentives contribute to non-market values, they may increase the efficiency of resource allocation, so long as the cost of the incentive is no greater than the marginal social value it produces.

Incentives have been widely advocated as a means of ensuring adequate provision of forest benefits, including biodiversity, game habitat, timber products, clean air, clean water, and recreation or open spaces (Schroeder et al. 1996, Sample 1995, Lippke 1992). Incentives may be introduced through administrative, legislative, or budgetary actions, and can take many forms; they may provide educational, technical, or financial assistance in modifying land management behavior. They can be designed to address any number of treatments that affect forest diversity such as planting, leaving more woody debris, retaining snags, providing for a mix of species, varying densities, providing larger trees or less frequent entries, varying the canopy, retaining pockets of reserves, maintaining certain structures, etc. The likelihood that incentives will succeed in modifying forest management strategies is directly related to whether they offset the cost to the landowner. Incentives can easily be structured around less costly treatment variations.

Programs have been developed to encourage small land owners to practise elementary stewardship, such as restocking, by providing incentives such as cost sharing. These programs are a close cousin to subsidies in that landowners receive the reward for something that they might have done anyway. Boyd and Hyde (1990) analyzed cost sharing and technical assistance programs and found no significant positive impact from cost-sharing programs. They concluded that 'technical assistance is generally more cost effective (and less inefficient than an equal amount of cost sharing . . .),' but neither has positive impacts on social welfare. In contrast, competitive bidding for incentive contracts to change specific forest structures could more efficiently produce the intended objective at the least cost, requiring no more compensation than is required to modify management.

For biodiversity incentives to be effective, they must not increase the risk of a regulatory taking, and competitive bidding for incentive contracts is almost a requirement. Interest in the potential for incentives has been growing (ECNRM 1989, Johnson *et al.* 1995, Keystone 1995, Fischer *et al.* 1994, Lippke and Fretwell 1996). Important conditions cited for effective contracts are summarized in Box 18.6.

BOX 18.6 **Contract requirements**
1. Compensation to offset costs or lost revenue.
2. Avoiding increased cash flow needs or facilitating cash availability (such as estate taxes that may require harvests to meet obligations as a conflict with long rotations for habitat goals).
3. Elimination of the risk of confiscation for achieving environmental goals, i.e., compensation at market value for any taking resulting from achieving habitat goals (such as critical habitat).
4. Buyback or penalty provisions for non-compliance or change in use (with the exit cost sufficient to purchase comparable biodiversity benefits in the market).
5. Flexibility to adapt to unexpected natural disturbances.
6. Sufficient scale in activity to support investment in needed infrastructure (such as sawmills to process high-quality wood).

Contracting agencies should determine and make known the total cost of each goal so that both biodiversity targets and payments have public support. Full evaluation of the impact of incentives or any other method of changing landowner management strategies requires consideration of the impact on the region as well as on the land owners and operators. Where impacts among different stakeholders vary there may be significant implications for public support.

Consumer incentives

As an alternative to a land owner incentive system, policy-makers could offer consumers a tax credit for voluntary contributions to organizations dedicated to investing in the production or maintenance of environmental values such the Nature Conservancy in the United States or the National Trust in the United Kingdom. Biodiversity values would then be represented in the market by increased purchases made by a range of organizations representing a variety of interests. Ideally, the efficiency of producing biodiversity values and the distribution of benefits would exceed that of government regulators.

IMPORTANCE OF REGIONAL IMPACTS TO POLICY DECISIONS

Increased management activity in treatments to retain or restore biodiversity provides an economic stimulus to the local economy comparable to economic development investments, even as it enhances biodiversity. An incentive to achieve biodiversity goals funded by some tax mechanism would increase economic activity locally, producing increased tax receipts and alleviating unemployment in distressed rural communities. These social benefits, supplemental to the biodiversity gains, may help to justify incentives.

Example of the impact of management incentives on tax receipts

The same biopathway treatment example used to illustrate cost curves (Figure 18.4) will be used to illustrate regional impacts. The first set of stand structure treatments involved thinnings which put the forest stands on a path toward more diverse structures but contribute little if any return to the land owner. Thinning treatments are labor intensive in rural communities. They result in earlier products flowing from the forest through the regional economy. Table 18.2 illustrates this impact for the sample treatment applied on the west side of the State of Washington (Lippke et al. 1996).

Table 18.2. *Economic impact of a first biopathway thinning treatment (25 cubic meter per hectare thinning on 7100 hectares at age 30, US Pacific Northwest, westside, USA)*

	Primary wood	Secondary wood	Pulp and paper	Total sector
Employment (person years)	2520	468	1188	4176
Gross product (US$ millions)	109	19	55	183
State and local tax receipts ($)	12	2	6	20
Federal tax receipts ($)	21	4	10	35
Reduced unemployment compensation (short term potential, $)				31
Estimated management incentive cost ($)				18

For this example, the increase in tax receipts, both regional and federal, exceeds the incentive cost needed to motivate the land owner to adopt the new management strategy, at least in the early years of the program. This can be considered a win/win solution in that society gains the increased biodiversity benefits and pays for the management change yet still sees improvements in the tax expenditures and receipts account. The incentive program may produce less net tax revenue per employee compared with the state average and may not be the best economic development investment that exists, but it is a relatively pain-free solution to enhance biodiversity benefits. These impacts will be treatment- and site-specific; in some settings the cost of the incentives may exceed the economic benefit, but might be justified by the biodiversity benefit.

Long-term regional impacts appear to be even more attractive, as long-term sustainable harvest volumes can be increased with longer rotations while also producing higher quality wood, both contributing to more processing activity.

With the incentive to change management strategy funded early in the forest rotation, large, long-term economic and biodiversity benefits might appear to come at no cost. However, in the intermediate period, harvests are delayed as the forest rotation is lengthened. A significant decline in economic activity during this transition period can be offset by harvests from temporary reserves as the aggregate measures of biodiversity improve.

The regional economic impact of alternative policies

A comparison of policy alternatives will generally reveal substantial efficiency differences. The Washington Forest Landscape Management project (Lippke *et al.* 1996) assessed the economic impact of restoring a certain level of biodiversity to 4 million hectares. Without reliance on reserves, the estimated annual incentive cost was $63 million per year, offset by increased tax receipts of $250 million for at least the first two decades, resulting in a net increase in tax receipts of $187 million per year. With 25% of the forest land in reserves, there was a revenue loss of $342 million offset by tax receipts of $85 million per year, a net loss in tax receipts of $257 million.

While these examples are instructive of the role of policy, economics, and management alternatives, there are very few regions of the world where sufficient data exist to perform such an analysis. The necessary inputs include: (a) a thorough economic analysis of a large number of forest management alternatives designed to support biological goals as well as commercial goals, (b) an analysis of production changes that would result from different management outputs, (c) the linkage of these production changes through a comprehensive regional model to simulate economic activity and tax accounts. Like all policy analysis, the simulations are hypothetical reactions to policy assumptions calibrated to baseline performance in a historical period. Whether they faithfully characterize the important aspects of a given situation is debatable.

Summary

Growing human populations and rising incomes in many countries have led to vast areas of natural forest being converted to agricultural or used for timber production. Human needs for food and other commodities have been served but at the cost of widespread loss of biological diversity and other non-market forest values. Pervasive market imperfections and policy failures hide the true environmental cost of forest land use from both producers and consumers, leading to inefficient land use and excessive loss of biodiversity. Institutional structures that guide market behavior have been a driving force in the decline of biodiversity and they must also contribute to any solution.

Because environmental values are difficult if not impossible to measure and compare with market costs and benefits, policy-makers often find it hard to determine the appropriate response to biodiversity loss. The challenge is to develop policies that internalize these values into market behavior, so that forest biodiversity and other environmental values are protected and provided efficiently. Even where the economic value of biodiversity is not known, useful information for forest managers and policymakers can be derived from estimates of the economic costs of alternative means of achieving biodiversity goals.

Totally protected areas (i.e., forest reserves) have an important role to play in biodiversity conservation, but they are a high-cost solution in some areas. Forest reserves reduce supplies of timber and increase producer costs. They can also stimulate increased harvests in other environmentally sensitive regions, and may lead consumers to switch to alternative products that cause even greater environmental harm. More importantly, reliance on such an approach does nothing to encourage forest land owners and managers to maintain or restore biodiversity outside of reserves.

One alternative to reserves is joint production of timber and biodiversity through improved forest management systems. New *biodiversity management pathways*, used in combination with conventional commercial management systems, can produce both timber and forest structures which mimic the diversity of mature natural stands, but at far less cost than reserves in some cases. The cost of biodiversity enhancement or restoration varies significantly depending upon the length of time allowed to reach a given target. Where timber values are high, such as the United States Pacific Northwest, relatively modest producer incentives may be sufficient to motivate management change if phased in over 50 to 100 years.

Managed alternatives to forest reserves appear to be most attractive where timber values, and thus the opportunity cost of reserves, are high. Conversely, reserves may be preferred where timber values are relatively low as is frequently the case in low population density regions. Land productivity and biodiversity values also vary across regions and within regions resulting in a need for mixed management strategies. Uncertainty about the importance of biodiversity and other non-market values, imperfect understanding of natural processes and of the environmental impacts of alternative forest management systems all suggest the need for a diversified strategy.

Further readings

A compendium of recent papers on environmental economics in forestry is available in *Forestry, Economics and the Environment* (Adamowicz et al. 1996). Many of the cost examples for biodiversity management pathways were derived from two reports of the Washington Forest Landscape Management Project: one focusing on the biological aspects of managing forests for multi-species habitat (Carey *et al.* 1996), and the other on economic issues (Lippke *et al.* 1996). For a thorough treatment of the legal basis for environmental damage see Ward and Duffield (1992). A fuller treatment of the theory and methods of environmental and natural resource economics is provided by Tietenberg (1996).

Literature cited

Adamowicz, W. L., P. C. Boxall, M. K. Luckert, W. E. Phillips, and W. A. White (eds). 1996. *Forestry, Economics and the Environment.* CAB International, Wallingford.

Arrow, K., R. Solow, P. Portney, E. Leamer, R. Radner, and H. Schuman. 1993. *Report of the NOAA panel on contingent valuation.* NOAA, Washington D.C.

Arrow, K., M. Cropper, G. Eads, R. Hahn, L. Bave, R. Noll, P. Portney, M. Russell, R. Schmalensee, V. K. Smith, and R. Stavins. 1996. *Benefit-Cost Analysis in Environmental, Health, and Safety Regulation: a Statement of Principles.* American Enterprise Institute, The Annapolis Center, and Resources for the Future. AEI Press. Washington, D.C. USA.

Barbier, E. 1994. The environmental effects of trade in the forestry sector. In *The Environmental Effects of Trade.* OECD: JSTEE, Washington DC.

Barbier, E. B. and B. A. Aylward. 1996. Capturing the pharmaceutical value of biodiversity in a developing country. *Environmental and Resource Economics* 8(2):157–81.

Barbier, E., J. Burgess, J. Bishop, and B. Aylward. 1994. *The Economics of the Tropical Timber Trade.* Earthscan Publications, London.

Boyd, R. G., and W. Hyde. 1989. Comparing the effectiveness of cost sharing and technical assistance programs. Pp. 48–77 in *Forestry Sector Intervention: The Impacts of Public Regulation on Social Welfare.* Iowa State University Press.

Boyce, S. G., and W. H. McNab. 1994. Management of forested landscapes: simulations of three alternatives. *Journal of Forestry* 92(1):27–32.

Carey, A. B., B. R. Lippke, J. Sessions, C. J. Chambers, C. D. Oliver, J. F. Franklin, and M. J. Raphael. 1996. *Pragmatic, ecological approach to small-landscape management: final report of the biodiversity pathways working group of the Washington Forest Landscape Management project.* Washington State Department of Natural Resources, Olympia, Washington.

Council of Economic Advisers (CEA). 1997. *Economic report of the President*. US Government Printing Office, Washington DC. ISBN 0-16-048501-0 (as well as earlier years).

Diamond, P., and J. Hausmann. 1994. Contingent valuation: is some number better than no number? *Journal of Economic Perspectives* **8**:4.

Eastin, I. 1996. The role of marketing in promoting sustainable trade in forest products in tropical regions. *Ghana Journal of Forestry* **V**(3):44–54.

Elway Research. 1995. *Regulation and Taxation Impacts on Family Forestry in Washington State: Survey of Members of WFFA*. Northwest Renewable Resource Center, Seattle, Washington.

Environment Committee on Natural Resource Management (ECNRM)-OECD. 1989. *Renewable Natural Resources: Economic Incentives for Improved Management*. OECD, Washington DC.

Fischer, H. (Project Director). 1994. *Building Economic Incentives into the Endangered Species Act*. Defenders of Wildlife, Washington, D.C.

Hahn, R., and G. Hester. 1989. Marketable permits: lessons for theory and practice. *Ecology Law Quarterly* **16**:361.

Hanley, N., and J. Milne. 1996. Ethical beliefs and behavior in contingent valuation surveys. *Journal of Environmental Planning and Management* **39**(2):255–72.

Harrison, D., Jr. 1994. *The Distributive Effects of Economic Instruments for Environmental Policy*. OECD, Washington DC.

Heissenbuttel, J., C. Fox, G. Gray, and G. Larsen. 1992. Combating deforestation. Chapter 11 in *Principles of sustainable management of global forests: review of the forest principles and Agenda 21*. Adopted at the United Nations Conference on Environment and Development. June 14, 1992, Rio de Janeiro, Brazil. Global Forestry Coordination and Cooperation Project.

Henderson, J., and R. Quandt. 1958. *Microeconomic Theory: a Mathematical Approach*. McGraw-Hill, New York.

Hunter, M. 1990. *Wildlife, Forests, and Forestry: Principles of Managing Forests for Biological Diversity*. Prentice Hall, Englewood Cliffs.

Hyde, W. F., G. S. Amacher, and W. Magrath. 1996. Deforestation and forest land use: theory, evidence, and policy implications. *The World Bank Research Observer*, **11**(2), August.

Jakobsson, D. M., and A. K. Dragun. 1996. *Contingent Valuation and Endangered Species: Methodological Issues and Applications*. Edward Elgar, Cheltenham. 269 pp.

Johnson, K. L., et al. 1995. *Building Forest Wealth: Incentives for Biodiversity, Landowner Profitability, and Value-added Manufacturing*. Washington Forestry Working Group, Northwest Policy Center, University of Washington, Seattle, Washington.

Joint Session of Trade and Environment Experts (JSTEE). 1994. *The environmental effects of trade for Environment Policy Committee and the Trade Committee*. OECD, Washington DC.

Kahn, J. R. 1995. *The economic approach to environmental and natural resources*. Dryden Press, Harcourt Brace College Publishers, New York.

Keystone. 1995. *The Keystone Dialogue on Incentives for Private Landowners to Protect Endangered Species (Final Report)*. The Keystone Center, Keystone, Colorado.

Lambert, T. 1995. *The Endangered Species Act: a train wreck ahead*. Center for the Study of American Business, PS # 126. Washington University, St. Louis, Missouri.

Lippke, B. R. 1992. *Managing landscapes: role of goals, regulations and incentives*. Prepared for the Conference on Managing Landscapes for Biodiversity, Forest Health, and Sustained Timber Production. CINTRAFOR Special Paper 14. College of Forest Resources, University of Washington, Seattle, Washington.

Lippke, B. R., and H. Fretwell. 1996. The market incentive for biodiversity. *Journal of Forestry* **95**(1):4–7.

Lippke, B. R., A. Carey, and J. Sessions. 1996. *Economic analysis of forest landscape management alternatives: final report of the economic analysis working group of the Washington Forest Landscape Management Project*. CINTRAFOR Special Paper 21. College of Forest Resources, University of Washington, Seattle, Washington.

Loomis, J. B. 1996. Measuring general public preservation values for forest resources: evidence from contingent valuation surveys. Pp. 91–103 in W. L. Adamowicz, P. C. Boxall, M. K. Luckert, W. E. Phillips, and W. A. White (eds). *Forestry, Economics and the Environment*. CAB International, Wallingford.

Munasinghe, M., and E. Lutz. 1993. Environmental economics and valuation in development decision-making. In Munasinghe, M. (ed.). *Environmental Economics and Natural Resource Management in Developing Countries*. Committee of International Development Institutions on the Environment, The World Bank. Washington, D.C.

Moffett, J., and B. R. Lippke. 1994. *Evaluating the cost and effectiveness of forest stand structure management alternatives to restore environmental values*. CINTRAFOR Working Paper 51. College of Forest Resources, University of Washington USA.

Moore, S. 1995. The coming age of abundance. Chapter 4 in R. Bailey (ed.) *The True State of the Planet*. The Free Press, Simon & Shuster, New York.

Oliver, C. D. 1992. A landscape approach: achieving biodiversity and economic productivity. *Journal of Forestry* **90**(9):20–5.

Parviainen, J., A. Schuck, and W. Bucking. 1994. A Pan-European system for measuring biodiversity, succession and structure of undisturbed forests and for improving biodiversity-oriented silviculture. In *The proceedings: Innovative Silviculture Systems in Boreal Forests*. Clear Lake Ltd., Edmonton, Alberta.

Pearce, D. 1996. Global environmental value and the tropical forests: demonstration and capture. Chapter 2 in W. L. Adamowicz, P. C. Boxall, M. K. Luckert, W. E. Phillips, and W. A. White (eds) *Forestry, Economics and the Environment*. CAB International, Wallingford.

Pearce, D., A. Markandya, and E. B. Barbier. 1989. *Blueprint for a Green Economy.* Earthscan Publications, London.

Perez-Garcia, J. 1994. *Global forestry impacts of reducing softwood supplies from North America.* CINTRAFOR Working Paper 43. College of Forest Resources, University of Washington, Seattle, Washington.

Perez-Garcia, J. 1995. Global economic and land use consequences of North American timberland withdrawals. *Journal of Forestry,* **93**(7). 34 pp.

Perez-Garcia, J. 1996. *An analysis of proposed domestic climate warming mitigation program impacts on international forest products markets.* CINTRAFOR Working Paper 50. College of Forest Resources, University of Washington, Seattle, Washington. 26 pp.

Sample V. A. 1995. *Building partnerships for ecosystem management on forest and range lands in mixed ownership.* Northeast Regional Workshop March 20–21, 1994. Manchester, NH. Published by Forest Policy Center, American Forests, Washington, D.C.

Schroeder, W. *et al.* 1996. *Incentives to encourage stewardship in forestry.* A report by the Forest Incentives Group to the Oregon Board of Forestry. Salem, Oregon.

Sedjo, R. 1995. Local logging global effects. *Journal of Forestry* **93**(7):25–7.

Simpson, D., R. Sedjo, and J. Reid. 1996. Valuing biodiversity for use in pharmaceutical research. *Journal of Political Economy* **104**(1). 163 pp.

Simula, M. 1994. *The Case of Timber.* OECD Documents: Trade and Environment: Processes and Production Methods. OECD, Washington DC.

Smith, V. K., and J. A. Espinosa. 1996. Theory and applications – environmental and trade policies: some methodological lessons. *Environment and Development Economics* **1**:19–40 (Cambridge University Press).

Tietenberg, T. 1996. *Environmental and Natural Resource Economics.* Harper Collins College Publishers, New York.

Upton, C., and S. Bass. 1996. *The Forest Certification Handbook.* St. Lucie Press Delray Beach, FL.

Ward, D. M., and J. W. Duffield. 1992. *Natural Resource Damages: Law and Economics.* John Wiley and Sons, New York.

Wibe, S. 1995. *Non-wood benefits in forestry: a survey of valuation studies.* UN-ECE/FAO Timber and Forest Discussion Papers, ECE/TIM/DP/2.

Willis, K. G., and G. D. Garrod. 1992. Amenity value of forests in Great Britain and its impact on the internal rate of return from forestry. *Forestry* **65**(3):331–46.

On a ranger district of a national forest in western South Carolina, forest management through timber harvest had come to a virtual halt in the late 1980s. Environmental groups, citing the need to protect the biological diversity of the hardwood forests in the area, filed appeals, initiated lawsuits, and staged demonstrations to protest attempts by the U.S.D.A. Forest Service and its private contractors to implement the timber harvest and regeneration provisions of the forest plan. Businesses dependent on national forest timber were angered and embarrassed by the protests, and they were prevented from exercising their contracts to harvest Forest Service timber. Environmental groups enjoyed a temporary surge of power, but looked ahead to unending battles over the same areas and same issues. The Forest Service, unable to carry out its traditional management activities, felt beleaguered by critics from all sides. All parties were suspicious of the motives of others.

In the 1970s in the hill country of northern India, villagers in the grassroots organization Chipko banded together to prevent harvesting in historically communally owned forests, at times chaining themselves to trees to prevent them from being cut down by commercial operators. These forests had supplied fuelwood, shelter, forage and food to local people, as well as being valued for their biological diversity (Gupta 1989). Similar scenes have been played out on private and public forestland in all regions of the United States, and in the forests of developing and developed countries worldwide. What are the common elements in these disputes over forest management? Why do they arise? How do they get resolved, if at all? Where are the linkages between the science of forestry and public and private values in these disputes, and in the methods used to resolve them?

My thesis is that these disputes arise because there are many people holding many different values who have a stake in how forestland is managed. The theme of this chapter is how a diversity of goals from a diversity of participants must be incorporated into forest management, for biodiversity and for other goals. I will use perspectives from social science to examine the values that underlie forest management disputes, the institutional and organizational contexts in which the disputes arise (and may be resolved), and the ways in which science and values may be integrated in forest management planning. I will emphasize the role of collaborative planning as a way to incorporate diverse public values, along with scientific analysis, in forest management. I will use the South Carolina case introduced above as the primary example. Although this example, and much of the work I use to interpret it, comes from public forest land management in North America, similar disputes afflict management of both public and private forests throughout the developed and developing world; I will call attention to a few of these instances along the way. In the chapter, I will (a) review the evolution of forest planning from a largely technocratic enterprise to a more truly public enterprise; (b) discuss the participation of public interest groups, technical experts, and forest managers in collaborative planning processes; (c) describe the integration of the social and ecological aspects of forest planning and their interaction with geographic scale; (d) illustrate collaborative planning with the South Carolina example; and (e) analyze the benefits and pitfalls of using collaborative planning processes to integrate science and values in forest management.

Evolution of forest planning

WHAT IS FOREST PLANNING?

Forest management, whether for biodiversity or for any other goals, requires decisions that are based on both scientific knowledge and social values. Whether on private or public land, in the developed world or in developing countries, these decisions are influenced by many goals advocated by many parties. Forest planning is a mechanism for decision-making that links social values with science.

Whether for a small, private forest landowner or for a large, public agency, whether done formally or informally, land management planning translates values into activities that will promote those values. Planning involves a blend of ecological and social systems, with the social side of planning just as complex, if not more so, than the ecological side. Forest management planning will not be successful if it flies in the face of the natural processes by which management actions are translated into ecological effects; nor will it be successful if it fails to produce the services and products that are desired by society. These may, of course, differ for different types of forests and different types of ownership.

Even for a small private landowner with a relatively narrow set of objectives, choosing among possible management scenarios involves a complicated calculus of alternative actions, projected outcomes, valuation of possible results, and tradeoffs among competing objectives. Where there are larger, public ownerships and many interested parties, with different sets of objectives and differing priorities even among shared objectives, this calculus becomes much more complex. Conservation of biodiversity is only one of many competing goals. Depending on whose goals you are examining, biodiversity may be viewed as an end in itself or as a means to some further end (such as ecological stability or new medicines). In any case, it takes its place among other values being pursued by the parties with an interest in the management decision. To achieve any measure of biodiversity conservation, management actions to maintain biodiversity must be proposed, the impacts of proposed actions on biodiversity anticipated, and tradeoffs with other forest management goals negotiated. The social and political settings in which this multiobjective planning takes place, and the procedures by which it may be carried out, are my focus in this chapter.

HOW HAS FOREST PLANNING CHANGED?

In recent years, pressure for more public involvement in forest planning, for both public and private land, has intensified. The early 1970s saw an increased interest in forest environmental issues by the general public. New laws, such as the National Forest Management Act and the National Environmental Protection Act (NEPA) in the United States, broadened the range of goals being pursued on public forestland and also mandated public participation in environmental decisions. These had the biggest impact on management of public lands, but with some impacts on private lands as well, particularly through laws such as the U.S. Endangered Species Act. These laws required that when federally funded projects were initiated, 'scoping' meetings were to be held to inform the general public of proposed activities and to hear their concerns. As project planning progressed and decision documents were drafted, the agencies provided opportunities for the public to comment on the documents (e.g., environmental impact statements, forest land management plans). These mechanisms allowed resource planners to learn about the multiplicity of goals being pursued by various segments of the public and, presumably, to do their best to incorporate those goals in planning for federally funded activities. Walker and Daniels (1996) describe this as 'traditional public participation', an agency-centered process where the agency makes decisions with input from public comments.

These initial forays into public participation in forest management decision-making have continued and matured. New players from outside the traditional timber-based interests have brought a wider range of goals into forest planning. Public demands that forests produce other values besides wood have been extended to private as well as public forestland, necessitating new partnerships among public and private entities. Maintaining biodiversity on forestland depends on management decisions for both publicly and privately held land and on the participation of public, private, and non-profit entities – both landowners and other interested parties. Although the range of goals being pursued on private land is often narrower than that for public lands, where multiple goals may be a mandate, the boundaries among public and private lands and values have become increasingly blurred. Private values, such as water for irrigation of private cropland, may be produced on public lands, such as national forest watersheds. Biodiversity, and other public values, are often produced on private lands, such as industrial timberland. Non-profit organizations, such as The Nature Conservancy, are private entities, but they are organized largely to serve public values, such as biodiversity. Particularly when biodiversity conservation is viewed from a regional perspective, these public and private interest groups and landowners must work together to make land management decisions. In the state of Washington, the Timber, Fish and Wildlife agreement, which guides forest practices on private land so that timber management will be more hospitable to healthy wildlife populations (Halbert and Lee 1990), is an example of management for public values on private lands, as are Habitat Conservation Plans under the U.S. Endangered Species Act. Increasingly, private corporations are joining public agencies in realizing that their ability to harvest from forests in the future depends on their attention to the multiple values of forestland that are important to their communities, both locally and more broadly (Kemmis 1990, p. 132). 'Green' certification of forest products that have been produced using an agreed-upon set of standards for sustainable forestry is one example of the influence of public values on the actions of private companies over a broad geographic scale.

There have been parallel pressures for public involvement in international development projects involving forestland. After a long history of imposing solutions created by western advisors and advocated by central authorities, development organizations like the World Bank and the U.S. Agency for International Development have begun to regard local participation in project design and decision-making as a necessity (e.g., Singh et al. 1995). Non-governmental organizations that provide support for development projects, such as the World Wide Fund for Nature, create and teach methods for obtaining public participation in environmental decisions (e.g., Margoluis and Salafsky 1996).

In parallel with, and no doubt prompted by, pressure for more active involvement by the public in forest management decisions, the range of forest planning styles has evolved from central control through public comment to active collaborative management. In the United States in the early 1960s to 1970s, planning was seen as a way to bring the power of rational analysis to bear on the implementation of complex policy goals. Lee (1993, p. 111) echoes this view of planning, describing it as 'the assembly of information and analytic skills able to describe the world shared by the parties and able to identify the uncertain consequences of action within it.' Since then, our expectations of what planning has to offer have evolved from technocratic rationality through adaptive management and, more recently, to conflict resolution. In technocratic rationality, the expression of values leads to an elaboration of alternatives, one of which can be shown to be best at meeting that suite of values. Adaptive management (e.g., Walters 1986) builds on that scheme by acknowledging uncertainty about how an apparently best alternative may turn out and prescribing an iterative scheme for monitoring the results of management and altering management if it fails to promote those values as anticipated. Conflict resolution (e.g., Fisher et al. 1991) further elaborates the role for values in this scheme by recognizing the multiplicity of values being pursued by different parties and offering a structure for negotiating solutions that will satisfy as many of the most important interests of all the parties as possible.

WHAT ROLE DOES THE PUBLIC PLAY?

The role of the public in articulating goals for land management and negotiating what management activities will be used to promote those goals has become more active. Rather than just receiving public input through scoping meetings and comments on draft documents, resource managers now engage in collaborative planning with representatives of interest groups and the general public, where groups of citizens may meet with agency representatives over a period of months, sharing the tasks of

setting goals, gathering information, developing and analyzing alternatives, and selecting a desired plan. This is true public participation, not
merely public input (Knopp and Caldbeck 1990); one description of this
style of public involvement in forest management is 'multiparty collaboration' (Walker and Daniels 1996). The ultimate decision authority still rests
with the agency proposing an activity, but the role of the public has
expanded greatly. Some examples of such participation include negotiated
rule-making for pesticide registration and labeling by the Environmental
Protection Agency (Schneider and Tohn 1985), and habitat conservation
plans under section 10 of the Endangered Species Act (Bean *et al.* 1991), as
well as recent negotiations of timber harvest practices on federal land in
the Pacific Northwest of the United States (Daniels and Walker 1995) and
community forest management in Nepal by forest user groups (Bartlett *et
al.* 1993). These more active collaborations may satisfy the desires of the
participants for a particular suite of services and products from forests,
but they also help address the process concerns of the participants, providing more opportunities for them to be heard and to influence land management decisions.

Studies of participant satisfaction with various styles of forest planning
have shown that centralized, technically based forest land management
has serious limitations. People care about substantive outcomes, but they
care as much, and sometimes more, about the processes by which agreements are reached (Lind and Tyler 1988). The main sticking points for
resolving forest management disputes are not technical uncertainty or the
difficulties of multi-objective optimization, but rather arguments over priorities among competing goals and how these are to be resolved. In the
words of Knopp and Caldbeck (1990, p. 14), '. . . the basic question is, how
do we fairly allocate resources among competing demands? Such decisions are more likely to involve subjective or normative values – and the
feelings and emotions of people, especially when dealing with recreational and preservation values.' Even on private lands, where the range of
goals may be narrower and where, in the United States at least, protection
of private property rights is near the top of the list, forest managers perceive public support as essential to their future success.

Public participation in collaborative planning

Although other schemes for forest planning are certainly still in
use, I will emphasize collaborative planning as a means of synthesizing

values and technical analysis that satisfies procedural as well as substantive concerns of the interested parties. The questions I want to address are: How does collaborative planning differ from more traditional forest management? What is the proper role of science and of learning in this process? And, what are the proper roles for technical experts, forest managers, and the public?

FROM CONTROL TO COLLABORATION

The experience of the U.S.D.A. Forest Service exemplifies the sometimes painful transition from central control to active collaboration. 'No longer are bureaucratic decision and planning processes simply a way for experts to choose the technically best ways of solving predefined problems or meeting already accepted objectives. Now, land management planning processes must establish a dialogue between political and social knowledge (located within social and political organizations) and technical knowledge (located within professionals from a diverse array of scientific disciplines)' (Shannon 1990, p. 236). 'Land management is not merely applied science but a complex public policy debate as well' (Daniels and Walker 1996, p. 80). Here is a view of forest planning quite different from the technocratic model, one where the interplay of science, values and multiple constituents is planning, rather than an annoying impediment to the true business of scientific land management. Although resource managers have traditionally called upon science to resolve management questions, now they must understand the values and perspectives of many interests as well. The U.S.D.A. Forest Service has departed from the traditional model with some reluctance, but considerable ingenuity.

When the New Perspectives program, and its later incarnation as Ecosystem Management, were first proposed by the Forest Service, it was in the hope that 'largely biologically conceived attempts to get the science 'right' 'would quell social and political foment' (Daniels and Walker 1995, p. 293). Ecosystem management emphasizes public participation in national forest management and the role of the Forest Service in local communities, as well as ecosystem science, but what this will mean to forest managers is only gradually becoming apparent. Increasingly, forest managers are being called upon to 'think of themselves as facilitators who apply their scientific, technical expertise to achieve socially defined management objectives developed in partnership with the public' (Manring 1993, p. 20). Even more challenging, public forest managers must function not only as facilitators, but also as interested parties themselves, with official mandates to satisfy. This tension between acting as a 'neutral' facilitator among disputing parties interested in national forest management, and simultaneously pursuing their own objectives, leaves public foresters in a delicate balancing act (Forester 1987).

ROLES FOR SCIENCE AND VALUES

If forest management is no longer just a matter of applying the best science to achieving previously agreed upon goals, where does that leave science? In the collaborative planning model, science is less the province of technical experts and more an integral part of the dialogue among forest managers and interested parties. One of the hallmarks of interest-based negotiation is joint fact-finding (Fisher *et al.* 1991), in which all parties exchange data and analyses that may help formulate a satisfactory plan. It is typical of public disputes that the parties may differ widely in technical expertise (Carpenter and Kennedy 1988); joint fact-finding helps to equalize power imbalances that might otherwise result. Many management planning protocols include some type of joint modeling exercise, whether formal and mathematical or informal and verbal, as a means of sharing information on a resource system and fostering a common conception of it (e.g., Bonnicksen's, 1985, use of scenario simulation in Initial Decision Analysis; Keeney's, 1992, use of means/ends networks in value-focused thinking; Bostrom *et al.*'s 1992 use of influence diagrams in the public debate on radon remediation; and Daniels and Walker's 1996 situation map). The learning in these situations is not just one way, from the expert to the public, but many ways, with managers learning as much about the values and mental models of the public as vice versa. This is the 'civic discovery' or 'civic science' that many (e.g., Lee 1993, Kemmis 1990) have touted as essential to truly democratic decision-making for resource management.

This view of forest management puts values at the center of the debate, with science in a supporting role. Conflicting values, rather than being seen as a negative burden for the manager, can then be viewed as a spur to creative management (Delli Priscolli 1989). The full participation of the many public groups interested in forest management is a necessity in this creative process, because it is in participation that interests and values take shape (Shannon 1990, Fischoff 1991). What do participating publics get out of this process, besides the opportunity to perhaps influence management decisions in the direction of their own interests? They can build influence for this and future decisions, gain the respect of other parties, and build better relationships with parties they are likely to meet again in the future (Crowfoot and Wondolleck 1991).

On the negative side, collaborative planning is time consuming for everyone, straining the resources of forest management organizations and excluding segments of the public who are unable or unwilling to invest so much time to participate. Both land managers and interested publics must decide which forest management decisions deserve the intense scrutiny of collaborative planning. Collaborative planning, and other consensus-focused dispute resolution processes, have sometimes been criticized for subverting the objectives of parties who become too focused on consensus, at the expense of pressing their own interests (Amy 1987). Other critics contend that collaborative planning dupes participants into believing that their input affects planning outcomes in situations where decision control remains with a land management authority.

Integrating the social and the ecological

Under the collaborative planning framework, forest ecosystem management emerges clearly as a social, as well as an ecological, enterprise. A sociological view of natural resource management includes both biophysical and sociocultural phenomena, and either can be viewed as the 'independent' variable, influencing the other (Firey 1990). Delli Priscolli (1989) describes water resource development planning as a process where resource management determines social behavior, which in turn affects water resources. This view emphasizes the interdependent status of the ecological and the social aspects of ecosystems.

CHOOSING SPATIAL AND TEMPORAL SCALES

Just as ecological systems operate at a hierarchy of spatial scales, so do social systems, from individuals through international endeavors. To make sense of forest management, we would like to choose appropriate and, if possible, compatible scales for viewing both the social and ecological parts of the decision process, although Lee et al. (1990) caution that there is often no good match between the scale of physical change and the human community that is interested in or depends on that physical change. Somewhere in the middle range of spatial scales seems most fruitful, particularly given our interest in biodiversity as one of the possible goals of forest management. From the ecological side, we might consider spatial scales ranging from a watershed up to a bioregion, admittedly spanning geographic scales that could range from a few hundred to several thousand square kilometers. From the sociological side, we might use the concept of a 'relationshed'. Yaffee and Wondolleck (1995) coined this term to describe the network of relationships encompassing a diverse set of individuals and groups with expertise needed to manage forests as ecosystems in the landscape. They describe a relationshed as a 'community of interests' oriented to a 'sense of place' at the ecosystem level. Matching the temporal scales of forest ecosystems and human decision-making is notoriously difficult; forests operate on time scales ranging from seasons to centuries, while humans often have trouble seeing further than the next political cycle or, at best, their own lifetimes and those of their children.

The network of human relationships that might constitute a 'relation-shed,' as Yaffee and Wondolleck (1995) have defined it, is a complex of interwoven social groups, with cultural, economic and political ties that may operate at very different spatial scales. The geographic scales suggested by these social networks may not coincide with each other, much less with the temporal and spatial scales of forest ecosystems. What implications do these multi-scale, interwoven cultural, economic and political systems have for the resolution of differences about the values to be pursued in forest ecosystem management? People meet and negotiate their differences in a variety of settings and organizational frameworks, from community-based groups (such as the working group of South Carolina residents I describe below) through regional commissions (such as the Northwest Power Planning Council; Lee 1993) and up to national and international congresses (such as the Seventh Forest Congress held in Washington, DC, in February 1996). How should these collaborative planning efforts be organized? At what geographic scale? Who should participate?

CHOOSING THE PARTICIPANTS AND THE PROCESS

Wondolleck (1988, p. 223) suggests that the appropriate spatial scale should be 'such that key interests can be meaningfully involved and the resource base under consideration be of manageable size.' As suggested above, scales ranging from a watershed to a bioregion seem about right. Lee (1993, p. 111) notes the importance of scale in negotiation, preferring face-to-face interactions not only among negotiators, but also between negotiators and the constituencies they may be representing.

This is often not possible in debates taking place at a national scale. Indeed, there may be a synergistic interaction between multi-party collaboration as a style of forest management and the scale of planning. In analyzing the resolution of appeals to national forest plans, Manring (1993) observes that willingness to negotiate with disputants helps the Forest Service keep decision-making authority at the local, rather than at a more central, level. Of course, not all forest management problems are local, calling for planning at a multiplicity of scales.

Who should participate in collaborative planning for forest ecosystems? Bonnicksen (1985) bases resource management planning on a 'biosocial systems model', consisting of a social subsystem and a resource support subsystem, and the linkages between them. The social subsystem includes 'claimant groups' with both 'direct' claims on natural resources, such as loggers, and 'indirect' claims, such as users of forest products. The principles of dispute resolution (Fisher *et al.* 1991) call for representation at the negotiating table of (a) all parties who have decision-making authority, (b) those who may be materially affected by any decisions taken, and (c) those who could impede, legally or otherwise, the implementation of any decisions taken. When it comes to forest management, particularly on public lands, this approach may seem to exclude no one, leading to an impossibly unwieldy process.

The issues of who should participate and at what scale the planning process should take place inevitably interact. In deciding who should be 'at the table' for collaborative forest planning, it is important to recognize that individuals are simultaneously members of cultural, economic, and political communities at various spatial scales. The way differences in values and disputes about management are resolved differ at these different scales. At the smaller scales, interactions tend to be face-to-face, rather than at a distance, and the same people and organizations tend to interact repeatedly. Under these circumstances, doing well in terms of getting what you want on the substantive issues is only part of what is important. It is also important that resolutions foster good working relationships among the parties to a given dispute, so that the next time they meet, as they surely will, they don't have a backlog of ill-will clouding the current dispute.

LOCAL VERSUS BROADER SCALES

There are forces pushing in the direction of small scales for collaborative planning, and some countervailing forces pressing for larger scales. On the one hand, there are good reasons for wanting to keep collaborative planning tied closely to the ecological and human communities of a relatively small geographic area. Kemmis (1990) argues eloquently for the role of attachment to place in forming the values that a group of citizens bring to collaborative planning: '... what holds people together long enough to discover their power as citizens is their common inhabiting of a single place' (p. 117), and '... there may be such things as 'natural units of habitation' which lend themselves to the political act of willing a common world' (p. 120). Kemmis sees the regulatory bureaucracy of federal land management as threatening collaborative solutions based on a common place (p. 126) and asks, 'Does it really make sense to speak of an economics or a politics of inhabitation which depends on the cooperation of those who are not genuine inhabitants?' (p. 128).

On the other hand, there are 'communities of affiliation in addition to communities of locality' (Machlis and Force 1990, p. 261), and these are not necessarily congruent. 'Rather than a discrete number of organized interest groups, we see a loose, fluid structure of social actors involved in and affected by forest planning decisions' (Shannon 1990, p. 236). Lee (1993, p. 130) describes an 'epistemic community' of experts who share a belief in the importance of an environmental management problem and a set of priorities for dealing with it, perhaps similar to Yaffee and Wondolleck's (1995) relationshed. These people are also participants in forest planning collaborations, although they may not be associated geographically with the area for which planning is taking place.

Some of the most heated disputes in forest management have arisen when members of various communities challenged each other's 'standing', or right to be a participant in the process. Sometimes these disagreements about right to participate center on proximity or longevity of residence in the planning area. This problem occurred in a meeting on management of the Shasta Costa area of the Siskiyou National Forest in the Oregon coast range, when industry and environmental participants judged the other's right to be present by entirely different standards, including disagreement about the importance of longtime residence in the area (Daniels and Walker 1995). Sometimes the disagreement stems from different standards regarding which interests are germane in forest disputes: only those associated with traditional consumptive uses, such as timber harvesting or hunting, or also those associated with more recently developed forest constituencies, such as forest biodiversity and non-consumptive recreation. One source of tension in forest management decision-making today is that the cultural systems that were once dominant have been joined, and sometimes supplanted, by other cultural systems which may operate under very different sets of 'rules' in pursuit of different social values. Biodiversity protection is one example of a social value that has been added to the forest management mix recently (Brown and Harris 1992), often by participants who are not part of the traditional culture of forestry decision-making. Traditional participants like to label the newcomers as 'special' interests, with the implication that they are not legitimately part of the forest planning process.

The tension between local and broader interests, and between traditional and non-traditional participants, may be inevitable in forest management planning, particularly on public lands. Lee (1993, p. 110) notes that since the appropriate definition of an ecosystem depends on the problem being addressed, there is no one answer to where the geographical boundaries should be, and inevitably, they won't coincide with political boundaries. He further observes that 'planning is centralized, implementation is decentralized', leading to a 'Tension between centralized knowledge and control and decentralized experience [that is] perennial.' National-level environmental policy can exert a strong influence on local environmental decisions, even on private lands. In the Shasta Costa case, a national policy initiative, introduction of the Ancient Forests bill to the U.S. Congress in the midst of negotiations, shifted the power balance among the participants by giving the environmentalists a better option outside the negotiation (Daniels and Walker 1995). Regional and national organizations often participate in local level planning, in part because of genuine interest in the outcome of planning in that particular area, in part because decisions taken locally may set precedents for similar decisions on a broader scale. Local chapters of regional and national organizations may experience conflicts between their interests at a local level and the broader interests of the parent organization. This conflict has often played out in the parent organization's greater willingness to risk losing in a local dispute through litigation for the potential benefit of winning a case that will set a precedent nationwide.

Further complicating these issues are decisions about direct versus indirect, or representative, participation. At the most local scales, participation is likely to be direct. However, even in very local disputes, the time and energy required for participation are likely to be borne by a few people representing, at least nominally, a larger constituency. In regional and national disputes, participation through representation is a necessity. In developing countries, particularly, where the gap between local parties likely to be affected by forest management decisions and the decision-makers responsible for those decisions may appear to loom especially large, non-governmental organizations play an important role in providing a voice, albeit a strongly filtered voice, for indigenous people. One example here is the role of the Natural Resource Defense Council negotiating with oil interests and the Ecuadorian government on behalf of the Waorani Indians in the Ecuadorian Amazon, a representation that was not endorsed by all the Waorani tribes (Kimerling 1991).

Cedar Creek case study

To illustrate some of the benefits and pitfalls of collaborative planning as a means of making forest management decisions, I will use the experience of the U.S.D.A. Forest Service in the South Carolina district mentioned above. The area involved is about 3250 hectares (8000 acres) running east from the Chauga River, which is designated in the forest plan as a scenic river (Figure 19.1). The area includes hardwood and mixed pine-hardwood stands ranging in age up to 160 years; loblolly pine (Pinus taeda) plantations; steep slopes; habitat for threatened species, including the smooth coneflower (Echinacea laevigata); and trout streams. Human uses of the area have been for timber harvest, mainly by clearcutting in recent years, and for dispersed recreation. The area illustrates the major resource management conflicts of forests in the southern Appalachians, and indeed nationally and internationally: disputes among timber interests, environmentalists, and the Forest Service over the best distribution of consumptive and non-consumptive uses of forest resources.

This area was chosen as the focus of an experimental collaborative planning process facilitated by the author and Dr F. Thomas Lloyd, a U.S.D.A. Forest Service researcher. The process had a research component, but it also filled a practical need for the Forest Service, which had been stymied in its attempts to harvest timber in the area due to concerns about biodiversity, water quality, and equitable treatment of traditional and non-traditional recreation interests. The two facilitators worked with a core group of interested citizens and Forest Service representatives to develop a 'consensus view' for managing this area over the next 10 years. The working group took the existing forest plan as background for its analysis and developed a vision for future management activities that could be implemented as individual projects approved through the usual NEPA processes. The members of the working group represented interest areas, such as timber, hunting, biodiversity, and local communities. They

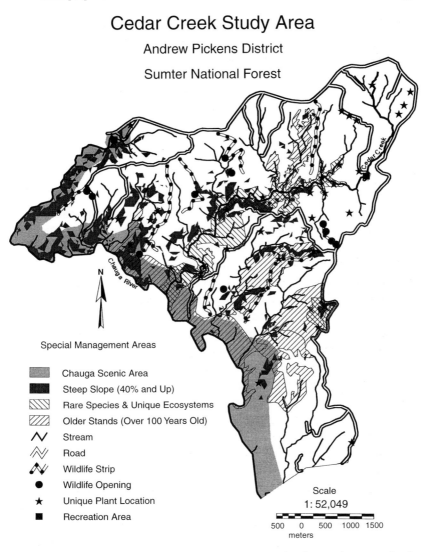

Cedar Creek Study Area

Andrew Pickens District

Sumter National Forest

Special Management Areas

- Chauga Scenic Area
- Steep Slope (40% and Up)
- Rare Species & Unique Ecosystems
- Older Stands (Over 100 Years Old)
- Stream
- Road
- Wildlife Strip
- ● Wildlife Opening
- ★ Unique Plant Location
- ■ Recreation Area

Scale
1 : 52,049

500 0 500 1000 1500
meters

Fig. 19.1. Map of Cedar Creek area, Pickens District, Sumter National Forest, in western South Carolina.

were selected by consensus of these constituencies during two large public meetings. All participants were residents of the area, but some were representatives of local chapters of regional or national organizations, providing a link to wider scale concerns. When an initial meeting failed to provide satisfactory representation of local residents concerned with traditional uses of the area, the facilitators made a special effort to solicit appropriate representatives. Obtaining proper representation of previously unorganized parties is frequently difficult in public disputes (Carpenter and Kennedy 1988). How much effort should be expended to ensure that the full span of public interests is included is a hard decision for convenors of collaborative planning processes. The meetings of the working group meetings were open to the general public, partly in deference to Federal Advisory Committee Act requirements, although the working group was not an official advisory committee.

GOALS AND WAYS TO REACH THEM

The working group developed a chart describing the goals important to each major constituency: timber, biodiversity, and recreation. We used the objectives hierarchy methodology from value-focused thinking (Keeney 1992) to develop and organize these goals (Figure 19.2a, b). These were combined into a common chart, to emphasize that the group was there to take a collaborative approach to solving a joint problem. The overall goal was 'to manage national forest land to meet social goals.' It is interesting that a group with such varied interests and educations perceived right away that all of the individual goals espoused by various parties, including timber harvest, preservation of rare ecological communities, or preservation of traditional lifestyles, should be considered social goals. Aspects of this overall goal included protecting the ecosystem, providing a variety of goods and services, preserving the quality of life, promoting economic well-being, and educating the public, among others (Figure 19.2a). Each of these was further broken down into specific subgoals that could be measured. For example, northern red oak sawtimber is a good whose output can be measured (Figure 19.2b). The initial focus on goals gave direction to later steps of the process, gathering and analyzing information and developing alternatives. It also served the important purpose of turning people's attention away from demands for action (or inaction, such as forbidding timber harvest), and toward the underlying goals toward which those actions were aimed. Understanding the underlying goals is an essential ingredient for developing solutions that meet the needs of multiple interests (Fisher *et al.* 1991).

The working group then developed 'means-ends' charts describing how management actions implemented on the ground would likely affect the goals identified previously (e.g., Figure 19.3). Unlike the process of identifying goals, describing the expected results of management actions requires technical expertise, which was supplied in part by the working

---

(a)

OVERALL:
Manage national forest land to meet social goals

- protect/restore ecosystem
- provide variety of goods/services
- preserve quality of life
- educate public
- promote economic well-being
- preserve options
- encourage research

(b)

Provide variety of goods/services

- timber
- sustained yield
    - indefinitely into future
    - predictable number of acres each year
    - variety of mature saw timber
        - hardwood (northern red oak)
        - pine
        - poplar

Fig. 19.2. (a) Fundamental goals for the Cedar Creek working group. (b) Subgoals and measures for part of the 'goods and services' branch of the fundamental goals.

group members themselves and in part by professionals from the Forest Service, universities, and state agencies. This work was done by 'mixed' subgroups, where representatives from different constituencies worked together to develop means-ends charts for the three main areas of recreation, timber, and biodiversity. Mixing membership in these subgroups promoted the goals of sharing information and mutual education, providing a common background for developing management proposals specific to the Cedar Creek area. Disagreements among the participants about how actions might affect forest resources suggested future research that might be undertaken to resolve these uncertainties.

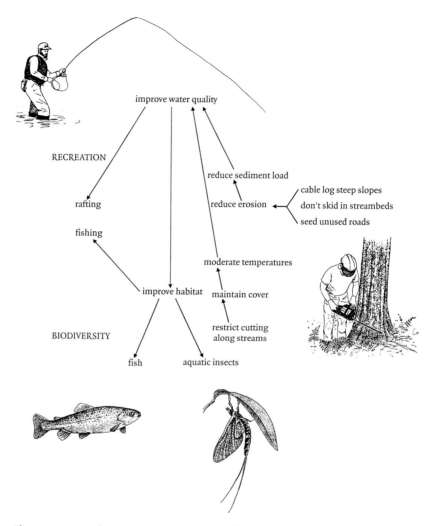

Fig. 19.3. An example means/ends network for the Cedar Creek area showing the impact of management actions on fundamental goals.

A CONSENSUS VIEW

Working in the same mixed subgroups, the working group began to develop a vision for management of the Cedar Creek area. This work was facilitated by access to a GIS database for summarizing and mapping forest resources in the area, including stand ages and types, locations of rare plants, areas of steep slope, and other areas of special concern (Figure 19.1). The ability to display this information visually, and then make simple calculations of the amounts of various resources in particular areas whose management was under discussion, was invaluable in working with a group of such varied technical backgrounds. Initial proposals from the three subgroups were integrated by the facilitators into a 'single negotiating text', which underwent a series of revisions before it was endorsed by nearly all working group members.

The resulting 'consensus view' requests that the Forest Service manage the area for a diversity of forest types, emphasizing native species, and for a range of traditional recreation uses. It distinguishes between the general forest area and 'special' areas, where unique resources may require special attention. The latter include situations where there is general agreement on what management techniques should be used to protect unique resources. For example, areas with special scenic importance (e.g., Chauga Scenic Area, visual retention areas) will be managed without timber harvest. Steep slopes may require special harvesting techniques, such as cable logging, to protect soil from erosion. In stream buffers, the amount of harvesting may be limited. In other areas with unique resources, including some rare plant habitats and areas to be managed for 'old growth' characteristics, there is far from general agreement on what management might be appropriate. In these situations contingent agreements, where disputing parties may not be able to agree immediately on what action should be taken, but where they can agree on a plan for gathering information and then choosing which actions should be taken based on that information, provide direction for resolving disputes (Lax and Sebenius, 1986). In the Cedar Creek case, jointly designed research and inventory projects will help resolve questions about how to manage for rare plants and old growth in the future. The state of Washington's Timber, Fish and Wildlife agreement makes similar use of shared uncertainty to develop explicit commitments to act differently once the uncertainty has been reduced by science (Halbert and Lee 1990).

The consensus view for the Cedar Creek area has strengths in recreation, research, and ongoing public involvement. Under recreation, there are suggestions for small-scale developments to improve access by the handicapped and elderly, as well as an expanded education program by the Forest Service and citizen groups on non-timber as well as timber uses of the forest. The research focus includes both short-term surveys and longer-term research. In the short term, surveys of rare plant and older stand locations will help outline a network of areas to provide old-growth forests. A socioeconomic study will examine the community consequences of both timber and non-timber uses of the forest. Longer-term research will identify management for rare plants and for areas in the old-growth network, specifying what types of timber management might be appropriate. Other research will examine the impacts on timber and non-timber resources of alternatives to clearcutting. Unlike many calls for research, which may be designed strategically to delay action (Daniels and Walker 1995), this one is well-focused to address the concerns raised by a broad constituency, so that resources can be protected without undue delays and uncertainties for the timber program. In both recreation and research, the consensus view contains specific plans for ongoing participation by citizen committees and volunteers.

IMPLEMENTATION

The consensus view was forwarded to the Forest Supervisor. He and his staff responded with proposals for items that could be undertaken immediately, those that required additional planning or funds, and those that would be considered in an upcoming revision of the forest plan. These activities have taken place: the Forest Service worked with citizens to secure matching funds and site a scenic trail; the Forest Service held a Saturday open house to meet with the public; research projects were initiated on management of smooth coneflower habitat, use of remotely sensed data to inform uneven-aged management, and characteristics of old growth; improvements were made to a rifle range in the study area; and timber sales were prepared to provide both commodity outputs and opportunities to test uneven-aged harvest techniques.

This collaborative problem-solving process required a substantial investment by citizens, the Forest Service, and facilitators. The working group met nine times over a nine month period, with additional work between meetings. It is possible that additional technical analysis might have made the consensus view more specific and more responsive to the goals of all parties, but the need to achieve closure and begin implementation precluded refining the document further. Although there are still tensions among interest groups and disputes about other Forest Service actions on the district, the fact that this group worked together to produce a credible plan, parts of which have been implemented, stands as at least a partial success for collaborative work.

Ups and downs of collaborative planning

A collaborative process for forest planning presents both opportunities for, and barriers to, the incorporation of multiple values from multiple parties in forest land management. On the plus side, such a framework has the potential to satisfy many of the procedural concerns important to participants' satisfaction with a decision-making process (Lind and Tyler 1988). It follows the principles of interest-based negotiation (Fisher et al. 1991). It provides a venue for exchanging and evaluating both scientific information and information on the values that guide forest management decisions. However, collaborative decision-making can fail to reach its potential for many reasons.

ARE THE RIGHT PEOPLE THERE?

As with any framework for multi-party decision-making, collaborative planning can fail to achieve its potential if it does not address satisfactorily issues such as equity, representation, voice and access. The opportunity for interested parties to present their views in front of other participants and the decision-making authority (in the Cedar Creek case, the Forest Service), either personally or via a representative they have helped to select, is one of the most important characteristics of procedures that are perceived to be just (Lind and Tyler 1988). In addition, presentation of the interests of the decision-makers and any affected parties is fundamental to interest-based negotiation as a problem-solving process (Fisher et al. 1991). Multi-criteria methods for analyzing and choosing among management alternatives depend on explicit statements of the many objectives being pursued by the participants, along with translation of those objectives into measurable, observable criteria that can be incorporated in technical analysis (Keeney 1992). To take advantage of both the procedural and substantive advantages of these elements of collaborative problem-solving, the right people must be present and they must be able to function effectively.

It is common in forest management disputes to have problems with both the perception and the reality of appropriate and equitable representation. Previously unorganized parties often have trouble mustering appropriate representation at the negotiating table. Sometimes these parties don't realize that a particular discussion should concern them. In our case study in South Carolina, longtime local residents did not turn out in force until someone started a rumor that the Forest Service planned to take the entire western tip of South Carolina by eminent domain and turn it into a wilderness area. That got their attention, but it took a lot of energy to quell the rumor and start working together constructively. Parties often differ in the ease with which they can participate in lengthy planning processes. Newcomers, who may often be retired professionals interested in the amenity values of forestland, may have more leisure to participate in collaborative planning than longtimers (Blahna 1990). In the Cedar Creek case, the fact that a private foundation made a grant in support of a local environmental group, thereby indirectly underwriting their participation in this and other forest management activities, rankled some other interests. As in other forest management disputes, participants in the Cedar Creek process sometimes disagreed about who had the 'right' to be represented, with long-standing presence in the community weighing heavily with some, technical expertise weighing heavily with others, and affiliation with national organizations weighing positively with some and negatively with others. This disagreement about standing surfaced in the designation of some of the more recent entrants to forest planning, such as biodiversity enthusiasts, as 'special interests' by some of the more traditional forest constituencies, such as timber operators. The facilitators tried to persuade the parties that all of them were special interests.

CAN THEY FUNCTION EFFECTIVELY?

Some of the participants in the Cedar Creek process did an excellent job of communicating from their constituencies to the negotiating group and vice versa. Others became preoccupied with expressing their personal goals, to the neglect of their broader constituencies. In any negotiation involving representatives from larger groups, there is tension between the representatives' identification with and loyalty to their constituencies and their identification as members of the negotiating group and their commitment to a negotiated solution (Kramer 1991). If they identify too strongly with the group, they risk becoming alienated from their larger constituency and agreeing to solutions that won't be accepted by that constituency. If they fail to identify with the group, they will lack the commitment to pursue a negotiated solution.

Parties differ in the technical and organizational expertise they bring to the negotiating table. Participants in the South Carolina process ranged from those with grade school educations to resource professionals with postgraduate degrees. Although joint fact-finding helps to equalize differences in expertise, it cannot totally eliminate them, or the power imbalances they may engender. On the other hand, mutual education was one of the most valuable parts of the Cedar Creek process. Citizen participants learned about Forest Service goals and regulations and came to appreciate why some things they may have wanted were, in fact, illegal for the Forest Service to do. All participants came away with a better understanding of each other's goals and interests.

The face-to-face negotiation typical of collaborative planning is a mixed blessing. It can help to promote sharing of information among parties and the development of mutual trust. On the other hand, public posturing in front of other parties can inhibit candid disclosure of the underlying interests that provide the raw material for creative solutions. Similarly, 'sunshine' laws requiring open meetings, despite their admirable goal of discouraging collusion between public decision-makers and private interests, can inhibit collaborative planning if a new set of participants is always present, slowing the development of trust among the parties. The presence of the news media can be a mixed blessing as well. When the media report positively on attempts at collaboration, they can help nurture these efforts. Too often they choose to focus on the inflammatory and conflictual elements of resource management.

IS A MEDIATOR NEEDED?

A facilitator or mediator is almost a necessity for forest planning disputes, with their many parties, complex technical issues, and long-standing mistrust. Maintaining 'neutrality' in both perception and fact is a challenge for any mediator. In many forest planning disputes, the decision-making agency, in the United States most often the Forest Service, fills the facilitator role, in addition to being an interested party in the dispute. This confounding of roles exacerbates the tendency of participants to doubt the neutrality of the mediator and suspect that the deck has been stacked in favor of what the Forest Service wanted in the first place. In the Cedar Creek case, although neither facilitator was a Forest Service manager, the fact that one was a research employee of the Forest Service and the other working under Forest Service funding (although not from the operations branch of the Forest Service) raised questions about their neutrality, which may have undermined the confidence of some participants.

Summary

Despite potential difficulties in implementation, collaborative planning seems a promising avenue for combining public values and technical expertise in pursuit of biodiversity conservation through forest management. Biodiversity is both a biophysical entity and a social value. In order to sustain it as a biophysical entity, we must maintain it as a social value. Forest planning processes that combine explicitly social values and scientific analysis offer the best opportunity to ensure that forest management will promote the values that participants hold dear.

Collaborative planning moves beyond traditional forest management to provide explicit mechanisms for public participation in integrating science and values in forest planning. Values are paramount in collaborative planning, and science serves the pursuit of those values by informing participants how management actions are likely to affect their goals. Technical experts have a role in collaborative planning, to provide scientific information to all participants, but the joint fact-finding and sharing of information among participants of different backgrounds is essential to the procedural success of forest planning. Forest managers often have a dual role to play in collaborative planning, as convenors or facilitators of the process and as representatives of their own publicly or privately mandated goals. The question of who should participate in a collaborative planning effort is intertwined with the choice of geographic scale. There are many advantages to small-scale planning with direct representation, but, particularly for public forestland, the constituencies interested in an area may extend far beyond its geographic boundaries.

Integrating people and their values in natural resource decision-making is both essential and desirable, but it is so complicated that the results thus far span the gamut from 'the thrill of victory to the agony of defeat.' Neither forest managers nor the public have been trained to participate in collaborative planning. There are institutional and psychological impediments to success. Nevertheless, here is a chance to return to the 'direct, face to face (republican) problem-solving' that characterized early experiments in participatory democracy (Kemmis 1990) and translate the many voices of those concerned with forest management into plans grounded both in deeply held values and in sound science.

Further readings

This chapter draws on an eclectic assortment of ideas. Fisher *et al.*'s *Getting to Yes* (1991) is the introduction to interest-based negotiation. Keeney's *Sloan Management Review* (1994) article provides a brief overview of objectives hierarchies and means-ends networks as ways of structuring values for collaborative decision-making. Carpenter and Kennedy's *Managing Public Disputes* (1988) offers practical advice on applying negotiation and planning in multi-party, public settings. *Community and Forestry: Continuities in the Sociology of Natural Resources* (1990), edited by Lee *et al.*, includes several chapters cited here that demonstrate the variety of approaches that sociologists bring to forest management.

Literature cited

Amy, D. J. 1987. *The Politics of Environmental Mediation*. Columbia University Press, New York.

Bartlett, A. G., M. C. Nurse, R. B. Chhetri, and S. Kharel. 1993. Towards effective community forestry through forest user groups. *Journal of World Forest Resource Management* 7:49–69.

Bean, M. J., S. G. Fitzgerald, and M. A. O'Connell. 1991. *Reconciling Conflicts Under the Endangered Species Act: The Habitat Conservation Planning Experience*. World Wildlife Fund, Washington, DC.

Blahna, D. J. 1990. Social bases for resource conflicts in areas of reverse migration. Pp. 159–78 in R. G. Lee, D. R. Field, and W. R. Burch, Jr. (eds). *Community and Forestry: Continuities in the Sociology of Natural Resources*. Westview Press, Boulder, Colorado.

Bonnicksen, T. M. 1985. Initial Decision Analysis (IDA): a participatory approach for developing resource policies. *Environmental Management* 9:379–92.

Bostrom, A., B. Fischhoff, and M. G. Morgan. 1992. Characterizing mental models of hazardous processes: a methodology and an application to radon. *Journal of Social Issues* 48(4): 85–100.

Brown, G., and C. C. Harris, Jr. 1992. National forest management and the 'Tragedy of the Commons': a multidisciplinary perspective. *Society and Natural Resources* 5:67–83.

Carpenter, S. L., and W. J. D. Kennedy. 1988. *Managing Public Disputes*. Jossey-Bass, San Francisco, California.

Crowfoot, J. E., and J. M. Wondolleck. 1991. *Environmental Disputes: Community Involvement in Conflict Resolution*. Island Press, Washington, DC.

Daniels, S. E., and G. B. Walker. 1995. Managing local environmental conflict amidst national controversy. *International Journal of Conflict Management* 6:290–311.

1996. Collaborative learning: improving public deliberation in ecosystem-based management. *Environmental Impact Assessment Review* **16**:71–102.

Delli Priscolli, J. 1989. Public involvement, conflict management: means to EQ and social objectives. *Journal of Water Resources Planning and Management* **115**:31–42.

Firey, W. 1990. Some contributions of sociology to the study of natural resources. Pp. 15–26 in R. G. Lee, D. R. Field, and W. R. Burch, Jr. (eds). *Community and Forestry: Continuities in the Sociology of Natural Resources.* Westview Press, Boulder, Colorado.

Fischoff, B. 1991. Value elicitation: Is there anything in there? *American Psychologist* **46**:835–47.

Fisher, R., W. Ury, and B. Patton. 1991. *Getting to Yes.* 2nd edition. Penguin Books, New York.

Forester, J. 1987. Planning in the face of conflict: negotiation and mediation strategies in local land use regulation. *American Planning Association Journal* **53**:303–14.

Gupta, R. 1989. *The Unquiet Woods.* University of California Press, Berkeley, California.

Halbert, C. L., and K. N. Lee. 1990. The Timber, Fish and Wildlife Agreement: implementing alternative dispute resolution in Washington State. *The Northwest Environmental Journal* **6**:139–75.

Keeney, R. L. 1992. *Value-focused Thinking.* Harvard University Press, Cambridge, Massachusetts.

Keeney, R. L. 1994. Creativity in decision making with value-focused thinking. *Sloan Management Review,* Summer: 33–41.

Kemmis, D. 1990. *Community and the Politics of Place.* University of Oklahoma Press, Norman, Oklahoma.

Kimerling, J. with the Natural Resources Defense Council. 1991. *Amazon Crude.* NRDC, New York.

Knopp, T. B., and E. S. Caldbeck. 1990. The role of participatory democracy in forest management. *Journal of Forestry* **88**(5):13–18.

Kramer, R. D. 1991. Intergroup relations and organizational dilemmas: the role of categorization processes. *Research in Organizational Behavior* **13**:191–228.

Lax, D., and J. K. Sebenius. 1986. *The Manager as Negotiator: Bargaining for Cooperation and Competitive Gain.* Free Press, New York.

Lee, K. N. 1993. *Compass and Gyroscope: Integrating Science and Politics for the Environment.* Island Press, Washington, DC.

Lee, R. G., W. R. Burch, Jr., and D. R. Field. 1990. Conclusions: past accomplishments and future directions. Pp. 277–89 in R. G. Lee, D. R. Field, and W. R. Burch, Jr. (eds). *Community and Forestry: Continuities in the Sociology of Natural Resources.* Westview Press, Boulder, Colorado.

Lind, E. A., and Tyler, T. R. 1988. *The Social Psychology of Procedural Justice.* Plenum Press, New York.

Machlis, G. E., and J. E. Force. 1990. Community stability and timber-dependent communities: future research. Pp. 259–76 in R. G. Lee, D. R. Field, and W. R. Burch, Jr. (eds). *Community and Forestry: Continuities in the Sociology of Natural Resources*. Westview Press, Boulder, Colorado.

Manring, N. J. 1993. Dispute systems design and the U.S. Forest Service. *Negotiation Journal* 9(1):13–21.

Margoluis, R. A., and N. N. Salafsky. 1996. *Measures of Success: A Systematic Approach to Designing, Managing, and Monitoring Community-Oriented Conservation Projects*. Biodiversity Support Program, 1250 24th Street, NW, Washington, DC.

Schneider, P., and E. Tohn. 1985. Success in negotiating environmental regulations. *Environmental Impact Assessment Review* 5(1):71–8.

Shannon, M. A. 1990. Building trust: the formation of a social contract. Pp. 229–40 in Lee, D. R. Field, and W. R. Burch, Jr. (eds). *Community and Forestry: Continuities in the Sociology of Natural Resources*. Westview Press, Boulder, Colorado.

Singh, J., D. Moffat, and O. Linden. 1995. *Defining an Environmental Development Strategy for the Niger Delta*. Industry and Energy Operations Division, West Central Africa Department, Africa Region, The World Bank. Washington, DC.

Walker, G. B., and S. E. Daniels. 1996. The Clinton administration, the Northwest Forest Conference, and managing conflict: when talk and structure collide. *Society and Natural Resources* 9:77–91.

Walters, C. 1986. *Adaptive Management of Renewable Resources*. Macmillan, New York.

Wondolleck, J. M. 1988. *Public Lands Conflict and Resolution: Managing National Forest Disputes*. Plenum Press, New York.

Yaffee, S. L., and J. M. Wondolleck. 1995. Building knowledge pools and relationsheds. *Journal of Forestry* 93(5):68.

Index

Note: page numbers in *italics* refer to figures and tables